Sex, Sexuality, Law, and (In)Justice

Sex, Sexuality, Law, and (In)Justice covers a wide range of legal issues associated with sexuality, gender, reproduction, and identity. These are critical and sensitive issues that law enforcement and other criminal justice professionals need to understand. The book synthesizes the literature across a wide breadth of perspectives, exposing students to law, psychology, criminal justice, sociology, philosophy, history, and, where relevant, biology, to critically examine the social control of sex, gender, and sexuality across history. Specific federal and state case law and statutes are integrated throughout the book, but the text moves beyond the intersection between law and sexuality to focus just as much on social science as it does on law. This book will be useful in teaching courses in a range of disciplines—especially criminology and criminal justice, history, political science, sociology, women and gender studies, and law.

Henry F. Fradella is a Professor in and Associate Director of the School of Criminology and Criminal Justice at Arizona State University.

Jennifer M. Sumner is an Assistant Professor of Criminal Justice Administration in the Department of Public Administration at California State University, Dominguez Hills (CSUDH).

Sex, Sexuality, Law, and (In)Justice

Henry F. Fradella and Jennifer M. Sumner
EDITORS

Routledge
Taylor & Francis Group

NEW YORK AND LONDON

First published 2016
by Routledge
711 Third Avenue, New York, NY 10017

and by Routledge
2 Park Square, Milton Park, Abingdon, Oxon, OX14 4RN

Routledge is an imprint of the Taylor & Francis Group, an informa business

Library of Congress Cataloging in Publication Data
  Sex, sexuality, and (in)justice / Henry F. Fradella and Jennifer M. Sumner.
  pages cm
  Includes bibliographical references and index.
  ISBN 978-1-138-85209-9 (hardcover : alk. paper) — ISBN 978-1-138-85211-2
  (pbk. : alk. paper) 1. Sex crimes—United States. 2. Sex and law—United States.
  3. Sex offenders—Legal status, laws, etc.—United States. I. Fradella, Henry F.,
  editor. II. Sumner, Jennifer Mortensen, editor.
  KF9325.S494 2016
  345.73′0253—dc23
  2015031366

ISBN: 978-1-138-85209-9 (hbk)
ISBN: 978-1-138-85211-2 (pbk)
ISBN: 978-1-315-72375-4 (ebk)

Typeset in Sabon and Trade Gothic
by Florence Production Ltd, Stoodleigh, Devon, UK

To Dr. Charles "Juda" Bennett and Dr. Ann Marie Nicolosi:

Thank you for inspiring me to learn about sex, gender, and sexuality; for teaching me; for helping me understand the role of educators in combatting LGBTQIA prejudice; for laughing with me; and for being wonderful friends.

With my eternal love and respect,

Hank

To the people who recognize their lives in these pages and those who fight on their behalf.

Jenn

CONTENTS

CONTRIBUTORS

Tod W. Burke received his B.A. in Criminal Justice from the University of Maryland, College Park, MD; his M.F.S. in Forensic Science from George Washington University, Washington, DC; and his M.Phil. and Ph.D. in Criminal Justice from the City University of New York (John Jay School of Criminal Justice). He currently serves as the Associate Dean for the College of Humanities and Behavioral Sciences and as a professor in the Department of Criminal Justice.

As of this writing, Dr. Burke has authored or co-authored approximately 140 publications, including journal articles (over 40 peer-reviewed), book chapters, encyclopedia entries, and other publications. Approximately 60 of the published articles have been co-authored with students. Dr. Burke is also the co-author of the Oxford University Press introductory criminal justice text titled, *Foundations of Criminal Justice* (second edition).

Dr. Burke's research interests can be classified into six broad areas, and sometimes overlapping categories, including: (1) policing, criminal investigation, and forensic science; (2) criminal justice policy; (3) mental health issues; (4) controversial legal issues; (5) victimology; and (6) criminal justice education and pedagogy. His research has been published in the *Journal of Criminal Justice Education*, *Journal of Contemporary Criminal Justice*, *Homicide Studies*, *Journal of Forensic Sciences*, *Journal of Police Studies*, *Journal of Police Science and Administration*, *The FBI Law Enforcement Bulletin*, and *The Police Chief*, to name just a few.

David Patrick Connor is an Assistant Professor in the Criminal Justice Department at Seattle University. In 2015, he received his Ph.D. in Justice Administration from the University of Louisville. Dr. Connor also holds a Master of Science in Justice Administration from the University of Louisville and a Bachelor of Arts in Radio/Television Broadcasting from Northern Kentucky University. His research interests include sex offender policy and treatment, institutional corrections, probation and parole, inmate reentry, social deviance and stigma, and qualitative methodology. Primarily recognized as an expert on sex offender legislation, Dr. Connor is regularly consulted by correctional agencies and interviewed by media outlets about such laws. His work often focuses on the experiences of individuals involved in the criminal justice system, including justice system actors, offenders, and their families. Specifically, Dr. Connor's current projects include qualitative examinations of parole board members and support partners of registered sex offenders. His most recent publications appeared in *Criminal Justice Review, Deviant Behavior, The Justice System Journal*, and *The Prison Journal*. At the University of Louisville, Dr. Connor was nominated for The Trustees Award in 2015 and received the Faculty Favorite Outstanding Professor Award in 2014 for his teaching. Classes that he teaches at Seattle University include Criminal Justice Legislation and Policy, Law and Social Control, and Prisons and Jails. Dr. Connor is an active member of the Academy of Criminal Justice Sciences and the American Society of Criminology. In his free time, he enjoys exploring new places, eating at restaurants, and relaxing with his wife and cats. Dr. Connor is a native of the Greater Cincinnati, Ohio area.

Elizabeth G. Dinkins is an Assistant Professor in the School of Education at Bellarmine University where she teaches classes in methods of literacy, and both instructional and qualitative research. She received her doctorate in English Education from the University of Virginia, her master's in Education from Peabody College of Vanderbilt University, and her bachelor's from The Evergreen State College. Her research interests utilize qualitative approaches to investigate how critical literacy can be used to help students read and write their worlds. Her work has focused on LGBTQ issues and identities in classroom instruction, the use of young adult literature to foster disciplinary thinking, critical representations of athletes and sports culture in literature, writing pedagogy, and approaches to teacher development and school-wide literacy. Her articles have been published in *Middle Grades Research Journal, Sex Education, English Journal*, and *Electronic Journal of Science Education*. She strives to produce scholarship that humanizes and empowers the youth and communities she represents and apprentices her doctoral students to do the same. Previously she taught English language arts and coordinated school-wide literacy instruction in an urban middle school. Before becoming an educator, she was a whitewater raft guide who pondered the significance of gender, sexuality, and bodies on the banks of rivers in the United States and Ecuador. She lives in Louisville, Kentucky with her husband and dog in an old house under constant renovation and spends her free time playing on rivers and in the woods as much as possible. She is an active ally for the LGBTQ community.

Patrick Englert is the Interim Assistant Vice President for Student Affairs and Multicultural Affairs at Bellarmine University where he oversees the areas of Career Development, Multicultural Affairs, and Student Engagement. He completed his master's in Education from the University of Louisville, and bachelor's from Western Kentucky University in English Literature. He is currently working to complete his Doctorate in Education and Social Change from Bellarmine University. His research interests focus on LGBTQ topics surrounding leadership and organizational constructs, community engagement within higher education, and critical inquiry of sexuality and gender. He has had articles published in the *AHEPPP Journal* and *Sex Education*. He has worked as a university administrator for nearly 15 years in roles such as Director of Residence Life and Assistant Dean of Students/Director of Student Engagement, which have contributed to his belief in holistic development and lifelong learning. Additionally he has taught for the past five years in the Interdisciplinary Core, a key program in the liberal arts tradition, which enables him to incorporate the co-construction of meaning within the classroom. He has taken his passion for working with college students in the diverse setting of higher education and focused on infusing a critical approach in his work with students and the community. Running provides an outlet for balance and reflexive thinking, which he uses to find balance as well as motivation.

Chantal Fahmy is a doctoral student and research assistant in the School of Criminology and Criminal Justice at Arizona State University. She received her bachelor's degree in Criminology, Law, and Society from the University of California, Irvine, and her master's degree in Criminal Justice from California State University, Long Beach. Her research interests include institutional corrections and reentry, offender social support and health, and biosocial criminology. Her recent work has appeared in the *Journal of Criminal Justice Education* and the *International Journal of Offender Therapy and Comparative Criminology*.

Henry F. Fradella earned a B.A. in psychology, *summa cum laude*, from Clark University, a master's in Forensic Science and a law degree from The George Washington University, and a Ph.D. in Interdisciplinary Justice Studies from Arizona State University. Dr. Fradella uses transdisciplinary theories and methods to examine the law's effects on human behavior and, conversely, how the social human condition affects the behavior of law. In particular, he specializes in the intersection of law with the social and forensic sciences, most frequently with emphases in either forensic psychology and psychiatry, or human sexuality. This includes research and teaching on the historical development of criminal and constitutional law (substantively, procedurally, and evidentially); the dynamics of legal decision-making (including the roles of politics, discretion, morality, and popular culture); and the nature, sources, and consequences of variations in legal institutions or processes (including law and social change).

In addition to being the lead editor and contributing author for this book, Dr. Fradella is also the author or co-author of eight other books including *Stop and Frisk* (New York University Press); *Mental Illness and Crime* (Sage); *The Foundations of Criminal Justice* (Oxford University Press); and four textbooks published by the Wadsworth Division of Cengage Learning. Dr. Fradella has also authored or co-authored more than 75 articles, book chapters, reviews, and scholarly commentaries that have appeared in outlets such as the *American Journal of Criminal Law*, *Criminal Justice Policy Review*, the *Criminal Law Bulletin*, the *Federal Courts Law Review*, *Journal of Contemporary Criminal Justice*, *Journal of Criminal Justice Education*, the *Journal of Law and Sexuality*, *The Justice Systems Journal*, and *Law and Psychology Review*. In addition, he has delivered more than a dozen invited lectures, 50 conference presentations, and has served as the editor of four scholarly journals.

Prior to entering academe, Dr. Fradella worked in both the private and public sectors as autopsy technician, a lawyer, and a judicial law clerk for the U.S. District Court for the District of Arizona. He then spent ten years holding faculty appointments of increasing rank at The College of New Jersey before becoming a professor in and chairperson of the Department of Criminal Justice at California State University, Long Beach. That university selected him as the 2014 award recipient for Distinguished Faculty Scholarly and Creative Activity. After his selection as a Fellow of the Western Society of Criminology (WSC) in 2009, Dr. Fradella served as the Society's vice-president in 2011; its president in 2012; and as the editor of its journal, *Criminology, Criminal Justice, Law & Society*, from 2013 to 2016. In 2014, he became a Professor in and Associate Director of the School of Criminology and Criminal Justice at Arizona State University, where he also holds affiliate appointments as a professor of law and psychology. Dr. Fradella is a member of the American Society of Criminology, the Academy of Criminal Justice Sciences, the Western Society of Criminology, the American Bar Association, the American Judicature Society, the American Psychological Association, the American Psychology and Law Association, the State Bar of Arizona, Alpha Phi Sigma, and Phi Beta Kappa.

Lauren E. Fradella is an attorney at a mid-sized law firm in Bergen County, New Jersey. Ms. Fradella is licensed to practice law in the State of New York and the State of New Jersey, as well as in U.S. District Court for the District of New Jersey. Ms. Fradella practices law in the areas of no-fault personal injury protection, commercial insurance litigation, worker's compensation, family law, as well as commercial litigation and transactional matters.

Ms. Fradella graduated from The College of New Jersey in 2007, *magna cum laude*, with double majors in criminology and women and gender studies. She was indicted into Phi Beta Kappa. Ms. Fradella earned her Juris Doctor from Seton Hall University Law School in 2011, with concentrations in intellectual property and entertainment law. To enhance her knowledge of law, Ms. Fradella spent a summer in Belgium and Ireland as part of Seton Hall Law's Pharmaceutical and Intellectual Property Program.

Kenneth Grundy earned an M.S. degree in criminal justice from California State University, Long Beach. At the time he wrote his portions of Chapter 6, he was employed by the Federal Investigative Service. He has since gone incognito.

Elisabeth Jandro graduated from law school (University of Vienna, Austria) in 2007. She then moved to Switzerland where she strengthened her legal skills by working for the prosecution, the courts, a law firm, and a legal insurance company. In 2012, she moved to Seattle, WA, to begin work on a master's degree in Criminal Justice at Seattle University. During her time at Seattle University, Ms. Jandro worked as a research assistant on a diverse set of projects, including a study on ideologically motivated homicides in the United States and Germany, the development of a public safety plan for a neighborhood in Seattle, and in the creation of problems and examples for multiple chapters in a statistics textbook. Ms. Jandro is member of Alpha Sigma Nu (Honor Society of Jesuit Colleges and Universities) and Alpha Phi Sigma (Criminal Justice Honor Society). She received the Norm Maleng Academic Excellence and Citizenship Award in 2015.

Ms. Jandro hails from a European country in which prostitution is legal. Comparing the dramatic differences in that legal system to the criminal regulation of prostitution in the United States inspired her to conduct research in this area. Her master's thesis is entitled "Exiting Prostitution: An Examination of Legal and Extralegal Factors." For it, she interviewed 42 people currently and formerly involved in prostitution. She presented her tentative findings at the annual conference of the American Society of Criminology in 2015. Ms. Jandro plans to defend her thesis and graduate with her master's degree during the fall semester of 2015.

Mary Maguire is a professor and the chair of the Division of Criminal Justice at California State University, Sacramento, and the director of the Center for the Study of Criminal Justice and Criminology. Her research interests include moral panic and public policy, as well as issues related to the incarceration movement in the United States, including drugs, race, class, and services for those at risk for offending. She is a member of the California State University's workgroup to develop a pipeline from California prisons to California universities for those who have been incarcerated. Selected publications include: *A False Sense of Security: Moral Panic Driven Sex Offender Legislation*, and *The Prevalence of Mental Illness in California Sex Offenders on Parole*. In addition to her co-edited text, *Critical Issues in Crime and Justice*, she has three editions of Annual Editions: *Drugs, Society, and Behavior*. Dr. Maguire served as the Book Review Editor for *Contemporary Justice Review* and as a past President of the Western Society of Criminology.

Weston Morrow is a postdoctoral scholar at Arizona State University's Center for Violence Prevention and Community Safety. He earned a B.S. in Social Science from California Polytechnic State University, San Luis Obispo; an M.S. in criminal justice from California State University, Long Beach; and a Ph.D. in criminology and criminal justice at Arizona State University. He has conducted research on the Fourth Amendment, police use of force, courts and sentencing, and juvenile justice. Dr. Morrow's work has appeared in the *American Journal of Criminal Law*, *Criminal Justice Studies*, the *Criminal Law Bulletin*, and the *Journal of Crime and Justice*. In addition to being a contributing author in this book, he has also contributed a chapter to the forthcoming New York University Press book, *Stop and Frisk*.

Ann Marie Nicolosi is an Associate Professor at the College of New Jersey where she holds a joint appointment in the Women's and Gender Studies Department and the History Department. She currently serves as chair of the Women's and Gender Studies Department. She earned a Ph.D. in U.S. History from Rutgers University with a specialization in women's history. Her research interests include twentieth-century women's social movements, lesbian history, and media representations of women. She teaches courses in U.S. Women's History, African-American History, Gay and Lesbian Studies, Feminist Theories, and Histories of Sexuality. She also teaches study abroad courses such as the Gendered History of Food in Italy, Gender and Irish Immigration in Ireland, and Documenting Women's History in London. Her work has appeared in scholarly journals such as *National Women's Studies Association Journal*, *Genders*, and *Gender Issues*. Her article, "The Most Beautiful Suffragette: Inez Milholland and the Political Currency of Beauty," appeared in the *Journal of the Gilded Age and Progressive Era* and was a finalist for the 2008 Fishel-Calhoun Article Prize. Her current research project is a study of how beauty product manufacturers and advertisers used the rhetoric and ideals of feminism and the women's movement to create a full sense of empowerment in order sell these products to women. Dr. Nicolosi resides in central New Jersey with her wife, Marisa—partners for more than 20 years, and their two dogs, Sadie and Rusty.

Thomas Nolan is an Associate Professor of Criminology and the Director of Graduate Programs in Criminology at Merrimack College in Massachusetts. Dr. Nolan was a police officer for 27 years in the City of Boston, Massachusetts. He joined the force in 1978. During his law enforcement career, he worked uniformed patrol for 10 years, including a stint in the department's elite Mobile Operations Patrol (motorcycle/SWAT) unit. In 1988, Nolan was promoted to sergeant, sergeant-detective in 1990, and lieutenant in 1995. As a sergeant and sergeant-detective, Dr. Nolan worked in the Youth Violence Strike Force and the Anti-Corruption Division of the Bureau of Internal Investigations—he spent his last 10 years as a uniformed lieutenant and shift commander in the patrol division.

   Dr. Nolan earned a doctorate at Boston University in 2000 and joined Boston University as an Associate Professor in Criminal Justice in 2004, where he taught courses in Forensic Behavioral Analysis, Crime and Punishment, Forensic Criminal Investigation, Criminal Procedure, Law Enforcement and Multiculturalism, Gender and Justice, and Policing the Urban Milieu. In 2011, Dr. Nolan accepted an appointment as a Senior Policy Advisor at the Department of Homeland Security's Office of Civil Rights and Civil Liberties in Washington, DC, and traveled throughout the United States providing training and consulting on civil rights and civil liberties issues for state and major urban area fusion centers.

Dr. Nolan's scholarly publications are in the areas of gender roles in policing, the police subculture, the influence of the popular culture on criminal justice processes, and sex-offender treatment. He writes regularly for the American Constitution Society in Washington, DC, as well as *The Daily Beast* and is frequently sought out for his expertise and commentary by local, national, and international media—print, radio, television, and the internet.

Stephen S. Owen is a Professor of Criminal Justice and Chair of the Criminal Justice Department at Radford University (Radford, Virginia). Dr. Owen holds a Bachelor of Science degree in Criminal Justice from Southeast Missouri State University and Master of Arts and Doctor of Philosophy degrees in Political Science from the University of Missouri—St. Louis. Dr. Owen is a recipient of the Radford University Distinguished Creative Scholar award and has authored numerous articles on the subjects of institutional corrections, criminal justice pedagogy, interpersonal violence, and criminal justice policy issues; he is also a co-author of the introductory text, *Foundations of Criminal Justice*. Dr. Owen teaches courses in criminal justice policy, corrections, emergency management, and environmental criminology, and has also taught law and sexuality courses in the criminal justice undergraduate and graduate programs and as part of the Radford University Core Curriculum program.

Megan Parry is a doctoral candidate in the School of Criminology and Criminal Justice. She received her Bachelor of Science in Criminal Justice from Weber State University and a Master of Science in Criminal Justice with a concentration in corrections from North Carolina Central University. Her research interests include issues of procedural justice and police legitimacy—particularly for under-represented populations; comparative systems of justice; moral reasoning; media effects on perceptions of crime and criminal justice.

James E. Robertson is Distinguished Faculty Scholar and Professor of Corrections at Minnesota State University, Mankato. In some 125 journal articles, essays, case notes, reviews, and book chapters, Professor Robertson has delineated and critiqued the constitutional rights of prisoners and the conditions of their confinement. His many journal articles on these topics have appeared in the *Journal of Criminal Law & Criminology*, *Harvard Journal on Legislation*, *North Carolina Law Review*, *American Criminal Law Review*, *Criminal Justice Review*, and other scholarly publications. From 2002 to 2015, Professor Robertson was editor-in-chief of the *Criminal Law Bulletin*, a scholarly journal published by Thomson Reuters; and from 2002 to 2015 he was a contributing editor to *Criminal Justice Review*. Presently, he is a contributing editor to the *Correctional Law Reporter*.

As a consultant, Professor Robertson has advised the California State Public Defender, the Federal Public Defender, and private counsel with regard to prison rape, custodial suicide, and other aspects of imprisonment. In turn, the *Los Angeles Times Magazine*, National Public Radio, the *Wall Street Journal*, the *Pittsburgh Post-Gazette*, and other media have sought his commentary.

Prior to his university appointment, Professor Robertson was a research associate at the American Justice Institute, the National Council on Crime and Delinquency, the National Consortium on Criminal Justice information and Statistics, and the Center for the Study of Law and Society at the University of California at Berkeley.

Professor Robertson received his undergraduate degree, with election to Phi Beta Kappa, from the University of Washington at Seattle; subsequently, he received a law degree from

Washington University at St. Louis, an M.A. in criminal justice from California State University at Sacramento, and, lastly, an advanced law degree from Oxford University.

Jennifer M. Sumner is an Assistant Professor of Criminal Justice Administration in the Department of Public Administration at California State University, Dominguez Hills (CSUDH). She completed her doctorate in Criminology, Law, and Society at the University of California, Irvine after obtaining an M.A. in Criminal Justice from Rutgers University, Newark, and a B.A. in Sociology from Boston University. Dr. Sumner's research examines how the criminal justice system constructs and deploys gendered and sexualized categories in its policies and practices, and how these processes affect different groups. This has included a focus on the experiences and treatment of transgender populations in the criminal justice system, including policies and practices developed to address the management and care of transgender prisoners. This work has also extended beyond correctional settings to focus on exclusion and inclusion of transgender law-enforcement professionals in the workplace, funded by the Palm Center. Her work has also been funded by the National Science Foundation to examine correctional policy in international settings.

Dr. Sumner has published in journals such as *Criminal Justice Policy Review*, *Critical Criminology*, *Deviant Behavior*, *Journal of Crime and Justice*, *Justice Quarterly*, and *Law & Social Inquiry*, as well as several edited volumes. She is also co-author of two reports to the California Department of Corrections and Rehabilitation on studies of violence and victimization in California prisons. In addition, Dr. Sumner works to connect research to policy and practice through collaboration with criminal justice professionals working in the field and advising criminal justice agencies on the development of policy for transgender populations. Dr. Sumner serves on the executive board of the Western Society of Criminology and is a member of the American Society of Criminology, the Law and Society Association, and the European Society of Criminology.

Jayn von Delden currently teaches in the School of Criminology and Criminal Justice at Arizona State University. She has earned a Ph.D. in Justice Studies from Arizona State University, a J.D. from The University of Iowa College of Law, and a B.S. in Philosophy from Oregon State University. Dr. von Delden has been a practicing attorney and a dedicated educator at both law schools and universities. Her research and writing interests include gender, sexuality, family, and the law. Previously, those interests led her to be a member of the 6th International Peace Education Conference in Poznan, Poland, and an NGO representative at the United Nations Working Group on Indigenous Populations and its parent body, the Commission on Human Rights, in Geneva, Switzerland.

PREFACE

This book is the result of more than 10 years of planning. A little more than a decade ago, Hank Fradella developed a course entitled "Law and Sexualities." It was designed to expose students to law, psychology, criminal justice, sociology, philosophy, history, and, where relevant, biology. Much to his dismay, finding books that allowed him to expose students to this range of materials proved to be quite challenging. He found fantastic books that focused on one (sometimes two) of these disciplines, but nothing that synthesized the literature across a wide breadth of disciplines in a manner that made the material accessible to undergraduate students. So, he decided he would create such a book. But life happens. For nine of the past 10 years, he has been consumed with administrative responsibilities—first as a department chair, then as the associate director of a large school. When it became clear to him that he needed to work with others to make this book a reality, he sought collaborators with whom he could work. Three co-editors later, he and Jennifer Sumner finally moved forward with making this book a reality. Both Hank and Jennifer owe much gratitude to the contributing authors who provided them with such first-rate chapters.

To our knowledge, this is the only book available that draws on law and related social sciences and humanities to critically examine the social control of sex, gender, and sexuality across history. The history explored throughout the book focuses on Western civilizations, although material from non-western cultures is included for comparative purposes where appropriate. The book references the common-law tradition of England, but primarily focuses on the law of the United States. Indeed, both federal and state case law and statutes are integrated throughout the book. But unlike some legal texts and casebooks that address the intersection between law and sexuality, this book focuses just as much on social science as it does on law. We believe the book will be useful in teaching courses in a range of disciplines—especially criminology and criminal justice, history, political science, sociology, women and gender studies, and law. To make sure the material is teachable over the course of a traditional semester, the book has been structured into 13 chapters.

To increase student engagement, we have included a number of pedagogical features.

Chapter Opener—Each chapter starts with an engaging case study that is drawn from an actual legal case or from a high-profile news story. These case studies present facts in a manner that exposes the reader to the "real world" implications of the material presented in the chapter.

Learning Objectives—Each chapter enumerates a list of measurable learning objectives using the language of Bloom's taxonomy.

"Law in Action" Boxes—Each chapter highlights a published judicial opinion on a controversial aspect of the chapter. Most chapters utilize U.S. Supreme Court decisions, although some use lower court decisions that illustrate a key point on which the authors want students to reflect. All "Law in Action" boxes include student engagement questions that can either be used to facilitate in-class discussions or can be used as homework assignments.

Additional Boxes—All chapters contain addition boxed features that highlight a topic that the authors believe will increase student engagement. These boxes were designed to get students thinking about the material in the chapter and engaging them in analysis and evaluation of the material through critical thinking questions. As with "Law in Action" boxes, these questions can either be used to facilitate in-class discussions or can be used as homework assignments.

Further Reading—At the end of each chapter, authors have provided a short list of references that readers (both professors and students) might consult to learn more about any of the topics discussed in the chapter. Faculty might consult these sources while "prepping" to teach; students might consult these sources when writing term papers.

Key Terms and Glossary—Each chapter presents key terms in-text. A glossary containing definitions of each key term appears at the end of each chapter.

We hope that you and your students find this book to be interesting and engaging.

Henry F. Fradella and Jennifer M. Sumner

ACKNOWLEDGEMENTS

We want to thank Steve Rutter for believing in this project enough to back its publication. We are indebted to the whole Routledge team. We also want to thank Dr. Kim Richman and Dr. Kate Talbot Fox for their thoughtful reads of the chapters with which we, as editors, needed some guidance from subject-matter experts. We thank our copy-editor, Neil Dowden, and the entire production team at Routledge. Finally, we appreciate the feedback from all of the anonymous reviewers selected by Routledge.

CHAPTER 1

An Overview of Sex, Gender, and Sexuality

Patrick Englert and Elizabeth G. Dinkins

In late May of 2011, Anthony Wiener, a U.S. Congressional Representative from New York, tweeted a photo of himself from the waist down in underwear to a 21-year-old college student. The photo showed his erect penis inside his underwear. He alleged that his Facebook (Wiener mistakenly referenced Facebook instead of Twitter) account was hacked and that he did not send the photo. Over the next several days, Wiener denied sending photos to women, despite another woman stepping forward with allegations that Wiener sent her several photos as well as having engaged in conversations of a sexual nature. In an interview with MSNBC (2011), he stated, "I'm not sure I want to put national, federal resources into trying to figure out who posted a picture . . . I'm not really sure it rises, no pun intended, to that level." On June 6, Wiener held a press conference where he admitted that he had engaged in relationships with six women over the course of three years, via Facebook, Twitter, and phone conversations. Wiener apologized for his actions and was adamant that the relationships were all via social media and were not physical in nature.

Democratic leaders such as Nancy Pelosi called for Wiener to resign as the turmoil was distracting from what many deemed as more pertinent topics. A photo of Wiener's penis appeared online on June 8, further fueling existing contention as to whether or not he should remain in office. President Obama was interviewed by Ann Curry on the June 11, 2011 edition of the *Today Show*, during which he shared this sentiment:

> Well, obviously what he did was highly inappropriate. I think he's embarrassed himself, he's acknowledged that, he's embarrassed his wife and his family. Ultimately there's going to be a decision for him and his constituents. I can tell you that if it was me, I would resign. Because public service is exactly that, it's a service to the public.

On June 16, 2011, Wiener stepped down from his position in Congress amidst his newly pregnant wife returning from a trip to Africa, as well as a former adult film star holding a press conference to discuss further allegations of online sexual interactions, and democratic leaders discussing ways to encourage Wiener to resign.

Anthony Wiener became a household name for a month as Americans were fascinated by the sexual subject matter that took over televisions, internet, and social media. Indeed, Wiener's actions highlight the role social media now plays with regard to social norms associated with sex and sexuality. Consider how this case frames the current state of sex, sexuality, and gender in the United States.

- What sexual behaviors or actions are accepted as norms within society?
- How have technology and social media impacted the ways in which we interact sexually? Can sex, sexuality, and gender be separated from portions of our everyday life?
- Would the impacts of a woman posting provocative photos be received differently?

LEARNING OBJECTIVES

1. Define the key terms sex, sexuality, and gender.
2. Compare and explore theoretical models of sex, sexuality, and gender.
3. Discuss the relationship between gender and societal structures.
4. Distinguish between transgender, cisgender, and genderqueer.
5. Discuss how sexuality is shaped.
6. Compare and contrast historical and contemporary perspectives toward sexuality.
7. Distinguish between lesbian, gay, bisexual, asexual, and pansexual identities.
8. Explore sex through biological, psychological, and societal perspectives.

DEFINING SEX, GENDER, AND SEXUALITY

Was the situation that led to Anthony Wiener's resignation from the U.S. House of Representatives about sex? The answer to that question depends, in part, on what the term means. Yet, for reasons that this chapter should make clear, it is difficult to craft a straightforward definition of the word *sex* because its range of meanings refers to a continuum of behaviors. And, as Figure 1.1 illustrates, *gender* and *sexuality* are similarly complicated concepts.

Sex

Sex refers to both biological characteristics, as well as certain acts through which we express desire or release sexual tension (Richardson, Smith, & Werndly, 2013).

Biological sex. When *sex* is used to refer to biology, we tend to think of humans as being male or female, depending on chromosomal expression (e.g., XY for males; XX for female); internal reproductive organs (e.g., the presence of ovaries, fallopian tubes, and a uterus in females; the presence of a prostate and testes in males); and external genitalia (e.g., a penis and scrotum for males; a vagina for females).

The male/female binary for sex is misleading because humans can be **intersexed**—a term referring to "medical conditions in which the development of chromosomal, gonadal, or anatomic sex varies from normal and may be incongruent with each other" and, therefore,

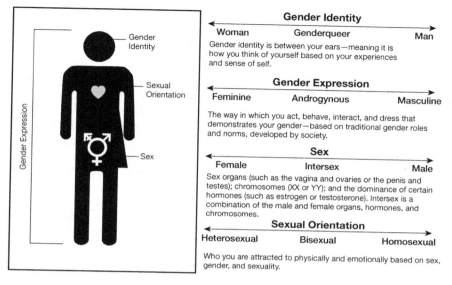

Figure 1.1 The continua of sex, gender, and sexuality expression

who do not fit the usual definitions of male or female (Allen, 2009, p. 25). For example, individuals whose 23rd pair of chromosomes (the sex chromosomes) are XXY occur in roughly one out of every 500 to 1,000 births (Colapinto, 2000; Wattendorf & Muenke, 2005). A small penis, small testes, low androgen secretion, and possible female breast development are characteristics of this chromosomal karyotype that is known as Klinefelter Syndrome (Wattendorf & Muenke, 2005). People with this condition typically live as men.

Intersexed individuals were once referred to as *hermaphrodites* based on the Greek god Hermaphroditus who was both male and female (Gurney, 2007). Today, there are at least 17 different intersex conditions, but most intersex individuals are classified as being either true hermaphrodites or pseudo-hermaphrodites. True hermaphrodites are rare; they possess both ovarian and testicular tissue, whereas pseudo-hermaphrodites occur more commonly—1 in 2,000 births (Colapinto, 2000)—and these individuals possess ambigu-

ous internal and external reproductive organs, but do possess the genitals of their dominant sex (Gurney, 2007). Research has suggested that while being intersexed is a result of biological outcomes, possessing ambiguous sexual anatomy is not a medical issue in most cases and medical interventions are not required (Preves, 2013). Social stigmas and familial pressure to categorize children into gender binaries typically drive normalizing surgeries that are conducted to remove or "correct" the body. Duality is feared and, therefore, parents feel a pressure to ensure that their child's gender and sex are as visually defined as possible (Preves, 2013).

Sex as a behavior. As previously mentioned, the word *sex* is not limited to biology; it also refers to behaviors. But this use of the word can be ambiguous (Sanders & Reinisch, 1999). Which acts qualify as "sex"? "For centuries, societies around the world adopted the view that sex means just one thing: penis-in-vagina intercourse within the context of marriage for the purpose of procreation" (Lehmiller, 2014, p. 2). Today, however, it is clear that sex—even when narrowly confined to the definition of penis-in-vagina intercourse—is no longer limited to the purpose of procreation within marriage. Regardless of the participants' marital status, penis-in-vagina intercourse offers pleasure, connection to others, expressions of love, exploration, and, for some, even the potential to earn money. Moreover, what is now classified as *sex* is not limited to penis-in-vagina intercourse. Indeed, the terms *oral sex* and *anal sex* specifically refer to sexual acts other than a vaginal penetration by a penis. And ponder whether penetration is even necessary for *sex*; if two people engage in mutual masturbation, is that *sex*?

Gender

People often use the words *sex* and *gender* interchangeably even though the terms have distinctive meanings. Unlike sex, which—at least in the biological context, tends to refer to a reductionist male/female binary, **gender** is a socially constructed category that reflects a set of behaviors, markers, and expectations associated with a person's biological sex and social norms concerning masculinity and femininity. A person's gender is usually represented in three ways (Parent, DeBlaere, & Moradi, 2013). The first is associated with physical appearance vis-à-vis secondary sex characteristics, such as the presence or absence of an Adam's apple, facial hair, the pitch of one's voice, and the like. The second concerns *gender identity*—how someone identifies in selecting a gender. And the third concerns *gender expression*—how people present themselves to others in their appearance, behaviors, actions, and interactions.

The first representation of gender is, in large part, a function of biology. For instance, one is either born with or without an Adam's apple. But other secondary sex characteristics are more malleable. Hormone therapy, for example, can alter the appearance of facial or body hair. The other two aspects of gender, however, are much more a function of the psychological and the social, both of which, to varying degrees, are partially dependent on social norms known as *gender roles*.

Gender roles are the behavioral, economic, and social roles that every society deems appropriate for members depending on their sex (Butler, 1999). Gender roles reflect societal norms concerning masculinity and femininity.

Social norms are societal rules. The norms that tell us what we *ought* to do—become educated; respect our elders; obey the law—are called *prescriptive norms*. The norms that tell us what we *ought not* to do—commit crimes, lie, drop out of high school—are called *proscriptive norms* (Anderson & Dunning, 2014).

Norms are based upon widely shared values regarding that which is "good" or "correct," and, conversely, that which is "bad" or "incorrect." Norms may be formal or informal. Formal norms, also known as *mores*, tend to have moral underpinnings. The values expressed in the Ten Commandments (e.g., not killing, stealing, committing adultery, etc.) or other religious doctrines, are examples of mores. In contrast, informal norms, also known as *folkways*, do not have as strong a moral foundation, but are social expectations nonetheless. Folkways include rules governing etiquette and acceptable standards of behavior, like how to dress for a particular occasion.

Norms vary across both situation and time. For example, language that may routinely be used while hanging out with your friends after school may be inappropriate to use at home with your family. Similarly, behaviors that may be considered perfectly acceptable by today's standards, such as teenage males wearing earrings, would have been taboo, or unacceptable, to many of our grandparents or great-grandparents.

Norms also vary across cultures. For example, belching at the dinner table is considered rude in many Western cultures, but is considered to be a compliment to the host or cook in some African and Asian countries.

(Owen et al., 2015, pp. 101–102)

Children learn gender roles as they grow up by watching and interacting with the world around them (Adler, Kless, & Adler, 1992). Traditional gender roles reflect congruence between biological sex and gendered behaviors that separate characteristics of men and women as aligned with their male or female biology. These traditional gender roles are the norms that families pass along to children. This can even occur before birth; consider, for example, that upon learning "It's a girl," parents may paint a room pink and adorn it with toys (e.g., certain types of dolls) and images (e.g., princesses) associated with femininity in little girls. These gender roles are reinforced by family, friends, school, media, and society-at-large. But those gender roles may not align with how one comes to perceive one's own gender because, unlike sex, gender is a psychological and sociological concept, not a biological one. A person's biological sex may lead to an assumption of gender, but that same person's gender identity may not reflect the biological sex assigned at birth. As one researcher stated, "Gender is between your ears and not between your legs" (Lehmiller, 2014, p. 116).

Gender identity is how one perceives oneself based on one's experiences and sense of self (Lehmiller, 2014). One's gender identity may or may not align with one's **gender expression**—how an individual expresses gender through dress, behavior, mannerisms, and actions. As with biological sex, gender identity and expression do not fit into binary classification systems.

Gender and sex commonly align such that a person who is assigned female at birth perceives her own gender identity as being a woman and, conversely a person who is assigned male at birth perceives his own

gender identity as being a man. **Cisgender** describes people who identify as and express the same gender they were assigned at birth based upon their perceived biological sex (Stryker, 2008).

Transgender, on the other hand, is a broad term used to refer to anyone who does not identify with or express gender norms that fit into traditional gender roles (Lehmiller, 2014; Stryker 2008). Transgender incorporates a range of identities, all of which do not conform to traditional gender expectations and presentations. **Trans*** has been used to represent the numerous identities that fit under the umbrella of being transgender. Trans* as a term does not stand alone, but may be used to describe a transgender person or identity. Transsexuals, cross-dressers, and genderqueer all fall under that category of transgender (Singer, 2015).

The term **transsexuals**[1] has been used to refer to individuals who have changed their bodies to reflect a gender identity that is different from what they were assigned at birth. Transsexuals may have undergone medical interventions, such as surgery or hormone therapy, to change their gender and fit the expectations of traditional gender presentation. The journey from one gender to the other is usually expressed as male-to-female (MTF) or female-to-male (FTM) transitions (Stryker, 2008).

Cross-dresser is used to describe an individual who wears clothes that are not traditionally assigned to their gender (Singer, 2015). An individual who dresses in drag for entertainment value would most likely not consider him or herself as transgender. However, some transgender individuals may opt not to have surgery or use hormones, but dress in clothing associated with the opposite sex that is more representative of their gender identity. Transvestitism is sometimes confused with cross-dressing. Transvestites cross-dress for sexual arousal and pleasure and research suggests that they tend to be heterosexual, married, men who do so in private

(Doctor & Prince, 1997). This may take place by wearing one garment, such as a bra or underwear, under clothing and is done for gratification and pleasure. Transvestitism does not fall under the collective umbrella of transgender identity; instead it is considered a fetish.

Gender queer is used by individuals who reject categories of gender altogether and wish to claim a space outside the traditional gender binary (Diamond & Butterworth, 2008; Lehmiller, 2014). Gender queer provides language for individuals who may present as masculine women or feminine men, who approach levels of **androgyny** by combining masculine and feminine presentation, or whose gender presentation shifts according to context and desire. Sexuality is not synonymous with gender identity. Research suggests that most transgender individuals are heterosexual (Chivers & Bailey, 2000; Ryan & Futterman, 1997). Despite this, it is important to remember that sexual orientation is not couched within gender identity; transgender individuals represent a range of sexual identities.

There is also a group of terms for individuals who identify by explaining who they are not, instead of by naming who they are. **Gender nonconforming** describes individuals who may not identify as transgender or gender-queer, but whose gender expression resists traditional gendered behaviors and intentionally rejects binaries by refusing to present traditional gender norms. **Gender questioning**, on the other hand, refers to individuals who are in the process of exploring various gender identities.

Sexuality

The expansive range of meanings associated with the words *sex* and *gender* also applies to the term *sexuality*. Sexuality encompasses the way we understand and feel about the process of sex, as well as the emotions, desires, attractions, and identities associated with the way we feel towards others (Beasley, 2005).

Sexuality is broadly defined as the "unique pattern of sexual and romantic desire, behavior, and identity that each person possesses" (Lehmiller, 2014, p. 145). As the definition states, sexuality comprises three dimensions: *sexual attraction* concerns the people one finds attractive and sexually desirable; *sexual behavior* concerns the people with whom one engages in sexual activity; and *sexual identity* refers to how one classifies one's sexuality, such as heterosexual, homosexual, or bisexual (Lehmiller, 2014).

Heterosexuality is a broad category used to describe individuals who are sexually attracted only to those who are of a different sex, whereas **homosexuality** describes individuals who are sexually attracted to only others of the same sex. The word "homosexual" in the current contexts is often considered offensive, thus the word **lesbian** is used to describe women who are attracted only to other women, and the word **gay** is used to describe men who are only attracted to men. Some lesbians, however, dislike that moniker and prefer to identify as gay or as a "gay woman." **Bisexuality** has been largely defined as sexual attraction not exclusive to the same or different sex. The experiences that define or comprise being bisexual have yet to be fully established by science and society (Diamond, 2008). Set parameters do not exist, which may make it confusing for an individual to associate with or identify as bisexual. Consider, for a moment, if an adolescent male masturbates with another male, but has sexual relationships for the remainder of his life with a female; is he bisexual? What if an adult fantasizes about same-sex sexual encounters, but engages in only opposite-sex sexual encounters; would he or she be considered bisexual?

The labels defined in the preceding paragraph might erroneously suggest that people are either heterosexual, gay, or bisexual. But sexuality is best conceptualized along a continuum that captures varying degrees of sexual attraction, behavior, and identity. We will return to the notion of a continuum of sexuality later in this chapter when addressing the psychology of human sexuality. For now, it suffices to state that the labels *heterosexual*, *gay*, or *bisexual* are reductionist because they ignore not only the potential fluidity of human sexuality (i.e., sexuality is not necessarily static), but also because they fail to capture the full range of human sexuality. For example, some people may be asexual. The **Asexuality** Visibility and Education Network (2014) describes an **asexual** person as "someone who does not experience sexual attraction. Unlike celibacy, which people choose, asexuality is an intrinsic part of who we are" (p. 1). Scholarly literature exploring asexuality is minimal, but expanding through the work of several researchers who have provided insights into the asexual identity (Bogaert, 2006; Prause & Graham, 2007; Scherrer, 2008). Other people identify as being pansexual, a term that is broader than bisexual. An individual who identifies as **pansexual** finds attraction to all genders and sexes. Bisexuality only focuses on attraction to men and women, whereas someone who is pansexual may engage in sexual activity or relationships with a range of gender and sexes.

What's in an Acronym?

You have likely seen or heard of the acronym "LGBT," which stands for *lesbian*, *gay*, *bisexual*, and *transgender*. In recent years, the acronym has grown longer to include the letters *Q*, *I*, and either one or two *A*s. The *Q* stands for *queer* (although it can also mean *questioning*); the *I* stands for *intersex*; and at least one *A* stands for *asexual*. When a second *A* is used, it refers to allies who do not identify as LGBTQIA, but who support the rights and safety of those who do identify as one of the letters in "the great alphabet soup of queer identity" (Tobia, 2013, para. 1).

Because we have already summarized the meaning of the words represented in the LGBTQIA acronym earlier in this chapter, it will strike some as odd that the acronym blends both gender and sexuality terms. We will revisit the reason for that blending later in this chapter after exploring queer theory and social constructionism, both of which can be used to explain the creation of a homosexual identity and its transformation first into a "gay community" and, later, into an "LGBTQIA community."

THEORETICAL PERSPECTIVES

Perspectives on sex, gender, and sexuality range from views that equate biological characteristics as static determinants for behaviors and attractions to views that embrace sex, gender, and sexuality as being unique and dynamic components of human existence. This range of views represents degrees of understanding that progress from rigid binaries to more fluid and changeable identities.

As Table 1.1 indicates, conservative perspectives tend to subscribe to dichotomous views that link biological sex characteristics to gender and sexual desire. More liberal perspectives recognize the role of society and individual autonomy in shaping understandings of gender and sexuality instead of establishing biology as a causal factor. As the theoretical perspectives move away from the conservative stance, the role of biology becomes less significant.

Essentialism

Essentialism is a theoretical perspective that posits any entity possesses a core set of attributes that are essential and, therefore, necessary to the entity's identity and function. With regard to sex, gender, and sexuality, the essen-

Table 1.1 Theoretical perspectives on gender

| | Conservative ← → Liberal | | | |
	Essentialism	Modernism	Social Constructionism	Queer Theory
Sex	Biological characteristics at birth dictate gender identity; biology and genetics determine sexuality	Biological characteristics at birth may not determine psychological identity; genetics may shape sexuality	Biological characteristics as distinct from psychological identity; societal factors inform gender and sexual identity	Recognizes that biological characteristics can be changed
Gender	Considers the "essence" of men and women to be different; embraces stable and dichotomous understandings of masculine and feminine	Psychologically determined; individuals can change their bodies to be coherent with their psychological gender; understands masculine and feminine to be distinct	Rejects strict dichotomous understandings of masculine and feminine; believes gender is constructed through interactions in social contexts; recognizes the pressure to conform to gender norms	Believes gender is fluid, multiple, and exists on a continuum; intentionally dismantles traditional gender categories to make new power dynamics possible; rejects dichotomous labels
Sexuality	Believes sexual desire is part of natural order; homosexuality and heterosexuality as natural desires	Recognizes bisexuality as part of sexual desire; recognizes that sexual desire exists on a continuum	Recognizes individuals make meaning in social contexts; desire is mutable and may expand beyond labels of heterosexual, homosexual, or bisexual; recognizes how societal pressures marginalize same-sex desires	Rejects categories and static understandings; views desire as fluid and changeable over time; recognizes sexuality as a layer of identity with socio-political power implications; rejects categories to make new power dynamics possible

tialist perspectives subscribe to the idea that people's sexuality and gender are innate parts of their being that are inherent (i.e., biologically determined) and universal (DeLamater & Hyde, 1998). In other words, biology—the sexual characteristics with which people are born—influences gender and sexuality (Heyman & Giles, 2006). Thus, essentialism rejects the idea of either gender or sexuality as stemming from psychological or social factors. Instead, essentialism asserts that both gender and sexuality are considered to be static traits with which individuals are born. This rigid understanding forces both gender and sexuality into binary categories: male or female, masculine or feminine, heterosexual or homosexual. Masculine and feminine identities are *normal* and any gender identity outside of these categories is considered *other* and at risk of being marginalized by society (Kumashiro, 2000). Moreover, essentialism asserts that masculine and feminine genders are inherently different based on intrinsic characteristics; the very nature—the *essence*—of what it means to be masculine is different than the very nature of what it means to be feminine.

For essentialists, sexuality is a core part of human nature. It is universal to everyone, genetically determined, and an essential part of the human life cycle (DeLamater & Hyde, 1998). Essentialists consider heterosexuality and homosexuality as natural states of desire created by combinations of hormones, genetics, and differences in brain composition; thus, individuals are born as either heterosexual or homosexual and both identities function to perpetuate and support human existence (DeLamater & Hyde, 1998; Heyman & Giles, 2006). Essentialism is, by far, the most conservative perspective on gender and sexuality; essentialism insists on the role of biological factors and, in doing so, it leaves little to no room for individual agency. Essentialism is explored in historical context in Chapter 2.

Modernism

Modernist perspectives embrace a less rigid relationship between biology and psychology and were the first to recognize how essentialist perspectives had used biology to determine different rights and affordances for men and women (Beasley, 2005). **Modernism** asserts that biological characteristics may differ from psychological characteristics and that both sexuality and gender consist of psychological factors—a key distinction in recognizing that biology does not automatically determine an individual's identity or capabilities. In other words, a person may have the biological sex of a man, but psychologically feel feminine or vice versa. Thus, a person's gender may differ from the sex assigned at birth.

The recognition of the discontinuity between biology and psychology opened the door for medical transformation (Lehmiller, 2014). Recall that transgender people may change their bodies to reflect their gender identity. This transition exemplifies the modernist perspective on gender; by changing their bodies, these individuals are able to embrace their true psychological identity and present a cohesive sense of self. Like essentialism, the modernist perspective views gender and sexuality as stable, but not congruous. Transgender individuals who opt to change their biological sex embrace a journey-like process, albeit an arduous one, where they reach their final destination (Lehmiller, 2014). For some transgender men and women, there is not a final destination and transitioning becomes a lifelong process. Though modernist perspectives embrace that individuals may change their assigned sex at birth to suit their psychological gender, they still insist on masculinity and femininity as distinct psychological characteristics.

Understandings of sexuality, on the other hand, expand beyond a dichotomous perspective. Modernist views of sexuality span a continuum that ranges from heterosexuality to homosexuality, including varying degrees of bisexuality as a component of sexual desire (Moe, Reicherzer, & Dupuy, 2011). By recognizing that psychological factors shaped sexual desire, modernist conceptions of sexuality were no longer stunted by connections to reproduction or evolutionary needs (Iasenza, 2010). How an individual thought and felt about desire and sex could evolve over time, establishing the power of individual agency in sexual attractions. Social constructionism and post-modernism/queer theory extend this foundation.

Social Constructionism

Social constructionism is a sociological theory of knowledge that explains "reality" as a function of jointly constructed understandings.

Social constructionists view the world as *created* through social interactions, not as *discovered* (see Schwandt, 2003). Instead of the rigid binary of essentialism's and modernism's belief in a "master plan" of gender and a continuum of sexual desire as innate, social constructionism asserts that gender and sexuality are socially created based on the actions and interactions of individuals in a particular context (Seidman, 2010). A person's understandings of history, cultural expectations, implicit and explicit societal traditions and rules all influence how one enacts gender and sexuality (Brickell, 2006; Lindsey, 2010). With this theoretical frame, gender and sexuality are mediated by societal pressures and cultural contexts instead of byproducts created through the biological or psychological domains. Understandings of femininity and masculinity, like understandings of heterosexuality, homosexuality, or bisexuality, are socially mediated (Parent, DeBlaere, & Moradi, 2013) and subject to pressures or norms. For example, as explained in more detail in Chapter 11, sexuality and gender expression can differ for many people when they are in jails and prisons (in comparison to their sexuality and gender expression when not incarcerated).

Social constructionism's dual emphasis on human agency and interactional context demonstrates the complex role of institutional policies, cultures, and stakeholders. The expression of gender and sexual identities is, in part, relational to the acceptance and expectations of social surroundings (Butler, 1993b). By prioritizing the role of context and social interactions, social constructionism highlights the prevalence of heteronormative contexts in institutions and cultures. **Heteronormativity** is the array of behaviors, interactions, and expectations that assume individuals are heterosexual and fit into traditional gender roles of masculine or feminine (Blackburn & Smith, 2010). If a context assumes and communicates expectations of traditional masculine or feminine gender and heterosexual identities,

individuals are more likely to work within those constraints—even if this is incongruent with their sense of self. In this sense, gender and sexual identity can function as an "obligatory masquerade" (Beasley, 2005, p. 24). If a particular social setting is open to non-traditional gender expression and diverse sexual identities, individuals may feel enabled to perform in non-traditional ways. In this way, social constructionism provides insight into implicit and explicit structural oppression that pushes individuals to fit into one box or the other (social constructionism is explored further in Chapter 2).

Queer Theory

Building on social constructionism's recognition that societal pressures and constructs influence how individuals present or perform gender, queer theory recognizes that gender and sexuality are two layers of identity that societies and institutions associate with power. **Queer theory** asserts that gender and sexual orientation are fluid aspects of identity that reject containment and consistencies (Giffney, 2009). Queer theory recognizes that identity is complex and changeable, and, as such, cannot be easily categorized. By rejecting categorization, queer theory also disrupts the social and cultural pressures for individuals to behave in particular ways. In this intentional disruption, queer theory challenges traditional political and social power dynamics. Queer theory dismantles categories of gender and sexual identity to reject symbols of power associated with these labels and make new power dynamics possible.

Gender and sexual orientation, like race/ethnicity, class, age, and geography, are individual layers that contribute to a person's identity. Each layer of identity, depending on the context, contributes to the level of power associated with that identity. Because society is structured as a series of hierarchies where power dynamics can be associated with a person's status and role, the same individual may be afforded different levels of power in different settings according to their relative position (Lindsey, 2010). Levels of power are constructed through socio-political actions over time. In terms of gender and sexuality, heterosexual men have been in positions of power long enough to establish a level of **hegemony**—a power structure in which positions have been used to oppress and limit options for women (regardless of sexuality) and all those whose sexuality, gender identity, and gender expression differ from heterosexual men. Although Western societies are shifting to more egalitarian perspectives (Lorber, 2013), gender and sexual orientation still play a role in defining power dynamics. As a theoretical perspective, queer theory rejects binary understandings of gender and sexuality as a means of disrupting hegemonic power structures. Extending the perspective of social constructionism, queer theory insists that gender and sexuality are fluid, multiple, and existing on a continuum for many people (Diamond & Butterworth, 2008). Queer theory's goal to reject labels and identities that have traditionally been used to exclude or limit the power of individuals who do not conform to gender or sexual norms creates an empowered space for individuals to embrace new identities (Beasley, 2005; Butler, 1993b). This perspective accepts that gender and sexuality can be embodied in multiple ways and change over time and that individuals can embody this fluidity as fits their personal and political identities. Gender and sexuality may interact to produce a variety of desires: the desire to embrace or reject particular power dynamics, the desire to embody or reject particular sexualities, the desire for congruence or incongruence with psychological feeling of gender and biological anatomy, or the desire to explore various masculine/feminine/heterosexual/homosexual/bisexual identities. Each of these possibilities reflects how queer theory asserts the dynamic and fluid nature of gender and sexuality.

Connecting the Pieces

Think back to the questions in the introduction to this section: How much power does an individual's biology exert on identity? To what degree do society and culture dictate behaviors or desires? How do either or both of these forces shape the levels of power individuals hold in particular contexts? Because sex, gender, and sexuality are complex concepts that shape our world, theoretical perspectives matter. According to the essentialists, identity is assigned at birth and the individual has minimal agency in this biological creation. According to modernists, a person's psychology may differ from a person's biological makeup—sexuality and gender are housed in the mind, not the body. According to social constructionists and queer theorists, gender and sexuality are created or selected according to individuals, interactions, contexts, and responses to power. Now consider these theories in relation to Title IX of the Educational Amendments of 1972 (Lopiano, 2000), which prohibits discrimination in education on the basis of sex and is credited with creating gender equality in women's athletics. When the law was enacted, essentialists and modernist perspectives defined gender and sexuality. The belief that women (regardless of sexual orientation) and non-heterosexual men were not capable or meant to participate in particular activities was prevalent. Today, social constructionism and queer theory complicate these views. Societal and cultural norms that categorize and limit the power and rights of individuals are questioned. As theoretical perspectives evolve, explicit and implicit societal and cultural norms shift and have real implications for the daily lives of individuals. How we understand sex, sexuality, and gender cannot be separated from how we understand the role of biology, psychology, or society and culture. Keep these theoretical perspectives in mind and refer to Tables 1.1 and 1.2 as you read the chapter.

EXPLORING SEX

As previously mentioned, the word *sex* elicits a range of meaning, contexts, and behaviors. These contexts range from the box to be checked on a survey that classifies individuals as male or female based on biological reproductive organs to the prominent presence of sex in television shows and movies to the impact of words through sexting and sexual images being Snapchatted every second across the country. The exploration and inundation of sex that has occurred in recent decades offers a more inclusive and broad definition of the behaviors associated with sex. Sex generates attention and evokes a range of emotion individually and collectively within cultures (Crooks & Baur, 2011).

Sexual interactions range in complexity and involvement from masturbation and "hook-up" culture—aided, in part, by apps such as Tinder and Grindr (Garcia et al., 2012)—to monogamous, committed sexual relationships between two people, and polyamorous relationships. People who identify as polyamorous engage in **polyamory**, which are sexually intimate relationships with more than one individual. This may be with people representing a range of gender or sexual identities, but is based upon commitment and trust (Crooks & Baur, 2011). Regardless of where on the spectrum of sexual activities and commitments a particular encounter or relationship falls, sexual acts do not merely occur. Rather, they are a result of several complex factors that include the social and cultural context in which we are immersed, genetics, historical perspectives, and our individual psychology.

Similar to gender and sexuality, sex is mediated by three influences: biological, psychological, and cultural/societal influences (Lehmiller, 2014; Richardson, Smith, & Werndly, 2013). These factors combine to strongly influence whether sex occurs or not and the varying purposes for and types of acts.

Sex and Biology

Biological and evolutionary influences related to sex may also be classified as the essentialist perspective. Essentialists believe that sex is a result of genetics, evolution, and biological factors. Research has linked the sex acts of humans to that of numerous animal species, which suggests very few of the sexual behaviors exhibited by humans are unique, ranging from homosexual acts to masturbation (Lehmiller, 2014). Hereditary factors have been suggested as being partly responsible for homosexuality (Dawood, Bailey, & Martin, 2009). The level of sex hormones present in the womb while a fetus is developing has been found to have impacts upon gender roles and identity (Beltz, Swanson, & Berenbaum, 2011). Garcia and colleagues (2010) found an association between the dopamine D4 receptor gene polymorphism (which is associated with risk-taking) and uncommitted sexual activity among both young men and young women.

Other examples of biological connections to sex and sexuality include studies conducted on finger length. Rahman and Wilson (2003) suggest that lesbians have ring fingers that are longer than their index finger, which is indicative of heterosexual males' finger patterns; further emphasizing the role of hormones and body chemistry.

Sex and Psychology

Attitudes, mood, and behaviors are just a few of the psychological influences that contribute to how and why we engage in sex. Some of these influences are static—such as personality traits—while others change often, such as moods. Consider the impact personality might have upon an individual's sexual exploration. Research suggests personality influences the type of sexual acts and frequency with which we engage (McCrae & Costa, 1987). An example of this is individuals with low conscientiousness tend to have higher levels of unprotected sex (Hoyle, Fejfar, & Miller, 2000). Markey & Markey (2007) found that extraverted individuals who display assertiveness and dominance have more sexual partners.

A person's mood and attitude towards sex directly impacts the frequency and interest in engaging in sex. If a person has a negative attitude or association towards sex, the likelihood of engaging in frequent sexual acts decreases. An example of this phenomenon might be someone who is stressed from work and has come home to a partner after a long work day. Such a person is less likely to want to engage in sex and will most likely experience lower levels of enjoyment (Lehmiller, 2014). Fisher et al. (1988) suggest through their research that individuals approach sex on a continuum ranging from *erotophilia*— or positively responding to sex, to *erotophobia*—negatively responding to sex. The implications of this continuum correspond to how likely someone is to enjoy sex and or engage in sexual activity.

Individuals who are predisposed to *sensation seek* tend to be more likely to pursue riskier sexual opportunities as a result of lower levels of dopamine being released in their brains. Dopamine is a brain chemical that appeals to our feel-good senses (Zuckerman, Eysenck, & Eysenck, 1978). Individuals who tend to sensation seek at high levels have more sexual partners than the average person and also engage in unprotected sex more often (Gullette & Lyons, 2005).

Sex and Society

Although psychological factors heavily influence the frequency and inhibitions attached to sex, societal influences regulate what is determined as the *norm* for a culture and how we as individuals engage in sex. Cultural and societal influences can be classified as social constructions. Society and culture develop normative behaviors and binaries that impact how concepts such as sex and sexuality are experienced and perceived. In the United States, norms have long focused on heterosexual, monogamous relationships (Beasley, 2005). For a long time, sex acts outside of heterosexual intercourse were viewed as taboo and abnormal because they counter what has been defined as "normal" (Crooks & Baur, 2011). But this sexual norm, like most other norms, varies across time, situation, and culture. Consider the Sambian tribe of New Guinea.

Sambian males engage in only male-to-male sexual acts from the ages of seven until their early twenties (Herdt, 1999). This comes from the cultural belief that males become great warriors and hunters through drinking as much semen from post-pubescent males as possible. Once a male has reached puberty, he no longer provides oral sex, but is the receiver of the fellatio until he is married. Upon being married to a female, the Sambian men generally engage in only heterosexual intimacy for the remainder of their lives (Herdt, 1999). The sexual practices of the Sambian people demonstrate the cultural and societal constructions of sex and sexuality when compared with United States norms.

One need not look, however, to the sexual practices of remote tribes to see how the sexual norms have changed in the United States since the Sexual Revolution of the 1960s and 1970s:

"Hookups," or uncommitted sexual encounters, are becoming progressively more engrained in popular culture, reflecting both evolved sexual predilections and changing social and sexual scripts. Hook-up activities may include a wide range of sexual behaviors, such as kissing, oral sex, and penetrative intercourse. However, these encounters often transpire without any promise of, or desire for, a more traditional romantic relationship. A review of the literature suggests that these encounters are becoming increasingly normative among adolescents and young adults in North America, representing a marked shift in openness and acceptance of uncommitted sex.

(Garcia et al., 2012, p. 161)

As the quote above suggests, changing sexual norms have not just affected the social acceptability of sex outside of monogamous relationships; the social acceptability of sex acts other than penis-in-vagina sexual intercourse—especially oral sex—has also increased (see Armstrong, England, & Fogarty, 2009; Reiber & Garcia, 2010). And, according to the National Survey of Sexual Health and Behavior (Herbenick et al., 2010), a much higher rate of both men and women have engaged in same-sex sexual behavior compared to those who identify as being gay or lesbian (see also Chandra et al., 2011).

Norms are developed within cultures based on religion, science, politics, law, and media (Seidman, 2010). With regard to sex, media of all forms—including magazines, blogs, television, music, social media applications, and more—have had a significant impact upon how sex and sexuality are defined. A study concerning sex on television found that media were cited as the primary basis for emerging adults' opinions about sex—a finding consistent with their content analysis result that 77% of prime-time television programs contained some sexual content (Kunkel et al., 2005). And, beyond mainstream media, pornography is more readily available now than ever before (see Chapter 8). As a result, people have access to explore a range of sexual interests via the privacy of their own home. The impact of more accessible pornography as an outlet to explore and understand sex and sexuality is still unclear; however, what is evident is that within each culture existing norms continue to remain, creating a divide between what is considered normal and what is considered deviant or abnormal (Richardson, Smith, & Werndly, 2013).

EXPLORING GENDER

Whether we like it or not, gender organizes our world (Lindsey, 2010; Parent, DeBlaere, & Moradi, 2013; Wharton, 2012). Enrollment forms, driver's licenses, and airline tickets give two boxes to select: male or female. Sports teams are divided by sex; college residence halls are often divided by sex, too. Yet, these divides presume segregation by sex constitutes segregation by gender when, in fact, it does not. Think of the image on countless bathroom doors: although the same round head with rounded hands and feet appears on both, one is depicted wearing a triangular skirt, the other is depicted wearing pants. Although this reference is far more historical than accurate, it symbolizes how quickly we associate behaviors and appearance with heteronormative gender identity. The process begins early in life when we often see gender stereotypes: toy aisles are filled with dolls and household appliances for girls and trucks and robots for boys. Even when marketers attempt cross-gender appeal, the distinction is made via color: pink and purple stethoscopes for girls; yellow and green for boys—occasionally, this stereotyping makes the news. In February 2014, a seven-year-old girl wrote a letter to the Lego Company requesting "more Lego girl people" who could "go on adventures and have fun" (Molloy, 2014, para. 10). The letter was picked up by social media and ignited a conversation about gender stereotypes, representation, and toys.

In both the child and adult domains, however, gender roles are frequently divided into two possibilities: one for men and boys and one for women and girls. What this division demonstrates is an inaccurate understanding of gender as associated with sexuality as well as the limited view that gender exists as a dichotomous, static state. Both understandings oversimplify gender and the role it plays in individual identity formation and societal constructs. The idea that sex is assigned at birth ("It's a boy!") means that an individual is supposed to identify as masculine or feminine from birth even though this approach reflects a narrow and inaccurate view of gender. Indeed, the assigned-at-birth binary ignores how gender develops and the role gender plays in the daily life of individuals.

Box 1.1 WHERE DO YOU GO IF YOU DON'T FIT EITHER CHOICE?

High-school bathrooms can be tense spaces for students of all genders, but a high school in Louisville, Kentucky, made bathroom access a controversial news topic when the school included gender identity in its nondiscrimination policy (Ross, 2014). By adding gender identity to the policy that already included race, ethnicity, disability, and sexual orientation, this school made school spaces, including bathrooms, a discrimination-free zone and gave transgender students the right to use whichever bathroom fit their self-identified gender. This school-based action sparked a flurry of legislation in Kentucky with a conservative senator drafting a bill that would limit transgender students' access to bathrooms and locker rooms across the state and making the previous high-school anti-discrimination action illegal. Although this bill died in the house, the debate garnered national attention (Kellaway, 2015). Although the policy change created conflict and tension for the school and school district, it mirrors a nationwide discussion about gender expression and access to public spaces (Knox, 2014).

As of 2015, this discussion is as far ranging as the American landscape. California, Texas, Missouri, Minnesota, and Florida have all debated whether or not individuals should be mandated to use bathrooms associated with their biology at birth (Kellaway, 2015). In 2014, California passed a bill enabling transgender students to use the bathroom of the gender they most identify with, but a year later the law is still being contested (Cadelago, 2015). News stories reporting this debate indicate that, from Utah to Maine to Texas, legislators, educators, and transgender students are mired in questions about biology, birth certificates, and gender identity (Knox, 2014). The debate has taken to Twitter with transgender individuals posting pictures under #WeJustNeedtoPee to show the jarring juxtaposition of someone who presents as one sex using the public facility designed for the opposite sex (Kellaway, 2015). Although some argue that separate bathrooms for transgender individuals would provide a safe space for these students, others assert that requiring transgender students to use a separate facility may make students more vulnerable as it calls attention to the difference in their gender. A significant number of LGBT students reported feeling unsafe in schools due to their gender expression and identified school bathrooms as the number one place of vulnerability (Kosciw et al., 2014).

- Should states legislate who uses what bathrooms?
- How would such legislation be enforced?
- Is forcing someone to use a certain bathroom a form of discrimination?
- What is the role of the state to protect children in public schools from discrimination?

Gender and Psychology

Modernist perspectives on gender bring a distinct separation between biological sex and psychological gender. People may be assigned one sex at birth but *feel* as if they belong to a different gender. This distinction is made clear in literature in novels like Virginia Woolf's *Orlando*, which explores a character that transitions between male and female form without a change in personality (Yazdani & Cheraghi, 2014). Modernist perspectives recognize the value in a person's psychological understanding of gender and embrace the idea that the body can be changed to better fit the mind (Beasley, 2005). A "master plan" of gender resides in a person's understanding of the self and identity and an individual should embrace this gender identity even when it does not fit with biological embodiment. Because the modernist perspective reflects the varying ways one can present psychological gender, this perspective embraces the idea of a range of masculine and feminine gender identities and rejects the idea that it is biologically determined. Shifting the focus of gender identity from the biological to the psychological has distinct significance for individuals who feel as if their bodies do not correspond to their gender. Individual agency plays a stronger role in modernism than the lack of role in essentialism, but the role is self-determined by the agency one takes over their physical presentation and body. Gender as a psychological concept is a defining feature of modernist perspectives, while still clinging to a binary understanding of masculinity and femininity.

Gender and Society

Gender functions as both a status and a role (Lindsey, 2010). As a status, gender influences how a person is perceived and treated by others. A person identifying as a man or a woman places himself or herself in a particular socio-demographic category that is frequently associated with specific power structures and relations. Feminist scholarship and activism have demonstrated how societal structures have historically limited the economic potential of women, their access to leadership roles, and their general underrepresentation in fields like science, medicine, and law (Beasley, 2005). Selecting or being placed in the category of man, on the other hand, historically places a person as a member of the dominant power structure (Lorber, 2013). As a role, gender reflects societal expectations in context. A person of

any status may function in varying roles depending on context. For example, a person identifying as a woman may function in the roles of mother, worker, and sister; in contrast, a person identifying as a man may function in the roles of father, worker, and brother. Each gender role reflects a unique set of societal expectations that pressure individuals to act within prescribed boundaries. In heteronormative contexts (contexts that assume individuals are attracted to the opposite sex and conform to traditional ideas of gender), gender status is frequently represented as a binary with categories like male and female or man and woman. This binary reflects the idea of gender as a label that limits a person's gender identity options to one of two possibilities. Gender roles, on the other hand, reflect the idea of gender as an experience that is learned through environment and socialization processes. These roles still tend to be defined as either masculine or feminine and may present dated perspectives that fail to reflect the changing nature of contemporary society. The idea that a woman should become a mother and run the household to ensure a nurturing environment for children represents a traditional understanding of gender roles.

Traditional southern culture where "gentlemen" are supposed to open doors for "ladies" is an example of such a marriage between context and expectations. This perspective embraces the notion of "doing" gender (Lindsey, 2010, p. 10), meaning an individual is not born with one gender or another, but instead learns to act in particular ways according to gender roles in different contexts. Butler (1993a) clarified that performing gender is not a voluntary choice that a person can change from day to day. Because of social pressures to conform and the prevalence of heteronormative contexts that assume individuals are heterosexuals fulfilling binary gender roles, these contexts create social constraints that pressure individuals to act in particular ways. Moreover, this traditional understanding appears to be quite outdated in an age in which many stay-at-home fathers serve as the primary care givers for children. As such, these social constraints operate to stifle gender expression and manipulate gender performance to reproduce socially accepted norms. An individual may perform femininity because the context requires/expects it even if that same person's sense of gender is more masculine. When the context dictates heteronormative interactions, gender performance is pressured to reflect these norms.

When understandings about gender and gender roles remain in a static binary, stereotypes are perpetuated and gender divisions produce structural power imbalances (Butler, 2004). Foucault (1979) established the tyranny of societal norms on human bodies—how we look, act, and interact—as a means of control (Richardson, Smith, & Werndly, 2013). The notion that men and women engage in different forms of work and have different responsibilities to families and society is an example of this. Gender statuses and roles that insist upon a dichotomous representation of what is woman/feminine and what is man/masculine reinforce hierarchies and gender inequality. Both research and societal understandings of gender have begun a shift towards more egalitarian and dynamic perspectives (Lindsey, 2010). Although essentialist and modernist theories of gender still subscribe to dichotomous understanding, theories of social constructionism, and queer theory provide frameworks for understanding gender as a more fluid and dynamic process. Because gender is a system that orders our world, labels individuals, and shapes power dynamics, shifts in our understanding of gender impact our understanding of the law and human societies.

In contrast to modernism's assertion that individuals can change their bodies to match their psychological gender, social constructionism recognizes that gender is produced and reproduced through individual, interactional, and societal understandings (Wharton, 2012). Rather than being a fixed concept, gender is fluid and potentially multiple. An individual may perform in a more feminine or masculine manner in one repressive/oppressive context and perform less so in another less oppressive setting. Social constructionism provides a kind of harbor for gender nonconforming individuals in that it recognizes gender as inherently unstable and existing on a continuum between masculine and feminine regardless of biological sex, but social constructionism also recognizes that human agency is contained, in part, by societal structures and norms.

Thinking about Gender

Because gender organizes our world, how we define gender and the theoretical perspective we embrace impacts our thinking about societal norms, behaviors, civil rights, protections, and institutions. Consider the bathroom symbol mentioned earlier. This omnipresent image can be defined in multiple ways even though its very presence assumes a binary that the essentialist perspective sees as assigned at birth. But according to modernists, a person's psychological gender can be identified and created. Moreover, according to social constructionists and queer theorists, gender is created or selected according to individuals, interactions, contexts, and responses to power. Definitions of gender determine access, funding, policy, and basic civil rights. In other words, definitions matter—and not just with regard to who uses which bathroom.

EXPLORING SEXUALITY

The relationship between sexuality and gender is elusive and complex. Although stereotypes exist that connect gender identities to straight, gay, and lesbian sexuality, the relationship between gender identity and desire

Box 1.2 SISTERHOOD TO SIBLINGHOOD: THE TRANSGENDER STUDENTS OF WELLESLEY

Wellesley College was founded in 1870, "To provide an excellent liberal arts education for women who will make a difference in the world" (Wellesley College, 2015, para. 1). Wellesley is one of about 50 women's colleges remaining from the nearly 300 that existed (Padawer, 2014). Women's colleges laud the opportunities for women to engage in leadership positions, be mentored by strong women professors and administrators, and pursue careers in fields largely dominated by men. Sisterhood, a concept that celebrates being a woman and being surrounded by women is an integral part of most women's colleges and a factor students often acknowledge as to why they select an all-female institution. Wellesley College is just one institution that has begun considering what it means to be a women's college as multiple sexual and gender identities are present on campus. It is approximated that a half dozen transgender students are enrolled at Wellesley (Padawer, 2014). Transgender students are challenging the current culture of Wellesley in numerous ways, such as pushing for gender-neutral language in university documents and assuming prominent leadership roles in student government and as resident assistants.

Women's colleges have approached inclusiveness of transgender students differently and with varying levels of acceptance. Mills College and Mount Holyoke College openly accept and support students who identify as women before applying or after admittance. Other schools, such as Hollins University, have drafted policies to assist students transitioning to find another institution because only those who present as female receive degrees from Hollins. Still other institutions have found a middle-of-the-road policy that requires only women be accepted to the institution and then places ownership on the students to navigate their identity within the university's culture.

Transgender students at Wellesley have been pushing for changing sisterhood to siblinghood a term that is considered more inclusive of all students enrolled. Although Wellesley may have been far ahead of many co-educational institutions in regards to ensuring unisex bathrooms are present in each academic building, most transgender students acknowledged feeling invisible in regard to campus care and support (Padawer, 2014). This invisibility came as a result of not acknowledging the presence of transgender students on campus. In 2015, however, Wellesley addressed many of these concerns and began admitting both cisgender and transgender women. Of course, the degree to which the larger campus community celebrates the full range of gender diversity remains a work in progress. But there can be little doubt that Wellesley is well ahead of most other U.S. colleges and universities in this regard.

- How do women's colleges honor traditions and the mission of serving women, but also maintain an inclusive spirit for transgender students?
- How do the experiences and rights of lesbian, gay, and bisexual students differ from those of transgender students?
- In what ways do private institutions such as Wellesley College and public co-ed institutions differ in regard to the way that they support transgender students?

cannot be reduced to such terms (Butler, 1993b). Sexuality, like gender, exists on a fluid continuum that reflects a range of behaviors, emotions, fantasies, and desires. Further, sex is considered a process to be studied as well as an identity produced through cultural production, simultaneously placing it in two distinct but equally complicated categories. Understanding the process of sex and enactment of sexual desire is not the same as understanding society's shifting views on the topic. The first is the domain of individuals engaged in intimate acts while the second reflects the interaction between individuals and cultural collectives. Because of this complexity, research on sexuality synthesizes multiple disciplines ranging from biology and sociology to history and psychology.

Heterosexual identities are defined as normal and therefore supported by government, policies, and laws. Normalcy is legitimized by the theories that men and women fit together naturally through physical and emotional connection, are able to reproduce, and ultimately contribute to the continuation of the human race (Seidman, 2010). We live in a society that functions on categorization and norms in regard to sexual identity. Sexual orientation is not easily defined and despite an individual's sexual orientation being composed of behavior, identity, romantic, and sexual desire (Lehmiller, 2014), often only singular elements of these categories are examined to better understand an individual's sexuality. This singular exploration skews understanding and limits the emergence and nuanced difference that exists among each individual.

Nonnormative Sexualities

The prevalence of lesbian and gay men in the United States has long been based on Alfred Kinsey's research and data that suggested 4% of men and 2% of women were homosexual in the United States (Kinsey, Pomeroy, & Martin, 1948). These data are dated and have been criticized for the collection methods (Crooks & Baur, 2011). The Williams Institute of Law at UCLA (Gates, 2011) endeavored to provide a more accurate representation as to the number of people identifying as lesbian, gay, bisexual, and transgender (LGBT) in the United States. Using multiple data sources from a variety of studies and from the U.S. Census, the Williams Institute (Gates, 2011) reported that:

- 1,359,801 (1.1%) of women self-identify as lesbian.

- 2,648,033 (2.2%) of women self-identify as bisexual.
- 2,491,034 (2.2%) of men self-identify as gay.
- 1,539,946 (1.4%) of men self-identify as bisexual.
- 697,529 (0.3%) of people self-identify as transgender.

It is important to note that these data only captured individuals who self-identify; they do not include individuals who engage in sexual activity with members of the same sex, but do not self-identify as being gay, lesbian, or bisexual.

Before 1970, bisexuality was not viewed as a sexual identity and was not supported by any formal organization. Seidman (2010) suggests three events that influenced bisexuality being recognized as an identity: support of bisexuality and the removal of sexuality and gender labels grounded in societal norms; the Sexual Freedom League and San Francisco Sex Information organizations promoted fluidity in sexuality and specifically encouraged bisexuality; and bisexuality was represented as an ideal by the lesbian and gay liberationists. These organizations believed bisexuality was viewed as an honored group of people who represented breaking free from binaries and categories. Despite being viewed in this way, identifying as bisexual was difficult due to the lack of understanding by most populations of people. While the lesbian and gay movement was pushing for being *out and proud*, bisexual individuals were exploring and developing a platform to promote. This created tension between the groups and assumptions that bisexual individuals have the luxury of sharing or hiding their identities. It was in the 1980s and 1990s when bisexual identities began to be recognized and bisexual organizations emerged, such as BiNet USA, which builds and supports bisexual communities, promotes visibility, and advocates and educates about bisexual identities. The bisexual community remains divided about the scope of the current movement. This divide exists among some bisexual individuals who want bisexuality to be recognized as a third category to be paired with heterosexuality and homosexuality. Other advocates feel this is not enough and seek to remove all categorization of sexuality and gender (Seidman, 2010). Despite many people experiencing a range or continuum of attraction, most people who find some attraction to the same sex do not identify as bisexual (Fairyington, 2008). The bisexual identity is not always evident, as people may assume an individual's sexual identity is based on the sex of the person the individual is currently in a relationship with, not considering or questioning if the individual may have a range of attraction (Plato, 2008).

The majority of research has approached exploring asexuality singularly as a behavior, lacking sexual acts or as desire, lacking desire for sexual acts (Scherrer, 2008). It is impor-tant to seek understanding of how desire and behavior are interrelated to better understand the decisions made between sexual and non-sexual that form the asexual identity. There is also a distinction between sex and romance within asexuality, which is counter to heterosexual norms that use the two terms interchangeably. Sex and romance may be independently interpreted by individuals identifying as asexual. Table 1.2 provides terminology and identifications for asexual people. These terms underscore that asexuality is a complex and individualized identity.

Sexuality and Psychology

Exploring and understanding theory is important because it challenges us to "radically question our understanding of sexuality, and hence enhance our ability to investigate critically popular culture in all of its forms" (Richardson, Smith, & Werndly, 2013, p. 19).

Table 1.2 Asexual identifications

Sex	**Sex-Positive:** Endorse sex as positive and may exhibit intellectual interest, but with no desire to engage in sex	**Asexual:** Does not experience sexual attraction
	Sex-Neutral: Uninterested in sex	**Demisexual:** Only experiences sexual attraction after a strong emotional bond exists
	Sex-Averse and Anti-Sex: A range of emotions and reactions from mild discomfort to severe disgust and distressing	**Greysexual:** Only occasionally experiences sexual attraction
Romance	**Aromantic:** No romantic attraction and no desire to pursue romantic relationships	**Heteromantic:** Romantically attracted to a different sex and/or gender
	Romantic: A romantic attraction to another person and interest in intimacy that does not include sexual relationships, but instead focuses on being close with another person	**Homoromantic:** Romantically attracted to the same sex and/or gender
		Biromantic: Romantically attracted to more than one sex and/or gender
		Panromantic: Romantically attracted to people regardless of sex or gender

Source: Carrigan (2011).

One of the earliest psychological theories developed to explore and explain sexual identity was a result of the works of Sigmund Freud (1905/2000). Freud believed an inborn, unconscious region of the mind called the id constantly sought to satisfy basic desires or impulses. The Id operates on the pleasure principle without regard to what is possible (which is the realm of reality, regulated by the ego) or what is proper (the constraints on activity imposed by the superego, the portion of the mind that develops over time akin to what may be thought of, for the sake of simplicity, as one's conscience).

Freud conceptualized five psychosexual stages of development: oral, anal, phallic, latent, and genital. As a child progresses through each stage, he or she must resolve specific developmental tasks in which id impulses must learn to be controlled with regard to what ego perceives as realistically possible, and what superego perceives is proper. According to Freud, how a child resolves particular tasks across the psychosexual stages of development impacts each person for life. For example, a child who is weaned too early from breastfeeding may develop orally fixated habits such as nail biting or overeating. Freud (1905/2000) suggests that in the phallic stage, the role of the mother and father has direct impact on the sexual development of the child. If the child becomes fixated due to an inability to identify with a rival parent, Freud believed the result could be homosexuality. Table 1.3 provides an overview of the model.

This progression offered insights as to how an individual may be categorized as heterosexual, bisexual, or homosexual. Freud posited that we are all polymorphously perverse; in other words, humans can derive sexual pleasure from most things. He drew upon the idea that sexual pleasure is inherently linked to sexual attraction. If humans are capable of deriving pleasure from almost anything, then Freud suggests that everyone is bisexual, finding attraction for men or women. Freud believed that individuals who progressed normally through the stages of psychosexual development became heterosexual. In contrast, homosexuality resulted from fixation on particular phases within the model, including distressing heterosexual experiences (Lehmiller, 2014).

Although Freud paved the way towards viewing sexuality on a continuum, few of his theories were grounded in empirical research. Studies by others failed to support his findings (Bell, Weinberg, & Hammersmith, 1981; Epstein, 2006). Bell and colleagues (1981)

Table 1.3 A summary of Freud's psychosexual stages of development

Stages	Erogenous Area	Developments	Adult Fixation
Oral (0–1 years)	The mouth – sucking or swallowing	Weaning off of breast or pacifier	Smoking, overeating, nail biting, habits using the mouth
Anal (1–3 years)	The anus – withholding or expelling feces	Toilet training	Orderliness or messiness
Phallic (3–6 years)	The penis or clitoris – Masturbation	Resolving Oedipus or Electra complex	Deviancy or sexual dysfunction
Latent (6–12 years)	Minimal or no sexual motivation	Developing defense mechanisms	Nothing
Genital (12–death)	The penis or vagina – Sexual intercourse	Sexual maturation	Sexually matured and healthy if all stages were met

presented a large body of work on sexual identity through their research involving a sample of 979 lesbian and gay identifying participants, as well as using a control group of 477 heterosexual participants. Their data suggest that Freud's psychosocial theory was incorrect insofar as it posited that unhealthy relationships with one's mother or father cause homosexuality. Bell and colleagues (1981) also debunked the seduction and contagion myths. The seduction myth posited that gay men and lesbians were able to seduce heterosexual individuals into becoming gay. The contagion myth hypothesized that an individual might become gay if he or she spent time with someone who identified as gay. Bell and colleagues (1981) were also able to dispel the theory that gay and lesbian identities were a result of having negative experiences in heterosexual relationships.

The biological-essentialist perspective recognizes that sexual desire and sexual drive are naturally occurring phenomena that have biological beginnings and places same-sex desire on the same footing as other-sex desire (Moe, Reicherzer, & Dupuy, 2011). Biological-essentialist perspectives believe that both biology and genetic combinations play a role in determining sexuality and assert that homosexuality is just as "natural" and normal as heterosexuality. Understanding both forms of sexuality as part of a natural order counters the idea that sexuality is environment driven and thus easily changed, but insists on a dichotomous understanding of sexuality as being one or the other: heterosexual or homo-sexual, without accounting for bisexuality or shifting sexual desires. Freud expressed the idea of bisexuality as an inherent part of sexual desire (Freud, 2000). This tenet was further established by the work of Kinsey and his colleagues (Kinsey, Pomeroy, & Martin, 1948) who established the prevalence of bisexuality (Iasenza, 2010). Ideas about sex are imparted to us through parents and family, religion, education, and numerous other sources. Each of these sources delivers a viewpoint that is grounded in the concept that sex is naturally inherited; we are sexual beings wired to engage in sexual acts just as we require the basics of eating, drinking, and sleeping (Seidman, 2010).

Although many people categorize sexual orientation into heterosexual, homosexual, or bisexual identities, Alfred Kinsey suggested that viewing sexuality via a continuum allows individuals to consider their sexuality in the fluid state it exists (Kinsey, Pomeroy, & Martin, 1948). The Kinsey Sexual Orientation Rating Scale acknowledges that sexual identity may change over time and that an individual may vary between homosexuality and heterosexuality throughout a lifetime. The Kinsey Scale laid the foundation for recognizing sexual orientations that are not static in nature, but complex and evolving. Kinsey's seven-point scale (Table 1.4) attempted to capture the continuum of sexuality by classifying individuals as ranging from exclusively heterosexual to exclusively homosexual. This work established that most individuals had the capacity for a range of sexual desire or

Table 1.4 Kinsey's sexual-orientation rating scale

(0) Exclusively heterosexual	(1) Mostly heterosexual/ incidentally homosexual	(2) Mostly heterosexual with significant homosexual experience	(3) Equally heterosexual and homosexual	(4) Mostly homosexual with significant heterosexual experience	(5) Mostly homosexual incidentally heterosexual	(6) Exclusively homosexual

sexual fluidity. Sexual fluidity provides space for sexual exploration. Although heterosexual individuals may feel attraction or engage in sexual activity ranging from mutual masturbation to intercourse with a same-sex sexual partner, they may not identify as bisexual. Therapists frequently communicate this potential to their clients in order to deconstruct the "loaded" (Iasenza, 2010, p. 292) nature of sexuality and create an open space where individuals can embrace making sense of themselves and their desires.

Sexuality and Society

Historical examinations of human sexuality have consistently documented the same-sex and other-sex desires of men and women for centuries, although the modern definition of homosexuality did not take root until the nineteenth century (Seidman, 2010). Understandings of sex, however, have always been "fundamentally social" (Seidman, 2010, p. 38) with societal constructs defining behaviors and desires as either acceptable or illicit. In this way, *how* sexuality is defined—as well as who defines it—reflects the production and reproduction of power dynamics as relative to societal norms. Foucault (1979) asserted that societal controls on sex, like societal controls on gender expression, enabled the management of populations and acted as a form of political and moral control (Richardson, Smith, & Werndly, 2013). Thus, perspectives on sexuality, like perspectives on gender, reflect a range from conservative essentialist viewpoints to liberal social construction and queer theory with expanding understandings of the fluid nature of sexuality emerging in the most recent research.

Chapter 2 will explore in more detail how sexuality was viewed, expressed, and changed over time rather dramatically. Consider that sexual relations between adult males and pubescent, adolescent boys were sanctioned in Ancient Greece and other societies that practiced pederasty, although prevailing gender roles at the time dictated that the older male take the active role and the younger male assume the passive role; today, however, such acts would constitute statutory rape (see Chapters 2 and 6). This is just one example (Chapter 2 presents additional examples in historical context) that illustrates how sexual acts come to be categorized as good and bad, leading to the creation of sexual norms. But *homosexuality* as an *identity* flowing from particular sexual acts performed within someone of the same sex is a relatively recent concept that has been created by Western thought between the 1860 and early 1900s (Foucault, 1979; Somerville, 1994), largely due to the work of the so-called early sexologists (see Chapter 2). Beyond becoming a distinct identity, homosexuality came to be viewed as a deviant and contagious disease between the 1930s and 1970s—yet another change that illustrates how views about human sexuality are socially constructed (Tierney & Dilley, 1998). Jump ahead to the present day and contemporary views on homosexuality differ significantly from the dominant ones over the past 150 years.

Starting in 1969, the modern gay rights movement (see D'Emilio, 1992) ushered in an era that undergirded research studies examining gay and lesbian identities and experiences (Renn, 2010). The 1970s opened the proverbial closet for lesbian and gay identities and acknowledged existing homophobia and discrimination. Indeed, the *identity perspective* (Tajfel, 1974), which is a sociological approach used to understand an individual's experience as a member of a marginalized group, emerged in the 1970s as people began to embrace the recognition of same-sex desire as part of an awakening of the self. This perspective was established as lesbian and gay communities formed to celebrate their shared identities and the public naming of their sexuality as a rejection of heterosexual culture and constraints.

The identity perspective grew and strengthened during the 1980s and 1990s, spurred, in large part, by AIDS awareness and political advocacy surrounding AIDS (Shilts, 2007). The AIDS epidemic was significant in building resilience for and support of "the gay community" (Herek & Greene, 1995). But it is important to contextualize that what appears to be, at least in hindsight, a period of great progress for gays and lesbians was, in fact, interjected with resistance. The strides made were a result of significant aggressions toward the gay community in the 1980s. Consider, for example, that in 1990, the Ryan White Care Act was enacted by Congress. It created a federally funded program for people living with AIDS (Eaklor, 2008; Kaiser, 2007). Although this program raised attention and support for AIDS patients, it failed to acknowledge or represent the gay community who fought for the better part of decade and lost nearly a 100,000 people to the disease. America was not ready to help gays living with AIDS; however, it was politically palatable to enact a law bearing the name of a teenager with hemophilia who was accidentally exposed to the virus through a blood transfusion.

The 1990s challenged heteronormativity through the emergence of queer theory (Alexander & Gibson, 2004). By the 2000s, more gays and lesbians held political offices, and both municipalities and Fortune 500 companies instituted anti-discrimination policies. And, as Chapter 9 will explore in greater detail, by the mid-2010s, marriage equality became the norm in much of the United States. This transformation ignited a backlash in some states as evidenced by the enactment of laws (reminiscent of Jim Crow laws) discriminating against LGBTQ people through refusal of service based on religious freedom (Walters, 2014). Walters discusses the progress of queer freedom in 2014, "The Progress Narrative, then, depends on a very gaudy pair of rose-colored glasses, through which continuing discrimination and inequity are either ignored or seen as remnants of a past we are about to put behind us" (p. B7).

These historical perspectives inform the current context of lesbian and gay identity.

A Return to the LGBTQIA Acronym

Consider the impact of queer theory and the larger gay rights movement through the lens of social constructionism. Similar to its understanding of gender as created through social action and interaction, social constructionism argues that sexuality is developed as individuals make meaning of their social and cultural worlds (Moe, Reicherzer, & Dupuy, 2011). Rather than subscribing to individuals identifying with a singular space on the continuum between heterosexuality and homosexuality, social constructionism acknowledges that an individual may occupy multiple spaces on that continuum depending on the meaning made in a particular context. LGBTQIA identities help to validate the struggle against being labeled in a way that does not acknowledge the continuum or fluidity along it—especially in the face of seemingly omnipresent contexts and entities that pressure all members of society to behave in heteronormative ways. Such pressure acts to marginalize same-sex desire through shaming and taboos (Butler, 1993b), while gay-, lesbian-, and bisexual-friendly contexts enable safe spaces for same-sex desires.

Critics of social constructionism fear that embracing the fluidity and mutability of sexual desire may lead to an abuse of power by heteronormative authorities and institutions that believe that re-socialization programs will change lesbian women and gay men to heterosexual women and men (see the "Law in Action" feature in Chapter 2). Despite the very real potential for this abuse, social constructionism embraces the idea that individuals can contain multiple types of desire that include—but may expand beyond—the labels of lesbian, gay, or bisexual.

In summary, sexual *desire* became sexual *identity*. Part of this transformation resulted from people with nonnormative sexuality

Law in Action *STATE V. RAVI* (2012)

On September 22, 2011 Tyler Clementi, a freshman at Rutgers University, committed suicide after his roommate, 18-year-old Dharun Ravi, secretly filmed and broadcasted Tyler having a sexual encounter with a man. Three days prior to his suicide Tyler asked Dharun to use their room for the evening in privacy. Dharun agreed, but left the webcam of his computer on as he went to a friend's room to watch a live stream of Tyler engaging in sexual relations with another man. Dharun proceeded to post the following to 150 followers on his Twitter account: "Roommate asked for the room till midnight. I went into Molly's room and turned on my webcam. I saw him making out with a dude. Yay" (Foderaro, 2010, p. A1). On September 21, Tyler read the Twitter post and discussed the situation with his resident assistant and two other university officials, ultimately requesting a room change. The same day, Dharun attempted to film his roommate again and informed friends in the campus community through texts and another Twitter post "daring" others to join the iChat session he had set up for the evening (Foderaro, 2010, p. A1). Tyler became aware of the tweet and unplugged the camera and the computer to prevent another recording from taking place. The next day, Tyler posted his plan to commit suicide and took his life by jumping off of the George Washington Bridge into the Hudson River. Dharun sent two apology emails within 15 minutes of the time Tyler posted his intention to commit suicide on Facebook. Dharun acknowledged guilt and his reasons for filming the first night; in the second email he explained he was not biased against gay people.

Dharun was found guilty of invasion of privacy, hindering apprehension, witness tampering, and biased intimidation pertaining to the second attempt to record his roommate. A jury found that Dharun did not act with a purpose to intimidate Tyler or his guest based on their sexual orientation.

- What role did sexuality have in this crime?
- Based on this case, is sexual fluidity a concept embraced or accepted in the United States?
- How does this case connect to the understanding of various sexual identities?

pushing a firm rejection of heterosexuality as the dominant culture, which, in turn, reshaped societal perspectives on sexual desire and acceptance (Moe, Reicherzer, & Dupuy, 2011; Woolfe, 2013). Adherence to labels as either lesbian or gay began as claiming of space and location on the continuum of sexuality with lesbians being women who desired women and gays being men who desired men. This mandate of identifying as either homosexual or heterosexual initially left no room for bisexual or transgender individuals and was critiqued by many for adherence to such strict naming of sexuality and gender (Butler, 2004; Diamond & Butterworth, 2008). Over time, the identity movement has become more inclusive—expanding from lesbian and gay identities to the LGBTQIA identities explained early in this chapter. As the acronym expanded, aspects of gender identity became conflated with sexual orientation. Transgender individuals, for example, may be attracted to same- or other-presenting genders, or both, a fact that emphasizes the fluidity of the sexual continuum (Parent, DeBlaere, & Moradi, 2013). Queer often refers to individuals who reject the categorization offered by the other options. Transgender and queer communities have advocated for terms like pansexual to capture the mutable and individual nature of sexual attraction (Diamond & Butterworth, 2008). In this sense, the evolution of the identity perspective has developed beyond requiring homosexual individuals to claim a space on the sexuality continuum as a stance against heteronormative dominance to include an understanding of sexuality as developing and changing over time.

CONCLUSION

As discussed in this chapter, the word *sex* elicits a range of meaning, contexts, and behaviors. These contexts range from the box to be checked on a survey that classifies individuals as male or female based on biological reproductive organs to the prominent presence of sex in television shows and movies to the impact of words through sexting and sexual images being Snapchatted every second across the country. The exploration and inundation of sex that has occurred in recent decades offers a more inclusive and broad definition of the behaviors associated with sex. Sex generates attention and evokes a range of emotion individually and collectively within cultures (Crooks & Baur, 2011).

The evolution of understanding sexual desire, sexual behaviors, and sexual identities continues to grow. It clearly has been established that desire falls along a continuum that changes and morphs over time and with experience. This transformation is shaped by biology, psychology, and society. Sexual identity begins to outline the possibilities of these desires but these identities fail to capture the nuances and complexities of which we are capable. Sexual practices, however, are not so easily labeled for they run the gamut of human desire.

Societal expectations regarding sex, gender, and sexuality are diverse. Moreover, these expectations pressure—and sometimes even demand—that people control aspects of emotional, physical, and relational sexuality within the constraints of social norms. Such norms are constructed through a belief system that is widely shared by many people in society. Some of these beliefs are embodied in laws that set forth formal expectations concerning expected behavior with regard to sex, sexuality, gender, and sexual identity. The remaining chapters in this book explore a wide variety of topics that lie at the intersection of law, sex, gender, and sexuality. As you read this book, keep in mind the theories presented in this chapter—especially those like social constructionism that suggest the validity of the assertions in any chapter of this book are not only subject to debate, but also are likely to change over time.

FURTHER READING

Bolin, A., & Whelehan, P. (2009). *Human sexuality: Biological, psychological, and cultural perspectives.* New York, NY: Routledge.

Clendinen, D., & Nagourney, A. (1999). *Out for good: The struggle to build a gay rights movement in America.* New York, NY: Touchstone.

Dabhoiwala, F. (2012). *The origins of sex.* New York, NY: Oxford University Press.

Diamond, L. (2008). *Sexual fluidity: Understanding women's love and desire.* Cambridge, MA: Harvard University Press.

Ferber, A., Halcomb, K., & Wentling, T. (2012). *Sex, gender, and sexuality: The new basics.* New York, NY: Oxford University Press.

Lehmiller, J. J. (2014). *The psychology of human sexuality.* Malden, MA: John Wiley & Sons.

Richardson, N., Smith, C., & Werndly, A. (2013). *Studying sexualities: Theories, representations, cultures.* New York, NY: Palgrave Macmillan.

Rosenthal, M. S. (2013). *Human sexuality: From cells to society.* Belmont, CA: Wadsworth/Cengage.

Ross, K. (Ed.). (2012). *The handbook of gender, sex, and media.* Malden, MA: Wiley-Blackwell.

Rudacille, D. (2006). *The riddle of gender.* New York, NY: Anchor Books.

Seidman, S. (2009). *The social construction of sexuality* (2nd ed.). New York, NY: Norton.

Stein, M. (2012). *Rethinking the gay and lesbian movement.* New York, NY: Routledge.

Stombler, M., Baunach, D. M., Simons, W., Windsor, E. J., & Burgess, E. O. (2013). *Sex matters: The sexuality and society reader* (4th ed.). New York: NY: Norton.

Taylor, J. K., & Haider-Markel, D. P. (2014). *Transgender rights and politics: Groups, issue framing, and policy adoption.* Ann Arbor, MI: University of Michigan Press.

Toulalan, S., & Fisher, K. (Eds.). (2013). *The Routledge history of sex and the body: 1500 to the present.* New York, NY: Routledge.

GLOSSARY

Androgyny: Combination of masculine and feminine presentation, or gender presentation that shifts according to context and desire.

Asexuality: Someone who does not experience sexual attraction.

Bisexuality: Sexual attraction not exclusive to the same or different sex.

Cisgender: Describes people who identify and express as the same gender they were assigned at birth based on their perceived biological sex.

Cross-dresser: Describes an individual who wears clothes that are not traditionally assigned to their gender.

Gay: Describes an individual who is attracted only to members of the same sex.

Gender: A socially constructed category that reflects a set of behaviors, markers, and expectations associated with a person's biological sex and social norms concerning masculinity and feminity.

Gender nonconforming: Describes an individual who may not identify as transgender or gender queer, but whose gender expression resists traditional gendered behaviors and intentionally rejects binaries by refusing to present traditional gender norms.

Gender queer: Used by individuals who reject categories of gender altogether and wish to claim a space outside the traditional gender binary.

Gender questioning: Refers to individuals who are in the process of exploring various gender identities.

Gender roles: The behavioral, economic, and social roles that every society deems appropriate for members depending on their sex.

Hegemony: A power structure in which positions have been used to oppress and limit options for women (regardless of sexuality) and all those whose sexuality, gender identity, and gender expression differ from heterosexual men.

Heteronormativity: The array of behaviors, interactions, and expectations that assume individuals are heterosexual and fit into traditional gender roles of masculine or feminine.

Homosexuality: A broad category used to describe individuals who are sexually attracted to only others of the same sex.

Intersexed: A term referring to "medical conditions in which the development of chromosomal, gonadal, or anatomic sex varies from normal and may be incongruent with each other" and, therefore, who do not fit the usual definitions of male or female.

Lesbian: Describes women who are attracted only to other women.

Pansexual: Describes an individual who is attracted to all genders and sexes.

Polyamory: Sexually intimate relationships with more than one individual.

Sex: (1) Biological characteristics (i.e., chromosomes, gonads, reproductive organs, external genitalia); (2) the act or process through which we express desire or release sexual tension.

Sexual fluidity: The notion that sexuality, like gender, exists on a fluid continuum that reflects a range of behaviors, emotions, fantasies, and desires.

Sexuality: The sexual and romantic emotions, desires, attractions, behaviors, and identities that each person possesses.

Trans*: Sometimes used to represent the numerous identities that fit under the umbrella of being transgender. Trans* as a term does not stand alone, but may be used to describe a transgender individual or identity.

Transexual: A term that has been used to describe individuals who have changed their bodies to reflect a gender identity that is different from what they were assigned at birth.

Transgender: A broad term used to refer to anyone who does not identify with or express gender norms that fit into traditional gender roles, expectations, and presentations.

NOTE

1 *Transsexual* originated as a medical term used in psychiatric diagnosis; later the term was spelled *transexual* as an act of reclamation and separation from the medical connotation (Rodriguez, 2015).

REFERENCES

Adler, P. A., Kless, S. J., & Adler, P. (1992). Socialization to gender roles: Popularity among elementary school boys and girls. *Sociology of Education, 65*(3), 169–187.

Alexander, J., & Gibson, M. (2004). Queer composition(s): Queer theory in the writing classroom. *JAC, 24,* 1–21.

Allen, L. (2009). Disorders of sexual development. *Obstetrics and Gynecology Clinics of North America, 36*(1), 25–45. doi:10.1016/j.ogc.2009.02.001

American Psychiatric Association. (2013). *Diagnostic and statistical manual of mental disorders, fifth edition*

(*DSM-5*). Washington, DC: American Psychiatric Association.

Anderson J. E., & Dunning D. (2014). Behavioral norms: Variants and their identification. *Social and Personality Psychology Compass*, 8, 721–738.

Armstrong, E. A., England, P., & Fogarty, A. C. K. (2009). Orgasm in college hookups and relationships. In B. J. Risman (Ed.), *Families as they really are* (pp. 362–377). New York, NY: Norton.

Asexuality Visibility and Education Network (2014, December 22). *Asexuality overview*. Retrieved from: http://www.asexuality.org/home/?q=overview.html

Beasley, C. (2005). *Gender and sexuality: Critical theories, critical thinkers*. Thousand Oaks, CA: Sage Publications.

Bell, A., Wienberg, M., & Hammersmith, S. (1981). *Sexual preference: Its development in men and women*. New York, NY: Simon & Schuster.

Beltz, A. M., Swanson, J. L., & Berenbaum, S. A. (2011). Gendered occupational interests: Prenatal androgen effects on psychological orientation to things versus people. *Hormones and Behavior*, 60, 313–317.

Blackburn, M., & Smith, J. (2010). Moving beyond the inclusion of LGBT-themed literature in English language arts classrooms: Interrogating heteronormativity and exploring intersectionality. *Journal of Adolescent & Adult Literacy*, 53(8), 625–634.

Bogaert, A. F. (2006). Toward a conceptual understanding of asexuality. *Review of General Psychology*, 10(3), 241–250.

Brickell, C. (2006). The sociological construction of gender and sexuality. *The Sociological Review*, 54(1), 87–113.

Butler, J. (1993a). *Bodies that matter: On the discursive limits of "sex."* London: Routledge.

Butler, J. (1993b). Critically queer. *GLQ: A Journal of Gay and Lesbian Studies*, 1(1), 17–32.

Butler, J. (1999). *Gender trouble*, London: Routledge.

Butler, J. (2004). *Undoing gender*. New York, NY: Routledge.

Cadelago, C. (2015, April 20). California transgender bill spurs initiative for "bathroom privacy." *The Sacramento Bee*. Retrieved from http://www.sacbee.com/news/politics-government/capitol-alert/article19064163.html

Carrigan, M. (2011). There's more to life than sex? Difference and commonality within the asexual community, *Sexualities*, 14(4), 462–478.

Chandra, A., Mosher, W. D., Copen, C., & Sionean, C. (2011). *Sexual behavior, sexual attraction, and sexual identity in the United States: Data from the 2006–2008 National Survey of Family Growth*. National Health Statistics Reports, No. 36. Hyattsville, MD: National Center for Health Statistics.

Chivers, M. L., & Bailey, J. M. (2000). Sexual orientation of female-to-male transsexuals: A comparison of homosexual and nonhomosexual types. *Archives of Sexual Behavior*, 29(3), 259–278.

Colapinto, J. (2000). *As nature made him: The boy who was raised as a girl*. New York, NY: HarperCollins.

Crooks, R., & Baur, K. (2011). *Our sexuality* (11th ed.). Belmont, CA: Wadsworth.

Dawood, K., Bailey, J. M., & Martin, N. G. (2009). Genetic and environmental influences on sexual orientation. In Y. Kim (Ed.), *Handbook of behavioral genetics* (pp. 269–280). New York, NY: Springer.

DeLamater, J. D., & Hyde, J. S. (1998). Essentialism vs. social constructionism in the study of human sexuality. *Journal of Sex Research*, 35(1), 10–18.

D'Emilio, J. (1992). *Making trouble: Essays on gay history, politics, and the university*. New York, NY: Routledge.

Diamond, L. (2008). *Sexual fluidity: Understanding women's love and desire*. Cambridge, MA: Harvard University Press.

Diamond, L. M., & Butterworth, M. (2008). Questioning gender and sexual identity: Dynamic links over time. *Sex Roles*, 59, 365–376.

Doctor, R., & Prince, V. (1997). Transvestitism: A survey of 1,032 cross-dressers. *Archives of Sexual Behavior*, 26(6), 589–605.

Eaklor, V. (2008). *Queer America: A GLBT history of the 20th century*. Westport, CT: Greenwood Press.

Epstein, R. (2006). Do gays have a choice? *Scientific American Mind*, February–March, 51–57.

Fairyington, S. (2008). Kinsey, bisexuality, and the case against dualism. *Journal of Bisexuality*, 8(3/4), 265–270.

Fisher, W. A., White, L. A., Byrne, D., & Kelley, K. (1988). Erotophobia-erotophilia as a dimension of personality. *Journal of Sex Research*, 25, 123–151.

Foderaro, L. M. (2010, September 29). Private moment made public, then a fatal jump. *The New York Times*, A1.

Foucault, M. (1979). *The history of sexuality: Volume 1, and introduction*. New York, NY: Vintage Books. (Original work published 1976.)

Freud, A. (2000). *Three essays on the theory of sexuality*. New York, NY: Basic Books Classic. (Original work published 1905.)

Garcia, J. R., MacKillop, J., Aller, E. L., Merriwether, A. M., Wilson, D. S., & Lum, J. K. (2010). Associations between dopamine D4 receptor gene variation with both infidelity and sexual promiscuity. *PLoS ONE*, 5, e14162. doi:10.1371/journal.pone.0014162

Garcia, J. R., Rieber, C., Massey, S. G., & Merriwether, A. M. (2012). Sexual hookup culture: A review. *Review of General Psychology*, 16(2), 161–176.

Gates, G. J. (2011). How many people are lesbian, gay, bisexual and transgender? Los Angeles, CA: The Williams Institute. Retrieved from http://williamsinstitute.law.ucla.edu/wp-content/uploads/Gates-How-Many-People-LGBT-Apr-2011.pdf

Giffney, N. (2009). Introduction: The "q" word. In N. Giffney & M. O'Rourke (Eds.), *The Ashgate research companion to queer theory* (pp. 1–13). Burlington, VT: Ashgate Publishing.

Gullette, D. L., & Lyons, M. A. (2005). Sexual sensation seeking, compulsivity, and HIV risk behaviors in college students. *Journal of Community Health Nursing, 22*(1), 47–60.

Gurney, K. (2007). Sex and the surgeon's knife: The family courts' dilemma . . . informed consent and the specter of iatrogenic harm to children with intersex characteristics. *American Journal of Law and Medicine, 33*(4), 625–661.

Herbenick, D., Reece, M., Schick, V., Sanders, S. A., Dodge, B., & Fortenberry, J. D. (2010). Sexual behavior in the United States: Results from a national probability sample of men and women ages 14–94. *Journal of Sexual Medicine, 7,* 255–265. doi:10.1111/j.1743-6109.2010.02012.x

Herdt, G. (1999). *Sambia sex culture: Essays from the field.* Chicago, IL: University of Chicago Press.

Herek, G. M., & Greene, B. (Eds.). (1995). *AIDS, identity, and community: The HIV epidemic and lesbians and gay men.* Thousand Oaks, CA: Sage.

Heyman, G. D., & Giles, J. W. (2006). Gender and psychological essentialism. *Enface, 58*(3), 293–310.

Hoyle, R. H., Fejfar, M. C., & Miller, J. D. (2000). Personality and sexual risk taking: A quantitative review. *Journal of Personality, 68,* 1203–1231.

Iasenza, S. (2010). What is queer about sex? Expanding sexual frames in theory and practice. *Family Process, 49*(3), 291–308.

Kaiser, C. (2007). *The gay metropolis: The landmark history of gay life in America.* New York, NY: Grove Press.

Kellaway, M. (2015, March 25). Kentucky's transphobic legislation dies after 'last ditch effort.' *The Advocate.* Retrieved from http://www.advocate.com/politics/transgender/2015/03/25/kentuckys-transphobic-legislation-dies-after-last-ditch-effort

Kinsey, A., Pomeroy, W. B., & Martin, C. E. (1948). *Sexual behavior in the human male.* Philadelphia, PA: Saunders.

Knox, A. (2014, February 4). Utah proposal dictates transgender bathroom use. *Huffington Post.* Retrieved from http://www.huffingtonpost.com/2014/02/04/utah-transgender-bathroom_n_4726397.html

Kosciw, J. G., Greytak, E. A., Palmer, N. A., & Boesen, M. J. (2014). *The 2013 National School Climate Survey: The experiences of lesbian, gay, bisexual and transgender youth in our nation's schools.* New York, NY: GLSEN.

Kumashiro, K. K. (2000). Toward a theory of anti-oppressive education. *Review of Educational Research, 70*(1), 25–53.

Kunkel, D., Eyal, K., Finnerty, K., Biely, E., & Donnerstein, E. (2005). *Sex on TV 4.* Menlo Park, CA: Henry J. Kaiser Family Foundation.

Lehmiller, J. J. (2014). *The psychology of human sexuality.* Malden, MA: John Wiley & Sons.

Lindsey, L. L. (2010). *Gender roles: A sociological perspective* (5th ed.). Boston, MA: Pearson Prentice Hall.

Lopiano, D. A. (2000). Modern history of women in sports: Twenty-five years of Title IX. *Clinics in Sports Medicine, 19*(2), 163–173.

Lorber, J. (2013). A world without gender. In A. L. Ferber, K. Holcomb, & T. Wentling (Eds.), *Sex, gender, and sexuality: The new basics* (2nd ed., pp. 401–409). New York, NY: Oxford University Press.

Markey, P. M., & Markey, C. N. (2007). The interpersonal meaning of sexual promiscuity. *Journal of Research in Personality, 41*(6), 1199–1212.

McRae, R. R., & Costa, P. T. (1987). Validation of the five-factor model of personality across instruments and observers. *Journal of Personality and Social Psychology, 52,* 81–90.

Moe, J. L., Reicherzer, S., & Dupuy, P. J. (2011). Models of sexual relational orientation: A critical review and synthesis. *Journal of Counseling and Development, 89,* 227–233.

Molloy, M. (2014, February 1). Girl, 7, praised for letter to Lego about gender stereotyping in toys. *Metro.* Retrieved from http://metro.co.uk/2014/02/01/charlotte-benjamin-girl-sends-letter-to-lego-about-gender-stereotypes-in-toys-4286634/

Owen, S. S., Fradella, H. F., Burke, T. W., & Joplin, J. (2015). *Foundations of criminal justice* (2nd ed.). New York, NY: Oxford University Press.

Padawer, R. (2014, October 19). Sisterhood is complicated: What is a women's college when gender is fluid? *The New York Times Magazine,* 34–39.

Parent, M. C., DeBlaere, C., & Moradi, B. (2013). Approaches to research on intersectionality: Perspectives on gender, LGBT, and racial/ethnic identities. *Sex Roles: A Journal of Research, 68,* 639–645.

Plato, C. (2008). Come out, come out, wherever you are! For bisexuals the lovely lifelong process of coming out is often twice as long—A double life long sentence if you will. *Curve, 18,* 62–72.

Prause, N., & Graham, C. A. (2007). Asexuality: Classification and clarification. *Archives of Sexual Behavior, 36*(3), 341–355.

Preves, S. (2013). Intersex narratives: Gender, medicine, and identity. In A. L. Ferber, K. Holcomb, & T. Wentling (Eds.), *Sex, gender, and sexuality: The new basics* (2nd ed., pp. 365–368). New York, NY: Oxford University Press.

Rahman, Q., & Wilson, G. (2003). Sexual orientation and the 2nd to 4th finger ratio: Evidence for organizing effects of sex hormones or developmental instability? *Psychoneuroendocrinology, 28,* 288–303.

Reiber, C., & Garcia, J. R. (2010). Hooking up: Gender differences, evolution, and pluralistic ignorance. *Evolutionary Psychology, 8,* 390–404.

Renn, K. (2010) LGBT and queer research in higher education: The state and status of the field. *Educational Researcher, 39*(2), 132–141.

Richardson, N., Smith, C., & Werndly, A. (2013). *Studying sexualities: Theories, representations, cultures.* New York: Palgrave Macmillan.

Rodriguez, S. (2015). LGBT: What's in a name—or an acronym? In M. Kimmel & The Stony Brook Sexualities Research Group (Eds.), *Sexualities: Identities, behaviors, and society* (2nd ed., pp. 326–327). New York, NY: Oxford University Press.

Ross, A. (2014, September 26). Atherton transgender policy stands after appeal. *The Courier-Journal.* Retrieved from http://www.courier-journal.com/story/news/education/2014/09/26/atherton-transgender-policy-stands-appeal/16272583/

Ryan, C., & Futterman, D. (1997). Lesbian and gay youth: Care and counseling. *Adolescent Medicine, 8*(2), 207–374.

Ryan White Care Act of 1990, Pub. L. No. 101–381, 104 Stat. 576 (August 18, 1990), *codified as amended* at 42 U.S.C. § 300ff *et seq.* (2015).

Sanders, S. A., & Reinisch, J. M. (1999). Would you say you "had sex" if . . . ? *JAMA, 281*(3), 275–277.

Scherrer, K. (2008). Asexual identity: Negotiating identity, negotiating desire. *Sexualities, 11,* 621–641.

Schwandt, T. A. (2003). Three epistemological stances for qualitative inquiry: Interpretativism, hermeneutics, and social constructionism. In N. Denzin & Y. Lincoln (Eds.), *The landscape of qualitative research: Theories and issues* (pp. 292–331). Thousand Oaks, CA: Sage.

Seidman, S. (2010). *The social construction of sexuality* (2nd ed.). New York, NY: Norton.

Shilts, R. (2007). *And the band played on: Politics, people, and the AIDS epidemic* (20th anniversary edition). New York, NY: St. Martin's Press.

Singer, T. B. (2015). The profusion of things, the "transgender matrix," and demographic imaginaries in U.S. public health. *TSQ: Transgender Studies Quarterly, 2*(1), 58–76.

Somerville, S. (1994). Scientific racism and the invention of the homosexual body. *The Journal of the History of Sexuality, 5*(2), 243–266.

Stryker, S. (2008). *Transgender history.* Berkley, CA: Seal Press.

Tajfel, H. (1974). Social identity and intergroup behavior. *Social Science Information, 13*(2), 65–93.

Tierney, W. G., & Dilley, P. (1998). Constructing knowledge: Educational research and gay and lesbian studies. In W. F. Pinar (Ed.), *Queer theory in education* (pp. 49–72). New York, NY: Routledge.

Tobia, J. (2013, March 2). LGBTQIA: A beginner's guide to the great alphabet soup of queer identity. *Policy.Mic* [blog]. Retrieved from http://mic.com/articles/28093/lgbtqia-a-beginner-s-guide-to-the-great-alphabet-soup-of-queer-identity

Walters, S. D. (2014, May, 23). Queer freedom and the tolerance trap. *The Chronicle Review,* B7.

Wattendorf, D. J., & Muenke, M. (2005). Klinefelter syndrome. *American Family Physician, 72*(11), 2259–2262.

Wellesley College Archives. (2015, April 10). *College History.* Retrieved from: http://www.wellesley.edu/about/collegehistory

Wharton, A. S. (2012). *The sociology of gender: An introduction to theory and research* (2nd ed.). Malden, MA: John Wiley & Sons.

Woolfe, K. (2013). It's not what you wear: Fashioning a queer identity. In A. L. Ferber, K. Holcomb, & T. Wentling (Eds.), *Sex, gender, and sexuality: The new basics* (2nd ed., pp. 365–368). New York, NY: Oxford University Press.

Yazdani, S., & Cheraghi, H. (2014). A modernist perspective: The concept of gender identity in Woolf's *Orlando,* from the viewpoint of SD Beauvoir. *Anthropologist, 18*(2), 469–476.

Zuckerman, M., Eysenck, S. B., & Eysenck, H. J. (1978). Sensation seeking in England and America: Cross-cultural, age, and sex comparisons. *Journal of Consulting and Clinical Psychology, 46,* 139–149.

Case

State v. Ravi, 11–04–00596 (N.J. Super. App. Div., May 21, 2012).

CHAPTER 2

Historical Perspectives

Ann Marie Nicolosi

In 1642 Massachusetts, William Bradford (the governor of Plymouth Colony) witnessed "Wickedness Breaking Forth" in the colony. Bradford, a strict Puritan and English Separatist, lamented that notorious sins such as "drunkenness and uncleanness" had broken out and threatened the sanctity of the colony. Bradford observed that not only "incontinency between persons unmarried" (for which they had been duly punished) plagued the colony, but also acts of "sodomy and buggery" (Bradford, 1952, p. 316). Bradford pondered the reasons for this debauchery and offered a few theories as to why his people committed sexual acts outside of the prescribed acceptable boundaries of Plymouth, which were based on biblical interpretations. Perhaps the devil was more spiteful against the godly? Maybe the strict laws of the colony acted much in the way that stopped-up waters did, releasing sin with a vengeance? Or maybe the denizens of Plymouth were no more licentious than any other persons, but because of the small size and the vigilance of the church and law (which were the same) proscribed sexual activities were more susceptible to discovery than elsewhere? Whatever the reasons, Bradford's account reveals the anxiety that sexual transgression caused, and even more importantly, the attempts of the church to define sexuality and control it. Sex that resulted in procreation was acceptable, even encouraged. Indeed, Bradford makes no distinction between heterosexual acts of sodomy or homosexual acts of sodomy. This illustrates—as historians such as John D'Emilio have argued—that prior to industrialization, there was no homosexual or heterosexual identity, only acceptable and unacceptable sexual acts (D'Emilio, 1983).

Although the church did not define sexual acts in terms of sexual identity, the punishments for those who committed acts of "perversion" were harsh and swift, even for the victims of sexual aggression. If found guilty of **fornication** (i.e., sexual intercourse outside of marriage; see Chapter 6), one could expect a public whipping, even if one (usually a woman) did not give consent. But for cases of sodomy,[1] or even public masturbation,[2] one could be executed as biblical scripture dictates. However, single charges of sodomy usually did not carry the sentence of execution in colonial New

England, although some were executed. When sexual violations transgressed human boundaries, as in cases of bestiality, punishment was swift and sure, as Thomas Granger unfortunately discovered.

In 1642, authorities executed servant Thomas Granger, a youth of about 16 or 17 years, who confessed to committing acts of "buggery" with "a mare, a cow, two goats, five sheep, two calves and a turkey" (Bradford, 1952, p. 320). Magistrates brought the poor animals before Granger and, as he identified them as the objects of his lust, they too were condemned to death. According to the exegesis of Leviticus 20:15, the animals were executed in front of Granger and his execution followed (Bradford, 1952).

The sexual prohibitions of colonial New England were no different than most of Europe in the seventeenth and eighteenth centuries. Although the scientific revolution of the sixteenth century and the Enlightenment challenged the control of organized religion on the lives of the faithful, Christianity still dominated the sexual lives, as well as other aspects, of most people. Strict biblical interpretations of what was sexually appropriate influenced the juridical and cultural sanctions or condemnation of sexual acts. These sanctions determined the punishments for sexual transgression—indeed they determined which sexual acts were trangressive. They were sex specific; women were vulnerable to harsher penalties for their sexual acts as the mere act of adultery violated and challenged the patriarchal structure of European society. One can see these harsh retributions in the witch-hunts of the medieval and early modern periods. Accusations of witchcraft against women frequently had at their core a reaction against some form of female independence, whether sexual, social, or economic—and this traveled to the New World. Historian Carol Karlsen has illustrated that most of the women accused during the Salem witch craze violated the passive acceptance of subordination (Karlsen, 1998).

The above cases illustrate the relationship between societies and the construction of sexual offenses. They also illustrate what constitutes a sexual offense and how the definitions of those offenses change over time. What is a sexual offense in one era is often no longer an offense in another. This chapter examines the historical perspectives in the development of sexual offending. It provides an understanding of how the construction of sexual acts as criminal offenses is rooted in the historical conditions of its time and place. It also discusses how these offenses can serve as a window into a society's ideology, religious beliefs, codes of morality, and structures of power and wealth.

1. What is the role of religion in the construction of sexual offending? How do religious beliefs determine what are acceptable and unacceptable sexual practices? How do religious beliefs indicate the changing definitions of sexual offenses?

2. What is the relationship between sexual practices that any given society approves or disapproves and social control? How might power and politics play a role in the acceptance or opposition of sexual practices?

LEARNING OBJECTIVES

1. Identify the historical construction of sexuality and sexual offenses.
2. Explain the historical relationship between social controls and sexual acts.
3. Distinguish between essentialism and social constructionism in the creation of sexual offenses.
4. Demonstrate an understanding of sexual politics and gender roles in the construction of sexual criminality and sexual deviance.
5. Appraise the relationship between the construction of historical sexual offenses and contemporary sexual offenses.

HISTORICIZING SEXUAL OFFENSES

What makes a sexual act, or sexual identity, a crime in one era and an accepted expression of sexuality in another? How can the same act or identity be construed as a criminal act or just another expression of sexuality? The answer lies in the historical moment. Sexual acts, definitions of sexuality, and by extension sexual offenses are rooted in their historical place and time. This can be observed in many sexual acts and sexual offenses, but perhaps it is most easily seen in the changing definitions of homosexuality as a *crime against nature* and the law and its evolution as a form of sexual expression. One only has to look at the history of punishment for homosexual acts and identity to understand that the act did not change; instead, the perception of the act changed. For much of world history, homosexuality (or acts of sodomy between members of the same sex) carried with it various religious and legal prohibitions, including the death penalty. Yet today many Western nations accept and recognize same-sex marriage (see Chapter 9), illustrating the protean perception of homosexuality and homosexual acts. We think of sex as biological—and the desire for sexual activity is—but the accepted forms of sexual expression are determined by a given society and are historically

specific—and this includes sexual offenses. Thus homosexual identity, or acts that may have resulted in the death penalty in one time and place, are now accepted as the basis for legal marriage just as heterosexual acts and identity.

Sexuality is not something that one thinks of as a historical topic. Our understanding of sexuality is something that is personal, emotional, and ahistorical. But sex and sexuality have a history. Behaviors that we sometimes mistakenly attribute to nature are really not natural at all, but are the result of complex societal expectations and conditioning (e.g., Pinker, 1997; Wegner & Wheatley, 1999). This is especially true of gender roles. Recall from Chapter 1 that **gender roles** are the behavioral and economic/social roles that every society deems appropriate for members depending on their sex (Butler, 1988). Every society determines what the proper roles are for its male and female members. These roles are socially constructed but sometimes perceived as natural (Lorber, 1995). Thus these roles change in different societies and different historical eras. Definitions of racial categories also change. Sociologists call this **social constructionism** and, as Allan G. Johnson argues, one can see the constructed nature of reality by how definitions of race, or gender roles, change (Johnson, 2006). So too is it for sexuality. Every society constructs sexuality to conform to the appropriate behaviors for the expression of sexual urges. It defines what are appropriate sexual expressions and acts and what are inappropriate, or deviant expressions. As such, they too change in ways that biological characteristics do not. In a very basic comparison, we can use the metaphor of food. All humans experience hunger—it is biological and necessary for survival. So is sex: although it is not necessary for the survival of the individual, it is necessary for the survival of the species. However, how one satisfies hunger is determined by what one's society deems as appropriate food. In the United States, dogs are pets and the thought of consuming Fido is distressing. In other areas of the world, dogs are either a delicacy or part of the staple diet. Religion also plays a large role in food choice. Christianity has few food prohibitions, while Islam, Hinduism, and Judaism have strict dietary laws. It is the same with sexuality, and because sexuality is constructed, it has a history.

As a historical and social construct, sexuality cannot be isolated from society. Thus, not only is sexuality historical, it is also political. We may think of sex as a private and personal act, but nothing could be farther from the truth. Sex is profoundly political and part of the **public discourse**—the discussions, media images, and writings of any society. Even in societies where sex is not openly discussed, the prohibitions against discussion constitute the discourse (Foucault, 1979). To understand how a seemingly private act is indeed a public one, just think of the debates in our own world. It is almost impossible to escape discussions of sexuality (Snitow, Stansell, & Thompson, 1983). One needs to live in isolation to ignore the current discourses of reproductive rights, same-sex marriage, pornography, and so on. So while your own sexual acts might be private, the context of those acts is public.

If sex has a history, then we should be able to use methods of historical inquiry to discover and understand that history. Essential to that inquiry is understanding the societies themselves, and how they rank sexual practices: which sexual practices are "good"—those that the society condones or holds in high regard—and which practices are "bad"—those frowned upon or liable for legal and social punishment. These rankings are key to understanding the wider political, economic, and social currents of any society. Anthropologist Gayle Rubin argues, "disputes over sexual behavior often become the vehicles for displacing social anxieties, and discharging their emotional intensity" (1993, p. 4). Thus we often see severe sexual sanctions and/or debates in eras of distress or contestations, eras in which social or government upheaval cause anxiety in a society's denizens. For example, the implementation of the Mann Act in 1910, which prohibited transporting women across state lines for immoral purposes, cannot be understood without an understanding of the anxieties large-scale immigration caused in the early twentieth century, especially against the Asian population. Late nineteenth-century and early twentieth-century moralists created a national frenzy with tales of "white slavery" and Chinese immigrants kidnapping American women and forcing them into a life of opium and debauchery. However, the Mann Act was used to control and punish those who challenged the status quo, either racially or morally. The most famous case was the prosecution of African-American fighter Jack Johnson, whose pugilistic success in the early twentieth century spawned race riots. Johnson was guilty of violating racial taboos of sexuality and sociality. He did not defer to White men, but probably more enraging were his relationships with White women. In 1913, the U.S. government charged Johnson with violating the Mann Act as he had crossed state lines with his White lovers. Johnson was not the only victim of the Mann Act. Actor and filmmaker Charlie Chaplin, was accused—although acquitted—of violating the Mann Act when he paid the train fare of his 24-year-old mistress. In 1913, Farley Drew Caminetti was convicted of violating the Mann Act when his wife notified authorities that her husband took his mistress from California to Nevada. Caminetti's case expanded the Mann Act to include non-commercial extra-marital sex consequently determining that consensual extra-marital sex fell within the definition of "immoral sex" (*Caminetti v. United States*, 1917).

The same relationship between politics and sexuality can be seen in the case of Smith College professor Newton Arvin. Arvin, by all accounts a reserved and scholarly man, was one of the foremost scholars of American literature in the 1950s. His scholarly biography and critical analysis of the writer Herman Melville won the National Book Award for Nonfiction in 1951. However, Arvin was also a closeted gay man in the era of Cold War witch-hunts. In 1960, Massachusetts State Police raided Arvin's apartment and found him in possession of male pornography, most of which were muscle magazines and tame by today's standards (milder than most advertisements and music videos). Under the new Massachusetts harsh obscenity law, possession of pornography was a felony punishable by up to five years in prison. Arvin eventually pleaded guilty, paid a substantial fine, and served one year of probation. Smith College also suspended Arvin from his teaching duties. Two other Smith professors, Edward Spofford and Raymond Joel Dorius, were dismissed. Although Smith paid Arvin a half salary until his retirement age, the scandal broke him and he was never the same (Werth, 2002). The same actions—possession of pornography that constituted a sexual offense—that destroyed the lives and careers of three professors are completely legal today (see Chapter 8). Indeed, the proliferation of pornography on the internet means that we all, in a figurative sense, are possessors of obscene material. In 2002, the trustees of Smith College acknowledged their actions and highlighted them to reaffirm the college's commitment to nondiscrimination. The college created The Dorius/Spofford Fund for the Study of Civil Liberties and Freedom of Expression, The Newton Arvin Prize in American Studies, and a national conference on the impact of the civil liberties crisis of the 1950s on the academy (Smith College, 2002).

It is clear from the few examples above that sex, and sexuality, have a history. However, writing and studying that history is a relatively recent area of scholarship, one that has its roots in the study of women's history and gender history. These areas of historical scholarship, women's history in particular, ushered in new methods of historical inquiry that understood the personal was as historical as the public. History is not only made in the public spheres of politics, economics, and military actions, but also in the bedrooms, living rooms, and kitchens (Scott, 1999). Central to women's history and gender history is the knowledge that people's historical experiences depend on their sex and gender, as much as it depends on their race and class. One's historical experience is shaped, in part, by whether he or she was born male or female—and how gender roles in his/her particular era either extended power and privilege, or constrained and controlled him/her. Gender historians, because they deal with private spheres as well as public spheres, have long understood how societies shape and use sexuality to determine access to power and privilege (Scott, 1996). For these historians, it is part of the tools of the trade. No one's historical experience can be adequately understood without an understanding of how sexuality shaped that experience. This is especially true for women as their status in U.S. history, and for the most part world history, has been dependent on their relationship to men. This is why most women did not vote in the United States until 1920. The United States adopted the concept of *femme couvert* (woman covered) from English common law, which defined women as their husband's property. Indeed, it defined women as part of their husband's political and economic body as Justice Joseph McKenna reiterated in the 1915 challenge to the Expatriation Act of 1907, defining women's citizenship as derivative. McKenna argued that the body of the husband and wife are one and reside in the body of the husband (*Mackenzie v. Hare*, 1915). For women, their roles as child bearers, and therefore as the transmitters of name and wealth, made them vulnerable to stronger control of their sexuality than their male peers. In addition, men's use of women as gifts for political alliances, or to consolidate power and money through marriage, have created a legacy in which female sexuality has long been available to serve the needs of a society or state. We can see this not only in the United States and in the distant past, but also in other countries such as France. At various points in the twentieth century, European countries used women's sexuality, specifically in the context of their reproductive abilities, in pronatalist movements to address the perceived problem of race suicide[3] and depopulation (Klaus, 1993).

Historians of sexuality, women, and gender allow us to interpret historical events, laws, and culture differently. They give us a view on the history of not only sexual acts and sexuality, but also how and why certain acts were criminal in a specific place and time. Using the lens of gender, we can achieve a more complete—and at times totally different—interpretation of history. For example, historian Judith Walkowitz examined the English Contagious Disease Acts of 1868 and 1869. London officials argued that these laws, which provided for medical and police inspection of prostitutes in port and garrison towns, were necessary to the health and well-being of the enlisted men who were their clients. Using traditional interpretations of historical documents, one could conclude that these acts were merely what the officials said they were—a way to safeguard the health of sailors and soldiers. However, when historians use a gendered lens, they ask different questions

of their sources. Walkowitz, in her examination of these acts, questioned why only women were subject to these medical examinations and police surveillance of their bodies. Why were the men who frequented prostitutes not also subject to examination? Questions such as these reveal much more complex narratives than superficial acceptance of the discourse surrounding the acts. They invite analysis of the cultural assumptions of sex and gender that underlie the impetus for such laws (Walkowitz, 1992).

In raising this question and others, Walkowitz argued that by imposing periodic genital examinations of prostitutes, but not their male clients, designers of these acts reinforced a double standard of morality for men and women. It reinforced the belief that men of all classes had the right of sexual access to women of the lower classes, as these women defied the accepted codes of female sexual behavior in the Victorian era. The acts constructed male desire and sexuality as natural, and female desire and sexuality as aberrant and criminal. They also reinforced the **binary** relationship imposed on female sexuality—that of good females and bad females, of "madonnas" and "whores"—categories that were highly classed and racialized. In addition, the laws helped to further entrench the Victorian ideology of proper womanhood and the constructions of "lady" that shaped and constricted the sexuality (and sexual expression) of middle- and upper-class women. Violation of these boundaries often resulted in shaming and loss of that status (and usually the economic support that accompanied that status). However, working class women were not "ladies" and were not susceptible to this type of pressure to conform to Victorian standards.

Walkowitz (1992) takes her point even further by focusing on the class implications of these laws. She argues that the acts

were part of institutional and legal efforts to contain the occupational and geographic mobility of the casual laboring poor, to clarify the relationship between the unrespectable and the respectable poor, and specifically to force prostitutes to accept their status as public women by destroying their private associations with the poor working-class community.

(p. 23)

Walkowitz's analysis illustrates the relationship between policy, law, and cultural mores in trying to contain female sexuality. It also reveals the complicated intersectionality of the multiple identities in nineteenth-century London, specifically gender and class. But Walkowitz goes even further. She reveals how the response of middle-class reformers, feminists, and radical workingmen defied the murky divisions of class in a rare instance of solidarity. In a campaign that brought masses of respectable women into the public space of the streets—"the shrieking sisterhood," in itself a transgression of the public/private boundaries of gender—these tenuous coalitions successfully repealed the Contagious Disease Acts.

Although the repeal of the Contagious Disease Acts indicates the power of the public to shape law, the law itself reveals a cultural shift in that the clients of these prostitutes, mostly military men or sailors, enjoyed the unspoken acknowledgement that their sexual violations were indeed not violations at all. Historian Matt Cook argues that in the attempt to regulate prostitution, the government tacitly accepted the sex trade and that the criminal acts were not really criminal at all, at least for the male customers (Cook, 2005).

Although women have been vulnerable to strict sexual control, so have men—primarily men whose sexual orientation or desires stood in opposition to the condoned sexual practices of their society. This is especially true for homosexual men as their sexual orientation challenges the model of heterosexuality that maintains a patriarchal tradition. In many aspects, the condemnation of homosexual

men and the criminalization of homosexual acts are more about a violation of gender roles than about the actual sexual experiences. This is why homosexual men who are the passive partners elicit more disdain, and at times even rage or violence (Kerns & Fine, 1994). As passive partners, others perceive them as "feminized," thus violating the code of masculinity. This is also why there is more outrage against homosexual men than lesbians. Lesbian invisibility is due to many factors, not the least of which is women's general invisibility in public discourse, but also because the perceived violation of masculine codes by gay men causes more discomfort than women's violation of traditional gender roles (Herek, 2002). The rage against homosexual men, especially against "feminized" men, is also indicative of how a society views women. Indeed, as scholar Suzanne Pharr argues, homophobia is more about **misogyny**—the hatred or dislike of women—than anything else as it reveals a disdain of the feminine (Pharr, 1997). In addition, many heterosexual men respond negatively to sex between men but eroticize sex between women (Herek & Capitanio, 1999). All of these factors are historical as they are fluid and changeable depending on the time and place of any society.

Despite much of the rampant homophobia that still exists, the enormous changes in the attitudes and laws towards homosexuality in recent years underscore the historical nature of sexuality. The dismantling of "Don't Ask, Don't Tell" challenged the view of homosexuals as deviant sex addicts that threatened troop cohesion as have the same-sex marriage debates. Even more indicative in the same-sex marriage debates is the age divide. A majority of younger Americans support same-sex marriage while many older Americans do not (Becker, 2011; Hook, 2015). Much of the debates surrounding sexual acts and identities, especially those that have evolved from criminal offenses to accepted expressions of sexuality, are rooted in the religious beliefs, or ideas about what is "natural." In order to fully explore and understand these debates, and the history of sexual offending, we need to understand how many laws and arguments are grounded in essentialist beliefs, when they are actually constructed.

ESSENTIALISM AND CONSTRUCTIONISM

Gender scholars have deconstructed the idea that sexuality is natural and fixed. This view, **essentialism**, dictates that sexual desires are based solely on the biological impulse to reproduce and reside within the individual. It is "essential" or innate, biological, and natural. While one cannot dispute the need for a species to reproduce in order for it to survive, this view does not take into account the other aspects of human sexuality, pleasure for example. Humans do not only have sex for procreation, they also have sex for other reasons, such as pleasure, intimacy, and dominance. How else can one explain the desire for sex when it is either impossible to reproduce (such as women past menopause) or undesirable to do so? Scholars John D'Emilio and Estelle B. Freedman (1997) have argued that the dominant meaning of sexuality changed in U.S. history from a primary association with reproduction (dating to before the birth of the nation and continuing, at least, through the 1950s) to the modern view of sexuality as being grounded in emotional intimacy and physical pleasure —especially as a result of the sexual revolution (see also Allyn, 2001). Essentialism ignores that sex and sexuality change and divorces human sexuality from the nonsexual aspects of society, such as economics and politics, which have framed the expressions of sexual desire. In viewing sex and sexuality as essential, it is impossible to see the historical aspects that have shaped human sexuality, especially societal ideas about gender, race, and class and what is or is not criminal. In order to easily see how

essentialism is problematic, one can use a simple test. If something is constant and never varies, despite its historic era or geographic area, then one can assume it is biological or fixed. For example, there is no place in recorded history or era in which women do not experience pregnancy and bear children; that is essential. However, how we define that experience—or motherhood—is socially constructed and subject to change in different places and times, often defined by race or class. So, for example, in the era of U.S. slavery motherhood for Black women was constructed quite differently from that of White women as it served the needs of the master or dominant class. Slaveholders argued that Black women did not have the same maternal instincts as White women and were incapable of loving their children in the same way. This view, essential to maintaining the system of slavery, permitted masters to sell children away from their mothers. If this view did not exist, then slaveholders would have to admit that they engaged in brutal behavior. Constructing Black motherhood as different and less substantial than White motherhood allowed slaveholders to assuage their guilt and negate the impact of their actions. The argument that motherhood was a natural or essential experience was manipulated to serve the needs of the society (Feldstein, 2000).

Social constructionism, in contrast, views sex and sexuality as something that society creates. It does not argue that society constructs the biological impulses of sexual desire, only how those desires manifest and are interpreted (although some theorists, such as Judith Butler (2006), argue that the desire itself is constructed). As constructs, they invite historical inquiry. If a society defines what sex and sexuality are, then those definitions are dependent on the historical changes, as are any other social aspects—such as economics, politics, and culture. Historians can, and do, ask the same type of questions about sex and sexuality that they do of any other social aspect, including questions about change and continuity. How have a society's ideas about sex changed over time? How have they remained the same? What defines certain sexual acts as criminal? What prompted those changes? What influence did those changes have on the society? What were the economic, political, and sexual confluences? How did members of the society interpret these changes?

Sometimes the easiest place to see these changes is in times of war or upheaval. Race relations are also a place to see them. For example, after the Civil War and emancipation, southerners lost control and ownership of Black men (at least legally). White southerners constructed an image of Black male sexuality as violent and out of control. Because they could no longer control Black men as easily as they had, they now needed to construct the Black male as a sexual predator and criminal who lusted after White women. This provided impunity for White southerners to inflict violence on Black men. Under the rubric of chivalry and defending the honor of White women, White men had carte blanche to perform acts of violence on Black men. Violent retribution for Black men's economic or political gains, or for simply not knowing their place, came under the chivalric code of protecting White women. This construction of a bestial and criminal Black sexuality is still evident in the myth of the Black rapist or the fallacy that Black men are better endowed than men of other races. For many Black men, their sexuality became criminalized as accusations of rape constructed a sexuality that had to be policed (Mercer, 1994).

Defining Sexuality and Sexual Acts

While most scholars of sexuality agree that sexuality is constructed and not innate or essential, there are others who dispute this. Historian Rictor Norton, in "Essentialism

and Queer History," argues that there is an essential homosexual history and that homosexuals existed as an identifiable group before the creation of a homosexual identity in the late nineteenth century. Norton (2002) argues that homosexuals understood themselves as an identifiable group before then. Scholars Virginia Rutter and Pepper Schwartz (2011) espouse an argument that comprises both views—sexuality is constructed, but does have biological components. They argue that using a solely essentialist approach or constructionist approach constrains an understanding of sexuality, and that a constructionist view is actually more powerful when it takes biology into consideration (Rutter & Schwartz, 2011). This disagreement among scholars is indicative of healthy debate and points to the slippery nature of defining sexuality in social and/or historical terms.

Sexual Scripts and Sexual Self-Schemas

One of the key aspects of constructing sexuality is the control of sexual expression. In every society there are laws, religious strictures, and societal mores and expectations regulating sex. Whether there are severe repercussions against certain forms of sexual acts, such as imprisonment for sodomy, or shaming, such as calling a woman a slut, these consequences are punishments for acting outside of those regulations. These regulations are called **sexual scripts**. According to scholars Susan Shaw and Janet Lee (2015), "sexual scripts reflect social norms, practices, and workings of power, and they provide frameworks and guidelines for sexual feelings and behaviors" (pp. 313–314). These sexual scripts differ in societies or in the different historical eras of the same society. They are historical and are dependent on the laws and customs of their place and era. We can see this in the way premarital sex, or any sex outside of marriage, has been viewed in the United States. In colonial New England, the church and court (often the same entity) imposed severe consequences for fornication, including levying fines and/or public whippings. Today, premarital sex in the United States is an accepted form of sexual expression (although there are still some religious prohibitions). Fornication evolved from a punishable crime to an accepted form of sexual expression. This change in sexual scripts reveals the historical nature of those scripts.

In contrast to sexual scripts, which are societal levels for regulation of expressions of human sexual expression, **sexual self-schemas** are individual. Shaw and Lee (2015) describe sexual self-schemas as "ideas and beliefs about sexual aspects of the self that are established from past and present experiences and that guide sexual feelings and behavior" (p. 314). Sexual self-schemas are personal, but individuals develop and experience these schemas within the context of their societies and their sexual scripts. Often, they are in contrast to accepted sexual scripts and what one person finds acceptable or desirable might be unacceptable or even repulsive to another. To again use the example of fornication, although a society might have laws and/or social stigmas against fornication, an individual may engage in this behavior and indeed find it desirable. This same act might be morally reprehensible to another person, even if they both live in the same society with the same set of sexual scripts.

Sexual scripts are very closely allied with the power structure of a society. In a patriarchal society (in which men have most of the economic and political power), sexual scripts will dictate the regulation of female sexual behavior as that society depends on that regulation to maintain its structure. **Patriarchal societies** are usually patrilineal—meaning that names, power, and property descend through the male line. In order to ensure this transmission, one must ensure that sexual access to women is closely guarded as they bear children. In the age before DNA testing, the only way to insure one's children's paternity was to make sure he was the only one who had access to his wife. In patriarchies, women are denied control of their own sexuality, whether through law, economics, or shaming (Walby, 1989). Sexual scripts reflect this. Even today, we judge women who have multiple sexual partners much more harshly than men who have multiple sexual partners. For men, sexual encounters can even act as a measure of masculinity and pride (i.e., a "stud"). For women, it is still a mark of promiscuity (i.e., a "slut"; see Armstrong et al., 2014).

All societies, present and historical, rank sexual acts on a scale of the condoned to the criminal—and these rankings change according to the society and the historical era. The law has a role in policing those rankings, as the law is key to regulating the relationship between the citizen and the state (Cook, 2005). Historian Michel Foucault, in his groundbreaking work *The History of Sexuality, Volume 1*, argued that ideas about sex, and also sexual identity, are determined by their time and place and reflect a shift from the church to the state (Foucault, 1979). Anthropologist Gayle Rubin (1993) has argued that in certain historical periods, there have been what she calls "sex panics," in which the state, the institutions of medicine, and the popular media have combined to control sexual acts, and to criminalize some of them, when they did not comply with contemporary models of sexual correctness. Rubin states that there "are historical periods in which sexuality is more sharply contested and more overtly politicized" (1993, p. 4). According to Rubin, most states judge sexual acts in a hierarchical system. A preliminary understanding of this hierarchy in modern Western society ranks married, consensual sex between opposite-sex partners for procreation at the top of the hierarchy. Envision a pyramid with this form of sexual expression at the apex. At the very bottom are forms of criminalized sexuality, with acts of child molestation or bestiality. In between is a range of different sexual expressions, which would change over time and by society. For example, in our society today sexual activity between same-sex persons (consenting adults) is no longer illegal. However, in the not so distant past, the same acts could result in criminal offenses and penal punishment, as well as being registered as a sexual offender. The higher an individual's sexual acts or behaviors rank on the pyramid, the more society affords him or her rewards such as a recognition of sound mental health, respectability, and legality. The lower one's behavior ranks, the more punitive the measures such as criminal charges, accusation of mental illness, and religious as well as social condemnation (Rubin, 1993).

The historical nature of sexuality can also be seen in the challenges women have made to control their sexuality. Societal views of rape and sexual harassment are vivid examples of these challenges and changes women have wrought. Prior to the feminist women's movement beginning in the 1960s, rape convictions were few and far between as it was almost impossible for a woman to prove she was raped and did not consent to sexual intercourse for the reasons explored in detail in Chapter 5. Courts permitted defense lawyers to interrogate rape victims on their sexual lives, past and present; how they dressed; and other factors irrelevant to sexual victimization in order to prove that they did not experience rape but secretly, or overtly, wanted it and/or gave consent. Rape was not about violence, but about male sexual desire that the woman somehow provoked in the man (Brownmiller, 1993). Marital rape was also impossible as the courts viewed sexual access to a wife, whether she wanted sexual relations or not, as the right of a husband (Frieze, 1983). This concept extended to the workplace as the term sexual harassment did not even legally exist until the 1980s (Stein, 1999). Challenges to these practices resulted in

changing the sexual scripts. Today we understand rape, legally and culturally, as an act of violence, not one of passion. We recognize that women have the right to control access to their bodies, even with their husbands, and it is now illegal to sexually harass women in the workplace or to create an uncomfortable working environment (Gregory, 2004).

The understanding of sexual harassment in the workplace as an offense did not exist prior to the 1980s and was a direct result of the changes the women's movement had on U.S. law and society (Rosen, 2000). Feminist lawyers and scholars pushed for the recognition of sexual harassment as a violation of Title VII of the Civil Rights Act of 1964 (Saguy, 2004). Although the 1980s saw the beginnings of sexual harassment court cases, it was not until the 1991 Senate Hearings for the nomination of U.S. Supreme Court Justice Clarence Thomas that the phrase *sexual harassment* became commonplace. During Thomas's nomination hearings, law professor Anita Hill, a former employee from the Equal Employment Opportunity Commission, accused Thomas of sexual harassment. The ensuing drama captivated television audiences and brought sexual harassment to the forefront of public dialogue and debate (Black, 2001). What was once a common practice in the workplace is now conduct that subjects people to civil liability.

How a society historically defines and constructs crimes such as rape and sexual harassment changes not only in time and place, but also with the rapist and victim, and who is actually defined as the victim. For Black female slaves, rape was a way of life, as masters (and other White men) had unlimited and uncontrolled access to slaves' bodies. The sexual abuse of slave women was not considered rape because slave women were legally defined as property and one could do with one's property as one wished. By denying slaves legal personhood, White men could do as they wished to slaves' bodies. Some historians, such as Deborah Gray White, have argued that because of this, slavery was often worse for women than for men; most male slaves did not experience sexual violation of their bodies, although some did (White, 1999). Sexual abuse of female slaves also had an economic incentive; the children of slaves followed the legal condition of the mother, thus providing for a system of slavery that replicated itself with every new birth. In other words, every child born to a female slave was also a slave. This legal status of property for the children of slaves had been codified as early as 1662 in the state of Virginia: "Be it therefore enacted and declared by this present grand assembly, that all children borne [sic] in this country shalbe [sic] held bond or free only according to the condition of the mother" (as quoted in Hening, 1969, p. 167). This law continued when the American colonies became the United States after the ratification of the Constitution until the end of the Civil War.

While White married women did not suffer the loss of personhood as did slave women, they were nonetheless at the mercy of a legal system that defined them as belonging to their husbands under the doctrine of *femme couvert*, the English common-law concept of coverture that subsumed the political and economic identity of a woman with that of her husband and limited women's economic and political rights (Nicolosi, 2001). This created a system in which White victims of rape were more often seen as victims of rape than Black women, but the legal victims were the husbands whose "property" had been violated. The criminality of the act of rape has changed over time and while we understand the crime of rape today as having sexual relations without a person's consent, for much of U.S. history that definition was murky at best, as it conflated issues of race, gender, property, and legal personhood.

We can also see the historical nature of sexuality and sexual acts in the different ways that cultures and societies view them. For example, our society has strict penalties against the practice of **pederasty**—sexual relations between an adult male and an adolescent male minor. However, this was accepted practice in ancient Greece, as long as an adult male did not take the passive position. For the youth, it was no shame to accept the sexual advances of an older male of the same or higher class. Ancient Greeks considered this part of the maturation process. An older male of higher status transferred his knowledge and power through the sexual act, whether by anal penetration or **intercrucial intercourse**—rubbing one's penis between the thighs of another. It was, however, shameful for an adult male to be the passive partner as it signified a loss of status or power. Once the youths became of age, they were expected to become the active partners to those younger than themselves. It was also acceptable for an adult free male to engage in sexual relations with a slave, as long as the free male was the active partner. None of these actions implied a homosexual identity as historians have shown that such an identity is a creation of the nineteenth and twentieth centuries. Although homosexual identity is relatively recent, homosexual acts have always occurred, as evidenced by the discussion and/or prohibitions from the Bible to the *Iliad*, and for Greek military power, sexual relations between men, as some argued, gave soldiers the bravery and desire to fight with their fellow soldiers (Keuls, 1985).

The conflicting interpretations of pederasty in ancient Greece and the modern-day United States could not be starker. In one society, it was an accepted mode of affection between adult and minor males who had reached puberty (Dover, 1978); in another, a punishable crime. One society saw it as a positive relationship; another sees it as criminal. Although the acts are the same, the interpretations and sanctions of the acts, and the criminal status, are specific to the society. Thus, sexual relations between adult males and post-pubescent minors constitute pederasty in one society, and statutory rape in another. The same analysis can be applied to marital relations in which a woman does not consent; what was considered a husband's right to his wife's body in one era in the same country is rape in a different era. If sexual acts and interpretations are "natural" or unnatural" or "biological" or "essential," then they would be constant and unchanging in different societies and eras. But they are not; societies construct these acts and imbue them with meaning. This has important repercussions for any society's penal system as it determines what sexual acts and/or relationships are legal and which are illegal and subject to punishment. In some countries today, adultery (at least for women) is still punishable, including death by stoning. In the United States, we consider this practice barbaric. But the act is the same. Although U.S. society may frown upon adultery, it does not impose the death penalty. However, in the American colony of Massachusetts in 1641, adultery was also a crime punishable by death. The law stated: "If any person committeth Adultery with a married or espoused wife, the Adulterer and Adulteresse shall surely by [sic] put to death (as quoted in Whitmore, 1889, pp. 128–129). Thus the act of adultery in colonial New England engendered different social responses and legal prohibitions than the act of adultery in the contemporary United States. In that earlier era, adultery was criminalized; today, as Chapter 6 explores in more detail, not only does the criminal law largely not concern itself with adultery, but also, the use of criminal sanctions to control such conduct may even be unconstitutional. Such radically diverse interpretations of the appropriate legal response lead to the questions: What does adultery mean? What does it denote in a society? How do sanctions and punishments for women's sexual transgressions reveal the status of women, socially, politically, and economically in a society? These questions expose the historical nature of acts many consider nat-

ural or unnatural—and not just adultery, as Box 2.1 illustrates.

The Politics of Sexuality

While all the examples in the previous section illustrate the historical nature of sexual scripts and sexuality schemas, they also point to what scholars call the "politics of sexuality" (see, e.g., Snitow et al., 1983; Collins, 2005). The politics of sexuality are the conflicts and discourse in the interpretations of sexual acts and sexuality. It also refers to the distribution of power in sexual relationships. The uneven power allocation occurs because these relationships do not take place outside of the society to which the individuals involved belong. Most societies, our own included, assign power based on gender as well as other systems of power and privilege, such as race and class. For example, in male and female sexual and emotional relationships, men usually have more power than women. In some cases, especially in cases of sexual consent, women may seem to have the power in the relationship (Langford, 1999). However, a closer look at these relationships illustrates that female power, based on consent and/or sexual access, has a very limited form of power, one that is short lived and available only to women whom society considers attractive. This form of power, while seemingly ubiquitous, is actually quite shallow and restricted, and is also dependent on male cooperation. Some males see this power as threatening and use either sexual abuse or the threat of sexual abuse to keep it in check, but for many men and women, this power is part of the dance of courtship (Wolf, 2002). However, taking a closer look into the power between men and women in relationships, one can see that in most relationships men hold more power as they usually (not always) are the higher earners and because of that they sometimes have more control in a relationship (Tichenor, 1999). Sexual politics is not only about the power in any given

Box 2.1 HISTORICAL CASE STUDY ON THE SOCIAL CONSTRUCTION OF "DEVIANT" SEXUAL ACTS

In 1905, Progressive Era reformer Florence Kelley asserted that a society must guarantee its children a "right to childhood." Kelley's admonition was part of a larger movement in the late nineteenth and early twentieth century that changed the definition of childhood from the years before adulthood in a person's life to a period of time in which society, and all its adult members, had the obligation to shield its younger members from labor, sexual abuse, and physical harm, as well as guarantee all children a right to an education. Although we take the rights of children for granted today, this was a radical change in their status and created a blueprint for social structure and hierarchy based on age. It also created a new class of criminals and sexual offenders. To wit, owners of businesses could be held accountable for violating child labor laws that did not exist previously. Similarly, those who had sexual relationships with young people came to face criminal prosecution even though the same conduct had been previously acceptable. Indeed, most states created statutory rape laws in the 1880s. These laws defined the legal age at which a minor could consent to sexual activity (see Chapter 6). Common law, inherited from England, defined the marriageable age for boys as 14 and 12 for girls. But changing perspectives of childhood challenged those definitions. As the nineteenth century progressed, Americans increasingly saw childhood as incompatible with sexual activity and the age of consent began to rise (Syrett, 2014). As an 1887, Illinois law made clear, "Every male person of the age of sixteen years and upwards, who shall have carnal knowledge of any female person under the age of fourteen years, either with or without her consent, shall be adjudged to be guilty of the crime of rape" (ILLINOIS CRIMINAL CODE § 237, 1887). In 1886, New York prosecuted for rape all men who had sexual relations with girls under the age of 16, adding statutory rape as a secondary charge (Robertson, 2002). By the middle of the twentieth century, Americans had clear boundaries on appropriate ages for sexual activity with children, as popular rock-and-roll entertainer Jerry Lee Lewis learned. Lewis's career and popularity plummeted after the 21-year-old married his 13-year-old cousin (Stein, 2013). These examples illustrate how an action can be perfectly legal at one point in time, and create a category of sexual offending, at another point in time.

1. How do these examples exemplify the construction of sexual offending?
2. Were the men who violated the statutory rape laws of the nineteenth and twentieth centuries rapists and sexual offenders if their sexual activities with young partners were legal in an earlier era?
3. What is the age of consent under the statutory rape law in your state?
4. How does the sexual offending category of a pedophile depend on changing legal definitions?

sexual relationship, but also the ways in which a society views relationships. This is especially true in reproductive politics and debates surrounding homosexuality and same-sex marriage.

Reproductive politics and criminalization of birth control are excellent places to understand the historical nature of sexuality and the role of power and dominance in any society. At the heart of all debates on reproduction is who controls female bodies. Do females control their own bodies, or does society—either though formal governmental control or socially constructed gender norms and sexual mores, or both? Are men entitled to female bodies? The debates over reproduction are so volatile because at their core they reveal the schisms in any society over gender roles—not only in sexual areas but all other aspects of life. In our own society, as well as many others in the world, we are still grappling with the changing of women's economic roles. Although most women still earn less than men (in 2013 full-time female workers made 82.1 cents for every dollar men earned) the ratio is becoming smaller and women now have more earning power than at any time in U.S. history (Hegwisch et al., 2014). There are more than economic factors responsible for this. Without access to safe and reliable birth control, women cannot have complete control over if and when they will bear children or how many they will bear. Without this control, women's economic lives would be controlled by their reproductive lives. Thus, a society that is struggling with changing gender roles, especially those of women, will often exhibit those anxieties in the discourse—or public debates—about reproduction and reproductive technologies. When historians look back at the debates surrounding the enactment of the Patient Protection and Affordable Health Care Act (2010), the mandate for birth control coverage for women will be especially informative (see *Burwell v. Hobby Lobby*, 2014).

The political nature of sexual acts can be seen in some important historical court cases regarding reproductive policies. Under the Comstock Act of 1873, birth-control advocate and Planned Parenthood founder Margaret Sanger was arrested in 1914 for her role in distributing information for birth control. The Comstock Act, named for U.S. postal inspector Anthony Comstock, made it a crime to distribute material or information about birth control through the U.S. mail. Comstock

argued that this information fell under the category of obscene materials, yet some historians have argued that this law must be understood not as protecting citizens from obscene material, but as a response to women's increased use of contraceptives to control their fertility. Despite this law, women—particularly middle-class women—continued to learn about contraceptives through their physicians and pharmacists (D'Emilio & Freedman, 1997). By the 1930s, it was clear that distributing contraceptive material was commonplace and in 1936 a federal appeals court overturned the anti-contraception provision of the law in *United States v. One Package* (1936). The deciding judge, Augustus Hand, argued that the authority of the medical community was not available in 1873 and it now had a role in safe and effective modern contraception. Thus, the criminal act Margaret Sanger committed in 1914 was no longer criminal in 1936 (D'Emilio & Freedman, 1997).

In 1961, the executive director of Planned Parenthood League of Connecticut, Estelle Griswold, and Dr. C. Lee Buxton were arrested and convicted as accessories to providing illegal contraception under an 1879 Connecticut state law that prevented the use of birth control. The law stipulated that "any person who assists, abets, counsels, causes, hires or commands another to commit any offense may be prosecuted and punished as if he were the principle offender" (CONN. GEN. STAT. § 54–196, 1958). Griswold and Buxton were fined $100 each and appealed their convictions. Two levels of state appellate courts in Connecticut affirmed their convictions. But the U.S. Supreme Court, under Chief Justice Earl Warren, overturned their convictions in the landmark case of *Griswold v. Connecticut* (1965). The Court determined that the use of birth control by legally married couples falls under the right to privacy implied by the First, Third, Fourth, Fifth, and Ninth Amendments of the U.S. Constitution. Therefore, it could not be criminalized, despite the history of criminalization of the dissemination and use of birth control under the Comstock Act and subsequent state laws to the same effect.

One can easily see how *United States v. One Package* and *Griswold v. Connecticut* are part of their historical moments or eras; today, birth control is widely available in supermarkets, pharmacies, and convenience stores. This has also been the case with sodomy laws as legal scholar Henry Fradella (2003) has shown. The *Lawrence v. Texas* decision had wide implications for the understanding of the political ramifications and criminalization of private behavior between homosexuals (Fradella, 2003; see also Chapter 6). In any society, legal language and the rhetoric of the courts can illustrate how sexual criminality and the construction of the victim are constituted (Cook, 2005).

THE ROLE OF RELIGION IN ESTABLISHING SEXUAL BOUNDARIES

At the core of perceived sexual transgressions are religious beliefs that established the boundaries of accepted sexual practices. For Western countries, Christianity (and its Judaic influences) was the dominant religion that spread across Europe at the end and after the fall of the Roman Empire. Although proper sexual conduct has always been regulated in criminal and civil law, Christianity has influenced the construction of those laws since the fourth century (Nye, 1999). Contemporary moral crusaders who seek to control the sexual behavior of others share a common ground with medieval moralists, which James Brundage (1987) calls "a system of legal theology rooted in medieval Catholicism but extending into modern statute law" (p. xix). Although there has been a loosening of the criminal retribution for many consensual sexual practices such as adultery, fornication, homosexuality, oral sex, and so on, Christian philosophy still dominates the discourse of what is acceptable sexual behavior.

The Foundations of Christian Beliefs about Sex

Christianity's central tenet—regardless of any of its sects—is the belief that Jesus Christ is the son of God and died to save humankind from its sins. To be a Christian is to accept Jesus Christ as your Savior. The earliest form of Christianity, Catholicism, dominated Christianity until the Protestant Reformation in the early sixteenth century, but all forms of Christianity adhere to the acceptance of Jesus Christ as the root of their faith or philosophy. The foundational texts of Christianity, the books of the New Testaments of the Bible, are interpretations of the life and teachings of Christ, as written by his chosen disciples. Combined with the Judaic Old Testament, the Bible serves not only as a code of appropriate behavior, but also as the perceived blueprint of Christian behavior, including sexual behavior. However, Jesus Christ said very little about sexual behavior, and sex was not central to his moral teachings and philosophy. Brundage (1987) argues that because Christ was not concerned with sexual behavior, Christian sexual morality is the result of a "complex assemblage of pagan and Jewish purity regulations, linked with primitive beliefs about the relationship between sex and the holy, joined to stoic teachings about sexual ethics, and bound together by a patchwork of doctrinal theories largely invented in the fourth and fifth centuries" (p. 3).

Historians Vern and Bonnie Bullough (1977) agree with the argument that Christian prohibitions against certain sexual acts predate Christianity. The Bulloughs contend that sex-negative ideas predate Christianity and include the pagan beliefs of the Greeks and Romans. They support the earlier work of scholar Morton Enslin (1930) in the conviction that it was not Christianity that made the world ascetic but "the world in which Christianity found itself strove to make Christianity ascetic" (Enslin, 1930, p. 180). In other words, this idea of certain sexual acts as unacceptable, or the ranking of sexual acts, exists well before Christianity became the dominant religion in the West. However, it is the spread of Christianity, which incorporated these mores, that creates a sexual code of hierarchy for what is good sex (moral, legal) and what is bad sex (immoral, illegal).

Scholars such as the Bulloughs trace the roots of Western hostility to certain sexual acts back to the Greek philosophies of dualism that divided the world into two opposite or binary forces, which they identified as the spiritual vs. the material. These philosophies argue that humans have two natures, and they are ranked as the higher and the lower. The higher is associated with the spiritual and the intellectual, the lower with the material, including the body. Another way to interpret this is the familiar tenets of Christianity in which humans have a soul and a body. In its adoption of this philosophy, Christian doctrine believes that the soul is incarcerated in the body and the goal and purpose of human existence is to achieve salvation by freeing the soul (allowing it to escape). As sexual acts are associated with the body and not the soul, and as sexual activity represents the assertion or dominance of the body over the soul (or spiritual), any form of sexual activity is an expression of the body—the material—winning out over the soul—the spiritual. The Christian adoption of the Platonic concept of duality shapes the Christian ideas of love in these opposing terms, which alternately were labeled the sacred and profane. Sacred came to mean one's occupation with the mind and character of one's beloved, and profane with lust and desire for one's beloved's body (Bullough & Bullough, 1977). "I know nothing which brings the manly mind down from the heights more than a woman's caresses and that joining of bodies without which one cannot have a wife" (St. Augustine, as quoted in Bullough & Bullough, 1977, p. 23).

Much of the sexual traditions of the Church can be traced back to the writings of St. Augustine. This early Christian philosopher and theologian was the bishop of Hippo Regius (in present-day Algeria) in the late fourth and early fifth centuries and his works, including *The City of God*, are the foundations of today's Catholic Church and much of the philosophy of all Christianity and Western religion. St. Augustine's influence on how Christianity has shaped Western ideas of sexuality cannot be overemphasized. Like most of the early Christian writings on sex, St. Augustine's codification of sexual morality was not based mostly on Biblical teaching but was derived from the intellectual and philosophical assumptions and ideology already in place at the birth of Christianity and can also be traced to the pre-Christian teachings of the Greeks and Romans (Bullough & Bullough, 1977). What made St. Augustine's work so influential is that he crafted a theology and philosophy of sex that included the biblical mandate found in Genesis that instructed Adam and Eve to populate the earth with the dualism of the material and the spiritual.

It is in the acknowledgement that sex is mandatory for procreation and biblical instructions for humans to "be fruitful and multiply" that Augustine needed to bring in line with the dualism of body/matter versus soul/mind. If he strictly adhered to the theories that abstinence was the preferred sexual state and one that was more "godly," then how could he reconcile the instructions in Genesis? The answer for Augustine, and for Christian-based societies that have followed, was the exception of sex for procreation within the marital relationship. However, although sex for procreation between men and women, as it was God's will, should be tolerated, it should not be enjoyed (Bullough & Bullough, 1977). Americans, like many other peoples whose national identities are derived from historically Christian-based nations, are the heirs to this tradition. Despite all the advances and progression in sexual thinking, our sexual conservatism, as witnessed in the public discourse of sex, is the remnant of this ideology.

"Natural" vs. "Unnatural"

Once the subject of the necessity of sex for procreation was settled, it was easy to create a hierarchy of sex and sexuality based on procreative sex as the apex of that hierarchy or the acknowledgement of that sexual act as "good" and other forms of sex or sexual expression as "bad." The equation of "good" with the term *natural*, and "bad" with *unnatural* (in terms of sexual acts and sexuality) was already in place by Augustine's day and was readily available to be codified in the Christian Church. The terms *natural* and *unnatural* can also be traced to the pre-Christian teaching of the Greeks and Romans; and in his letters to the Romans, Paul establishes the terms natural and unnatural to define the boundaries of sexual activity (Romans 1:26–27). It is easy to understand the establishment of sexual acts resulting in procreation (within the confines of marriage) as natural and those acts outside of marital procreation as unnatural. Thus, according to Augustine, anything that did not result in procreation fell in to the category as "unnatural" (Bullough & Bullough, 1977). The legacy of these terms is evident in American laws that, in the past, identified some sexual acts or transgressions as "crimes against nature" or "not fit to be named" (Bullough & Bullough, 1977, p. 24; see also Fradella, 2002).

From Biblical Teachings to Law

How did biblical teachings on sexuality become the foundation of laws and punishment regulating sexual acts and sexuality? After all, the U.S. Constitution separates church and state, mandating that religion has no role in defining American civic status or identity. How, then, do U.S. laws regulating sexual behavior come to pass? The answer is in the history of canon law and how that law became the basis of European societies and nations, and consequently, laws in the Americas.

In the sixth century, the Roman Emperor Justinian embarked on an ambitious goal of the codification of Roman law, which would become the foundation for canon law and eventually the legal framework for Western European countries. Combining his desire for codification of Roman law, with his quest to reunite the fractured Roman Empire into his Christian Empire, Justinian sought to erase any boundaries between civil and criminal legislation, and ecclesiastical legislation (Millar, 2008). It is under Justinian that the terms of *natural* and *unnatural* become codified into law, foreshadowing the legal use of these terms to define and to criminalize sexual acts, including the equation of homosexuality with unnaturalness (Bullough & Bullough, 1977).

Although we can trace the usage of the terms *natural* and *unnatural*, what exactly was understood as unnatural and natural is much more nebulous, as medieval Church Fathers tacitly acknowledged. This, in turn, prompted efforts to define the specific conduct that fell within each word's ambiguous ambit. As the legal profession grew in the medieval ages, lawyers sought answers and guidance from Church Fathers for how to define *natural* and *unnatural*. In the late eleventh and early twelfth centuries, Ivo, the Bishop of Chartres, based his justification for punishment of *natural* and *unnatural* acts on St. Augustine's teachings. He identified *unnatural* acts as those for which the "member" was not designed (Bullough & Bullough, 1977, p. 33). In contrast, Ivo's designation of acts that were *natural* was quite vague. Procreative sex within marriage was natural (and lawful), but unnatural (and unlawful) outside of marriage: "To act against nature is always unlawful and beyond doubt more flagrant and shameful than to sin by a natural use in fornication or adultery" (as quoted in Bullough & Bullough, 1977, p. 33). Thus, Ivo defined sex inside of marriage as legal and sex outside of marriage as illegal but still *natural* (Bullough & Bullough, 1977).

It fell to Gratian, the "father of the science of Canon Law" (Bullough & Bullough, 1977, p. 33), for further clarification of natural and unnatural sex in the mid-twelfth century. Gratian conceived of his treatise *Concordia Discordantium Canonum* (*Concordance of Discordant Canons*) as the universal work on canon law. This treatise, published circa 1140, was the product of his meticulous research in the intricacies of Roman law, the canons of Church councils, papal and royal ordinances, and biblical, liturgical and penitential texts. When it came to matters of sex, Gratian adopted the premises of natural and unnatural sex that St. Augustine and the Bishop of Chartres had articulated earlier, but added his own judgments, concluding that any act *contra naturam* (against nature) was always unlawful and more shameful than adultery and fornication. He created four categories of sexual sins, each more shameful than the previous one: fornication, adultery, incest, and those against nature. In defining those against nature, he implemented St. Augustine's and the Bishop of Chartre's classifications—"using a member not intended for that purpose" (Bullough & Bullough, 1977, p. 33). Gratian still left the term ambiguous and his term "sin against nature" became the standard for identifying sexual acts that precluded the goal of avoiding conception. It also came to include any sexual position other than the "missionary" position (female on her back) and using any orifice other than the vagina for intercourse. Gratian later included a section referencing the crime of abducting and corrupting boys, which he argued was fitting for capital punishment if the sexual act was completed (Bullough & Bullough, 1977). Thus "sin against nature" entered both legal and religious parlance and remained firmly in place for over the next eight centuries.

FROM SIN TO DEVIANCE

Although the ideologies and concepts of *natural* and *unnatural* dominated legal discourse for centuries, things began to change in the nineteenth century. The concept of deviance began to displace *natural* and *unnatural*, reflecting a shift from the religious foundations of legal definitions to those of the sciences, especially the social sciences and the rise of disciplines such as criminology, sexology, and psychology. By the first third of the twentieth century, deviance became the standard definition for describing sexual criminal behavior. Sexual acts and identities that once carried the imprimatur of sin became medical pathologies and sexual offenders became "sick," "degenerates," and "perverts." Although medical experts may have come into direct rivalry with religion, sexologists did not so much as challenge the morality and sexual guidelines of Judeo-Christianity as incorporate it into a scientific discourse that preserved the concepts of sin, discipline, punishment, and redemption (Nye, 1999). Incorporating religious and juridical ideas about sexuality, in particular homosexuality, science was able to impart a veil of impartiality and objectivity (Terry, 1999).

Historians of sexuality argue that much of this shift must be discussed in the context of the industrialization of the West. As unified nations proliferated, the notion took hold that a healthy populace equaled a healthy nation. They believed that diseases and weakness associated with sexual activity such as prostitution and promiscuity weakened the nation state as well as threatened the spread of empire (Nye, 1999). By the nineteenth century, problems such as venereal disease, prostitution, and masturbation fell under the domain of the medical experts. However, they had never been grouped together as *sexual problems* (Nye, 1999). Such a taxonomy had significant implications for the criminalization of certain sexual acts, identities, and behaviors. Whatever the causes, one thing is certain: the medicalization of sexual practices and sexuality were part of a broader movement in the nineteenth century of classifying human behavior (see Conrad & Schneider, 1992).

Indeed, medical experts followed in the footsteps of other scientists who had been developing systems of taxonomies for the material and natural worlds. Some of these scientists measured skulls (e.g., Gall & Spurzheim, 1810–1819; Gall, 1835; Morton, 1839, 1844); explored intelligence (Binet, 1905/1916); or classified—and even ranked—races, ethnicities, and body types (e.g., Linnaeus, 1735/2003; Sheldon, 1942; for a historical overview of medieval and premodern concepts of race and ethnicity, see Bartlett, 2001). And those who studied human sexual behavior, as explored in the next section, laid the foundation for creating categories of sexual offenses.

Early Sexology

In the 1880s, Austrian-German psychiatrist Richard von Krafft-Ebing (1866/1965) published what became the definitive text of sexual offending: *Psychopathia Sexualis* (*Sexual Psychopathy: A Clinical-Forensic Study*). Krafft-Ebing was one of the early practitioners of the science of psychiatry. He was also one of the influential social scientists who created a new body of study, **sexology**. Sexologists studied human sexuality in its variations and determined what the parameters of healthy human sexuality were. The efforts of sexologist scientists focused on their controversial work of examining aspects of sexual disease. Initially designated as a science that created an elaborate system of classification for a range of sexual types and behaviors, sexology and sexologists had enormous influence on the criminalization of sexual behaviors and acts (Bristow, 1997). In an odd twist, their work and legacy defined generations of men and women as deviants, degenerates, and criminal perverts—even as they also advocated for more humane treatment, arguing that mental state or physical aberrations should be taken in context when meting out punishments for criminal sexual offenders.

Krafft-Ebing's book *Psychopathia Sexualis* became *the* forensic reference book for judges, psychiatrists, and physicians for decades. *Psychopathia Sexualis* popularized many of the terms that are now commonplace, such as heterosexuality, homosexuality, and sadism. In addition, Krafft-Ebing, along with other prominent sexologists, both in Europe and the United States, established a medical model of sexuality, one that located sexual desires and acts along a **continuum**—a system in which there is a space between the polar ends that exist in a binary system—of "deviance" and "normalcy." What had previously been classified by religious guidelines and prohibitions and categories of "natural" and "unnatural" now fell into the realm of physical and mental health. The consequences of this shift are still evident in our social and judicial systems today as sexual acts that fall outside standard accepted sexual practices are still termed as perversions or crimes. However, as noted earlier, what denotes a standard accepted sexual practice changes and fluctuates in different eras and societies. This medicalization of sexuality had the effect of creating a network of physicians and psychiatrists in the late nineteenth and twentieth centuries who devoted their practices to understanding, diagnosing, and "treating" diseases of sexuality. This medicalization of sexuality was reflective of the changes in the organization and the ideology of sexuality (Chauncey, 1989).

Diagnosing sexual disease was, at best, a precarious business. Many sexual desires, acts, and behaviors that today are classified as perfectly normal were medical conditions earlier. This can be seen in the changing diagnosis of homosexuality. In 1973, the American Psychiatric Association removed the diagnosis of homosexuality as a sociopathic personality disorder from its *Diagnostic and Statistical Manual of Mental Disorders*. Thus, homosexuality was a mental disorder one day, and a normal variation of sexual behavior on the next (Eaklor, 2008). Categorizing sexual behavior, then as now, depended on accepted ideologies of sexuality. One area especially vulnerable to prevailing social norms was female sexuality.

As noted earlier, in a patriarchal and patrilineal society, wealth and property descend through the male line. In the age before DNA testing, the only way men could be sure that their sons were theirs was to control the sexuality of women. This is why virginity was so valued (and, to some extent, still is today). Making sure that no other man had sexual access to one's wife ensured that one's children were indeed his. Ideological justification for limiting and controlling female sexuality was the foundation for the construction of female desire as less powerful than male desire. Women's sexual desire was romantic and related to their desire for children. Acknowledging female sexual desire as autonomous and outside the purview of male control was a threat to society and its structure. Thus, women who exhibited sexual desire outside of male control became sexual deviants. Indeed, there was great fear of out-of-control female sexuality. As Krafft-Ebing warned in *Psychopathia Sexualis*, "woe unto the man who falls into the meshes of such an insatiable Messalina, whose sexual appetite is never appeased" (Krafft-Ebing, 1866/1965, p. 403). Oversexed women (and that could mean any woman who desired sex) had "nymphomania" and were patients for medical practitioners to cure.

As the following case illustrates, ideas of "normal" female sexuality influenced the treatment of women. Physician Charles K. Mills (1885) published one of the cases in the *Philadelphia Medical Times*. His article "A Case of Nymphomania with Hystero-Epilepsy and Peculiar Mental Perversions —the Results of Clitoridectomy and Oophorectomy—The Patient's History as Told by Herself" described his treatment of a 29-year-old woman whose "morbid disposition" resulted in her repeated masturbation. This poor woman was tormented by what she understood as pathological desires and

subjected herself to a **clitoridectomy** (removal of the clitoris) and an **oophorectomy** (removal of the ovaries). Despite these drastic measures, she was still plagued by her sexual desire in her sleep as she sometimes "felt something like an orgasm taking place" (Mills, 1885, p. 536).

Historian Carol Groneman argues that much more was at play in this case than just a young woman's presumably excess sexual desire. This young woman was emblematic of women who were beginning to bristle against the strict constraints of Victorianism and agitating for access to education and political rights. There was, as the famous criminologist Cesare Lombroso noted, a connection between lesbians, nymphomaniacs, and prostitutes—and by extension—suffragists—in that they were not only diseased, but also dangerous (Groneman, 1994).

Although women were favorite targets of early sexologists, homosexuality—and homosexuals—provided a vast subject of study. Early sexologists, such as Krafft-Ebing and Carl Friedrich Otto Wesphal, provided the language with which to describe men and women who experienced same-sex desire. In the nineteenth century, sexologists solidified the categories of homosexuality and heterosexuality. Before then, homosexual acts were acknowledged, but as some historians such as Michel Foucault have argued, a homosexual identity was not (Foucault, 1979). The shift from homosexual acts to homosexual identity had a broad impact on the criminalization of the homosexual. As Foucault states: "The sodomite had been a temporary aberration; the homosexual was now a species" (1979, p. 43). Not all of the early sexologists were anti-homosexual or understood it as a perversion. Some, such as German physician Magnus Hirschfeld, could be considered early gay rights activists. Hirschfeld, with a few fellow scientists, founded the Scientific Humanitarian Committee with the intent of researching homosexuality in order to help repeal the infamous Paragraph 175 of the

German penal code, which criminalized it (Garton, 2004). However, most sexologists wrote about homosexuals and same-sex desire—as well as other sexual practices outside the accepted social mores—as aberrations, perversions, or pathologies. Some argued, such as the famous British sexologist Havelock Ellis, that homosexuals were "inverts," in that their sexual desire was the invert of heterosexual desire. These physicians, psychiatrists, and social commentators, who ranged from early practitioners such as Krafft-Ebbing in the 1880s to Sigmund Freud, whose theories dominated the field of psychology and psychiatry well into the mid-twentieth century, created a body of literature that influenced how sexual offending came to be defined.

Treatment of Sexual "Perversions"

As the story about Charles Mills's patient demonstrates, sexual desires and practices that deviated from accepted norms needed to be treated. For women, the most common treatment was hysterectomy, although as Mills made clear, physicians sometimes employed the drastic practice of clitoridectomy to prevent women from experiencing "excess" sexual desire. In addition, these treatments were used to "cure" lesbianism. Lesbianism defied all of the Victorian notions of a "passionless" female sexuality that responded only to desire for motherhood. In their same-sex desire, lesbians undermined the reproductive foundations of female sexuality and sexual practices. Thus, lesbians joined the ranks of sexually promiscuous women and prostitutes in the class of deviants. Historian George Chauncey (1989) found a sudden growth of the discussion of lesbianism or "inversion" in the medical literature in the late nineteenth century. Chauncey argues that this was a response from the medical profession to women challenging the sex/gender system of the period. Chauncey states that designating sexual inversion as a disease "allowed male

doctors to explain the phenomenon in a non-threatening way and to stigmatize as deviant behavior which could be avoided by 'healthy' women" (1989, p. 104). Of course, female inversion did not only mean sexual desire for another woman, but sexologists and physicians also labeled women who defied the cultural norms of established gender roles as inverts.

While some women were subjected to medical "treatment" for their sexual indiscretions, many were either incarcerated or institutionalized. Numerous inmates in women's prisons were there because of sexual crimes. In New York's Bedford prison, more than 55% of the women committed in 1915 were there for sexual crimes ranging from prostitution to solicitation to violating the Tenement House Laws[4] (Potter, 2004). For women, much of the treatment inflicted on them was defined not only by gender, but also by class and race. Middle-class women whose families sought treatment for them usually received treatment at the hand of private physicians or practitioners; working-class women, poor women, and African-American women swelled the ranks of the incarcerated. Class also played an important role in visibility. As women of the middle and upper classes lived their lives in the relative seclusion of the private sphere, they were less apt to appear in the public discourse of sex offending. Poorer women lived more of their lives in the streets, especially in urban areas and the public spaces where many sexual interactions took place. This is evident in the shift of heightened public discourse about female sexuality and deviance during the World War II years and beyond, as the war necessitated women's access to the public spaces of war work and the lessening of male oversight. During the war years and their aftermath, there is increased discussion of female (especially juveniles) sexual delinquency. In 1955, Dr. Frank Caprio (1955) linked lesbianism and "psychic masculinization" in women to the rise of female independence. Caprio posited that this "masculinity complex" and turn to female homosexuality was the result for women who were "sex-starved" (p. 164).

The increased visibility of female sexuality and sexual behavior in the mid-twentieth century brought with it a more acute examination of lesbianism. As Cold War anxieties about homosexuality rose, lesbians, as well as gay men, came under closer scrutiny. With that closer policing of sexuality came increased cases of "treatment" for lesbians, including institutionalization shock therapy, aversion therapy, and psychoanalysis. As lesbians claimed more public space for themselves, criminalization of gender transgression and lesbian activity increased. As Elizabeth Lapovsky Kennedy and Madeline D. Davis (1993) have shown, lesbians—especially butch lesbians—were routinely captured in police raids in Buffalo, New York. Police would check their attire to make sure that they had on at least three articles of women's clothing, as it was a crime to wear any less than that (Kennedy & Davis, 1993).

Modern Sexology

Although much of the criminalization or "treatment" for female sexual deviance was based on the construction of passive female sexuality in the early twentieth century, sexologists in the mid-twentieth century began to change this interpretation. Scientists such as Alfred Kinsey, William Masters, and Virginia Johnson challenged not only the ideology of female sexual passivity and sexual deviance, but also particular sexual practices in general. What these sexologists found was that despite the accepted sexual scripts of the era, sexual schemas and practices were quite different and much more open and fluid.

Alfred Kinsey's work, in particular, had a profound impact on the understanding of sexual practices. Kinsey's 1948 study on male sexual behavior and his 1953 study on female sexual behavior "propelled sex into the public eye in a way unlike any previous book or event had done" (D'Emilio & Freedman, 1997, p. 285). In these studies, based on over 18,000 case histories, Kinsey laid bare the most elaborate descriptions of the sexual histories of Americans, albeit without sufficient regard to racial and ethnic diversity in his sample. Nonetheless, Kinsey's work revealed that most Americans engaged in masturbation and premarital sex, and that a significant amount had experienced extramarital affairs and homosexual experiences (D'Emilio & Freedman, 1997). The following decade, Masters and Johnson's research stressed the significance of sexual pleasure and sexual response for women, undermining the ideology that women merely tolerated sex (Bristow, 1997). The work of mid-twentieth-century sexologists provided an intellectual and scientific foundation for reexamining the construction of acceptable and unacceptable sexual practices, including sexual offending. One historian has called this period of sexual study "the golden age of sexual science" (Allyn, 2001, p. 166). These scientists were part of the changing social forces that provided the foundation for the sexual revolution of the 1960s, and the changing sexual attitudes toward women, but also towards men and sexual minorities.

Although it is clear that all the cures and criminalization of female sexual activities and behavior caused untold pain and destroyed countless lives, the focus on male sexual criminal behavior has been much more stringent. This is for a number of reasons, not the least of which is the historical visibility of male sexual lives and men's easy access to the public sphere and public places. Men lived their lives in ways that few women had the opportunity to and the vigilance of policing female sexual behavior by their male relatives left women, especially middle-class women, much fewer opportunities to express their sexual desires and acts outside the confines of socially sanctioned outlets such as heterosexual relations and marriage. But men had much greater latitude in their lives. With this freedom came visibility, and higher numbers of cases of male sexual offending with attendant cures and punishments. Treatment for male sexual offending in the past often included castration (physical and chemical). Sterilization by other methods was frequently employed. Indeed, many men—as well as women—who were not sex offenders, but who had been adjudicated "insane" were sterilized without their knowledge (Reilly, 1991).

Castration, physical and chemical, of male sexual offenders has a long history and even today there are many who believe this to be an effective punishment and deterrent for sexual offenses. However, the predominant form of cure in the twentieth century has been psychiatric and psychoanalytical, with the attendant behavior modifications aimed at changing a sex offender's drive (Gordon, 2008). One of the most popular behavior modification practices has been aversion therapy, in which unpleasant stimuli are applied to patients when they view images that provoke inappropriate sexual responses. This has been a frequent method of trying to "cure" homosexuality, as well as current sexual offending.

In more recent years, **conversion therapy** (also known as *reparative therapy* or *sexual reorientation therapy*) has been used to try to "cure" homosexuality. Many of these so-called "treatments" are promoted by "ex-gay ministry" groups that "have close ties to religious institutions and organizations" (Just the Facts Coalition, 2008, p. 2; see also Glassgold et al., 2009). But conversion therapy has been discredited and rejected by nearly all leading American medical, psychological, and professional counseling organizations, including the American Academy of Child and Adolescent Psychiatry, the American Association for Marriage and Family Therapy, the American Academy of Pediatrics, the American Counseling Association, the American Medical Association, the American Psychiatric Association, the American Psychological Association, and the National Association of Social Workers—and not just because homosexuality has not been viewed as a mental illness in the United States since 1973 (e.g., Linqiardi & Drescher, 2003; Just the Facts Coalition, 2008; Beckstead, 2012). Conversion, or reparative, therapy causes social harm by disseminating "unscientific information" about sexual orientation (Glassgold et al., 2009, p. 53). Not only is conversion therapy considered unethical since there is no reliable data that sexual origination can be changed (e.g., Shidlo & Schroeder, 2002), but also the "treatments" utilized in conversion therapy can cause harm to the person undergoing efforts to change their sexual orientation, including "increased anxiety, depression, suicidality, and loss of sexual functioning in some participants" (Glassgold et al., 2009, p. 67). As a result, several U.S. jurisdictions, including California, New Jersey, Oregon, and Washington, DC, have enacted legislation banning conversion therapy for minors (Movement Advancement Project, 2015). These bans have been challenged in court; but, as the "Law in Action" box below explores, the courts have upheld the laws thus far. As of the writing of this book, the U.S. Supreme Court has refused to hear any appeals from the courts that upheld the constitutionality of these bans.

Law in Action ARE LAWS BANNING CONVERSION THERAPY CONSTITUTIONAL?

In August of 2013, a New Jersey statute took effect that prohibited all state-licensed providers of professional counseling services from treating minors using methods of Sexual Orientation Change Efforts (SOCE), more commonly known as "gay conversion therapy." In Section 1 of the statute, the New Jersey State Legislature declared that "[b]eing lesbian, gay, or bisexual is not a disease, disorder, illness, deficiency, or shortcoming. The major professional associations of mental health practitioners and researchers in the United States have recognized this fact for nearly 40 years" (N.J. STAT. ANN. 45:1–54, § 1[a]). The Legislature then went on to state that "[m]inors who experience family rejection based on their sexual orientation face especially serious health risks," and that "[s]uch directed efforts [at changing sexual orientation] are against fundamental principles of psychoanalytic treatment and often result in substantial psychological pain by reinforcing damaging internalized attitudes" (N.J. STAT. ANN. 45:1–54, §§ 1[m], [j][2]). In support of its determination, the legislature cited many of the position statements and resolutions of medical, psychological, and counseling associations, including those that have concluded that there is little or no evidence of the efficacy of SOCE. Moreover, the legislature cited the American Psychological Association in support of its finding that SOCE can cause "confusion, depression, guilt, helplessness, hopelessness, shame, social withdrawal, suicidality, substance abuse, stress, disappointment, self-blame, decreased self-esteem and authenticity to others, . . . [and] a feeling of being dehumanized" (N.J. STAT. ANN. 45:1–54, § 1[b]).

Similarly—and particularly relevant to minors—the legislature cited an American Academy of Pediatrics journal article when concluding that "[t]herapy directed at specifically changing sexual orientation is contraindicated, since it can provoke guilt and anxiety while having little or no potential for achieving changes in orientation" (N.J. STAT. ANN. 45:1–54, § 1[f]). The legislature also quoted an American Academy of Child and Adolescent Psychiatry journal article, which states,

> [c]linicians should be aware that there is no evidence that sexual orientation can be altered through therapy, and that attempts to do so may be harmful. . . . Indeed, there is no medically valid basis for attempting to prevent homosexuality, which is not an illness. On the contrary, such efforts may encourage family rejection and undermine self-esteem, connectedness and caring, important protective factors against suicidal ideation and attempts. Given that there is no evidence that efforts to alter sexual orientation are effective, beneficial or necessary, and the possibility that they carry the risk of significant harm, such interventions are contraindicated.

> (N.J. STAT. ANN. 45:1–54, § 1[k])

Two therapists filed a lawsuit challenging the constitutionality of laws, joined by the American Association of Christian Counselors and the National Association for Research and Therapy of Homosexuality, an ex-gay group devoted to promoting reparative therapies with strong ties to fundamentalist religious organizations. These plaintiffs alleged that the statute violated their state and federal First Amendment rights to free speech by prohibiting clinicians from counseling a minor with regard to certain viewpoints on "unwanted" same-sex sexual attractions. They also alleged the law infringed on their state and federal First Amendment rights to the free exercise of religion by infringing on their sincerely held religious beliefs that changing same-sex attraction or behavior is possible.

The court rejected the free speech challenge to the law because it does not prevent

licensed professionals from voicing their opinions on the appropriateness or efficacy of SOCE, either in public or private settings. Indeed, [the statute] does not prevent a licensed professional from, for example, lecturing about SOCE at a conference or providing literature to a client on SOCE; the statute only prohibits a licensed professional from engaging in counseling for the purpose of actually practicing SOCE . . . [thereby regulating] conduct, not speech. [If that were not the case] . . ., taken to its logical end, it would mean that any regulation of professional counseling necessarily implicates fundamental First Amendment free speech rights, and therefore would need to withstand heightened scrutiny to be permissible. Such a result runs counter to the longstanding principle that a state generally may enact laws rationally regulating professionals, including those providing medicine and mental health services.

(*King v. Christie*, 2014, pp. 314, 318–319)

The court then upheld the law over the free exercise of religion claim, reasoning as follows:

To begin, there can be no serious doubt that the Legislature enacted [the law] because it found that SOCE "poses critical health risks" to minors. By doing so, the Legislature exercised its regulatory powers to prohibit licensed mental health professionals in New Jersey from engaging in SOCE. There is no indication in the record that religion was a motivating factor in the passage of [the statute]. In fact, Plaintiffs have not suggested that the Legislature was motivated by any religious purpose. From its plain language, the law does not seek to target or burden religious practices or beliefs. Rather, [it] bars all licensed mental health providers from engaging in SOCE with minors, regardless of whether that provider or the minor seeking SOCE is motivated by religion or motivated by any other purpose. Plainly, [the statute] is neutral in nature. Because of the statute's neutrality, even if [it] disproportionately affects those motivated by religious belief, this fact does not raise any Free Exercise concerns.

(*King v. Christie*, 2014, p. 332)

On appeal, the U.S. Circuit Court of Appeals for the Third Circuit agreed with the district court on the free exercise of religion claim, but disagreed with the district court that "speech" was not at issue in the case, only conduct. Indeed, the appeals court determined that the statute did implicate First Amendment free speech rights. It determined, however, that "a licensed professional does not enjoy the full protection of the First Amendment when speaking as part of the practice of her profession" (*King v. Governor of New Jersey*, 2014, p. 232).

[S]peech occurring as part of SOCE counseling is professional speech. SOCE counselors provide specialized services to individual clients in the form of psychological practices and procedures designed to effect a change in the clients' thought patterns and behaviors. Importantly, [the statute] does not prevent these counselors from engaging in a public dialogue on homosexuality or sexual orientation change—it prohibits only a professional practice that is, in this instance, carried out through verbal communication. While the function of this speech does not render it "conduct" that is wholly outside the scope of the First Amendment, it does place it within a recognized category of speech that is not entitled to the full protection of the First Amendment.

(*King v. Governor of New Jersey*, 2014, p. 333)

After determining that the law in question implicated the free speech protections of the First Amendment, the court likened professional speech from a medical or counseling professional to commercial speech—as classification of speech that the U.S. Supreme Court has long held may be subject to regulation that other types of speech may not (see *Bigelow v. Virginia*, 1975). The Third Circuit upheld the law as a valid consumer protection restriction on professional speech:

> The legislative record demonstrates that over the last few decades a number of well-known, reputable professional and scientific organizations have publicly condemned the practice of SOCE, expressing serious concerns about its potential to inflict harm. . . . Many such organizations have also concluded that there is no credible evidence that SOCE counseling is effective. We conclude that this evidence is substantial. Legislatures are entitled to rely on the empirical judgments of independent professional organizations that possess specialized knowledge and experience concerning the professional practice under review, particularly when this community has spoken with such urgency and solidarity on the subject. . . .

(*King v. Governor of New Jersey*, 2014, p. 239)

1. Like the Third Circuit, the Ninth Circuit upheld a California state law banning licensed counseling professionals from engaging in conversion therapy in that state (see *Pickup v. Brown*, 2013). But like the district court in *King*, the Ninth Circuit found that the ban did not involve speech, but conduct. With which court's approach do you agree more? Why?

2. The plaintiffs in *King* asserted that the ban was overly burdensome because the state's objectives could be accomplished in a less restrictive manner, such as by requiring minor clients to give informed consent before undergoing SOCE counseling. The Third Circuit rejected this argument because minors constitute "an especially vulnerable population" and, therefore, "may feel pressured to receive SOCE counseling by their families and their communities despite their fear of being harmed" (p. 240). Do you agree? Explain your reasoning.

3. The U.S. Supreme Court rejected appeals from those challenging conversion therapy bans before the Ninth Circuit in *Pickup v. Brown* (2013) and the Third Circuit in *King v. Governor of New Jersey* (2014). As of the writing of this book, no court has invalidated laws banning conversion therapy for minors on the grounds that they infringe on the First Amendment's guarantee of the free exercise of religion. Laws usually withstand such challenges so long as they are rationally related to a legitimate government objective, even though they have "the incidental effect of burdening a particular religious practice" or group (*Church of the Lukumi Babalu Aye, Inc. v. City of Hialeah*, 1993, p. 531). Assess these bans under this standard. Do you feel that they are rationally related to a legitimate government objective? Why or why not? Assume that conversion therapy bans are rationally related to a legitimate government objective—at least with respect to minors under the age of 18. Explain whether you believe they incidentally burden a particular religious practice or group.

4. In *Ferguson v. Jews Offering New Alternatives for Healing* ([JONAH], 2015), four young men filed a civil lawsuit against a conversion therapy group. The plaintiffs alleged that the organization violated the State of New Jersey's Consumer Fraud Act (CFA) by peddling bogus psychological services on the premise that homosexuality was a mental disorder that could be cured. In the first ever of its kind ruling, a New Jersey Superior Court judge held that, "it is a misrepresentation in violation of the CFA, in advertising or selling

conversion therapy services, to describe homosexuality, not as being a normal variation of human sexuality, but as being a mental illness, disease, disorder, or equivalent thereof" (*Ferguson*, 2015a, p. 1). The judge also ruled that the CFA is violated if conversion therapy providers offer specific success statistics when "client outcomes are not tracked and no records of client outcomes are maintained" because "there is no factual basis for calculating such statistics" (p. 1). In a related order in the case, the judge ruled that because the overwhelming weight of medical and behavioral science has established, as a matter of law, that homosexuality is not a disease or disorder, expert testimony to the contrary is inadmissible as unreliable pseudoscience (*Ferguson*, 2015b). If the plaintiffs in Ferguson are ultimately successful in obtaining a judgment against JONAH, do you think this case spells the death-knell for conversion therapy, considering that all 50 states have consumer protection laws that bar advertising a good or service that does not work by pretending that it does?

CONCLUSION

Sexual offending, like sex and sexuality, has a history. The definition of what constitutes a sexual offense is one that changes in different times and different places. What is an accepted sexual practice in one era is a crime in another era, illustrating that sexual offenses, like laws and all other social structures and systems, are constructed. The construction of these offenses and what are acceptable and unacceptable sexual variations, behaviors, acts, and identities have been influenced, and in a large part determined, by the dominant ideologies and social institutions of a given period. The enormous influence of religion before the modern era dictated sexual acceptability according to scripture interpretation while the early study of the natural world added to this influence in determining what practices were natural or unnatural. The modern era of scientific discovery and the ascendency of the status of scientists and scientific inquiry, as well as the creation of social sciences, created an environment that led to the medicalization of sexual acts and sexuality. Each of these influences helped to determine what sexual practices are acceptable and legal, and those that are not. As the influences shift and develop, so does the definition of sexual offending. For every shift, there are those practices that become criminalized and those that become decriminalized as well as new categories of criminals.

FURTHER READING

Bristow, J. (1997). *Sexuality*. New York, NY: Routledge.

Brundage, J. A. (1987). *Law, sex, and Christian society in medieval Europe*. Chicago, IL: University of Chicago Press.

Bullough, V. L., & Bullough, B. (1977). *Sin, sickness and sanity*. New York, NY: Garland.

Butler, J. (2006). *Gender trouble: Feminism and the subversion of identity*. New York, NY: Routledge.

D'Emilio, J., & Freedman, E. (1997). *Intimate matters: A history of sexuality in America* (2nd ed.). Chicago, IL: University of Chicago Press.

Eaklor, V. L. (2008). *Queer America: A people's GBLT history of the United States*. New York, NY: The New Press.

Garton, S. (2004). *Histories of sexuality: Antiquity to sexual revolution*. New York, NY: Routledge.

Nye, R. (1999). *Sexuality*. New York, NY: Oxford University Press.

Peiss, K. (2002). *Major problems in the history of American sexuality*. New York, NY: Houghton Mifflin Company.

GLOSSARY

Binary: A system of classification in which characteristics or individuals are divided into two, usually one positive and one negative.

Clitoridectomy: Removal of a woman's clitoris, usually to reduce female sexual pleasure; also known as female circumcision.

Continuum: A system in which there is a space between the polar ends that exist in a binary system.

Conversion therapy: Also known as reparative therapy, these discredited and potentially dangerous interventions seek to "cure" homosexuality by changing a person's sexual orientation to be heterosexual.

Essentialism: The philosophy that there is an innate set of characteristics for specific entities that all members possess; that many social behaviors are biological.

Femme couvert: The legal status of a married woman, whose rights and identity are derived from her husband.

Fornication: Voluntary sexual intercourse, usually in reference to between a male and female, outside of marriage.

Gender roles: Social, sexual, economic, and political roles a given society determines are appropriate for males and females who are members of that society.

Intercrucial intercourse: Non-penetrative sex in which a male places his penis between the thighs of a partner.

Intersectionality: The study of intersections between forms or systems of oppression, domination, or discrimination.

Misogyny: The hatred or dislike of women.

Oophorectomy: Surgical removal of one or both ovaries.

Patriarchal societies: Societies that favor men over women and in which men have more power, privilege, and access to resources than women.

Pederasty: A sexual relationship between an adult male and adolescent or pubescent boy.

Public discourse: The discussions, media images, and writings on any given topic that take place within the context of a culture.

Sexology: The study of human sexual life and relationships.

Sexual self-schemas: Cognitive generalizations about sexual aspects of the self.

Sexual scripts: The social and cultural definitions and/or mores of appropriate sexual behaviors for members of a given society, usually dependent on their sex.

Social construction: The philosophy or understanding that aspects once believed to be essential, such as sexual behavior, knowledge, gender roles, and mores, are socially constructed.

NOTES

1 Sometimes called *buggery* or the "crime against nature," sodomy included oral or anal sex between human adults, or any act of sexual penetration with an animal (i.e., bestiality). For more information on these offenses, see Chapter 6.

2 Sex acts in public, whether committed alone or with others, are traditionally subsumed under the crimes of "public sexual indecency" or "lewd and lascivious conduct." For more information on these offenses, see Chapter 6.

3 A term applied to pressure women to procreate in order to prevent the extinction of a racial or ethnic population as a function of the birth rate falling below the death rate.

4 Tenement laws were one of the reforms of the Progressive Era. The first such law was enacted in New York City; it banned construction of poorly lit and poorly ventilated buildings that lacked toilets and fire safeguards. Women who either ran away from or were disowned by their families, and women who were abandoned by their husbands, lacked the financial resources to rent better housing. So, many flocked to apartments that violated the tenement laws (see DeForest & Veiller, 1903).

REFERENCES

Allyn, D. (2001). *Make love, not war: The sexual revolution: An unfettered history.* New York, NY: Routledge.

Armstrong, E. A., Hamilton, L. T., Armstrong, E. M., & Seeley, J. L. (2014). "Good girls": Gender, social class and slut discourse on campus. *Social Psychology Quarterly, 77*(2), 100–122.

Bartlett, R. (2001). Medieval and modern concepts of race and ethnicity. *Journal of Medieval and Early Modern Studies, 31*(1), 39–56.

Becker, A. B. (2011). New voters, new outlook? Predispositions, social networks, and changing politics of gay civil rights. *Social Science Quarterly, 92*(2), 324–345.

Beckstead, A. L. (2012). Can we change sexual orientation? *Archives of Sexual Behavior, 41*(1), 121–134.

Binet, A. (1916). New methods for the diagnosis of the intellectual level of subnormals. In E. S. Kite (Trans.), *The development of intelligence in children* (pp. 37–90). Baltimore, MD: Williams & Wilkins. (Original work published 1905.)

Black, A. E. (2001). Tracing the legacy of Anita Hill: The Thomas/Hill hearings and media coverage of sexual harassment. *Gender Issues, 19*(1.4), 33–52.

Bradford, W. (1952). *Of Plymouth plantation, 1620–1647.* S. E. Morison (Ed.). New York, NY: Knopf.

Bristow, J. (1997). *Sexuality.* New York, NY: Routledge.

Brownmiller, S. (1993). *Against our will: Men, women and rape.* New York, NY: Ballantine Books.

Brundage, J. A. (1987). *Law, sex, and Christian society in medieval Europe.* Chicago, IL: University of Chicago Press.

Bullough, V. L., & Bullough, B. (1977). *Sin, sickness and sanity.* New York, NY: Garland.

Butler, J. (1988). Performative acts and gender constitution: An essay in phenomenology and feminist theory. *Theatre Journal, 40*(4), 519–531.

Butler, J. (2006). *Gender trouble: Feminism and the subversion of identity*. New York, NY: Routledge.

Caprio, F. (1955). *Variations in sexual behavior: A psychodynamic study of deviations in various expressions of sexual behavior*. New York, NY: Citadel Press.

Chauncey, G. (1989). From sexual inversion to homosexuality: The changing medical conceptualization of female "deviance." In K. A. Peiss (Ed.), *Passion and power: Sexuality in history* (pp. 87–117). Philadephia, PA: Temple University Press.

Collins, P. H. (2005). *Black sexual politics: African Americans, gender, and the new racism*. New York, NY: Routledge.

Comstock Act of 1873. Ch. 258, Sect. 2, 17 Stat. 598 (1873), *codified as amended at* 18 U.S.C. § 1461 (1994).

CONNECTICUT GENERAL STATUTES § 54–196 (1958), invalidated by *Griswold v. Connecticut*, 381 U S. 479 (1965).

Conrad, P., & Schneider, J. W. (1992). *Deviance and medicalization: From badness to sickness* (2nd ed.). Philadelphia, PA: Temple University Press.

Cook, M. (2005). Law. In M. Houlbrook & H. G. Cocks (Eds.) *Palgrave Advances in the Modern History of Sexuality* (pp. 64–86). London: Palgrave Macmillan.

D'Emilio, J. (1983). *Sexual politics, sexual communities*. Chicago, IL: Chicago University Press.

D'Emilio, J., & Freedman, E. (1997). *Intimate matters: A history of sexuality in America* (2nd ed.). Chicago, IL: University of Chicago Press.

DeForest, R. W., & Veiller, L. (1903). *The tenement house problem*. Norwood, MA: J. S. Gushing & Co.

Dover, J. K. (1978). *Greek homosexuality*. Cambridge, MA: Harvard University Press.

Eaklor, V. L. (2008). *Queer America: A people's GBLT history of the United States*. New York, NY: The New Press.

Enslin, M. S. (1930). *The ethics of Paul*. New York, NY: Harper.

Expatriation Act of 1907, ch. 2534, §§ 6, 7; Pub. L. No. 59–193, § 2; 34 Stat. 1228 (1907), *codified as amended* at 8 U.S.C. §§ 1–18, *repealed by* 54 Stat. 1172, 8 U.S.C. § 904 (1940).

Feldstein, R. (2000). *Motherhood in Black and White: Race and sex in American liberalism, 1930–1965*. Ithaca, NY: Cornell University Press.

Foucault, M. (1979). *History of sexuality, Volume 1: An introduction*. New York, NY: Vintage Books.

Fradella, H. F. (2002). Legal, moral, and social reasons for decriminalizing sodomy. *Journal of Contemporary Criminal Justice, 18*(3), 279–301.

Fradella, H. F. (2003). *Lawrence v. Texas*: Genuine or illusory progress for gay rights in America? *Criminal Law Bulletin, 39*(5), 597–607.

Frieze, I. (1983). Investigating the causes and consequences of marital rape. *Signs, 8*(3), 532–553.

Gall, F. J. (1835). *On the functions of the brain and of each of its parts: with observations on the possibility of determining the instincts, propensities, and talents, or the moral and intellectual dispositions of men and animals, by the configuration of the brain and head* (W. Lewis, Jr., Trans.). Boston, MA: Marsh, Capen, & Lyon).

Gall, F. J., & Spurzheim, J. G. (1810–1819). *Anatomie et physiologie du système nerveux en général et du cerveau en particulier* (4 vols.). Paris, France: E. Schoell.

Garton, S. (2004). *Histories of sexuality: Antiquity to sexual revolution*. New York, NY: Routledge.

Glassgold, J. M., Beckstead, L., Drescher, J., Greene, B., Miller, R. L., Worthington, R. L., & Anderson, C. W. (2009). *Report of the American Psychological Association Task Force on Appropriate Therapeutic Responses to Sexual Orientation*. Washington, DC: American Psychological Association. Retrieved from http://www.apa.org/pi/lgbt/resources/therapeutic-response.pdf

Gordon, H. (2008). The treatment of paraphilias: An historical perspective. *Criminal Behavior and Mental Health, 18*, 79–87.

Gregory, R. F. (2004). *Unwelcome and unlawful: Sexual harassment in the American workplace*. Ithaca, NY: Cornell University Press.

Groneman, C. (1994). Nymphomania: The historical construction of female sexuality. *Signs, 19*(2), 337–367.

Hegwisch, A., Williams, C., Hartmann, H., & Hudiberg, S. K. (2014). *The gender wage gap: 2013; Differences by race and ethnicity, no growth in real wages for women*. Washington, DC: Institute for Women's Policy Research.

Hening, W. W. (Ed.). (1969). *The statutes at large: Being a collection of all the laws of Virginia, 1619–1792*. Charlottesville, VA: Jamestown Foundation/University Press of Virginia.

Herek, G. M. (2002). Gender gaps in public opinions about lesbians and gay men. *The Public Opinion Quarterly, 66*(1), 40–66.

Herek, G. M., & Capitanio, J. P. (1999). Sex differences in how heterosexuals think about lesbians and gay men: Evidence from survey context effects. *The Journal of Sex Research, 36*(4), 348–360.

Hook, J. (2015, March 10). Support for gay marriage hits all-time high—WSJ/NBC News poll. *The Wall Street Journal*. Retrieved from http://blogs.wsj.com/washwire/2015/03/09/support-for-gay-marriage-hits-all-time-high-wsjnbc-news-poll/

Johnson, A. G. (2006). *Privilege, power, and difference*. New York, NY: McGraw Hill.

Just the Facts Coalition. (2008). *Just the facts about sexual orientation and youth: A primer for principals, educators, and school personnel*. Washington, DC: American Psychological Association. Retrieved from http://www.apa.org/pi/lgbt/resources/just-the-facts.pdf

Karlsen, C. (1998). *The devil in the shape of a woman: Witchcraft in colonial New England.* New York, NY: W.W. Norton & Company.

Kelley, F. (1905). *Some ethical gains through legislation.* New York, NY: Macmillan.

Kennedy, E. L., & Davis, M. D. (1993). *Boots of leather, slippers of gold: The history of a lesbian community.* New York, NY: Penguin Books.

Kerns, J. G., & Fine, M. A. (1994). The relation between gender and negative attitudes toward gay men and lesbians: Do gender role attitudes mediate this relation? *Sex Roles, 31*(5/6), 297–307.

Keuls, E. C. (1985). *The reign of the phallus: Sexual politics in ancient Athens.* Berkeley, CA: University of California Press.

Klaus, A. (1993). Depopulation and race suicide: Maternalism and pronatalist ideologies in France and the United States. In S. Koven & S. Michel (Eds.), *Mothers of a new world: Maternalist politics and the origins of the welfare states* (pp. 188–212). New York, NY: Routledge.

Krafft-Ebing, R. F. v. (1965). *Psychopathia sexualis* (H. E. Wedeck, Trans.). New York, NY: G.P. Putnam's Sons. (Original work published 1886.)

Langford, W. (1999). *Revolutions of the heart: Gender, power and the delusions of love.* New York, NY: Routledge.

Linnaeus, C. (2003). *Systema naturae* [A photographic facsimile of the first volume of the tenth edition]. (G. R. De Beer, Ed. & Trans.). Woodland Hills, CA: Rudolph William Sabbot. (Original work published 1735.)

Linqiardi, V., & Drescher, J. (Eds.). (2003). *The mental health professions and homosexuality.* Binghamton, NY: The Haworth Medical Press.

Lorber, J. (1995). *Paradoxes of gender.* New Haven, CT: Yale University Press.

Mann Act, ch. 395, § 3, 36 Stat. 825 (1910), *codified as amended at* 18 U.S.C. §§ 2421–2424 (2006).

Mercer, K. (1994). *Welcome to the jungle: New positions in black cultural studies.* New York: NY: Routledge.

Millar, F. (2008). Rome, Constantinople, and the Near Eastern Church under Justinian: Two synods of C.E. 526. *The Journal of Roman Studies, 98,* 62–82.

Mills, C. K. (1885). A case of nymphomania with hystero-epilepsy and peculiar mental perversions—the results of clitoridectomy an oophorectomy—the patient's history as told by herself. *Phildalephia Medical Times, 15,* 534–540.

Morton, S. G. (1839). *Crania Americana, or, A comparative view of the skulls of various aboriginal nations of North and South America.* Philadelphia, PA: Dobson.

Morton, S. G. (1844). *Crania Aegyptiaca, or, Observations on Egyptian ethnography derived from anatomy, history and the monuments.* London: J. Pennington.

Movement Advancement Project. (2015). *Conversion therapy laws.* Retrieved from http://www.lgbtmap.org/equality-maps/conversion_therapy

New Jersey Statutes Annotated 45: 1–54, § 1 (2013).

Nicolosi, A. M. (2001). "We do not want our girls to marry foreigners": Gender, race, and American citizenship. *National Women's Studies Association Journal, 13*(3), 1–21.

Norton, R. (2002). Essentialism and queer history. In K. Peiss (Ed.), *Major problems in the history of American sexuality* (pp. 10–16). New York, NY: Houghton Mifflin Company.

Nye, R. (1999). *Sexuality.* New York, NY: Oxford University Press.

Patient Protection and Affordable Health Care Act of 2010. Pub. L. No. 111–148, 124 Stat. 119, *codified at* 42 U.S.C. §§ 300gg *et seq.* (2010).

Pharr, S. (1997). *Homophobia: A weapon of sexism.* Berkeley, CA: Chardon Press.

Pinker, S. (1997). *How the mind works.* New York, NY: Norton.

Potter, S. (2004). "Undesirable relations": Same-sex relations and the meaning of sexual desire at a women's reformatory during the progressive era. *Feminist Studies, 30*(2), 394–415.

Reilly, J. (1991). *The surgical solution: A history of involuntary sterilization in the United States.* Baltimore, MD: Johns Hopkins University Press.

Robertson, S. (2002). Age of consent law and the making of modern childhood in New York City, 1886–1921. *Journal of Social History, 35*(4), 781–798.

Rosen, R. (2000). *The world split open: How the modern women's movement changed America.* New York, NY: Penguin Books.

Rubin, G. (1993). Thinking sex: Notes for a radical theory of the politics of sexuality. In H. Abelove, M. A. Barale, & D. M. Halperin (Eds.), *The lesbian and gay studies reader* (pp. 3–44). New York, NY: Routledge.

Rutter, V., & Schwartz, P. (2011). *The gender of sexuality: Exploring sexual possibilities* (2nd ed.). New York, NY: Rowan & Littlefield.

Saguy, A. (2004). What is sexual harassment? From Capitol Hill to the Sorbonne. *Thomas Jefferson Law Review, 27*(1), 46–56.

Scott, J. (Ed.). (1996). *Feminism and history.* Cambridge: Oxford University Press.

Scott, J. (1999). *Gender and the politics of history.* New York: Columbia University Press.

Sexual Orientation Change Efforts, Pub. L. 2013, ch. 150, A.B. 3371 (2013), *codified at* N.J. Stat. Ann. 45:1–54 (2015).

Shaw, S. M., & Lee, J. (2015). *Women's voices, feminist visions* (6th ed.). New York, NY: McGraw-Hill Education.

Sheldon, W. H. (1942). *The varieties of temperament.* New York, NY: Harper & Brothers.

Shidlo, A., & Schroeder, M. (2002). Changing sexual orientation: A consumers' report. *Professional Psychology: Research and Practice, 33*(3), 249–259.

Smith College. (2002, March 26). *Actions of the Smith College Board of Trustees regarding issues of civil liberties past and present.* Retrieved from http://www.smith.edu/newsoffice/releases/01-085.html

Snitow, A., Stansell, C., & Thompson, S. (Eds.). (1983). *Powers of desire: The politics of sexuality.* New York, NY: Monthly Review Press.

Stein, J. S. (2013). Early to wed: Teenage marriage in postwar America. *The Journal of the History of Childhood and Youth, 6*(2), 359–382.

Stein, L. (1999). *Sexual harassment in America: A documentary history.* Westport, CT: Greenwood Publishing Group.

Syrett, N. L. (2014). The contested meanings of child marriage in the turn-of-the-century United States. In J. Marten (Ed.), *Children and youth during the gilded age and progressive era* (pp. 145–165). New York, NY: New York University Press.

Terry, J. (1999). *An American obsession: Science, medicine, and homosexuality in modern society.* Chicago, IL: University of Chicago Press.

Tichenor, V. J. (1999). Status and income as gendered resources: The case of marital power. *Journal of Marriage and Family, 61*(3), 638–650.

Walby, S. (1989). Theorizing patriarchy. *Sociology, 23*(2), 213–234.

Walkowitz, J. R. (1992). *City of dreadful delight: Narratives of sexual danger in late Victorian London.* Chicago, IL: University of Chicago Press.

Wegner, D. M., & Wheatley, T. (1999). Apparent mental causation: Sources of the experience of will. *American Psychologist, 54,* 480–492.

Werth, B. (2002). *The scarlet professor: Newton Arvin: A literary life shattered by scandal.* New York, NY: Anchor Books.

White, D. G. (1999). *Ar'n't I a Woman? Female slaves in the plantation south* (rev. ed.). New York, NY: W.W. Norton and Company.

Whitmore, W. H. (Ed.). (1889). *The colonial laws of Massachusetts.* Boston, MA: City Council of Boston.

Wolf, N. (2002). *The beauty myth: How images of beauty are used against women.* New York, NY: Harper Perennials.

Cases

Bigelow v. Virginia, 421 U.S. 809 (1975).
Burwell v. Hobby Lobby, 134 S. Ct. 2751 (2014).
Caminetti v. United States, 242 U.S. 470 (1917).
Church of the Lukumi Babalu Aye, Inc. v. City of Hialeah, 508 U.S. 520 (1993).
Ferguson v. Jews Offering New Alternatives for Healing (JONAH), HUD-L-5473–12, Order Granting Plaintiffs' Motion for Partial Summary Judgment (N.J. Super. Ct., Law. Div., Feb. 5, 2015a).
Ferguson v. Jews Offering New Alternatives for Healing (JONAH), 2015 N.J. Super. Unpub. LEXIS 236 (Law Div., Feb. 5, 2015b).
Griswold v. Connecticut, 381 U.S. 479 (1965).
King v. Christie, 981 F. Supp. 2d 296 (D.N.J. 2013), *aff'd,* 767 F.3d 216 (3rd Cir. 2014), *cert. denied,* 2015 U.S. Lexis 3122 (May 4, 2015).
King v. Governor of New Jersey, 767 F.3d 216 (3rd Cir. 2014), *cert. denied,* 2015 U.S. Lexis 3122 (May 4, 2015).
Mackenzie v. Hare, 239 U.S. 299 (1915).
Pickup v. Brown, 740 F.3d 1208 (9th Cir.), *cert. denied,* 134 S. Ct. 2871 (2014).
United States v. One Package, 86 F.2d 737 (2nd Cir. 1936).

CHAPTER 3

Sex and the Fourteenth Amendment: Part I: Due Process of Law

Stephen S. Owen and Tod W. Burke

In 2000, the U.S. Court of Appeals for the Third Circuit issued its opinion in the case of *Sterling v. Minersville*. The facts of the case were summarized in the opinion of the court:

> On April 17, 1997, 18-year old Marcus Wayman and a 17-year old male friend were parked in a lot adjacent to a beer distributor. The car and its occupants were observed by . . . [a police officer, who] was concerned about previous burglaries of the beer distributor and was suspicious of the fact that the headlights on the car were out. [The officer] called for back-up and, shortly thereafter, . . . [a second officer] arrived at the scene.
>
> The officers' investigation did not show any sign of a break-in at the business, but it was apparent to the officers that the young men had been drinking alcohol. The boys were also evasive when asked what they were doing in the parking lot. When an eventual search uncovered two condoms, [the officer] questioned whether the boys were in the parking lot for a sexual assignation. [The officer] testified that both Wayman and his companion eventually acknowledged that they were homosexuals and were in the parking lot to engage in consensual sex, but we note that the 17-year old denied making such admissions.
>
> The two boys were arrested for underage drinking and were taken to the Minersville police station. At the station, [the officer] lectured them that the Bible counseled against homosexual activity. [The officer] then warned Wayman that if Wayman did not inform his grandfather about his homosexuality that [the officer] would take it upon himself to disclose this information. After hearing this statement, Wayman confided to his friend that he was going to kill himself. Upon his release from custody, Wayman committed suicide in his home.
>
> (pp. 192–193)

- What does this case suggest about the relationship between law and morality?
- The court held that the officer's "threat to disclose Wayman's suspected homosexuality suffices as a violation of Wayman's constitutionally protected privacy interest" (p. 197). Do you agree with the court that Wayman's privacy rights were violated? What about his friend's privacy rights? Explain your reasoning with regard to both Wayman and his companion.
- Did the officer(s) follow proper and appropriate procedures in handling this case?

LEARNING OBJECTIVES

1. Compare and contrast the philosophies of law as expressed through the harm principle, legal moralism, legal positivism, and legal paternalism.
2. Distinguish between minimal scrutiny and strict scrutiny as they apply to the resolution of due process cases pertaining to law and sexuality.
3. Explain the concept of substantive due process and how it relates to law and sexuality, including cases related to privacy and the right to association.
4. Explain the concept of procedural due process and how it relates to law and sexuality, including legal principles and cases related to entrapment, void-for-vagueness, courtroom proceedings, and punishment.
5. Describe how the legal system has addressed issues related to hate crime.
6. Assess the legal reasoning in court cases pertaining to law and sexuality, considering the strength of the arguments and their implications.
7. Apply legal principles and precedents from the chapter to the resolution of scenarios related to chapter content.

The **Fourteenth Amendment** to the U.S. Constitution was enacted in 1868, in the aftermath of the Civil War. Although the Amendment includes numerous provisions about citizenship, apportionment of representation, qualifications for holding public office, and postwar debt, the following is the section most frequently referenced in contemporary jurisprudence:

No State shall make or enforce any law which shall abridge the privileges or immunities of citizens of the United States; nor shall any State deprive any person of life, liberty, or property, without due process of law; nor deny to any person within its jurisdiction the equal protection of the laws.

The variety of issues that may potentially be addressed by the Fourteenth Amendment is very broad.

• The **Due Process Clause** requires that states must follow both procedural and substantive due process. As its name suggests, *procedural due process* refers to the rules the state or federal govern-ment must follow in both civil and criminal proceedings before denying any person of a constitutionally protected right that concerns the person's life, liberty, or property. *Substantive due process* refers to the protection of rights that are articulated in the Constitution, itself, or that are determined by the courts to be fundamental rights, freedoms, or liberties that are worthy of protection even if they are not listed or identified in the text of the Constitution.

• The **Equal Protection Clause** requires that all similarly situated people be treated in a similar manner under the law. Of course, this is a complex endeavor, as the law does permit some circumstances in which full equality is not required (consider differences in the rights of adults, as opposed to juveniles, or the rights of those who are imprisoned, as opposed to those who are not).

Given the breadth and complexity of due process and equal protection as they relate to issues of sex and sexuality, this chapter explores the scope of the Due Process Clause, especially with regard to privacy rights, and Chapter 4 explores how the Equal Protection Clause operates to prevent arbitrary or irrational classifications based on sex, gender, or sexuality.

We will begin by considering philosophical perspectives on the role of law in society, with a particular emphasis on its role in the regulation of sexual activity. In doing so, we must consider the relationship between law and morality. As you read about the Hart–Devlin debate on philosophy of law, think about the *Sterling v. Minersville* case (the case study at the start of this chapter), and the philosophical issues it raises. Thereafter, we will turn to an in-depth study of procedural and substantive due process rights. In presenting the topics in this chapter, we emphasize the importance of understanding the depth of legal reasoning and analysis as it pertains to key legal opinions—usually from the U.S. Supreme Court—that address the nexus of law and sexuality. While it is impossible to survey the entirety of the field in a single chapter, the cases presented here are some of the "classics" of law and sexuality. As you read, we challenge you to ask yourself two questions about each case: First, how would you critically assess the legal reasoning? Do you think the logic and argumentation are sound? Go beyond a reaction based on your opinion of the issue in question, to instead reflect upon how the law was applied in the court case. Second, in what way might the case serve as precedent for future cases and issues? Work to discern the rule of law that was established by the case, and how it would apply to other issues. The boxes in the chapter will help you to do so by posing real and hypothetical legal scenarios for you to analyze.

THE HART–DEVLIN DEBATE AND THE LAW OF SEXUALITY

In the mid-twentieth century, British legal philosophers H. L. A. Hart and Patrick Devlin engaged in a vibrant exchange about the role of morality in the law, which subsequently came to be known as the Hart–Devlin debate. The debate was prompted by a report commissioned by British Parliament that offered a series of recommendations about how the law should address prostitution and homosexuality. Before considering the arguments made by Hart and Devlin, we will first turn to the work of John Stuart Mill.

John Stuart Mill and the Harm Principle

In the nineteenth century, British philosopher John Stuart Mill wrote a treatise titled *On Liberty* (1989/1859), in which he argued that the government's role in regulating human behavior should be a minimal one. Mill subscribed to the concept of liberty as a core value that merited the strongest of protection. Mill conceptualized liberty as the right of an individual to engage in whatever behavior he or she may please, so long as it does not directly harm another person. This has come to be known as the **harm principle**—a philosophical test that Mill advocated using to determine whether the government had exceeded its power. That is, if the government were to pass a law that prohibited a behavior that did not directly harm another person, Mill would view that law as being improper.

Of course, this begs the question as to what it means for an act to directly harm another person. Mill was careful to draw two distinctions. The first was that acting contrary to another person's morality was *not* a sufficient harm for the law to regulate. Although Mill saw it as acceptable to impose social sanctions on an individual who was perceived as acting immorally (e.g., through informal social control), he did not believe it was the law's purview to do so. Related was Mill's strong support for the freedom of speech, as he found noxious any attempts by the law to regulate the expression of ideas. In fact, Mill saw positive value in disagreements over ideas, as opposed to conformity (whether imposed by the law or by notions of morality). In fact, Mill argued that disagreement, and the resulting debates, were necessary to allow new ideas to be promulgated and tested.

Mill cites as an example an issue related to sexuality, namely polygamy. Writing contemporaneously with the development of the Mormon (Church of Jesus Christ of Latter-Day Saints) religion, Mill argued that polygamy—the practice of a man having more than one wife—need not be punished (see Chapter 6). Although Mill did find it acceptable for individuals to attempt to censure the practice, or to express their opinions about it, he did not find it appropriate for the law to intervene. Mill held this to be true even if polygamy was contrary to an individual's moral perspectives. As a coda to this discussion, Mill's essay was written in 1859; within 20 years, the U.S. Supreme Court upheld laws against polygamy as practiced by Mormons in the then-territory of Utah (*Reynolds v. United States*, 1878). One central premise of the Court's opinion was the moral opposition that had historically been accorded to polygamy.

The second distinction drawn by Mill was between direct and indirect harm. Mill saw any behavior that directly harmed another to be within the purview of state regulation through the law. However, Mill did not see indirect harm caused by a behavior as being sufficient to prohibit that behavior. To further illustrate, Mill uses drinking as an example:

> No person ought to be punished simply for being drunk; but a soldier or a policeman should be punished for being drunk on duty. Whenever, in short, there is a definite damage, or a definite risk of damage, either to an individual or to the public, the case is taken out of the province of liberty, and placed in that of morality or law.
> (p. 82)

In other words, just because a behavior might cause secondary (indirect) harms is not sufficient reason, from Mill's perspective, to

prohibit it. Taken as a whole, Mill's philosophy of the harm principle has the effect of narrowly prescribing those issues that can be regulated by the law, excluding those whose only basis lies in moral approbation or in a concern for indirect effects.

Taken as a whole, the above suggests that the key question for Mill would be whether or not an act causes a direct harm to others. Debates on other grounds would be irrelevant to the question of whether an act should be permitted or prohibited. To return to polygamy as an example, Mill would likely entertain evidence as to whether or not the practice does actually cause harm (for an exchange on this matter, see Beaman, 2006; Kent, 2006), and on that basis, absent morality, make the decision for how the law should respond.

The Wolfenden Report and Patrick Devlin's Response

Should homosexual conduct and prostitution be criminalized? In England, the Committee on Homosexual Offences and Prostitution considered this question in the 1950s. The Committee's report, also known as the **Wolfenden Report** (named for the committee chairman), was issued in 1957 (and reprinted in 1963) and made recommendations that reflected Mill's harm principle perspective.

Homosexual conduct was prohibited in England at the time. The Committee recommended decriminalizing consensual homosexual activity that occurred between adults in private. The rationale was grounded in an argument emphasizing "the importance which society and the law ought to give to individual freedom of choice and action in matters of private morality" (Committee on Homosexual Offences and Prostitution, 1963, p. 48). The Committee recommended the toleration of prostitution activities occurring in private, while maintaining a prohibition against those occurring in public. In doing so, the Committee was most concerned about "those activities which offend against public order and decency or expose the ordinary citizen to what is offensive or injurious" (p. 143). Note the connection to Mill's perspectives. The Wolfenden Report focused on maintaining liberty to engage in activities that did not cause direct harm, with little emphasis on the preservation of public morality as a rationale for the law.

British legal scholar Patrick Devlin disagreed with the Wolfenden Report's conclusions, for reasons he laid out in a series of lectures and writings. The philosophy articulated by Devlin has come to be known as **legal moralism**, as Devlin argued that the government had an obligation to pass laws designed to guarantee morality. To Devlin, morality was based on religion, so the law would invariably reflect religious concepts of morality. This does leave a question as to how legislators will know what issues are of significant enough moral concern to warrant regulation through law. Devlin (1977/1965) suggested that society would use its "collective judgement" (p. 55) to distill those moral principles that were significant enough to result in legislation.

The most significant moral issues were those "about which any twelve men or women drawn at random might after discussion be expected to be unanimous" (p. 61). But Devlin's method for assessment of morality (or of the immorality of that which was to be regulated) went beyond mere public opinion. In reaching their conclusions, the public was to be guided by feelings of "intolerance, indignation, and disgust" (p. 62), identifying those practices or behaviors that "lie beyond the limits of tolerance" (p. 62). Note, then, that Devlin's ideas about the law are more discriminating than simply suggesting that anything anyone believes to be immoral should be regulated. The bar Devlin sets is one that requires strong feelings against the practice in question. This was important to Devlin, as he did acknowledge that morally based laws should be carefully crafted, with attention given to preserving individual freedoms when possible—so long as (even private) acts do not violate the principles of morality identified through the above processes.

Also note that Devlin's legal philosophy is based on feeling and opinion, rather than requiring demonstrable evidence as to the impact or harm caused by an act. This is because Devlin saw immorality as a harm to society, in its own right. More specifically, Devlin argued that "societies disintegrate from within more frequently than they are broken up by external pressures" (p. 59). This is because Devlin saw a shared morality as a necessary foundation to society, and if that shared morality was to be eroded, the foundation of society would erode with it, potentially leading to its collapse. To be immoral, then, was to threaten social stability and the legislature therefore not only had the right, but also the obligation, to legislate morality.

Devlin's position is antithetical to Mill's. Mill argued that a wide variety of opinions should be heard and behaviors tolerated; Devlin advocated for a single concept of morality shared among the members of a society. Mill argued that freedoms should be maximized by allowing persons to engage in those activities that they desired and which did not pose a direct harm; Devlin supported restrictions even on those private activities that did not pose direct harms if public sentiment was that they were immoral. This dichotomy in legal philosophies, between a focus on harm versus a focus on morality, is relevant to many questions of law and sexuality. For instance, how would Devlin assess private and consensual activities, such as sex between unmarried heterosexual couples (see Chapter 6), sex between same-sex couples (see Chapter 6), or the viewing of pornography in the home (see Chapter 8)? How would Devlin assess activities that are more commercial, such as prostitution (see Chapter 7) or the production of pornography—or, for that matter, the depiction of suggestive sexual content in the mainstream media (see Chapter 8)? Then, consider how Mill would respond to each of the same questions. By engaging in this type of inquiry, you can approximate the competing perspectives on many of the policy debates surrounding contemporary issues of law and sexuality. This often corresponds to political ideology, as many conservative arguments have some basis in legal moralism, and many liberal arguments have some basis in the harm principle. Of course, this dichotomy is perhaps overly simplistic, leading into the more nuanced perspective articulated by H. L. A. Hart.

H. L. A. Hart Responds to Devlin

British legal philosopher H. L. A. Hart entered into this fray, challenging the propositions advanced by Devlin. Hart's (1958) arguments embodied concepts of **legal positivism**, which holds that the law is a human creation, separate from considerations of morality. Legal positivism also suggests that the law should be based on empirical (i.e., data-driven) facts, such as about the harms and impacts actually caused by a behavior or what the actual impact of a particular law would be.

Hart (1971/1959) explicitly rejected Devlin's arguments in response to the Wolfenden Report, raising the rallying cry, "Morality, what crimes may be committed in thy name!" (p. 54). By this, he meant to emphatically stress that a reliance on morality alone, without further empirical analysis of the behavior to be regulated, could pose significant negative consequences. His reference to "crimes" is metaphorical, suggesting that it would be unjust and violative of rights to impose laws and regulations solely based on morality, to the detriment of the persons who were affected. Instead, Hart recommended consideration of a series of questions before passing a law with its initial roots in a concern for social morality:

> Surely, the legislator should ask whether the general morality is based on ignorance, suspicion, or misunderstanding; whether there is a false conception that those who practise what it con-

demns are in other ways dangerous or hostile to society; and whether the misery to many parties, the blackmail and the other evil consequences of criminal punishment, especially for sexual offences, are well understood.

(p. 54)

Hart advocated this caution because he disagreed with Devlin's fundamental propositions about the regulation of morality. For instance, Hart was concerned about the potential for morally based laws to infringe upon individual freedoms, and also about the harms posed by morally based laws that remain on the books after society's view of morality changes. As an example of the latter point, consider laws prohibiting fornication (i.e., premarital sex; see Chapter 6). Once a staple of state legal codes, the earliest fornication statutes were morally driven (see D'Emilio & Freedman, 1988). However, over time, premarital sexuality became more common, with a notable increase in the early twentieth century. As D'Emilio & Freedman (1988) described, "What was daring and nonconformist in the earlier period appeared commonplace a generation later . . . as attitudes and ideals altered, so too did aspects of sexual activity" (p. 256). Research suggests that by the late twentieth century, public opinion toward premarital sexuality had become more favorable (Harding & Jencks, 2003); its practice had become "highly normative," as "almost all individuals of both sexes" had engaged in premarital sexuality by their early thirties (Finer, 2007, p. 76); and media depictions of premarital sexuality had increased (Malamuth & Impett, 2001). Yet, laws against fornication remained, though largely unenforced, in state codes. The implication is that persons engaging in fornication, once much more proscribed than currently is the case, could nonetheless remain under the threat of criminal prosecution for doing so. Hart's concern reflects a view of morality as an entity that changes over time based on new social norms and understandings.

Hart also did not agree with Devlin in terms of the degree of threat posed by activities labeled by society as immoral, when there were no other direct harms associated with them. Hart specifically found this to be the case when considering consensual, private sexual activities, writing "we have ample evidence for believing that people will not abandon morality . . . merely because some private sexual practice which they abominate is not punished by the law" (Hart, 1971/1959, p. 53). To Hart, there was not the same slippery slope that Devlin warned of, as society's foundation would not be likely to crumble if sexual freedoms were permitted.

While Devlin and Mill were at two opposite points on a spectrum, Hart falls somewhere in between—though certainly closer to Mill than to Devlin. Although Hart did not believe that morality, by itself with no other considerations, was sufficient as a basis for the law, he was willing to accept legislation that reached more broadly than Mill's somewhat narrow harm principle—so long as it was clear that there was a legitimate empirical basis for it.

Another Perspective: The Law as Protector

What if the analysis of an act or behavior suggests that, while not posing a direct harm to others, it poses a harm to those who choose voluntarily to engage in it? If this is empirically demonstrated, as Hart would require, would a legislature be justified in prohibiting the act? Here, morality is not (directly, anyway) part of the analysis, as the question turns on the extent to which the law should prevent persons from engaging in those actions that may cause them harm, even if voluntarily undertaken. This is a philosophy known as **legal paternalism**.

Joel Feinberg (1971) wrote about legal paternalism, and noted that there is risk inherent in virtually all choices that individuals make on a day-to-day basis. The first ques-

tion then becomes which acts are risky enough to merit the attention of the law. If an act is sufficiently risky, Feinberg describes two types of paternalism: weak and strong. *Weak paternalism* is essentially about informed consent—that is, ensuring that a person is informed about potential risks and then, with this knowledge, still chooses to consent to voluntarily engage in the behavior. *Strong paternalism* occurs when the state chooses to criminalize a behavior not because it can harm others, but in the interest of preventing persons from engaging in dangerous activities through which they could harm themselves.

One of the most common examples of legal paternalism focuses on seat belts. The state's interest in promoting seat-belt use is to protect drivers who might risk injury if seat belts are not worn. Weak paternalism might be accomplished through an awareness campaign emphasizing the value of seat belts and the risks involved with not wearing them; strong paternalism would be accomplished by mandating seat-belt usage, and issuing tickets to drivers who do not wear them.

An example more directly related to law and sexuality may be found in the debates surrounding prostitution. One perspective argues that prostitution must be criminalized to protect prostitutes from suffering harm at the hands of clients or pimps (e.g., Dempsey, 2010). A countervailing perspective argues that prostitution should be legalized, as government regulation can serve to reduce violence to prostitutes (e.g., Brents & Hausbeck, 2005). Note that these justifications for prostitution law—whether to criminalize or legalize prostitution—apply even if a prostitute has freely and voluntarily entered into sex work as a means for making money. That is, the focus is on protecting individuals from consequences (e.g., violence) that result from their activities, even if consensua (but note that persons are sometimes coerced into prostitution rather than making a free choice to participate).

The philosophies presented in this section explicitly or implicitly underlie many debates about what should or should not be regulated under the law. As such, the ideas of Mill, Devlin, Hart, and Feinberg serve as paradigms for the role of law in society (for an interesting discussion applying the Hart–Devlin debate to Arthur Miller's play *The Crucible*, see Samuelson, 1998). At the same time, there are many debates, particularly in the area of law and sexuality, about which of these philosophies ought to serve as the law's primary function. As we move to the next sections of the chapter, we will see how the law, and the Fourteenth Amendment, in particular, helps to resolve disputes about how sexual activity should be regulated.

OVERVIEW OF FOURTEENTH AMENDMENT DUE PROCESS STANDARDS OF REVIEW

Recall from earlier in this chapter that the Fourteenth Amendment was enacted in 1868, in the aftermath of the Civil War. But the interpretation of its language has evolved over time. Indeed, although one purpose of the Amendment was to protect the rights of African-Americans who had been newly invested with citizenship following the abolition of slavery (Boyer et al., 1993), the Amendment's impact on the American legal landscape has actually been much broader. As noted by Epps (2007), viewing the scope of the Fourteenth Amendment as limited to

Box 3.1 MARDI GRAS FLASHERS

Mardi Gras is a celebration held on Fat Tuesday, which is the day before Ash Wednesday. New Orleans is arguably the U.S. city most closely associated with Mardi Gras, known for its elaborate parades, costumes, and festive street parties. Sociologist Craig Forsyth (1992) observed that "[o]n Mardi Gras day in New Orleans, many things normally forbidden are permitted" (p. 395). One act for which the street celebrations have acquired a reputation is the practice of flashing, in which (primarily female) revelers show their breasts in exchange for being thrown strands of beads.

Section 14:106 of the Louisiana Revised Statutes prohibits "Exposure of the . . . female breast . . . in any public place or place open to the public view . . . with the intent of arousing sexual desire or which appeals to prurient interest or is patently offensive." However, as Forsyth suggests, laws such as those prohibiting flashing for beads may not be as vigorously enforced during Mardi Gras as during other times of year. Although the law does not go entirely unenforced, as some indecent exposure arrests are made (e.g., McConnaughey, 2000), this does pose the question as to whether there is ever a justification to relax enforcement of the laws.

- Considering the example of flashing for beads during Mardi Gras, how do you think Mill, Devlin, Hart, and Feinberg's philosophies would address laws against indecent exposure?
- How do you think they would address differential enforcement of the law, based on whether it is, or is not, within the context of Mardi Gras street celebrations?

post-Civil War, Reconstruction-era issues "robs the Amendment of a rich set of meanings that might directly apply to current constitutional controversies" (p. 442). Indeed, consider the depth of the impact that Epps (2007) attributes to the Fourteenth Amendment: "The Amendment was not only designed to protect citizens within the states from overreaching majorities or undemocratic elites, but also to protect the federal government against what today we would call 'capture' by states that did not honor the spirit of republican government" (p. 453).

Take a moment to reflect upon the power of the above concepts. Comprising only a single sentence, the section of the Fourteenth Amendment quoted earlier may be invoked when any person in the United States, citizen or otherwise, believes his or her due process or equal protection rights have been violated. This allows the Amendment to protect individuals and for the federal government, via the courts, to require that state law is consistent with notions of equality and with the protection of those rights that have been deemed fundamental or that are constitutionally required. The Fourteenth Amendment has, in fact, touched upon a variety of controversial issues whose currency extends past the mid-nineteenth century. For instance, debates and legal cases concerning abortion, interracial marriage, gender equality, sexual orientation, and privacy, in general, have invoked the Fourteenth Amendment. Therefore, one way in which the Fourteenth Amendment has evolved is through the variety of controversies, current to any given period in history, to which it has been applied. Another way that the Fourteenth Amendment has evolved lies in the methods through which judges and justices resolve Fourteenth Amendment cases.

The text of the Fourteenth Amendment itself does not provide much guidance in terms of what "due process" or "equal protection" mean. Over the past century, the U.S. Supreme Court has clarified Fourteenth Amendment decision-making through the identification of three levels of judicial scrutiny known as **standards of review**. Shaman (2001) emphasizes the importance of the levels of scrutiny: "Determining the level of scrutiny to be utilized in a particular case has a greater impact on its outcome than deciding what constitutional provision will be applied to it . . . what really matters is what level of scrutiny will be chosen" (pp. 72–73). This is because the standard of review establishes the criteria for decision-making that are applied in Fourteenth Amendment (and other constitutional) cases, and some levels (e.g., strict scrutiny) require much more stringent criteria than others (e.g., minimal scrutiny).

Constitutional standards of review have developed over time. It is important to acknowledge that the levels of scrutiny are a judicially created framework, rather than something specified in the Constitution itself. This is important because it means that the application of the standards of review are continually evolving, so our understanding of levels of scrutiny may be very different in 20 years than it is today.

There are currently three constitutional standards of review, each of which calls for judges to apply a different level of judicial scrutiny to the law being challenged. Stated another way, the particular standard of review informs the judge reviewing the constitutionality of a law how exacting she should be in requiring the government to justify its intrusion on the rights of citizens. In the early twentieth century, minimal scrutiny—sometimes known as rational basis review—was the primary tool for constitutional analysis. Over time, it became clear that some issues merited closer examination than minimal scrutiny allowed, and strict scrutiny was developed. Still later, it became clear that there needed to be a middle level of analysis, and intermediate scrutiny emerged (for a more detailed history and discussion of constitutional

Table 3.1 Constitutional standards of review and their associated levels of scrutiny

Standard of Review	Legislative Deference	Relationship to State Interest	Relationship between Means and Ends	Burden of Proof
Strict Scrutiny	Not Deferential	"Compelling"	"Absolutely Necessary"	State
Intermediate Scrutiny	Somewhat Deferential	"Important or Substantial"	"Close, though not perfect, Fit"	State
Minimal Scrutiny	Highly Deferential	"Rational"	"Reasonably Related"	Challenger

Source: Adapted from Shaman (2001: Chapter 3).

standards of review and the levels of scrutiny each requires, see Shaman, 2001). Table 3.1 provides a summary of each level of scrutiny. This chapter will address minimal scrutiny and strict scrutiny. Intermediate scrutiny, which applies primarily to equal protection issues, will be discussed in Chapter 4.

Minimal Scrutiny: The Rational Basis Test

We will begin with the oldest form of scrutiny, minimal scrutiny, which is also known as the rational basis test. Most issues are presumed to fall under minimal scrutiny; it is the method used to resolve disputes about any issues that are not specifically identified as falling under strict or intermediate scrutiny. Let's assume that a law is being challenged under minimal scrutiny. The court will begin with a presumption of legislative deference, meaning that it will presume the law to be valid as drafted by the legislature. In granting deference, the court acknowledges that it is the legislature, and not the judicial system, that is best positioned to study societal concerns and arrive at the appropriate solutions to them. This is also an indication of a legal philosophy known as judicial restraint, which suggests that the role of the court should be limited (or restrained), respecting the judgments of the legislature and overturning them only if there is a clear and patently imper-

missible violation of due process or equal protection. The law under review will be upheld as constitutional so long as (1) the law bears some rational relationship to a legitimate state interest; and (2) the law is "reasonably related" to accomplishing that state interest (Shaman, 2001, p. 72). It is the challenger who bears the burden of persuading the court that the above criteria are not the case—that is, that the law does not have a "rational basis" related to some legitimate state interest, or the law is not reasonably related to accomplishing some legitimate state interest.

Dobbins v. Los Angeles (1904) illustrates how the rational basis test works in substantive due process cases. The Los Angeles City Council enacted an ordinance making it illegal to construct gasworks facilities outside of designated zones within the city. The plaintiff in *Dobbins* applied for a permit to engage in construction of a gasworks facility within one of the designated areas. During construction, however, the city council amended the ordinance, causing the plaintiff's construction project to lie outside the appropriate zone. The U.S. Supreme Court acknowledged that the city council had a legitimate governmental interest for amending its ordinance—namely "making regulations to promote the public health and safety" (pp. 235–236). In spite of the fact that the plaintiff had already invested a considerable amount of money in the construction project, the Court emphasized that the city could still use its ordinance-making authority to regulate the project in question to promote the health, safety, and welfare of people in the city. Yet, the Court declared the ordinance violated due process because the ordinance was not rationally related to these permissible governmental interests. In fact, the area in which the plaintiff had begun construction was no different from the areas in which the amended ordinance permitted new construction. Thus, the ordinance lacked a rational basis because its terms, as applied to the plaintiff's construction project, were not reasonably related to accomplishing the legitimate governmental interests of promoting health, safety, and welfare.

Perhaps the leading substantive due process case applying the rational basis test to an issue of law and sexuality is *Lawrence v. Texas* (2003). *Lawrence* invalidated the nation's remaining sodomy laws, which had once criminalized oral or anal sex performed in private between consenting adults, on the grounds that such laws violated the Fourteenth Amendment. *Lawrence* is discussed in greater detail later in this chapter. For now, it is sufficient to note that the Court found there was no rational basis for upholding sodomy laws because they further "no legitimate state interest which can justify . . . intrusion into the personal and private life of the individual" (p. 578).

Strict Scrutiny

For many years, minimal scrutiny was applied in such a way that laws were rarely overturned. However, over time, it became clear that there were some issues that required a more critical analysis than minimal scrutiny allowed (Shaman, 2001). The origins of strict scrutiny are generally attributed to a footnote in *United States v. Carolene Products* (1938), a case about a law regulating the interstate transportation of milk products. Footnote 4 speculates that there may be some instances in which "more exacting judicial scrutiny

under the general prohibitions of the Fourteenth Amendment" (p. 153) may be appropriate. From this inauspicious beginning, the concept of strict scrutiny emerged (Jackson, 2011). In strict scrutiny, legislative deference is absent; that is, the court need not begin with the presumption that the law is inherently valid. Indeed, in order to be upheld, the law must meet a much higher bar than minimal scrutiny. Not only does the government bear the burden of showing that the law is valid, but it must also meet two criteria to do so. The first is that the law must address a state interest that is more than legitimate; it must be a "compelling." The second is that the law, itself, must be "absolutely necessary" to accomplish the state interest (Shaman, 2001, p. 72). This is generally interpreted to mean that the law must be narrowly tailored and impinge upon the smallest number of rights possible in order to achieve its desired goal. This is a high bar to meet; indeed, because this standard of review begins with the presumption that the law is unconstitutional until the government proves otherwise, legal scholars debate whether it is "strict in theory and fatal in fact" (Gunther, 1972, p. 8; cf. Winkler, 2006).[1]

Strict scrutiny is not applied to all cases. The most typical triggers for strict scrutiny analysis are when a fundamental right or a suspect class is involved. In this chapter, we focus on the due process analyses attendant to fundamental rights. In Chapter 4, we will examine suspect classifications as part of our study of equal protection.

A **fundamental right** is one that is not necessarily listed in the Constitution or Bill of Rights, but which has great and historical significance and merits protection, nonetheless. In *Washington v. Glucksberg* (1997), fundamental rights were defined as follows:

We have regularly observed that the Due Process Clause specially protects those fundamental rights and liberties which are, objectively, "deeply rooted in this Nation's history and tradition," and "implicit in the concept of ordered liberty," such that "neither liberty nor justice would exist if they were sacrificed." [Also], we have required in substantive due process cases a "careful description" of the asserted fundamental liberty interest.

(p. 721)

Clearly, this is reserved for those rights and liberties deemed most important to protect, such as free speech, the free exercise of religion, freedom of association, the right to travel, the right to vote, the right to run for office, and the rights subsumed under the notion of "substantive due process" (Winkler, 2006). Substantive due process includes the amorphous right to privacy, discussed later in this chapter. And it also encompasses certain "liberty interests," such as,

> infringements on the right to "bodily integrity," which encompasses denials of bail to aliens detained pending deportation, forced civil commitment of sexual predators, and compulsory medical treatment of criminal defendants ... [as well as] restrictions on parents' rights to control their children's upbringing.
>
> (Winkler, 2006, p. 864)

However, a full enumeration of all fundamental rights, especially those protected by substantive due process, is likely not possible because, as also noted in the *Glucksberg* case, fundamental rights analyses are "a process" in which "the outlines of the 'liberty' specially protected by the Fourteenth Amendment" are "never fully clarified, to be sure, and perhaps not capable of being fully clarified" (p. 722). Indeed, history and tradition "guide and discipline" any constitutional inquiry regarding fundamental rights, "but do not set its outer boundaries" thereby allowing us to learn from history "without allowing the past alone to rule the present" (*Obergefell v. Hodges*, 2015, p. 2598).

> [T]he full scope of the liberty guaranteed by the Due Process Clause cannot be found in or lim-

ited by the precise terms of the specific guarantees elsewhere provided in the Constitution. This "liberty" is not a series of isolated points pricked out in terms of the taking of property; the freedom of speech, press, and religion; the right to keep and bear arms; the freedom from unreasonable searches and seizures; and so on. It is a rational continuum which, broadly speaking, includes a freedom from all substantial arbitrary impositions and purposeless restraints, . . . and which also recognizes, what a reasonable and sensitive judgment must, that certain interests require particularly careful scrutiny of the state needs asserted to justify their abridgment.

> (*Planned Parenthood of Southeastern Pa. v. Casey*, 1992, p. 849, quoting *Poe v. Ulman*, 1961, p. 543, Harlan, J., dissenting)

Let's turn to a more concrete example that illustrates strict scrutiny for a fundamental rights question.

In *Loving v. Virginia* (1967), the U.S. Supreme Court considered a challenge to a Virginia law that prohibited interracial marriages. The Court considered both an equal protection and a due process challenge to the law, and unanimously found that the law was unconstitutional on both counts. Here, our interest is on the due process argument. Chief Justice Warren's opinion for the Court was explicit in its conclusion that (heterosexual) marriage is a fundamental right, thus meriting protection under the Due Process Clause: "The freedom to marry has long been recognized as one of the vital personal rights essential to the orderly pursuit of happiness by free men. Marriage is one of the 'basic civil rights of man,' fundamental to our very existence and survival" (p. 12). Note how this corresponds to the description of fundamental rights provided above. Marriage is not enumerated within the Constitution, itself, but its historical role and significance as a "vital personal right" would deprive significant liberty if it were not permitted. As such, it is a fundamental right, the abrogation of which

Box 3.2 PHARMACIST REFUSAL CASES

You are the judge in a case challenging a state law that allows pharmacists to refuse to fill prescriptions for birth control pills and to refuse to sell the so-called "morning after pill," which may prevent pregnancy if taken shortly after sexual intercourse, if doing so violates their conscience (for an overview of such laws, see National Conference of State Legislatures, 2012). The plaintiff in the case claims that the law violates her rights under the Due Process Clause by denying access to medication.

- What standard of review would you apply—the rational basis test or strict scrutiny? Why?
- What conclusion would you reach? If you feel that additional information is necessary, specify what information and how it would affect your decision.
- How does your answer reflect philosophical principles from Mill, Devlin, Hart, or Feinberg?

would violate notions of substantive due process as embodied in the Fourteenth Amendment (*Obergefell v. Hodges*, 2015).

The significance of marriage being designated as a fundamental right is illustrated in a subsequent case, *Turner v. Safley* (1987). This case challenged limits that were placed on the right of prison inmates to marry, through a Missouri Department of Corrections regulation that specified inmates could "marry only with the permission of the superintendent of the prison, and . . . that such approval should be given only 'when there are compelling reasons to do so' " (p. 82). Because marriage is a fundamental right, strict scrutiny applies, and such an analysis requires (as noted in Table 3.1) that the measure is the "absolutely necessary" means to accomplish the state's desired ends. Here, the state argued that the regulation was necessary for security and rehabilitative purposes. In ruling the measure unconstitutional, Justice O'Connor's opinion for the Court held that it was "an exaggerated response to . . . security objectives" and that "the rule sweeps much more broadly than can be explained by petitioners' penological objectives" (p. 98) for rehabili-

tation. Therefore, the regulation was viewed by the Court as not being the "absolutely necessary," or narrowly enough tailored, means for accomplishing the Department of Corrections' goals. Note that, were marriage not a fundamental right, the Court would have likely granted deference to the Department of Corrections under minimal scrutiny: "Courts will defer to prison officials when they can show that a restriction is related to legitimate correctional goals, particularly facility security" (Silverman, 2001, p. 333). It is the strict scrutiny analysis of fundamental rights that required closer analysis of the issue. (For more information on marriage, see Chapter 9.)

SUBSTANTIVE DUE PROCESS

The Fourteenth Amendment is one of the most significant parts of the Constitution for the field of law and sexuality. Although the initial concepts addressed under the Fourteenth Amendment Due Process Clause may appear simple on the surface, this belies a complexity in both the meaning and the application of the Amendment.

Substantive due process protects individual rights and liberties, meaning that it identifies protected areas into which the law may not intrude. Another way of conceptualizing substantive due process is by imagining those rights, behaviors, forms of expression, and so on, to which all persons should be entitled. If protected under the Fourteenth Amendment Due Process Clause, no state may make laws that infringe upon rights, behaviors, forms of expression, and so on, unless there is a compelling state interest at stake, and the law is narrowly tailored to achieve that interest. In this section, we will discuss several areas of substantive due process related to law and sexuality. It is important to realize, however, that substantive due process involves many more issues than can be considered in the course of one chapter. For instance, some discussions will be reserved for other chapters, such as rights related to freedom of speech and expression (see Chapter 8) and same-sex marriage (see Chapter 9). Here, we will focus primarily on privacy and on the right to association.

The Right to Privacy

Nowhere in the U.S. Constitution, including in the Bill of Rights, is there specifically stated any guarantee of a "right to privacy"; in fact, the word "privacy" does not appear anywhere in the Constitution. However, the right to privacy has been upheld by the courts and is at the very heart of many debates surrounding issues of law and sexuality.

The Early Roots of Privacy

Although not pertaining to law and sexuality, it is important to note the role of two U.S. Supreme Court cases from the early twentieth century in building toward the concept of a right to privacy, both grounded in the concept of due process. In 1923, the Court decided *Meyer v. Nebraska*, a case challenging a state law that prohibited foreign language instruction to students who had not yet completed the eighth grade. In addition to questioning the rational basis for the law, the Court found that it was contrary to the presumed "power of parents to control the education of their" children (p. 401). Accordingly, the Court rejected the law under the Due Process Clause of the Fourteenth Amendment.

Two years later, in 1925, the Court heard another case pertaining to education. In *Pierce v. Society of Sisters*, the Court overruled a law that required students to attend public schools. While the law did allow for some exceptions to be made, it essentially prohibited instruction at private or parochial schools. Again, the Court questioned the rational basis for the law and, citing *Meyer*, concluded that the law "unreasonably interferes with the liberty of parents and guardians to direct the upbringing and education of children under their control" (pp. 534–535).

Although on the surface *Meyer* and *Pierce* were about education, their legacy runs much deeper. Both address issues of substantive due process and suggest that parents and guardians have an entitlement to privacy in determining the appropriate education for their children—a privacy that the U.S. Supreme Court held to be protected. And, both were cited in the landmark case of *Griswold v. Connecticut*, discussed below, which reconceptualized how privacy was viewed by the courts.

Griswold: Privacy and Contraception

A Connecticut law provided: "Any person who uses any drug, medicinal article or instrument for the purpose of preventing conception shall be fined not less than fifty dollars or imprisoned not less than sixty days nor more than one year or be both fined and imprisoned" (p. 480). In other words, birth control was illegal, and the prohibition applied to all persons in Connecticut, whether married, partnered, or single. Also illegal was the provision of advice and information about birth control, because that was viewed as aiding and abetting in the commission of an offense.

Estelle Griswold was Executive Director of the Planned Parenthood League of Connecticut, and did precisely what was proscribed by Connecticut law—she counseled married couples on the use of contraception. Griswold was fined $100 for the offense, and appealed. In a 7–2 decision, the U.S. Supreme Court ruled in *Griswold v. Connecticut* (1965) that there was a constitutional right to marital privacy, although the justices disagreed on the constitutional basis for the right. The perspectives offered by the justices are presented below. As you read, consider the arguments set forth, and consider which you find to be the most persuasive rationale.

The majority opinion of the Court was delivered by Justice Douglas, and set forth a creative but complex rationale for supporting marital privacy. The argument was based on the concept of a *penumbra*, which essentially refers to an extension of a previously identified right that, in turn, supports the concept of marital privacy. Rather than identifying one specific place where the right to privacy was housed, then, the opinion suggested that it was supported by the accumulation of multiple penumbras that led to a "zone of privacy created by several fundamental constitutional guarantees" (p. 485). Aspects of the First, Third, Fourth, Fifth, and Ninth Amendments suggest a privacy interest. Respectively, these include the right to choose with whom one associates (discussed further below), the protection against the military requiring private homeowners to house troops, the protection against illegal search of a home, the right to not disclose incriminating information, and the protection of rights not otherwise listed. Taken as a whole, these previously enumerated rights suggest that the Constitution implies a zone of privacy, which then extends to also protect marital privacy.

Importantly, Justice Douglas's opinion conceptualizes marital privacy as a fundamental right because the rights on which marital privacy is based—that is, those within the penum-

bras and zone of privacy—are identified as fundamental. But perhaps this begs a question, namely, how do we know when privacy protections should or should not be extended? Another way of asking this question is, why did the Court agree to extend the existing privacy rights to the protection of marital privacy in a case about birth control? The answer lies in the opinion's description of the quality of marital privacy:

> Would we allow the police to search the sacred precincts of marital bedrooms for telltale signs of the use of contraceptives? The very idea is repulsive to the notions of privacy surrounding the marriage relationship. We deal with a right of privacy older than the Bill of Rights—older than our political parties, older than our school system. Marriage is a coming together for better or for worse, hopefully enduring, and intimate to the degree of being sacred.
>
> (p. 486)

Recall the definition of fundamental rights provided earlier. Note how the above passage corresponds to the notions of what a fundamental right is. It appears that the argument in the Court's opinion could actually be upheld on two premises—the first based on the concept of penumbras and the zone of privacy, and the second based on casting marital privacy as a fundamental right, on its own. Taken together, both perspectives shaped the *Griswold* decision.

Three justices wrote concurring opinions in the case, agreeing with the outcome, but with different legal reasoning. Justice Goldberg grounded his analysis in the Ninth Amendment, seeing it as something of a "catch all" amendment that allows for the protection of fundamental rights not explicitly listed in the Constitution. The Ninth Amendment states the following: "The enumeration in the Constitution, of certain rights, shall not be construed to deny or disparage others retained by the people." Of course, this raises a question, to wit: How does one identify the unlisted rights that are sufficiently important to be "retained by the people" and protected? Justice Goldberg addresses this question by returning to the concept of fundamental rights, arguing that marital privacy qualifies as fundamental and, therefore, merits protection:

> The fact that no particular provision of the Constitution explicitly forbids the State from disrupting the traditional relation of the family—a relation as old and as fundamental as our entire civilization—surely does not show that the Government was meant to have the power to do so. Rather, as the Ninth Amendment expressly recognizes, there are fundamental personal rights such as this one, which are protected from abridgment by the Government though not specifically mentioned in the Constitution.
>
> (*Griswold*, 1965, pp. 495–496, Goldberg, J., concurring)

The Ninth Amendment analysis is one that Abramson, Pinkerton, and Huppin (2003) argue is unappreciated in matters of law and sexuality, and as a result they argue for the Ninth Amendment to be rediscovered and applied to matters of sexuality. They further argue that the founders were very aware of sexuality and the significance of sexual freedom, but did not include sexual rights within the Constitution because they assumed their presence as "retained by the people" and protected under the provisions of the Ninth Amendment.

Justice Harlan argued that the Fourteenth Amendment was sufficient, on its own, to protect marital privacy. In fact, Justice Harlan did not feel that the Court needed to consider any other areas of the Constitution or Bill of Rights, noting simply that "The Due Process Clause of the Fourteenth Amendment stands, in my opinion, on its own bottom" (p. 500). In other words, the substantive due process rights embodied in the Fourteenth Amendment were sufficient to Justice Harlan to support protection of marital privacy as a fundamental right.

Finally, Justice White offered yet another perspective, this one grounded in an analysis of the basis for the law. Justice White's opinion is the closest to a traditional strict scrutiny analysis. Consistent with the strict scrutiny criteria, Justice White notes that "an examination of the justification offered [for the law] . . . cannot be avoided" (p. 503). The task would then be to determine how compelling the state interest was and whether the law in question is narrowly enough suited to accomplish it.

The explanation for the law offered by Connecticut was that it "serve[s] the State's policy against all forms of promiscuous or illicit sexual relationships, be they premarital or extramarital" (p. 505), which Justice White recognized as a *legitimate* state interest, although not necessarily a *compelling* interest. In other words, Connecticut argued that allowing anyone, even married couples, access to contraception could promote or encourage other forms of prohibited sex (e.g., adultery, prostitution, premarital sex), as persons would be more willing to engage in such activities if they knew that the risk of pregnancy was diminished. Justice White did not feel the need to determine if these legitimate state interests rose to the level of being compelling because, even if they were, Justice White found that the law, as constructed, was too broad, stating that "I find nothing in this record justifying the sweeping scope of this statute, with its telling effect on the freedoms of married persons, and therefore conclude that it deprives such persons of liberty without due process of law" (p. 502). This does leave open the question of how Justice White would have ruled had the law been more narrowly written.

Griswold is described in such detail because of the central role that it has played in subsequent privacy analyses. It is also a good illustration of the complexities of legal reasoning. What seems like an initially simple question (i.e., should married persons be permitted to use birth control) in fact turns into a multifaceted legal analysis, as substantive due process jurisprudence requires careful consideration of fact patterns and how legal principles may be applied to them. And, it is rare to find a unanimous decision. Here, Justices Black and Stewart dissented from the majority. Both expressed concern that the Supreme Court was exceeding its power by identifying a right to privacy that was not stated in the Constitution; although Justice Stewart did label the law as "uncommonly silly" (p. 527), he nonetheless believed that the matter of whether to support or repeal the law was best left to the legislature.

Griswold applied to contraception for married persons. The court later explored the right of contraception for unmarried persons in a case that we will consider when discussing equal protection in Chapter 4 (*Eisenstadt v. Baird*, 1972). But in what other cases has *Griswold* served as precedent, extending notions of the right to privacy?

Stanley: *The Home as Private*

In 1969, the U.S. Supreme Court gave its ruling in the case, *Stanley v. Georgia*, which considered whether individuals could possess obscene materials in the privacy of their own homes. Important to note is that materials labeled as "obscene" (see Chapter 8 for a discussion of obscenity) receive no First Amendment protection, and their sale and distribution can be criminalized. But the possession of obscene materials in a private home raises privacy concerns. Delivering the opinion of a unanimous Court, Justice Marshall held that individuals could possess these materials in their homes: "States retain broad power to regulate obscenity; that power simply does not extend to mere possession by the individual in the privacy of his own home" (p. 568).

How far does, or should, *Stanley*'s holding extend? A footnote to the decision itself noted, "What we have said in no way infringes upon the power of the State or Federal Government to make possession of other items, such as narcotics, firearms, or stolen goods, a crime" (p. 568). In *Osborne v. Ohio* (1990), the Court did not extend *Stanley* to include child pornography, on the basis that the prohibition of possession of child pornography, even in a private home, was necessary to protect children who would be harmed in the creation of the materials. The Court also expressed concern that promoting a market for child pornography, as would occur if its private possession were permitted, would put children at risk. In *United States v. Thirty-Seven Photographs* (1971), the Court refused to extend *Stanley* to permit the importation of obscene materials, even if intended for private use. And in *Paris Adult Theatre v. Slaton* (1973), the Court drew a distinction between private homes and commercial establishments, noting that *Stanley* did not extend to the latter. Lower courts have also refused to extend *Stanley* to private clubs (*31 West 21st Street Associates v. Evening of the Unusual*, 1984) or to prostitution, even when it occurs in a private home (e.g., *Blyther v. United States*, 1990). This is another valuable lesson for legal reasoning, as one challenging task is to determine when and why a precedent may or may not be applied to a different fact pattern. Doing so requires a careful analysis of the scope of the decision and the reasoning for it, which is another important reason for carefully reviewing the holding as stated in the opinion of each case.

Roe: *Privacy and Abortion Law*

Perhaps the most controversial area into which *Griswold* has reached, related to privacy rights, is abortion. *Roe v. Wade* (1973) is widely known as the first Supreme Court case to rule on the issue of abortion.

Roe v. Wade (1973) was an appeal based on a Texas law prohibiting all abortions, the only exception being for medical necessity for the life of the mother. Roe, a woman from

Texas, was pregnant and filed the appeal on the grounds that she was unable to procure a safe, legal abortion in Texas and did not have the means of traveling to another state to do so. In a 7–2 decision, the Court struck down the Texas law and established guidelines for what type of state regulation was permissible at each trimester of pregnancy. Writing the opinion of the court, Justice Blackmun provided an historical survey of the development of abortion law, noting that in the early years of American history "abortion was viewed with less disfavor than under most American statutes currently in effect" (p. 140). Justice Blackmun then noted that three reasons could explain why there was an increased regulation on abortion beginning in the 1800s: Victorian-era perceptions of the immorality of sexuality; concerns about the safety of abortion procedures, resulting in laws regulating them to protect pregnant women; and "protecting prenatal life" (p. 150).

In *Roe*, the Court located the right to privacy within the Due Process Clause of the Fourteenth Amendment. From the perspective of legal reasoning, *Roe* was significant because it expanded the scope of *Griswold* beyond "marital privacy" and because it resolved the source of privacy rights that led to so much confusion in the *Griswold* opinions. Because privacy was held to be a fundamental right, the analysis of the constitutionality of the Texas abortion law proceeded following strict scrutiny.

The Court's ruling in *Roe* was in some ways a compromise between the arguments of Roe, who challenged the law, and the state, who sought to have the law upheld. Roe argued that abortion fell entirely within the right to privacy, which would exempt it from any government control. Texas argued that its compelling state interest in the protection of life entitled it to regulate abortion at any time. The Court rejected both interpretations, instead identifying two compelling state interests that could be served if the abortion law

was narrowly enough tailored: protection of the mother's health and protecting "potential life" (p. 154). The degree of state regulation permitted was based on the trimester of pregnancy. In the first trimester, state law could not restrict abortion, as it was to be construed as a private medical decision. In the second trimester, state law could regulate abortion to accomplish its interest in protecting the mother's health, so long as the regulations "are reasonably related to maternal health" (p. 164). In the third trimester, state law could regulate abortion to accomplish its interest in protecting potential life, and the Court noted that it could, in fact, prohibit third trimester abortions so long as there was an exception "for the preservation of the life or health of the mother" (p. 165).

It would be illogical to leave the discussion of *Roe v. Wade* without noting the significant controversy that it has generated, abortion being one of the most controversial (and divisive) modern political issues (e.g., Clarke, 1999; Norrander & Wilcox, 2001). For instance, Justice Rehnquist's dissent in *Roe* argued that abortion should not be viewed as a fundamental right and that the ruling ran counter to national sentiment, as illustrated through state laws in existence at the time. Perhaps Justice Blackmun anticipated the range of views that would lead to controversy in abortion law when he noted in the Court's opinion:

> One's philosophy, one's experiences, one's exposure to the raw edges of human existence, one's religious training, one's attitudes toward life and family and their values, and the moral standards one establishes and seeks to observe, are all likely to influence and to color one's thinking and conclusions about abortion.
>
> (p. 116)

Planned Parenthood of Southeastern Pennsylvania v. Casey (1992) reaffirmed *Roe* almost 20 years later. *Casey* is a significant case for precisely that reason—because of the reaffirmation of the Court's holding in *Roe* 19 years earlier. The opinion of the Court held that "the essential holding of *Roe v. Wade* should be retained and once again reaffirmed" (p. 846), the rationale coming from a substantive due process analysis based on the Fourteenth Amendment. The Court also dismissed moral arguments, writing "Men and women of good conscience can disagree, and we suppose some always shall disagree, about the profound moral and spiritual implications of terminating a pregnancy, even in its earliest stage ... Our obligation is to define the liberty of all, not to mandate our own moral code" (p. 850).

The opinion brings a fairly lengthy analysis of why *Roe* should be maintained, noting that it has not been unworkable; that it is established within modern culture and overturning it would pose a hardship to "those who have relied reasonably on the rule's continued application" (p. 855); and that neither case law after *Roe* nor scientific developments have rendered *Roe*'s provisions moot.

Casey did, however, diminish the reliance on the trimester scheme articulated in *Roe*. In the Court's opinion, Justice O'Connor described the protected right as:

> a recognition of the right of the woman to choose to have an abortion before viability and to obtain it without undue interference from the State. Before viability, the State's interests are not strong enough to support a prohibition of abortion or the imposition of a substantial obstacle to the woman's effective right to elect the procedure.
>
> (p. 846)

Note that this modifies the interpretation in *Roe*. In this regard, the Court held that the point at which the fetus becomes viable is the point at which states may prohibit abortion, which was previously defined as the third trimester in *Roe*. The *Casey* opinion emphasized that this principle remained in force, although with medical advances, the actual

point at which viability occurs may change. This suggests that it is not the third trimester that is the definitive point at which state prohibition of abortion may occur, but rather it is at the point of fetus viability.

Having rejected *Roe*'s trimester framework, the Court in *Casey* instead announced that an "undue burden" standard should be employed to assess the constitutionality of restrictions placed on abortions.

> A finding of an undue burden is a shorthand for the conclusion that a state regulation has the purpose or effect of placing a substantial obstacle in the path of a woman seeking an abortion of a nonviable fetus. A statute with this purpose is invalid because the means chosen by the State to further the interest in potential life must be calculated to inform the woman's free choice, not hinder it. And a statute which, while furthering the interest in potential life or some other valid state interest, has the effect of placing a substantial obstacle in the path of a woman's choice cannot be considered a permissible means of serving its legitimate ends.
>
> (p. 877)

Justice Rehnquist wrote a dissenting opinion in *Casey*, in which he argued similarly as he had in *Roe* that abortion is not a fundamental right, which would remove it from strict scrutiny Fourteenth Amendment analysis. Justice Rehnquist also questioned in dissent why subsequent "cases must be decided in the same incorrect manner as was the first case [*Roe*] to deal with the question" (p. 955), having found the Court's argument for retaining *Roe* to be unpersuasive.

Abortion law has not remained static, but rather has changed over time. In fact, in *Casey*, the Court allowed a requirement that:

> a woman seeking an abortion give her informed consent prior to the abortion procedure, and specifies that she be provided with certain information at least 24 hours before the abortion is

performed . . . For a minor to obtain an abortion the Act requires the informed consent of one of her parents, but provides for a judicial bypass option if the minor does not wish to or cannot obtain a parent's consent.

(p. 844)

However, the *Casey* ruling struck down a provision requiring that married women notify their husbands prior to an abortion.

Subsequently, one key area of debate has surrounded partial-birth abortion procedures. In *Stenberg v. Carhart* (2000), the Supreme Court considered a Nebraska law that defined partial-birth abortion as a "procedure in which the person performing the abortion delivers vaginally a living unborn child before killing the unborn child and completing the delivery" (p. 922). The Court ruled the law unconstitutional, because it did not provide an exception for the mother's health, as required by *Roe* (although there was an exception for the life of the mother). Also, the legislation was counter to *Casey* in that the Court found it imposed an undue burden on women seeking an abortion because the language of the statute did not satisfactorily differentiate which medical procedures were prohibited. This imposed a burden because the law could have been construed to prohibit abortion procedures that were not within the intent of the ban on partial-birth abortions.

Seven years later, the Court upheld a federal law prohibiting partial-birth abortion in *Gonzales v. Carhart* (2007). The Court found that the description of the procedure was sufficiently detailed and constructed in a way that did not pose an undue burden on women seeking abortions. In addition, the Court overturned its position in *Stenberg* and found that the law was not unconstitutional for lacking a health of the mother exception. The Court recognized that there was disagreement in the medical community on whether partial-birth abortions would be necessary for preservation of health, which led to the conclusion that:

"The Act is not invalid on its face where there is uncertainty over whether the barred procedure is ever necessary to preserve a woman's health, given the availability of other abortion procedures that are considered to be safe alternatives" (pp. 166–167). In upholding the law, the Court also took into consideration the state's interest in preservation of life, including the life of a fetus past the point of viability.

The above discussion illustrates how the law evolves, in this case considering the scope and limits of the constitutional right to privacy. Of course, privacy law is not fixed in place, but is constantly shaped as new issues and interpretations emerge in litigation.

The Right of Association

The second area of substantive due process that we will consider also has significant implications for law and sexuality, and that is the right of association. It is a right that groups invoke when determining who to include, or as the issue more subject to litigation, who not to include, in their membership and associations. The 1958 case of *NAACP v. Alabama* provided an overview of the right to association, which it defined as a fundamental right under the Fourteenth Amendment's Due Process Clause:

Effective advocacy of both public and private points of view, particularly controversial ones, is undeniably enhanced by group association, as this Court has more than once recognized by remarking upon the close nexus between the freedoms of speech and assembly. It is beyond debate that freedom to engage in association for the advancement of beliefs and ideas is an inseparable aspect of the 'liberty' assured by the Due Process Clause of the Fourteenth Amendment, which embraces freedom of speech. Of course, it is immaterial whether the beliefs sought to be advanced by association pertain to political, economic, religious, or cultural matters, and state action which may have the effect of curtailing the freedom to associate is subject to the closest scrutiny.

(p. 461)

Therefore, the right of association is what groups use to ensure that their membership is able to achieve the "advocacy" and "advancement of beliefs and ideas" that the group desires. The above statement was made in a case in which the state of Alabama required the NAACP (National Association for the Advancement of Colored Persons) to submit its membership list to the state. The Court ruled the requirement unconstitutional, because of the chilling effect it would have on the right of association, without a compelling justification for doing so.

In applying the right of association to issues of law and sexuality, consider the questions in Box 3.3. First, each question raises a point related to the right to association, in that each considers the extent to which groups can determine their membership by limiting it based on gender (cases 1 and 2) or sexual orientation (cases 3 and 4). Second, in each case,

the dispute is shaped by the presence of a state law banning discrimination, creating a material conflict between a group's argument in favor of a right to association and a state's argument that discrimination should be prohibited. This requires the courts to make a judgment as to which interest is the stronger one, and should therefore prevail. Third, the state nondiscrimination laws require a showing that the group in question functions as a public accommodation or business establishment. Perhaps it is easier to conceptualize the latter than the former; but in civil rights law, the notion of public accommodation is an essential element.

The Civil Rights Act of 1964 is a federal law that prohibits "discrimination or segregation on the basis of race, color, religion, or natural origin" (42 U.S.C. § 2000a) in places of public accommodation, which are somewhat narrowly defined as lodging, dining, and entertainment venues, or those that serve persons in those venues (42 U.S.C. § 2000a). Similarly, the 1990 Americans with Disabilities Act (ADA) prohibits discrimination in places of public accommodation against

Box 3.3 JUDICIAL RULINGS ON THE RIGHT OF ASSOCIATION

1. Under the right of association, may the Jaycees, (a nonprofit civic organization) national headquarters enforce upon its chapters a rule that limits membership to men, when a state law prohibits gender discrimination in places of public accommodation (*Roberts v. United States Jaycees*, 1984)?

2. Under the right of association, may Rotary International (a nonprofit civic organization) enforce upon its chapters a rule that limits membership to men, when a state law prohibits gender discrimination in "business establishments" (*Rotary International v. Rotary Club of Duarte*, 1987, p. 542)?

3. Under the right of association, may a private organization that sponsors a public parade exclude a gay organization within the parade, when there is a state law against discrimination based on sexual orientation in places of public accommodation (*Hurley v. Irish-American Gay, Lesbian and Bisexual Group of Boston*, 1995)?

4. Under the right of association, may the Boy Scouts of America exclude from membership gay males, when there is a state law against discrimination based on sexual orientation in places of public accommodation (*Boy Scouts of America v. Dale*, 2000)?

persons with disabilities, but with a much more expansive definition of public accommodation. The ADA's definition includes those facilities listed in the Civil Rights Act, but also adds retail, service, transportation, recreational, and educational establishments (42 U.S.C. § 12181). The law pertaining to the first case in Box 3.3 provided a still broader conceptualization of public accommodation: "a business, accommodation, refreshment, entertainment, recreation, or transportation facility of any kind, whether licensed or not, whose goods, services, facilities, privileges, advantages or accommodations are extended, offered, sold, or otherwise made available to the public" (*Roberts v. United States Jaycees*, 1984, p. 615). Therefore, one central inquiry in each case in Box 3.3 must be whether the organization in question is or is not considered within the scope of a public accommodation, based on each state's definition of what public accommodation means, as that is one criterion on which the analysis will turn.

The four cases in Box 3.3 were heard by the U.S. Supreme Court. The Court answered the first two questions, pertaining to gender, in the negative. The Court answered the second two questions, pertaining to sexual orientation, in the positive. Let's consider the argumentation that was brought to each.

Association and Gender

In *Roberts v. United States Jaycees* (1984), Justice Brennan delivered the unanimous opinion of the Court. The Jaycees are a civic organization oriented toward young professionals, and at the time of the case, only males were entitled to full membership. However, women were permitted to hold a non-voting associate membership, but were ineligible to hold office. Several chapters in Minnesota made the decision to allow women full membership in their chapters. As a result, the national headquarters pursued a revocation of these chapters' charters. The affected chapters then filed a discrimination complaint with the Minnesota Human Rights Department, which ruled that the Jaycees were a place of public accommodation requiring the admission of women, thereby sustaining the Minnesota chapters' decisions to include women as full members of the organization. It was on the basis of this ruling that the national headquarters filed its own lawsuit, which was ultimately heard by the U.S. Supreme Court.

The Court analyzed two forms of freedom of association: "Choices to enter into and maintain certain intimate human relationships" (p. 617) and the "right to associate for purpose of engaging in those activities protected by the First Amendment" (p. 618). The Court analyzed each in turn.

In regard to the first type of freedom of association, the Court noted that freedom of association applied to family or domestic relationships, or also those "deep attachments and commitments to the necessarily few others with whom one shares not only a special community of thoughts, experiences, and beliefs, but also distinctively personal aspects of one's life" (p. 620). The Court noted that the Jaycees are a large organization and that it has (with the exception of gender) been a fairly open organization to join. Also, even as associate members, women were permitted to participate in many of the organization's activities, other than holding office. Cumulatively, these findings led the Court to reject the notion of an intimate group whose associational rights would be violated by admitting women.

In regard to the second type of freedom of association, the Court did acknowledge how intrusive it would be to require "the group to accept members it does not desire" (p. 623). At the same time, the Court acknowledged that the prevention of gender discrimination was a compelling state interest. Key to the analysis was the Court's holding that the Jaycees are a public accommodation, as the opinion cited the Minnesota Supreme Court's conclusion (referring to the definition of public accommodation provided above) that "noted the various commercial programs and benefits offered to members, and stated that '[l]eadership skills are "goods," [and] business contacts and employment promotions are "privileges" and "advantages" ' " (p. 626).

The Court further held that admitting women would not have an adverse impact on the ability of the Jaycees "to disseminate its preferred views" (p. 627), meaning that the provision was suitably focused, and with minimum detriment, to meet the compelling state interest. Although the group would be permitted "to exclude individuals with ideologies or philosophies different from those of its existing members" (p. 627), the Court rejected any concern that women would have different enough opinions on substantive issues about which the Jaycees express an interest to alter the group's expression. However, note that this does suggest an avenue along which restrictions on group membership could be upheld, if evidence does suggest that admitting certain persons to a group would lead to changes in the positions it advocates.

In *Rotary International v. Rotary Club of Duarte* (1987), the Court considered a similar case, focused on the Rotary Club. While the Jaycees were established as a group focused on young professionals, the Rotary Club is an assembly of persons holding leadership positions in their fields. Also, unlike the Jaycees, Rotary Clubs utilized a membership vetting process that limited the number of persons from each occupational area and which screened applicants on a variety of criteria prior to membership. Like the Jaycees, Rotary Clubs limited membership to men, but women were "permitted to attend meetings, give speeches, and receive awards. Women relatives of Rotary members may form their own associations, and are authorized to wear the Rotary lapel pin" (p. 541). The justification offered for the exclusion of female membership was that it was necessary to preserve "an 'aspect of fellowship . . . that is enjoyed by the present male membership,'

and also allows Rotary to operate effectively in foreign countries with varied cultures and social mores" (p. 541).

As in the Jaycees case, a local chapter, this time in California, chose to allow women as members, resulting in a revocation of its charter by the international Rotary organization. The club and two female members filed suit for violation of California's anti-discrimination law, which applied to "business establishments" (p. 542). The Court proceeded with an analysis of the same two aspects of the right to association as in *Roberts*.

Justice Powell delivered the opinion of a unanimous Court. Considering the right to association in an intimate group, the Court rejected the notion that the Rotary Club provided this kind of environment, noting that individual chapters may be large and with a constant flow of membership (some members leaving, new members joining). Furthermore, the Court observed that the organization was designed to be inclusive, that visitors may attend meetings, and that chapter activities may be publicized. Therefore, it was a larger and more open and public organization than the Court was willing to recognize as intimate.

Considering the right to associate for free expression, the Court again noted that the state has a compelling interest in preventing gender discrimination. Furthermore, the Court noted that admission of women as full members would not impair the organization's ability to accomplish its goals. For instance, the group does "not take positions on 'public questions,' including political or international issues" (p. 548), so the possibility of gender-based changes in the organization's viewpoints on these matters is not at issue. In fact, the Court noted that, by admitting female members, "Rotary Clubs are likely to obtain a more representative cross-section of community leaders with a broadened capacity for service" (p. 549).

The Court did not take up the issue of whether the Rotary Club was a business establishment, but did indicate that the California Court of Appeals found that it was in an earlier decision on the case, noting "its complex structure, large staff and budget, and extensive publishing activities" (p. 542).

A common thread runs through both cases. In each, the presence of a gender nondiscrimination statute was deemed sufficient to require the organizations to accept female members, because the state interest was compelling and the intrusion on the organization was minimal, as it did not fundamentally change the expressive activities of the group.

Association and Sexual Orientation

The next two cases focus on sexual orientation, rather than gender, and involve groups that raise claims of deeper intrusions into their expressive activities. This led the Court to take a different approach than in the prior cases. Rather than using the two-part freedom of association analysis applied in *Roberts* and *Rotary International*, the Court first begins with a consideration of how expression would be impacted by the inclusion of sexual minorities in the organizations.

We will first consider *Hurley v. Irish-American Gay, Lesbian and Bisexual Group of Boston* (1995). Since 1947, the South Boston Allied War Veterans Council, a private entity, organized Boston's St. Patrick's Day Parade; the council started arranging the parade when the city ceased doing so. In 1992 and 1993, the Irish-American Gay, Lesbian, and Bisexual Group of Boston applied to march in the parade, but the Council denied the request. The group subsequently filed suit, alleging violation of a state law prohibiting discrimination in public accommodations based on sexual orientation.

The unanimous opinion of the Court, written by Justice Souter, began by noting that "Parades are . . . a form of expression, not just motion" (p. 568), because they are organized to include "marchers who are making some sort of collective point" (p. 568). The Court emphasized that the expressive nature of a parade was not diminished by having a broad or multifaceted message or set of messages, nor was it diminished by including messages promoted by entities other than the parade organizers. Indeed, both were the case, as multiple and diverse groups, conveying a variety of messages, participated in the parade, subject to approval by the Council. Likewise, the Court held that, were the gay group to march in the parade, it would be expressive, seeking to convey that group's ideas.

The Court noted that there was a state interest in preventing discrimination, but opined that in this case, the "law has been applied in a peculiar way" (p. 572). The Court's opinion suggests that if individual gay, lesbian, or bisexual persons had been denied the right to participate in the parade, there could have been a justifiable claim against the Council. However, in this case, the Court held, there was not. Requiring the gay group to be permitted to march in the parade would "requir[e] petitioner [i.e., the Council] to alter the expressive content of their parade" (p. 572). In so ruling, the Court drew a distinction between public accommodations (which they did not find the parade to be) and expression (which they did find they parade to be):

> On its face, the object of the law is to ensure by statute for gays and lesbians desiring to make use of public accommodations what the old common law promised to any member of the public wanting a meal at the inn, that accepting the usual terms of service, they will not be turned away merely on the proprietor's exercise of personal preference. When the law is applied to expressive activity in the way it was done here, its apparent object is simply to require speakers to modify the content of their expression to whatever extent beneficiaries of the law choose to alter it with messages of their own.
>
> (p. 578)

Because the Court found it violative of free expression to require parade organizers to change the expressive content of the parade by allowing the gay group to march, the Court allowed the Council to exclude the group from the parade (although in 2015, 20 years after the decision was issued, parade organizers did allow two groups representing the gay, lesbian, bisexual, and transgender community to participate in the parade; see Seelye & Bidgood, 2015).

The ruling in *Hurley* stands in notable contrast to those in *Roberts* and *Rotary Club*, the significant difference being the amount of organizational expression that would be curtailed. Although the Court held the effect to be minimal for the Jaycees and Rotary Club, the Court found that the impact would be more significant if a same-sex organization was permitted to participate in a parade. All three of the above cases served as precedents to what has been the highest-profile right of association case in the past 20 years, centering on the Boy Scouts of America. After reading the facts below, consider which (if any) of the above cases should be controlling precedents. The majority opinion suggested one answer, and the dissents another.

Boy Scouts of America v. Dale was decided in 2000. James Dale was an Eagle Scout and assistant scoutmaster. A college student, Dale was also co-president of the Lesbian/Gay Alliance at Rutgers University. After being featured in a newspaper article about issues related to gay teenagers, Dale was removed from the Boy Scouts, because the organization "specifically forbid[s] membership to homosexuals" (p. 645). Dale brought suit against the Boy Scouts of America, on the grounds that the action violated a New Jersey law that "prohibits . . . discrimination on the basis of sexual orientation in places of public accommodation" (p. 645).

The New Jersey Supreme Court ruled in favor of Dale, based on analyses similar to those offered in the *Roberts* and *Rotary Club* cases. That is, it found that the organization was not intimate, negating the first prong of right to association analysis as stated in those cases. The New Jersey court also found that the Boy Scouts were a public accommodation, that the state had a compelling interest in preventing discrimination, and that the inclusion of gay persons in the organization would not impair its abilities to achieve its goals.

The U.S. Supreme Court, in an opinion written by Justice Rehnquist, disagreed, and held that the Boy Scouts have the right to exclude homosexuals from membership. The Court's opinion stated that "Forcing a group to accept certain members may impair the ability of the group to express those views, and only those views, that it intends to express" (p. 648). The reasoning of the opinion was as follows: (1) the Boy Scouts of America is an expressive group, focused on teaching a set of values to its youth members; (2) based on deference to the explanations of the Boy Scouts of America, the organization has as one of its values a sincere belief that homosexuality is contrary to its values; (3) the presence of a homosexual in the organization "would, at the very least, force the organization to send a message, both to the youth members and the world, that the Boy Scouts accepts homosexual conduct as a legitimate form of behavior" (p. 692); and (4) drawing upon the analysis in *Hurley*, the "state interests . . . do not justify such a severe intrusion on the Boy Scouts' rights to freedom of expressive association" (p. 659). Again, note the emphasis on group expression that sets this case apart from those based on gender, discussed earlier.

The case was not a unanimous opinion of the Court, but was a 5–4 decision. Two justices wrote dissents. Justice Stevens, like the New Jersey Supreme Court, argued that the *Roberts* and *Rotary Club* precedents should be controlling here. Justice Stevens was not willing to grant deference to the Boy Scouts' explanation of their stance on homosexuality, arguing that "unless one is prepared to turn the right to associate into a free pass out of antidiscrimination laws, an independent inquiry is a necessity" (p. 688). Based on his independent reading of Boy Scout documents, Justice Stevens found that the organization did not "make its position clear" or "connect its alleged [anti-homosexual] policy to its expressive activities" (p. 677). Therefore, even if the Boy Scouts engage in expressive activity, Justice Stevens suggested that admission of homosexuals would not impair its ability to achieve organizational goals. Justice Souter also wrote a dissent, agreeing with Justice Stevens that the Boy Scouts did not adequately demonstrate the significance of messages about sexual orientation to the organization's expressive goals. It should be noted that, as with the *Hurley* case, perspectives have changed since 2000. In 2013, the Boy Scouts permitted gay youths to be members of the organization. In 2015, the ban on adult gay leaders was relaxed, as "the national organization will no longer allow discrimination against its paid workers or at . . . [its] facilities," but "local troops and councils will be permitted to decide for themselves whether they will allow openly gay volunteer leaders" (Boorstein, 2015, para. 2).

It is easy to read these four cases as illustrating a dichotomy between how gender and sexual orientation are addressed under the law. Perhaps there is some merit to that observation; at the very least, as indicated in the discussion of levels of scrutiny, gender does receive a higher (intermediate) scrutiny than the minimal level of scrutiny generally accorded to sexual orientation in most analyses (see Chapter 4). At the same time, these cases illustrate other balances that the courts attempt to strike when considering right of association cases. Think about what test you think is most appropriate for addressing right of association issues, with the attendant considerations that must balance freedom of expression, compelling state interests in preventing discrimination and promoting equality, and determining what is or is not a public accommodation. Needless to say, it becomes a complex area of substantive due process inquiry, perhaps masked by what may seem, on the surface, to be straightforward questions.

Privacy Revisited: Sodomy

Substantive due process and the debates surrounding it are not static. Rather, they continue to evolve as new issues emerge. Sometimes, the same issue is even reconsidered as legal interpretations, or social understandings of an issue as reflected through the law, change. This has occurred in areas of jurisprudence outside of law and sexuality, such as allowing a state to set a minimum wage (*West Coast Hotel Co. v. Parrish*, 1937, overturning *Adkins v. Childrens Hospital*, 1923), determining that states cannot force students to salute the flag and recite the pledge of allegiance (*West Virginia Board of Education v. Barnette*, 1943, overturning *Minersville School District v. Gobitis*, 1940), or instituting marriage equality for same-sex couples (*Obergefell v. Hodges*, 2015, overturning *Baker v. Nelson*, 1972). Let's examine an issue on which the modern Supreme Court has reversed itself over time.

For many years, state legal codes contained laws prohibiting "crimes against nature," which was generally understood to mean sodomy—that is, oral or anal sex (see Chapter 6). Over time, the language became more precise, as legal codes specifically identified the types of activities that were prohibited. By the late twentieth century, states could be roughly classified into one of three groups: those in which sodomy laws were in place, and applied to both homosexual and heterosexual encounters; those in which sodomy laws were in place, but applied only to homosexual encounters; and those in which there were no sodomy laws, prior laws having been repealed or ruled unconstitutional in state courts (for a comprehensive history, see Eskridge, 2008; Fradella, 2002).

Bowers: *A Retreat from Sexual Privacy as Part of Substantive Due Process*

The U.S. Supreme Court has twice heard challenges to sodomy laws. The first time was in

1986, in *Bowers v. Hardwick*. In August of 1982, an Atlanta police officer was serving an arrest warrant at the apartment of Michael Hardwick. The officer was allowed into the residence by a houseguest who informed the officer that he was unsure whether Hardwick was currently inside the residence. While searching the residence for Mr. Hardwick, the officer noticed that the bedroom door was slightly ajar. When the officer entered, he observed Hardwick and a male companion engaged in consensual oral sex. Both men were placed under arrest and charged for violating the Georgia sodomy statute. Georgia law defined sodomy to include both oral and anal sex between same-sex or opposite-sex partners.

Eskridge (2008) provides additional information about the facts in the case. The warrant for Michael Hardwick was actually invalid at the time the officer entered his apartment, the matter (drinking in public) having already been resolved. In fact, the prosecuting attorney declined to prosecute the sodomy charge. However, Hardwick felt an obligation to challenge the law, having the opportunity to do so, and he filed suit against Georgia Attorney General Michael Bowers.

Hardwick challenged the Georgia sodomy law on the basis that it violated his substantive due process rights under the Fourteenth Amendment. In a 5–4 ruling, the Supreme Court upheld the constitutionality of the law, even in private encounters between consenting adults, holding that sodomy is not a fundamental right. According to Justice White, who wrote the opinion of the Court: "to claim that a right to engage in such conduct is 'deeply rooted in this Nation's history and tradition' or 'implicit in the concept of ordered liberty' is, at best, facetious" (p. 194). He further noted that:

Even if the conduct at issue here is not a fundamental right, respondent asserts that there must be a rational basis for the law and that there is none in this case other than the pre-

sumed belief of a majority of the electorate in Georgia that homosexual sodomy is immoral and unacceptable. This is said to be an inadequate rationale to support the law. The law, however, is constantly based on notions of morality, and if all laws representing essentially moral choices are to be invalidated under the Due Process Clause, the courts will be very busy indeed. Even respondent makes no such claim, but insists that majority sentiments about the morality of homosexuality should be declared inadequate. We do not agree, and are unpersuaded that the sodomy laws ... should be invalidated on this basis.

(p. 196)

Justice Blackmun, writing in dissent, focused squarely on protections of the right to privacy: "Indeed, the right of an individual to conduct intimate relationships in the intimacy of his or her own home seems to me to be the heart of the Constitution's protection of privacy" (p. 208). Unpersuaded by arguments about morality, Blackmun also noted that "I cannot agree that either the length of time a majority has held its convictions or the passions with which it defends them can withdraw legislation from the Court's scrutiny" (p. 210).

Blackmun's dissent foreshadowed the Court's analysis in *Lawrence v. Texas* (2003), the second challenge to sodomy laws heard by the Supreme Court. *Lawrence* overturned *Bowers*, in an opinion that starkly criticized the *Bowers* Court's ruling. The ruling in *Lawrence* is notable for its impact on the jurisprudence of sexuality and as an extension of substantive due process rights to privacy.

Lawrence: *The Rebirth of Sexual Privacy as Part of Substantive Due Process*

It is little exaggeration to say that *Lawrence v. Texas* (2003) is one of the most important U.S. Supreme Court cases to have been decided within the past 50 years in the field of law and sexuality. The direct subject matter of the case was a challenge to Texas's sodomy law, but its implications are significantly more far-reaching. The key theme of the case centers on the right to sexual privacy as protected through the Fourteenth Amendment.

The case began with the nighttime report of a disturbance occurring at an apartment in a gated complex. Earlier that evening, three men, including John Lawrence and Tyron Garner, returned to Lawrence's apartment after having dinner out. Later, one of the men left and made a false 911 call to the Harris County Police Department. "According to the police dispatcher, the caller claimed that 'a black man was going crazy in the apartment and he was armed with a gun'" (Eskridge, 2008, p. 300). The call was made after the man's boyfriend, Garner, indicated that he did not want to leave, and Lawrence indicated that he could stay. Police responded quickly to the call, entering the apartment through an open door. Moving from room to room, the police eventually entered the bedroom, where they found Lawrence and Garner engaged in sexual activity. They were arrested for violation of the Texas sodomy law and were fined $200 each, having pled *nolo contendere* (no contest) to the charges and also having preserved their right to appeal (Eskridge, 2008).

Because the Texas law being challenged prohibited only homosexual sodomy, the Court could have ruled it unconstitutional under the Equal Protection Clause (see Chapter 4) since it treated homosexuals and heterosexuals differently with regard to private, consensual sexual activity. But in a 6–3 opinion written by Justice Kennedy, the Court concluded that the law was unconstitutional based on the Fourteenth Amendment's Due Process Clause.

> [The] Equal Protection Clause [presents] . . . a tenable argument, but we conclude the instant case requires us to address whether *Bowers* itself has continuing validity. Were we to hold the statute invalid under the Equal Protection

Clause, some might question whether a prohibition would be valid if drawn differently, say, to prohibit the conduct both between same-sex and different-sex participants. Equality of treatment and the due process right to demand respect for conduct protected by the substantive guarantee of liberty are linked in important respects, and a decision on the latter point advances both interests.

> (pp. 574–575)

The Court then reconsidered and rejected the due process holding in *Bowers v. Hardwick.*

The *Lawrence* Court began its substantive discussion in *Bowers* as follows:

> "The issue presented is whether the Federal Constitution confers a fundamental right upon homosexuals to engage in sodomy and hence invalidates the laws of the many States that still make such conduct illegal and have done so for a very long time." That statement, we now conclude, discloses the Court's own failure to appreciate the extent of the liberty at stake. To say that the issue in *Bowers* was simply the right to engage in certain sexual conduct demeans the claim the individual put forward, just as it would demean a married couple were it to be said marriage is simply about the right to have sexual intercourse. The laws involved in Bowers and here are, to be sure, statutes that purport to do no more than prohibit a particular sexual act. Their penalties and purposes, though, have more far-reaching consequences, touching upon the most private human conduct, sexual behavior, and in the most private of places, the home. The statutes do seek to control a personal relationship that, whether or not entitled to formal recognition in the law, is within the liberty of persons to choose without being punished as criminals. This, as a general rule, should counsel against attempts by the State, or a court, to define the meaning of the relationship or to set its boundaries absent injury to a person or abuse of an institution the law protects. It suffices for us to acknowledge that adults may

choose to enter upon this relationship in the confines of their homes and their own private lives and still retain their dignity as free persons. When sexuality finds overt expression in intimate conduct with another person, the conduct can be but one element in a personal bond that is more enduring. The liberty protected by the Constitution allows homosexual persons the right to make this choice.

(pp. 566–567)

Texas attempted to justify its homosexual sodomy law by arguing it served the legitimate governmental interests of promoting morality. The Court had accepted such an argument as satisfying the rational basis test in *Bowers*. But the Court reversed itself in *Lawrence* and made it clear that even though homosexual conduct may be condemned by some as immoral based on their "religious beliefs, conceptions of right and acceptable behavior, and respect for the traditional family," people may not "use the power of the State to enforce these views on the whole society through operation of the criminal law" (p. 571). The Court then explicitly overruled *Bowers* by saying it "was not correct when it was decided, and it is not correct today. It ought not to remain binding precedent" (pp. 578).

The opinion concluded with a strong statement:

The present case does not involve minors. It does not involve persons who might be injured or coerced or who are situated in relationships where consent might not easily be refused. It does not involve public conduct or prostitution. It does not involve whether the government must give formal recognition to any relationship that homosexual persons seek to enter. The case does involve two adults who, with full and mutual consent from each other, engaged in sexual practices common to a homosexual lifestyle. The petitioners are entitled to respect for their private lives. The State cannot demean their existence or control their destiny by making their private sexual conduct a crime. Their right to liberty under the Due Process Clause gives them the full right to engage in their conduct without intervention of the government. It is a promise of the Constitution that there is a realm of personal liberty which the government may not enter. The Texas statute furthers no legitimate state interest which can justify its intrusion into the personal and private life of the individual.

(p. 578)

Lawrence v. Texas has generated, and will likely continue to generate, significant discussion. Box 3.4 identifies several questions to consider pertaining to *Bowers* and *Lawrence*.

PROCEDURAL DUE PROCESS

Recall from earlier discussion that there are two types of due process: procedural and substantive. In this section, we will focus on **procedural due process**. As previously mentioned, procedural due process refers to the rules the state or federal government must follow in both civil and criminal proceedings before denying any person of a constitutionally protected right that concerns the person's life, liberty, or property. Procedural due process exists to help ensure *procedural justice*, which may be defined as "the fairness of the processes used when applying the law. Procedural justice is grounded in the idea that fair procedures are the best guarantees for fair outcomes" (Owen et al., 2015, p. 211). In other words, civil and criminal justice system actors and processes must comply with certain rules that are designed to ensure fairness for all.

The Fifth Amendment to the Constitution guarantees due process of law in *federal* proceedings, but it does not apply to the states. It was the Fourteenth Amendment that required states to also guarantee due process in their proceedings. Note the language of the

Box 3.4 REFLECTING ON BOWERS AND LAWRENCE

Consider the facts, holding, and rationale in both *Bowers* and *Lawrence* and then answer the following questions:

1. How do you think the history of the legal regulation of sodomy illustrates aspects of the Hart–Devlin debate?
2. Justice Scalia felt that Texas's morality argument was a sufficiently legitimate state interest to support the law. Thus, in his dissent in *Lawrence*, Scalia stated that, "This effectively decrees the end of all morals legislation" (p. 599). Do you agree or disagree? Explain your answer.
3. Eskridge (2008) suggests that, through *Lawrence*, "the Court committed the Constitution to an important principle—that there is a tolerable range of sexual variation that the state cannot persecute, either through criminal prohibitions or pervasive civil exclusions" (p. 333). But how far does *Lawrence* extend? Do you think the *Lawrence* precedent would apply to laws against fornication (i.e., consensual sex between unmarried adults), bigamy (i.e., having multiple spouses), adultery, prostitution, incest, or the sale of sexual devices? Explain your reasoning. (See Chapter 6 for more information on these offenses and cases address their constitutionality in the wake of *Lawrence*.)

Fourteenth Amendment cited earlier in this chapter—it directly specifies that *states* may not abridge the due process of any person. This can become tricky, in terms of legal doctrine. The Bill of Rights lists many protections to which persons are entitled in legal proceedings; it is through the Fourteenth Amendment that most of these have been applied to the states (though not all—for instance, the right to a grand jury is an exception; for more on the rights selectively incorporated by the Due Process Clause, see Henkin, 1963). Other due process rights are not explicitly listed in the Constitution, but have been applied to the states through the Fourteenth Amendment in appellate court cases, in which the argument would be as follows: This right is necessary for due process; the Fourteenth Amendment requires states to provide due process; therefore, the states must guarantee this right. Thus, the Fourteenth Amendment's Due Process Clause is not intended as a definitive listing of what constitutes due process, but rather is the vehicle through which due process is required of state governments.

As the above discussion might suggest, there is a complexity to procedural due process that goes beyond the scope of this chapter, both in terms of how rights are identified and in terms of what those rights actually are. For the purposes of this chapter, we will consider procedural due process as a concept, exploring the types of issues that have raised debates about fairness in the enforcement of law related to sexuality. In the sections that follow, we will address selected procedural due process issues that have relevance to law and sexuality, but this should not be construed as an exhaustive list limited to Fourteenth Amendment cases. Here, we will focus on entrapment (related to police procedures), ruling laws void for vagueness (related to lawmaking), the confrontation clause and court testimony (related to courtroom procedures), and proportionality of punishment (related to correctional alternatives). Rather than providing definitive answers—which is likely impossible to do—we will instead consider questions and the considerations that might affect how they are answered.

Entrapment: Can Police Practices Entice Persons to Commit Crimes?

Entrapment is a due process issue for law enforcement. The most basic conceptualization of entrapment is that it entails "government agents getting people to commit crimes they wouldn't otherwise commit" (Samaha, 2002, p. 309). This violates notions of due process because it violates one of the basic concepts of justice, as defined by philosopher David Schmidtz (2006): "justice concerns what people are due" (p. 7). If an individual is coerced into committing a crime that he or she would otherwise not have committed, had it not been for the coercion, is it fair to say that individual is due a punishment? The courts have indicated that the answer to this question is "no." While not a Fourteenth Amendment issue, per se, defendants in criminal cases have the right to offer entrapment as a defense to their charges, because a conviction based on entrapment would be contrary to an understanding of what due process means, conceptually. It is usually an affirmative defense, meaning that the defendant bears the burden of proving that entrapment occurred (Samaha, 2002). The availability and use of the entrapment defense restrains police agencies from engaging in such conduct.

Defining Entrapment

How do we know when entrapment has occurred? Police agencies routinely use undercover investigations, and it is through such operations that entrapment claims often arise. In the course of undercover work, police officers may engage in the "encouragement" of an illegal act, for the purpose of obtaining evidence that can then be used against the offender (Samaha, 2002, p. 309). But how much encouragement is too much?

The subjective test for entrapment is the one used by most (though not all) jurisdictions, including the federal government, and it is the one we will consider here. It is summarized as follows: "A defendant must prove, by a preponderance of the evidence, that he was actively induced or encouraged to commit the charged crime by the police or someone acting in cooperation with the police, and that he was not predisposed to committing the crime" (*Pinter v. City of New York*, 2010, p. 434). The fact pattern of a case can help in establishing what role, if any, the police played in inducing or encouraging commission of an offense. Perhaps more difficult is showing, or refuting, predisposition to commit an offense. There are several factors that may be considered in such an inquiry, including:

> (1) The defendant's character or reputation; (2) whether the government initially suggested the criminal activity; (3) whether the defendant engaged in the criminal activity for profit; (4) whether the defendant evidenced a reluctance to commit the offense that was overcome by government persuasion; and (5) the nature of the inducement or persuasion by the government.
>
> (*United States v. Blassingame*, 1999, p. 281)

Jacobson v. United States

In *Jacobson v. United States* (1992), the defendant mail-ordered two magazines that contained pictures of nude boys. At the time the magazines were ordered, it was legal to do so. The law was changed shortly thereafter, and government agents learned of the defendant's prior purchase of these materials (see Chapter 8). "There followed over the next 2½ years repeated efforts by two Government agencies, through five fictitious organizations and a bogus pen pal, to explore petitioner's willingness to break the new law by ordering sexually explicit photographs of children through the mail" (p. 543). The fictitious organizations were creations of the government, designed to ascertain the defendant's interest in, and to solicit his purchase of, child pornographic materials. Among other things, the mailings from the fictitious organizations included a survey, unclear references as to whether items were or were not child pornography, political statements (e.g., "Not only sexual expression but freedom of the press is under attack. We must be ever vigilant to counter attack right wing fundamentalists who are determined to curtail our freedoms," p. 545), and a pen-pal exchange with an undercover government agent, in which the defendant wrote, "I like good looking young guys (in their late teens and early 20's) doing their thing together" (p. 545).

The question posed in *Jacobson* is whether the facts of the case constituted entrapment. Using the subjective test, the Court held that entrapment had occurred. The majority opinion, by Justice White, observed that there was insufficient evidence of the defendant's predisposition to purchase child pornography in violation of the new law, and that it was through government inducement that he did so. The opinion noted, "The evidence that petitioner was ready and willing to commit the offense came only after the Government had devoted 2½ years to convincing him that he had or should have the right to engage in the very behavior proscribed by law" (p. 553). In a statement justifying the importance of being vigilant for entrapment, Justice White wrote, "When the Government's quest for convictions leads to the apprehension of an otherwise law-abiding citizen who, if left to his own devices, likely would have never run afoul of the law, the courts should intervene" (p. 554).

Entrapment and Sexual Solicitation

After work, the defendant in *Pinter v. City of New York* (2010) stopped at a store that rented adult videos. In the section of the store where adult videos were housed, the defendant noticed a "younger man staring at him from the end of the aisle" (p. 412). The two smiled at each other, moved toward each other, and complimented each other's looks. The record indicates that the younger man initiated these activities, and he also asked the defendant "What do you like to do," to which the defendant responded that "he both enjoyed—and was good at—fellatio" (p. 413). The younger man expressed reservations about engaging in sexual activity at the store, but mentioned that his car was outside. The defendant moved to exit the store and was followed by the younger man. The judge inferred that this indicated that the two men had "reached an agreement for consensual, gratuitous sex and took steps in furtherance of that agreement" (p. 413). On their way out of the store, the younger man said, "I want to pay you $50 to suck your dick" (p. 413), to which the defendant did not respond. Outside of the store, the two men walked down a sidewalk, engaging in flirtatious conversation. The defendant "never told [the younger man] that he did not wish to have oral sex with him or to receive money in exchange for it" (p. 414), and the record also has no indication that the defendant verbally accepted the offer of $50; in fact, the defendant later reported that, after the financial offer was made, he decided that "any possibility of really engaging in anything . . . was over" (p. 414), although he did not tell the younger man that. As it turns out, the younger man was an undercover police officer. On the basis of the above, the defendant was arrested for prostitution.

Although there were a number of legal issues involved with this case, and the conviction was ultimately vacated, the U.S. District Court for the Southern District of New York opined that entrapment had occurred here. Key to the judge's opinion was the fact that the agreement to engage in sexual activity had been made prior to any offer of money, which suggests that the defendant was not predisposed to engage in prostitution, and the situation was initiated by the undercover officer. The judge minced no words, in writing, "If true, these circumstances not only reek of entrapment; they are unsettling and inappropriate" (p. 436). Indeed, the case attracted media attention critical of the New York Police Department's tactics (e.g., Hauser, 2009).

The examples above illustrate the nature of entrapment, which centers on the concern that it would be unfair to penalize persons who are enticed to commit an act that they would not have otherwise committed. It is for this reason that entrapment is contrary to the notions of fairness embodied within the concept of due process.

Ruling Laws Void for Vagueness or Overbreadth

When crafting legislation and policy, lawmakers and policymakers have the obligation to ensure that measures are clearly written and easily understood. If laws lack specificity and are open to multiple interpretations, they cannot give adequate notice as to what conduct is prohibited. The meaning of the law would then be left open for police officers, prosecuting attorneys, and judges to individually interpret in their own ways, causing inconsistency in application and lack of clarity as to meaning of the law. This is a due process concern because the above situations would contravene ideas about fairness. Is it fair to punish an individual for violating a law whose meaning is not, or cannot be, uniformly understood? The courts have answered that it is not fair. In such situations, a law may be struck down as being **void for vagueness**. This occurs when, for the law in question, "men of common intelligence must necessarily guess at its meaning and differ as to its application" (Robinson, 2005, p. 356).

The doctrine of **overbreadth** is closely related to the vagueness doctrine insofar as both require criminal statutes to be precisely worded. Just as a law may be too vague to provide notice of what conduct is prohibited, a law can be too broad in what is prohibits. When a criminal statute prohibits conduct that is constitutionally protected as well as that which is unprotected, it is unconstitutionally overbroad.

Defining Solicitation: Is the Meaning Clear and Sufficiently Precise?

One concern about vague laws is that they can be disproportionately applied toward groups or persons that have been stereotyped or discriminated against, which can then further serve to negatively label those groups (Owen et al., 2015). As an example, consider one state's solicitation and sodomy laws. In relevant part, they read as follows:

> For criminal solicitation: "Any person who commands, entreats, or otherwise attempts to persuade another person to commit a felony other than murder, shall be guilty of a Class 6 felony."
> (Va. Code § 18.2–29, 2002)

> For sodomy: "If any person . . . carnally knows any male or female person by the anus or by or with the mouth, or voluntarily submits to such carnal knowledge, he or she shall be guilty of a Class 6 felony."
> (Va. Code § 18.2–361, 2002)

Now consider the fact patterns of two cases.

In *Ford v. Commonwealth* (1990), the defendant approached a car with its windows down at a fast-food restaurant's drive-through window. The defendant, a male employee of the restaurant, leaned against the car and engaged in brief conversation with the female driver. After the defendant "mumbled something," the driver asked him what he wanted. He replied that he "wanted to perform oral sex on her" (p. 604).

In *Singson v. Commonwealth* (2005), the defendant was in a public restroom. He "approached a stall occupied by an undercover police officer," and "peered into [the] stall through the crack in the stall door" (p. 684). The officer and defendant then engaged in a dialogue during which the defendant stated that he wanted to perform oral sex on the undercover officer in the handicap stall of the bathroom.

In both the *Ford* and *Singson* cases, Virginia charged the defendants with solicitation for the commission of sodomy. The defendant in *Ford* was found guilty, and the defendant in *Singson* pled guilty, but reserved his right to appeal. The defendants in both cases appealed their convictions. The court reversed the conviction in *Ford*, but upheld the conviction in *Singson*. In *Ford*, the court reasoned that the defendant's "statements were no more than the expression of his own desire and did not constitute a command, entreaty, or attempt to persuade either [passenger in the car] to engage in oral sodomy" (*Ford*, 1990, p. 605). In *Singson*, however, the court observed that the defendant "approached a stranger in a public restroom in a public department store during business hours, and he proposed to commit sodomy in that restroom" (*Singson*, 2005, p. 689).[2] Here, the distinction appears to be in the meaning of the terms in the solicitation statute. In both cases, the defendants used sexually explicit language to explain their desire to perform oral sex—language that left nothing to the imagination and little doubt as to their intent. But what does the solicitation statute mean when it criminalizes attempting to "command, entreat, or otherwise attempt to persuade" someone to commit a felony? Is this provision too vague to comply with procedural due process? Is this language so broad that it reaches both constitutionally protected conduct and conduct that may be constitutionally proscribed?

In invalidating the conviction in *Ford*, the court did not discuss whether the language of the solicitation statute was unconstitutionally vague or overbroad because the court was able to resolve the appeal without addressing any constitutional concerns. The court ruled

that the defendant's statements merely expressed his desire to perform oral sex on the female driver in the case and, as such, his statements "did not constitute a command, entreaty or attempt to persuade" the driver to engage in oral sex. In contrast, there was little doubt in *Singson* that the defendant tried to convince the undercover officer to allow the defendant to perform oral sex on the officer. Accordingly, the court had to address the defendant's arguments that the solicitation statute was unconstitutional because it potentially "chilled" an individual from requesting a private act of sodomy. The court rejected this argument, stating that

> the statute's "legitimate sweep" encompasses not only public sodomy, but also other forms of conduct that lack constitutional protection, specifically, non-consensual sodomy, incestual sodomy, sodomy with a minor, committing sodomy in exchange for money, and engaging in acts of bestiality. In our view, the incidental, hypothetical effect of the statute on speech requesting an act of private, consensual sodomy "cannot, with confidence, justify invalidating [the] statute on its face and so prohibiting a State from enforcing the statute against conduct that is admittedly within its power to proscribe."
> (*Singson*, 2005, p. 693)

It would be unusual to find a solicitation statute that did not leave some room for interpretation, which is an important lesson to take away. Not every statute with unclear language or some latitude for interpretation is struck as being void for vagueness or overbreadth, as there is some leeway to permit legal reasoning that focuses on the meanings of the words (known as the plain meaning rule) and on an examination of the purpose of the law as intended by the legislature (see Porto, 1998), reflecting the concept of deference described earlier. Indeed, it is difficult to imagine a statute that does not need some interpretation. At the same time, the two cases raise the question as to why the outcomes differed.

Was it the context (car at a drive-through versus public restroom)? Was it uncertainty as to what activity was intended? Was it the duration of the conversation? Was it the heterosexual versus the homosexual nature of the encounter? Or was it some other factor or factors? Whatever the answer, the broader point is that the more specific and narrowly tailored the law can be, the better. The less specific, the less consistently applied, and the less known the law may be, the more the law might raise concerns about procedural due process concerns about the fundamental fairness of the administration of justice.

Probation Conditions against Adult Materials

When people are sentenced to probation, they are required to follow certain rules, known as conditions. Some *general conditions* apply to all persons on probation (e.g., report to the probation officer when required, don't violate the law), but some *special conditions* are ordered by the judge specifically for individual offenders, based on the nature of their offense, their criminal history, their rehabilitative needs, and so on. Consider the two following conditions, which applied to individual offenders: A prohibition "from possessing 'all forms of pornography, including legal adult pornography'" (*United States v. Loy*, 2001, p. 253); and "You will not possess or view any pornographic or sexually explicit material—including books, magazines, computer images, internet files, photographs, VCR cassettes, film or other materials" (*Foster v. Indiana*, 2004, p. 1237).

The court ruled that the first condition, regarding "all forms of pornography," was void for vagueness. The rationale turned in part on the finding that there was no precise definition of pornography. Although the U.S. Supreme Court has provided a working framework for defining *obscenity* in *Miller v. California* (1973), that term is not synonymous

with—and is in fact considerably more narrow than—pornography (see Chapter 8). Regarding a ban on pornography as a condition of probation, the court held that the probationer "can hardly be expected to be able to discern, in advance, which materials are prohibited" (*Loy*, 2001, p. 264). This, in turn, allowed too much discretionary authority to the probation officer, meaning the condition "may ultimately translate to a prohibition on whatever the officer personally finds titillating" (p. 266). The court did recommend creating a more precise definition that clarified the type of materials, specifically, that were to be prohibited.

The second condition listed above appears to do so, by specifying that "sexually explicit material" is banned, and in what forms. Is this enough? In this case, the probationer had his probation revoked for the possession of *Stuff for Men* and *Maxim* magazines, which were thought to violate the condition. The court ruled the condition void for vagueness, because it "does not define sexually explicit or pornographic" and therefore "is not sufficiently clear to inform [the probationer] of what conduct would result in his being returned to prison" (*Foster v. Indiana*, 2004, p. 1239). The condition was also overbroad because it reached material such as *Maxim* magazine. This is noteworthy, as it raises the question as to what level of detailed description would be sufficient to allow a probation condition prohibiting the possession of pornography to stand.

It is important to recognize that most void for vagueness or overbreadth challenges are not upheld because the plain meaning, legislative intent, or precedent from other cases are used to interpret questioned passages. For instance, the definition of what is or is not "public" has been challenged in a number of court cases (e.g., *Weideman v. Indiana*, 2008; *Richmond v. Corinth*, 2002). In one such challenge to an indecent exposure law, the Supreme Court of Mississippi held that "public place" was a clear concept, as "this Court will apply the statute according to its plain meaning" (*Richmond v. Corinth*, 2002, p. 378) and that "a common sense reading of the statute adequately provides an individual of common intelligence an understanding and notice of what conduct is acceptable or prohibited" (p. 379). Judge for yourself by reviewing the Law in Action box in which you can consider how to define "public" and whether a definition would be sufficiently clear to resolve actual cases where the meaning has been in dispute.

Law in Action WHAT IS PUBLIC?

Sometimes there are terms that defy easy definition, which can cause confusion in the application of law. Certainly, one of those terms is "public." This becomes important for law and sexuality, because of the various prohibitions on public sexuality such as indecent exposure, public sexual indecency, and lewd and lascivious conduct (see Chapter 6). First, develop and justify your own definition of "public." Then, consider the following scenarios from actual legal cases. For each, determine whether or not you think it is "public" (note that "it depends" is a fair answer, in which case you should specify what additional information you need, or what circumstances would make a difference in your decision).

1. A "public beach [that] was 'remote' and 'secluded' and 'could not easily be seen from adjacent property'" where a group of approximately 100 nudists had gathered. "The nudists apparently picked this particular beach . . . because it was not easily accessible to the public" (*Lacour v. Texas*, 2000, p. 671). The court ruled the secluded area of the beach was "public." Would it make a difference if it was officially designated as a nude beach, with a sign? Would it make a difference if it was unofficially designated as a nude beach, with a sign? What if no sign was used, but locals knew it to be a nude beach?
2. A secluded area of a subway platform, not in the immediate view of other persons on the platform, as a location to engage in sexual activity (*New York v. Frank S. et al.*, 2000). The court ruled the subway platform was "public." In this case, there were other persons on the subway platform. Does this make a difference to the analysis?
3. In a parked car, engaging in sexual activity (*New York v. McNamara et al.*, 1991). The court ruled the car was not "public" because there was no evidence that someone could see into the car. Would it matter if the car had been parked in a well-lit place? Would it make a difference where the car was parked—on a residential street, commercial street, public parking lot, private parking lot, driveway, and so on?
4. The operator of a tractor-trailer truck was driving nude, discovered when a state police officer approached the truck at a weigh station and asked the operator to open the door for a routine inspection. The driver indicated "that he was in too big a hurry to get dressed," and that "characterizing his truck as a 'home on wheels' [the driver] argues that he was not in a public place" (*Whatley v. Indiana*, 1999, p. 67). The court ruled this was "public." Would your opinion differ if it were not a tractor trailer, but any other type of vehicle being operated on a highway? Should the height of the cab, and associated likelihood as to the ease with which the driver could be observed, make a difference?

5. Police officers conducting surveillance of a unit in an apartment building noticed that "a light came on in the back bedroom, and the officers approached the building. The wind parted the curtains at the open window to the back bedroom and one of the deputies, stationed near the window, saw [defendant], nude, talking on the telephone" (*Everett v. Virginia*, 1973, p. 565). The court ruled this was not public. Would it make a difference whether the observation was made of the unit under surveillance, or of another adjacent unit? Would it make a difference how widely the curtains were parted or how completely the curtains covered the window?

6. "Defendant's dining room . . . was visible through sliding glass doors . . . [an] officer (with his naked eye) observed the defendant, with a light overhead, stand up from the dining room table and, without any attempt to veil the glass doors, throw his bathrobe back behind his hips [and] expose his nude thigh and crotch area" (*Illinois v. Legel*, 1974, p. 166). The court ruled this was "public." Note that the defendant repeated this action several times in a half-hour time period. Should this matter?

7. Defendant, "while a guest in a private home, suddenly exposed his genitals to three other people in the room, who were not family members and who were deeply offended by that conduct. There was no evidence whether anyone outside the home did see or could have seen what he had done" (*Wisneski v. Maryland*, 2007, p. 274). The court ruled this "public." Does it matter whether or not any of the witnesses in the room were minors?

8. "Undercover [police] officers . . . paid a $10.00 admission fee" to enter an adult theater, where they observed individuals engaging in a variety of sexual activities in the view of other persons in the theater. "No customers within the theater appeared to the officers to be shocked or alarmed by this open sexual activity" (*Massachusetts v. Can-Port Amusement*, 2005, pp. 3–4). The court ruled this "public." What if the facility was a private club instead of a theater with an admission charge?

9. Participation in sexual activity using a hole cut between two private viewing booths in an adult video store (*Liebman v. Texas*, 1983). The court ruled that there is an expectation of privacy in one booth, but not the other, so the activity occurred in "public." Note that in this case, the walls of each booth were seven feet tall, but did not go all the way to the ceiling, meaning that there was an open area above each booth. Does this make a difference?

Confrontation Clause and Court Testimony: When Must Defendants Have the Right to Confront Their Accusers?

The Sixth Amendment to the United States Constitution contains what is known as the **Confrontation Clause**. It reads as follows: "In all criminal prosecutions, the accused shall enjoy the right . . . to be confronted with the witnesses against him." In short, this means that witnesses testifying at a trial must be present at the trial and available for cross-examination. In other words, if the prosecution in a case wishes to present testimony from a witness, that witness must appear in the courtroom to offer the testimony and must be available for defense counsel to question after the prosecution has concluded their questions. In *Mattox v. United States* (1895), the U.S. Supreme Court identified the purpose of the Confrontation Clause as permitting the accused:

a personal examination and cross-examination of the witness in which the accused has an opportunity, not only of testing the recollection and sifting the conscience of the witness, but of compelling him to stand face to face with the jury in order that they may look at him, and judge by his demeanor upon the stand and the manner in which he gives his testimony whether he is worthy of belief.

(p. 243)

Doing so ensures that the accused has due process of law at trial. But does this mean that the Confrontation Clause is without limits? The answer is "no," and there are two exceptions of particular interest in the field of law and sexuality. The first is the enactment of rape shield laws, which limit the scope of questions that may be asked of rape victims at trial. Generally, these laws are rules of evidence that prohibit asking about the victim's past behavior unrelated to the current case. These laws are discussed in greater detail in Chapter 5. For now, it is sufficient to say that rape shield provisions have withstood Confrontation Clause challenges, largely because the defendant can still confront the victim at trial, but the scope of cross-examination is narrowly limited in ways that promote public policy through the introduction of relevant evidence and the exclusion of irrelevant or highly prejudicial evidence (see *Gagne v. Booker*, 2012). The second Confrontation Clause exception that is highly relevant to law and sexuality concerns delivery of witness testimony via closed-circuit television (CCTV) technology for cases of child sexual abuse.

CCTV Testimony

Testifying at trial can be a traumatic experience for child victims who may have to face their accusers in the courtroom. In *Maryland v. Craig* (1990), the U.S. Supreme Court upheld the use of CCTV for victims of child sexual abuse, when certain conditions are met.

In the case, the defendant was charged with the sexual and physical abuse of a child who had attended a private education center that she operated. An expert witness testified that the victim would experience "emotional distress" (p. 842) and would be unable to communicate effectively if she was asked to testify in front of the defendant. As a result, the judge allowed the testimony to be conducted via CCTV, which was permitted under state law at the time. Specifically, the child witness, prosecuting attorney, and defense attorney would relocate to another room, where the presentation of testimony and cross-examination would take place and be broadcast back to the courtroom, in view of the judge, defendant, and jury. The defendant argued that this procedure violated the Confrontation Clause.

Justice O'Connor's opinion for the Court upheld the use of CCTV in this case. The analysis turned on two observations, which express the criteria that must be met in order for such CCTV testimony of child witnesses to be lawful. The first is that the method utilized must permit an "oath, cross-examination, and observation of the witness' demeanor," in such a way that is "functionally equivalent to . . . live, in-person testimony" (p. 851). The second is that a determination must be made specifically for each child in each case to determine when CCTV is necessary to protect a child's well-being. There cannot be an assumption that all child victims will testify via CCTV, and the state must show there is a need to do so for the child in question. In addition, the justification must be based on the potential trauma of testifying in front of the defendant; a general discomfort or fear of the courtroom setting is not sufficient. The level of distress caused by testifying must be shown to be "more than de minimis, i.e., more than 'mere nervousness or excitement or some reluctance to testify' " (p. 856).

The Court's opinion found that protecting child witnesses was a compelling state interest and that the procedure was narrowly enough tailored to meet that state interest. However, the opinion was not unanimous. Writing for the dissent, Justice Scalia expressed concern that the ruling abrogated the Confrontation Clause's guarantee to "what it explicitly says: the 'right to meet face to face all those who appear and give evidence at trial' " (p. 844). This interpretation turns on a broader questions of how the Constitution and its provisions should be interpreted, such as what it means "to be confronted," and what role modern technology ought to play.

It is important to distinguish *Maryland v. Craig* from a prior case, in which Justice Scalia wrote the opinion for the Court: *Coy v. Iowa* (1988). Here, too, child witnesses were provided an alternative to testifying in front of the defendant, although there did not appear to be a specific finding as to the level of emotional distress of the witnesses in question. Also, rather than CCTV, a visual barrier (screen) was placed between the witnesses and the defendant, and the courtroom lighting was adjusted so the witnesses would have no view of the defendant. In the Court's opinion, Justice Scalia argued: "The face-to-face presence may, unfortunately, upset the truthful rape victim or abused child; but by the same token it may confound and undo the false accuser, or reveal the child coached by a malevolent adult. It is a truism that constitutional protections have costs" (p. 1020).

Most states allow child abuse victims to offer testimony through CCTV systems (see Brancatelli, 2009). Furthermore, research suggests that the manner in which testimony is given may not affect juror determinations of verdict. Ross and colleagues (1994) conducted a mock jury experiment of a child sexual abuse case, using three different conditions – one in which the child victim's testimony was given in open court, one in which it was presented through CCTV, and one in which a screen was utilized. Regardless of how the victim testified, at the conclusion of the trial, conviction rates were consistent.

Proportionality of Punishment: How Much Is Too Much?

When a defendant is convicted of a crime, there are constitutional limits to the punishment that can be imposed. We will consider three punishment-related issues and how the courts have handled them: Civil commitment of sex offenders, probation conditions prohibiting procreation, and the death penalty for rape of a minor. In each case, the court had to issue a judgment as to whether these punishments were consistent with notions of due process and fairness.

Civil Commitment of Sex Offenders

In 1994, Kansas passed a law that allowed "the civil commitment of persons who, due to a 'mental abnormality' or a 'personality disorder,' are likely to engage in 'predatory acts of sexual violence' " (*Kansas v. Hendricks*, 1997, p. 350). Note that this is a *civil* court process. This means that, after an offender's prison sentence as handed down by a *criminal* court has been completed, the state may petition to have the individual sent to a secure facility for treatment. If the civil court agrees that the offender meets the criteria for commitment, then he or she is committed. The facility is not a prison, but in order to be released, the offender would have to demonstrate that he or she is no longer likely to engage in predatory sexual offending.

Involuntary civil commitment programs for sex offenders have been controversial, largely because of their high cost and because few persons are actually released, having completed treatment. There are also criticisms that the persons who are civilly committed are not the most dangerous of sex offenders. At the same time, proponents of the policies argue that the programs help to promote public safety (see Davey & Goodnough, 2007). In the late 1990s and early 2000s, the fairness of state sex offender civil commitment laws was challenged and appealed to the U.S.

Supreme Court. In all cases, the Court has upheld the laws.

The first challenge was in *Kansas v. Hendricks* (1997), in which the U.S. Supreme Court held that the Kansas civil commitment law passed constitutional muster. The Court was clear to distinguish that the law was not intended as a punishment, but was indistinguishable from any other circumstance in which persons are confined in a mental institution in order to promote their own safety and welfare, or because they pose a threat to that of others. The law does not violate the principle of *double jeopardy* (broadly defined as a second prosecution or punishment for the same criminal offense) because it is not a second criminal proceeding; again, it is fully in the jurisdiction of civil court. *Seling v. Young* (2001) challenged the state of Washington's civil commitment law. The Court again noted that the law was a civil, not criminal, matter, but did emphasize the importance of treatment. Because the law specified "the right to adequate care and individualized treatment" (p. 254) for those who had been committed, if that was not provided, the Court noted that offenders would have an avenue for legal action.

In 2002, the Court ruled on another challenge to the Kansas law, *Kansas v. Crane*. At issue was whether the state had to show that offenders could not control their behavior in order to initiate the civil commitment process. The Kansas Supreme Court had previously held that "the State *always* [had] to prove that a dangerous individual is *completely* unable to control his behavior" (p. 411); the U.S. Supreme Court found this to be too rigid a criterion. However, the Court did hold that the state was obligated to provide "proof of serious difficulty in controlling behavior" (p. 413). If this was not required, the Court was concerned that civil commitment might too easily be applied without proper assessment, devolving more into punishment than treatment. (For more information on the civil commitment of sexually dangerous persons, see Schug & Fradella, 2015.)

Prohibiting Procreation on Probation

What if a condition of probation—that is, a rule that a person on probation must follow to avoid being sent to prison—conflicts with a fundamental right guaranteed by the Due Process Clause? The first case to recognize procreation as a fundamental right was *Skinner v. Oklahoma*, in 1942. Subsequent cases, including some discussed earlier in this chapter, have extended individual rights to control procreative choices.

Consider the following case: The defendant "was initially charged with intentionally refusing to pay child support for his nine children he has fathered with four different women . . . His repeat offender status stemmed from intimidating two witnesses in a child abuse case – where one of the victims was his own child" (*Wisconsin v. Oakley*, 2001, p. 453). As a result, the defendant's sentence included a probation term, with the following condition: "while on probation, [the defendant] cannot have any more children unless he demonstrates that he had the ability to support them and that he is supporting the children he already had" (p. 454). On appeal, the defendant argued that strict scrutiny should apply to the review of the probation condition, because procreation is a fundamental right. The defendant further argued that the condition would fail strict scrutiny, because it is not a narrowly enough tailored means to accomplish the state's interest in ensuring payment of child support.

The Wisconsin Supreme Court disagreed, finding that by virtue of being a convicted offender under correctional supervision of the state, some rights are limited. As a result, the court applied a rational basis analysis to the condition, and found that it passed muster by meeting a legitimate state interest and being reasonably related to that interest. The decision did spark some measure of controversy, as critics voiced concerns including: An observation that even if birth control was used, a failure of birth control could lead to a revocation of probation (Miles, 2002); that strict scrutiny should be utilized to place a check on judges making decisions based on personal values and to ensure probation's rehabilitative goals are supported by the conditions offenders are required to meet (Corneal, 2003); and that it could encourage abortion should a sexual partner become pregnant (Roth, 2004).

In fact, some courts have gone farther, including as a condition of probation a prohibition on sexual activity, whether or not it leads to procreation (Roth, 2004). Regulation of procreation as a probation condition appears to be an instance in which the courts have fairly wide latitude, with such penalties assessed at a lower level of scrutiny as applied to persons under correctional control.

Capital Punishment for Rape of a Child

The final issue we will consider is the use of the death penalty for rape of a child. The analysis here turns on the Eighth Amendment's prohibition of cruel and unusual punishment, which is applied to the states through the Fourteenth Amendment. Punishments deemed too severe violate notions of due process, because proportionality is one of the criteria on which "fair" punishment is determined.

The death penalty is, without question, the most controversial of sanctions, and one which has generated numerous legal questions about to whom it can be applied. The state of Louisiana authorized use of the death penalty for the rape of a child who was under 12 years of age, and a Louisiana offender who had committed aggravated rape against his eight-year-old stepdaughter was sentenced to death. The case was appealed to the Supreme Court, on the grounds that the punishment was in violation of the Eighth Amendment (*Kennedy v. Louisiana*, 2008).

The opinion of the Court, written by Justice Kennedy, held that the punishment was a violation of the Eighth Amendment. The argument relied on several premises, but two of

the most central were the nature of offenses for which the death penalty is appropriate and national trends in the use of the death penalty for child rape. As to the former, the Court held that evolving standards of decency require that the death penalty be applied with restraint, and that no matter how traumatic and horrific child rape is, the death penalty does not provide a proportional punishment. The Court also noted a concern that there could be unanticipated negative consequences of allowing the death penalty for child rape, such as psychological harm to the child witness who would be involved with the lengthier court processes that capital punishment entails; an increased willingness for offenders to kill their victims, since both rape and murder would be capital offenses; and a concern for wrongful executions in the event that a child falsely accused an individual of rape. As to national trends, the Court observed that only a small number of states authorized capital punishment for child rape, and that since 1964 there had been no executions and only two sentences of death for child rape. This suggested to the Court that national legal sentiment was not supportive of the death penalty for child rape, rendering it an exception rather than an accepted practice of capital punishment.

The Supreme Court's decision was 5–4, and Justice Alito wrote for the dissenting Justices. The dissent offered a critique of the analysis of national trends, suggesting that they instead signaled a willingness to expand the death penalty to include child rape, but that actual drafting of new statutes had been precluded by logistic hurdles or by misreading of prior Supreme Court precedent on the death penalty. The dissent also suggested that it was fallacious to argue that the death penalty was always a disproportionate punishment for child rape, instead arguing that it depends on the circumstances of an individual offense.

Clearly, the use of the death penalty for child rape is a controversial issue, and *Kennedy v. Louisiana* was an equally controversial decision, prompting much commentary. As you read this, you likely find yourself agreeing with one side more than the other, depending on your perspectives about the Eighth Amendment, the death penalty, proportionality, and so on. Due process analysis rarely results in unanimous opinions, given the weight of the issues involved.

The purpose of the discussion of punishment has been to suggest that, even after a crime has been committed and an offender found guilty, due process analysis must continue, to assess the fairness of prescribed punishments. As you see above, it can be a complicated undertaking.

CONCLUSION

Both substantive and procedural due process focus on questions of fairness. Substantive due process concerns itself with the substance of a law in terms of what the government can and cannot criminalize. Procedural due process addresses issues related to fair enforcement, interpretation, and punishment under a law once it has been enacted. This chapter provided a brief overview of a sampling of due process issues that routinely surface in cases related to law, sex, and sexuality. There are certainly other due process rights—especially in the area of constitutional criminal procedure, such as the right to be free from unreasonable searches and seizures, the privilege against self-incrimination, and the right to effective assistance of counsel—that are beyond the scope of this chapter (for detailed coverage of such rights, see Ferdico, Fradella, & Totten, 2016). In the next chapter, we explore the other part of the Fourteenth Amendment that is of critical importance to laws, policies, and procedures concerning the legal regulation of sex and sexuality: the Equal Protection Clause.

FURTHER READING

D'Emilio, J., & Freedman, E. B. (1997). *Intimate matters: A history of sexuality in America* (2nd ed.). Chicago, IL: University of Chicago Press.

Eskridge, W. N., Jr. (2008). *Dishonorable passions: Sodomy laws in America, 1861–2003*. New York, NY: Viking.

Grossman, J. L., & Friedman, L. M. (2011). *Inside the castle: Law and the family in 20th century America*. Princeton, NJ: Princeton University Press.

Hull, N. E. H., & Hoffer, P. C. (2010). *Roe v. Wade: The abortion rights controversy in American history* (2nd ed.). Lawrence, KS: University Press of Kansas.

Johnson, J. W. (2005). *Griswold v. Connecticut: Birth control and the constitutional right of privacy*. Lawrence, KS: University Press of Kansas.

Jones, J., Grear, A., Fenton, R. A., & Stevenson, K. (Eds.). *Gender, sexualities and law*. New York, NY: Routledge.

Senjo, S. R. (2011). *Sexual deviance and the law: Legal regulation of human sexuality*. Dubuque, IA: Kendall Hunt Publishing.

Stychin, C. F. (1995). *Law's desire: Sexuality and the limits of justice*. New York, NY: Routledge.

GLOSSARY

Confrontation Clause: The portion of the Sixth Amendment to the U.S. Constitution which guarantees that, in a trial, witnesses must provide testimony in open court and be subject to cross-examination.

Due Process Clause: The rules the state or federal government must follow in both civil and criminal proceedings before denying any person of a constitutionally protected right that concerns the person's life, liberty, or property.

Entrapment: Occurs when government agents entice persons to commit crimes they would not otherwise commit.

Equal Protection Clause: The provision in the Fourteenth Amendment to the U.S. Constitution that serves to guarantee equality, requiring that the law treat persons equally, without discrimination.

Fourteenth Amendment: Guarantees citizens due process and equal protection of the law.

Fundamental right: The rational continuum of rights, whether specified in the text of the constitution or impliedly flowing therefrom, that have such great or historical significance that they merit the highest levels of judicial protection against substantial, arbitrary impositions and purposeless restraints on them.

Harm principle: The idea advanced by British philosopher John Stuart Mill that the law should regulate only those actions that pose a direct harm to others.

Legal moralism: The idea that popular notions of morality should influence decisions about what behaviors the law should regulate. This was the perspective held by British legal scholar Patrick Devlin during the Hart–Devlin debate.

Legal paternalism: A legal theory holding that the government should create and enforce laws to protect individuals from engaging in risky behaviors that might harm them.

Legal positivism: A philosophy that views the law solely as a human creation rather than as an attempt to enforce higher moral standards. This was the perspective held by H. L. A. Hart during the Hart–Devlin debate.

Levels of scrutiny: See standards of review.

Overbreadth: The doctrine that renders a law invalid when it is too broad such that it deters constitutionally protected conduct as well as unprotected conduct.

Procedural due process: Also known as procedural justice; concerns the fairness of the processes used when applying the law. It is grounded in the idea that fair procedures are the best guarantee for fair outcomes.

Standards of review: The criteria for decision-making that are applied to Fourteenth Amendment cases. There are three levels of scrutiny: minimum scrutiny (also known as the rational basis test), intermediate scrutiny (also known as the heightened scrutiny test), and strict scrutiny (requiring the highest level of critical analysis of the issues).

Substantive due process: Protects against governmental infringement of fundamental rights.

Void for vagueness: Laws that are so vague that persons must guess as to their meaning, rendering them unenforceable. Based on the principle that laws must provide clear descriptions of the conduct that is prohibited.

Wolfenden Report: A report issued by a British government commission in 1957 regarding the legal status of homosexuality and prostitution. The report formed the basis for the Hart–Devlin debate.

NOTES

1   According to Professor Adam Winkler (2006), strict scrutiny is not necessary "fatal in fact" when laws are evaluated by the federal courts; "context matters" (p. 869).

> Of the five rights protected by strict scrutiny, courts clearly apply a much more lenient version of strict scrutiny in religious liberty cases, in particular those involving claims for exemptions from generally applicable laws. In addition to doctrinal differences, the courts are acutely attuned to the identity of the governmental actor behind a law. Courts are far more likely to uphold federal laws than state and, especially,

local laws. This federalism effect is particularly profound in suspect class discrimination and free speech cases—the latter an area of law where the prevailing scholarly literature ignores federalism as a factor in judicial review. Courts are also more likely to uphold judicial orders that burden constitutional rights than legislation or executive action, and tend to uphold prison policies but not those of educational institutions. Strict scrutiny review is institutionally sensitive.

> Within discrete areas of law, strict scrutiny varies even more with the underlying context and courts have identifiable tendencies to uphold or reject particular types of laws. In suspect classification cases, courts are relatively likely to uphold law enforcement affirmative action policies and reject public contracting and redistricting laws—with Democrats being far more likely than Republicans to vote to uphold any use of race. In freedom of speech cases, strict scrutiny is relatively easy to overcome for laws or court orders limiting access to judicial proceedings or regulating charitable solicitation. By contrast, courts systematically invalidate sign ordinances, viewpoint discriminatory access denials to public forums, and a range of other speech limitations. Campaign speech restrictions are capable of surviving, but do not do so at an inordinately high rate and, surprisingly, strict scrutiny did not prove unusually lenient when applied to contribution limits. Strict scrutiny is always fatal to laws intentionally discriminating against religion and to limitations on the right to vote, but capable of being overcome in substantive due process, right to travel, and freedom of association cases.

(p. 870)

2   Note that *Singson* was decided three years after the decision in *Lawrence v. Texas* (2003). But *Lawrence* legalized sodomy between consenting adults in private; it does not permit people to engage in sex acts in public (see Chapter 6).

REFERENCES

Abramson, P. R., Pinkerton, S. D., & Huppin, M. (2003). *Sexual rights in America: The Ninth Amendment and the pursuit of happiness.* New York, NY: New York University Press.

Americans with Disabilities Act, Definitions, 42 U.S.C. § 12181 (1990).

Beaman, L. G. (2006). Who decides? Harm, polygamy and limits on freedom. *Nova Religio, 10*(1), 43–51.

Boorstein, M. (2015, July 27). Boy Scouts of America votes to end controversial ban on openly-gay scout leaders. Washington Post. Retrieved from https://www.washingtonpost.com/news/acts-of-faith/wp/

2015/07/26/the-boy-scouts-are-slated-to-lift-ban-on-openly-gay-adult-leaders/

Boyer, P. S., Clark, C. E., Jr., Kett, J. F., Salisbury, N., Sitkoff, H., & Woloch, N. (1993). *The enduring vision: A history of the American people* (2nd ed.). Lexington, MA: D. C. Heath and Company.

Brancatelli, M. (2009). *Facilitating children's testimony: Closed circuit television* (Update report 21(11). Retrieved from National Center for Prosecution of Child Abuse website: http://www.ndaa.org/pdf/update _vol_21_no_11.pdf

Brents, B. G., & Hausbeck, K. (2005). Violence and legalized brothel prostitution in Nevada: Examining safety, risk, and prostitution policy. *Journal of Interpersonal Violence*, 20(3), 270–295.

Civil Rights Act of 1964, Prohibition against Discrimination or Segregation in Places of Public Accommodation, Pub. L. 88–352, 78 Stat. 243, (July 2, 1964), *codified as amended at 42 U.S.C. § 2000a et seq. (1964)*.

Clarke, S. E. (1999). Ideas, interests, and institutions shaping abortion politics in Denver. In E. B. Sharp (Ed.), *Culture Wars and Local Politics* (pp. 43–62). Lawrence, KS: University Press of Kansas.

Committee on Homosexual Offences and Prostitution. (1963). *The Wolfenden Report: Report of the Committee on Homosexual Offences and Prostitution*. New York, NY: Stein and Day. (Original work published 1957.)

Corneal, D. A. (2003). Limiting the right to procreate: State v. Oakley and the need for strict scrutiny of probation conditions. *Seton Hall Law Review*, 33(2), 447–478.

Criminal Solicitation, Penalty, VIRGINIA CODE ANNOTATED § 18.2–29 (2002).

D'Emilio, J., & Freedman, E. B. (1988). *Intimate matters: A history of sexuality in America*. New York, NY: Perennial Library.

Davey, M., & Goodnough, A. (2007, March 4). Doubts rise as states hold sex offenders after prison. *The New York Times*. Retrieved from http://www.nytimes.com/2007/03/04/us/04civil.html?pagewanted=all&_r=0

Dempsey, M. M. (2010). Sex trafficking and criminalization: In defense of feminist abolitionism. *University of Pennsylvania Law Review*, 158(6), 1729–1778.

Devlin, P. (1977). Morals and the criminal law. In K. Kipnis (Ed.), *Philosophical issues in law* (pp. 54–65). Englewood Cliffs, NJ: Prentice Hall. (Original work published 1965.)

Epps, G. (2007). Interpreting the Fourteenth Amendment: Two don'ts and three dos. *William and Mary Bill of Rights Journal*, 16(2), 433–463.

Eskridge, W. N., Jr. (2008). *Dishonorable passions: Sodomy laws in America, 1861–2003*. New York, NY: Viking.

Feinberg, J. (1971). Legal paternalism. *Canadian Journal of Philosophy*, 1(1), 105–124.

Ferdico, J. N., Fradella, H. F., & Totten, C. (2016). *Criminal procedure for the criminal justice professional* (12th ed.). Belmont, CA: Wadsworth/Cengage.

Finer, L. B. (2007). Trends in premarital sex in the United States, 1954–2003. *Public Health Reports*, 122(1), 73–78.

Forsyth, C. J. (1992). Parade strippers: A note on being naked in public. *Deviant Behavior*, 13(4), 391–403.

Fradella, H. F. (2002). Legal, moral, and social reasons for decriminalizing sodomy. *Journal of Contemporary Criminal Justice*, 18(3), 279–301.

Gunther, G. (1972). The Supreme Court, 1971 term – Foreword: In search of evolving doctrine on a changing court: A model for a newer equal protection. *Harvard Law Review*, 86(1), 1–48.

Harding, D. J., & Jencks, C. (2003). Changing attitudes toward premarital sex: Cohort, period, and aging effects. *Public Opinion Quarterly*, 67(2), 211–226.

Hart, H. L. A. (1958). Positivism and the separation of law and morals. *Harvard Law Review*, 71(4), 593–629.

Hart, H. L. A. (1971). Immorality and treason. In R. A. Wasserstrom (Ed.), *Morality and the Law* (pp. 49–54). Belmont, CA: Wadsworth. (Original work published 1959.)

Hauser, C. (2009, February 14). Among gay men, arrests spark concern about being singled out. *The New York Times*. Retrieved from http://www.nytimes.com/2009/02/15/nyregion/15arrests.html

Henkin, L. (1963). "Selective incorporation" in the Fourteenth Amendment. *Yale Law Journal*, 73(1), 74–88.

Jackson, J. D. (2011). Putting rationality back into the rational basis test: Saving substantive due process and redeeming the promise of the Ninth Amendment. *University of Richmond Law Review*, 45(2), 491–548.

Kent, S. A. (2006). A matter of principle: Fundamentalist Mormon polygamy, children, and human rights debates. *Nova Religio*, 10(1), 7–29.

Malamuth, N. M., & Impett, E. A. (2001). Research on sex in the media: What do we know about its effects on children and adolescents? In D. G. Singer & J. L. Singer (Eds.), *Handbook of children and the media* (pp. 269–287). Thousand Oaks, CA: Sage.

McConnaughey, J. (2000, February 28). Police warn on Mardi Gras flashing, bead tossing. *The Pittsburgh Post-Gazette*, p. A6.

Miles, R. L. (2002). Criminal consequences for making babies: Probation conditions that restrict procreation. *Washington and Lee Law Review*, 59(4), 1545–1584.

Mill, J. S. (1989). On liberty. In S. Collini (Ed.), *J.S. Mill: On Liberty and other writings* (pp. 1–116). New York, NY: Cambridge University Press. (Original work published 1859.)

National Conference of State Legislatures. (2012). *Pharmacist conscience clauses: Laws and information.*

Retrieved from http://www.ncsl.org/issues-research/health/pharmacist-conscience-clauses-laws-and-information.aspx

Norrander, B., & Wilcox, C. (2001). Public opinion and policymaking in the states: The case of post-*Roe* abortion policy. In C. Z. Mooney (Ed.), *The public clash of private values: The politics of morality policy* (pp. 143–159). New York, NY: Chatham House Publishers.

Obscenity, Louisiana Revised Statutes § 14–106 (2012).

Owen, S. S., Fradella, H. F., Burke, T. W., & Joplin, J. J. (2015). *Foundations of criminal justice* (2nd ed.). New York, NY: Oxford University Press.

Porto, B. (1998). *The craft of legal reasoning*. New York, NY: Harcourt Brace College Publishers.

Robinson, P. H. (2005). Fair notice and fair adjudication: Two kinds of legality. *University of Pennsylvania Law Review, 154*(2), 335–398.

Ross, D. F., Hopkins, S., Hanson, E., Lindsay, R. C. L., Hazen, K., & Eslinger, T. (1994). The impact of protective shields and videotape testimony on conviction rates in a simulated trial of child sexual abuse. *Law and Human Behavior, 18*(5), 553–566.

Roth, R. (2004). "No new babies?" Gender inequality and reproductive control in the criminal justice and prison systems. *Journal of Gender, Social Policy, and the Law, 12*(3), 391–425.

Samaha, J. (2002). *Criminal law* (7th ed.). Belmont, CA: Wadsworth.

Samuelson, D. R. (1998). Hart, Devlin, and Arthur Miller on the legal enforcement of morality. *Denver University Law Review, 76*(1), 189–216.

Schmidtz, D. (2006). *Elements of justice*. New York, NY: Cambridge University Press.

Schug, R., & Fradella, H. F. (2015). *Mental illness and crime*. Thousand Oaks, CA: Sage.

Seelye, K. Q., & Bidgood, J. (2015, March 15). Boston celebrates end of ban as gays march in St. Patrick's parade. *New York Times*. http://www.nytimes.com/2015/03/16/us/boston-celebrates-end-of-ban-as-gays-march-in-st-patricks-parade.html

Shaman, J. M. (2001). *Constitutional interpretation: Illusion and reality*. Westport, CT: Greenwood Press.

Silverman, I. J. (2001). *Corrections: A comprehensive view* (2nd ed.). Belmont, CA: Wadsworth.

Winkler, A. (2006). Fatal in theory and strict in fact: An empirical analysis of strict scrutiny in the federal courts. *Vanderbilt Law Review, 59*(3), 793–871.

Cases

31 West 21st Street Associates v. Evening of the Unusual, 480 N.Y.S.2d 816 (N.Y.C. Civ. Ct. 1984).

Adkins v. Childrens Hospital, 261 U.S. 525 (1923).

Baker v. Nelson, 409 U.S. 810 (1972), *overruled by Obergefell v. Hodges*, 135 S. Ct. 2584 (2015).

Blyther v. United States, 577 A.2d 1154 (D.C. 1990).

Bowers v. Hardwick, 478 U.S. 186 (1986).

Boy Scouts of America v. Dale, 530 U.S. 640 (2000).

Coy v. Iowa, 487 U.S. 1012 (1988).

Dobbins v. City of Los Angeles, 195 U.S. 223 (1904).

Eisenstadt v. Baird, 405 U.S. 438 (1972).

Everett and Wright v. Virginia, 200 S.E.2d 564 (Vir. 1973).

Ford v. Commonwealth, 391 S.E.2d 603 (Vir. Ct. App. 1990).

Foster v. Indiana, 813 N.E.2d 1236 (Ind. Ct. App. 2004).

Gagne v. Booker, 680 F.3d 493 (6th Cir. 2012).

Gonzales v. Carhart, 550 U.S. 124 (2007).

Griswold v. Connecticut, 381 U.S. 479 (1965).

Hurley v. Irish-American Gay, Lesbian and Bisexual Group of Boston, 515 U.S. 557 (1995).

Illinois v. Legel, 321 N.E.2d 164 (Ill. Ct. App. 1974).

Jacobson v. United States, 503 U.S. 540 (1992).

Kansas v. Crane, 534 U.S. 407 (2002).

Kansas v. Hendricks, 521 U.S. 346 (1997).

Kennedy v. Louisiana, 554 U.S. 407 (2008).

Lacour v. Texas, 8 S.W.3d 670 (Tex. Ct. Crim. App. 2000).

Lawrence v. Texas, 539 U.S. 558 (2003).

Liebman v. Texas, 652 S.W.2d 942 (Tex. Ct. Crim. App. 1983).

Loving v. Virginia, 388 U.S. 1 (1967).

Maryland v. Craig, 497 U.S. 836 (1990).

Massachusetts v. Can-Port Amusement, 19 Mass L. Rep. 562 (Mass. Super. Ct. 2005).

Mattox v. United States, 156 U.S. 237 (1895).

Meyer v. Nebraska, 262 U.S. 390 (1923).

Miller v. California, 413 U.S. 15 (1973).

Minersville School District v. Gobitis, 310 U.S. 586 (1940).

NAACP v. Alabama, 357 U.S. 449 (1958).

New York v. Frank S., et al., 705 N.Y.S.2d 171 (N.Y.C. Crim. Ct. 2000).

New York v. McNamara et al., 78 N.Y.2d 626 (N.Y. 1991).

Obergefell v. Hodges, 135 S. Ct. 2584 (2015).

Osborne v. Ohio, 495 U.S. 103 (1990).

Paris Adult Theatre v. Slaton, 413 U.S. 49 (1973).

Pierce v. Society of Sisters, 268 U.S. 510 (1925).

Pinter v. City of New York, 710 F. Supp. 2d 408 (S.D.N.Y. 2010).

Planned Parenthood of Southeastern Pennsylvania v. Casey, 505 U.S. 833 (1992).

Poe v. Ullman, 67 U.S. 497 (1961).

Reynolds v. United States, 98 U.S. 145 (1878).

Richmond v. Corinth, 816 So. 2d 373 (Miss. 2002).

Roberts v. United States Jaycees, 468 U.S. 609 (1984).

Roe v. Wade, 410 U.S. 113 (1973).

Rotary International v. Rotary Club of Duarte, 481 U.S. 537 (1987).

Seling v. Young, 531 U.S. 250 (2001).

Singson v. Commonwealth, 621 S.E.2d 682 (Vir. Ct. App. 2005).

Skinner v. Oklahoma, 316 U.S. 535 (1942).

Stanley v. Georgia, 394 U.S. 557 (1969).

Stenberg v. Carhart, 530 U.S. 914 (2000).

Sterling v. Minersville, 232 F.3d 190 (3rd Cir. 2000).

Turner v. Safley, 482 U.S. 78 (1987).

United States v. Blassingame, 197 F.3d 271 (7th Cir. 1999).

United States v. Carolene Products, 304 U.S. 144 (1938).

United States v. Loy, 237 F.3d 251 (3rd Cir. 2001).

United States v. Thirty-Seven Photographs, 402 U.S. 363 (1971).

Washington v. Glucksberg, 521 U.S. 702 (1997).

Weideman v. Indiana, 890 N.E.2d 28 (Ind. Ct. App. 2008).

West Coast Hotel Co. v. Parrish, 300 U.S. 379 (1937).

West Virginia Board of Education v. Barnette, 319 U.S. 624 (1943).

Whatley v. Indiana, 708 N.E.2d 66 (Ind. Ct. App. 1999).

Wisconsin v. Oakley, 629 N.W.2d 200 (Wis. 2001).

Wisneski v. Maryland, 921 A.2d 273 (Md. 2007).

CHAPTER 4

Sex and the Fourteenth Amendment: Part II: Equal Protection of the Law

Stephen S. Owen and Tod W. Burke

Laws against **statutory rape** have a long history in the American states, dating back to legal codes from the colonial era. "Today's statutory rape laws prohibit sexual intercourse with an unmarried person under the age of consent, which varies depending on the state" (Cocca, 2004, p. 9). It is important to note that statutory rape laws prohibit even consensual sexual activity, if one of the participants is under the age of consent.

Through the 1970s, state laws defined the age of consent fairly rigidly. In the 1800s, the age was typically 10–12 years, but by the early decades of the twentieth century, the legal age of consent had increased to 16–18 years. In the 1970s, though, state laws began to change, once again. Beginning in 1971, states began adopting "age-span, or age-differential, provisions" (Cocca, 2004, p. 19). These laws, sometimes known as Romeo and Juliet provisions (named for the young lovers in Shakespeare's play), "required that one partner be a certain number of years older than the other for the crime of statutory rape to occur" (Cocca, 2004, p. 19). This was based on the argument that teenagers of similar ages may engage in relationships that involve consensual sexual activity, which do not deserve as strict a punishment as accorded to statutory rape. While sexual activity between teenagers may still remain illegal, under age-span provisions it is not labeled as statutory rape, instead carrying lesser charges and punishments (Cocca, 2004).

Age-span provisions quickly became popular modifications to statutory rape laws. While individual states defined their measures differently, by 1983, half of the states had adopted age-span provisions. By 1998, 43 states had done so (Cocca, 2004). In 1999, Kansas passed its age-span law, which defined the following as "unlawful sexual relations" rather than as statutory rape:

> voluntary sexual intercourse, sodomy, or lewd touching when, at the time of the incident, (1) the victim is a child of 14 or 15; (2) the offender is less than 19 years of age and less than 4 years older than the victim; (3) the victim and offender are the only ones involved; and (4) the victim and offender are members of the opposite sex.
>
> (*Kansas v. Limon*, 2005, p. 24)

The differences are stark, as illustrated in the Kansas Supreme Court case, *Kansas v. Limon*. In that case, an 18-year-old male and a 14-year-old male engaged in consensual oral sex, which occurred "at a school for developmentally disabled children where [both] were residents" (p. 24). The first three points in the Kansas law applied to this encounter; the last did not, as the sexual contact was between two persons of the same sex. Based on his juvenile criminal history, the 18-year-old in this case was sentenced to 206 months in prison and five years of supervision after release. In addition, he had to register as a sex offender. Had the same encounter occurred between two persons of the opposite sex, with the same criminal history, the sentence would have been 13 to 15 months of imprisonment without having to register as a sex offender.

Consider the questions raised by this case. Does the law provide unequal treatment based on whether the couple is same sex or opposite sex? The answer is clearly "yes." Is there a justification for the law to do so? And, how does the law make that determination? These are the questions that generated debate in the case, and both lay squarely within the realm of the Fourteenth Amendment to the U.S. Constitution.

Upon appeal, the Kansas Supreme Court held that the law lacked a rational basis for excluding same-sex couples from the age-span provisions of Kansas law. As a result, the court held that the law violated the Equal Protection Clauses of both the U.S. and Kansas Constitutions. The court required that the language about being members of the opposite sex be struck from the law, and that the sentence given in the case was accordingly in violation of equal protection.

LEARNING OBJECTIVES

1. Distinguish between the three standards of review (i.e., the rational basis test, intermediate scrutiny, and strict scrutiny) as they apply to the resolution of cases pertaining to law and sexuality when challenged under the Equal Protection Clause of the Fourteenth Amendment to the U.S. Constitution.
2. Explain the concept of equal protection and how it is promoted by the Fourteenth Amendment and Title VII of the Civil Rights Act of 1964.
3. Describe how the legal system has addressed issues related to hate crime.
4. Assess the legal reasoning in court cases pertaining to law and sexuality, considering the strength of the arguments and their implications under the Equal Protection Clause.
5. Apply legal principles and precedents from the chapter to the resolution of scenarios related to chapter content.

Recall from Chapter 3 that the Fourteenth Amendment to the U.S. Constitution provides that "No State shall . . . deny to any person within its jurisdiction the equal protection of the laws." This section of the Fourteenth Amendment is referred to as the **Equal Protec-**tion Clause. This provision was included in the post-Civil War amendments to the U.S. Constitution to enshrine the principle that all people, regardless of their race, should be treated the same by the law (Boyer et al., 1993). But as explained in Chapter 3, the

Table 4.1 Constitutional standards of review and their associated levels of scrutiny

Standard of Review	Legislative Deference	Relationship to State Interest	Relationship between Means and Ends	Burden of Proof
Strict Scrutiny	Not Deferential	"Compelling"	"Absolutely Necessary"	State
Intermediate Scrutiny	Somewhat Deferential	"Important or Substantial"	"Close, though not perfect, Fit"	State
Minimal Scrutiny	Highly Deferential	"Rational"	"Reasonably Related"	Challenger

Source: Adapted from Shaman (2001: Chapter 3).

Amendment's impact on the American legal landscape was actually much broader. For instance, the Amendment has framed debates and legal cases concerning abortion, interracial marriage, gender equality, sexual orientation, and privacy.

The plain language of the Fourteenth Amendment limits the authority of the states. In addition, the Equal Protection Clause also constrains the power of the federal government through the operation of the Due Process Clause of the Fifth Amendment to the U.S. Constitution (see *Bolling v. Sharpe*, 1954).[1] In other words, the concept of "fundamental fairness" embodied in the notion of "due process" includes the principle that all similarly situated persons be treated in a similar manner under both state and federal laws.

OVERVIEW OF EQUAL PROTECTION STANDARDS OF REVIEW

Chapter 3 introduced two standards of review that are commonly used in due process cases: the rational basis test (i.e., minimal scrutiny) and strict scrutiny. Both are also used in equal protection cases. In addition, equal protection litigation employs a third standard of review (that is not used in due process cases) called

intermediate scrutiny. Table 4.1 summarizes the three levels of judicial scrutiny courts use to analyze equal protection claims.

Minimal Scrutiny: The Rational Basis Test

The rational basis test works the same way for equal protection cases as it does for due process cases. Under this highly deferential standard of review, a law will be upheld as constitutional so long as (1) the law bears some rational relationship to a legitimate state interest; and (2) the law is "reasonably related" to accomplishing that state interest (Shaman, 2001, p. 72). It is the challenger who bears the burden of persuading the court that the above criteria are not the case—that is, that the law does not have a "rational basis" related to some legitimate state interest, or that the law is not reasonably related to accomplishing some legitimate state interest. The U.S. Supreme Court case of *Romer v. Evans* (1996) illustrates how the rational basis test applies to equal protection claims concerning law and sexuality.

In 1992, voters in the state of Colorado approved by a margin of 53% to 47% a ballot initiative to amend the state constitution. The amendment stated:

Neither the State of Colorado, through any of its branches or departments, nor any of its agencies, political subdivisions, municipalities or school districts, shall enact, adopt or enforce any statute, regulation, ordinance or policy whereby homosexual, lesbian or bisexual orientation, conduct, practices or relationships shall constitute or otherwise be the basis of or entitle any person or class of persons to have or claim any minority status, quota preferences, protected status or claim of discrimination. This Section of the Constitution shall be in all respects self-executing.

The impetus for the ballot initiative stemmed from several Colorado cities—such as Boulder, Aspen, and Denver—having enacted nondiscrimination ordinances that included sexual orientation. Once passed by the voters, the ballot initiative became Amendment 2 to the Colorado Constitution and had the immediate effect not only of repealing these local ordinances, but also prohibiting sexual minorities from seeking any legislative, executive, or judicial action that might protect them from discrimination. A group of plaintiffs that included lesbian, gay, and bisexual people, then filed a lawsuit, *Romer v. Evans* (1996), which sought to have Amendment 2 declared unconstitutional. Both a state trial court and the Colorado Supreme Court ruled that Amendment 2 violated the Equal Protection Clause of the Fourteenth Amendment to the U.S. Constitution because the amendment infringed on the rights of gays, lesbians, and bisexuals to participate equally in the political process. In its first-ever case of the modern era adjudicating the rights of gays and lesbians as a class of people, the U.S. Supreme Court agreed with the Colorado courts and invalidated Amendment 2.

One of the key issues in *Romer v. Evans* was the standard of review that should be applied to Amendment 2. Ultimately, the U.S. Supreme Court never ruled on the proper level of scrutiny that courts should apply when reviewing the constitutionality of laws that discriminate on the basis of sexual orientation. Rather, the Court left that question open because Amendment 2 could not even pass constitutional muster under the lowest, most deferential standard of review—the rational basis test:

Sweeping and comprehensive is the change in legal status effected by this law. So much is evident from the ordinances that the Colorado Supreme Court declared would be void by operation of Amendment 2. Homosexuals, by state decree, are put in a solitary class with respect to transactions and relations in both the private and governmental spheres. The amendment withdraws from homosexuals, but no others, specific legal protection from the injuries caused by discrimination, and it forbids reinstatement of these laws and policies. . . .

Amendment 2 confounds this normal process of judicial review. It is at once too narrow and too broad. It identifies persons by a single trait and then denies them protection across the board. The resulting disqualification of a class of persons from the right to seek specific protection from the law is unprecedented in our jurisprudence. . . .

It is not within our constitutional tradition to enact laws of this sort. Central both to the idea of the rule of law and to our own Constitution's guarantee of equal protection is the principle that government and each of its parts remain open on impartial terms to all who seek its assistance. Equal protection of the laws is not achieved through indiscriminate imposition of inequalities. Respect for this principle explains why laws singling out a certain class of citizens for disfavored legal status or general hardships are rare. A law declaring that in general it shall be more difficult for one group of citizens than for all others to seek aid from the government is itself a denial of equal protection of the laws in the most literal sense.

(pp. 627, 633)

The Court went on to say that Amendment 2 raised "the inevitable inference that the disadvantage imposed is born of animosity toward the class of persons affected" (p. 634). In fact, the Court found that Amendment 2 was "inexplicable by anything but animus toward the class that it affects" (p. 632). "If the constitutional conception of 'equal protection of the laws' means anything, it must at the very least mean that a bare . . . desire to harm a politically unpopular group cannot constitute a *legitimate* governmental interest" (p. 634; emphasis added). Stated differently, the Court found that a bias against— or dislike for—gay and lesbian persons was the primary factor motivating the law and such bias or dislike cannot serve as a "legitimate governmental interest" that satisfies the rational basis test in Equal Protection Clause cases. Accordingly, the Court held that "Amendment 2 classifies homosexuals not to further a proper legislative end, but to make them unequal to everyone else. . . . A State cannot so deem a class of persons a stranger to its laws. Amendment 2 violates the Equal Protection Clause. . ." (p. 635).

In his dissenting opinion, Justice Scalia argued that there was a rational basis to the law. At the time of this case, some states still criminalized sodomy (generally conceptualized as same-sex sexual conduct), as *Lawrence v. Texas* (2003) had not yet ruled such laws unconstitutional. Scalia suggested the following rational basis for the Colorado law: "If it is rational to criminalize the conduct, surely it is rational to deny special favor and protection to those with a self-avowed tendency or desire to engage in the conduct" (*Romer v. Evans*, 1996, p. 642, Scalia, J., dissenting). The dissenting opinion also suggests a role for morality, arguing that the Colorado law "is rather a modest attempt by seemingly tolerant Coloradans to preserve traditional sexual mores against the efforts of a politically powerful minority to revise those mores . . ." (p. 636, Scalia, J., dissenting). This suggests that the echoes of the Hart–Devlin debate continue (see Chapter 3), as societal debates on same-sex issues often include political and policy debates driven by the politics of morality (see Haider-Markel & Meier, 1996).

Kansas v. Limon (2005), the case discussed at the beginning of this chapter, also illustrates the application of the rational basis test in an Equal Protection Clause case. The Kansas Supreme Court applied minimal scrutiny to the question of whether the age-span provisions of the state's statutory rape laws could be accorded to two persons of the opposite sex, but denied to two persons of the same sex.[2] Thus, the court considered six possible reasons offered by the State of Kansas for excluding same-sex encounters from the age-span provisions:

(1) the protection and preservation of traditional sexual mores of society; (2) preservation of the historical notions of appropriate sexual development of children; (3) protection of teenagers against coercive relationships; (4) protection of teenagers from the increased health risks that accompany sexual activity; (5) promotion of parental responsibility and procreation; and (6) protection of those in group homes. (pp. 33–34)

The court rejected each of these reasons, finding that they did not provide a rational basis, under the law, for treating the same behavior (in this case, oral sex) differently based on whether it occurred between two persons of the opposite sex or two persons of the same sex. As a result, the court struck down the provision of the law relating to sexual orientation, so the Kansas age-span statute would apply without reference to the gender or sexual orientation of the participants.

Strict Scrutiny

Recall from Chapter 3 that Due Process Clause challenges to laws are reviewed under the rational basis test unless a fundamental right is involved, which triggers the exacting level of judicial review known as strict scrutiny. A similar logic applies to Equal Protection Clause challenges to laws. As a rule, classifications between groups or classes of people (e.g., minors versus adults; people with a history of a felony conviction versus people never convicted of a felony) are reviewed under the rational basis test. But higher levels of judicial scrutiny are warranted when the classification concerns a fundamental right or is based on a characteristic that has historically been subject to systematic discrimination. The most exacting standard of review, strict scrutiny, is reserved for distinctions made on the basis of a suspect classification.

A **suspect class** is a group that has historically experienced prejudice, as demonstrated through four criteria:

> They include: A) whether the class has been historically "subjected to discrimination"; B) whether the class has a defining characteristic that "frequently bears no relation to ability to perform or contribute to society"; C) whether the class exhibits "obvious, immutable, or distinguishing characteristics that define them as a discrete group"; and D) whether the class is "a minority or politically powerless."
>
> (*Windsor v. United States*, 2012, p. 181)

In shorthand, the definition of a suspect class can be conceptualized as having experienced tangible discrimination, while having the ability to make contributions to society, with the discrimination being based on an immutable (i.e., unchangeable) characteristic, and with one result being political marginalization. Race constitutes a suspect class. The Equal Protection Clause "prohibits all racial distinctions and . . . strict scrutiny ensures that state actors limit their consideration of race to the pursuit of compelling objectives" (Hutchinson, 2014, p. 991). Classifications based on national origin or alienage similarly are reviewed under strict scrutiny since, like race-based classification, laws that make distinctions on such grounds historically "reflect prejudice and antipathy—a view that those in the burdened class are not as worthy or

deserving as others" (*City of Cleburne v. Cleburne Living Center*, 1985, p. 440).

Should sexual orientation be treated with strict scrutiny, defining gays and lesbians as a suspect class? Courts have struggled with this question for decades. Some courts ruled that, unlike race, sexual orientation is not an immutable characteristic (e.g., *High Tech Gays v. Defense Industrial Security Clearance Office*, 1990). Today, however, most courts reject that view, instead arguing

> Sexual orientation is fundamental to a person's identity and is a distinguishing characteristic that defines gays and lesbians as a discrete group. . . . Individuals do not generally choose their sexual orientation. No credible evidence supports a finding that an individual may, through conscious decision, therapeutic intervention or any other method, change his or her sexual orientation.
>
> (*Perry v. Schwarzenegger*, 2010, pp. 963–964, 966; see also *Windsor*, 2012, p. 182)

Courts have also differed on the political power of sexual minorities. Consider two U.S. Courts of Appeals cases from the 1980s in which plaintiffs unsuccessfully challenged the then-active ban on gays and lesbians serving in the U.S. military. In *Ben-Shalom v. Marsh* (1989), the Seventh Circuit found that gays and lesbians were not a suspect class because they did not lack political power. The court's dubious reasoning, however, rested on two news articles that pointed to isolated incidents at a time when gays and lesbians could still go to prison for engaging in same-sex sexual conduct with each other:

> Homosexuals are not without political power. *Time* magazine reports that one congressman is an avowed homosexual, and that there is a charge that five other top officials are known to be homosexual. Support for homosexuals is, of course, not limited to other homosexuals. *The Chicago Tribune* . . . reported that the Mayor

of Chicago participated in a gay rights parade. (*Ben-Shalom*, 1989, p. 466 n. 9)

In contrast, the Ninth Circuit initially ruled that gays and lesbians constituted a suspect class in *Watkins v. United States Army* (1988). The ruling in *Watkins* (1988) was based on the principles of suspect-class identification listed above. Specifically, the court observed that gay and lesbian persons have been discriminated against in society and that "sexual orientation plainly has no relevance to a person's 'ability to perform or contribute to society' " (p. 1346). The court also found sexual orientation to be an immutable characteristic, using a definition of immutable to include traits where "changing it would involve great difficulty, such as requiring a major physical change or a traumatic change of identity" (p. 1347). Finally, the court held that prejudice or discrimination against homosexuality could "deter many gays from openly advocating pro-homosexual legislation, thus intensifying their inability to make effective use of the political process" (p. 1348), and that even if gays and lesbians were to be politically active, "the general animus toward homosexuality may render this participation wholly ineffective" (p. 1348). Taking these factors together, the court determined that sexual orientation should be defined as a suspect class, and therefore subject to strict scrutiny under the Fourteenth Amendment. Although the decision was later vacated (see *Watkins v. United States Army*, 1989), the argument foreshadowed subsequent discussion on the subject.

The U.S. Supreme Court has never ruled on whether gays, lesbians, and bisexuals constitute a suspect class. In his dissent in *Romer v. Evans* (1996), however, Justice Scalia clearly indicated that distinctions based on the basis of sexual orientation should be reviewed under the rational basis test:

[B]ecause those who engage in homosexual conduct tend to reside in disproportionate numbers in certain communities, have high disposable income, and, of course, care about homosexual-rights issues much more ardently than the public at large, they possess political power much greater than their numbers, both locally and statewide. Quite understandably, they devote this political power to achieving not merely a grudging social toleration, but full social acceptance, of homosexuality.

(*Romer*, 1996, pp. 645–646, Scalia, J., dissenting)

As these cases indicate, the question of political power tends to be very narrowly construed by judges. Moreover, judicial assumptions about gays and lesbians often appear to be rooted in stereotypes that portray them as powerful, well educated, and wealthy and, therefore, able to achieve their desired political wishes without the need for the courts to protect them from discrimination (see Hutchinson, 2014; Schacter, 1994). But this stereotype is not supported by actual data:

Several empirical studies, however, debunk the myth of gay and lesbian wealth. These studies show that gay or lesbian sexual identity negatively impacts employment opportunities and income. Other studies show acute economic deprivation for many gays and lesbians. For example, many studies find that well over 30 percent of homeless teenagers in large urban centers are gay or lesbian. Family conflict over sexual orientation is a leading cause of homelessness among gay and lesbian youth. These teens often turn to sex work and criminal behavior in order to survive. Predictably, many of them also suffer from untreated mental illnesses, which can lead to substance abuse, alcoholism, and suicide. They also suffer from physical abuse and are very susceptible to contracting HIV and other infections. Many existing homeless shelters that offer services for youth are ill-prepared to address the special needs of this population. Other empirical studies have examined the impact of poverty, homophobia, and racism upon low-income gays and lesbians of color.

For example, the rate of HIV and AIDS among black gay and bisexual men is the highest of any gay and bisexual demographic group. The rate among Latino gay and bisexual men is also disproportionately high. Some researchers attribute this higher rate of infection to emotional distress that results from exposure to multiple sources of disempowerment, such as racism, xenophobia, homophobia, and poverty.

Although some gays and lesbians undoubtedly have wealth and power, the class as a whole suffers economic detriment due to societal discrimination. Many persons in the class, moreover, live in conditions of extreme deprivation. They are not politically powerful. Instead, they are a prime example of a powerless minority that needs protection from an abusive political process.

(Hutchinson, 2014, pp. 1021–1022)

Perhaps partly in response to fallacious judicial reasoning with regard to the political power of gays, lesbians, and bisexuals, some scholars who study issues of sexuality have argued that the better framework for analyzing how the courts should review legal distinctions on the basis of sexual orientation should involve intermediate scrutiny—the standard of review for quasi-suspect classifications (see Eskridge, 2010). Notably, state high courts and federal appellate courts agree and have taken this route (*Windsor v. United States*, 2012; *Varnum v. Brien*, 2009; *Kerrigan v. Commissioner of Pub. Health*, 2008).

Intermediate Scrutiny

Minimal scrutiny and strict scrutiny are two opposing ends of a scale. In its consideration of two landmark cases related to gender (*Reed v. Reed*, 1971; *Craig v. Boren*, 1976), the U.S. Supreme Court suggested a new level of scrutiny that requires a more stringent analysis than required by minimal scrutiny, but not quite as stringent as that required by strict scrutiny. This is known as **intermediate scrutiny**, and its application is fairly limited in Equal Protection Clause litigation to quasi-suspect classes. The identification of a quasi-suspect class appears to be similar to that of a suspect class, with the distinction being a matter of degree. A quasi-suspect class may be one in which some, but not all, of the elements of a suspect class are met, or it may be one in which the cumulative weight of the evidence is sufficient to indicate an equal protection concern, but not at the highest level of scrutiny.

In intermediate scrutiny, the state must show that the law being challenged is related to an "important or substantial" state interest, and that the law is a "close, though not perfect, fit" as a means to achieve that state interest (Shaman, 2001, p. 72). This requires more than simply showing a rational basis for the law, but is not as demanding as the exacting requirements specified under strict scrutiny.

Intermediate (also known as heightened) scrutiny is the most recently developed of the three levels, and as such, is perhaps the least well specified. As noted by Eskridge and Hunter (2004), "The Supreme Court has applied, sometimes rather weakly and sometimes quite strongly, . . . heightened scrutiny to sex-based classifications" (p. lviii). There is considerable flexibility in how intermediate scrutiny can be applied. Let's consider an example from one of the cases that established the notion of intermediate scrutiny.

In *Craig v. Boren* (1976), the U.S. Supreme Court considered the constitutionality of a gender-based difference in the age at which alcoholic beverages could be purchased. An Oklahoma law prohibited "the sale of 'non-intoxicating' 3.2% beer to males under the age of 21 and to females under the age of 18" (p. 192). The justification proffered by the state was that the measure was necessary for traffic safety, due to males' greater propensity to drink and drive. The opinion, written by Justice Brennan, challenged the statistical findings that the state used to justify the law, and held that the showing offered by the appellees does not satisfy us that sex represents a legitimate, accurate proxy for the regulation of drinking and driving . . . the relationship between gender and traffic safety becomes far too tenuous to satisfy [the] requirement that the gender-based difference be substantially related to achievement of the statutory objective.

(p. 204)

It is the last phrase that illustrates intermediate scrutiny. Referring to the elements of intermediate scrutiny in Table 4.1, it would be difficult to argue that traffic safety, and the prevention of drinking and driving, is not an "important or substantial" state interest. However, it is the relationship between the means and the ends where the constitutional difficulty emerges. The means specified in the law (here, the differential age at which males and females could purchase the 3.2% beer) must be closely related to the accomplishment of the state interest, (here, traffic safety), and in this case the Court ruled they were not.

Scholars debate whether sexual orientation constitutes a quasi-suspect class that triggers application of intermediate scrutiny. Consider the landmark case of *United States v. Windsor* (2013), which invalidated a section of the federal Defense of Marriage Act (DOMA, 1996) defining marriage exclusively as a union between one man and one woman. When decided by the U.S. Court of Appeals for the Second Circuit, the court specifically ruled that sexual orientation was a suspect class.

Analysis of these four factors supports our conclusion that homosexuals compose a class that is subject to heightened scrutiny. We further conclude that the class is quasi-suspect (rather than suspect) based on the weight of the factors and on analogy to the classifications recognized as suspect and quasi-suspect. While homosexuals have been the target of significant and long-standing discrimination in public and private spheres, this mistreatment is not sufficient to require our most exacting scrutiny.

(p. 185)

When the case was appealed to the U.S. Supreme Court, the justices did not reach the question of the applicable standard of review. Perhaps even though the Court did not explicitly declare sexual orientation to be a quasi-suspect class, it nonetheless treated sexual orientation as if it were a quasi-suspect classification by employing heightened scrutiny because DOMA was rooted in **animus** that marginalized sexual minorities. Most scholars, however, argue that *Romer*, *Lawrence* (to a lesser degree) and *Windsor* (to the clearest degree yet) represent an enhanced form of rational basis review—"one with 'bite' or 'teeth'"—that allows the Court to offer equal protection to those subjected to animus-motivated lawmaking without having to engage in "the arduous task of articulating just what about sexual orientation would classify it as suspect under the traditional tiered scrutiny of equal protection jurisprudence" (Ho, 2014, p. 56). And, as will be discussed in more detail in Chapter 9, although the U.S. Supreme Court's decision in *Obergefell v. Hodges* (2015) legalized marriage equality for same-sex couples on both due process and equal protection grounds, the Court was silent as to the specific standard of review it applied.[3]

EQUAL PROTECTION OF THE LAW

In this section, we will explore how the law ensures equal protection to all persons, regardless of factors such as gender, marital status, sexual orientation, transgender status, and more. In doing so, we will not be limited to a discussion of the Fourteenth Amendment. Many federal laws have also been instrumental in facilitating equality under law, including Title VII of the Civil Rights Act of 1964. We will consider how the Fourteenth Amendment has been applied to equal protection challenges to state law, and how Title VII has been applied to sexual harassment and bona fide occupational qualifications in the workplace. Taken together, it will become clear that the law has been structured to prevent discrimination in areas related to sexuality.

We have already considered some Fourteenth Amendment U.S. Supreme Court cases in the discussion of levels of scrutiny. These included ruling unconstitutional a gender-based distinction in drinking age based on intermediate scrutiny (*Craig v. Boren*, 1976), and two cases using the rational basis test—perhaps "with bite"—one ruling unconstitutional a measure that would have banned protections against sexual orientation discrimination (*Romer v. Evans*, 1996) and the other invalidating the provision in DOMA that prohibited the federal government from recognizing same-sex marriages legally performed in certain states (*United States v. Windsor*, 2013). Certainly, these are three of the more significant equal protection cases the Court has heard in the area of law and sexuality. We also discussed the debate about which level of scrutiny should be utilized when processing sexual orientation cases, a conversation that will likely continue as courts continue to address equal protection issues related to sexual orientation. Continuing a discussion of equal protection, we will consider how the Fourteenth Amendment's equal protection guarantees have been applied to marital status, gender, sexual orientation, and transgender status.

Marital Status

Recall from Chapter 3 that in 1965, the U.S. Supreme Court heard the case of *Griswold v. Connecticut*, which was instrumental to due process privacy rights. *Griswold* involved a challenge to a Connecticut law that prohibited the use of contraceptives by married couples. The Court held that this law was unconstitutional, largely because the justices determined that the use of contraceptives was protected under the right to marital privacy. The Court left unresolved whether unmar-

ried persons had a similar right to contraception. Seven years later, the Court took up this question in *Eisenstadt v. Baird* (1972). After a presentation at Boston University, speaker William Baird provided contraceptive material to an unmarried student. This was done in violation of Massachusetts state law, which only allowed married persons to be given devices intended to prevent pregnancy (interestingly, the law did allow the delivery of contraceptive devices for the purpose of preventing disease).

In a 6–1 decision, Justice Brennan delivered the opinion of the Court (two justices were unable to participate in the case). The Court first rejected the notion that the basis for the law lied in the prevention of fornication or the protection of public health, as others had argued. The Court then held that there was no rational basis for preventing contraceptive access to unmarried persons, as opposed to married persons, and that the law violated the Equal Protection Clause of the Fourteenth Amendment. In doing so, the Court made clear that the right to sexual privacy extends beyond marriage. Although access to contraceptives is no doubt a significant interest to many unmarried persons, the significance of *Eisenstadt* lies in its reasoning and in the use of the Equal Protection Clause to expand the concept of privacy. Justice Brennan wrote:

> It is true that in *Griswold* the right of privacy in question inhered in the marital relationship. Yet the marital couple is not an independent entity with a mind and heart of its own, but an association of two individuals each with a separate intellectual and emotional makeup. If the right to privacy means anything, it is the right of the *individual*, married or single, to be free from unwarranted governmental intrusion into matters so fundamentally affecting a person as the decision whether to bear or beget a child. (p. 453)

Consider the impact of this holding. While *Griswold* arguably focused on locating privacy rights for marriage as an institution, *Eisenstadt* applied privacy to individuals. A truly landmark case for this reason, *Eisenstadt*'s legal reasoning was motivated not by a substantive due process concern for privacy, but rather by an emphasis on the importance of ensuring that all persons, married or single, were equally granted privacy rights.

Chief Justice Burger dissented, focusing primarily on a portion of the law that was not at the center of the majority opinion, which required that only certain medically qualified personnel distribute contraceptives. As such, the equal protection question was not the primary focus of Justice Burger's dissent, in which he suggested that the majority opinion of the Court would "seriously invade the constitutional prerogatives of the States, and regrettably hark back to the heyday of substantive due process" (p. 467).

This illustrates a debate that may still be seen today, as there is sometimes a tension between interpretations of the Fourteenth Amendment (whether due process or equal protection) and arguments in favor of states' rights, suggesting that the states should have the right to enact whatever measures they believe appropriate, with minimal intrusion by the courts when a law is challenged. By way of illustration, consider the following comment that was made in opposition to the Connecticut Supreme Court's ruling that the state must permit same sex marriage: "This is about our right to govern ourselves . . . It is bigger than gay marriage" (McFadden, 2008, para. 10). The sentiment expressed by the speaker is grounded in the states' rights perspective, as it suggests that the issue is not so much same-sex marriage as it is the right of a state to enact its own laws.

Gender

In the area of gender, the U.S. Supreme Court has made a number of rulings that have upheld equality between men and women. We have already seen one example in *Craig v. Boren* (1976). The Supreme Court has also addressed gender discrimination in jury selection, holding that gender-based peremptory challenges are unacceptable, even if based on the rationale that women's views of the case will differ from those of men (*J.E.B. v. Alabama*, 1994). In jury selection, the prosecution and defense are each allocated a number of peremptory challenges in which jurors may be dismissed without specifying cause. The use of peremptory challenges is one element underlying scientific jury selection, in which each side attempts to maximize the number of jurors likely to be sympathetic to its presentation, but these cannot be used in a discriminatory fashion by dismissing persons based on their gender (likewise, the Supreme Court has ruled that peremptory challenges cannot be applied on the basis of race, *Batson v. Kentucky*, 1986; individual states may also identify other protected classifications).

In two cases, the Supreme Court prohibited gender-based restrictions in the admission of students to universities. In *Mississippi University for Women v. Hogan* (1982), the Court held that it would violate the Equal Protection Clause to deny men admission to the school's nursing program. In *United States v. Virginia* (1996), the Court held that it would violate the Equal Protection Clause to deny women admission to the all-male Virginia Military Institute. In each case, the Court was unpersuaded by arguments that the school's tradition was for single-sex education, and by arguments that other alternatives were available to the excluded sex (i.e., other in-state public institutions offering nursing degrees in *Hogan*, and the Virginia Women's Institute for Leadership in *Virginia*). Key to these rulings was that the controversy centered on requirements for equal access to public institutions. Were these private institutions, the issue would be viewed differently, from a legal perspective. This is because the Equal Protection Clause applies to state laws and actions (such as admission policies at state-supported universities), in which cases the courts use intermediate scrutiny to resolve claims of gender discrimination.

Before leaving a discussion of gender equality under the Fourteenth Amendment, it is instructive to consider a case in which the Supreme Court upheld a law that treated males and females differently. The case, a controversial one, involves the issue of statutory rape. Recall from the chapter introduction that statutory rape criminalizes even consensual sexual activity involving persons under the age of majority (for more on the topic, generally, see Chapter 6). Here, the controversy centered on the gender of the offender. *Michael M. v. Superior Court of Sonoma County* (1981) challenged a California law that prohibited "unlawful sexual intercourse," defined as that "accomplished with a female not the wife of the perpetrator, where the female is under the age of 18 years" (p. 466). Note that this offense does not require forcible sexual activity, but also prohibits consensual sexual activity between a male and a female under 18 years of age. In *Michael M.*, a 17-year-old male engaged in sexual intercourse with a 16-year-old female. The male was charged with the criminal offense of unlawful sexual intercourse. The focal question in the case was whether the law's presumption of the female as victim and the male as perpetrator in statutory rape cases was permissible under the Fourteenth Amendment.

The Court in *Michael M.* upheld the law. The majority opinion, by Justice Rehnquist, outlined the reasoning in the Court's 5–4 decision. Following principles of intermediate scrutiny, the Court identified the purpose of the law as the prevention of teenage pregnancy, and further held "that the State has a strong interest in preventing such pregnancy" (p. 470). As required by intermediate scrutiny, the Court further held that the law was appropriately constructed to accomplish the state's objective. Consider the reasoning:

> Because virtually all of the significant harmful and inescapably identifiable consequences of teenage pregnancy fall on the young female, a legislature acts well within its authority when it elects to punish only the participant who, by nature, suffers few of the consequences of his conduct. It is hardly unreasonable for a legislature acting to protect minor females to exclude them from punishment. Moreover, the risk of pregnancy itself constitutes a substantial deterrence to young females. No similar natural sanctions deter males. A criminal sanction imposed solely on males thus serves to roughly 'equalize' the deterrents on the sexes.
>
> (p. 473)

While considering the Court's reasoning, note that the criminal offense of unlawful sexual conduct did not require a pregnancy to occur, as any sexual activity by any male involving a female under 18 would be a violation of the law. In dissent, Justices Brennan and Stevens questioned the rationale for the law, finding that it was not defensible for a variety of reasons. Whether the modern Court would, in the wake of subsequent decisions related to gender, uphold the ruling in *Michael M.* is unclear, but it does stand to illustrate a counterpoint to other cases described above. The case also illustrates the potential for inconsistencies between state and federal law, as *Michael M.* stands in contrast to the *Kansas v. Limon* decision described in the chapter introduction.

Sexual Orientation

The U.S. Supreme Court's attention to issues involving equal protection based on sexual orientation has been fairly limited, addressed in *Romer v. Evans* (1996), discussed earlier in the chapter, and *United States v. Windsor* (2013), invalidating a portion of DOMA. Further discussion of marriage is provided in Chapter 9. Here, we will briefly consider Justice O'Connor's concurring opinion in *Lawrence v. Texas* and we will survey a sampling of state court marriage cases.

Recall that *Lawrence v. Texas* (2003) invalidated a Texas law prohibiting sodomy (oral and anal sex) between persons of the same sex. Justice Kennedy's majority opinion, described in Chapter 3, focused on substantive due process. However, Justice O'Connor's concurring opinion focused on equal protection, holding that the law could not stand because it failed to meet the rational basis test

as applied to discrimination against gay and lesbian persons. Justice O'Connor's reasoning began with the observation that the law had the effect of treating differently "people who have a same-sex sexual orientation and thus are more likely to engage in the behavior prohibited" (p. 581) by the law. This would result in harms to gay and lesbian persons, including harms imposed directly

Box 4.1 GENDER AND PRISON CONDITIONS

The following scenario is drawn from the case *Klinger v. Department of Corrections*, a 1994 case addressing conditions in Nebraska state prisons. Only one prison in the state housed female inmates—the Nebraska Center for Women. Inmates there filed an equal protection claim on the basis that, compared with male inmates in Nebraska State Prison, they "receive inferior 'vocational, educational, and employment opportunities and programs, rehabilitation programs, exercise, and recreational programs and facilities, visiting privileges, legal programs, medical, dental and psychological services, and treatment associated with security classifications'" (p. 729).

"The Equal Protection Clause generally requires the government to treat similarly situated people alike" (p. 730). However, if two groups are not similarly situated, then they do not have to be treated alike. The cases discussed previously have presumed that females and males are similarly situated, for purposes of equal protection analysis. However, in this case that notion was challenged. The female inmates argued that they were similarly situated to male inmates, and therefore should receive the same resources and opportunities as male inmates. Counter to this was the argument that male and female inmates were not similarly situated, because, compared to Nebraska State Prison, the Nebraska Center for Women was a smaller prison, at a lower security level, and with inmates serving shorter sentences. In addition, it was argued that male and female inmates differed, as females "are more likely to be single parents with primary responsibility for child rearing" and "are more likely to be sexual or physical abuse victims," while "male inmates, in contrast, are more likely to be violent and predatory than female inmates." (p. 732)

How would you rule in this case? First consider whether you think female and male inmates in this case were similarly situated, explaining why. If not, the analysis is concluded, and equal protection does not apply. If so, apply intermediate scrutiny (as this is an issue based on gender) to determine whether there is an equal protection violation. If you feel that additional information is necessary, specify what information and how it would affect your decision.

The U.S. Court of Appeals for the Eighth Circuit ruled that the female and male inmates were not similarly situated, due to differences such as those listed above; as a result, the court did not find an equal protection violation. However, for a counterpoint, see Carroll-Ferrary's (2006/07) argument that the criteria considered in this case were "constitutionally irrelevant, arbitrary, and inconsistent with the purposes of incarceration" (p. 608), and that male and female inmates should have been viewed as similarly situated.

through criminal prosecution and punishment as well as harms imposed indirectly by the labeling of gay and lesbian persons as criminal, thereby "making it more difficult for homosexuals to be treated in the same manner as everyone else" (p. 581). Acknowledging that the rationale offered by Texas for the law was "the promotion of morality" (p. 582), Justice O'Connor concluded: "But the State cannot single out one identifiable class of citizens for punishment that does not apply to everyone else, with moral disapproval as the only asserted state interest for the law" (p. 584). In fact, Justice O'Connor goes so far as to suggest promotion of morality is never sufficient to sustain an equal protection challenge. Justice Scalia disagreed, reserving part of his dissenting opinion for a refutation of Justice O'Connor's analysis. In his dissent, Justice Scalia argued that morality was sufficient to uphold the rational basis analysis applied to issues of sexual orientation discrimination.

Concurring opinions do not hold the force of law, as they are not the majority opinion of the Court. However, the concurring opinion in *Lawrence* was important because it signaled that sexual orientation was a classification in need of protection through the Fourteenth Amendment, and that legal moralism was not a sufficient basis for the restriction of sexual privacy (see Chapter 3). This places Justice O'Connor's opinion squarely in the center of the debate about the relationship between law and the promulgation of morality. Indeed, as explored in Chapter 3, this is a central issue in discussions of legal philosophy, as courts must resolve disagreements about what does or does not constitute a rational basis for the law.

Also recall the discussion of *Loving v. Virginia* (1967), which overturned a Virginia law that prohibited marriage between persons of different races. We have already discussed the Court's ruling that marriage was a fundamental right under substantive due process, and that the Virginia law could not

survive the strict scrutiny applied to fundamental rights. At the same time, the Court also noted that the law failed because it violated the Equal Protection Clause, by imposing racial classifications that did not survive strict scrutiny applied to suspect classes. The most recent wave of cases related to sexual orientation and equal protection focus on marriage, involving the question of whether it is a violation of equal protection to deny same-sex couples the right to marry.

State courts have been split in their rulings on this matter. *Baker v. Vermont* (1999) was a landmark case, as it was the first to require same-sex couples to be accorded the same rights as opposite-sex couples, though through civil unions instead of marriage. In *Baker*, the Vermont Supreme Court held that the state's equal protection provisions required it. Other state courts followed suit, but holding that full marriage equality was required of same-sex and opposite-sex couples based on state equal protection provisions, in cases including *Goodridge v. Department of Public Health* in Massachusetts (2003), *Kerrigan v. Commissioner of Public Health* in Connecticut (2008), and *Varnum v. Brien* in Iowa (2009). These decisions teach an important secondary lesson about due process and equal protection, namely, that states may choose (although they are not required to do so) to provide more stringent rights and protections than the federal government, through state constitutions and state law. Although several cases were cited above that have upheld gay marriage under equal protection provisions, it is important to observe that other state appellate courts have upheld defense of marriage provisions that limit the definition of marriage to a union between a man and a woman (e.g., *Andersen v. King County*, 2006; *Morrison v. Sadler*, 2005).

In the June 2015 court case *Obergefell v. Hodges*, the U.S. Supreme Court invalidated all state laws and state constitutional amendments banning legal recognition of marriages between members of the same sex (*Obergefell v. Hodges*, 2015). Most of the decision in *Obergefell* is devoted to a discussion of the due process components of marriage—namely marriage as fundamental right. Although the Court also based its decision on the Equal Protection Clause, it did not address the question of whether gays and lesbians constitute a suspect or quasi-suspect class. Rather, the Court reasoned that laws prohibiting the legal recognition of same-sex marriages

> abridge central precepts of equality. Here the marriage laws enforced by the respondents are in essence unequal: same-sex couples are denied all the benefits afforded to opposite-sex couples and are barred from exercising a fundamental right. Especially against a long history of disapproval of their relationships, this denial to same-sex couples of the right to marry works a grave and continuing harm. The imposition of this disability on gays and lesbians serves to disrespect and subordinate them. And the Equal Protection Clause, like the Due Process Clause, prohibits this unjustified infringement of the fundamental right to marry.
> (*Obergefell v. Hodges*, 2015, p. 2604)

For more information on same-sex marriage, see Chapter 9.

Transgender Persons

A new frontier in Fourteenth Amendment analysis is in litigation related to rights of transgender persons (see Chapters 1 and 9 for a discussion of transgender status). This is not an issue that has been heavily litigated under the Fourteenth Amendment, as transgender rights have more commonly been addressed under Title VII. However, we will consider *Glenn v. Brumby*, a 2011 case from the U.S. Court of Appeals for the Eleventh Circuit. In this case, the appellant, Glenn, was a transwoman. Upon notifying her employer that "she was ready to proceed with gender transition and would begin coming to work as a woman and was also changing her legal name" (p. 1314), Glenn was fired by her supervisor. The rationale offered by her supervisor was that the "intended gender transition was inappropriate, that it would be disruptive, that some people would view it as a moral issue, and that it would make Glenn's coworkers uncomfortable" (p. 1314).

The Court of Appeals first considered whether discrimination against transgender individuals constituted sex discrimination as prohibited under the Fourteenth Amendment, and held that it did. Following from a discussion of gender stereotyping, the court held that, "There is a congruence between discriminating against transgender and transsexual individuals and discrimination on the basis of gender-based behavioral norms. Accordingly, discrimination against a transgender individual because of her gender nonconformity is sex discrimination" (p. 1317).

This holding is significant, as it conceptualizes sex discrimination as encompassing gender role stereotypes for the purposes of Fourteenth Amendment analysis. The court then proceeded following the criteria of intermediate scrutiny, consistent with prior case law on sex discrimination. First, the court found that Glenn's firing was discriminatory based on gender norm stereotypes. Second, the court considered whether there was the substantial state interest required by intermediate scrutiny analysis. The state interest offered to the court was a concern about Glenn's use of the women's restroom facilities at her place of employment, which the court found not to constitute the requisite level of state interest. As a result, Glenn prevailed, and the court did not have to consider whether the state action (in this case, termination from employment in a public agency) was narrowly enough tailored to meet the (in this case, nonexistent) compelling state interest.

The above discussion provides a sampling of the types of issues that have been raised related to the Fourteenth Amendment's Equal Protection Clause for issues of law and sexuality. As with many other issues in this chapter, case law will continue to clarify the meaning of equal protection, particularly in the still-developing areas of sexual orientation and transgender status.

TITLE VII OF THE CIVIL RIGHTS ACT OF 1964

The Civil Rights Act of 1964 was a landmark piece of legislation enacted by Congress and signed by President Johnson with the purpose of preventing discrimination. The act was largely focused on the prohibition of racial discrimination, but its measures also included prohibitions of discrimination based on sex. **Title VII of the Civil Rights Act of 1964** addressed employment discrimination, noting that no employer could, on the basis of an individual's sex, "fail or refuse to hire or to discharge any individual, or otherwise to discriminate against any individual with respect to his compensation, terms, conditions, or privileges of employment" (42 U.S.C. § 2000e-2) or "limit, segregate, or classify his employees or applicants for employment in any way which would deprive or tend to deprive any individual of employment opportunities or otherwise adversely affect his status as an employee" (42 U.S.C. § 2000e-2). While the Fourteenth Amendment applies to state governments and their laws and policies, Title VII applies to private businesses with 15 or more employees.

In many ways, then, Title VII provides similar types of protections in the private workplace that the Equal Protection Clause provides for state actions. Individuals who feel that their rights under Title VII have been violated may bring the matter to the attention of the Equal Employment Opportunity Commission (EEOC). The EEOC, in turn, investigates and attempts to resolve complaints; if a complaint cannot be resolved, the EEOC may choose to file a lawsuit on behalf of the complainant against the party alleged

to have violated the Title VII rights (see U.S. Equal Employment Opportunity Commission, n.d.). Because the law is constructed to apply to private employment, the investigation does not have to consider the same elements as a Fourteenth Amendment proceeding. Specifically, all that must be shown is that a prohibited action, as listed in the prior paragraph, was made on the basis of the individual's sex. There is no requirement for showing a substantial government interest or that the decision was tailored in a particular way to advance that interest. Title VII has been interpreted, among other things, to prohibit discrimination on the basis of gender role stereotypes (*Price Waterhouse v. Hopkins*, 1989); to prohibit discrimination on the basis of sexual orientation, when that discrimination is grounded in gender role stereotypes (*Prowel v. Wise Business Forms*, 2009); to prohibit discrimination based on transgender status (*Macy v. Holder*, 2012); and to prohibit fetal protection policies, in which a business "exclude[s] a fertile female employee from certain jobs because of its concern for the health of the fetus the woman might conceive" (p. 190), such as due to exposure to hazardous materials (*Automobile Workers v. Johnson Controls*, 1991).

BFOQs and the Limits of Title VII

Although the Title VII ban on workplace discrimination is fairly broad, there are circumstances in which differential treatment based on sex may be permitted. Title VII provides exemptions for "those certain instances where . . . sex . . . is a bona fide occupational qualification reasonably necessary to the normal operation of that particular business or enterprise" (42 U.S.C. § 2000e-2). Indeed, one debate that often emerges in Title VII litigation is whether a measure that provides differential treatment based on sex is a **bona fide occupational qualification** (BFOQ), which thereby begs the question of how the idea of a BFOQ should be defined, understood, and applied.

The Code of Federal Regulations (CFR) provides guidelines ("Sex as a Bona Fide ...", 2012, 29 C.F.R. § 1604.2) for interpreting BFOQs based on sex. Several principles emerge from a review of these guidelines: Provisions allowing sex-based BFOQs "should be interpreted narrowly"; neither general characteristics presumed of all men or all women nor gender stereotypes are acceptable justifications for a BFOQ; "the preferences of coworkers, the employer, clients, or customers" are generally not sufficient justifications for a BFOQ; convenience to the employer (e.g., avoiding hiring women if female restrooms are not available at a business location, in those states whose laws require separate restrooms to be provided to male and female employees) is not an acceptable justification for a BFOQ; and providing employment benefits to one sex but not the other is not justifiable under BFOQs. In fact, the guidelines specify only one situation in which a BFOQ based on an individual's sex will be upheld, which is "where it is necessary for the purpose of authenticity or genuineness." As suggested by the guidelines, an example would be casting only females in a female role in a play. As guidelines, these principles do not hold the force of law, but courts can and do utilize them in resolving BFOQ claims (see Manley, 2009).

In an analysis of BFOQs related to an individual's sex, Manley (2009) summarizes three tests that are used by courts to assess claimed BFOQs. These tests are broader than the CFR guidelines, offering frameworks through which particular BFOQs may be analyzed to determine whether they are acceptable. The first test, known as the "all or substantially all" test, asks whether " 'all or substantially all women' [or men] would be unable to fulfill the requisite job duties" (p. 174). In considering this test, though, note that the CFR guidelines would require more than presumptions or stereotypes to be utilized in making this determination. The second test, known as the "essence of the business" test, asks

whether "gender is absolutely essential to the business' primary function and that members of the opposite gender could not successfully perform the duties" (p. 175). Note that this test first requires ascertaining what the primary function of the business actually is, a question about which there may not be an agreed-upon answer. The third test asks if a "reasonable, less discriminatory alternative exists" (p. 176) that would make it unnecessary to define an individual's sex as a BFOQ. As such, an affirmative answer to this test could discount a BFOQ even if either of the first two tests would otherwise allow it.

Taken together, the CFR guidelines and the tests summarized by Manley (2009) set a high bar for BFOQs to meet. Refer to the "Law in Action" box to read about sex-based employment decisions that were claimed as BFOQs. Think about how you would decide each case, and then compare your decision to the court's actual ruling.

Sexual Harassment

The first **sexual harassment** case heard by the U.S. Supreme Court, *Meritor Savings Bank v. Vinson* (1986), centered on whether hostile work environment sexual harassment was actionable under Title VII. In that case, the individual bringing the sexual harassment complaint alleged a pattern of behaviors that she argued met the definition for sexual harassment. The trial court held that there had been no sexual harassment because there was no quid pro quo exchange (e.g., offering workplace benefits in exchange for sexual activity); to the contrary, the victim had received several merit-based job promotions. The Supreme Court did not seek to determine the veracity of the sexual harassment complaint, itself, but instead addressed the question as to whether sexual harassment could exist in the absence of a quid pro quo situation. In an opinion written by Justice Rehnquist, a unanimous Court held that it could, and in turn remanded the case to a lower court for

Law in Action BONA FIDE OCCUPATIONAL QUALIFICATION (BFOQ) OR EMPLOYMENT DISCRIMINATION?

Each of the following scenarios is an actual situation in which a BFOQ was claimed. Review the facts for each and consider the criteria described in the text of the chapter. Based on the criteria, do you think each is a legitimate BFOQ that should permit differential treatment based on an individual's sex? Provide your answer with justification. You can compare your results to those of the courts that actually addressed each case.

1. Under Alabama Department of Corrections policy, female correctional counselors were not assigned to positions in which they would have to be in close contact with male inmates in maximum security settings. This excluded women from the majority of correctional counselor assignments in the state's correctional system. The state claimed a BFOQ, based on the unique characteristics of Alabama's correctional facilities at the time of the regulation, described as: "In a prison system where violence is the order of the day, where inmate access to guards is facilitated by dormitory living arrangements, where every institution is understaffed, and where a substantial portion of the inmate population is composed of sex offenders mixed at random with other prisoners, there are few visible deterrents to inmate assaults on women custodians" (*Dothard v. Rawlinson*, 1977, pp. 335–336). Upheld as BFOQ.

2. Following news that a female inmate in a Nevada state prison for women had become pregnant after having sex with a male correctional officer, the state commissioned a full investigation. The investigation revealed a pattern of sexual activity between male correctional officers and female inmates at that facility, including sex in exchange for privileges and contraband items. The report found that the activity was facilitated by a "lack of effective supervisory management oversight and control." This generated significant negative publicity for the Department of Corrections. The facility had been operated by a private prison provider, but that provider cancelled its contract and the state took over the operation of the facility. When it did so, the state set certain employment parameters, including the decision "to hire only women in . . . three correctional lieutenant positions." Lieutenants "are shift supervisors and are the senior employees on duty seventy-five percent of the time" (*Breiner v. Nevada Department of Corrections*, 2010, p. 1205). Rejected as BFOQ.

3. A hospital prohibited male nurses from working "in the labor and delivery section." The reason offered centered on patient privacy, referring to that section of the hospital as "unique" because "there are few duties which a registered nurse can perform in relation to an obstetrical patient which are not sensitive or intimate." The hospital "contends that if a male nurse is performing these duties, the patient's constitutional right to privacy is violated." Other considerations included that patients who were subjected to a male nurse and accordingly uncomfortable would go to other hospitals in the future, and that the only safeguard would be to assign a female nurse to work with all male nurses in that section of the hospital, which would duplicate job responsibilities and lead to increased costs (*Backus v. Baptist Medical Center*, 1981, p. 1193). Upheld as BFOQ.

4. The Southwest Airlines policy of "hiring only females for the public contact positions of flight attendant and ticket agent" is at question in this case. The airline justifies this as a BFOQ with the argument that "its attractive female flight attendants and ticket agents

personify the airline's sexy image and fulfill its public promise to take passengers skyward with 'love.' Defendant claims maintenance of its female-only hiring policy is crucial to the airline's continued financial success." Further information considered by the court included that "Southwest projects an image of feminine spirit, fun, and sex appeal. Its ads promise to provide 'tender loving care' to its predominantly male, business passengers." In addition, "the airline also encourages its attendants to entertain the passengers and maintain an atmosphere of informality and 'fun' during flights" (*Wilson v. Southwest Airlines*, 1981, pp. 293–295). Rejected as BFOQ.

5. The Playboy Club of New York was staffed by female employees known as "Bunnies," who were described as "the cornerstone of its business." Women employed as "Bunnies" were required to meet certain standards of appearance, and were evaluated on a four point scale. The endpoints of the scale were "A flawless beauty" and "Has lost Bunny Image." A "Bunny" employee was dismissed after a "loss of weight and because she did not meet acceptable standards in reference to physical proportions." The Playboy Club contends that its "business would be destroyed were they required to abandon the Bunny Image." Accordingly, the question is whether the "Bunny Image" is a BFOQ for the Playboy Club (*St. Cross v. Playboy Club*, 1971; quotations cited in *Aromi v. Playboy Club*, 1985, pp. 5–7). Upheld as BFOQ.

further consideration about whether hostile work environment harassment had occurred.

In reaching this decision, the Court focused upon the section of Title VII addressing the "terms, conditions, or privileges of employment." Even if sexual harassment was not quid pro quo, the Court held, it could still have an impact on working conditions. The Court was careful to note that not every sexually motivated comment constitutes sexual harassment. The type of hostile work environment harassment prohibited by Title VII must be "sufficiently severe or pervasive 'to alter the conditions of [the victim's] employment and create an abusive working environment' " (p. 67). In addition, the criterion for determining whether sexual harassment had occurred was that it must be "unwelcome" (p. 68) to the victim. This is important because even behavior in which the victim voluntarily participates can still be unwelcome, and thus elevate to prohibited conduct. For instance, in the *Meritor* case, the complainant reportedly went on a date and engaged in sexual activities with the individ-

ual against whom the sexual harassment complaint was directed, all voluntarily, but more significant would be her perceptions of whether the conduct at issue in the complaint was unwelcome.

The criteria for identifying hostile work environment sexual harassment were further clarified by the U.S. Supreme Court in *Harris v. Forklift Systems* (1993). The complainant in the case alleged that her supervisor, the owner of the company, made comments such as "you're a woman, what do you know," "we need a man as the rental manager," and when working with a customer on a deal, "What did you do, promise the guy . . . some [sex] Saturday night" (p. 19). In addition, the owner was also alleged to have "asked Harris and other female employees to get coins from his front pants pocket" (p. 19) and to have "made sexual innuendos about Harris' and other women's clothing" (p. 19), among other issues referenced by the complainant. The trial court held that the facts did not elevate to the level of hostile work environment sexual harassment, because it was not shown that the victim experienced abuse, intimidation or psychological harm. As in *Meritor*, the Court did not seek to resolve whether or not sexual harassment had actually occurred, but instead clarified the criteria on which hostile work environment claims are to be assessed, and remanded the case to the lower court for further consideration as to whether harassment had occurred.

Justice O'Connor delivered the opinion of a unanimous Court and noted that conduct did not have to cause psychological harm in order to be considered sexual harassment. At the same time, as noted in *Meritor*, not every comment constitutes sexual harassment. In order for a claim to proceed, the Court held that it must meet both an subjective and objective standard. For the former, the victim must perceive the environment as hostile. For the latter, the fact pattern must constitute "an environment that a reasonable person would find hostile or abusive" (p. 21). But this does not address the question of where the dividing line is, between environments that do and do not elevate to constituting sexual harassment. The Court determined that the totality of circumstances in a case must be considered to make the determination as to whether an allegation of hostile work environment sexual harassment is objectively reasonable.

> These may include the frequency of the discriminatory conduct; its severity; whether it is physically threatening or humiliating, or a mere offensive utterance; and whether it unreasonably interferes with an employee's work performance. The effect on the employee's psychological well-being is, of course, relevant to determining whether the plaintiff actually found the environment abusive. But while psychological harm, like any other relevant factor, may be taken into account, no single factor is required.
>
> (p. 23)

As you can see, hostile work environment sexual harassment is not something that can be defined with precision, but rather must be evaluated in the unique context of each case. Although the cases above have involved opposite-sex sexual harassment, it is important to note that the U.S. Supreme Court has confirmed that same-sex sexual harassment is also actionable under the same standards described above (see *Oncale v. Sundowner Offshore Services*, 1998). And, all cases of sexual harassment—quid pro quo or hostile work environment—are prohibited under Title VII of the Civil Rights Act of 1964, and subject to legal action.

ENDA

The Employment Non-Discrimination Act (ENDA) is a proposed piece of legislation that has been introduced in multiple sessions of Congress, but which has not yet passed. Even though the ENDA remains unenacted at the time of this writing, it is an important measure to consider in a discussion of employment law pertaining to sexual orientation and gender identity. Were it to be passed, the ENDA "would ban employers from firing, refusing to hire or discriminating against workers or job applicants based on their sexual orientation or gender identity" (O'Keefe, 2013, para. 2). As such, this would provide a consistent nationwide prohibition against sexual orientation and gender identity discrimination in the workplace, replacing the more fragmented state-by-state (and in some cases, city-by-city) policies that provide varying protections, or sometimes none at all. It remains to be seen whether Congress will ultimately pass the ENDA, but if so, Title VII remedies would apply when sexual orientation or gender identity discrimination was detected (see Employment Non-Discrimination Act of 2013).

Controversy has surrounded the ENDA. While the measure received some bipartisan support when it passed in the Senate in 2013, it was then stalled in the House of Representatives amidst political disagreements (Fox,

2014). Other concerns (see O'Keefe, 2014) have centered on religious exemptions to the ENDA's provisions, which specify that it "shall not apply" to "religious employer[s]" (Employment Non-Discrimination Act of 2013, Section 6a). The courts have also upheld exemptions to federal law based on religious belief pertaining to issues of sexuality. The 2014 U.S. Supreme Court case of *Burwell v. Hobby Lobby* exempted certain employers from provisions in the Affordable Care Act (the "Obamacare" law) regarding contraceptives, for family-owned businesses in which the owners felt the provisions violated their sincerely held religious beliefs. In the wake of the *Burwell* decision, some have suggested that ENDA provisions could likewise be exempted from any business in which an owner claimed religious disapproval of gay, lesbian, bisexual, or transgender identification or behavior (O'Keefe, 2014). The *Burwell* decision also leaves unanswered—and for future courts to interpret—how protections already established under cases such as *Romer*, *Lawrence*, and *Windsor* will be balanced with rights pertaining to religious freedom.

In the midst of debates about the ENDA, in 2015 the U.S. Equal Employment Opportunity Commission (EEOC) issued a memorandum, which may have the effect of providing de facto Title VII protections for sexual minorities, even if the ENDA remains unenacted. Specifically, EEOC offices have been instructed that claims of discrimination based on "sexual orientation," "transgender status," and "gender-identity" "should be accepted under Title VII and investigated as claims of sex discrimination" (U.S. Equal Employment Opportunity Commission, 2015, p. 1). The full effect of this memorandum remains to be seen; while not an action with the full force of law (future memorandums could revise or even rescind the provisions), it is a sign of growing awareness of gay, lesbian, transgender, and gender-identity-related discrimination concerns.

HATE-CRIME LEGISLATION AND SEXUAL MINORITIES

The Equal Protection Clause of the Fourteenth Amendment and Title VII of the Civil Rights Act of 1964 serve to ensure that individuals are treated equally under the law and in the workplace. This signals a governmental and social concern for promoting equality. Related to this is a governmental and social concern for reducing bias, and especially that bias which results in the commission of criminal offenses. To respond to those instances in which victims of crime are selected because of a bias against the groups of which they are a member or with which they identify, the federal government and state governments have enacted laws to address **hate crime**.

Defining Hate Crime

There is no single definition of hate crime. The Federal Bureau of Investigation (FBI) is charged with maintaining data about the number of hate crimes annually, by recording information about hate crimes that were reported to local law enforcement agencies. The definition utilized by the FBI in its data collection process is the following: "Criminal offenses that were motivated, in whole or in part, by the offender's bias against a race, gender, gender identity, religion, disability, sexual orientation, or ethnicity, and were committed against persons, property, or society" (Federal Bureau of Investigation, n.d., para. 1).

Most pertinent to law and sexuality are hate crimes based on gender, gender identity, and sexual orientation. Each of these categories is protected under current federal hate-crime legislation. The Matthew Shepard and James Byrd, Jr., Hate Crime Prevention Act of 2009 (18 U.S.C. § 249) prohibits the following:

Willfully causing bodily injury (or attempting to do so with fire, firearm, or other dangerous weapon) when ... the crime was committed because of the actual or perceived religion, national origin, gender, sexual orientation, gender identity, or disability of any person and the crime affected interstate or foreign commerce or occurred within federal special maritime and territorial jurisdiction.

(U.S. Department of Justice, n.d., para. 2–3)

It is important to note that this is a federal law with a very specific jurisdiction. As a general rule, the development and enforcement of criminal law is a power held primarily by the states. This reflects the principle of federalism, in which state and federal governments may each enact their own legislation. Federal criminal laws, such as the hate-crime law quoted above, apply in limited circumstances, primarily when an action "substantially affects" (*United States v. Lopez*, 1995, p. 559) interstate commerce (see generally Brickey, 1996). This is sometimes a challenging inquiry, as federal prosecutors would have to show that an action had implications for, drew upon resources from, or involved movement between one or more other states. While not specific to issues of sexuality, the same federal law also prohibits hate crimes based on race, color, religion, and national origin, regardless of jurisdiction, even if interstate commerce is not affected.

In addition, states may enact their own hate-crime laws, and may choose which categories to include or not to include in their legislation. As of this writing, 31 states have hate-crime laws that include sexual orientation and 27 states have hate-crime laws that address gender (Anti-Defamation League, 2011). One conclusion to draw is that there is not a uniform understanding of what "hate crime" is. The definitions from the FBI for data collection, from the Hate Crimes Prevention Act, and from the various state laws may differ, but the theme underlying them all is that a hate crime is one in which the motive or the selection of the victim is based on some type of bias or prejudice.

Hate Crime Victimization

Attention to hate crime, and to the development of legislation against hate crime, has increased in the wake of high-profile incidents. One tragic example was the 1998 murder of Matthew Shepard, for whom the federal law quoted above was named. Shepard, a student at the University of Wyoming, was abducted, beaten, and tied to a fence post. Left for dead, Shepard was discovered the following day and he was hospitalized for his injuries. However, Shepard's injuries left him in a coma from which he never recovered, and he died five days after the incident. Evidence suggested that the crime was motivated, in part, by anti-gay bias directed against Shepard (see Kaufman, 2001; Loffreda, 2001). James Byrd, Jr., for whom the law was also named, was the victim of another high-profile and tragic 1998 incident, in which three men beat him and then dragged him to his death behind a pickup truck. The incident was quickly identified as a hate crime, as the evidence suggested that the crime was racially motivated; Byrd was African-American and two of the assailants had connections to white supremacist groups (see King, 2003; Temple-Raston, 2002).

Sadly, there are many other examples of hate crimes. The Southern Poverty Law Center (n.d.) maintains an annotated list of hate incidents, grouped by year and by state. Data from the FBI found that there were 5,928 incidents of hate crime reported to police agencies in 2013. Approximately 21% of these incidents stemmed from bias based on sexual orientation. Most (approximately 98%) were anti-homosexual, with the greatest proportion (approximately 61%) directed against gay males (Federal Bureau of Investigation, 2014).

The FBI data are limited in that they count only those hate crimes that are reported to the police. The National Crime Victimization Survey (NCVS) is an alternate means of measuring the amount of crime in the United States, by asking persons to self-report any offenses that were committed against them, regardless of whether or not they were reported to the police. NCVS data suggest that, in 2012, there were 293,790 hate crime victimizations. Of these, 13% were based on sexual orientation and only 34% of hate crime victimizations were reported to the police (Wilson, 2014).

The above data suggest that hate crime based on sexual orientation is a concern, and one that has the potential to affect many victims. Victimization can further be exacerbated through the actions of the criminal justice system, especially when agencies are not sensitive to issues of gender and sexuality. Consider the case of *Brandon v. County of Richardson* (2001), heard by the Supreme Court of Nebraska. The case was filed in response to a 1993 incident in which three people were murdered. Teena Brandon was biologically female but identified with the male gender, dressing as a male and dating a female. Two acquaintances of Brandon's girlfriend, "in an attempt to prove ... that Brandon was a female ... pulled Brandon's pants down" (p. 611) in front of his girlfriend. Later that day, the same acquaintances assaulted and raped Brandon. Upon reporting these crimes to the police, Brandon was questioned about the incident and about his gender identity. The questioning took on biased tones, with the sheriff referring to Brandon as "it" and asking questions such as "Why do you run around with girls instead of guys being you're a girl yourself? Why do you make girls think you're a guy?" (p. 613). In addition, the language used in the questioning was "crude and dehumanizing" (p. 622) and the "tone throughout the interview was demeaning, accusatory, and intimidating" (p. 622). Brandon also expressed a fear that the perpetrators would retaliate for his having reported the crimes, as they had threatened

to do, but the sheriff's office did not provide protection to Brandon during the time when the investigation was underway and the alleged offenders were still free in the community. The assailants did subsequently kill Brandon and two other persons at the home where he was staying.

The Supreme Court of Nebraska held that the sheriff's "conduct was extreme and outrageous, beyond all possible bounds of decency, and is to be regarded as atrocious and utterly intolerable in a civilized community" (p. 621). The court further held "that the county's negligence was a proximate cause of Brandon's death" (p. 628). This case was significant, as the court's holding requires criminal justice agencies to protect, and to treat without bias, sexual minorities. At the same time, the case is an unfortunate reminder of the discrimination that sexual minorities sometimes encounter from those charged with public service. (For more information on victimization, see Chapter 13.)

Hate-Crime Legislation

In each of the incidents referenced above—Matthew Shepard, James Byrd, Jr., and Teena Brandon—the offenders were apprehended and sentenced for their roles in the murders. In the Matthew Shepard case, both offenders were sentenced to life in prison; in the James Byrd case, two offenders were sentenced to death and one was sentenced to life in prison; and in the Teena Brandon case, one offender was sentenced to death and one was sentenced to life in prison. In these cases, the offenders were tried and sentenced for the crime of homicide. This leads to the question of why jurisdictions, whether state or federal, choose to enact laws against hate crime, when existing laws (e.g., against assault and murder) can be used, and are used, to charge and punish those who commit such criminal acts.

Gerstenfeld (2004) summarized several rationales that underlie the passage of hate-crime laws. The first is that hate crimes are more damaging than equivalent acts based on motives other than hate. Such damages may include enhanced psychological trauma to victims due to the stigma of being targeted based on identity or personal characteristics. There is some indication that acts committed in bias-motivated incidents are more violent than others, as well. Another harm that can be attributed to hate crimes, setting them apart from other crimes, is the impact that they have on other members of the group against which the bias is directed. This conceivably creates a vicarious victimization in which individuals, even if not directly harmed by an incident, may indirectly suffer from fear or emotional distress as a result of it, which would not be as likely experienced after other incidents. The second argument for passing legislation related to hate crime is that it may have a deterrent effect, leading to the prevention of such acts. The third argument is that hate-crime laws, even if imperfect, serve to symbolically demonstrate the government's opposition to bias motivation and concern for those who are targeted by it. This subsequently serves as an affirmation of the government's emphasis on equality as a social value.

It is important to acknowledge that each of the above points has been debated, as hate-crime laws tend to generate controversy. Jacobs and Potter (1997) note several arguments critical of hate-crime laws. One asks whether the act itself, rather than the motivation for the crime, is what ought to be addressed by the law. Relatedly, this suggests the difficulty of establishing causality sufficient to prove a hate crime, a challenge for investigators and for the courts: "Must the criminal conduct have been wholly, primarily, or slightly motivated by the disfavored prejudice?" (p. 4). Another concern is whether hate-crime legislation treads into areas protected by the First Amendment, if individuals are punished or subjected to higher punishments because of their expressed opinions. Finally, Jacobs and Potter (1997) express concern about whether hate-crime laws can be divisive in society, by affording to some groups special protections or different definitions of criminal acts than would apply to others.

Even with the critiques that have been levied, hate-crime laws have been upheld by the courts. Generally speaking, hate-crime laws can be classified into two broad categories (see also Jacobs & Potter, 1997): those which define new offenses based on bias motivation, and those which provide increased penalties for offenses committed due to a bias motivation. The federal Hate Crime Prevention Act is an example of the former, as it specifies a new criminal offense for acts of violence committed due to bias against one of the protected categories. The law was upheld in *United States v. Jenkins*, heard by the U.S. District Court for the Eastern District of Kentucky in 2012. In what has been identified as the first federal hate-crime prosecution based on sexual orientation (Cratty, 2012), two individuals were charged with kidnapping and with violation of the Hate Crimes Prevention Act on the basis of an assault against a gay male. The victim was kidnapped and transported via automobile to a location where the two perpetrators "restrained and 'brutally beat [the victim] . . . while yelling anti-homosexual comments' " (*United States v. Jenkins*, 2012, p. 3).

The court considered, and overruled, a number of challenges to the law. One challenge was that the accused persons had not engaged in interstate commerce, since the crime was committed entirely in the state of Kentucky, without crossing state lines. However, the court ruled that the use of an automobile traversing a federal highway was, consistent with prior court opinions, sufficient to show a relation to interstate commerce. Another challenge was that the law "creates special protection for a class of individuals based on the victim's sexual orientation, which violates the equal protection component of the Fifth Amendment" (p. 34;

note that the Fifth Amendment applies to federal actions, such as a federal prosecution, and the Fourteenth Amendment applies to the actions of state governments). The court found this not to be the case, as the law applies to all persons and prohibits crime based on any sexual orientation, whether homosexual, heterosexual, or any others. Against other challenges, the court also held that the law did not violate freedom of speech, as assault was the action prohibited by the law, and that the law was not void for vagueness. On the basis of *United States v. Jenkins* (2012), then, the federal government's law against crimes of violence motivated by bias based on sexual orientation was constitutional, generally, and as applied to this prosecution. However, while convicted by a jury for the crime of kidnapping, the accused in this case were acquitted of the hate crime charges (Cratty, 2012).

The second category of hate-crime legislation is that which provides for heightened, or enhanced, penalties for those crimes that can be shown to have been committed due to a bias motivation. The U.S. Supreme Court upheld this type of law in *Wisconsin v. Mitchell* (1993). Pursuant to a law allowing sentence enhancements for crimes committed on the basis of race, the defendant was sentenced to seven years in prison (instead of the two years that would otherwise be authorized) for an assault in which the victim was selected for being white. At issue was whether the sentence enhancement law punishes "bigoted thought" (p. 482), which would have First Amendment protection, or whether it "punishes only conduct" (p. 482), in this case the assault. Justice Rehnquist wrote the opinion for a unanimous Court, which upheld the sentencing enhancement law and found that it did not violate the First Amendment. Noting that a consideration of motive has traditionally been incorporated into sentencing decisions, the Court held that "The First Amendment ... does not prohibit the evidentiary use of speech to establish the elements of a crime or to prove motive or intent" (p. 489). While not directly related to law and sexuality, this case does affirm that sentence enhancements can be given for bias-motivated offenses, and the sentencing enhancement law that was upheld did include sexual orientation as a protected category.

The cases described above have as a common theme the presence of a prohibited action – such as kidnapping or assault. It is important to distinguish hate crime from **hate speech**, which refers to expressive activities that are directed against an individual or group based upon bias or discrimination. When the only matter in question is speech, courts have been reluctant to permit restrictions, as expression of ideas, even ideas that some may find offensive, is protected under the First Amendment (note that this is another example of substantive due process, applied to the states through the Fourteenth Amendment). For instance, in *Snyder v. Phelps* (2011), the U.S. Supreme Court held that a lawful funeral protest that conveyed anti-gay messages (including "God Hates Fags" and "Fags Doom Nations," p. 1216) was protected under the First Amendment. At the same time, the U.S. Supreme Court has held that expressive activities can be restricted in some cases. In *Virginia v. Black* (2003), the Court upheld a Virginia law prohibiting "cross burning carried out with the intent to intimidate" (p. 347). The "intent to intimidate" provision would have to be proven in a successful prosecution. Because speech and expressive activities are protected through the First Amendment, with many types of expression recognized as a fundamental right, intermediate and strict scrutiny must be applied to the analysis of laws that restrict them. It is much more difficult to regulate hateful speech than it is to use the law to respond to crimes that are committed due to a bias motivation. As you can see, equal protection concerns are multifaceted and involve many elements of law, ranging from the Fourteenth Amendment to Title VII to hate-crime legislation.

Box 4.2 SEXUAL HARASSMENT AND HATE CRIME

A student in a course visits his professor during her office hours. While there, he tells several sexist jokes and asks his professor for a date. She refuses, explaining that she maintains a policy of not dating students in her courses. She also indicates that she would prefer that he not tell sexist jokes in her presence. The student leaves, but returns the following day, again asking for a date and sharing his ideas about what she should wear "to spice things up" when teaching class. The professor explains to the student that she is interested neither in dating nor in fashion tips. Over the course of the next week, the student leaves notes under his professor's door, continuing to ask for a date and including comments like, "Teach 'em babe," "Hot outfit, hot lecture," and "Nominated you for porn teacher's edition." The comments being unwanted, the professor pursues a sexual harassment complaint against the student (for further analysis of student sexual harassment of teachers, see Shane, 2009). Later, and in retaliation for the complaint, the student paints on his professor's office door and car windshield a series of derogatory comments about, and unflattering illustrated images of, women. Although none of the comments or images specifically reference the professor, she reports that they made her feel uncomfortable. The student was arrested when he posted a photo of himself next to the images on a social-media site, which has also resulted in numerous other students posting a variety of potentially offensive comments. The student is charged with vandalism, and the incident is further charged as a hate crime under the state's law that recognizes gender as a protected classification. The student argues that his actions constitute neither sexual harassment nor a hate crime. You are the judge; how do you rule? If you feel that additional information is necessary, specify what information and how it would affect your decision.

The common theme of each is the emphasis on ensuring that all persons are treated equally under the law, free from discrimination or intimidation based on unlawful biases. Consider how you would address the hypothetical case presented in Box 4.2.

CONCLUSION

The Fourteenth Amendment guarantees equal protection of the law and due process under the law. The seeming simplicity of these concepts is juxtaposed against a complex framework with multiple levels of scrutiny, each with its own criteria for determining when Fourteenth Amendment violations have occurred. One enduring issue, both within and beyond the Fourteenth Amendment, is

ensuring that all persons are treated equally, without prejudice and without receiving unlawful discrimination in either public or private settings. Whether through the Equal Protection Clause, the provisions of Title VII, or legislation against hate crime, the law strives to achieve the principles embodied within the Fourteenth Amendment's protections of equality.

FURTHER READING

Cochran, A. B., III. (2004). *Sexual harassment and the law: The Mechelle Vinson case.* Lawrence, KS: University Press of Kansas.

D'Emilio, J., & Freedman, E. B. (1997). *Intimate matters: A history of sexuality in America* (2nd ed.). Chicago, IL: University of Chicago Press.

Gerstenfeld, P. B. (2010). *Hate crimes: Causes, controls, and controversies* (2nd ed.). Thousand Oaks, CA: Sage Publications.

Grossman, J. L., & Friedman, L. M. (2011). *Inside the castle: Law and the family in 20th century America.* Princeton, NJ: Princeton University Press.

Kaufman, M. (2001). *The Laramie Project.* New York, NY: Vintage Books.

Murdoch, J., & Price, D. (2001). *Courting justice: Gay men and lesbians v. the Supreme Court.* New York, NY: Basic Books.

Strebeigh, F. (2009). *Equal: Women reshape American law.* New York, NY: W. W. Norton.

Strum, P. (2002). *Women in the barracks: The VMI case and equal rights.* Lawrence, KS: University Press of Kansas.

GLOSSARY

Animus: Prejudice against a group and its members.

Bona fide occupational qualification (BFOQ): Serving as an exception to Title VII of the Civil Rights Act of 1964, the bona fide occupational qualifications provision allows employers to consider factors that would otherwise be deemed discriminatory (e.g., applicant's gender) when related to the essential duties of the job.

Equal Protection Clause: The provision in the Fourteenth Amendment to the U.S. Constitution that serves to guarantee equality, requiring that the law treat persons equally, without discrimination.

Hate crime: Criminal offenses that are motivated, in whole or in part, by the offender's bias against a race, religion, sexual orientation, ethnicity/national origin, or disability and are committed against persons, property, and society.

Hate speech: Expressive activities directed against an individual or group based upon bias or discrimination.

Intermediate Scrutiny: A judicial standard of review for determining the constitutionality of laws in which the state must show that the law being challenged is related to an "important or substantial" state interest, and that the law is a "close, though not perfect, fit" as a means to achieve that state interest (Shaman, 2001, p. 72).

Sexual Harassment: Prohibits workplace actions that offer benefits in exchange for sexual activity (quid pro quo harassment) or that create an unwelcome and sexually motivated hostile work environment.

Statutory rape: Laws prohibiting sexual activity, even if consensual, with a person under the age of majority; the age of majority and statutory rape laws vary by jurisdiction.

Suspect Class: A group that has the ability to make contributions to society, yet historically has been subjected to discrimination on the basis of an immutable characteristic such that the group has experienced political marginalization.

Title VII of the Civil Rights Act of 1964: A landmark piece of legislation enacted by Congress and signed by President Johnson with the purpose of preventing discrimination in the workplace.

NOTES

1 The U.S. Constitution contains two Due Process Clauses. The one in the Fifth Amendment constrains the power of the federal government. The one in the Fourteenth Amendment constrains the power of state and local governments. The practical effect of each is virtually identical with regard to the substantive and procedural rights these Clauses guarantee to U.S. citizens.

2 At the time *Kansas v. Limon* (2005) was decided, it remained an open question—as it still does as of the writing of this chapter—whether sexual orientation constitutes a suspect or quasi-suspect classification, either of which would warrant a heightened standard of review (either strict scrutiny or intermediate scrutiny, respectively). Without U.S. Supreme Court precedent specifically directing the use of a more exacting standard of review, the Kansas Supreme Court decided that *Romer v. Evans* (1996) and *Lawrence v. Texas* (2003) suggested that equal protection claims based on sexual orientation should be subject to rational basis review.

3 Presumably, because the Court reiterated its longstanding rationale that marriage is a "fundamental right," strict scrutiny was applied in that case, although that is not specifically specified in the decision. Moreover, the decision did not utilize any language traditionally associated with strict scrutiny, such as whether the state has a compelling government interest in limiting marriage to members of different sexes.

REFERENCES

Anti-Defamation League. (2011). *Anti-Defamation League state hate crime statutory provisions.* Retrieved from http://www.adl.org/assets/pdf/combating-hate/state_hate_crime_laws.pdf

Boyer, P. S., Clark, C. E., Jr., Kett, J. F., Salisbury, N., Sitkoff, H., & Woloch, N. (1993). *The enduring vision: A history of the American people* (2nd ed.). Lexington, MA: D. C. Heath and Company.

Brickey, K. F. (1996). The commerce clause and federalized crime: A tale of two thieves. *Annals of the American Academy of Political and Social Science, 543*(1), 27–38.

Carroll-Ferrary, N. L. (2006/07). Incarcerated men and women, the Equal Protection Clause, and the requirement of "similarly situated." *New York Law School Law Review, 51*(3), 595–617.

Cocca, C. E. (2004). *Jailbait: The politics of statutory rape laws in the United States.* Albany, NY: State University of New York Press.

Cratty, C. (2012, October 26). Men found guilty in kidnapping of gay man, but acquitted of hate crime. *CNN.* Retrieved from http://www.cnn.com

Defense of Marriage Act (DOMA), Pub. L. 104–199, 110 Stat. 2419 (1996), *codified at* 28 U.S.C. § 1738C (2014), *abrogated by Obergefell v. Hodges,* 135 S. Ct. 2584 (2015).

Employment Non-Discrimination Act of 2013, S. 815, 113th Cong. (2013).

Eskridge, W. N., Jr., (2010). Is political powerlessness a requirement for heightened equal protection scrutiny? *Washburn Law Journal, 50*(1), 1–31.

Eskridge, W. N., Jr., & Hunter, N. D. (2004). *Sexuality, gender, and the law* (2nd ed.). New York, NY: Foundation Press.

Federal Bureau of Investigation. (2014). *Uniform Crime Report hate crime statistics, 2013.* Retrieved from http://www.fbi.gov/about-us/cjis/ucr/hate-crime/2013/topic-pages/incidents-and-offenses/incidentsandoffenses_final.pdf

Federal Bureau of Investigation. (n.d.). *Hate crime statistics 2013: Methodology.* Retrieved from https://www.fbi.gov/about-us/cjis/ucr/hate-crime/2013/resource-pages/methodology/methodology_final

Fox, L. (2014, June 16). GOP House leaders still oppose ENDA. *U.S. News and World Report.* Retrieved from http://www.usnews.com/news/articles/2014/06/16/gop-house-leaders-still-oppose-enda-despite-obama-action

Gerstenfeld, P. B. (2004). *Hate crimes: Causes, controls, and controversies.* Thousand Oaks, CA: Sage Publications.

Haider-Markel, D. P., & Meier, K. J. (1996). The politics of gay and lesbian rights: Expanding the scope of conflict. *Journal of Politics, 58*(2), 332–349.

Ho, J. A. (2014). Weather permitting: Incrementalism, animus, and the art of forecasting marriage equality after *U.S. v. Windsor. Cleveland State Law Review, 62*(1), 1–74.

Hutchinson, D. L. (2014). "Not without political power": Gays and lesbians, equal protection, and the suspect class doctrine. *Alabama Law Review, 65*(4), 975–1034.

Jacobs, J. B., & Potter, K. A. (1997). Hate crimes: A critical perspective. *Crime and Justice, 22,* 1–50.

Kaufman, M. (2001). *The Laramie Project.* New York, NY: Vintage Books.

King, J. (2003). *Hate crime: The story of a dragging in Jasper, Texas.* New York, NY: Pantheon Books.

Loffreda, B. (2001). *Losing Matt Shepard.* New York, NY: Columbia University Press.

Manley, K. (2009). The BFOQ defense: Title VII's concession to gender discrimination. *Duke Journal of Gender Law and Policy, 16*(1), 169–210.

Matthew Shepard and James Byrd, Jr., Hate Crime Prevention Act, Pub. L. 111–84, 123 Stat. 2838, 2842 (2009), *codified as amended at* 18 U.S.C. § 249 (2015).

McFadden, R. D. (2008, October 10). Gay marriage is ruled legal in Connecticut. *The New York Times.* Retrieved from http://www.nytimes.com/

O'Keefe, E. (2014, July 8). Gay rights groups withdraw support of ENDA after *Hobby Lobby* decision. *Washington Post.* Retrieved from http://www.washingtonpost.com/blogs/post-politics/wp/2014/07/08/gay-rights-group-withdrawing-support-of-enda-after-hobby-lobby-decision/

O'Keefe, E. (2013, November 4). ENDA, explained. *Washington Post.* Retrieved from http://www.washingtonpost.com/blogs/the-fix/wp/2013/11/04/what-is-the-employment-non-discrimination-act-enda/

Schacter, J. S. (1994). The gay civil rights debate in the states: Decoding the discourse of equivalents. *Harvard Civil Rights—Civil Liberties Law Review, 29*(2), 283–317.

Sex as a Bona Fide Occupational Qualification, 29 C.F.R. § 1604.2 (2012).

Shaman, J. M. (2001). *Constitutional interpretation: Illusion and reality.* Westport, CT: Greenwood Press.

Shane, R. D. (2009). Teachers as sexual harassment victims: The inequitable protections of Title VII in public schools. *Florida Law Review, 61*(2), 355–377.

Southern Poverty Law Center. (n.d.). *Hate incidents.* Retrieved from http://www.splcenter.org/get-informed/hate-incidents

Temple-Raston, D. (2002). *A death in Texas: A story of race, murder and a small town's struggle for redemption.* New York, NY: Henry Holt and Company.

Title VII of the Civil Rights Act of 1964, Unlawful Employment Practices, Pub. L. 88–352, 78 Stat. 255 (1964), *codified as amended at* 42 U.S.C. § 2000e-2 (2015).

U.S. Department of Justice. (n.d.). *Matthew Shepard & James Byrd, Jr., Hate Crimes Prevention Act of 2009.* Retrieved from http://www.justice.gov/crt/about/crm/matthewshepard.php

U.S. Equal Employment Opportunity Commission. (2015, February 3). Memorandum: Update on intake and charge processing of Title VII claims of sex discrimination related to LGBT status. Retrieved from http://www.hrdefenseblog.com/files/2015/02/eeoc-lgbt-field-guidance.pdf

U.S. Equal Employment Opportunity Commission. (n.d.). *Overview.* Retrieved from http://www.eeoc.gov/eeoc/index.cfm

Wilson, M. M. (2014, February). *Hate crime victimization, 2004–2012 – statistical tables.* Washington, DC: Bureau of Justice Statistics. Retrieved from http://www.bjs.gov/content/pub/pdf/hcv0412st.pdf

Cases

Andersen v. King County, 138 P.3d 963 (Wash. 2006).

Aromi v. Playboy Club, No. CS-32986–74 (N.Y. Exec. Dep't Div. Hum. Rts. 1985).

Automobile Workers v. Johnson Controls, 499 U.S. 187 (1991).

Backus v. Baptist Medical Center, 510 F. Supp. 1191 (E.D. Ark. 1981).

Baker v. Vermont, 744 A.2d 864 (Vt. 1999).

Batson v. Kentucky, 476 U.S. 79 (1986).

Ben-Shalom v. Marsh, 881 F.2d 454 (7th Cir. 1989).

Bolling v. Sharpe, 347 U.S. 497 (1954).

Brandon v. County of Richardson, 624 N.W.2d 604 (Neb. 2001).

Breiner v. Nevada Department of Corrections, 610 F.3d 1202 (9th Cir. 2010).

Burwell v. Hobby Lobby, 134 S. Ct. 2751 (2014).

City of Cleburne v. Cleburne Living Center, 473 U.S. 432 (1985).

Craig v. Boren, 492 U.S. 190 (1976).

Dothard v. Rawlinson, 433 U.S. 321 (1977).

Eisenstadt v. Baird, 405 U.S. 438 (1972).

Glenn v. Brumby, 663 F.3d 1312 (11th Cir. 2011).

Goodridge v. Department of Public Health, 798 N.E.2d 941 (Mass. 2003).

Griswold v. Connecticut, 381 U.S. 479 (1965).

Harris v. Forklift Systems, 510 U.S. 17 (1993).

High Tech Gays v. Defense Industrial Security Clearance Office, 895 F.2d 563 (9th Cir. 1990).

J.E.B. v. Alabama, 511 U.S. 127 (1994).

Kansas v. Limon, 122 P.3d 22 (Kan. 2005).

Kerrigan v. Commissioner of Public Health, 957 A.2d 407 (Conn. 2008).

Klinger v. Department of Corrections, 31 F.3d 727 (8th Cir. 1994).

Lawrence v. Texas, 539 U.S. 558 (2003).

Loving v. Virginia, 388 U.S. 1 (1967).

Macy v. Holder, Appeal No. 0120120821 (U.S. Equal Employment Opportunity Commission 2012).

Meritor Savings Bank v. Vinson, 477 U.S. 57 (1986).

Michael M. v. Superior Court of Sonoma County, 450 U.S. 464 (1981).

Mississippi University for Women v. Hogan, 458 U.S. 718 (1982).

Morrison v. Sadler, 821 N.E.2d 15 (Ind. Ct. App. 2005).

Obergefell v. Hodges, 135 S. Ct. 2584 (2015).

Oncale v. Sundowner Offshore Services, 523 U.S. 75 (1998).

Perry v. Schwarzenegger, 704 F. Supp. 2d 921 (N.D. Cal. 2010), aff'd, 671 F.3d 1052 (9th Cir. 2012), vacated and remanded for lack of standing by Hollingsworth v. Perry, 133 S. Ct. 2652 (2013).

Price Waterhouse v. Hopkins, 490 U.S. 228 (1989).

Prowel v. Wise Business Forms, 579 F.3d 285 (3rd Cir. 2009).

Reed v. Reed, 404 U.S. 71 (1971).

Romer v. Evans, 517 U.S. 620 (1996).

Snyder v. Phelps, 131 S. Ct. 1207 (2011).

St. Cross v. Playboy Club, Case No. CSF-22618–70, Appeal 773 (N.Y. Hum. Rts. App. Bd. 1971).

United States v. Jenkins, 909 F. Supp. 2d 758 (E.D. Ky. 2012).

United States v. Lopez, 514 U.S. 549 (1995).

United States v. Virginia, 518 U.S. 515 (1996).

United States v. Windsor, 133 S. Ct. 2675 (2013).

Varnum v. Brien, 763 N.W.2d 862 (Iowa 2009).

Virginia v. Black, 538 U.S. 343 (2003).

Watkins v. United States Army, 847 F.2d 1329 (9th Cir. 1988).

Watkins v. United States Army, 875 F.2d 699 (9th Cir. 1989).

Wilson v. Southwest Airlines, 517 F. Supp. 292 (N.D. Tex. 1981).

Windsor v. United States, 699 F.3d 169 (2d Cir. 2012), aff'd, 133 S. Ct. 2675 (2013).

Wisconsin v. Mitchell, 508 U.S. 476 (1993).

CHAPTER 5

Rape and Related Offenses

Henry F. Fradella and Chantal Fahmy

On the night of August 11, 2012, a 16-year-old girl from Weirton, West Virginia was raped by a group of her peers in Steubenville, Ohio, many of whom shared their actions on social-media websites. The convicted rapists, Trent Mays (17) and Ma'lik Richmond (16), played on Steubenville High School's legendary football team. Overall, these two well-rounded athletes, as well as all the other football players, were considered heroes in this small, poverty-stricken town that revolved around Friday-night games.

The young girl, visibly intoxicated and stumbling at the first party of the night, left with several Steubenville High football players to a second party where they only stayed briefly before ending at the third party of the night. Over the course of the evening, witnesses say she had vomited multiple times and could not walk. Other witnesses claim that Mays had flashed her breasts, penetrated her with his fingers, and tried to force her to perform oral sex on him while Richmond was simultaneously penetrating her. The naked and unconscious victim was photographed and videotaped in compromising positions, many of which were circulated on social media and via text messages.

Despite Twitter and Facebook posts, Instagram photos, and cell-phone videos disseminating among the teenagers who were at the parties that night, the police officers assigned to the case had difficulty retrieving clear, physical evidence of the rape. The story gained national headlines and began a discourse on rape culture as well as the major role social media played in the development of the tragedy. Mays was sentenced to at least two years in the juvenile justice system and Richmond must serve at least one year, but both could end up incarcerated until at least age 21.

- What might explain the actions of these young men? Were these young men driven by sexual desire? Were they trying to dominate or subjugate a vulnerable woman?
- In a landmark cross-cultural study, Sanday (1981) reported that rape is a rare phenomenon in some cultures, while other societies appear to be "rape-prone" either because "the incidence of rape is high, rape is a ceremonial act, or rape is an act by which men punish or threaten women" (Sanday, 1981, p. 9). In such rape-prone societies,

rape is linked with an overall pattern of violence and that part of this pattern includes the concept of woman as property. . . . [R]ape is the playing out of a socio-cultural script in which the expression of personhood for males is directed by, among other things, interpersonal violence and an ideology of toughness.

(Sanday, 1981, pp. 20, 24)

Might there be something about contemporary U.S. culture that can explain the actions of the Steubenville football players? Were they trying to prove strength or masculinity? Were they trying to feel accepted by their peer group by "playing along"? Such questions regarding motives for rape may not have definitive answers, but this chapter traces the legal development of the crime of rape and explores a number of bio-psycho-social theories that help to explain why people commit the crime.

The Steubenville High School football rape case did not receive significant media attention until after Deric Lostutter, a member of the hacker collective Anonymous, obtained and disseminated tweets, photos, and videos pertaining to the case. Lostutter claimed he had attempted to bring justice to the Steubenville case by exposing the football coach, school superintendent, and other pertinent adults who may have covered up, or at least ignored the inappropriate behavior. Lostutter was convicted of hacking into a public computer system and was sentenced to ten years in prison. What does it say about the criminal justice system that Lostutter's sentence was so much more severe than those of Mays and Richmond for their acts of sexual assault?

Sources: Macur & Schweber, 2012; Oppel, 2013.

LEARNING OBJECTIVES

1. Trace the evolution of the crime of rape from its common-law origins to its contemporary legal elements.
2. Analyze the ambiguities in modern rape law concerning the *mens rea* for the crime.
3. Compare and contrast the distinction between rape laws that define the crime as requiring the use of force and those that define the crime as requiring a lack of consent.
4. Discuss the purpose of rape shield laws.
5. Explain how alcohol and other drugs contribute to sexual assault victimization.
6. Compare and contrast the traditional crime of rape to post-penetration rape.
7. Explain how modern sexual assault and battery laws differ from the traditional crime of rape, as well as how they differ from each other.
8. Discuss how child molestation laws are a distinct form of the crime of rape.
9. Evaluate the leading theoretical perspectives on the causes of sexual assaults.
10. Analyze how male and female victims of sexual assault differ from each other.

According to the National Crime Victimization Survey administered by the U.S. Department of Justice (Truman & Langton, 2014), approximately 300,000 rapes and sexual assaults of U.S. residents age 12 or older occur each year, only about 35% of which are ever reported to the police. To put that in context, a sexual assault occurs nearly every two minutes in the United States. As a result, the U.S. Centers for Disease Control and Prevention (CDC) reports that nearly 20% of U.S. women and 1.7% of U.S. men are raped in their lifetime (Breiding, Smith, Basile, Walters, Chen, & Merrick, 2014). These victimizations are not evenly distributed across sexual orientations. "Approximately 1 in 8 lesbian women (13.1%), nearly half of bisexual women (46.1%), and 1 in 6 heterosexual women (17.4%) have been raped in their lifetime" (Walters, Chen, & Breiding, 2013, p. 10). The distribution of male rapes across sexual orientations is too unreliable for the CDC to report, although the CDC reports that roughly "4 out of 10 gay men (40.2%), half of bisexual men (47.4%), and 1 in 5 heterosexual men (20.8%) in the United States have experienced sexual violence other than rape at some point in their lives" (Walters, et al., 2013, p. 11). Regardless of the sex or sexual orientation of the victim, it should be noted that statistics concerning sexual victimization underestimate the number of rapes that occur each year due to under-reporting to the police, irregular reporting practices by police, and the methodological shortcomings of self-report survey data concerning sexual victimization (Kruttschnitt, Kalsbeek, & House, 2014; Yung, 2014).

Sexual assaults represent a particularly traumatic type of criminal victimization.

> These crimes are devastating, extending beyond the initial victimization to such consequences as unwanted pregnancy, sexually transmitted infections, post-traumatic stress disorder, depression, flashbacks, sleep disorders, eating dis-

orders, post-incident substance abuse, self-harm, and even suicide. The effects are often long lasting and can lead to health and work productivity issues for years. Using analyses from three different studies of the cost of crime, Heaton (2010) estimated that the victim-related costs for nonlethal rape and sexual assault are between $150,000 and $283,626 per victim.
>
> (Kruttschnitt, et al., 2014, p. 15)

In an attempt to explore the complexities of the crime of rape, this chapter begins by exploring the history of the offense of rape and its evolution into modern-day statutes governing sexual assaults and related crimes. The second half of the chapter is devoted to exploring the possible causes of sexual assault. Prison-based rapes are discussed in Chapter 11, and victims of sexual assault are discussed in Chapter 13.

THE CRIME OF RAPE[1]

In 2012, Tracy, Fromson, Long, and Whitman delivered a report to the National Research Council of the National Academies that began with the following statement:

> Rape and sexual assault laws are complex and evolving. Rape originated as a crime against property, not a crime against a person. As such, the crime related to patriarchal inheritance rights and a female's reproductive capacity and, therefore, was limited to a crime against unmarried virgins and included only forcible penile/vaginal penetration. These laws have evolved but retain vestiges of their archaic origins. The result is inconsistency and variability in sex crime terminology and elements from state to state as well as anomalies.
>
> (Tracy, et al., 2012, p. 1)

Ancient civilizations considered rape to be a form of theft because a young virgin was the property of her parents and a married woman was considered the property of her husband (Brownmiller, 1975; Conley, 1986; Pistono, 1988). Thus, in Ancient Greece, rape was punishable merely by a fine, whereas seduction could be legally avenged through justifiable homicide (Pistono, 1988). Ancient Babylonian and Hebrew laws "punished" a man who committed a rape against an unbetrothed girl or woman by requiring him to pay a certain amount of silver to a girl's father (Brownmiller, 1975; Conley, 1986). The Code of Hammurabi did not recognize the rape of a married woman. Rather, such an act was considered adultery that justified both the rapist and his victim being put to death by drowning. Ancient Hebrew law similarly interpreted rape of a married woman to be akin to adultery and, therefore, provided for death by stoning for both the married woman who was raped and her rapist (Brownmiller, 1975; Pistono, 1988).

Ancient Roman law also treated females as the property of males. Hence, "[s]tealing away a woman from her parents or guardians and debauching her, was made equally penal whether she consented or not" (Stephen, 1890, p. 78). Consent was of no concern to the Romans because they assumed that women "never go astray, without the seduction and arts of the other sex" (Stephen, 1890, p. 78). In contrast, both Saxons and Normans "treated rape as a crime of violence with consent a crucial factor" (Conley, 1986, p. 520). The penalty for rape was death and dismemberment until William the Conqueror changed the punishment to one of castration and the loss of the rapist's eyes (MacFarlane, 1993). Notably, this punishment was premised upon a belief that rape was motivated by uncontrolled lust. Indeed, Lord Bracton (1968/c. 1250–1260) explained the rationale for these punishments by saying, "Let him thus lose his eyes which gave him sight of the maiden's beauty for which he coveted her. And let him lose as well the testicles which excited his hot lust" (pp. 414–415).

Common-Law Rape

Many contemporary notions surrounding the legal intricacies of rape stem from the common-law understanding of the crime. In his *Commentaries on the Laws of England*, Sir William Blackstone (1979/1765–1769) defined **rape** as the *unlawful carnal knowledge of a woman by a man not her husband, without her effective consent*. Before exploring the technicalities of this definition, it is important to note that, as legal scholar Susan Estrich (1986) explained, the common-law definition of rape differs significantly from most other common-law crimes.

> The traditional way of defining a crime is by describing the prohibited act (*actus reus*) committed by the defendant and the prohibited mental state (*mens rea*) with which he must have done it. We ask: What did the defendant do? What did he know or intend when he did it?
>
> The definition of rape stands in striking contrast to this tradition, because courts, in defining the crime, have focused almost incidentally on the defendant—and almost entirely on the victim. . . . [T]raditionally at least, the rules associated with the proof of a rape charge . . . placed the victim as much on trial as the defendant. Such a reversal also occurs in the course of defining the elements of the crime. *Mens rea*, where it might matter, is all but eliminated; prohibited force tends to be defined according to the response of the victim; and nonconsent—the *sine qua non* of the offense—turns entirely on the victim's response.
>
> (p. 1094)

Actus Reus and Attendant Circumstances for Common-Law Rape

Every crime sets forth some conduct that is prohibited, either a voluntary act or state of possession that the criminal law prohibits, or an omission—a failure to act when the law imposed a legal duty to do so. The conduct proscribed under a penal statute is called the *actus reus*, Latin for the "evil act" (Dressler, 2006). Some crimes require an *actus reus* to be committed under certain *attendant circumstances* before giving rise to criminal liability. Consider the crime of criminal speeding, defined as "operating a motor vehicle on a public roadway in exceed of 25 miles per hour over the posted speed limit." The *actus reus* for the crime is speeding. There are two attendant circumstances. First, the vehicle must have been operating on a public roadway. Thus, a car being operated on a private racetrack would not be violating the criminal speeding law. Second, even if a vehicle were being operated on a public roadway, it would have to be traveling at least 25 miles per hour over the posted speed limit for the offense to be criminal speeding; a car traveling 10 miles per hour over the speed limit would merely be committing a civil motor vehicle infraction, not a crime.

The *actus reus* and attendant circumstances for common-law rape were defined as *the unlawful carnal knowledge of a woman by a man not her husband* (Dressler, 2006). Several words in this phrase require detailed explanation.

NECESSARY PARTIES

The common law's restrictive attendant circumstances for the crime of rape produced two principles of a function of logic. First, "only a female could be the victim of a rape and only a male could be the perpetrator" (Duncan, 2007, p. 1093). Second, the concept of marital rape was not recognized by the common law. Sir Matthew Hale explained the sexist and paternalistic logic underlying the marital exclusion to rape in his treatise *History of the Pleas of the Crown* (1778): "A husband cannot be guilty of a rape committed by himself upon his lawful wife, for by their mutual matrimonial consent and contract the wife hath given up herself in this kind unto her husband, which she cannot retract" (p. 628). In other words, by the nature of the marital contract as understood in an era when

a wife was viewed as her husband's property, sexual intercourse between husband and wife was always lawful, even if the husband used force or violence to accomplish it (Futter & Mebane, 2001; Hasday, 2000).

VAGINAL PENETRATION

Over time, the *actus reus* element of *unlawful carnal knowledge* came to be defined as forcible penetration, however slight, of a woman's vagina by a man's penis (Dressler, 2006). Thus, nonconsensual sexual acts other than penile-vaginal penetration fell outside the definition of rape and were, therefore, punished as other crimes, such as forcible sodomy (Dressler, 2006).

The inclusion of the qualifier "however slight" meant that that penile penetration from the opening of the vulva to the cervix of the uterus was unnecessary. Rather, even partial penetration of the labia was sufficient to constitute the *actus reus* of rape (e.g., *State v. Montgomery*, 1999; see also Dressler, 2006). Once a nonconsensual penile penetration of the vagina occurred, however slight, the *actus reus* for the crime of rape was complete; ejaculation was not necessary (e.g., *People v. Wallace*, 2008).

FORCE AND RESISTANCE

Neither force nor threats of force were technically required as part of *actus reus* for the common-law crime of rape (Berger, 1977). Rather, the law merely required that the penetration be without the effective consent of the victim. But proving nonconsent in the absence of force-induced physical injuries was almost always difficult. In fact, women's allegations of rape were viewed with such suspicion that Sir Matthew Hale wrote: "Rape is . . . an accusation easily to be made and hard to be proved, and harder to be defended by the party accused, tho never so innocent" (Hale, 1778, p. 635). As a result, the common law evolved over time such that, by the end of the 1600s, the nonconsent of the victim came to be interpreted as requiring proof of force as either part of the *actus reus* for rape or an attendant circumstance to the crime (MacFarlane, 1993; see also, e.g., *Moran v. People*, 1872).

Threats of force were included in the definition of "force" for the purposes of proving nonconsent, but "claims of threatened use of force were rarely persuasive" (MacFarlane, 1993, p. 19). This, in turn, gave rise to the common-law requirement that the victim of a rape needed to resist "to the utmost" to provide physical evidence of her nonconsent. The *resistance to the utmost* standard effectively required a woman to be physically brutalized while being sexually brutalized. Bishop (1902, as quoted in MacFarlane, 1993), explained the standard by quoting a nineteenth-century appellate judge as follows: "The resistance must be up to the point of being overpowered by actual force, or of inability, from loss of strength, longer to resist, or, from the number of persons attacking, resistance must be dangerous or absolutely useless, or there must be dread or fear of death" (pp. 18–19). As a result, medical evidence of forcible penetration, documented injuries caused by violence, or proof of venereal infection linked to the accused became the hallmarks of evidence of rape under the common law (p. 19). But nineteenth-century medicine was often complicit in protecting men by perpetuating the belief that "absent extraordinary force and violence, it was impossible to commit a rape upon a grown woman who had full possession of her faculties" (p. 20).

The utmost resistance requirement almost always produced one of two unacceptable outcomes. Either the requirement proved to be "an invitation to danger of death or serious bodily harm" to the woman (MODEL PENAL CODE § 213.1 cmt., 1980, p. 305), or it provided a rapist with a defense to his crime. Consider the case of *Brown v. State* (1906). The victim in the case was a 16-year-old who was attacked by her neighbor. At trial, she testified: "I tried as hard as I could to get away. I was trying all the time to get away just as

hard as I could. I was trying to get up; I pulled at the grass; I screamed as hard as I could, and he told me to shut up, and I didn't, and then he held his hand on my mouth until I was almost strangled" (p. 537). Although the jury convicted the defendant, that conviction was overturned because the appellate court found that the victim had not resisted the attack to her utmost ability. In so ruling, the court reasoned that "[n]ot only must there be entire absence of mental consent or assent, but there must be the most vehement exercise of every physical means or faculty within the woman's power to resist the penetration of her person, and this must be shown to persist until the offense is consummated" (p. 538).

It is important to note that rape was the only crime that "required the victim to resist physically in order to establish nonconsent" (Estrich, 1986, p. 1090).

> [T]he injection of a concept of "force," over and above the coercion implicit in denying freedom of sexual choice, led to the rather illogical idea that the victim had to "resist to the utmost." Thus, an offense whose gravamen was non-consent acquired a gloss that shifted the focus from the woman's subjective state of mind, as affected by the man's actions, to her behavior in response. By contrast, in a crime like robbery, also "a nonconsensual and forcible version of an ordinary human interaction," the law imposes no special burden of opposition: It simply inquires whether the accused took something from another person by violence or intimidation.
>
> (Berger, 1977, p. 8)

The Mens Rea for Rape

The term *mens rea* is Latin for "evil mind." It refers to the level of criminal intent that must accompany the commission of an *actus reus*. Consider the common-law crime of larceny, a form of theft. It criminalized the taking and carrying away of another's personal property with the intent to steal it. If an actor had the owner's permission to take the property at issue, or if the actor accidentally took the property believing it to be his own, then the *mens rea* element—intent to steal—would not be present and, hence, no theft crime occurred. The level of *mens rea* entertained by a person is often what differentiates an accident from a crime, or serious crimes from petty ones.

At common law, the *mens rea* for rape was quite ambiguous since the offense was a general-intent crime. This means that a defendant need not have entertained any specific intent to rape, but rather need only have acted with a general sense of moral blameworthiness (Dressler, 2006; Duncan, 2007). At first blush, it might seem bizarre to think that a man might not know whether he was raping a woman and, therefore, could be without moral blame. But the restrictively narrow definition of rape under the common law made it virtually unnecessary to grapple with the question of *mens rea*. As Susan Estrich (1986) explained,

> It is difficult to imagine any man engaging in intercourse accidentally or mistakenly. It is just as difficult to imagine an accidental or mistaken use of force, at least as force is conventionally defined. But it is not at all difficult to imagine cases in which a man might claim that he did not realize that the woman was not consenting to sex. He may have been mistaken in assuming that no meant yes. He may not have bothered to inquire. He may have ignored signs that would have told him that the woman did not welcome his forceful penetration.
>
> (p. 1097)

In effect, the *mens rea* for rape was all but eliminated by the common law's focus on the victim's nonconsent as expressed through her utmost resistance. Thus, in sharp contrast to other crimes, the central issue at a rape trial rarely, if ever, concerned the man's criminal intent, but rather focused on the victim's response to his actions. In essence, proof of the woman's resistance established the nec-

essary *mens rea* that the man acted with a morally blameworthy state of mind sufficient to satisfy the *mens rea* requirement for a rape conviction. The twofold legacy of this refocusing of responsibility from the defendant to the victim has been tragic on two fronts. First and foremost, it created situations in which the victim of a rape was basically put on trial, rather than the accused rapist (Berger, 1977). Not only would the woman be subjected to a grueling cross-examination about the amount of resistance she offered, but also to humiliating innuendo about her character, dress, demeanor, and sexual history in the hopes that such character assassination would lead the jury to entertain reasonable doubt with regard to whether she consented to sex (Berger, 1977; Schultz, 1975). Second, as explored in greater detail later in this chapter, it created such confusion with regard to the requisite *mens rea* for rape that many U.S. states have yet to clarify this aspect of their criminal law even to this day (see Fradella & Brown, 2005; Kinports, 2001).

Rape Law Reform

Starting in the 1960s, feminists began to challenge much of the outdated reasoning behind the common-law definition of rape (Berger, Searles, & Neuman, 1988). Advocacy efforts led to reform of rape laws in every U.S. state by the mid-1980s (Horney & Spohn, 1991). As a result, nearly all U.S. jurisdictions presently define the crime of rape using a definition similar to this one: "a sexual intercourse accomplished without the consent of the victim" (Berger, et al., 1988; Horney & Spohn, 1991; Fradella & Brown, 2005). This change in terminology reflected several important developments in the law of rape.

Changes to the Actus Reus and Attendant Circumstances for Rape

First, by eliminating the phrase "unlawful carnal knowledge of a woman" and replacing it with the broader term of nonconsensual "sexual intercourse," legislatures expanded the definition of rape beyond nonconsensual vaginal penetrations. Thus, under most modern rape laws, the penetration of any sexual orifice (i.e., the mouth, the anus, and the vagina) constitutes rape. Moreover, the penetration need not be by a penis to qualify as a rape; the crime now includes digital penetration or penetrations using a foreign object (Berger, et al., 1988; Horney & Spohn, 1991; Reyes, 2003). Thus, this broader definition of rape recognizes that most types of forcible sexual penetrations violate the victim, regardless of the victim's sex (see Capers, 2011).

Second, many modern rape laws have eliminated, either wholly or in part, the spousal exemption to rape in recognition of the sad reality that spousal rapes do occur. Accordingly, a husband who sexually assaults his wife can now be criminally prosecuted for rape in all U.S. jurisdictions (Hasday, 2000; Klarfeld, 2011). But the approaches to marital rape taken by U.S. states vary greatly, ranging from criminalizing "a narrower range of offenses if committed within marriage," to subjecting marital rape "to less serious sanctions," and/or creating "special procedural hurdles for marital rape prosecutions" (Hasday, 2000, p. 1375). In sum, "[t]he current state of the law represents a confusing mix of victory and defeat for the exemption's contemporary feminist critics" (p. 1375).

NONCONSENT, FORCE, AND RESISTANCE

When many, but not all, U.S. state legislatures revised their rape laws, they placed primary emphasis on the assaultive nature of the crime. In fact, many states abandoned the term "rape" and instead adopted laws against **sexual assault** or **sexual battery**. In doing so, these states relied on the definitions of nonsexual criminal assaults and batteries, neither of which requires the application of force. Rather, a criminal assault places a victim in a state of reasonable apprehension of imminent bodily harm, while a criminal battery conviction may be sustained for any unwanted, offensive touching in the absence of any "force" as commonly understood (see Dressler, 2006). Criminal liability for these crimes hinges on the defendant's state of mind, not the victim's reaction. Thus, when legislatures adopted terminology that emphasized the affinity between sexually-based assaults and batteries and nonsexual forms of assault and battery, they purposefully changed the scope of rape law to avoid the historic focus on resistance by the victim.

The requirement of resistance "to the utmost" has been eliminated in all U.S. jurisdictions (Berger, et al., 1988; Bryden, 2000; Estrich, 1986). The 1980 comments to the Model Penal Code presented the rationale for this change as follows:

> To some degree, . . . [various formulations of the resistance requirement] share common faults. First, resistance may prove an invitation to danger of death or serious bodily harm. Second, it is wrong to excuse the male assailant on the ground that his victim failed to protect herself with the dedication and intensity that a court might expect of a reasonable person in her situation. As a practical matter, juries may require resistance to show that the male compelled her to submit, but there is little reason to encase this generalization in a rule of law. Where the proof establishes that the actor did compel submission to intercourse by force, the failure of a weak or fearful victim to display "utmost" or even "earnest" resistance should not be exculpatory.
>
> (MODEL PENAL CODE § 213.1 cmt., 1980, p. 305)

Thus, no longer does a rape victim have to fight back to the utmost and thereby risk being subjected to even further brutalization.

Shifting the focus from the victim's level of resistance to either the perpetrator's use of forcible compulsion or the victim's lack of consent has not produced any uniform rules on what is required to prove rape. Some jurisdictions continue to require that the victim undertook "some resistance"—defined as "whatever resistance is appropriate under the circumstances" (Fradella & Brown, 2005, p. 6; see also Decker & Baroni, 2011). Other states do not require any resistance at all; simply saying "no" is technically sufficient. However, since force or compulsion remains an element of rape in many U.S. jurisdictions, the removal of any formal resistance requirement may be form over substance, producing an illusory removal of the resistance requirement (see Artherton, 2012). A prosecutor interviewed by Horney and Spohn (1991) explained why this is: "Juries still expect some resistance or some explanation as to why there was none. This is especially true if it was a date gone sour; if we can't show some resistance in this case we're in a lot of trouble" (p. 139). In other words, courts usually "insist on something more than the movements that are customary in sex. Thus, most jurisdictions, in effect, require 'reasonable' resistance" (Bryden, 2000, pp. 358–359). It should be noted, though, that this approach is flawed for the following reason:

> All intercourse, or at least all unwanted intercourse, can be thought of as forcible, because penetration requires some force. As Professor Robin West puts it, "unwanted, undesired penetration of a woman who has expressed a refusal, by a man who then ignores her refusal, is a violent act. It is a physical intrusion of one's body, it causes pain. . . ." Why doesn't that amount to "force"?
>
> (Bryden, 2000, p. 372)

Recognizing this shortcoming, a few courts have held that the minimal "force" necessary to accomplish a customary act of sexual penetration is sufficient for rape liability, even in the absence of any resistance by the alleged victim (see Law in Action Box). This approach, however, is clearly a minority view, as the "overwhelming majority of jurisdic-

tions in this country continue to require proof of both force and lack of consent to support a rape conviction" (Kinports, 2001, p. 757).

ADDITIONAL ATTENDANT CIRCUMSTANCES EVIDENCING COMPULSION OR NONCONSENT

Nearly all U.S. states have modern rape or sexual assault laws that statutorily recognize at least three or four attendant circumstances that demonstrate the victim's lack of consent even in the absence of the use or threatened use of force or any resistance thereto. First, the youthful age of the victim is the most common of such attendant circumstances. Depending on how young the victim may be, the crime may be deemed rape or child molestation (see later in this chapter) or statutory rape (see Chapter 6).

Second, incapacitation is another common attendant circumstance demonstrating nonconsent. Such incapacitation can be a function of the victim being asleep, being impaired by alcohol or other drugs (either legal or illicit), or being cognitively impaired due to some mental condition that either prevents the victim from understanding the distinctively sexual nature of the conduct or impairs the victim's ability to understand or exercise the right to refuse to engage in the conduct with another (Falk, 2002; Schulhofer, 1998).

Third, some states criminalize sex as rape if consent was fraudulently induced by one of two types of deceptions: impersonation and phony medical "treatment" (Bryden, 2000; McJunkin, 2014). As one might imagine, impersonation of a spouse or lover occurs infrequently; it requires sufficient similarity between the imposter and the victim's spouse or lover such that the victim consents to engaging in sexual intercourse honestly and reasonably believing that the sexual acts were being performed with his or her spouse or lover (Schulhofer, 1998). False treatment ruses also involve fraud. In such schemes, the victim is intentionally deceived as to the nature of the act, such as when someone impersonates a physician by pretending to conduct a gynecological exam (Bryden, 2000). Barring one of these types of frauds, most states do not otherwise criminalize sex induced by deception. Thus, the gullible should be wary in the face of false promises to marry, fake declarations of love, or untruthful representations of status ranging from being single or on birth control, to having been a war hero or an Olympic gold medalist (see McJunkin, 2014).

Finally, there is one type of deception, whether affirmatively voiced as a lie or passively made through nondisclosure, many states have criminalized: failure to warn about one's known status as carrying a sexually transmitted infection (STI). These laws typically criminalize engaging in sexual conduct with another person (the *actus reus*) knowing (the *mens rea*) that one is positive for a STI (attendant circumstance) without first disclosing his or her STI-positive status to the other person prior to engaging in sexual conduct (attendant circumstance). Few states have laws that view this type of deception as vitiating consent in a manner that would give rise to rape liability (see Kaplan, 2012). Instead, the intentional spread of such diseases can be prosecuted as assault, battery, reckless endangerment, and even under homicide statutes (see Waldman, 2011). But more than 30 states have adopted separate "knowing transmission" statutes to criminalize such conduct (Ayres & Baker, 2005; Kaplan, 2012). This offense is discussed in detail in Chapter 6.

Continued Confusion over the Mens Rea for Rape

Unfortunately, the reforms to the law of rape did not necessarily include fixing the ambiguities concerning the requisite *mens rea* for the crime. The *mens rea* for rape today differs by jurisdiction.

In the United States, many modern rape laws mirror the old common law insofar as they do not mention any *mens rea* require-

ment (Fradella & Brown, 2005; Kinports, 2001). When statutes are silent with regard to *mens rea*, the courts must grapple with the issue. They have come up with very different approaches. Some courts have held rape to be a specific intent crime; thus, the prosecution must prove that the defendant purposefully or intentionally used force or threats of force to effectuate nonconsensual sexual intercourse. Others have read into their rape statutes a requirement of knowledge even in the absence of statutory language to that effect, although sometimes this requirement attaches to the use of force, while other times it attaches to knowing that the victim did not actually consent. And still other courts have followed the Model Penal Code Section 2.02(3), which requires proof of at least recklessness in cases where a criminal statute fails to specify a *mens rea* requirement (Fradella & Brown, 2005; Kinports, 2001).

States with statutes that do specify a level of criminal intent are not in agreement. A minority of states designates rape as a specific intent crime requiring at least a *mens rea* level of knowledge. Colorado, Hawaii, Indiana, Montana, and Texas all fall into this category by having statutory language paralleling Arizona's: "A person commits sexual assault by intentionally or knowingly engaging in sexual intercourse or oral sexual contact with any person without consent of such person" (ARIZ. REV. STAT. § 13–1406, 2015). Delaware, Ohio, and Wyoming require the even higher level of *mens rea* of purpose, using such language as, "No person shall engage in sexual conduct with another when the offender purposely compels the other person to submit by force or threat of force" (OHIO REV. CODE ANN. § 2907.02[A][2], 2014). But even among these states that have designed rape a specific intent crime requiring purpose or knowledge, there is no uniformity with regard to which specific element of rape the *mens rea* must attach. Some jurisdictions require the *mens rea* to attach to either performing sexual intercourse or using of force—

Law in Action HOW MUCH FORCE? IN RE M.T.S.

Around 11:30 p.m. one night, C.G., a 15-year-old girl, went to bed wearing underpants, a bra, shorts, and a shirt. Earlier that day, M.T.S., a 17-year-old male house guest, teased C.G. that he "was going to make a surprise visit up in [her] bedroom." According to C.G., she did not take M.T.S. seriously because he frequently teased her. At approximately 1:30 a.m., she awoke to use the bathroom. As she was getting out of bed, she said that she saw M.T.S., fully clothed, standing in her doorway. According to her, M.T.S. then said that "he was going to tease [her] a little bit." She "didn't think anything of it" and, therefore, walked past him, used the bathroom, returned to bed, and fell asleep within fifteen minutes. The next event C.G. claimed to recall of that morning was waking up with M.T.S. on top of her, her underpants and shorts removed. She said "his penis was into [her] vagina." As soon as C.G. realized what had happened, she said, she immediately slapped M.T.S. once in the face, then "told him to get off [her], and get out." She did not scream or cry out. She testified that M.T.S. "jumped right off of [her]" and left her room. C.G. did not know how long M.T.S. had been inside of her before she awoke. She "fell asleep crying" because "[she] couldn't believe that he did what he did to [her]." C.G. later explained that she did not immediately tell her mother or anyone else in the house of the events of that morning because she was "scared and in shock," although she did tell her mother later that morning.

M.T.S. told a different version of events. He testified that at exactly 1:15 a.m., he entered C.G.'s bedroom as she was walking to the bathroom. He said C.G. soon returned from the bathroom, and the two began "kissing and all," eventually moving to the bed. Once they were in bed, he said, they undressed each other and continued to kiss and touch for about five minutes. M.T.S. and C.G. proceeded to engage in sexual intercourse. According to M.T.S., who was on top of C.G., he "stuck it in" and thrust three times before C.G. pushed him off of her while saying "stop, get off." M.T.S. claimed he "hopped off right away."

Following a two-day trial on the sexual assault charge, M.T.S. was adjudicated delinquent. After reviewing the testimony, the court concluded that the victim had consented to a session of kissing and heavy petting with M.T.S. The trial court did not find that C.G. had been sleeping at the time of penetration, but nevertheless found that she had not consented to the actual sexual act. He appealed.

Under New Jersey law, a person who commits an act of sexual penetration using physical force or coercion is guilty of second-degree sexual assault. The sexual-assault statute, however, does not define the words "physical force." Because there was no evidence or even a suggestion that M.T.S. used any unusual or extra force or threats to accomplish the act of penetration, the appellate court reversed the adjudication of delinquency. The state then appealed, arguing that the element of "physical force" could be met simply by an act of nonconsensual penetration involving no more force than necessary to accomplish that result. The New Jersey Supreme Court agreed. The court reasoned as follows:

> The understanding of sexual assault as a criminal battery, albeit one with especially serious consequences, follows necessarily from the Legislature's decision to eliminate non-consent and resistance from the substantive definition of the offense. Under the new law, the victim no longer is required to resist and therefore need not have said or done anything in order for the sexual penetration to be unlawful. The alleged victim is not put on trial, and his or her responsive or defensive behavior is rendered immaterial. We are thus satisfied that an interpretation of the statutory crime of sexual assault

to require physical force in addition to that entailed in an act of involuntary or unwanted sexual penetration would be fundamentally inconsistent with the legislative purpose to eliminate any consideration of whether the victim resisted or expressed non-consent.

We note that the contrary interpretation of force—that the element of force need be extrinsic to the sexual act—would not only reintroduce a resistance requirement into the sexual assault law, but also would immunize many acts of criminal sexual contact short of penetration. The characteristics that make a sexual contact unlawful are the same as those that make a sexual penetration unlawful. An actor is guilty of criminal sexual contact if he or she commits an act of sexual contact with another using "physical force" or "coercion." That the Legislature would have wanted to decriminalize unauthorized sexual intrusions on the bodily integrity of a victim by requiring a showing of force in addition to that entailed in the sexual contact itself is hardly possible.

Because the statute eschews any reference to the victim's will or resistance, the standard defining the role of force in sexual penetration must prevent the possibility that the establishment of the crime will turn on the alleged victim's state of mind or responsive behavior. We conclude, therefore, that any act of sexual penetration engaged in by the defendant without the affirmative and freely-given permission of the victim to the specific act of penetration constitutes the offense of sexual assault. Therefore, physical force in excess of that inherent in the act of sexual penetration is not required for such penetration to be unlawful.

1. Do you agree with the court's decision in the case? Why or why not?
2. Concern about acquaintance rape played a significant role in the court's decision. Had the viewpoint of the intermediate court of appeals been adopted (i.e., if the statute had been interpreted as requiring more force than that inherent in the act of sexual penetration), what do you think the effect would be on rape prosecutions generally, and acquaintance rape prosecutions, in particular? Explain your reasoning.
3. Why do you think that the approach taken in New Jersey is the minority approach? In other words, why do you think most states require "some amount of force" to be proven beyond that force inherent in sexual penetration? Should a lack of affirmative and freely given permission be sufficient for criminal liability? Why or why not?

purposefully or knowingly using force to achieve penetration; others apply the *mens rea* element to the issue of knowing the victim did not consent (Charlow, 2002; Fradella & Brown, 2005; Kinports, 2001).

Most states continue the common-law tradition of rape being a general intent crime. They differ, however, on whether criminal recklessness or negligence will suffice for a conviction. Recklessness refers to the situation in which a defendant is subjectively aware of a substantial risk that the victim has not consented to sex, but in spite of the conscious awareness of that risk, the defendant unjus-tifiably disregards the risk and engages in the sex act anyway (Charlow, 2002). But a recklessness standard for the crime of rape can lead to situations in which the "willfully blind" or "stupid" can escape criminal liability (Taslitz, 2005). The holding in the highly controversial 1975 British case of *Director of Public Prosecutions v. Morgan* illustrates this point.

The defendant Morgan was a lieutenant in the Royal Air Force. While out drinking, he invited enlisted men to his home to have sexual intercourse with his wife. Morgan explained to his friends that she would protest, but her resistance would be feigned because she was "kinky" and living out a rape fantasy, complete with struggling, would really get her "turned on" (*Director of Public Prosecutions v. Morgan*, 1975, p. 354). The four men went to the Morgan house where they found Mrs. Morgan asleep on a cot in one of her children's bedrooms. They dragged her out of her bed by her hands and feet and brought her to another room with a double bed where each of the four men took turns in having forcible intercourse with Mrs. Morgan over her vocal protestations and in spite of the resistance she offered—resistance that was substantial enough that she sustained physical injuries requiring hospital treatment. "Mrs. Morgan testified that the defendants held her down the entire time. At one point when she yelled to her children to call the police, the defendants held her nose and mouth shut until she couldn't breathe (Alexander, 1995, p. 210).

As odd as it may seem considering the hundreds of years of common-law history before the *Morgan* case, no case law precedent had been decided on the *mens rea* for rape in Great Britain prior to 1975 (Alexander, 1995). Following the usual law that factual mistakes cannot be defenses to crimes unless both honestly held based on reasonable grounds, the trial court judge directed the jury that the defendants' belief in consent had to be reasonably held (*Director of Public Prosecutions v. Morgan*, 1975, p. 356). The jury convicted them, finding that no reasonable person could believe the victim had consented in light of her vocal and physical resistance. The defendants appealed, contending there was no requirement that their belief in her consent had to be reasonable. A three to two majority of members of the House of Lords sided with the defendants, holding a subjectively held belief that the other party to a sexual intercourse had consented, even if objectively unreasonable and factually untrue, is a defense to rape (p. 347). However, the lords dismissed the appeal without setting aside the men's convictions on the grounds that no reason-

able jury could have found that the men held honest beliefs that Mrs. Morgan had consented (pp. 353–362).

The decision in *Morgan* stands in sharp contrast to the rule of law applied to other crimes that a mistake of fact can only negate the *mens rea* if the mistake was honestly held (a subjective standard) and objectively reasonable; unreasonable mistakes usually cannot serve as defenses to crimes (see Alexander, 1995). Professor Andrew Taslitz (2005) wrote the following when criticizing the case:

> Even if the men were not fully consciously aware of Mrs. Morgan's nonconsent, . . . my students are suspicious that the men knew at some level that they were violating her desires. They chose not to confront their lurking suspicions of nonconsent, both because it would have spoiled their orgy and because they did not want to challenge the credibility or authority of their superior officer. Even if these men were so stupid or gullible that the wrongness of their actions never even momentarily crossed their minds, however, the students remain equally offended, for such gullibility can be dangerous. Barring some mental impairment, it was easily within the power of these men to have more sharply honed their moral sensibilities. Their ignorance was thus in some sense "willful," a stupidity chosen or allowed to fester to serve a variety of less-than-laudable personal goals.
>
> (p. 400)

To avoid the problems with a subjective approach to the *mens rea* for rape, many U.S. states—indeed the majority of them—have opted for a negligence standard (Taslitz, 2005). In contrast to a recklessness standard that requires proof that an actor consciously disregarded a substantial and unjustified risk of nonconsent, the negligence approach uses an objective standard. One who acts with criminal negligence and, therefore, would be guilty of rape may not have been subjectively aware of a risk of nonconsent, but, under the circumstances, should have been aware of such a risk. In other words, a rape conviction is proper when it is proven that the defendant entertained an objectively unreasonable belief that the victim consented (Duncan 2007; Taslitz, 2005).

Conversely, one who has a subjectively honest belief that sex is consensual is not guilty of rape if that belief is also objectively reasonable under the totality of the circumstances (see Alexander, 1995). Professor Taslitz (2005) argued in favor of this approach, particularly in terms of its benefits in acquaintance rape cases if "reasonableness" is defined in both jury instructions and common understanding "as a duty of reasonable inquiry to determine an intended sexual partner's desires" (p. 446). This, in turn, would be "an effective way to combat male self-deception" that a partner consented to sex when, in fact, that partner had not (p. 446).

Reynolds v. State (1983) illustrates how an objective standard of reasonableness can be applied. The victim in *Reynolds* alleged that the defendant "forced her to enter his apartment and used a key to close a deadbolt lock and pocketed the key, effectively preventing her from leaving" (p. 622). She engaged in sexual intercourse with him "against her will," driven by fear of a handgun in plain view of the defendant's bed. She testified that although she objected verbally, she offered no physical resistance due to the presence of the gun. She conceded that the defendant never threatened her and "never touched or even mentioned the handgun" (p. 622). The presence of the gun led an Alaska appellate court to affirm his conviction, reasoning that the defendant "should have known" the gun would have intimidated the victim into compliance, even though he never otherwise used any force against her person (p. 630).

Finally, two or three U.S. jurisdictions appear to have adopted a strict liability approach to rape. As Kinports (2001) explains, this is somewhat paradoxical.

[I]n *State v. Reed* [1984] the Maine Supreme Court noted that the crime of forcible rape was "defined without reference to the actor's state of mind," concluding that "the legislature . . . clearly indicated that rape compelled by force or threat requires no culpable state of mind." But the court went on to remark that "one person cannot accidentally or innocently compel another to submit to sexual intercourse," thereby suggesting that its view is more in line with the courts that consider rape a general intent crime.

The states that apply strict liability to rape usually apply it only to the element of consent. In these jurisdictions, a defendant's honest and reasonable mistake with regard to whether the victim consented is not a defense (Kinports, 2001). This approach is quite rare. If one generalization can be made about the *mens rea* of rape, it is that some level of general intentionality is implicit in the crime—even when the statute is "silent on the subject" (see *People v. Williams*, 1993, 736; see also Duncan, 2007).

Rape Shield Laws

Rape prosecutions present unique difficulties for the justice system. According to the Bureau of Justice Statistics, rape remains one of the most under-reported of all crimes, as only 36% of sexual assault victims report the crime to the police. Of the just over one-third of rapes that are reported to law enforcement, cases are cleared by arrest in fewer than 42% of cases. Data on rape conviction rates vary significantly by study and range from a shockingly low 4% to 5%, to 20%, to a high of 73%. In spite of the wide variability in conviction rates, it certainly seems that rape defendants enjoy a significantly higher rate of acquittal than those charged with other serious felonies, as the conviction rate for murder stands at 80%, driving related offenses at 73%, motor vehicle thefts at 68%, burglaries at 66%, and drug trafficking at 64%.

(Fradella & Brown, 2007, pp. 1–2 [internal citations omitted])

As the statistics in the quote above suggest, proving rape is very difficult. Often, forensic evidence is not particularly helpful because the defendant admits that some sex act took place, but defends on the grounds that the act was consensual. Even when there is some evidence of a struggle, a "rough-sex" defense can create reasonable doubt (see Rayburn, 2006).

Another tactic that was often used by the defense in rape cases was to put the victim on trial. Factual issues such as the victim's past sexual conduct and/or the victim's manner and style of dress were made the focal points of the trial by the defense in an attempt to create reasonable doubt with regard to the matter of consent (Anderson, 2002; Wells & Motley, 2001). Starting in the 1970s, some U.S. jurisdictions began to enact **rape shield laws** designed to prevent the victim and his or her past sexual conduct from being put on trial, thereby attempting to focus attention at trial on the facts of the incident in question (Estrich, 1986; Futter & Mebane, 2001). Today, rape shield laws have been adopted in federal criminal law, the military, and all U.S. states (Flowe, Ebbesen, & Putcha-Bhagavatula, 2007).

Generally speaking, rape shield laws prohibit the introduction of any evidence of the alleged victim's past sexual conduct. Most jurisdictions, however, recognize exceptions to this general bar and admit evidence of the alleged victim's past sexual conduct with the accused, reasoning the past sexual history between the accused and the accuser is highly relevant (Flowe, et al., 2007). Similarly, most U.S. jurisdictions allow evidence of the alleged victim's prior sexual conduct to refute physical or scientific evidence, such as the victim's virginity, the origin of semen found, the presence of disease or pregnancy, or the source of injuries (Anderson, 2002; Flowe, et al., 2007). Some states also admit evidence of the alleged victim's prior sexual conduct when the defendant argues that the alleged victim consented to an act of prostitution or that the alleged victim had made an unsubstantiated charge

of rape in the past (Anderson, 2002; Flowe, et al., 2007). Finally, many states also include a "catch-all" exception to admit prior sexual conduct evidence when the trial judge agrees that it is "relevant" (Anderson, 2002; Flowe, et al., 2007). Such an exception seemingly undermines the purpose underlying the existence of rape shield laws, but a failure to allow a defendant to introduce relevant, probative evidence at trial can violate the accused's Sixth Amendment rights to a fair trial and/or to conduct a reasonable cross-examination (Price, 1996).

Although rape shield laws have routinely been upheld, defendants continually challenge their constitutionality as applied to their particular cases if they operate in such a manner as to interfere with a defendant's constitutional rights. Box 5.1 presents the case of *Williams v. State* (1997), in which such a challenge was unsuccessful. But the unique facts of any particular case might tip the balance in favor of the admissibility of evidence that is typically excluded by rape shield laws. For example, in *State v. DeLawder* (1975), the defendant was convicted of rape after he was not permitted to show the alleged victim had a reason to fabricate her charge of rape against him. He contended that at the time of the alleged rape, the victim had engaged in sexual activity with her boyfriend and had gotten pregnant. She feared telling her family of this, so she claimed she was raped by the defendant and was pregnant as a result of the rape. His conviction was reversed on appeal on the grounds that excluding evidence of the alleged victim's past sexual history with her boyfriend denied the defendant a fair trial.

At times, courts struggle with what constitutes "prior sexual conduct." Does flirtatious behavior count? In *State v. Garron* (2003), the New Jersey Supreme Court held that the victim's prior flirtations with the defendant should not have been excluded at his rape trial. These flirting incidents included suggestive comments, such as, "if your wife's never around let me know . . . I can take care of you" (p. 249). Witnesses of the flirtation testified that they had seen the victim brush her breasts against the accused on one occasion and had seen her grab the defendant's buttocks and give him a passionate kiss on another occasion. But a significant amount of time had passed from these events to the date of the alleged rape; some had occurred months earlier while others had occurred over six years in the past. Nonetheless, the high court ruled that all the excluded testimony of past flirting—most especially those that could be offered by the victim's former co-workers who were "disinterested witnesses"—should have been admitted into evidence to assure a fair trial for the defendant (p. 259). Critics of the decision pointed out that past flirting—even flirting that indicates a willingness to have sex at one point in time—does not indicate a willingness to have at any point (Johnston, 2005, p. 198; for additional critiques of rape shield laws, see Capers, 2013).

Box 5.1 HOW RAPE SHIELD LAWS OPERATE—*WILLIAMS V. STATE*

During the early morning hours on January 9, 1993, the victim was working as a topless dancer at a nightclub in downtown Indianapolis. When she finished work at approximately 2:45 a.m., she walked out into the parking lot and asked two strangers, defendants Williams and Edmondson, for a ride home. The two men agreed and she got into the car. Williams did not drive the car directly to the victim's home. Instead, he told her that "they had to make a stop." He drove into an alley behind a different club where Edmondson exited the car. The victim then attempted to run away, but Edmondson grabbed her arms and pulled her into the back seat of the car. As the victim struggled with Edmondson in the car, Williams drove to a public park and stopped the car in a dark area of its parking lot. The two then ordered the victim to engage in sexual acts with them. Edmondson pulled a gun out of his pocket and placed it on the arm rest of the front seat. He then removed the victim's shoe and sock and pulled her right pants leg off. The victim managed to grab the gun, open the car door, and run away. As she ran, she fired the gun behind her and, although she apparently had never fired a weapon before, shot Edmondson in the jaw. Williams and Edmondson were subsequently arrested and charged with several counts, including attempted rape.

At their joint trial, the state sought to exclude evidence of the victim's sexual history pursuant to Indiana's rape shield rule, as well as her history of cocaine use. The trial court granted these motions, but sustained a defense objection with regard to the victim's drug use on the day of the incident. Later during the trial, both Williams and Edmondson testified that the victim wanted the men to locate some cocaine for her and when they could not find any, the men agreed to give her money in exchange for sex. Williams requested that the trial court lift its proscription on testimony as to prior drug use because the victim's prior drug use and alleged acts of prostitution were now at issue. The trial court denied the request. Defense counsel then made an offer of proof that a friend of the victim would testify that the victim had previously committed acts of prostitution in exchange for money or cocaine. This evidence was also excluded by the trial court and the two defendants were convicted.

The Supreme Court of Indiana affirmed the trial court's exclusion of the victim's drug history because there was no evidence of the victim's inability to recall the incident as a function of prior drug use; thus, the court deemed that evidence irrelevant. The court also affirmed and excluded the friend's testimony that, on prior occasions, the victim had committed acts of prostitution in exchange for money or cocaine, finding such evidence was barred by the state rape shield law. When balancing the purpose of protecting the victim from the disclosure of potentially embarrassing and prejudicial evidence concerning past sexual history against the accused's right to present relevant evidence, the court reasoned that:

> The allegation of prostitution does not affect this calculus. . . . It is intolerable to suggest that because the victim is a prostitute, she automatically is assumed to have consented with anyone at any time . . . . In this case, there was no restriction on the ability of the defense to present evidence of the incident. The trial court allowed both defendants to testify that the victim agreed to perform sex acts in exchange for money. The jury was informed through testimony of the defendants and the victim that the victim voluntarily entered a car with two strange men at 2 a.m. in the parking lot of a topless club.
>
> Whatever her initial motive, at some point, according to her, she clearly communicated her lack of consent to proceeding as the men directed. Whatever her sexual past, if the jury accepted that story, conviction was proper. As noted above, the excluded evidence did not serve to explain any physical evidence. Under these facts, exclusion of the victim's past sexual experiences with third persons is not unconstitutional. We do not agree that an alleged prostitute's prior sexual history becomes fair game simply by reason of her prior actions, or that there is any constitutional right to present evidence of past consensual sex with other persons for that reason alone. Accordingly, [the defendants'] constitutional right to present witnesses was not violated.
>
> (pp. 200–202)

1. Indiana's rape shield law did not bar the evidence of the alleged victim's drug use; another rule of evidence was used to exclude it based upon the court's determination that it was not relevant to the issue of rape. The defendants argued, though, that her history of drug use was relevant to her credibility and was relevant to her ability to recall facts and details accurately. Do you agree with the court's ruling on this issue? Why or why not?
2. The court reasoned that in rape cases, the status of the victim as being a prostitute is not relevant to determining the issue of consent. Do you feel the fact that an alleged victim is a prostitute has any relevance on the issue of consent in a rape prosecution? (Consider the ongoing debates presented in Chapter 7 regarding choice and coercion in prostitution.) When such an allegation is made, should the jury be informed that the accuser is a prostitute, or would such information unfairly bias the jury? Explain your answers.

Drugs, Alcohol, and Sexual Assault

Women who are sexually assaulted after the voluntary or involuntary ingestion of some substance, either alcohol or other drugs, or a combination of both, are victims of **drug-facilitated sexual assault (DFSA)**. The commonly yet inappropriately designated term "date rape" is inaccurately applied in the context of describing these types of sexual assaults. In 2010, Lawyer, Resnick, Bakanic, Burkett, and Kilpatrick studied 314 college-student females and discovered that "29.6% (n = 93) of the respondents reported a drug-related sexual assault or rape; 5.4% (n = 17) reported a forcible sexual assault or rape" (p. 453). The most commonly administered drugs used in DFSA are flunitrazepam (Rohypnol), gamma-hydroxybutyrate acid

(GHB), Ketamine, and MDMA (Ecstasy) (Pope & Shouldice, 2012). Rohypnol rapidly induces sleep and is an extremely potent sedative and muscle relaxant; it is ten times more potent than Valium. "These effects, coupled with anterograde amnesia and relatively low cost, make Rohypnol very attractive for a potential perpetrator" (Pope & Shouldice, 2012, p. 81).

According to the Drug Enforcement Administration (DEA), GHB has no currently accepted medical use and is produced illegally in clandestine labs as well as in the home. GHB also causes anterograde amnesia (no memory of what occurred after ingestion), and in sufficient doses can cause sedation, hypersuggestibility, and unconsciousness, thus rendering those who ingest it vulnerable to sexual assault.

Ketamine is a commonly used anesthetic that reduces pain and causes amnesia and in sufficiently high doses can be used to facilitate DFSA incidents. "Higher doses may lead to a feeling of detachment from the surroundings and floating" (Pope & Shouldice, 2012, p. 82). It is undetectable through the use of commonly available testing technologies.

MDMA (methylene-dioxy-methamphetamine) does not cause anterograde amnesia and it is a stimulant drug and not a depressant, yet it has nonetheless been linked to use in DFSA incidents. Some researchers argue that MDMA induces an elevated sense of empathy, sensuality, disinhibition, and heightened sexuality that can lead to DFSA incidents, although there is some level of disagreement with these conclusions (Eiden, et al., 2013).

The consumption of alcohol is commonly linked to incidents of DFSA; Lawyer and colleagues (2010) discovered that the "majority of drug-related assaults (96.1%) involved alcohol consumption prior to assault" and that "[v]oluntary incapacitation preceded 84.6% of drug-related assaults and involuntary incapacitation preceded 15.4% of drug-

related assaults" (p. 453). These authors also draw the distinction between DFSA "as unwanted sexual contact or intercourse that occurs when the victim is too intoxicated or high from alcohol and/or a drug given to her without her consent or against her wishes," and **incapacitated sexual assault** as unwanted sexual contact or intercourse that occurs after the victim is too intoxicated or high to provide consent after voluntarily consuming alcohol and/or drugs (Lawyer, et al., 2010, p. 454).

In 2014, the U.S. Bureau of Justice Statistics released a report on the incidence of rape and sexual assault among college-age females that found "for both college students and nonstudents, the offender was known to the victim in about 80% of rape and sexual assault victimizations" (Sinozich & Langton, 2014, p. 1). These were well-known or casual acquaintances in 50% of the DFSA incidents involving college students; 24% were intimate partners of the victims. In about 20% of DFSA incidents, the women reported that they were assaulted by strangers (Sinozich & Langton, 2014, p. 7).

Sexual assault and rape can and do occur within the context of a dating or courtship relationship and rape and sexual assault can and do also occur in a marriage. Miethe, McCorkle, & Listwan (2006) identify five different types of date or courtship rape:

1. Beginning date rapes occur during a couple's first few dates.
2. Early date rapes happen after several dates but before a couple has established sexual ground rules.
3. Relational rape takes place after these sexual ground rules have been established (and violated).
4. Rapes within sexually active couples are the fourth type of sexual assault.
5. Rapes within formerly sexually active couples who previously had consensual sexual relationships.

(Miethe, et al., 2006, p. 54)

These authors go on to identify a number of risk factors present for date or courtship rape to occur:

1. The male initiating and maintaining a dominant role during a date.
2. Miscommunication of verbal and other cues regarding sex.
3. Heavy alcohol or other drug use.
4. "Parking" (or being in an isolated place).
5. Male acceptance of traditional sex roles, interpersonal violence, adversarial attitudes regarding relationships, and rape myths.
6. Perpetrators' previous experiences as victims of childhood or adolescent sexual abuse.

(Miethe, et al., 2006, p. 54)

POST-PENETRATION RAPE[2]

As described previously, the crime of rape specifically targeted a nonconsensual, vaginal penetration by a penis for hundreds of years. And although modern criminal law has expanded the definition of rape to include other types of sexual penetrations, the common law and contemporary rape statutes shared a requirement of a lack of consent *at the time of initial penetration*, at least until fairly recently (Fradella & Brown, 2005). But several cases over the past 25 years or so have highlighted a problem with which the common law did not deal: is the crime of rape committed if someone consents to a sexual penetration and then, later, withdraws consent, yet the sexual act continues? In 1991, a law student, Amy McLellan, termed this phenomenon **post-penetration rape**.

Very few courts had confronted the question of post-penetration before the 1990s. And only a few more have addressed the issue since then. Some of these courts held that "the presence or absence of consent at the moment of initial penetration appears to be the crucial point in the crime of rape" (*People v. Vela*, 1985, p. 242; see also *State v. Way*, 1979). These courts typically reasoned that,

the essence of the crime of rape is the outrage to the person and feelings of the female resulting from the nonconsensual violation of her womanhood. When a female willingly consents to an act of sexual intercourse, the penetration by the male cannot constitute a violation of her womanhood nor cause outrage to her person and feelings. If she withdraws consent during the act of sexual intercourse and the male forcibly continues the act without interruption, the female may certainly feel outrage because of the force applied or because the male ignores her wishes, but the sense of outrage to her person and feelings could hardly be of the same magnitude as that resulting from an initial nonconsensual violation of her womanhood. It would seem, therefore, that the essential guilt of rape . . . is lacking in the withdrawn consent scenario.

(*People v. Vela*, 1985, p. 243)

In 2000, a different appellate court in California came to the opposite conclusion than the *Vela* court (*People v. Roundtree*, 2000). The *Roundtree* court sided with the decisions of only five other appellate courts in the United States that had recognized post-penetration rape between 1985 and 2000 (*McGill v. State*, 2001; *State v. Crims*, 1995; *State v. Jones*, 1994; *State v. Robinson*, 1985; *State v. Siering*, 1994). With the split of authority within California between the *Vela* and *Roundtree* decisions, the California Supreme Court agreed to hear *In re John Z.* (2003). That case drew both legal and scholarly attention to the issue of post-penetration rape, although not necessarily in a manner that resolved matters with any logical clarity.

A juvenile court found John Z. responsible for rape. The California Court of Appeals and the California Supreme Court affirmed John Z.'s conviction. Both courts held that rape is committed when a victim withdraws her consent during an act of sexual intercourse but is forced to complete the act. Although commentators praised the court for clarifying the law in this manner (e.g., Fradella & Brown,

2005), the unique facts of the case caused many to question whether John Z.'s conviction was appropriate.

First, the victim's withdrawal of consent in the *John Z.* case was ambiguous; she never told John Z. to stop. Instead, she repeatedly told John Z. that she needed to go home. According to the dissent, this statement clearly established that she felt she was in a hurry to get home "so [her] mom wouldn't suspect anything" (p. 190, Brown, J., dissenting). John Z. could have mistaken her words as a demand for speed in completing the sex act. Such a mistake of fact would have been both honest and reasonable given the ambiguity of the victim's words.

Second, even if it were assumed, for the sake of argument, that the victim had clearly withdrawn her consent to continuing the sex act, it does not appear that all of the requirements for the crime of rape were proved under California law. The relevant provision of the California Penal Code defines rape as a sexual intercourse "accomplished against a person's will by means of force, violence, duress, menace, or fear of immediate and unlawful bodily injury on the person or another" [CAL. PENAL CODE § 261(a)(2), 2003]. But as the dissent points out, "[I]t is not clear that Laura was forcibly compelled to continue. All we know is that John Z. did not instantly respond to her statement that she needed to go home. He requested additional time. He did not demand it. Nor did he threaten any consequences if Laura did not comply" (p. 190, Brown, J., dissenting).

Finally, the rather unique facts of the case called into doubt whether John Z. was physically incapable of forcing Laura to have sex with him against her will. During intercourse, there was approximately a five-minute interval during which Laura claimed she had withdrawn consent; yet, during this time John was on his back while Laura was on top of him in the female superior position. Laura testified that she "kept . . . pulling up, trying to sit up to get it out . . . [a]nd he grabbed my hips and pushed me back down" (p. 190, Brown, J., dissenting). But it is undisputed that one of John's hands was in a cast. And since there was no bruising or other evidence of John having used force with this other arm—indeed, Laura conceded on cross-examination that John did not use his good hand in a manner that she even experienced any pressure from it, there is reasonable doubt that Laura's continued intercourse with John was anything other than consensual.

Bad Public Policy?

Critics argued that the *John Z.* opinion created unnecessary ambiguities in the law of rape (Fradella & Brown, 2005). First and foremost, the majority in *John Z.* relied heavily on the fact that John did not immediately discontinue sexual intercourse after Laura had requested him to stop. As previously discussed, though, it is unclear whether the victim ever even made such a request and, even if she did, whether John could have reasonably interpreted her ambiguous statements as demands for speed. But assume the victim had said something much clearer—something like, "Stop. I don't want to have sex with you anymore." Had John then forced her to continue intercourse, a post-penetration rape would have unquestionably occurred. But the defense in *John Z.* insisted that even under such circumstances, the court should grant a "reasonable amount of time" for the male to withdraw (*In re John Z.*, 2003, p. 187). This argument was also raised in the one post-penetration rape case from Kansas reported after *John Z.* was decided (*State v. Bunyard*, 2003). Unfortunately, both cases failed to reject this proposition for the absurdity it is. Rather, the court in *John Z.* concluded that the defendant exceeded this standard by continuing intercourse for four to five minutes after Laura told him she "needed to go home" (*In re John Z.*, 2003, p. 187). The *Bunyard* case, citing *John Z.*, similarly concluded that the defendant's actions failed the "reasonableness test" because he continued intercourse for five to ten minutes after the victim had clearly communicated her withdrawal of consent (*State v. Bunyard*, 2003, p. 754). In so holding, the courts in *John Z.* and *Bunyard* created an ambiguity in the law concerning post-penetration rape.

How long after a clearly communicated request to cease sexual intercourse is it reasonable for a male to continue? Consider the dissent's comments on this point in the *John Z.* case:

> The majority relies heavily on John Z.'s failure to desist immediately. But, it does not tell us how soon would have been soon enough. Ten seconds? Thirty? A minute? Is persistence the same thing as force? And even if we conclude persistence should be criminalized in this situation, should the penalty be the same as for forcible rape? Such questions seem inextricably tied to the question of whether a reasonable person would know that the statement "I need to go home" should be interpreted as a demand to stop. Under these circumstances, can the withdrawal of consent serve as a proxy for both compulsion and wrongful intent?
>
> (*In re John Z.*, 2003, p. 190, Brown, J., dissenting)

Neither the majority in *John Z.* nor *Bunyard* answer any of these questions raised by the dissenting justice. Several commentators have answered the "reasonable time" question by stating that there should be no "reasonable period of time" for someone engaged in intercourse to complete the act once the other party withdraws consent; rather, sex should cease immediately upon a clearly communicated request to do so (see Fradella & Brown, 2005; Palmer, 2004).

Fradella and Brown (2005) contend that the *John Z.* court's rationale is dangerous (see also Palmer, 2004). They argue that the court should have held, in no uncertain terms, that the law requires a participant in a sexual intercourse to stop immediately upon being clearly requested to do so. They argue that it is absurd to suggest that some base animalistic instinct renders men incapable of conforming their conduct to the requirement of law. Suggesting otherwise would be quite paradoxical: it seems contradictory that an objective standard—in this instance, that of "reasonable time"—would be used to judge the behavior of someone under the control of a primal urge that rendered him unreasonable in the first place.

The primal urge theory espoused by the defense in *John Z.* is also factually suspect. For example, suppose an 18-year-old male engages in sexual intercourse with his girlfriend in her parents' house. Both he and his girlfriend believe they have the house to themselves. If one of her parents unexpectedly enters the room, would it not be a certainty that the sex act would end immediately? Surely, the girl's parent would not think it necessary that he be provided with a reasonable period of time to finish the sex act. Thus, the court should have dismissed the primal urge theory outright. By failing to do so, they have invited future defendants in a post-penetration rape case to argue the alleged reasonability of the period of time he took to withdraw upon a request to do so. And that has, in fact, occurred. In *State v. Flynn* (2011), for example, an appellate court in Kansas applying *Bunyard* reversed a rape conviction and remanded the case for a new trial on the grounds that the jury in the case should have been provided with a special jury instruction that the defendant had a reasonable amount of time to end the intercourse after the alleged victim withdrew her consent. But more reasonable minds prevailed when the *Flynn* case was appealed to the Supreme Court of Kansas. The court overturned *Bunyard* and reversed the holding of the intermediate appellate court (*State v. Flynn*, 2014). Thus, criminal liability for post-penetration rape in Kansas includes "nonconsensual sexual intercourse occurring when a person communicates his or her withdrawal of consent after penetration and the other person continues the intercourse through compulsion" (p. 431). A person is no longer "entitled to a reasonable time in which to act after consent is withdrawn and communicated to the defendant" (p. 431).

The Current Status of Post-Penetration Rape

Since 2003, three more states have recognized post-penetration rape. In *State v. Baby* (2008), a Maryland court held that "the withdrawal of consent negates initial consent for the purposes of sexual offense crimes and, when coupled with the other elements, may constitute the crime of rape" (p. 493). Since, however, Maryland law requires both the use or threatened use of force and some resistance on behalf of the victim in order to sustain a rape conviction, the *Baby* court limited its holding to "the continuation of vaginal intercourse by force or the threat of force" after consent has been withdrawn (p. 486). Still, the case is noteworthy because unlike in *John Z.*, the court did not adopt a "reasonable time to withdraw" approach. Rather, the court upheld a rape conviction against a defendant who continued for "about five or so seconds" after consent was withdrawn (p. 467). But, as with *John Z.*, the question of initial consent was more than ambiguous.

Massachusetts law also requires the use or threatened use of force to sustain a rape conviction (*Commonwealth v. Lopez*, 2001). Thus, the court in *Commonwealth v. Enimpah* (2012) upheld the conviction of a defendant who, after a clearly communicated withdrawn consent, forcibly continued to have intercourse with a victim despite her pleas for him to stop and her efforts to get away from him.

The most interesting development since *In re John Z.* concerns the State of Illinois—the only U.S. state to have adopted explicit legislation criminalizing post-penetration rape as a less serious crime than rape.[3] Thus, as suggested by various legal commentators (Duncan, 2007; Fradella & Brown, 2005;

McLellan, 1991), the statute recognizes a qualitative difference between a traditional rape in which no consent existed at the time of initial penetration and post-penetration rape in which initial consent is subsequently withdrawn. Courts applying this statute have been more diligent than the *John Z.* court was when analyzing ambiguous behavior. For instance, in *People v. Denbo* (2007), the defendant inserted a hand into the victim's vagina during otherwise consensual sexual relations. The victim pushed the defendant twice—harder the second time—intending to signify that she no longer consented to the sexual penetration. The defendant removed her hand from the victim's vagina on the second push. She was subsequently arrested, tried, and convicted for post-penetration rape for failing to stop the penetration after the first push. In reserving her conviction, the appeals court reasoned that even looking at the evidence in a light most favorable to the prosecution, "no rational trier of fact could find, beyond a reasonable doubt, that the first push objectively communicated to defendant a withdrawal of consent" (p. 358).

SEXUAL ASSAULT/SEXUAL BATTERY STATUTES

Roughly half of U.S. states continue to use the term "rape," while the other half have statutes that "replaced the word 'rape' with terms such as 'sexual assault,' 'sexual battery,' or 'criminal sexual conduct'" (Robinson, 2008). As explained earlier, such changes in terminology were made with two primary goals in mind: (1) "to shift the focus from the sexual aspect to the violent aspect of the crime"; and (2) to facilitate changes in the pervasive prejudices, preconceptions, and stigma concerning rape (pp. 573–574; see also Bryden & Lengnick, 1997). As the following sections illustrate, most of these statutes differentiate various degrees of sexual assault or battery.

Rape as Sexual Assault or Sexual Battery

The modern definition of rape—sexual penetration without the consent of the victim—is often, but not always, subsumed in the definition of sexual assault in the first degree (e.g., ALASKA STAT. ANN. § 11.41.410(a)(1), 2015). In contrast, some jurisdictions differentiate between degrees of sexual assault or sexual battery not based on the amount of force used. Colorado (COLO. REV. STAT. ANN. § 18–3–402, Supp. 2014), for example, defines sexual assault as a fourth-degree felony when accomplished through coercion without the use or threatened use of physical force or violence. The crime is elevated to a third-degree felony if physical force or violence is used or threatened, or if a drug or intoxicant was used to induce submission. And sexual assault climbs to a second-degree felony under three circumstances: if the attacked was aided or abetted by one or more other people; if the victim suffers serious bodily injury; or if a deadly weapon was used.

Other U.S. jurisdictions have retained the word "rape" while differentiating degrees of it depending on the amount of force that was used. Consider the structure of Tennessee's criminal code:

§ 39–13–502. Aggravated rape

(a) Aggravated rape is unlawful sexual penetration of a victim by the defendant or the defendant by a victim accompanied by any of the following circumstances:

(1) Force or coercion is used to accomplish the act and the defendant is armed with a weapon or any article used or fashioned in a manner to lead the victim reasonably to believe it to be a weapon;

(2) The defendant causes bodily injury to the victim;

(3) The defendant is aided or abetted by one (1) or more other persons; and

(A) Force or coercion is used to accomplish the act; or

(B) The defendant knows or has reason to know that the victim is mentally defective, mentally incapacitated or physically helpless.

§ 39–13–503. Rape

(a) Rape is unlawful sexual penetration of a victim by the defendant or of the defendant by a victim accompanied by any of the following circumstances:

(1) Force or coercion is used to accomplish the act;

(2) The sexual penetration is accomplished without the consent of the victim and the defendant knows or has reason to know at the time of the penetration that the victim did not consent;

(3) The defendant knows or has reason to know that the victim is mentally defective, mentally incapacitated or physically helpless; or

(4) The sexual penetration is accomplished by fraud.

Lesser Forms of Sexual Assault or Sexual Battery

In contrast to nonconsensual penetrations, sexual assault or battery in the second degree is often defined as the "sexual contact with another person without the consent of that person" (e.g., ALASKA STAT. ANN. § 11.41.420(a)(1), 2014). For the purposes of second-degree sexual assault or battery statutes, "sexual contact" is typically defined broadly to include an "offensive touching" of an "intimate part" or "private part" of the body. The following provision in the U.S. Uniform Code of Military Justice is typical of such statutes:

touching, or causing another person to touch, either directly or through the clothing, the genitalia, anus, groin, breast, inner thigh, or buttocks of any person, with an intent to abuse, humiliate, or degrade any person; or any touching, or causing another person to touch, either directly or through the clothing, any body part of any person, if done with an intent to arouse or gratify the sexual desire of any person.

(UNIFORM CODE MIL. JUST. art. 120(g)(2), 2012)

It should be noted that statutory language in sexual assault laws, like the one quoted above from military law, is troublesome. As discussed later in this chapter, the etiology of rape is complicated. Some explanations for sexual assaults theorize they are crimes of violence and power, not ones committed for sexual gratification (Mitchell, Angelone, Kohlberger, & Hirschman, 2009). Proving the requisite statutory intent of sexual gratification may, therefore, be problematic in some cases (see Wencelblat, 2004).

Some states have avoided the problem of motivation by enacting laws that omit any such references. Arizona, for example, has a statute that criminalizes *sexual abuse*, defined as "intentionally or knowingly engaging in sexual contact [defined as any direct or indirect touching, fondling, or manipulating of any part of the genitals, anus, or female breast by any part of the body or by any object or causing a person to engage in such contact] with any person who is fifteen or more years of age without consent of that person or with any person who is under fifteen years of age if the sexual contact involves only the female breast" (ARIZ. REV. STAT. §§ 13–1401 & 13–1404, 2014).

Child Molestation

In many states, the age of the victim may be the factor that determines the degree of a rape or sexual assault, regardless of the level of force or violence that may have been used or threatened. South Dakota, for example, defines rape in the first degree only as those perpetrated against a child less than 13 years of age and designates second-, third-, and fourth-degree rapes based on other factors, such as whether an intoxicant was used or whether the victim was physically or mentally incapacitated such that valid consent could not be given (S.D. STAT. § 22–22–1, 2014). Some states, though, have created a special statutory offense that punishes a sexual act on a child under a particular age more severely than other forms of sexual assault. For example, Arizona's **statutory rape** (see Chapter 6) law punishes non-forcible sexual intercourse with a minor between the ages of 15 and 18 as a class 6 felony (ARIZ. REV. STAT. § 13–1405, 2014). In contrast, sexual intercourse or sexual contact with a minor under the age of 15 is considered **child molestation**, and is punished as a class 2 felony (ARIZ. REV. STAT. §§ 13–1405 & 13–1410, 2014). Moreover, the state provides a sentencing enhancement if a sexual penetration occurred and the child victim was 12 years of age or younger such that a sentence of life imprisonment is mandated with the possibility of parole until after the perpetrator has served at least 35 years of the sentence (ARIZ. REV. STAT. § 13–705, 2014).

Still other states incorporate other factors, in addition to a child's age, to grade child molestation. Indiana, for example, differentiates degrees of child molestation based on the level of force used, whether a deadly weapon was used, whether the child sustained serious bodily injury, and whether an intoxicant was administered (IND. CODE § 35–42–4–3, 2014).

CHARACTERISTICS OF RAPISTS

At first blush, rapists appear to share similar sociodemographic characteristics as others in the general prison population: "Generally, rapists tend to be characterized by low socioeconomic status, poor education, and employment in unskilled professions (Gannon, Collie, Ward, & Thakker, 2008). Their criminal histories, however, share much more in common with other violent offenders than property offenders or child molesters (Simon, 2000; Smallbone, Wheaton, & Hourigan, 2003). In fact, "rape is often part of a wider array of generalist offending that includes prolific histories of violence" (Gannon, et al., 2008, p. 984).

Unsurprisingly, developmental assessments of rapists reveal personal histories marred by poor family relationships, neglect, as well as physical and sexual abuse (e.g., Haapasalo & Kankkonen, 1997). These childhood experiences are thought to impair their ability to interact appropriately in adult intimate relationships, especially insofar as rapists often display a dismissive, hostile, and suspicious interpersonal style (Ward, Hudson, & Marshall, 1996). It should be noted, however, that similar developmental deficits are not unique to rapists or the larger class of sex offenders; indeed, these childhood experiences characterize a range of criminal offenders (in addition to adults who do not commit crimes in spite of such developmental disadvantages).

Personality assessments of rapists (such as those using the Minnesota Multiphasic Personality Inventory [MMPI]) "show marked heterogeneity on . . . profiles and scale scores, making it impossible to detect reliable between-group differences" (Gannon, et al., 2008, p. 98). In other words, there does not appear to be a "typical" rapist profile with regard to general psychopathology (Marshall & Hall, 1995). Rapists, however, tend to exhibit higher levels of psychopathic traits (the hallmark of which is a lack of empathy) compared with other types of sex offenders (Abracen, Looman, Di Fazio, Kelly, & Stirpe, 2006; Hare, 1999). There is also some neurobiological research suggesting that rapists exhibit "impaired neurological functioning in the form of a structural deficit, neurotransmitter or hormonal imbalance, or other neural

functioning impairment" (Gannon, et al., 2008, p. 986). But these nascent findings stem from small samples or from studies using techniques that have not been sufficiently validated. Future neurobiological studies may shed light on whether brain structures or functioning play some role in sexual offending.

THEORETICAL PERSPECTIVES ON THE CAUSES OF SEXUAL ASSAULT

Sexual assault is a controversial subject that becomes even more contentious when the question of *why* people rape is debated (Brownmiller, 1975; Conley, 1986). Recall that William the Conqueror changed the punishment for rape to castration and the loss of the rapist's eyes because it was assumed that uncontrolled lust was the cause of rape (Bracton, 1968/c. 1250–1260; MacFarlane, 1993). Although the approach of the Saxons and Normans acknowledged a woman's ability—indeed right—to refuse to engage in sexual intercourse, it had the paradoxical effect of making the offense difficult to prove since consent vitiated the crime. Thus, trials at English common law often centered around not whether a woman affirmatively consented to sex, but rather whether sexual intercourse occurred "forcibly and against her will" (18 Eliz. I, c. 7, as cited in Conley, 1986; see also MacFarlane, 1993). Even when the circumstances of a sexual assault clearly established that force was used to overcome the victim's will, English common law made numerous exceptions to the usual rules of criminal liability for rape. Consider, as previously discussed, that the law specifically exempted spousal rape (Conley, 1986; Fradella & Brown, 2005). Similarly, the law categorically presumed males under the age of 15 could not commit a rape. And even when a young man was of age to be convicted of the crime, judges made allowances for male sexual impulses and "youthful exuberance" such that rapes by teenage boys "were rarely perceived as criminal" and, even when prosecuted, judges often imposed lenient sentences (Conley, 1986, p. 533). The view that male sexual aggression was "normal, healthy, and inevitable" (Conley, 1986, p. 532) remained the primary motivational theory for rape until psychology became established as a significant social science.

Until the 1970s, most explanations for rape were grounded in theories of psychology. After World War II, psychologists began combining rapists in a diverse group with other sex offenders, which also included homosexuals, pedophiles, and people with a range of paraphilias (Bryden & Grier, 2011). Unsurprisingly, most psychological explanations of the day were rooted in Freudian psychoanalytic theory (Check & Malamuth, 1985).

Psychoanalytic Explanations

Early Approaches

Sigmund Freud (1925/1959) asserted that, on the whole, women were masochistic. One of Freud's ardent followers, Helene Deutsch (1944), used this premise to posit that women could satisfy their self-destructive impulses—which she characterized as "painful longing[s]" and "wish[es] to suffer for the lover" (often unknown)—either through rape fantasies or through actual sexual victimization (p. 225). Karen Horney (1926) similarly argued that women's masochism led to rape fantasies and, sometimes, actual rapes. But she viewed the masochism as a psychological response to cultural norms concerning men's aggression. Put another way, women internalized men's fantasies about women in ways that led most women to accept masochistic tendencies as being "normal." These views on the etiology of rape strongly contributed to the persistent rape myth that the crime is victim-precipitated by advocating the proposition that women desired to be sexually violated.

These profoundly influential psychoanalytic thinkers did not discuss rape as a real occurrence carried out by men. Instead, they focused on the role of rape fantasies in the lives of ideally masochistic women. In this sense, actual physical rape was the natural outcome of the female's pain-inflicting psyche.

(Albin, 1977, p. 424)

In addition to perpetuating the notion that a woman was responsible for her own rape, psychoanalytic theory also contributed to another myth concerning widespread false accusations of rape. Separate and apart from concerns of purposefully falsified claims of rape, psychodynamic theory discounted rape as a real act of violence by explaining "sexual delusions of rape" as a function of neurotic fantasy or full-blown hysteria/"gynecological pathology" (Gavey, 2005, p. 22). Deutsch's (1944) work, in particular, maintained that women's psychosexual delusions of rape were so common that "even the most experienced judges are misled in trials of innocent men accused of rape by hysterical women" (p. 254).

Later Approaches: Rapists as Mental Patients

In contrast to early psychoanalysts who generally ignored perpetrators in their etiological explanations for rape, subsequent psychoanalytic theorists assumed that rapists suffered from some form of mental illness as conceptualized at the time. Regardless of whether rapists were "perverted," "psychopathic," or "neurotic," "aberrations in the psychosexual development of men were typically viewed as the 'cause' of these criminal tendencies" (Albin, 1977, pp. 424–425). For example, research on sex offenders conducted during the 1950s reported that they exhibited higher levels of castration anxiety than other types of criminal offenders (e.g., Hammer & Glueck, 1957; Lindler, 1953). Freud (1938/2005) had used the term *castration anxiety* to describe situations in which a little boy believed that young girls were once boys whose fathers had castrated them. Most males grow out of this belief, but psychoanalytic theorists posited that rapists did not. Thus, in an effort to overcome the fear of castration, rapists prove their "masculinity" by sexually dominating their victims, often while placing them in degrading roles (Bromberg, 1948; Toner, 1977). Notably, Bromberg's (1948) analysis, though not valid by contemporary standards, paved the way for a causal explanation of rape rooted in hostility towards women, rather than just a function of repressed sexual desire (Bryden & Grier, 2011; Cowan, 2000).

Hammer and Glueck (1957) opined that rape served as a means for proving masculinity in an effort to overcome "enduring underlying feelings of phallic inadequacy" (Albin, 1977, p. 425). Indeed, a plethora of studies, many of which were methodologically unsound, reported that sex offenders "were fearful, inadequate, sensitive, shy, impulsive, irresponsible, expected too much sex, lacked social skills, had a self-concept confused in psychosexual areas of identification, and were unable to evaluate the consequences of their own behavior" (Albin, 1977, p. 426). Some theorists hypothesized that rapists' lack of confidence in dealing with women or crippling doubt that women are not attracted to them led to rape as a means of overcoming anxieties about their masculinity (Mathis, 1972; Rada, 1978). Given the foundational beliefs of Freudian psychodynamic theory, most psychologists of the time explained such psychological dysfunction as a function of bad parenting techniques—especially inconsistent and overbearing mothers or overly harsh, inaccessible fathers (McCaldon, 1967; Rada, 1978)—that interfered with a child's ability to successfully navigate the stages of psychosexual development.

Rapists were often viewed as being less sick than other types of sex offenders because most rapists studied were adult men who engaged in forcible genital intercourse against an adult woman. As such, they were viewed as less sexually abnormal than offenders who committed acts of oral sex, anal sex, bestiality, or offenses against children (see Rada, 1978). In fact, many psychologists in the 1950s basically viewed rapists as essentially "normal" men who needed to learn to control their sexual urges (Check & Malamuth, 1985; Malamuth, 1984; Rada, 1978). Nonetheless, the notion that rape is a product of mental illness remains a pervasive myth today (Cowan, 2000; Cowan & Campbell, 1995; Cowan & Quinton, 1997).

The Fall of Psychoanalysis

In spite of the powerful influence of psychodynamic theories through the 1950s and 1960s, the latter half of the twentieth century ushered in a new era in which scientific objectivity was redefined. Case studies, especially those involving subjective clinical judgments, fell into comparative disrepute to more "objective" methods of inquiry, such as survey research and experiments—especially those based on randomized controls. Indeed, replicability—research that was *reproducible*—increasingly came to be a prerequisite for any knowledge being considered *science* (Popper, 1959). This movement contributed to the overwhelming demise of psychoanalytic theory as a credible, scientific approach to the study of human behavior.

With regard to sex offenders in particular, critics pointed out that psychoanalytic concepts had not only failed to garner empirical support—especially with regard to a lack of reliability in constructs (see Eysenck & Wilson, 1973)—but also had not produced prevention or treatment programs that worked (e.g., Lanyon, 1991; Scully & Marolla, 1985). In contrast, competing paradigms of psychology, notably those rooted in behavioral theories, gained influence as a function of their testability through replicable experiments.

Behavioral Theories

The behavioral paradigm holds as its central assumption that all human actions and mental processes are determined by our life experiences, more specifically the result of learning. People behave in response to both encountered stimuli and experienced rewards and punishments that together act to shape the individual (Bandura, 1986; Bandura & Walters, 1963; Pavlov, 1897; Skinner, 1948; Thorndike, 1905; Watson, 1913, 1930).

Early behavioral explanations for rape posited that situational "rape cues" produced sexual arousal (Abel, Blanchard, Becker, & Djenderedjian, 1978; Amir, 1971). As with psychodynamic explanations, these behavioral etiologies focused on sexual stimuli, rather than on the important role aggression plays in rape. Subsequent behavioral theorists integrated aggression into how rape cues function (e.g., Barbaree & Marshall, 1991; Malamuth, 1986), but few of these approaches abandoned sexual arousal as a partial explanation for rape. Thus, these explanations are subject to some of the same criticisms as psychodynamic explanations for emphasizing rape as a sexual act, rather than a violent one (see Baron & Straus, 1987; Brownmiller, 1975), especially those behavioral models that explain rape as a function of actions by victims that decrease rapists' prosocial inhibitions (such as wearing provocative clothing, using alcohol or other drugs, being alone at night, and so on).

Most behavioral explanations for rape are subject to most of the same criticism that may be levied at the entirety of the behavioral paradigm, ranging from assuming the human mind is *tabula rasa* (a blank slate) to being reductionist insofar as it explains behavior as a function of learning in environment through reinforcement without regard to physiological, biochemical, or cognitive processes—especially free will. But some of the more complex, integrated biosocial behavioral views of rape attempt to overcome these shortcomings by taking both environmental and biological situational determinants into account. For example, Marshall and Barbaree (1984, 1990) developed a theory of rape that draws on biological, psychological, sociocultural, and situational factors, especially as they relate to adolescent development. The theory posits that "some males will have a strong tendency to rape because they did not acquire proper socialization, either because of innately unusual levels of testosterone, or because of parental mismanagement, or a combination of both these factors" (Marshall & Barbaree, 1984, p. 70). Moreover, the theory recognizes mediating factors:

> The acquisition of constraints is not an all or nothing procedure; the degree of control over the tendency to rape will range along a continuum from virtually no control to complete control, with most men probably falling somewhere near the middle. Of course a tendency to rape (or to control rape) is just that: a tendency, which will require certain environmental events for its release. Therefore, the strength of the acquired constraints will determine the strength of the situational disinhibitors required to release the tendency to sexually aggress. Available evidence indicates that momentary anger (particularly toward a woman), or intoxication, both disinhibit the arousal of nonrapists to forced sex, as do prior sexual arousal, permissive instructions indicating that rape is an acceptable act, and negative attitudes toward women.

(Marshall & Barbaree, 1984, p. 70)

Notably, the three mediating factors Marshall and Barbaree (1984) specified take into consideration a range of societal norms upon which feminist scholars first expounded. For example, double standards regarding "yes meaning no" (Burt, 1980; Marshall & Barbaree, 1984) and social views that value hypermasculinity both contribute to social justifications for rape. Similarly, pornography—especially if violent or degrading—visually reinforces notions that "sex involves coercion and violence," thereby contributing to beliefs that disinhibit rape (Marshall & Barbaree, 1984, p. 71; for more information on pornography, see Chapter 8). Although this theory has garnered significant empirical support (e.g., Smallbone & Dadds, 1998), especially as it has been refined (see Marshall & Marshall, 2000), like all other theories of sexual aggression, it has some gaps, especially in its ability to explain "why some offenders begin to display sexually aggressive behaviors later in adulthood or the existence of offenders who appear to have high (yet unstable) self-esteem" (Gannon, et al., 2008. p. 994).

Feminist Theory

During and beyond the 1970s, feminists began to develop new theories of rape, in contrast to the psychologists that came before them (Check & Malamuth, 1985). The feminist perspective for the causes of rape stemmed from a patriarchal framework (Baron & Straus, 1987; Check & Malamuth, 1985; Vandermassen, 2011). Rape, therefore, is a function of social control in patriarchal societies that exists as a way for men to assert power over women (Baron & Straus, 1987; Brownmiller, 1975; Herman, 1990). In contrast to earlier explanations on why rape occurs, feminists began listening to their victims' stories, rather than from the rapist's perspective. Similar to their anti-war and pro-civil rights counterparts, feminists began to point at social structural injustices in the system as a basis for patriarchal violence. Thus, from the feminist standpoint, rape is *power motivated*, not sexually motivated (Griffin, 1971).

Stranger Rape

The early stereotypes regarding rapists conceived them strictly as strangers to the victims. This, coupled with the lack of punishment and/or lack of recognition that acquaintances, amongst others, can rape as well, allowed feminist scholarship to criticize

the then popular idea that only strangers raped (Frieze, 1983; Russell, 1975). Feminists took issue with the fact that non-stranger rape was not considered "real" rape and this idea was further exacerbated by cultural norms and gender roles (Griffin, 1971; Russell, 1975). Directing attention to the patriarchy embedded in society at the time, Griffin (1971) noted that the "same culture which expects aggression from the male expects passivity from the female" (p. 27).

Some research even hypothesized a direct, inverse relationship between gender equality and the number of rape incidences in a given community (Baron & Straus, 1987). In this way, feminists were able to argue that our culture encourages rape or, at the very least, creates an easily targetable and perfect victim who is likely to concede to the demands of the rapist (Check & Malamuth, 1985). In fact, consistent with this viewpoint, Baron and Straus (1987) found that in a society with a higher ratio of males to females, rape reflects the "low valuation of women and contributes to their subordinate position" in the social (and sexual) stratification structure (p. 481).

Acquaintance Rape

When women reported an acquaintance rape, they were often blamed and otherwise treated poorly by authorities (Russell, 1975). Victim blaming increased under circumstances in which the victim's conduct or clothing suggested "unladylike" conduct, especially for women who were violating traditional norms of sexual chastity, which were expected of them at the time (Russell, 1975). This posed significant problems for women who reported an acquaintance rape during the late 1960s and 1970s, as premarital sex was still considered promiscuous behavior at that time (Laumann, Gagnon, Michael, & Michaels, 1994).

Feminist scholars such as Brownmiller (1975) and Griffin (1971) essentially rejected the notion of victim precipitation in sexual assault cases. Brownmiller (1975), citing the National Commission on the Causes and Prevention of Violence, noted that claims of precipitant behavior included an invitation of sexual relations vis-à-vis language and gestures (which, as previously discussed, formed the foundations of many "rape cues" in behavioral explanations for rape). Brownmiller debunked this line of thought by equating White supremacy to patriarchy. Specifically, she argued that both racists and rapists seek to maintain their supremacy over the groups they seek to dominate. Using this parallel, Brownmiller argued that any victim precipitation or sexual suggestion is irrelevant because the overall cause of sexual assault is nonsexual and only seeks to subjugate women. Indeed, research today typically relegated the notion of female precipitation as nothing more than a rape myth, however widespread it may be, that blames the victim and absolves the rapist (Cowan, 2000; Cowan & Campbell, 1995). By demonstrating that rapists' motives are grounded in patriarchal aggression and power, Brownmiller argued that there are no reasons to forgive rape offenders in the same ways that patients with serious mental illness might be excused. In so arguing, she and other feminist scholars (Griffin, 1971; Russell, 1975) undercut the approach taken by many psychoanalytic and behavioral psychologists. Indeed, feminist theories of rape have "robustly challenged etiological notions based on offender psychopathology" (Polaschek, Ward, & Hudson, 1997, p. 126).

Proving Masculinity

Recall that some psychoanalytic theorists adopted a "proving masculinity" hypothesis as a possible cause of rape. Some feminist theorists agree, at least to some extent (Baron & Straus, 1987; Brownmiller, 1975; Frieze, 1983). According to this view, outward displays of physical aggression toward and dominance of women are ways for men to express their masculinity (Baron & Straus, 1987).

Baron and Straus (1987) note that this assertion of masculinity may be exacerbated in societies that lack appropriate avenues for economic success.

Although incarcerated rapists have been shown to be overly concerned with their masculinity, others appear to be so hypermasculine that claims they rape in an attempt to prove their own masculinity seem questionable. Nonetheless, being hypermasculine and feeling the need to prove masculinity are not necessarily mutually exclusive. One may possess overtly masculine traits, yet still feel the urge to exhibit these traits in particular contexts. Consider that in a study about the causes of marital rape, Frieze (1983) found that nearly 80% of the wives in the sample attributed their rapes to their husbands trying to prove their masculinity. Frieze (1983) notes that sexual assault is most likely to occur in marriages wrought with violence in many other ways, not just rape. Some have noted that the men in this group of aggressors are typically those who are aroused by violent sexual stimuli (McKibbin, et al., 2008).

The "proving masculinity" hypothesis plays a particularly influential role in explaining gang rape (Baker, 1997; Sanday, 2007). Kanin (1967) indicated that acceptance among one's peer group may influence not only aspirations for sexual gratification, but also physical attempts to attain sex. College men who felt pressured or compelled by their peers to engage in sex more use coercive techniques (Felson, 2002; Kanin, 1967; Sanday, 2007).

Patriarchal Images and Values

Feminist theories of rape as a form of male social control are generally interested in social attitudes that contribute to acceptance of rape myths that breed rape acceptance (Burt, 1980). It should come as no surprise, then, that proponents of the feminist views of rape tend to be ardent critics of media since media perpetuate patriarchal views, generally, and rape myths, in particular, that reinforce violence against women (see Burt, 1980; Check & Malamuth, 1985). But feminist theory struggles to explain why such a culture causes some men to commit acts of sexual aggression and not others. Indeed, most feminist scholarship on rape does not deal with any of the individual factors that might account for rape. Similarly, feminist theory offers little in explaining three types of rape that seem to defy patriarchal explanations: women who rape men, same-sex rapes (especially those committed by women against other women), and rape of women by men who are "oblivious to the harm caused to women following rape and do not appear to use rape to consciously intimidate women" (Gannon, et al., 2008, p. 989; see also Scully, 1990).

Evolutionary Theories

Some scholars have advanced evolutionary theories to explain rape (e.g., Ellis, 1991; Quinsey & Lalumière, 1995; Thornhill & Palmer, 2000). Evolutionary psychologists believe that both our minds and bodies are shaped by evolutionary principles such as natural selection. Thus, certain behaviors adapt over time, including those that foster reproductive success (Malamuth, 1998; McKibbin, Shackelford, Goetz, & Starratt, 2008; Thornhill & Palmer, 2000). Evolutionary theorists posit that men's reproductive success is predicated on having many sexual encounters that allow them to spread their genes; in contrast, it is far less advantageous for women to be sexually promiscuous because they have a finite number of eggs and pregnancy cycles during fertile years, as well as maternal demands on them for nursing and caring for their offspring (Goetz, et al., 2008; McKibbin, et al., 2008; Vandermassen, 2011). As a result, it is hypothesized that women evolved to be much more selective about their choice in sexual partners than men are (Malamuth, 1998; Thornhill & Palmer, 2000).

Extrapolating from these premises, evolutionary theorists argue that men are predisposed to spread their genes as efficiently as possible via frequent sex, even if doing so involves aggression or coercion (McKibbin, et al., 2008). Supporters of this viewpoint often cite examples in the animal kingdom where forced copulation is commonplace (e.g., Galdikas, 2005). In other words, this theoretical explanation suggests an evolutionary adaptation that drives some men to be sexually violent, especially toward women in their late teens through late 20s since that represents peak female fertility (McKibbin, et al., 2008).

> [S]ome theorists hypothesize that rape is the product of a direct adaptation that occurred in our ancestral past (e.g., male ancestors who raped were highly successful, reproductively, as a direct outcome of forced copulation) while others hypothesize that rape is the product of an indirect adaptation . . . it was promiscuous sex that was directly selected for and forced copulation is simply an associated by-product of this selection process.
>
> (Gannon, et al., 2008, p. 990)

Few, if any, evolutionary theorists assert this argument as one of *biological determinism*. In other words, this approach does not posit that men are biologically programmed to commit rape. Rather, it is that the inherited drive to reproduce by force is one of many sexual strategies men use (largely unconsciously), "when they are unable to secure sexual access through social status, or attractiveness, when the relative costs of raping appear low, and when men are in a position of ultimate physical control over the woman" (Gannon, et al., 2008, p. 990; see also Thornhill & Palmer, 2000). For example, strands of such evolutionary psychological theory are evident in the so-called *mate deprivation model*, which posits that men with limited or no access to sex are more likely to engage in coercive sex (Felson, 2002; Malamuth, 1998; Thornhill & Palmer, 2000). This construct, however, has mixed empirical support. Consider that Kanin

(1967) found that among the college men in his sample, those who had the *most* sexual experience were the same men who more often sexually coerced women. Similarly, other studies have found that men with overall higher sexual aspirations were more likely to engage in sexual intercourse on a regular basis—whether or not the sex was coercive (Felson, 2002; Frieze, 1983; Kanin, 1967; Lussier, Leclerc, Cale, & Proulx, 2007). McKibbin and colleagues (2008) argue that sexually experienced men who commit rapes tend to be domineering, aggressive, and exhibit high levels of self-esteem—many of the same qualities psychopaths exhibit.

Sex drive aside, research suggests that rejection by women or a feeling of deep distrust of women because of previously hurt feelings, may be a cause of rape (e.g., Kanin, 1965). Malamuth (1998) grounded this theoretical explanation in an evolutionary perspective, claiming that frequent rejections by women or delay of sexual access may interfere with a man's mating patterns. Stermac and Quinsey (1986) noted that the interpersonal functioning of rapists may be a cause of several variables simultaneously interacting, which do not facilitate submissive sexual rejections by women, and hence lead men to seek sex through force.

Rape as Violence vs. Rape as Sex

Comparisons of the psychological and feminist explanations for rape highlight an important question concerning the etiology of rape: is it crime motivated by anger, power, dominance, and violence, or is it a crime primarily driven by abnormal sexual desire? The question does not have a definitive answer, even within a particular theoretical paradigm. Consider that some feminist scholars agree with Brownmiller (1975) that rape is "a conscious process of intimidation by which all men keep all women in a state of fear" (p. 6), while other feminist scholars argue that sexual motives explain some aspects of rape (e.g.,

Baker, 1997; Muehlenhard, Danoff-Burg, & Powch, 1996).

Felson (2002) argued that the sexual component of rape is inherent to the act much like robbers typically have a financial motivation to steal. The sex cannot be fully separated from the rape. A study by Jewkes, Sikweyiya, Morrell, and Dunkle (2014) of rape in South Africa lends support to this notion. They reported that the most common motivation for rapists—nearly two thirds of the sample—was a sense of sexual excitement or entitlement, the combination of which expresses both sexual motivations and intentions to dominate. This combination is rarely discussed in the literature. Raping out of anger or to instill punishment was a motivation for more than half of the non-stranger rapes (e.g., girlfriends or wives). Additionally, the authors specify that a portion of their sample raped young girls specifically to punish a third party close to the girl, such as her mother (Jewkes, et al., 2014). Caution must be taken to parallel these findings with that of the United States since rape in South Africa is far more prevalent and perpetrated by a wider range of men (Jewkes, et al., 2014). Nonetheless, this research adds credence to the proposition that the etiology of rape is unlikely to be an "either/or" proposition. Thus, many contemporary theories of rape rely on multi-factor models that integrate bio-psycho-social variables.

Select Multi-Factor Theories

At first blush, the feminist and evolutionary approaches to explaining rape seem diametrically opposed. But Smuts (1995) argued that the two viewpoints can be reconciled if feminists accepted that the coercive function of sexual psychology is part of an evolutionary process, rather than being society specific. In other words, "the drive to gain control of female sexuality, and the willingness to use force or violence to that end (i.e., rape) evolved because it contributed to male reproductive success" which is males' ultimate evolutionary goal (Vandermassen, 2011, p. 738).

Confluence Model of Sexual Aggression

Neil Malamuth and colleagues developed the *confluence model of sexual aggression* (Malamuth, 1986, 1996; Malamuth, Heavey, & Linz, 1993), which draws on both the feminist and evolutionary perspectives. In short, this theory posits that evolutionary forces explain men's "*propensity* for sexual aggression," but that genetic predisposition is mediated by a "confluence of risk factors . . . that motivate, disinhibit, and provide the context for sexual offending to occur (Gannon, et al., 2008, p. 992). These risk factors incorporate constructs from both psychological and feminist perspectives, including hostility toward women, acceptance of rape myths and rape-supportive attitudes, and sexual excitement by violent sexual scripts. Although this theory has garnered significant empirical support (e.g., Lim & Howard, 1998; Wheeler, George, & Dhal, 2002), there are some concerns about the theory having been developed and validated primarily by using samples of male college students, a population which may differ from incarcerated rapists. Moreover, the model is complex and the relationship between the risk factors and the pathways to offending are not always clear (see Gannon, et al., 2008).

Quadripartite Model of Sexual Aggression

The *Quadripartite Model of Sexual Aggression* (Hall & Hirschman, 1991) draws upon a variety of perspectives. The theory attempts to explain rape as a function of four factors, all of which contribute to sexual violence, but any one of which may prove to be more dominant in a particular offender: "physiological sexual arousal, cognitive distortions, affective dyscontrol, and personality traits that arise from developmental experience" (Gannon, et al., 2008, p. 994).

First, for the *physiologically driven rapist* rape is most likely to occur in the presence of sexual fantasies or sexually aggressive stimuli such as pornography. . . . For the *cognitively driven rapist*, rape is more likely to occur in situations where offense relevant stimuli mitigate or justify rape (i.e., if the victim is wearing "provocative" dress), or where legal and societal condemnation are perceived to be low (i.e., date or acquaintance rape). . . . For the *affectively driven rapist*, sexual aggression is hypothesized to be the product of unplanned, impulsive behavior, that may involve violence and be precipitated by anger (towards others or women). Such offenders are characterized by severe emotion regulation difficulties (i.e., either total regulation failure or maladaptive regulatory attempts). . . . Finally, for the *personality driven rapist*, rape is hypothesized to be the product of long-term and pervasive personality problems that stem from developmental difficulties (i.e., poor childhood attachments). Individuals characterized by this factor are likely to offend violently, show adult attachment problems, and be generally antisocial in nature.

(Gannon, et al., 2008, p. 994)

Although this theory explains the wide range of differences across rapists, it has been criticized for lacking "conceptual clarity (or explanatory depth) concerning core constructs within the model (e.g., cognition, affect, inhibitory thresholds) and how they develop" (Gannon, et al., 2008, p. 994). Perhaps that explains why it has received little attention for validation.

Integrated Theory of Sexual Offending

Ward and colleagues (Ward & Beech, 2005; Ward, Polaschek, & Beech, 2006) developed the *Integrated Theory of Sexual Offending* (ITSO) by combining validated portions of other theories into a single, unified model. They argued that

sexual aggression stems from three main causal factors which interact continuously and dynamically. These are: *biological factors* (i.e., genetics, evolutionary factors and brain development), proximal and distal *ecological niche factors* (i.e., the physical, social, and cultural environment and personal context), and three fundamental neuropsychological systems associated with assorted brain structures: (a) *motivation–motion*, (b) *action–control*, and (c) *memory–perception*. (Gannon, et al., 2008, p. 995)

The strength of this theory is that it integrates bio-psycho-social factors into a model, which recognizes that the factors are dynamic, not static. Moreover, because the theory incorporates ecological factors, it addresses Sanday's (1981) important findings on the role that sociocultural forces play in rape-prone societies (see the opening case study at the start of this chapter). On the other hand, this theory is quite complex and has yet to be empirically validated as a unified theory.

Contemporary Rapists Typologies

The growing emphasis on empiricism during the 1970s contributed to the rise of *diagnostic psychiatry* (see Houts, 2000; Mayes & Horwitz, 2005). Until the 1970s, psychology and psychiatry did not concern themselves too much with specific diagnoses.

> Dynamic explanations posited that symptoms were symbolic manifestations that only became meaningful through exploring the personal history of each individual. The focus of analytic explanations and treatment, therefore, was the total personality and life experiences of the person that provided the context for the interpretation of symptoms. . . . [Diagnostic manuals, therefore,] made little effort to provide elaborate classification schemes, because overt symptoms did not reveal disease entities but disguised underlying conflicts that could not be expressed directly.
>
> (Mayes & Horwitz, 2005, pp. 249–250)

Psychology's evolution as an empirical science and the corresponding rise of diagnostic psychiatry led to a system for classifying mental disorders not on etiology, but rather on observable symptoms that could be used to promote reliable clinical diagnoses (Fradella, 2008). Perhaps as a function of the classification movement, Neo-Freudians emphasized that they did not advocate any link between specific diagnostic categories and specific types of sex offenders. Indeed, they conceded that sex offenders rarely exhibited classic symptoms of severe mental illness, but rather evidenced a wide range of "character neuroses, character disorders, and more severe borderline and psychotic states" (Cohen, Garofalo, Boucher, & Seghorn, 1971, as cited in Albin, 1977, p. 430). Nonetheless, they developed their own classification system for rapists, albeit one rooted in psychodynamics: "those with aggressive aims, sexual aims, and sex-aggression diffusion" (Albin, 1977, p. 430). But as classification systems grew in popularity (and as psychoanalytic theory continued its decline), social psychology and its focus on empirical methods grew to be the dominant lens through which rapists, motivations were analyzed. This led to the development of various typologies of rapists that merely describe common motivational traits among an otherwise heterogeneous group of offenders. This typology includes *anger rapists*, *power rapists*, *sadistic rapists*, and *opportunistic rapists* (see Groth, 1979; Knight & Prentky, 1990). Rapist typologies are explored in detail in Chapter 12 in the context of possible treatments for rapists.

Rape as a Bias Crime?

Bias crimes (sometimes called "hate crimes") are typically thought of as criminal offenses that are committed against victims because of their race, ethnicity, religion, gender, sexual orientation, or disability (Gerstenfeld, 2011; Lawrence, 1999). The U.S. federal government and nearly all U.S. states have enacted some form of bias-crime laws; some criminalize bias-motivated violence and intimidation while others provide sentencing enhancements for traditional crimes that are motivated by bias (Bell, 2007; Gerstenfeld, 2011). In *Wisconsin v. Mitchell* (1993), the U.S. Supreme Court upheld the authority of states to create statutes aimed at the act of intentional selection of a victim because of his or her status as a member of a protected class.

Some have advocated that rape should be treated as a bias crime because offenders target women on the basis of their gender in ways that "subordinate women as a group" (Pendo, 1994, p. 172; see also Brownmiller, 1975; Carney, 2001; Miller & Biele, 1993; Rothschild, 1993). But McPhail and DiNitto (2005) documented that prosecutors of both sexes find this suggestion puzzling and unnecessary. Pokorak (2006) pointed out that such a paradigm presented theoretical and reporting problems for same-sex rapes. And Bryden and Grier (2011, p. 262) have argued that defining rape as a bias crime is "unwise" because they

> see no reason to impose longer rape sentences on men who seem to have an animus against women than on those who are "merely" selfish, callous, and aggressive sexual (and often general) predators. In either case, the rapist may cause great anguish to his victim and other women; whether potential victims fear him will be determined by what he did, where he did it, and how much publicity it received—not by his motive.
>
> (p. 263)

Jones (1999) similarly questioned whether rape should be conceptualized as a bias crime since "biobehavioral theories suggest that view may be overly optimistic" (p. 924). One commentator, though, offered an interesting middle ground. Perhaps as a function of these arguments or perhaps as function of resistance to change, rape is rarely prosecuted as a bias crime unless the victim is also a member of another protected class. For example, the gang rape of a woman by two men and two teenage boys who taunted her during the attack for being a lesbian was charged as a hate crime ("California: 4 arrests in gang rape called a hate crime," 2009).

Male Victims of Rape

Nearly all of the scholarly research on rape concerns female victimization by men. Sexual assaults of men have long been assumed to be uncommon outside of very limited circumstances that were explained as a function of asserting anger, power, and dominance, rather than an act primarily driven by sexual gratification motives (Bullock & Beckson, 2011; Groth & Burgess, 1980; King, 1990). Indeed, rapes of men by other men, especially by heterosexual men, have "long been recognized as a means used by conquering soldiers to humiliate opponents, as a feature of sexual torture or aggression [including as a form of gay-bashing against victims perceived to be homosexual], or as a sexual outlet in institutions where heterosexual activity is impossible" such as in prisons, certain military settings, and one-sex boarding schools (King, 1990, p. 1345).

> "Often, male survivors may be less likely to identify what happened to them as abuse or assault because of the general notion that men always want sex," says Jennifer Marsh, the vice president for Victim Services at RAINN, an anti-sexual violence organization.
>
> "Males have the added burden of facing a society that doesn't believe rape can happen to them . . . at all," says psychotherapist Elizabeth Donovan.
>
> She says gender roles dictate that males are expected to be strong and self-reliant—men are viewed as those who seek sexual conquests instead of those who "fend them off."
>
> (LeTrent, 2013, paras. 15–17)

Non-heterosexual men report higher rates of sexual victimization than heterosexual men (Peterson, Voller, Polusny, & Murdoch, 2011; Walters, Chen, & Breiding, 2013), further adding stigma to men who come forward as victims of sexual aggression.

Just as rape myths permeate societal views concerning female victims of sexual assault, rape myths also plague both social and legal understanding of male victimization of rape, including

> that men in the civilian community simply cannot be victims of sexual assault; that the incidence of sexual assault of males is so rare as not to merit attention; that male victims are more responsible for their assault than female victims; and that male victims are more likely to be homosexual and therefore actually wanted the assault. Complicating these misperceptions is the status and meaning of erectile and ejaculatory behavior in men and the erroneous assumption that, when present, these physiological occurrences signify consent by the victim.
>
> (Bullock & Beckson, 2011, p. 200)

Relatively recently, research began to document that male sexual victimization is not nearly as uncommon as once presumed. Indeed, as rape laws evolved, and in the wake of the Federal Bureau of Investigation changing its definition of rape to be gender neutral in 2012 for the purposes of gathering official crime statistics, researchers began to gather reliable data about male victims of rape. Approximately 1.7% of U.S. men have been raped, a figure that translates to approximately 2 million victims (Breiding, et al., 2014). But these statistics only include men who were forcibly penetrated, either orally or anally. Another 6.7% of men (about 7.6 million) reported that they had been "made to penetrate" another person either vaginally, orally, or anally. And another 5.8% of U.S. men experience some form of nonphysical sexual coercion in their lifetimes, such as being

pressured into sex via threats to end a relationship or spread rumors (Breiding, et al., 2014). And contrary to common misconception, many of these sexual victimizations are committed by women.

Male sexual assault victimizations appear to be more prevalent during high school and college. Indeed, young men between the ages of 16 and 24 have the highest rates of sexual victimization (Walker, Archer, & Davies, 2005). Anderson and Aymami (1993) reported that 15.9% of the male college students in their sample ($n = 128$) indicated at least one instance of nonconsensual sexual contact following a woman's use of physical force. Struckman-Johnson (1988) similarly found that 16% of the college males in her sample experienced forced sexual intercourse while on a date, a rate almost as high as the 22% she reported from the college women in her study. French, Tilghman, and Malebranche (2014) reported an 18% rate of physical coercion and a 7% rate of substance coercion. And Tewksbury and Mustaine (2001) found that nearly a quarter of male undergraduate students at 12 universities had been the victim of some form of sexual assault. These studies report much higher incidence levels of sexual assault than some other studies that found a high rate of sexually coercive behaviors on college campuses, but much lower levels of sexual assaults involving threats, force, or impairment due to alcohol or other drugs (see Larimer, Lydum, Anderson, & Turner, 1999; O'Sullivan, Byers, & Finkelman, 1998). Most research suggests a male victimization rate of between 2.8% and 5.2% for both rapes and attempted rapes—levels that are much higher than in the general population (see Krahé, Scheinberger-Olwig, & Bieneck, 2003; Spitzberg, 1999). Notably, because upwards of 95% of these sexual assaults against adolescent and emerging adult males are committed by women (French, et al., 2014), most of the traditional theoretical explanations for why men sexually assault women or other men cannot explain this phenomenon.

Only one—a desire for sexual gratification—appears applicable.

Sexual Assault in the Military

Between 1991 and 2003, a number of high-profile sexual assault cover-up scandals rocked several braches of the U.S. armed forces (Turchik & Wilson, 2010). Since then, the media, Congress, and the military itself have focused on the fact that the military presents a unique environment for both the commission of sexual assaults and responding to them.

According to the U.S. Department of Defense ([DOD], 2013), U.S. service members reported 3,374 sexual assaults in fiscal year 2012. There is little doubt that this number vastly underrepresents the true scope of the problem in the military (Government Accountability Office, 2008; Turchik & Wilson, 2010). In fact, that same DOD (2013) report contained the results of a survey that led the DOD to conclude that only 34% of military women and 24% of military men reported their sexual victimization that year, leading the DOD to estimate the actual number of sexual assaults in the military that year likely approximated 26,000. It should be noted that that number includes "unwanted sexual contacts" that do not necessarily involve a penetration, such as nonconsensual groping. Additionally, the sampling methodology and statistical techniques used in the DOD survey have been criticized (e.g., Burris, in press). Nonetheless, it is clear that sexual assault in the military is a serious problem, one that appears to occur at much higher rates—perhaps as high as double the rate that exists among civilians.

Sexual assaults in the military pose special problems for a number of reasons. First and foremost, military culture emphasizes violence, deindividualization, hypermasculinity, and a language that is often highly sexualized (Hunter, 2007; Turchik & Wilson, 2010). Second, both military laws and culture have long perpetuated a culture of victim-blaming and acceptance of rape myths (Hunter, 2007; Service Women's Action Network [SWAN], n.d.). Third, and perhaps most importantly, the structure of the Uniform Code of Military Justice places charging decisions in the hands of commanding officers who lack any significant legal training or expertise. These officers have the power to decide which sexual assault cases to investigate and bring to courts-martial, resulting in a structure that builds-in conflicts-of-interest, rather than vesting charging decisions in the sound discretion of legally trained, independent prosecutors outside the chain of command. Worse yet, commanders have the legal authority to overturn convictions. Collectively, these quirks of military law have perpetuated a lack of accountability by preventing survivors from reporting incidents to their commanding officers and by preventing perpetrators from being properly disciplined (Hunter, 2007; SWAN, n.d.; Turchik & Wilson, 2010). Finally, "service members are prevented from bringing lawsuits against members of the military who either perpetrated these crimes against them or may have mishandled their cases" (SWAN, n.d., para. 2).

The psychological effects of sexual victimization are discussed in Chapter 13. For now, however, it should be noted that in addition to the traditional and well-documented effects of depression, substance abuse, sexual dysfunction, shame, and post-traumatic stress (Turchik & Wilson, 2010), there are also special concerns about male-on-male sexual assaults in the military. Unlike in civilian life, more than half of sexual assault victims in the military are men (DOD, 2013; Penn, 2014). Turchik and Wilson (2010) reported that "one problem that may be unique for men is confusion concerning sexual identity, masculinity, and sexual orientation after an assault, especially if the perpetrator is a man," and that "homosexual victims may . . . feel that the assault was a punishment for being gay, whereas heterosexual victims may feel confused about sexuality and masculinity, especially if their body sexually responded during the assault" (p. 269; see also Penn, 2014).

Reports of sexual assaults rose to over 5,061 in fiscal year 2013, a more than 50% increase (Crawford, 2014). The military argued that the increase in reporting rate demonstrates that their efforts to encourage victims to come forward have been partially successful. U.S. Senator Kirsten Gillibrand (D-NY) has led efforts to have Congress change the way that sex crimes are reported and prosecuted in the military. As of the writing of this book, however, such efforts have proven unsuccessful.

CONCLUSION

Bryden and Grier (2011) concluded their study of the "real motives for rape" by acknowledging that there seem to be many motives for rape. Indeed, given the heterogeneity of rapists, it is logical to deduce that multiple causal factors motivate sexual violence. As scientists continue to study the etiology of rape with more advanced methodologies, perhaps new empirical evidence will help shed light on why people rape. For now, as Bryden and Grier (2011) stated, perhaps even the most plausible of motivational approaches is not as important as "reaching sound conclusions about public policies" (p. 278). Clearly, laws criminalizing sexual assaults still require modification to achieve their public policy aims.

FURTHER READING

Brownmiller, S. (1993). *Against our will: Men, women, and rape* (rev. ed.). New York, NY: Fawcett/Ballantine. (Original work published 1975.)

Buchwald, E., Fletcher, P., & Roth, M. (Eds.). (2005). *Transforming a rape culture* (2nd ed.). Minneapolis, MN: Milkweed.

Estrich, S. (1988). *Real rape* (reprint ed.). Cambridge, MA: Harvard University Press.

Reddington, F. P., & Kreisel, B. W. (2009). *Sexual assault: The victims, the perpetrators, and the criminal justice system* (2nd ed.). Durham, NC: Carolina Academic Press.

Spohn, C. C., & Tellis, K. (2013). *Policing and prosecuting sexual assault: Inside the criminal justice system*. Boulder, CO: Lynne Rienner.

Warshaw, R. (1994). *I never call it rape: The Ms. Report on recognizing, fighting, and surviving date and acquaintance rape*. New York, NY: HarperCollins.

GLOSSARY

Child molestation: A form of sexual assault committed against a child below a certain age. That age is usually set between 12 and 14 since such ages correspond to the onset of puberty, thereby differentiating the offense from statutory rapes (against post-pubescent adolescents) and various degrees of sexual assaults/sexual batteries against victims over the age of consent for sex.

Drug-facilitated sexual assault (DFSA): The term used to describe the situation when a victim is sexually assaulted after the involuntary ingestion of some substance, either alcohol or other drugs, or a combination of both.

Incapacitated sexual assault: Any unwanted sexual contact or intercourse that occurs after the victim has voluntarily consumed alcohol or other drugs such that the victim is too intoxicated or high to provide effective legal consent to engage in sexual activity.

Post-penetration rape: A form of sexual assault that occurs when someone initially consents to a sexual penetration, but subsequently withdraws consent, yet the sexual act continues contrary to the victim's wishes that the sex activity stop.

Rape: At common law, the crime of rape was defined as "the unlawful carnal knowledge of a woman by a man not her husband, without her effective consent." The common-law definition of rape required a vaginal penetration by a penis. Today, most rape laws define the crime as the "penetration, no matter how slight, of the vagina or anus with any body part or object, or oral penetration by a sex organ of another person, without the consent of the victim." In about half of all U.S. jurisdictions, rape has been renamed as *sexual assault* in the first degree.

Rape shield laws: The term given to rules of evidence that prohibit (or significantly limit) the introduction of any evidence concerning the past sexual conduct of an alleged sexual assault victim.

Sexual assault/sexual battery: In jurisdictions that use this nomenclature, sexual assaults or sexual batteries are usually graded offenses. In the first degree, these offenses generally mirror the modern definition of the crime of *rape*. In the second degree, these offenses involve non-penetrative forms of sexual contact with another person without the consent of that person.

Statutory rape: Nonforcible sex between a legally consenting adult and a minor whose youth renders him or her unable to grant legal consent to engage in sex.

NOTES

1   Portions of this section of the chapter are taken from Fradella, H. F., & Brown, K. (2005). Withdrawal of consent post-penetration: Redefining the law of rape. *Criminal Law Bulletin, 41*(1), 3–23. Used with the gracious permission of West/Thompson Reuters and the *Criminal Law Bulletin.*

2   Portions of this section of the chapter are taken from Fradella, H. F., & Brown, K. (2005). Withdrawal of consent post-penetration: Redefining the law of rape. *Criminal Law Bulletin, 41*(1), 3–23. Used with the gracious permission of West/Thompson Reuters and the *Criminal Law Bulletin.*

3   "A person who initially consents to sexual penetration or sexual conduct is not deemed to have consented to any sexual penetration or sexual conduct that occurs after he or she withdraws consent during the course of that sexual penetration or sexual conduct" (720 ILL. COMP. STAT. § 11–1.70[c], 2015).

REFERENCES

720 ILL. COMP. STAT. § 11–1.70(c) (2015).

Abel, G. G., Blanchard, E. B., Becker, J. V., & Djenderedjian, A. (1978). Differentiating sexual aggressives with penile measures. *Criminal Justice and Behavior, 5*, 315–332.

Abracen, J., Looman, J., Di Fazio, R., Kelly, T., & Stirpe, T. (2006). Patterns of attachment and alcohol abuse in sexual and violent nonsexual offenders. *Journal of Sexual Aggression, 12*, 19–30.

ALASKA STATUTES ANNOTATED §§ 11.41.410(a)(1), 11.41.420(a)(1) (2015).

Albin, R. S. (1977). Psychological studies of rape. *Signs, 3*(2), 423–435.

Alexander, D. F. (1995). Twenty years of *Morgan*: A criticism of the subjectivist view of *mens rea* and rape in Great Britain. *Pace International Law Review, 7*, 207–246.

Amir, M. (1971). *Patterns of forcible rape.* Chicago, IL: University of Chicago Press.

Anderson, M. (2002). From chastity requirement to sexuality license: Sexual consent and a new rape shield law. *George Washington Law Review, 70*, 51–165.

Anderson, P. B., & Aymami, R. (1993). Reports of female initiation of sexual contact: Male and female differences. *Archives of Sexual Behavior, 22*(4), 335–343.

ARIZONA REVISED STATUTES §§ 13–705, 13–1401, 13–1404, 13–1405, and 13–1410 (2015).

Artherton, A. C. (2012). "Raped, but not by a rapist": The Arkansas rape statute provides no legal recourse to some victims. *Arkansas Law Review, 65*, 317–341.

Ayres, I., & Baker, K. K. (2005). A separate crime of reckless sex. *University of Chicago Law Review, 72*, 599–666.

Baker, K. K. (1997). Once a rapist? Motivational evidence and relevancy in rape law. *Harvard Law Review, 110*(3), 563–624.

Bandura, A. (1986). *Social foundation of thought and action: A social cognitive theory.* Englewood Cliffs, NJ: Prentice Hall.

Bandura, A., & Walters, R. H. (1963). *Social learning and personality development.* New York, NY: Holt, Rinehart, & Winston.

Barbaree, H. E., & Marshall, W. L. (1991). The role of male sexual arousal in rape: Six models. *Journal of Consulting and Clinical Psychology, 59*(5), 621–630.

Baron, L., & Straus, M. A. (1987). Four theories of rape: A macrosocial analysis. *Social Problems, 34*(5), 467–489.

Bell, J. (2007). Hate thy neighbor: Violent racial exclusion and the persistence of segregation. *Ohio State Journal of Criminal Law, 5*, 47–76.

Berger, R. J., Searles, P., & Neuman, W. L. (1988). The dimensions of rape reform legislation. *Law and Society Review, 22*, 329–353.

Berger, V. (1977). Man's trial, woman's tribulation: Rape cases in the courtroom. *Columbia Law Review, 77*, 1–103.

Blackstone, W. (1979). Of offenses against the persons of individuals. In T. A. Green (Ed.), *Commentaries on the laws of England* (Vol. IV, Ch. XV, pp. 205–219). Chicago, IL: University of Chicago Press. (Original work published 1765–1769.)

Bracton, H. (1968). *De legibus et consuetudinibus Angliae libri quinq* [*Bracton on the laws and customs of England*] (Vol. II, G. E. Woodbine, Ed. & S. E. Thorne, Trans.). Cambridge, MA: Harvard University Press. (Original work published circa 1250–1260.)

Breiding, M. J., Smith, S. G., Basile, K. C., Walters, M. L., Chen, J., & Merrick, M. T. (2014). Prevalence and characteristics of sexual violence, stalking, and intimate partner violence victimization—national intimate partner and sexual violence survey, United States, 2011. *Surveillance Summaries, 63*(SS08), 1–18.

Bromberg, W. (1948). *Crime and the mind: A psychiatric analysis of crime and punishment.* New York, NY: The Macmillan Company.

Brownmiller, S. (1975). *Against our will: Men, women, and rape.* New York, NY: Fawcett/Ballantine.

Bryden, D. P. (2000). Forum on the law of rape: Redefining rape. *Buffalo Criminal Law Review, 3*, 317–512.

Bryden, D. P. & Grier, M. M. (2011). The search for rapists' "real" motives. *Journal of Criminal Law and Criminology, 101*, 171–278.

Bryden, D. P. & Lengnick, S. (1997). Rape in the criminal justice system. *Journal of Criminal Law and Criminology, 87*, 1194–1384.

Bullock, C. M., & Beckson, M. (2011). Male victims of sexual assault: Phenomenology, psychology, physiology. *Journal of the American Academy of Psychiatry and the Law, 39*(2), 197–205.

Burris, M. (in press). Thinking slow about sexual assault in the military. *Buffalo Journal of Gender, Law, and Social Policy, 23*, 21–72.

Burt, M. R. (1980). Cultural myths and supports for rape. *Journal of Personality and Social Psychology, 38*, 217–230.

California: 4 arrests in gang rape called a hate crime. (2009, January 2). *The New York Times* Retrieved from http://www.nytimes.com/2009/01/02/us/02brfs-4ARRESTSINGA_BRF.html

CALIFORNIA PENAL CODE § 261(A)(2) (2003).

Capers, B. (2011). Real rape too. *California Law Review, 99*, 1259–1308.

Capers, B. (2013). Real women, real rape. *UCLA Law Review, 60*, 826–882.

Carney, K. (2001). Rape: The paradigmatic hate crime. *St. John's Law Review, 75*, 315–355.

Charlow, R. (2002). Bad acts in search of a *mens rea*: Anatomy of a rape. *Fordham Law Review, 71*, 263–327.

Check, J. V. P., & Malamuth, N. (1985). An empirical assessment of some feminist hypotheses about rape. *International Journal of Women's Studies, 8*, 414–423.

Cohen, M. L., Garofalo, R., Boucher, R., & Seghorn, T. (1971). The psychology of rapists. *Seminars in Psychiatry, 3*, 307–327.

COLORADO REVISED STATUTES ANNOTATED § 18-3-402 (2014).

Conley, C. A. (1986). Rape and justice in Victorian England. *Victorian Studies, 29*(4), 519–536.

Cowan, G. (2000). Beliefs about the causes of four types of rape. *Sex Roles, 42*(9/10), 807–823.

Cowan, G., & Campbell, R. R. (1995). Rape causal attitudes among adolescents. *The Journal of Sex Research, 32*(2), 145–153.

Cowan, G., & Quinton, W. J. (1997). Cognitive style and attitudinal correlates of the perceived causes of rape scale. *Psychology of Women Quarterly, 21*(2), 227–245.

Crawford, J. (2014, May 1). Reports of military sex assault up sharply. CNN.com. http://www.cnn.com/2014/05/01/politics/military-sex-assault/

Decker, J. F., & Baroni, P. G. (2011). "No" still means "yes": The failure of the "non-consent" reform movement in American rape and sexual assault law. *Journal of Criminal Law & Criminology, 101*, 1081–1169.

Deutsch, H. (1944). *The psychology of women: Motherhood.* New York, NY: Grune & Stratton.

Dressler, J. (2006). *Understanding criminal law* (4th ed.). Newark, NJ: Matthew Bender & Co.

Duncan, M. J. (2007). Sex crimes and sexual miscues: The need for a clearer line between forcible rape and nonconsensual sex. *Wake Forest Law Review, 42*, 1087–1139.

Eiden, C., Cathala, P., Fabresse, N., Galea, Y., Mathieu-Daude, J., Baccino, E., & Peyriere, H. (2013). A case of drug-facilitated sexual assault involving 3,4-methylene-dioxy-methylamphetamine. *Journal of Psychoactive Drugs, 45*(1), 94–97.

Ellis, L. (1991). A synthesized (biosocial) theory of rape. *Journal of Consulting and Clinical Psychology, 59*, 631–642.

Estrich, S. (1986). Rape. *Yale Law Journal, 95*, 1087–1184.

Eysenck, H. J., & Wilson, G.D. (1973). *The experimental study of Freudian theories.* New York, NY: Routledge.

Falk, P. J. (2002). Rape by drugs: A statutory overview and proposals for reform. *Arizona Law Review, 44*, 131–212.

Felson, R. B. (2002). *Violence and gender reexamined.* Washington, DC: American Psychological Association.

Flowe, H. D., Ebbesen, E. B., & Putcha-Bhagavatula, A. (2007). Rape shield laws and sexual behavior evidence: Effects of consent level and women's sexual history on rape allegations. *Law and Human Behavior, 31*, 159–175.

Fradella, H. F. (2008). *Forensic psychology: The use of behavioral sciences in civil and criminal justice* (2nd ed.). Belmont, CA: Wadsworth/Cengage.

Fradella, H. F., & Brown, K. (2005). Withdrawal of consent post-penetration: Redefining the law of rape. *Criminal Law Bulletin, 41*(1), 3–23.

Fradella, H. F., & Brown, K. (2007). The effects of using social scientific rape typologies on juror decisions to convict. *Law and Psychology Review, 31*, 1–19.

French, B. H., Tilghman, J. D., & Malebranche, D. A. (2014, March 17). Sexual coercion context and psychosocial correlates among diverse males. *Psychology of Men & Masculinity.* Advance online publication. http://dx.doi.org/10.1037/a0035915

Freud, S. (1959). Some psychical consequences of the anatomical distinction between the sexes. In J. Stachey (Ed. and Trans.), *Standard edition of the complete psychological works of Sigmund Freud* (Vol. 20, pp. 173–179). London: Hogarth Press. (Original work published 1925.)

Freud, S. (2005). Three contributions to the theory of sex. *Nervous and Mental Disease Monograph Series, 7*, 1–73. (Original work published 1938.)

Frieze, I. H. (1983). Investigating the causes and consequences of marital rape. *Signs: Journal of Women in Culture and Society, 8*(31), 532–553.

Futter, S., & Mebane, Jr., W. R. (2001). The effects of rape law reform on rape case processing. *Berkeley Women's Law Journal, 16*, 72–139.

Galdikas, B. M. F. (2005). Subadult male orangutan sociality and reproductive behavior at Tanjung Putting. *American Journal of Primatology, 8,* 87–99.

Gannon, T. A., Collie, R. M., Ward, T., & Thakker, J. (2008). Rape: Psychopathology, theory, and treatment. *Clinical Psychology Review, 28,* 982–1008.

Gavey, N. (2005). *Just sex? The cultural scaffolding of rape.* New York, NY: Routledge.

Gerstenfeld, P. B. (2011). *Hate crimes: Causes, controls, and controversies.* Thousand Oaks, CA: Sage.

Goetz, A. T., Shackelford, T. K., & Camilleri, J. A. (2008). Proximate and ultimate explanations are required for a comprehensive understanding of partner rape. *Aggression and Violent Behavior, 13*(2), 11–123.

Government Accountability Office. (2008, August 29). DOD's and the Coast Guard's sexual assault prevention and response programs face implementation and oversight challenges. Retrieved from http://www.gao.gov/new.items/d08924.pdf

Griffin, S. (1971, September). Rape: The all-American crime. *Ramparts Magazine,* 26–35.

Groth, A. N. (1979). *Men who rape: The psychology of the offender.* New York, NY: Plenum Press.

Groth N., & Burgess, A. W. (1980). Male rape: Offenders and victims. *American Journal of Psychiatry, 137,* 806–810.

Haapasalo, J., & Kankkonen, M. (1997). Self-reported abuse among sex and violent offenders. *Archives of Sexual Behavior, 26,* 421–431.

Hale, M. (1778). *The history of the pleas of the crown* (vol. 1). London: T. Payne.

Hall, G. C. N., & Hirschman, R. (1991). Toward a theory of sexual aggression: A quadripartite model. *Journal of Consulting and Clinical Psychology, 59,* 662–669

Hammer, E. F., & Glueck, B. C. (1957). Psychodynamic patterns in sex offenders: A four-factor theory. *Psychiatric Quarterly, 31*(14), 325–345.

Hare, R. D. (1999). Psychopathy as a risk factor for violence. *Psychiatric Quarterly, 70,* 181–197.

Hasday, J. E. (2000). Contest and consent: A legal history of marital rape. *California Law Review, 88,* 1373–1505.

Herman, J. L. (1990). Sex offenders: A feminist perspective. In W. L. Marshah, D. R. Laws, & H. E. Barbaree (Eds.), *Handbook of sexual assault: Issues, theories, and treatment of the offender* (pp. 117–193). New York, NY: Plenum.

Horney, J. & Spohn, C. (1991). Rape law reform and instrumental change in six urban jurisdictions. *Law and Society Review, 25,* 117–153.

Horney, K. (1926). The flight from womanhood: The masculinity complex in women as viewed by men and women. *International Journal of Psychoanalysis, 3,* 324–339.

Houts, A. C. (2000). Fifty years of psychiatric nomenclature: Reflections on the 1943 War Department Technical Bulletin, Medical 203. *Journal of Clinical Psychology, 56*(7), 935–967.

Hunter, M. (2007). *Honor betrayed: Sexual abuse in America's military.* Fort Lee, NJ: Barricade Books.

INDIANA CODE § 35-42-4-3 (2015).

Jewkes, R., Sikweyiya, Y., Morrell, R., & Dunkle, K. (2014). Why, when and how men rape: Understanding perpetration in South Africa. *South African Crime Quarterly, 34,* 23–31.

Johnston, J. B. (2005). How the confrontation clause defeated the rape shield statute: Acquaintance rape, the consent defense, and the New Jersey Supreme Court's ruling in *State v. Garron. Southern California Review of Law and Women's Studies, 14,* 197–233.

Jones, O. D. (1999). Sex, culture and the biology of rape: Toward explanation and prevention. *California Law Review, 87,* 827–941.

Kanin, E. J. (1965). Male sex aggression and three psychiatric hypotheses. *The Journal of Sex Research, 1*(3), 221–231.

Kanin, E. J. (1967). An examination of sexual aggression as a response to sexual frustration. *Journal of Marriage and Family, 29*(3), 428–433.

Kaplan, M. (2012). Rethinking HIV-exposure laws. *Indiana Law Journal, 87,* 1517–1570.

King, M. B. (1990). Male rape; victims need sensitive management. *BMJ, 301*(6765), 1345–1346.

Kinports, K. (2001). Rape and force: The forgotten *mens rea. Buffalo Criminal Law Review, 4,* 755–799.

Klarfeld, J. (2011). Striking disconnect: Marital rape law's failure to keep up with domestic violence law. *American Criminal Law Review, 48,* 1819–1841.

Knight, R. A., & Prentky, R. A. (1990). Classifying sexual offenders: The development and corroboration of taxonomic models. In W. L. Marshall, D. R. Laws, & H. E. Barbaree (Eds.), *Handbook of sexual assault: Issues, theories, and treatment of the offender* (3rd ed., pp. 23–52). New York, NY: Plenum Press.

Krahé, B., Scheinberger-Olwig, R., & Bieneck, S. (2003). Men's reports of nonconsensual sexual interactions with women: prevalence and impact. *Archives of Sexual Behavior, 32*(5), 165–175.

Kruttschnitt, C., Kalsbeek, W. D., & House, C. E. (Eds.). (2014), *Estimating the incidence of rape and sexual assault.* Washington, DC: National Academies Press.

Lanyon, R. I. (1991). Theories of sex offending. In C. R. Hollin & R. Howells (Eds.), *Clinical approached to sex offenders and their victims* (pp. 35–54). Chichester: Wiley.

Larimer, M. E., Lydum, A. R., Anderson, B. K., & Turner, A. P. (1999). Male and female recipients of unwanted sexual contact in a college student sample: Prevalence rates, alcohol use, and depression symptoms. *Sex Roles, 40,* 295–308.

Laumann, E. O., Gagnon, J. H., Michael, R. T., & Michaels, S. (1994). *The social organization of sexuality: Sexual practices in the United States.* Chicago, IL: University of Chicago Press.

Lawrence, F. M. (1999). *Punishing hate: Bias crimes under American law.* Cambridge, MA: Harvard University Press.

Lawyer, S., Resnick, H., Bakanic, V., Burkett, T., & Kilpatrick, D. (2010). Forcible, drug-facilitated, and incapacitated rape and sexual assault among undergraduate women. *Journal of American College Health, 58*(5), 453–460.

Lazzarini, Z., Bray, S., & Burris, S. (2002). Evaluating the impact of criminal laws on HIV risk behavior. *Journal of Law, Medicine, and Ethics, 30*, 239–252.

LeTrent, S. (2013, October 10). Against his will: Female-on-male rape. *CNN Living.* Retrieved from http://www.cnn.com/2013/10/09/living/chris-brown-female-on-male-rape/

Lim, S., & Howard, R. (1998). Antecedents of sexual and non-sexual aggression in young Singaporean men. *Personality and Individual Differences, 25*, 1163–1182.

Lindler, H. (1953). The Blacky Pictures Test: A study of sexual offenders and non-sexual offenders. *Journal of Projective Techniques, 17*, 79–84.

Lussier, P., Leclerc, B., Cale, J., & Proulx, J. (2007). Developmental pathways of deviance in sexual aggressors. *Criminal Justice and Behavior, 34*(11), 1441–1462.

MacFarlane, B. A. (1993). Historical development of the offence of rape. In J. Wood & R. C. C. Peck (Eds.), *100 years of the criminal code in Canada; Essays commemorating the centenary of the Canadian criminal code.* Ottawa, ON: Canadian Bar Association.

Macur, J., & Schweber, N. (2012, Dec. 16). Rape case unfolds on web and splits city. *The New York Times.* Retrieved from http://www.nytimes.com/2012/12/17/sports/high-school-football-rape-case-unfolds-online-and-divides-steubenville-ohio.html

Malamuth, N. M. (1984). Aggression against women: Cultural and individual causes. *Pornography and Sexual Aggression.* In N. M. Malamuth & E. Donnerstein (Eds.), *Pornography and sexual aggression* (pp. 19–52). Orlando, FL: Academic Press.

Malamuth, N. M. (1986). Predictors of naturalistic sexual aggression. *Journal of Personality & Social Psychology, 54*, 953–962.

Malamuth, N. M. (1996). The confluence model of sexual aggression: Feminist and evolutionary perspectives. In D. B. Buss & N. M. Malamuth (Eds.), *Sex, power, conflict: evolutionary and feminist perspectives* (pp. 269–295). New York, NY: Oxford University Press.

Malamuth, N. M. (1998). An evolutionary-based model integrating research on the characteristics of sexually coercive men. In J. G. Adair, D. Belanger, & K. L. Dion (Eds.), *Advances in psychological science*, Vol. 1 (pp. 151–184). Hove: Psychology Press Ltd.

Malamuth, N. M., Heavey, C. L., & Linz, D. (1993). Predicting men's antisocial behavior against women: The interaction model of sexual aggression. In G. C. N. Hall, R. Hirschman, J. R. Graham, & M. S. Zaragoza (Eds.), *Sexual aggression: Issues in etiology, assessment and treatment* (pp. 63–97). Washington, DC: Taylor & Francis.

Marshall, W. L., & Barbaree, H. E. (1984). A behavioral view of rape. *International Journal of Law and Psychiatry, 7*(1), 51–77.

Marshall, W. L., & Barbaree, H. E. (1990). An integrated theory of sexual offending. In W. L. Marshall, D. R. Laws, & H. E. Barbaree (Eds.), *Handbook of sexual assault: Issues, theories and treatment of the offender* (pp. 363–385). New York, NY: Plenum

Marshall, W. L., & Hall, G. C. N. (1995). The value of the MMPI in deciding forensic issues in accused sexual offenders. *Sexual Abuse: A Journal of Research and Treatment, 7*, 205–219.

Marshall, W. L., & Marshall, L. E. (2000). The origins of sexual offending. *Trauma, Violence, and Abuse, 1*, 250–263.

Mathis, J. L. (1972*). Clear thinking about sexual deviations.* Chicago, IL: Nelson-Hall Company.

Mayes, R., & Horwitz, A. V. (2005). DSM_III and the revolution in the classification of mental illness. *Journal of the History of the Behavioral Sciences, 41*(3), 249–267.

McCaldon, R. J. (1967). Rape. *Canadian Journal of Corrections, 9*, 37–59.

McJunkin, B. A. (2014). Deconstructing rape by fraud. *Columbia Journal of Gender and Law, 28*, 1–47.

McKibbin, W. F., Shackelford, T. K., Goetz, A. T., & Starratt, V. G. (2008). Why do men rape? An evolutionary psychological perspective. *Review of General Psychology, 12*(1), 86–97.

McLellan, A. (1991). Post-penetration rape—Increasing the penalty. *Santa Clara Law Review, 31*, 779–808.

McPhail, B. A., & DiNitto D. M. (2005). Prosecutorial perspectives on gender-bias hate crimes. *Violence Against Women, 11*, 1162–1185.

Miethe, T., McCorkle, R., & Listwan, S. (2006). *Crime profiles: The anatomy of dangerous, persons, places, and situations* (3rd ed.). Los Angeles, CA: Roxbury Publishing.

Miller, P., & Biele, N. (1993). Twenty years later: The unfinished revolution. In E. Buchwald, P. Fletcher, & M. Roth (Eds.), *Transforming a rape culture* (pp. 48–53). Minneapolis, MN: Milkweed Editions.

Mitchell, D., Angelone, D. J., Kohlberger, B., & Hirschman, R. (2009). Effects of offender motivation, victim gender, and participant gender on perceptions of rape victims and offenders. *Journal of Interpersonal Violence, 24*(9), 1564–1578.

MODEL PENAL CODE § 213.1, *Rape and related offenses* (1980). Philadelphia, PA: American Law Institute.

Muehlenhard, C. L. Danoff-Burg, S., & Powch, I. G. (1996). Is rape sex or violence? Conceptual issues and implications. In D. M. Buss, & N. M. Malamuth. (Eds.). *Sex, power, conflict: Evolutionary and feminist perspectives* (pp. 119–137). New York, NY: Oxford University Press.

Ohio Rev. Code Ann. § 2907.02(A)(2) (2014).

Oppel, R. A. (2013, March 17). Ohio teenagers guilty in rape that social media brought to light. *The New York Times*. Retrieved from http://www.nytimes.com/2013/03/18/us/teenagers-found-guilty-in-rape-in-steubenville-ohio.html?pagewanted=all

O'Sullivan, L. F., Byers, E. S., & Finkelman, L. (1998). A comparison of male and female college students' experiences of sexual coercion. *Psychology of Women Quarterly, 22*, 177–195.

Palmer, E. G. (2004). Antiquated notions of womanhood and the myth of the unstoppable male: Why post-penetration rape should be a crime in North Carolina. *North Carolina Law Review, 82*, 1258–1278.

Pavlov, I. P. (1897). *The work of the digestive glands*. London: Griffin.

Pendo, E. A. (1994). Recognizing violence against women: Gender and Hate Crimes Statistics Act. *Harvard Women's Law Journal, 17*, 157–183.

Penn, N. (2014). Military sexual assault: Male survivors speak out. GQ.com. http://www.gq.com/longform/male-military-rape

Peterson, Z. D., Voller, E., Polusny, M. A., & Murdoch, M. (2011). Prevalence and consequences of adult sexual assault of men: Review of empirical findings and state of the literature. *Clinical Psychology Review, 31*, 1–24.

Pistono, S. P. (1988). Susan Brownmiller and the history of rape. *Women's Studies, 14*, 265–276.

Pokorak, J. J. (2006). Rape as a badge of slavery: The legal history of, and remedies for, prosecutorial race-of-victim charging disparities. *Nevada Law Journal, 7*, 1–54.

Polaschek, D. L. L., Ward, T., & Hudson, S. M. (1997). Rape and rapists: Theory and treatment. *Clinical Psychology Review, 17*(2), 117–144.

Pope, E., & Shouldice, M. (2012). Drugs and sexual assault: A review. In C. Bartol, & A. Bartol (Eds.), *Current perspectives in forensic psychology and criminal behavior* (pp. 80–83). Thousand Oaks, CA: Sage Publications.

Popper, K. R. (1959). *The logic of scientific discovery*. London: Hutchinson.

Price, J. M. (1996). Constitutional law—Sex, lies, and rape shield statutes: The constitutionality of interpreting rape shield statutes to exclude evidence relating to the victim's motive to fabricate. *Western New England Law Review, 18*, 541–576.

Quinsey, V. L., & Lalumière, M. L. (1995). Evolutionary perspectives on sexual offending. *Sexual Abuse: A Journal of Research and Treatment, 7*, 301–315.

Rada, R. T. (1978). *Clinical aspects of the rapist*. New York, NY: Grune & Stratton, Inc.

Rayburn, C. (2006). To catch a sex thief: The burden of performance in rape and sexual assault trials. *Columbia Journal of Gender and Law, 15*, 437–484.

Reyes, I. B. (2003). The epidemic of injustice in rape law: Mandatory sentencing as a partial remedy. *UCLA Women's Law Journal, 12*, 355–378.

Robinson, L. D. (2008). It is what it is: Legal recognition of acquaintance rape. *Ave Maria Law Review, 6*, 627–663.

Rothschild, E. (1993). Recognizing another face of hate crimes: Rape as a gender-bias crime. *Maryland Journal of Contemporary Legal Issues, 4*, 231–285.

Russell, D. E. H. (1975). *The politics of rape: The victim's perspective*. Lincoln, NE: iUniverse, Inc.

Sanday, P. R. (1981). The socio-cultural context of rape: A cross-cultural study. *Journal of Social Issues, 37*(4), 5–27.

Sanday, P. R. (2007). *Fraternity gang rape: Sex, brotherhood, and privilege on campus*. New York, NY: New York University Press.

Schulhofer, S. J. (1998). *Unwanted sex: The culture of intimidation and the failure of law*. Cambridge, MA: Harvard University Press.

Schultz, L. G. (Ed.). (1975). *Rape victimology*. Springfield, IL: Charles Thomas.

Scully, D. (1990). *Understanding sexual violence: A study of convicted rapists*. Boston, MA: Unwin.

Scully, D., & Marolla, J. (1985). Rape and vocabularies of motive: Alternative perspectives. In A. W. Burgess (Ed.), *Rape and sexual assault: A research handbook* (pp. 294–312). New York, NY: Garland.

Service Women's Action Network. (n.d.). Military sexual violence: Rape, sexual assault and sexual harassment. Retrieved from http://servicewomen.org/military-sexual-violence/

Simon, L. M. J. (2000). An examination of the assumptions of specialization, mental disorder, and dangerousness in sex offenders. *Behavioral Sciences and the Law, 18*, 275–308.

Sinozich, S., & Langton, L. (2014). *Rape and sexual assault among college-age females, 1995–2013*. Washington, DC: U.S. Department of Justice Office of Justice Programs, Bureau of Justice Statistics. Retrieved from http://www.bjs.gov/content/pub/pdf/rsavcaf9513.pdf

Skinner, B. F. (1948). *Walden two*. New York, NY: Macmillan.

Smallbone, S. W., & Dadds, M. R. (1998). Childhood attachment and adult attachment in incarcerated adult male sex offenders. *Journal of Interpersonal Violence, 13*, 555–573.

Smallbone, S. W., Wheaton, J., & Hourigan, D. (2003). Trait empathy and criminal versatility in sexual offenders. *Sexual Abuse: A Journal of Research and Treatment, 15*, 49–60.

Smuts, B. (1995). The evolutionary origins of patriarchy. *Human Nature*, 6(1), 1–32.

SOUTH DAKOTA STATUTES § 22–22–1 (2015).

Spitzberg, B. H. (1999). An analysis of empirical estimates of sexual aggression victimization and perpetration. *Violence and Victims*, 14(3), 241–60.

Stephen, H. J. (1890). *Mr. Sergeant Stephen's new commentaries on the laws of England* (Vol. IV). London: Butterworths.

Stermac, L.E., & Quinsey, V.L. (1986). Social competence among rapists. *Behavioral Assessment*, 8, 171–185.

Struckman-Johnson, C. (1988). Forced sex on dates: It happens to men, too. *Journal of Sex Research*, 24, 234–241.

Taslitz, A. E. (2005). Willfully blinded: On date rape and self-deception. *Harvard Journal of Law and Gender*, 28, 381–446.

TENNESSEE CRIMINAL CODE §§ 39–13–502, 39–13–502 (2014).

Tewksbury, R., & Mustaine, E. E. (2001). Lifestyle factors associated with the sexual assault of men: A routine activity theory analysis. *Journal of Men's Studies*, 9, 153–182.

Thorndike, E. L. (1905). *The elements of psychology.* New York, NY: Seiler.

Thornhill, R., & Palmer, C. T. (2000). *A natural history of rape: Biological bases of sexual coercion.* Cambridge, MA: MIT Press.

Toner, B. (1977). *The facts of rape.* London: Hutchinson.

Tracy, C. E., Fromson, T. L., Long, J. G., & Whitman, C. (2012). Rape and sexual assault in the legal system. Paper commissioned by the National Research Council Panel on Measuring Rape and Sexual Assault in the Bureau of Justice Statistics Household Surveys. Retrieved from http://www.womenslawproject.org/resources/Rape%20and%20Sexual%20Assault%20in%20the%20Legal%20System%20FINAL.pdf

Truman, J. L., & Langton, L. (2014). *Criminal victimization, 2013.* Washington, DC: U.S. Department of Justice Office of Justice Programs, Bureau of Justice Statistics. Retrieved from http://www.bjs.gov/content/pub/pdf/cv13.pdf

Turchik, J., & Wilson, S. (2010). Sexual assault in the U.S. military: A review of the literature and recommendations for the future. *Aggression and Violent Behavior*, 15(4), 267–277. doi:10.1016/j.avb.2010.01.005

UNIFORM CODE OF MILITARY JUSTICE art. 120(g)(2) (2012).

U.S. Centers for Disease Control and Prevention (2011). *Sexually transmitted disease surveillance, 2010.* Atlanta, GA: U.S. Department of Health and Human Services, Centers for Disease Control and Prevention. Retrieved from http://www.cdc.gov/std/stats10/surv2010.pdf

U.S. Department of Defense (2013). Annual report on sexual assault in the military, fiscal year 2012. Retrieved from http://www.sapr.mil/public/docs/reports/FY12_DoD_SAPRO_Annual_Report_on_Sexual_Assault-volume_one.pdf

Vandermassen, G. (2011). Evolution and rape: A feminist Darwinian perspective. *Sex Roles*, 64(9/10), 732–747.

Waldman, A. E. (2011). Exceptions: The criminal law's illogical approach to HIV-related aggravated assaults. *Virginia Journal of Social Policy and the Law*, 18, 550–605.

Walker, J., Archer, J., & Davies, M. (2005). Effects of rape on men: A descriptive analysis. *Archives of Sexual Behavior*, 34, 69–80.

Walters, M. L., Chen, J., & Breiding, M. J. (2013). *The National Intimate Partner and Sexual Violence Survey (NISVS): 2010 findings on victimization by sexual orientation.* Atlanta, GA: Centers for Disease Control and Prevention. Retrieved from http://www.cdc.gov/violenceprevention/pdf/nisvs_sofindings.pdf

Ward, T., & Beech, T. (2005). An integrated theory of sexual offending. *Aggression and Violent Behavior*, 11, 44–63.

Ward, T., Hudson, S. M., & Marshall, W. L. (1996). Attachment style in sex offenders: A preliminary study. *Journal of Sex Research*, 33, 17–26.

Ward, T., Polaschek, D. L. L., & Beech, A. R. (2006). *Theories of sexual offending.* Chichester: Wiley.

Watson, J. B. (1913). Psychology as the behaviorist views it. *Psychological Review*, 20, 158–178.

Watson, J. B. (1930). *Behaviorism* (rev. ed.). Chicago, IL: University of Chicago Press.

Wells, C.E., & Motley, E. E. (2001). Reinforcing the myth of the crazed rapist: A feminist critique of recent rape legislation. *Boston University Law Review*, 81, 127–198.

Wencelblat, P. (2004). Boys will be boys? An analysis of male-on-male heterosexual sexual violence. *Columbia Journal of Law and Social Problems*, 38, 37–66.

Wheeler, J. G., George, W. H., & Dahl, B. J. (2002). Sexually aggressive college males: Empathy as a moderator in the "confluence model" of sexual aggression. *Personality and Individual Differences*, 33, 759–777.

Yung, C. R. (2014). How to lie with rape statistics: America's hidden rape crises. *Iowa Law Review*, 99, 1197–1250.

Cases

Brown v. State, 106 N.W. 536 (Wis. 1906).

Commonwealth v. Enimpah, 966 N.E.2d 840 (Mass. App. Ct. 2012).

Commonwealth v. Lopez, 745 N.E.2d 961 (Mass. 2001).

Director of Public Prosecutions v. Morgan, 2 All E.R. 347 (H.L. 1975).

In re John Z., 60 P.3d 183 (2003).

In re M.T.S., 609 A.2d 1266 (N.J. 1992).

McGill v. State, 18 P.3d 77 (Alaska Ct. App. 2001).

Moran v. People, 25 Mich. 356 (1872).

People v. Denbo, 868 N.E.2d 347 (Ill. App. 2007).

People v. Roundtree, 77 Cal. App.4th 846 (2000).

People v. Vela, 172 Cal. App.3d 237 (1985), *overruled by In re John Z.*, 60 P.3d 183 (2003).

People v. Wallace, 189 P.3d 911 (Cal. 2008), *as modified*, (Oct. 22, 2008) and *cert. denied*, 556 U.S. 1223 (2009).

People v. Williams, 614 N.E.2d 730 (N.Y. 1993).

Reynolds v. State, 664 P.2d 621 (Alaska Ct. App. 1983).

State v. Baby, 946 A.2d 463 (Md. 2008).

State v. Bunyard, 75 P.3d 750 (Kan. App. 2003).

State v. Crims, 540 N.W.2d 860 (Minn. Ct. App. 1995).

State v. DeLawder, 344 A.2d 446 (Md. 1975).

State v. Flynn, 257 P.3d 1259 (Kan. App. 2011), *rev'd* 329 P.3rd 429 (Kan. 2014).

State v. Flynn, 329 P.3rd 429 (Kan. 2014).

State v. Garron, 827 A.2d 243 (N.J. 2003).

State v. Jones, 521 N.W.2d 662 (S.D. 1994).

State v. Montgomery, 974 P.2d 904 (Wash App. 1999).

State v. Reed, 479 A.2d 1291 (Me. 1984).

State v. Robinson, 496 A.2d 1067 (Me. 1985).

State v. Siering, 644 A.2d 958 (Conn. App. Ct. 1994).

State v. Way, 254 S.E.2d 760 (N.C. 1979).

Williams v. State, 681 N.E.2d 195 (Ind. 1997).

Wisconsin v. Mitchell, 508 U.S. 476 (1993).

CHAPTER 6

The Criminal Regulation of Sex Acts: The Limits of Morality and Consent

Henry F. Fradella and Kenneth Grundy

Jerry Sandusky spent more than 30 years as a leading Division I college football coach, leading Penn State University to two national championships. He was also the founder of a widely respected charity for underprivileged boys and a dedicated provider of service to local high schools' football programs. But his legacy was forever tarnished when he was convicted of 45 criminal counts for having sexually assaulted 10 boys over a 15-year period of time, making Sandusky one of the most high-profile, child-molesting pedophiles in the nation.

Sandusky spent his undergraduate years at Pennsylvania State University, where he played football during his four years of college and landed a position as a graduate assistant for the football program shortly thereafter. A short stint teaching physical education and coaching football at a nearby community college preceded Sandusky obtaining a spot as an assistant coach under the Hall of Fame coach Joe Paterno. He later met and married his wife Dorothy, and together they adopted six children.

Sandusky then founded Second Mile, the nonprofit organization through which Sandusky "allegedly fit a pattern of 'grooming' " boys into sexual victimization (Viera, 2011, para. 6). This pattern involved buying the boys gifts, bringing them to football games, inviting them to his home, and showering with them before initiating sexual contact. The milder offenses included placing his hands on boys' legs as they drove with him in the car, putting his hands under their clothing, and cracking the boys' backs as they lay face-to-face on top of him. More seriously, one victim recounted the dozens of times he was forced to perform oral sex on Sandusky or be the recipient of oral sex performed on him by Sandusky. One of the more egregious acts in this pattern of sexual offenses occurred when Mike McQueary, a graduate assistant with Penn State's football program, walked in on Sandusky anally raping one of his victims in the school's locker-room showers. McQueary reported this behavior to his supervisors, not realizing they would downplay the report, enabling Sandusky to victimize young boys for nearly another decade (Sandusky Grand Jury Presentment, 2011). The grand jury indictment detailed the accounts of eight of Sandusky's victims; that number grew to 10 at trial, with additional victims surfacing after the jury reached its verdict of "guilty." Sandusky was ultimately sentenced to a term of between 30 and 60 years in prison.

Under contemporary mores and legal standards, pedophilia is a reviled affliction, and Sandusky is the embodiment of the public's conception of a predatory pedophile. The Second Mile charity allowed Sandusky access to hundreds of boys over decades. Further, according to the task force investigating the Penn State administration's negligence, the suppression of reports of his activities by his supervisors (in the hope that the school's athletic programs would not be compromised) gave him the unfettered ability to carry out his sexually deviant desires. Penn State's failure to act resulted in a series of civil lawsuits against the university. Ultimately, Penn State's board agreed to pay $59.7 million to 26 sexual abuse victims to settle their claims against the university. And three top administrators—University President Graham Spanier, Athletic Director Tim Curley, Vice President for Finance and Business Gary Schultz—were criminally charged for either lying to the police or turning a blind eye to children in harm's way. Spanier resigned from the university's presidency. The NCAA placed Penn State's football program on five years of probation, banned the university from post-season play for four years, stripped Penn State of some scholarship funding, and vacated more than 100 wins between 1998 and 2011, causing the university to lose some of its Big Ten titles.

As a result of Penn State's multiple failures to protect dozens of children from Jerry Sandusky, the State of Pennsylvania instituted mandatory reporting laws for all public employees who come into contact with children. As a result, every grammar school, high school, college, and university employee—regardless of the employee's job classification—are required to report all suspected child abuse. Other states also instituted similar mandatory reporting laws for all public employees.

Sources: Freeh, Sporkin, & Sullivan, LLP, 2012; "Jerry Sandusky," 2012

LEARNING OBJECTIVES

1. Explain how sexual mores and laws governing the criminal regulation of non-forcible sexual behavior vary across time and culture.
2. Trace the history of criminal laws against sodomy, adultery, and fornication.
3. Evaluate the actual and potential impact of *Lawrence v. Texas* on the criminal regulation of a wide range of sexual activities, including public sexual indecency, prostitution, bestiality, incest, obscenity, bigamy, adultery, fornication, statutory rape, and laws governing the known transmission of sexually transmitted infections.
4. Analyze how non-forcible sex crimes have targeted lesbian, gay, bisexual, and transgender groups.
5. Compare and contrast how and why consent serves as defense to certain sex crimes and not others.

Sexual behaviors vary across cultures (Bhugra, Popelyuk, & McMullen, 2010; Davis & Whitten, 1987). For instance, certain tribal communities in Africa engage in sex as a means of maintaining physical and spiritual health, or of cleansing their bodies (Agunbiade & Ayotunde, 2012; Ayikukwei, Ngare, Sidle, Ayuku, Baliddawa, & Greene, 2007). In other cultures, sexual acts are rites of passage that are viewed as promoting growth and strength. For example, the Sambian tribe of New Guinea believes that boys must be removed from the "polluting" influence of their mothers before they turn 10 years old and start performing oral sex on older adolescent boys and ingest their semen (Herdt, 1984, 2000). By ingesting the "life force" of young men, the Sambians believe that prepubescent boys will develop strong bones, muscles, and reproductive strength. Once adolescent boys sexually mature, they become the recipients of oral sex performed on them by younger boys until such time as the adolescent male marries, usually in his late teens or early 20s, when his participation in such rituals generally ends and his sexual activity is primarily confined to acts with his wife (Herdt, 1999).

Other cultures ascribe little or no significance to sex other than pleasure. Nonetheless, some cultural sexual practices seem odd by contemporary Western standards, especially those involving children. Consider that in New Guinea, children in the Trobriand tribe routinely engage in sexual behaviors between the ages of six and 12 (Martinson, 1994). And on the small South Pacific Island of Mangaia, 13-year-old boys have sex with older women who teach the boys how to please sexual partners (Marshall, 1971). In contrast, other cultures are incredibly sexually repressive. For instance, the World Health Organization reports that in some areas of western Africa, the practice of *female genital mutilation*—the removal or mutilation of a female's clitoris that is sometimes referred to as female circumcision—is routinely performed in hopes of reducing a girl's ability to

enjoy sex, thereby improving her purity, fertility, and marriage prospects (Sipsma, Chen, Ofori-Atta, Ilozumba, Karfo, & Bradley, 2012).

Even among adults in Western cultures, some of the acts that bring sexual stimulation or satisfaction range from the innocuous to the bizarre. Some of these behaviors are legal, such as role-playing. Others are legal, albeit potentially harmful. For example, some males inject saline or air into their scrotums—a practice dubbed "scrotal inflation"—even though such a practice can cause permanent damage to the genitalia or even death from an air embolism (Summers, 2003). Other sexual behaviors are criminally proscribed, some of which involve acts that are the products of **paraphilias**—psychiatric conditions in which sexual arousal and gratification depend on fantasizing about or engaging in behaviors that are considered to be extreme and atypical of "normal" human sexuality because they involve either nonhuman objects, the suffering or humiliation of oneself or one's partner, or children or other nonconsenting persons (see Chapter 12). Examples include *pedophilia*—sexual attraction to or activity with prepubescent children, as was the case with Jerry Sandusky (Seto, 2008); *frotteurism*—rubbing one's genitals against an unsuspecting and nonconsenting person (Guterman, Martin, & Rudes, 2011); *bestiality*—copulating with animals (Ascione, 2005); *exhibitionism*—exposing oneself to nonconsenting strangers (Kenworthy & Bloem, 2005); and *sadism* that, when taken to extremes, involves living-out violent sexual fantasies of torture, rape, and even murder (White, 2007).

Recall from Chapters 3 and 4 that philosophers have long debated the appropriateness of using the law to regulate morality (compare Hart, 1959/1971; with Devlin, 1965/1977). But such philosophical arguments notwithstanding, it is undebatable the law has been—and continues to be—used as a tool for the formal social control of sex and sexuality.

Since the earliest period of recorded history, lawmakers have tried to set boundaries on how people take their sexual pleasure, and they have doled out a range of controls and punishments to enforce then, from the slow impalement of unfaithful wives in Mesopotamia to the sterilization of masturbators in the United States. At any given point in time, some forms of sex and sexuality have been encouraged while others have been punished without mercy. Jump forward or backward a century or two, or cross a border, and the harmless fun of one society becomes the gravest crime of another.

(Berkowitz, 2012, p. 7; see also Frank, Camp, & Boutcher, 2010)

Historically, criminal sanctions have been especially unkind to those who engage in sex that is non-traditional, non-heterosexual, or that is not for the purpose of procreation (Cantor, 1964; Fradella, 2002). This chapter explores the criminal regulation of a variety of such sexual acts.

SODOMY

Most historians agree that "no Western legal or moral tradition—civil or ecclesiastical, European, English, or Anglo-American—has ever attempted to penalize or stigmatize a 'homosexual person' apart from the commission of external acts" (Boswell, 1993, p. 40). Thus, it has not been the status of being a homosexual per se that has been condemned throughout history, but rather the acts in which the homosexual engages. These acts, which are usually taken to include both oral and anal intercourse and subsumed under the general term **sodomy** have been proscribed by either civil or ecclesiastical laws for centuries.

The History of Sodomy Laws

Sodomy laws have existed since biblical times; indeed, even the term *sodomy* comes from the Bible, in the story of the destruction of Sodom

(Genesis 19:1–29). And Judaic law specifically prohibited sodomy (Brooks, 1985, citing Leviticus 18:22). But there is scholarly literature that suggests the story of Sodom in Leviticus may not be aimed at condemning sodomy, but rather at condemning inhospitality (Boswell, 1993). But even if we accept the text as a condemnation of homosexuality, it is clear that sodomy has not always been considered a crime. For example, sodomy played a large part in ancient Greek and Roman culture since both societies not only condoned acts of sodomy, but also seemed to encourage them (Ellis, 1964; Font, 2000).

Paiderastia, which should not be confused with pedophilia, . . . [involved] younger males . . . [who] had reached puberty. Such relationships were governed by centuries of tradition handed down from father to son, ratified in an extensive philosophical, heroic, and erotic literature, and, it is claimed, ordained in law by Solon the lawgiver himself, who decreed that before marrying, a citizen had the obligation to take as a lover and pupil a younger male and train him in the arts of war and citizenship.

(Dover, 1978, p. 19)

Western civilization, however, especially with the spread of Christianity in Europe, was revolted by homosexuality and punished sodomy as an ecclesiastical offense (Brooks, 1985, p. 648). Sodomy was made a crime against the state at common law in the sixteenth century by Henry VIII (25 Hen. VIII, c. 6, 1533, *repealed by* 9 Geo. 4, c. 31, 1828). By the Victorian era, the mass suppression of sexuality of all types led to the criminalization of all acts of sodomy, whether homosexual or heterosexual (Brooks, 1985, p. 648). The Puritans brought the sodomy laws with them to the colonies. As the country grew, sodomy laws spread as a part of common law and were in effect in all 50 states. Up until the mid-1960s, these sodomy laws facially applied to both heterosexual and homosexual sodomy, although the targets of prosecution were usually homosexuals (Eskridge, 1997; Leslie, 2000), and judicial construction of the apparently gender-neutral statutes was often targeted at homosexuals. For example, in *Bowers v. Hardwick* (1986), the majority opinion of the U.S. Supreme Court "described the Georgia law solely as a prohibition on 'homosexual sodomy' despite the fact that the statute was gender-neutral and applied to all sodomy" (Leslie, 2000, p. 112).

As society became more sexually open through the 1960s and 1970s, a number of states altered their sodomy statutes so heterosexual acts of sodomy would be beyond the reach of the criminal law, officially making sodomy statutes apply only to acts of same-sex sodomy (Eskridge, 1997; Leslie, 2000). These laws

> establish gay men and lesbians as a legally distinct 'other.' Gay sexuality is proscribed as criminal while similar conduct between heterosexuals is permitted. Thus, while the woman who performs fellatio is expressing herself sexually, the man who performs fellatio is a felon, subject to fines and imprisonment. By their clear text, these statutes set up gay men and lesbians as a criminal class.
>
> (Leslie, 2000, p. 111)

Early English law prohibited only anal sex. But as Barnhart (1981) explained in her analysis of the history of sodomy laws, the definition was broadened in most U.S. jurisdictions either by legislation or judicial construction to include both oral sex as well as bestiality (i.e., sexual contact with an animal). Laws against such conduct have not only been designated as sodomy laws, but have also generated various neologisms: "the infamous crime against nature," the "abominable and detestable crime against nature," "buggery," "unnatural intercourse," and "deviate sexual intercourse" (Barnhart, 1981, p. 254). Kane (2007) succinctly notes that "[t]hough most sodomy statutes criminalized these activities between different-sex partners, sodomy laws

always criminalized these forms of sexual activity between same-sex partners" (p. 213, italics in original).

Bowers v. Hardwick Rejects the Right to Privacy in Context of Sodomy Laws

In 1986, the U.S. Supreme Court issued a direct attack on the privacy arguments against sodomy statutes in *Bowers v. Hardwick* (1986). The Court explicitly ruled on the constitutionality of sodomy statutes, holding that the right to privacy does not protect consensual sexual acts of sodomy between homosexuals. Recall from Chapter 4 that in *Bowers*, the police had legally entered the home of the defendant, Michael Hardwick, to serve an unrelated warrant upon him. When the police entered, they discovered him engaging in oral sex with another man, and they arrested him. Hardwick was never prosecuted for the crime, but in fear of such prosecution, he brought suit claiming that Georgia's sodomy law violated his rights to privacy, due process, and freedoms of expression and association. The federal district court dismissed the case, but the Eleventh Circuit Court of Appeals reversed, holding that the Ninth Amendment and the Due Process Clause of the Fourteenth Amendment to the U.S. Constitution guaranteed Hardwick the privacy to engage in private consensual sexual conduct (*Hardwick v. Bowers*, 1985). On appeal to the U.S. Supreme Court, Justice White, writing for the majority in a five-to-four decision, held that the right to privacy did not protect homosexual sodomy from criminal prosecution (*Bowers v. Hardwick*, 1986).

Justice White began by explaining that the situation presented in the case was not covered by what had been heretofore generally thought of as sexual privacy cases: *Griswold v. Connecticut* (1965), which struck down an anti-contraceptive law as an "impermissible intrusion on the right of the association protecting the marital relationship, [the] enforcement of [which] threatens police intrusion into the marital bedroom"; *Eisenstadt v. Baird* (1972), which extended *Griswold*'s holding to unmarried persons on Equal Protection Clause grounds; and *Roe v. Wade* (1972), which held the right to privacy guaranteed a woman's right to choose to have an abortion during the first trimester of pregnancy. Justice White distinguished these cases as dealing with the family, marriage, and procreation. He reasoned that homosexual sodomy did not concern any of these issues, and, therefore, was outside the realm of the constitutional right to privacy these three key cases collectively represented.

The majority opinion in *Bowers* was sharply criticized as having framed the issues much too narrowly (e.g., Goldstein, 1988; *Harvard Law Review*, 1986). These critics took issue with the way in which the majority chose to frame the issue as being one pertaining to homosexual sodomy when the statute in question prohibited all forms of sodomy, whether heterosexual or homosexual. If the Court had looked at the case as one of sexual privacy, it could easily have fit the facts into the line of precedent descending from *Griswold* and held the statute unconstitutional. This is especially true since *Griswold*, *Eisenstadt*, and *Roe* can be interpreted as guaranteeing that adults have a right "to engage in non-procreative sexual relations, even outside the traditional setting of marriage" (Williamson, 1989, p. 1310).

The Supreme Court has also been criticized for defining fundamental rights as those "deeply rooted" in history. The Constitution itself has no objective meaning in the Due Process or Equal Protection Clauses when it comes to defining the scope of privacy—a word that does not even appear in the text of the Constitution. The Supreme Court's reliance on history and tradition is found in the text as an act of interpretation, not of an inherent objective quality in the text. For examples, the right to contraceptives established in *Griswold*, and the right to choose an abortion established in *Roe*, are both

notions that were found within the scope of the right to privacy despite the fact that neither contraceptives nor abortion were rights "deeply rooted" in history and tradition. The editors of the *Harvard Law Review* (1986) deconstructed this inconsistency as follows:

> [R]elying on history involves a value choice in that the Court selects which history it will base its decision on. The Court could have decided to rely on recent history: for example, a majority of states no longer outlaw sodomy, and homosexual leaders now occupy prominent positions in local, state, and federal elective office. The historic persecution of homosexuals should not have been used to deter the current societal trend of recognizing that individuals have a fundamental right to define their own sexual identities. Such reliance on past discrimination to justify future discrimination harkens back to the days when historical tradition was used to justify long since condemned laws supporting slavery and the so called separate but equal treatment of Blacks.
>
> (pp. 218–219)

Accordingly, many commentators viewed the decision in *Bowers* as homophobic, as the Court did not similarly limit its interpretation of the right to privacy when faced with the heterosexual privacy concerns raised in *Griswold*, *Eisenstadt*, and *Roe* (Fradella, 2002; Harrison, 2000).

Lawrence v. Texas Rejects Sodomy Laws on Liberty Grounds

In 1961, every state in the United States had a criminal sodomy law (*Bowers*, 1986). Between 1961 and the decision in *Bowers*, many states decriminalized sodomy through legislative repeal or through state court judicial action (Fradella, 2003). Over the course of 17 years following the *Bowers* decision, 12 more states decriminalized sodomy (Fradella, 2003; Leveno, 1994). Thus, at the time the U.S. Supreme Court decided *Lawrence v.*

Texas in 2003, 13 U.S. states still criminalized sodomy—a fairly remarkable number since, in the wake of the European Convention on Human Rights calling for the decriminalization of sodomy, many other countries in the free world—even former Soviet republics and staunchly religious Ireland—had invalidated their sodomy laws by the turn of the twenty-first century. The United States joined these countries with its decision in *Lawrence v. Texas* (2003).

Lawrence concerned two men who had been convicted of violating Texas's sodomy law when police found them engaged in sex upon entry into their apartment upon a complaint of a weapons disturbance. It turns out there was no such disturbance; the story was fabricated by someone trying to harass Lawrence. The Supreme Court ultimately overturned the convictions, but the way in which it did so is perplexing, to say the least.

As explained earlier, the U.S. Supreme Court had tied the constitutional right to privacy to the Due Process Clause of the Fourteenth Amendment of the U.S. Constitution and, more specifically, to the liberty interests it protects. Recall from Chapter 3 that challenges to laws based on the Due Process Clause are reviewed by federal courts under one of two standards. If the law at issue involves a *fundamental right*, then courts apply a standard of review known as strict scrutiny. Fundamental rights are those that are "deeply rooted in the Nation's history and tradition" or those that are "fundamental to the concept of ordered liberty" (*Bowers*, 1986, pp. 191–192). Applying the exacting standard of strict scrutiny, a law impinging on a fundamental right will be invalidated unless it is narrowly tailored to achieve a compelling governmental interest. For example, after deciding the right to marry was a fundamental right, the U.S. Supreme Court invalidated the nation's miscegenation laws in *Loving v. Virginia*. Similarly, finding the decision to "bear or beget" a child was similarly found to be a fundamental right leading to

the invalidation of laws banning access to contraceptives in *Griswold* and abortions in *Roe*.

When no fundamental right is at issue, the courts use a much less exacting test for determining the constitutionality of a law under the Due Process Clause called the *rational basis test*. Recall from Chapter 3 that under this lenient standard of review, federal courts defer to legislative decisions so long as the law at issue is not arbitrary or capricious in its application, and there is a rational basis for the connection between the law and the state interest avowed. Any permissible police power objectives, such as regulating public health, safety, or welfare generally suffices. *Ferguson v. Skrupa* (1963) is an example of the rational basis test in action. Kansas had enacted a statute making it a criminal offense for anyone other than a licensed attorney to engage in debt adjustment. In upholding the law, the U.S. Supreme Court explained,

> We conclude that the Kansas Legislature was free to decide for itself that legislation was needed to deal with the business of debt adjusting. Unquestionably, there are arguments showing that the business of debt adjusting has social utility, but such arguments are properly addressed to the legislature, not to us. We refuse to sit as a super-legislature to weigh the wisdom of legislation, and we emphatically refuse to . . . use the Due Process Clause to strike down state laws . . . because they may be unwise, improvident, or out of harmony with a particular school of thought. . . . The Kansas debt adjusting statute may be wise or unwise. But relief, if any be needed, lies not with us but with the body constituted to pass laws for the State of Kansas.
>
> (*Ferguson v. Skrupa*, 1963, pp. 731–732)

Bowers similarly involved the application of the rational basis test. As previously explained, the *Bowers* majority determined no fundamental right was at issue since sodomy was neither "deeply rooted in our Nation's history or tradition," nor "implicit in the concept of ordered liberty." Applying the rational basis test, the Court upheld the constitutionality of criminalizing sodomy since such laws were rationally related to the legitimate governmental interest of regulating morality. Although the Court stated it was not passing judgment "on whether laws against sodomy between consenting adults in general, or between homosexuals in particular, are wise or desirable" (*Bowers*, 1986, p. 190), it clearly endorsed the notion that "sodomy is immoral and unacceptable" when it refused to declare that purpose an insufficient rational basis upon which to criminalize the act (*Bowers*, 1986, p. 196). In fact, the *Bowers* Court concluded its opinion with this sentiment:

> The law ... is constantly based on notions of morality, and if all laws representing essentially moral choices are to be invalidated under the Due Process Clause, the courts will be very busy indeed. Even respondent makes no such claim, but insists that majority sentiments about the morality of homosexuality should be declared inadequate. We do not agree, and are unpersuaded that the sodomy laws of some 25 States should be invalidated on this basis.
> (*Bowers*, 1986, p. 196)

Lawrence v. Texas (2003), however, overruled the decision in *Bowers* and invalidated the nation's remaining sodomy laws on Fourteenth Amendment substantive due process grounds. The *Lawrence* majority acknowledged that the framing of the issue in *Bowers* was mistaken in that it failed "to appreciate the extent of the liberty [interest] at stake" (*Lawrence*, 2003, p. 567). *Lawrence* recognized that sodomy laws "seek to control a personal relationship that ... is within the liberty of persons to choose without being punished as criminals" (p. 567).

It should be noted that, by the plain language used in *Lawrence*, the scope of its protections are limited to private acts that occur between adults who truly consent to such sexual activities. *Lawrence* does not apply to acts of sodomy that are nonconsensual or that involve minors (e.g., *In re R.L.C.*, 2007; *McDonald v. Commonwealth*, 2006).

Public Sexual Indecency Law Unchanged by Lawrence

Lawrence acknowledged that sodomy laws did more than criminalize a particular act. They had "more far reaching consequences, touching upon the most private human conduct, sexual behavior, and in the most private of places, the home" (*Lawrence*, 2003, p. 567). It should come as no surprise, then, that by its plain terms, *Lawrence* does not apply to sexual acts that take place in public. As a result, the host of laws that existed prior to the decision in *Lawrence* that were designed to socially control sex and sexuality in public remain viable. Such laws include:

- **Indecent exposure** – Knowing exposure or exhibition of the genitals, anus, or female nipples in a public place or on the private premises of another, or so near thereto as to be seen from such private premises, in a vulgar or indecent manner, or to be naked in public except in any place provided or set apart for that purpose. In the past, such laws did not exclude breast-feeding, but today, the laws of nearly all states specifically exempt breast-feeding from the definition of indecent exposure (FLA. STAT. ANN. § 800.02, 2014; REV. CODE WASH. 9A.88.010, 2014).
- **Lewd and lascivious conduct** – Committing an act of sexual gratification, either by oneself or with another person, with knowledge or reasonable anticipation that the participants are being viewed by others (e.g., KAN. STAT. ANN. § 21–3508(1), 2014).

- **Public sexual indecency** – Intentionally or knowingly engaging in any [sexual acts], if another person is present, and the defendant is reckless about whether such other person, as a reasonable person, would be offended or alarmed by the act (e.g., ARIZ. REV. STAT. § 13–1403, 2014).

Not all U.S. jurisdictions have these distinct offenses. For example, both indecent exposure and public sexual indecency can be subsumed within the definition of lewd and lascivious conduct (e.g., MASS. GEN. LAWS c. 272, § 16, 2014).

Sting Operations

Prior to the mid-twentieth century, given the stigma of non-heterosexuality—not the least of which was the criminalization of acts of sodomy—and the lack of any other social institutions, those who sought to engage in sexual activity with members of the same sex "existed outside mainstream society" and, therefore, often sought such encounters in public places like movie-theater balconies, public restrooms, parks, and all-night diners or cafeterias (Escoffier, 1998, p. 69).

Starting in the 1950s and 1960s, however, establishments catering to gays, lesbians, and bisexuals began to flourish, thereby creating spaces and opportunities for socializing, bonding, and finding intimacy or sex (Escoffier, 1998; Woods, 2009).

Police officers often turned a blind eye and tolerated these establishments as "practical solutions to difficult law enforcement problems of controlling sex in public places." The controlled ghettoization of gay sex to underground bathhouses and isolated bars was viewed as the solution to having men engage in sex acts in public or semi-public places. Some establishments even paid law enforcement and organized crime bodies for protection. Not all police officers, however, turned a blind eye to gay bars

and bathhouses. As fears of communism swept America during the 1950s, politicians and law enforcement waged moral crusades aimed to protect the morals, health, and safety of the American public. Gays and lesbians found themselves labeled as sexual psychopaths, deviates, and communists. This anti-homosexual panic caused gay bathhouses and bars to become primary targets of police sting operations in order to preserve public morale. Police used stings to harass gay men and lesbians and to increase law enforcement's public image by preserving public morality.

(Woods, 2009, pp. 551–552)

Contemporary Discriminatory Enforcement

Even today, there is little doubt that laws against public sexual indecency are selectively enforced against gays and lesbians. Consider that polls suggest men and women of all sexual orientations engage in public sex acts.

A 2006 MSNBC.com survey found that 22% of Americans had sex in public during the previous year. In an informal survey conducted by *New York Magazine*, almost 100% of the people interviewed in New York had a tale of public or semi-public lewdness. According to one opposite-sex twenty-something couple interviewed by *New York Magazine*, "we've done it on rooftops, in empty subway cars, in the backseat of cabs, in bar and restaurant bathrooms, in our offices, under a blanket in Central Park." [But many] of these locations are primary targets of stings directed exclusively against men who engage in public sex acts with other men.

(Woods, 2009, pp. 565–566)

Some people who engage in public sex meet with diagnostic criteria for *exhibitionism* (see Chapter 12). Others do not; they are merely careless or are trying to "spice up" their sex lives. It is clear, though, that same-sex couples and opposite-sex couples are not treated the same way when they are caught. In contrast to same-sex actors who typically find themselves arrested for such acts, when opposite-sex couples are caught engaging in public sex, a Los Angeles Sheriff's Department sergeant is quoted as telling in Amnesty International (2005) that "officers usually check to make sure there is not a serious crime occurring (such as rape) and then send them on their way. The parties are told to take it to a hotel or take it home" (p. 21; see also Mogul, Ritchie, & Whitlock, 2011).

Claims of discriminatory enforcement of public sex laws are not new. Critics have long charged that laws against public sex have been discriminatorily enforced against gays, lesbians, and bisexuals (e.g., Berube, 2003; Rosen, 1981), especially in areas in which police surveillance ostensibly tried to combat **tearoom trade**—sex in easily accessible public locations where homosexuals purportedly engaged in sex (Sklansky, 2012). Sociologist Laud Humphreys studied such activities in the late 1960s when he

> spent several months observing, primarily in an unnamed Midwestern city, the conduct and norms of men who had sex with other men in public bathrooms, in particular those located in public parks. Humphreys concludes that whether a public bathroom serves as a "tearoom," that is, whether it functions as a site where men can potentially have anonymous sex with other men, depends on the extent to which the site affords them privacy. If a particular site can protect the sexual actors from unwilling gazers and unwilling gazers from the sexual actors, then it can be transformed from a mundane bathroom into a sexualized site.
>
> (Ball, 2008, pp. 16–17)

Humphreys published his research in a book he titled *Tearoom Trade: Impersonal Sex in Public Places* (1970). Since then, other researchers have also chronicled how people (mostly men) cruise for sex in public places, which can transformed into semi-private areas (e.g., Hollister, 1999). Tewksbury (1995,

2008) catalogued such spaces and dubbed them *erotic oases*—centralized cruising locations where sex occurs between men, including public parks, secluded walkways, or any place where there is an attainable measure of privacy (Tewksbury, 1995). To increase privacy in such areas, Tewksbury and Polley (2007) found that cruisers signal to one another with various signs in an attempt to discern other cruisers from undercover police and general passersby. Apostolopoulos, Sonmez, Shattell, Kronenfeld, Smith, and Stanton (2011) documented how cruising also frequently occurs at truck stops, with truckers who ordinarily identify as straight occasionally engaging in semi-public sex with other men.[1] And a significant body of literature documents how people in predominantly single-sex environments, such as prisons, sex-segregated boarding schools, and, to a lesser degree, even the military, seek out sexual activity with those who are available—a practice dubbed *situational homosexuality* (for a review, see Rodriguez-Rust, 2000).

Some scholars and activists argue that there is a world of difference between sex in public—where nonconsenting people are likely to view such activity—and sex in places that, although technically not private, are nonetheless locations in which people might enjoy a reasonable expectation of privacy. Ball (2008), for instance, maintains that certain spaces—"specific public bathrooms in parks and rest stop areas along highways, as well as commercial establishments (such as sex clubs and adult movie theaters) that make available designated areas within their facilities where individuals may engage in sexual conduct"—should not automatically fall outside the constitutional protections offered by *Lawrence* and other key privacy precedents (p. 8).

> [I]it is possible to delink the concept of privacy from the privateness or publicness of the sites where sexual conduct takes place. Such a delinking does not require questioning the proposition that individuals have a legitimate interest

in not having to observe sexual conduct by others unless they consent. Instead, the delinking simply recognizes the fact that, as the sociological literature shows, those who engage in public sex frequently and effectively privatize public sex sites.

(Ball, 2008, pp. 58–59)

Nonetheless, courts have not embraced such arguments. Laws against public nudity and public sexual indecency remain enforceable just as the majority in *Lawrence v. Texas* (2003) specified they should.

The Impact of *Lawrence* on Other Laws Criminally Regulating Sex

What specific right was announced in *Lawrence* remains unclear. Narrowly read, the liberty interest announced in *Lawrence* is for consenting adults to engage in private acts of oral or anal sex, regardless of their marital status or sexual orientation. Some courts have clearly given *Lawrence* such a narrow read when they upheld the constitutionality of applying sodomy laws to acts between adults in situations in which consent may be tainted by a power imbalance, such as between a therapist and a client (e.g., *United States v. McClelland*, 2006), a clergy member and a congregant (e.g., *State v. Bussmann*, 2007), a teacher and student (e.g., *Berkovsky v. State*, 2006; *State v. Clinkenbeard*, 2005; *Talbert v. State*, 2006), or between military personnel of different ranks (*United States v. Marcum*, 2004).

Nonetheless, the broad language in *Lawrence* suggests a more far-reaching result than certain sex acts. Indeed, the opinion seems to be concerned with privacy rights. Consider the Court's introduction to the case:

Liberty protects the person from unwarranted government intrusions into a dwelling or other private places. In our tradition the State is not omnipresent in the home. And there are other spheres of our lives and existence, outside the home, where the State should not be a dominant presence. Freedom extends beyond spatial bounds. Liberty presumes an autonomy of self that includes freedom of thought, belief, expression, and certain intimate conduct. The instant case involves liberty of the person both in its spatial and more transcendent dimensions.

(p. 562)

To many scholars and commentators, the language used in *Lawrence* presents a paradox. On one hand, the decision used broad language concerning the importance of concepts like liberty, privacy, and autonomy. Yet the Court did not declare any specific right to be a fundamental one. The Court could have clearly announced that the right of consenting adults to engage in private, sexual acts was a fundamental right—a decision so private that is should generally be beyond the regulation of the government. Had the Court done so, then strict scrutiny would be applied to laws infringing upon this zone of privacy in the future, thereby allowing governmental regulation only when it is narrowly tailored to achieve a compelling governmental interest. In applying strict scrutiny to the Texas sodomy law at issue in the case, then the Court could have held that regulating morality absent actual injury to others is not a valid, compelling governmental interest. But the Court did not take such an approach. Instead, the Court applied the lowest standard of review in invalidating the Texas sodomy law when it simply concluded that the "Texas statute furthers no legitimate state interest which can justify its intrusion into the personal and private life of the individual" (*Lawrence v. Texas*, 2003, p. 578).

Because the Court invalidated sodomy laws under the rational basis test, the majority may have deemed it unnecessary to engage in a more exacting strict scrutiny analysis that would have led to the same end result in the case. But one could also view the Court's language as intentionally narrow—a specific refusal to have declared sexual privacy rights to be fundamental ones and thereby declining to hold that future challenges concerning this right should be reviewed under strict scrutiny. Yet, if that was the Court's intention, it is perplexing that it would go to such great lengths to have used broad, inclusive language such as, "[o]ur obligation is to define the liberty of all, not to mandate our own moral code" (*Lawrence v. Texas*, 2003, p. 571). In fact, the Court's dismissive handling of the issue of morality led the dissenting justices to suggest the majority had opened Pandora's Box. Consider the point raised in Justice Scalia's dissent with regard to active euthanasia. In *Washington v. Glucksberg* (1997), the Court applied the rational basis test when it held that substantive due process did not include the right to assisted suicide. Since *Lawrence* counsels against making moral arguments, why do the principles of privacy, autonomy, and self-determination get construed under rational basis review in a manner that allows someone to be free from unwanted governmental regulation with regard to having an abortion or engaging in oral or anal sex, yet, at the same time, those same principles of privacy, autonomy, and self-determination do not serve as rational bases for allowing assisted suicide? The majority never addresses this question.

If morality is truly no longer a rational basis for legislation, many laws may be affected by *Lawrence* (see Strader, 2011). Justice Scalia's dissent makes mention of a number of such laws. "State laws against bigamy, same-sex marriage, adult incest, prostitution, masturbation, adultery, fornication, bestiality, and obscenity are likewise sustainable only in light of *Bowers'* validation of laws based on moral choices" (*Lawrence v. Texas*, 2003, p. 590, Scalia, J., dissenting).

Justice Scalia was correct that *Lawrence*, when considered with other relevant precedent, paved the way for the federal recognition of state-recognized same-sex marriages in *United States v. Windsor* (2013), and, subsequently, the legalization of same-sex marriage by numerous states and several federal circuit courts of appeal (*Baskin v. Bogan*, 2014; *Bostic v. Schaefer*, 2014; *Kitchen v. Herbert*, 2014; *Latta v. Otter*, 2014), and ultimately, by the U.S. Supreme Court itself (*Obergefell v. Hodges*, 2015; see Chapter 9 for more detail on same-sex marriage). And, as described later in this chapter, he was also correct about the impact of *Lawrence* on fornication laws (*Martin v. Ziherl*, 2005). But Justice Scalia clearly overstated his point.

First of all, masturbation is not criminally prohibited in any state today, provided that such acts are not performed in public (Carpenter, 2004; Cruz, 2005). In fact, no state has ever criminalized masturbation (Koppelman, 2004), although at least one court upheld a prison regulation against masturbation (*Rodgers v. Ohio Dep't of Rehab and Correction*, 1993).

Second, there are reasons other than morality to prohibit prostitution, bestiality, and incest. Public health would seem to be the most obvious reason, but there are other reasons as well.

Prostitution

The crime of **prostitution** involves engaging in a sexual act in exchange for compensation (FLA. STAT. 796.01, 2014). The compensation is usually money, but it could be drugs or any item of value (e.g., N.J. STAT. ANN. § 2C:34–1, 2014). Some oppose prostitution because it "objectifies, exploits, and ultimately dehumanizes women; others decry it for precipitating social ills, such as the proliferation of communicable diseases, crime, rape, and" human trafficking (Streit, 2007, pp. 729–730). These arguments are discussed at length in Chapter 7. Here, suffice it to say that prostitution laws have remained viable since *Lawrence* was decided in 2003. In addition to the public health rationale—which, in and of itself, is a rational basis supporting laws against prostitution—courts also distinguish prostitution on the grounds that *Lawrence* was concerned with private conduct, not activity for hire (*State v. Freitag*, 2006; *State v. Green*, 2013; *State v. Romano*, 2007; *United States v. Thompson*, 2006).

Bestiality

Bestiality, sometimes called *zoophilia*, is a crime involving human sexual activity with an animal. Depending on the jurisdiction, bestiality may be its own criminal offense, may be subsumed in the definition of sodomy, or may be prosecuted under statutes that prohibit cruelty to animals. As of the writing of this book, bestiality constitutes a misdemeanor in approximately 19 states and a felony in about 17 states; in the remaining 14 states and the District of Columbia,[2] bestiality is not illegal (Animal Legal Defense Fund, 2014; Turcios, 2014).

As with prostitution, there are public health reasons for prohibiting such acts, especially preventing the spread of disease. But there is an important additional argument that places bestiality beyond the scope of *Lawrence*. An animal cannot grant legally valid consent to engage in sexual activity with a human. Accordingly, acts of bestiality can continue to be criminally prosecuted and punished under sodomy laws or animal cruelty laws without running afoul *Lawrence*'s central holding, although states differ as to whether offenders must register as sex offenders. An appellate court in Kansas ruled that a man who had sex with a Rottweiler was required to register as a sex offender (*State v. Coman*, 2009), whereas an appellate court in Michigan reached the opposite conclusion in a case involving a man who had multiple convictions for having sex with sheep (*People v. Haynes*, 2008).

Incest

Incest is the marriage or sexual activity between people related within a certain degree of kinship. Again, there are public health rea

sons to prevent incest, especially to prevent in-breeding, a practice that increases the likelihood of offspring being born with harmful genetic mutations that negatively affect health. Additionally, incest laws are intended to deter coercion, protect the integrity of the family unit, and prevent the significant psychological harm that incest can cause (e.g., *Lowe v. Swanson*, 2009; *Muth v. Frank*, 2015; *People v. McEvoy*, 2013; *State v. Freeman*, 2003; *State v. Lowe*, 2007; see also Strader, 2011).

Obscenity

Chapter 8 explores legal regulation of obscene materials. Although morality undoubtedly underpins the legal regulation of sexually explicit materials, there are other reasons why obscene materials fall outside the scope of First Amendment protections for free expression, especially when dealing with child pornography. Thus, courts have routinely held that even when the age of consent for sexual activity is below age 18, any photography, filming, or video-recording of such acts when one of the participants is younger than 18 may be criminally regulated (see *State v. Senters*, 2005; *People v. Hollins*, 2012; *State v. Hughes*, 2011).

On the other hand, a federal district court dismissed obscenity charges (not involving child pornography) on the grounds that *Lawrence* barred Congress from using the criminal law to enforce a "moral code" (*United States v. Extreme Associates*, 2005, p. 586). A federal appeals court, however, reversed that decision by dismissing the question of morals legislation as irrelevant to the regulation of the allegedly obscene materials in the case, especially since *Lawrence* dealt with intimate relationships and what occurs within them while in private, not sexual stimulation or pleasure, per se. Some scholars and commentators have argued that current obscenity laws are no longer viable after *Lawrence*.

The Court's holding in *Lawrence* is hard to reconcile with retaining the state's authority to ban the distribution to adults of sexually explicit materials identified by, among other things, their supposed appeal to what those in power regard as "unhealthy" lust, or the state's power to punish adults for enjoying such materials in private, whether alone or in the company of other adults.

(Tribe, 2004, p. 1945; see also
Glazer, 2008; Kaplan, 2014)

Others argue that the potential harms related to obscenity discussed in Chapter 8 justify providing only limited constitutional protections for obscene materials, but allowing for regulations that are akin to those governing commercial speech (Huppin & Malamuth, 2012). As of the writing of this book, however, no federal appellate courts have interpreted *Lawrence* in ways that have undercut the law of obscenity laws as set forth in Chapter 8.

Bigamy

The crime of **bigamy** is the condition of having or purporting to marry two or more spouses at the same time. In most U.S. jurisdictions, the crime requires *scienter*—knowledge that oneself is still legally married to another person or, alternatively, knowledge that the person one purports to marry is still legally married to another person (e.g., 720 ILL. COMP. STAT. 5/11–45, 2014; MINN. REV. STAT. 609.355, 2014). The *scienter* requirement means that someone is not guilty of the crime of bigamy if he or she neither knows nor had reason to know that his or her spouse was already legally married to another person. The *scienter* requirement also means that one is not guilty of bigamy if he or she reasonably believes that his or her own previous marriage was dissolved by death, divorce, or annulment.

Criminal trials for the crime of bigamy are relatively infrequent, primarily because few people purport to marry someone while still married to another person. When the crime occurs, it is usually part of a fraudulent scheme to obtain someone's property or as part of some other type of criminal scheme. The other situation that prompts bigamy prosecutions concerns the activities of splinter religious groups that continue the practice of polygamy to this day in spite of fact that the mainstream religions from which these offshoots broke away prohibit polygamy. Consider that even though the Church of Jesus Christ of Latter-day Saints officially abandoned the practice in 1890, the Mormon sect known as the Fundamentalist Church of Jesus Christ of Latter-day Saints still advocates and practices plural marriage. Bigamy prosecutions of these fundamentalist sects often arise from situations like those described in Andrea Moore-Emmet's (2004) book *God's Brothel: The Extortion of Sex for Salvation in Contemporary Mormon and Christian Fundamentalist Polygamy*, or in Wright and Richardson's (2011) book *Saints Under Siege*. These books document how a warped view of religion is used by some fundamentalist sects to justify rape, incest, orgies, and violence—even against young girls who are taken as "wives" at remarkably young ages.

In *Reynolds v. United States* (1879), the U.S. Supreme Court ruled that Utah's criminalization of bigamy (a law Utah was required to enact before it was admitted to the Union) was constitutionally permissible in spite of the First Amendment right to the free exercise of religion. *Reynolds* has never been overruled. Moreover, defendants convicted of violating bigamy laws have not been successful in arguing that *Lawrence* changed the legal landscape. In *State v. Holm* (2006), for instance, the Utah Supreme Court said,

> First, the behavior at issue in this case is not confined to personal decisions made about sexual activity, but rather raises important questions about the State's ability to regulate marital relationships and prevent the formation and propagation of marital forms that the citizens of the State deem harmful. . . .

Moreover, marital relationships serve as the building blocks of our society. . . . The people of this State have declared monogamy a beneficial marital form and have also declared polygamous relationships harmful. As the Tenth Circuit stated . . . Utah "is justified, by a compelling interest, in upholding and enforcing its ban on plural marriage to protect the monogamous marriage relationship". . . . The distinction between private, intimate sexual conduct between consenting adults and the public nature of polygamists' attempts to extralegally redefine the acceptable parameters of a fundamental social institution like marriage is plain.

(pp. 743–745; see also *State v. Fischer*, 2008)

In some states, the crime of bigamy also includes cohabiting or living with someone other than his or her lawful spouse under circumstance that give the appearance that the cohabiting couple are legally married when, in fact, they are not (TEX. PENAL. CODE § 205.014, 2014; UTAH CODE ANN. § 76–7–101, 2014). Such a law was challenged in 2013 in a civil lawsuit brought by Kody Brown and his four wives after they appeared on the television show *Sister Wives*. That case is explored in the Law in Action box.

Law in Action *SISTER WIVES* AND *BROWN V. BUHMAN*

Unlike the bigamy laws in most states, Utah's bigamy law contains a provision concerning cohabitation (i.e., living together). The statute provides, "A person is guilty of bigamy when, knowing he has a husband or wife or knowing the other person has a husband or wife, the person purports to marry another person or cohabits with another person" (UTAH CODE ANN. § 76-7-101(1), 2013). In a *Brown v. Buhman* (2013), a federal district court declared the cohabitation portion unconstitutional under the First Amendment to the U.S. Constitution.

Kody Brown lived with his "sister wives" and allowed a cable television channel to document their lives together. Unsurprisingly, this drew a lot of attention to the stars of the reality television show, especially because they lived in Utah. As the court recognized, the case was "fraught with both religious and historical significance for the State of Utah because it deals with the question of polygamy, an issue that played a central role in the State's development and that of its dominant religion, The Church of Jesus Christ of Latter-Day Saints" (*Brown v. Buhman*, 2013, p. 1180). Although Brown and his "sister wives" were not members of the LDS Church, they adhered "to the beliefs of a fundamentalist church that shares its historical roots with Mormonism" (p. 1180). In ruling in their favor, the court first rejected the notion the *Lawrence* and other privacy cases created a right to engage in the practice of polygamy.

The court went on, however, to invalidate the portion of the Utah bigamy statute aimed at cohabitation.

The relationship at issue in this lawsuit, which the court has termed "religious cohabitation," has been aptly described by then Chief Justice Durham of the Utah Supreme Court. Religious cohabitation occurs when "[t]hose who choose to live together without getting married enter into a personal relationship that resembles a marriage in its intimacy but claims no legal sanction." Those who choose to live in these relationships "intentionally place themselves outside the framework of rights and obligations that surrounds the marriage institution." A defining characteristic of such cohabitation as lived by Plaintiffs and those similarly situated is that, in choosing "to enter into a relationship that [they know] would not be legally recognized as marriage, [they use] religious terminology to describe the relationship," and this terminology—'marriage' and 'husband and wife'—happens to coincide with the terminology used by the state to describe the legal status of married persons." Stated succinctly, Plaintiffs "appropriate the terminology of marriage, a revered social and legal institution, for [their] own religious purposes," though not purporting "to have actually acquired the legal status of marriage."

(pp. 1197–1198)

The court then went on to analyze the plaintiffs' right under the First Amendment to live in religious cohabitation with each other.

In the religious cohabitation at issue in this case, however, the participants have consciously chosen to enter into personal relationships that they knew would not be legally recognized as marriage even though they used religious terminology to describe the relationships. They make no claim to having entered into legal unions by virtue of their religious cohabitation, having instead intentionally placed themselves outside the framework of rights and obligations that surround the marriage institution. In light of this, despite any applicability of *Reynolds* to actual polygamy (multiple purportedly legal unions), the cohabitation prong of the Statute is not operationally neutral or of general applicability because of its targeted effect on specifically religious cohabitation. It is therefore subject to strict scrutiny under the Free Exercise Clause and fails under that standard. Also, . . . following *Lawrence* and based on the arguments presented by Defendant in both his filings and at oral argument, the State of Utah has no rational basis under the Due Process Clause on which to prohibit the type of religious cohabitation at issue here; thus, the cohabitation prong of the Statute is facially unconstitutional, though the broader Statute survives in prohibiting [actual] bigamy.

(p. 1190)

- *Lawrence* was aimed at private, consensual sexual conduct between two consenting adults. Do you think that Brown and his "sister wives" should be legally able to enter into a plural marriage that is legally recognized by the state if they all consented to do so? Why or why not?
- The plaintiffs in *Brown v. Buhman* were members of a fundamentalist sect of the Mormon faith that subscribed to plural marriages even though the mainstream Mormon Church had abandoned polygamy in the late 1800s. Do you think that the law needs to accommodate all sincerely held religious beliefs? Explain your reasoning. What about religious beliefs that may not be sincerely held? Where would you draw the line? Who is to determine what is—and is not—a legitimate faith or a sincerely held religious belief?

Adultery and Fornication Laws

In barbarian times, wrongful acts were considered private wrongs against the victim and his kinship group (Weinstein, 1986). The remedy for a private wrong at this early time was for the victim or a member of his kinship group to extract "blood-vengeance" by killing a member of the wrongdoer's kinship group. Through time, quasi-legal systems developed to keep the peace. In early England, certain acts became punishable by the throne in order to keep the "king's peace":

The king[] assert[ed] that a violent act, a breach of the peace, was a wrong to him. The growth of strong government gave the king a special interest in preserving peace and preventing homicides and personal injuries, apart from the interests of his individual subjects. What was formerly a private wrong exclusively against an individual came to be seen as a public wrong against the domestic order and therefore against the state.

(Weinstein, 1986, p. 198)

As Britons adopted the traditions of Germanic tribes, monogamy being among them, adultery came to be viewed "as a serious wrong that invaded a husband's 'rights' over his wife" (Weinstein, 1986, p. 200). In the late ninth century, Alfred of Wessex codified one of the first Anglo-Saxon Codes. It made adultery and fornication illegal, and punished the offenses by imposing a fine. By the end of the twelfth century, adultery and fornication—considered "illicit unions" in the same category as prostitution—had evolved into public wrongs, punishable as crimes (Weinstein, 1986, p. 203). The state had become the enforcer of morality.

After the Norman invasion in 1066, adultery and fornication became ecclesiastical offenses, now under the jurisdiction of the Church. It remained in the exclusive jurisdiction of the Church until the Statute of Labourers was passed to remedy the labor shortage caused by the Black Death (Weinstein, 1986). The statute made it a crime to entice, retain, or harbor deserting servants. Gradually, the ability to sue for the taking of a person in whom the "owner" had a property interest came to cover the loss of consortium in a marital relationship, or the loss of one's daughter's virginity to someone other than her husband. Thus, adultery and fornication were not only punishable under canon law, but also gave the husband of the adulterous wife or the father of the fornicating female a civil remedy against the person with whom the wife or daughter was having an affair. In other words, neither adultery nor fornication were common-law crimes. As explained by Blackstone in his famous *Commentaries*,

In the year 1650, when the ruling power found it for their interest to put on the semblance of a very extraordinary strictness and purity of morals, not only incest and willful adultery were made capital crimes; but also the repeated act of keeping a brothel, or committing fornication, were made felony without benefit of clergy. But at the restoration, when men, from an abhorrence of the hypocrisy of the late times, fell into a contrary extreme of licentiousness, it was not thought proper to renew a law of such unfashionable rigor. And these offenses have been ever since left to the feeble coercion of the spiritual court, according to the rules of the canon law.
(1979/1765–1769, pp. 64–65)

As Blackstone states, the offenses became less severely punished by institutions as the importance of Church declined. Privately, however, adultery and fornication were considered immoral, and often carried severe consequences within the community and within the household. The law did not need to turn adulterers and fornicators into pariahs; these acts were sins which society punished more severely than any court would. When the Puritans settled in North America, however, they were unhappy with the lack of institutional punishment that existed in England. Accordingly, they made adultery and fornications crimes in the colonies. By this time, neither offense was necessarily viewed as a wrong against a husband or father, but rather as "an offense against morality and chastity" (Weinstein, 1986, p. 212).

Following the lead of the colonial Puritans, adultery and fornication became crimes in almost every U.S. jurisdiction. "Most of those statutes were enacted in the 1800s and were vigorously enforced" (Sweeny, 2014, p. 130). In 1955, the American Law Institute's Model Penal Code recommended that adultery be decriminalized, but not fornication. As many states adopted variations of the Model Penal Code thorough the 1960s and 1970s, they opted to decriminalize both adultery and fornication. Adultery remains a crime, however, in approximately 20 states.[3] It is usually a misdemeanor, but in some jurisdictions, it is still punishable as a felony (Falco, 2004; Sweeny, 2014). In those jurisdictions that continue to classify **adultery** as a crime, it is usually defined as sexual intercourse between consenting persons during a time when at least one of the participants is married to someone else. It is distinguished from **fornication**, which is sexual intercourse between unmarried, consenting persons.

"Modern" Adultery Statutes

The statutes that currently criminalize adultery are as varied as the states that criminalize it. There are two approaches, though, that are common. In many states, a single act of sexual intercourse outside of the marital relationship is insufficient to warrant criminal sanction. For instance, adultery is defined in South Carolina as having "habitual carnal intercourse" with someone who is married to another person (S.C. CODIFIED LAWS §16-15-70, 2014). Similarly, some statutes explicitly state that adultery is only criminal when "open and notorious" (e.g., 720 ILL. COMP. STAT. 5/11–35).

Another common approach to adultery defines the crime by limiting the enforceability of the statute by the criminal justice system. For example, in Arizona "[n]o prosecution for adultery shall be commenced except upon complaint of the husband or wife" [ARIZ. REV. STAT. § 13–1408(B)]. A North Dakota court summarized the rationale underlying this approach as follows:

> Laws of this character are evidently enacted for the purpose of protecting the sanctity of the home, and in recognition of the principle that the crime of adultery is a crime peculiarly infringing upon the rights of the innocent par-

ties to the marriage relation, and that if such innocent parties see fit to condone the offense, and from a desire to avoid scandal and humiliation, and to preserve the integrity of the home, and prevent the disgrace of children and relatives, refuse to prosecute, the public is not sufficiently interested or injured to justify the institution of criminal proceedings, as in other cases, by any member of the community.

(*State v. Wesie*, 1908, p. 21)

On the other hand, this approach can provide a legal mechanism for coercing a cheating spouse into accepting certain divorce settlement terms on the threat of criminal prosecution or, even worse, blackmailing an unfaithful spouse with regard to other criminal activity (Sweeny, 2014).

Although 20 states still have criminal laws against adultery, prosecutions under these laws are quite rare (Sweeny, 2014). In fact, they are so uncommon that

> when a Wisconsin district attorney actually prosecuted someone for adultery in 1990, the story rated the front page of *The New York Times*. More recently, in 2004 in Virginia, the jilted lover of John R. Bushey, Jr. turned him in for violating Virginia's adultery statute. In response, Bushey planned to take his case to the Supreme Court, and the American Civil Liberties Union agreed to represent him. Bushey, however, changed his mind and agreed to perform 20 hours of community service as punishment.

(Annuschat, 2010, p. 1164, n. 21)

Most contemporary criminal prosecutions for adultery occur in military courts when the act is "prejudicial to good order and discipline" or otherwise brings "discredit upon the armed forces" (Annuschat, 2010, p. 1177, quoting Joint Service Commission on Military Justice, 2008, p. 62). Given these types of harms that are unique to the military setting, compounded by the military interests in preserving honor, challenges to adultery courts martial based on *Lawrence* have been unsuccessful (e.g., *United States v. Orellana*, 2005). Outside the military context, it remains an open question whether or not adultery laws can survive constitutional scrutiny on the grounds that they serve a legitimate governmental interest in promoting healthy marriages and preserving the integrity of the family.

"Modern" Fornication Laws

Prior to the decision in *Lawrence v. Texas* (2003), a number of states maintained statutes that criminalized sexual intercourse between unmarried persons, a crime known as *fornication*. As originally proscribed, however, this occurred when an unmarried adult female engaged in consensual sexual intercourse, showing the sexist nature of the offense. Even today, Massachusetts, Virginia, Georgia, Idaho, Mississippi, North Carolina, Utah, and South Carolina still have fornication laws on their books. Prosecutions under these laws, are virtually nonexistent. If they were to occur, Justice Scalia's dissent in *Lawrence v. Texas* (2003) accurately predicted that the decision sounded the death knell for fornication laws since they simply prohibit unmarried adults from engaging in consensual sexual conduct with each other on the basis of the perceived immorality of premarital sex. In *Martin v. Ziherl* (2005), the Virginia Supreme Court relied on *Lawrence* when it declared Virginia's fornication law unconstitutional.

Several months before *Lawrence* was decided, the Supreme Court of Georgia had invalidated that state's fornication law on state constitutional grounds. That case is notable because the defendant was a minor. He was 16 years of age and charged with violating the fornication law for having consensual sex with his girlfriend, another 16-year-old, after the girl's mother found the boy in her daughter's bed in the wee hours of the morning (*In re J.M.*, 2003). Because the case involved two minors, *Lawrence* would not apply.

THE SOCIAL CONTROL OF MINORS' SEXUALITY: STATUTORY RAPE

Statutory rape laws criminalize sex between adults and underage minors. The crime was first codified in English law in 1275, when the Statute of Westminster I provided "[T]he King prohibiteth that none do ravish, nor take away by force, any Maiden within Age" (3 Edw. 1, c. 13, as quoted in Eidson, 1980). The age of consent was initially 12 years of age, but it was lowered to 10 in 1576 (Oberman, 2004–2005). That same age of 10 was incorporated into early American laws, but rose to 18 or even 21 during the 1800s (Oberman, 2004–2005). Today, all U.S. jurisdictions continue to have criminal laws penalizing sexual conduct with someone under their specified age of consent. Thirty U.S. states and the District of Columbia set the age of consent at 16; the remaining states set the age of consent at 17[4] or 18.[5]

For most of their existence, statutory rape laws were not gender-neutral. They penalized only sex with an underage female, not with underage males, largely because girls were viewed as "special property in need to special protection" (Oberman, 2004–2005, p. 120). Unlike most crimes that require criminal intent, statutory rape has been a strict liability crime for most of its existence. In other words, a bona fide mistake of fact with regard to the age of girl was irrelevant. In fact, "it did not matter whether the victim looked older than the age of consent, that she consented, or even that she initiated sexual contact" (Oberman, 2004–2005, p. 120). Moreover, because some jurisdictions recognized a so-called promiscuity defense—meaning the crime of statutory rape occurred only when the victim was a virgin—critics argue that the real purpose behind statutory rape laws was to protect virginity, rather than to punish those who pressure young into engaging in sex. Nonetheless, these laws persist today, largely because society has a compelling interest in protecting youth, especially those with raging hormones during puberty, from exploitative or predatory sexual relationships (Findholt & Robrecht, 2002), a situation that has been exacerbated in the digital age (see Jacobs, 2012). Hence, the law sets an age at which youth are presumed old enough to grant effective legal consent to engage in sexual activity. Youth under the age of consent are legally incapable of granting consent. In other words, age is presumed to be a measure of sexual maturity that "acts as a proxy for a power differential that is suspect of coercion" (Cocca, 2004, p. 19).

Starting in the mid-1960s, a minority of U.S. states changed their laws to recognize an honest and reasonable mistake of fact with regard to the victim's age as a defense to a charge of statutory rape. To this day, however, a mistake of fact regarding age is not a defense to statutory rape in 37 states and the District of Columbia.[6] However, nearly all states have changed their statutory rape laws such that they are now gender-neutral, recognizing that underage males can also be the victims of a statutory rape.

Approximately 30 states have amended their statutory rape laws to decriminalize sex acts between people close in age (e.g., within two, three, or four years of each other's ages, even if one is over the age of consent and the other is younger than the age of consent). These so-called "Romeo and Juliet" provisions are designed to make sure that statutory rape laws are not used to prosecute normal teenage sexual experimentation. As a result, statutory rape laws are typically used to prosecute offenders who exploit an age gap or in cases "in which there is insufficient evidence to sustain a heightened criminal sexual assault charge (e.g., felony rape) because prosecutors lack proof that intercourse was nonconsensual" (Oberman, 2004–2005, p. 133). That being said, statutory rape laws can still be used discriminatorily in attempts to perpetuate heteronormativity, as the case of *Kansas v. Limon* (2005) illustrates (see

Chapter 3). Indeed, some states only exempt opposite-sex sexual activity in spite of the apparent equal protection barriers to enforcing age-gap exceptions to statutory rape laws only to Romeo and Juliet, but not Romeo and Romeo or Juliet and Juliet (see Higdon, 2008). But even when such exceptions are neutral with regard to sexual orientation, police are more likely to arrest—and prosecutors are more likely to charge—cases involving same-sex statutory rape. "If it's two boys and they're both young or it's two girls, there's a tendency to assume it's abuse. With opposite genders, they're more likely to say 'Well, you know, they're experimenting'" (Meidinger, 2012, p. 421).

Discriminatory enforcement across sexualities aside, in states that have not adopted such age-gap provisions, statutory rape law can lead to bizarre consequences:

> Shane Sandborg cannot drop his daughter off for her first day of school. He cannot coach his son's little league team. He cannot attend any of his children's birthday parties. Due to his oldest daughter's birth, Shane cannot do any of these things. After Shane's 16-year-old fiancée gave birth to their now seven-year-old daughter, Shane was investigated, charged, and convicted of criminal sexual abuse. He was just 15 months older than his fiancée. Shane was required to register on the Illinois Sex Offender Registry, and the label "sex offender" has haunted him ever since.
>
> (Franklin, 2012, pp. 309–310)

As was the case for Shane Sandborg, most contemporary statutory rape cases, indeed upwards of 75% of them, are prosecuted when a parent—usually, but not always, the parent of an underage girl—reports the case to the police (Elstein & Davis, 1997). Troup-Leasure and Snyder (2005) found that of the roughly 7,550 statutory rape incidents reported to police between 1996 and 2000, 95% involved female victims and nearly all of the offenders were men. The median age difference between the female victim and male offenders was six years. Of the 5% of male victims of statutory rape, 94% of the corresponding offenders were female.

> The research confirms stereotypes about the risk for teenage girls: that statutory relationships carry higher risks of pregnancy, single-parenthood, and other psychosocial problems . . . with poverty, family dysfunction, parent–child relationships, and/or other antisocial behaviors that precede the commencement of the statutory relationship.
>
> (Hines & Finkelhor, 2007, pp. 303–304)

SEXUALLY TRANSMITTED DISEASES AND THE CRIMINAL LAW

After reading this chapter and Chapter 5, the importance of the concept of effective *consent* in sexual relations should be evident. Sexual activity without effective legal consent may constitute a range of criminal offenses from statutory rape (if the sex involves a minor who is unable to give consent due to his or her youthful age) all the way up to sexual assault in the first degree (rape). But what exactly does the ordinary, reasonable, prudent person consent to when he or she consents to have sex with another person? Does someone who consents to sex assume the risk of exposure to treatable sexually transmitted infections (STIs) like chlamydia, gonorrhea, and syphilis? What about potentially life-threatening STIs, like hepatitis or HIV?

Knowing Transmission Statutes Impose a Duty to Disclose

The Ryan White Comprehensive AIDS Resources Emergency Act of 1990 was an important piece of legislation enacted, in large part, to provide the states with federal funding for the prevention and treatment of HIV/AIDS. At the time the Ryan White Act was initially enacted, the HIV/AIDS epidemic was relatively young. In fact, the first recognized cases of AIDS came to light in 1981 and the virus that causes AIDS—the human immunodeficiency virus (HIV)—was not discovered until 1983 (Gallo & Montagnier, 2003). More importantly, in the 1980s, effective treatments for HIV had not yet been discovered; as Table 6.1 illustrates, an HIV infection was a death sentence for the overwhelming majority of people.

The Ryan White Act required states to certify that criminal laws were adequate to prosecute individuals who knowingly exposed another person to HIV. According to the CDC (2014), this caused a number of states to implement "HIV-specific criminal exposure laws [that] impose criminal penalties on people living with HIV who know their HIV status and who potentially expose others to HIV" (para. 1).

According to an analysis by CDC and Department of Justice researchers (CDC, 2014; Lehman, Carr, Nichol, Ruisanchez, Knight, Langford, Gray, & Mermin, 2014), by 2011, 67 laws focusing on people living with HIV had been enacted in 33 states:

> HIV-specific criminal laws impose criminal penalties on persons who know that they have

Table 6.1 Number and percentage of people with AIDS

	1981–1987	1988–1992	1993–1995	1995–2000
Living	2,103 (04.2%)	20,572 (10.2%)	96,998 (37.7%)	203,192 (76.9%)
Deceased	47,993 (95.5%)	181,212 (89.5%)	159,048 (61.8%)	59,807 (22.6%)

Source: U.S. Centers for Disease Control and Prevention ([CDC], 2001).

HIV and engage in certain behaviors, most commonly sexual activity without prior disclosure of their status. HIV-specific criminal laws are a controversial policy and some prosecutions under them have received widespread local and national media attention. In some cases, prosecutions were based on documented HIV transmission; some were based on behaviors with an increased likelihood of HIV transmission; and others were based on behaviors posing little or only theoretical risk of transmission, such as biting or spitting.

(Lehman et al., 2014, para. 2)

Of the 33 states with criminal laws regulating people with HIV, 24 states criminalize sexual activity by persons with HIV who do not disclose their STI-positive status to their sexual partners (Lehman et al., 2014). Such statutes are commonly referred to as **knowing transmission laws** and they typically contain three elements:

1. a *mens rea* requirement that the defendant must know he or she is HIV-positive;
2. an *actus reus* requirement that an HIV-positive defendant engage in certain prohibited conduct; and
3. an attendant circumstance requirement that the defendant's sexual partner must not be aware of the defendant's HIV-positive status.

(Kaplan, 2012, p. 1519)

Not all states limit their knowing transmissions laws to HIV. Some states include forms of hepatitis and classify the offense as a felony (e.g., NEB. REV. STAT. § 28–934, 2014; TENN. CODE ANN. § 39–13–109, 2014; see also Fan, 2012a, 2012b; Lehman et al., 2014; Wolf & Vezina, 2004). Other states have knowing transmission statutes targeting a full array of STIs that grade the severity of the crime dependent on the diagnosis, typically making the offense a misdemeanor if it involves chancroid, gonorrhea, genital herpes, syphilis, or chlamydia, and designat-

ing it a felony if it involves HIV or hepatitis (e.g., ALA. CODE § 22–11A-21(c); CAL. HEALTH & SAFETY CODE § 120291(a), 2014; N.J. STAT. ANN. § 2C:34–5, 2014; see also Fan, 2012a, 2012b; Lazzarini, Bray, & Burris, 2002; Lehman et al., 2014; Wolf & Vezina, 2004). Regardless of whether such statutes target HIV or STIs more broadly, most of the states with such laws require proof of nondisclosure as an element of the crime that the prosecution must prove beyond a reasonable doubt. In eight states, however, disclosure is an affirmative defense that the defendant must prove, "even though evidence of such disclosure during a sexual encounter and/or needle-sharing may be limited" (Lehman et al., 2014, para. 16).

The "prohibited conduct" includes more than vaginal or anal sex in many states; other "prohibited conduct," depending on the state, includes oral sex; needle-sharing; engaging in acts of prostitution; biting, spitting, and throwing bodily fluids, especially in correctional institutions; and donating blood, tissue, or bodily fluids (Lehman et al., 2014). Four states also criminalize sharing sex objects/toys and one, Colorado, bars mutual masturbation (Lehman et al., 2014). Thus, many states fail to differentiate between high-risk (e.g., vaginal or anal intercourse), low-risk (e.g., oral sex), and negligible-risk behaviors (e.g., mutual masturbation). Consider, for instance, that "there are no documented cases of HIV transmission from spitting" (Lehman et al., 2014, p. 19). And few states take into account behaviors that significantly reduce the risk of transmission, such as condom use (a defense in only four states), antiretroviral therapy, or pre-exposure prophylaxis (Lehman et al., 2014). Nonetheless, most of the laws lump all such "prohibited conduct" together and classify the offenses as felonies, with 18 states imposing sentences up to 10 years, 7 states imposing sentences between 11 and 20 years, and 5 states imposing sentences of more than 20 years (Fan, 2012a, 2012b; Lehman et al., 2014; Wolf & Vezina, 2004).

Consider the case of *State v. Hinkhouse* (1996). Hinkhouse had unprotected sex with several women while HIV-positive. He lied to several of them to conceal his seropositive status. Hinkhouse engaged in rough sex, including anal intercourse that, at times, was so rough that he made his partners bleed. At trial, the prosecution elicited testimony that Hinkhouse disclosed his HIV-positive status to his fiancée and used a condom to prevent transmitting the virus to her. By contrasting his behavior with his fiancée with the women with whom Hinkhouse had unprotected sex, prosecutors were able to prove that his actions demonstrated a specific intent to spread HIV. For these acts, Hinkhouse was convicted of ten counts of assault and attempted murder.

Beyond Knowing Transmission Laws

Even in states without specific laws targeting the behavior of people with STIs, the criminal law can still be used to prosecute people who knowingly expose others to HIV and other serious STIs. Indeed, because a failure to disclose one's status as HIV-positive may vitiate consent to sex (see Ginn, 2000), such actions may even constitute the crime of rape in jurisdictions that define rape in terms of the absence of consent, rather than by the use of force (see Chapter 5). But because rape by fraud is a tricky prosecutorial enterprise even more so than "regular" rape cases (see Rubenfeld, 2013), other criminal laws—such as reckless endangerment, aggravated assault, and even homicide and attempted homicide laws—are more commonly used to prosecute knowing exposure to STIs. For example, *State v. Neatherlin* (2007) affirmed a conviction for assault with a deadly weapon in a case involving a defendant infected with the Hepatitis C virus who bit a woman and then said that he hoped she would die.

The *mens rea* for crimes like attempted murder or aggraded assault with intent to kill requires specific intent to cause the death of one's victim. *Boyer v. Belleque* (2011) illus-

trates how such intent may be inferred from the defendant's actions. Boyer was an AIDS patient in his mid-30s. He was convicted of more than 20 counts of sodomy, sexual assault, and attempted murder. Although Boyer did not dispute that he engaged in the predicate sexual acts, he argued that he did not intend to cause the deaths of his victims, a material element of any attempted murder charge. In upholding his conviction, the Ninth Circuit Court of Appeals reasoned as follows:

> Boyer knew that he had developed full-blown AIDS by 1993 and he believed his condition to be terminal; Boyer understood that he could transmit the disease through even a single instance of unprotected sex, regardless of whether or not he ejaculated, and his partner consequently could develop AIDS and die as a result; Boyer targeted extremely vulnerable victims, indeed children, over a period of several months, through deliberate "grooming" and predatory activities; Boyer sexually abused B.B. and R.M., anally penetrating each of them once without a condom, despite knowing that he had full-blown AIDS; Boyer concealed from his victims and lied to his victims about the fact that he had AIDS; when Boyer raped R.M. and had anal sex with B.B., he knew his viral count was high, which increased the likelihood of transmission; Boyer's sexual encounters with his victims were rough and violent, as he raped R.M., and his anal penetration of B.B. was painful; and Boyer bragged about raping R.M. The facts here are strikingly similar to those recognized in *Hinkhouse* as probative of intent. Accordingly, we do not think that Boyer's case can be fairly distinguished from the facts of *Hinkhouse*. If there was sufficient evidence to sustain the element of intent to kill in *Hinkhouse*'s attempted murder conviction, then we conclude that there was also adequate evidence to sustain that of Boyer.
>
> (*Boyer v. Belleque*, 2011, p. 968)

The approach taken in *Hinkhouse* and *Boyer* poses a quandary in cases of so-called *bug chasing*. As Gauthier and Forsyth (1999) explained, some individuals actively seek out HIV-positive partners, called *gift-givers* and engage in unprotected sex with them with the intent of contracting the virus (see also Freeman, 2003).

> Four explanations have been proffered for this phenomenon. Some believe that bug chasing has emerged as a function of some gay men's yearning to be accepted by a community, to be included in the greater HIV-positive "brotherhood" . . . Others contend infection has become substantially more sustainable and livable and as a corollary, HIV has become a virtually meaningless hindrance toward "sexual nirvana" . . . A third perspective argues that this phenomenon is merely a psychological reactance effect (Brehm & Brehm, 1981), where the bombardment of safe-sex information and anti-infection "propaganda" has created a psychological and behavioral reversal in some in the community . . . Gay men are simply exhausted. The preponderance of awareness posters and safe sex warnings has fatigued the vitality of prophylaxis. . . . And last, some believe that these gay men have come to think that infection is an inevitable result of their lifestyle—that bug chasing increases the locus of control regarding imminent infection. Bug chasers want to be able to choose who infects them and under what circumstances they are infected; and similar to the Pygmalion effect, they believe that because it *will* happen, they should play an active role in its occurrence as a means to increase autonomy and recapture their fate.
>
> (Moskowitz & Roloff, 2007, pp. 22–24)

Moskowitz and Roloff (2007) rejected all four of these explanations and instead posited that bug chasing is a symptom of sexual addiction because the behavior meets the definition of "engaging in persistent and escalating patterns of sexual behavior acted out despite increasing negative consequences to self and others" (Moskowitz & Roloff, 2007, p. 24).

Specifically, they found evidence that bug chasing is a masochistic paraphilia (see Chapter 12) in which the relinquishment of sexual control becomes an aphrodisiac. "Chasing becomes the ultimate expression of subjugation, humiliation, and passivity—all of which are simply not voiced by the bareback community, all of which are incredibly arousing for chasers" (Moskowitz & Roloff, 2007, p. 35).

Bug chasers are a small part of the LGBT community; indeed, most gay men view bug chasers as "outsiders" to the gay community (Cole, 2007). Additionally, they do not seek death. Rather, they see infection with HIV as freeing themselves from fear under terms that allow them to manage a chronic disease with drugs that were not available a generation ago. But many bug chasers, especially younger gay men, are unaware of the toxic side effects of medications used to treat HIV. Moreover, many do not understand that they "could be infected or re-infected by a drug-resistant strain of the virus and that drugs might not be an option. Many thought that once they had the virus, they could have unprotected sex without worry that they could get any sicker" (Hogarth, 2003, para. 3).

Their wishes notwithstanding, it is unlikely that bug chasers can give effective legal consent to engage in unprotected sex with someone who is HIV positive. Just as there are limits to the ability of someone to consent to serious bodily harm during sadomasochistic sex (see Chapter 12), "consent by the victim is not a valid defense when the conduct is of a nature to be injurious to the public as well as to the party assaulted" (*United States v Johnson*, 1988, p. 804). This mirrors the usual doctrine of consent in criminal law that consent is not a valid defense to any form of homicide, mutual combat, or aggravated assaults or batteries (see Beale, 1895; Bohlen, 1924; Chiesa, 2011; see also *Commonwealth v. Burke*, 1983). Similarly, as previously discussed in this chapter, this approach to consent aligns with the applicability of consent to sex crimes like incest or statutory rape.

Even in the wake of *Lawrence v. Texas* (2003), informed consent to be infected with HIV is unlikely to be legally valid since "any court sincerely interpreting *Lawrence* would probably find the public health risk too slight to allow such a broad infringement on consensual intimate conduct" (Weiss, 2006, p. 408).

Bad Public Policy?

The use of criminal law to regulate the sexual behavior of people with STIs was initially justified on two grounds: as a means of deterring risky sexual behaviors and as a way of exacting retributive punishment on those who engaged in such behaviors (Wolf & Vezina, 2004). These laws were enacted to serve a public health goal. Consider that accordingly to the U.S. Centers for Disease Control and Prevention ([CDC], 2011), those between the ages of 15 and 24 experience roughly half of all STIs even though this age range represents only 25 percent of the sexually experienced population. By requiring disclosure, STI rates can be reduced since it is much more likely that uninfected people would insist on engaging in safer sex, such as using condoms, to prevent disease transmission to themselves if they knew that potential sex partners carried STIs (Fan, 2012a).

But research indicates that these laws do little to change the behaviors of people who are HIV-positive (Burris, Beletsky, Burleson, Case, & Lazzarini, 2007; Galletly, Glasman, Pinkerton, & DiFranceisco, 2012; Galletly & Pinkerton, 2008; Horvath, Weinmeyer, & Rosser, 2010). Moreover, these laws may actually be damaging public health efforts by increasing "stigma towards persons living with HIV"; reducing "the likelihood of disclosure to sexual or needle-sharing partners" and the "frequency of HIV testing since knowledge of status is required for culpability" and perpetuating "inflammatory or ill-informed media coverage that may perpetuate misinformation regarding modes of HIV transmission" (Lehman et al., 2014, para. 5; see also Fan, 2012a, 2012b; McElroy, 2010).

To prevent over-inclusive criminalization that potentially rises to the levels of due process violations, several scholars have called for revising knowing transmission laws (e.g., Grant, 2009; Waldman, 2011). At minimum, they argue that safer sex practices "are so important and so relevant to the risk of transmission of HIV that the criminal law should distinguish between protected and unprotected sex in HIV exposure and nondisclosure cases (Waldman, 2011, p. 605).

Box 6.1 A CRIME OF RECKLESS SEX?

In a provocative article, Ayres and Baker (2005) propose the creation of a new crime called "reckless sexual conduct." Recklessness, in legal parlance, is defined as the conscious disregard of a known risk. In other words, one acts recklessly when he or she knows or should have known that his or her behavior could result in some substantial and unjustifiable harm, but nonetheless engages in the risky behavior. Using this standard of recklessness, Ayres and Baker propose the following model statute:

(1) A person is guilty of reckless sexual conduct when the person intentionally engages in unprotected sexual activity with a person other than his or her spouse and these two people had not on an occasion previous to the occasion of the crime engaged in sexual activity.

(2) Affirmative Defense: Notwithstanding Section (1), it shall be an affirmative defense to any action brought under this article that the person with whom the defendant had unprotected sex expressly

asked to engage in unprotected sexual activity or otherwise gave unequivocal indications of affirmatively consenting to engage in sexual activity that is specifically unprotected.

(3) Definitions:

(a) "Sexual activity" means penile penetration of a vagina or anus accomplished with a male or female.

(b) "Unprotected sexual activity" means sexual activity without the use of a condom.

(c) "Occasion of the crime" includes the twelve-hour period after the two people engage in sexual activity for the first time.

(4) Sanctions:

(a) Sentence: The crime of reckless sexual conduct is punishable by imprisonment . . . for up to three months, or a fine.

(b) Sexual Offender Status: The court shall not register a person as a sexual offender because the person was found guilty of reckless sexual conduct.

Ayres and Baker argued that such a statute would serve several goals, two of which are particularly important. First, it would decrease unprotected sex, thereby decreasing the rate of transmission for STIs. Second, the crime would decrease nonconsensual sex.

For other couples, the break in the action caused by the attempt to put on a condom will present an opportunity for the parties (primarily women) to better express whether or not they truly consent. The result of this improved communication will be to more explicitly inform men that sex (either protected or unprotected) is not wanted. Studies suggest that at least some acquaintance rapists will not proceed if they truly learn the woman is not consenting. This reduction in the amount of unprotected, nonconsensual sex . . . would be clear progress in the fight against acquaintance rape. At other times, the opportunity for clearer communication will lead to better evidence of genuine consent. This condom-induced opportunity for communication is an opportunity for a conversation about sex that may make both parties feel more in control of their decisions. Thus some of the unprotected, ambiguously consensual sexual encounters in the shadow of the new crime will become protected, consensual sexual encounters.

(p. 636)

1. Unlike knowing transmission laws that require the defendant to have known that he or she has a transmissible STI, a defendant who does not know he or she has an STI can be guilty of reckless sexual conduct. Would this approach serve public health interests by encouraging people to get tested regularly for STIs? Or is this approach over-inclusive such that it imposes an unnecessary health regulation, as Ferzan (2006) argued?

2. Given the proposed affirmative defense built into the statute, the crime of reckless sexual conduct would seemingly change the law with regard to informed consent as it applied to bug chasers. What do you think about that? Why?

3. If this proposal were enacted into law, what evidence would be available to prove the affirmative defense that the unprotected sex was engaged in consensually?

4. Do you think that, if adopted, the proposed crime would actually decrease the incidence of acquaintance rape as Ayres and Baker contend? Why or why not?

5. Compare and contrast any other benefits and drawbacks you see about the proposed crime. Explain your reasoning.

CONCLUSION

Like sexual mores, the criminal laws that seek to regulate sexual activities have changed over time. Historically, criminal laws have not only been used to deter and punish nonconsensual sexual—such as rape and child molestation (see Chapter 5), but also have been used for the social control of sex-related behaviors that are consensual. Sex crimes that fall into the latter category generally involve the deterrence and punishment of sexual conduct,

1. in which one of the participants cannot or may not be able to give knowing, intelligent, and voluntary consent, such as sex acts with post-pubescent teenagers or animals;
2. because the behavior has the potential to cause secondary harm to others, such as the aggrieved spouse when a married person commits adultery or a startled onlooker who observes sex acts in public;
3. that has public health consequences, such as laws barring incest, prostitution, or the knowing transmission of sexually transmitted diseases; or
4. that is viewed as damaging to widely shared views on public morality at any given time, even if the conduct was truly "victimless" because the sexual behavior involved consenting adults acting in private, such as laws criminalizing fornication and non-forcible sodomy.

Criminal laws continue to be used today to serve all four of these goals. But after the U.S. Supreme Court's decision in *Lawrence v. Texas* (2003), the fourth objective may not serve as the *sole* basis justifying the exercise of governmental police power. The *Lawrence* decision counsels "against attempts by the State, or a court, to define the meaning of" a private, intimate, relationship between consenting adults or "to set its boundaries absent injury to a person or abuse of an institution the law protects" (p. 567). The Court recognized that many people—perhaps even a majority—might view particular sexual conduct as immoral even when the behavior occurs between consenting adults in private. Nonetheless, perceived immorality does not, without more, justify the use of "the power of the State to enforce these views on the whole society through operation of the criminal law" (p. 571).

History has yet to determine the full scope of the impact from the *Lawrence* decision. Although seemingly neutral on their face, there can be no serious debate that crimes regulating consensual sex have had a disparate impact on those who are not heterosexual. *Lawrence* began to remedy this inequality, but there is still a long way go. Beyond disparate impact on LGBT people, thus far, *Lawrence*'s impact on criminal laws against fornication and cohabitation appears to render these laws unconstitutional for the same privacy-rights reasons the *Lawrence* decision invalidated criminal laws against sodomy in private between consenting adults. Whether that logic extends to criminal laws proscribing bigamy or adultery remains to be seen. As more fully explored in Chapter 8, obscenity laws may be the most vulnerable, although as of the writing of this book, courts have not interpreted *Lawrence* as affecting the constitutional validity of obscenity laws. It is clear, however, that most other criminal laws targeting consensual sexual acts remain viable, including those involving minors or others "who are situated in relationships where consent might not easily be refused" (p. 578), those involving public conduct or prostitution, and those involving significant public health concerns.

FURTHER READING

Aggrawal, A. (2009). *Forensic and medico-legal aspects of sexual crimes and unusual sexual practices.* Boca Raton, FL: CRC Press.

Hickey, E. W. (Ed.). (2005). *Sex crimes and paraphilia*. Upper Saddle River, NJ: Pearson.

Mogul, J.L., Ritchie, A. J., & Whitlock, K. (2011). *Queer (in)justice: The criminalization of LGBT people in the United States*. Boston, MA: Beacon Press.

Zilney, L. J., & Zilney, L. A. (2009). *Perverts and predators: The making of sexual offending laws*. Lanham, MD: Rowman & Littlefield.

GLOSSARY

Adultery: Sexual intercourse between consenting persons during a time when at least one of the participants is married to someone else.

Bestiality: Sexual contact between a human and an animal.

Bigamy: The condition of having or purporting to marry two or more spouses at the same time.

Fornication: Consensual sex between two unmarried persons.

Incest: The marriage of or sexual activity between people related within a certain degree of kinship.

Indecent exposure: Knowing exposure or exhibition of the genitals, anus, or female nipples (other than during breast feeding) in a public place or on the private premises of another, or so near thereto as to be seen from such private premises, in a vulgar or indecent manner, or to be naked in public except in any place provided or set apart for that purpose.

Knowing transmission laws: Laws that criminalized sex when people know they have HIV, hepatitis, or another sexually transmitted infection and, in spite of such knowledge, fail to disclose their STI-positive status to sexual partners in advance of engaging in sexual activity.

Lewd and lascivious conduct: Committing an act of sexual gratification, either by oneself or with another person, with knowledge or reasonable anticipation that the participants are being viewed by others.

Paraphilias: Psychiatric conditions in which sexual arousal and gratification depend on fantasizing about or engaging in behaviors that are considered to be extreme and atypical of "normal" human sexuality because they involve either nonhuman objects, the suffering or humiliation of oneself or one's partner, or children or other nonconsenting persons.

Prostitution: Engaging in a sexual act in exchange for money or any item of value.

Public sexual indecency: Intentionally or knowingly engaging in any sexual acts, if another person is present, and the defendant is reckless about whether such other person, as a reasonable person, would be offended or alarmed by the act.

Sodomy: Oral or anal sex between two individuals; in some jurisdictions, it also includes *bestiality*.

Statutory rape: Nonforcible sex between a legally consenting adult and a minor whose youth renders him or her unable to grant legal consent to engage in sex.

Tearoom trade: Anonymous sex in public places in which some semblance of privacy might be achieved, such as in public restrooms.

NOTES

1 Cruising also occurs online in a variety of forms (Fernández, Warren, Varga, Prado, Hernandez, & Bowen, 2007; Grov, Parsons, & Bimbi, 2007). Tikkanen and Ross (2003) provide an interesting account of Swedish men visiting same-sex internet chat rooms; the anonymity and extensive access to the internet mirror the excitement of physically cruising various locales. But with the advent of online cruising chatrooms, websites, and even mobile apps, much of the risk that once existed for cruising in public places has been significantly mitigated, if not entirely eliminated.

2 Arkansas, Hawaii, Kentucky, Montana, Nevada, New Hampshire, New Jersey, New Mexico, Ohio, Texas, Vermont, Virginia, West Virginia, and Wyoming.

3 Alabama, Arizona, Florida, Georgia, Idaho, Illinois, Kansas, Maryland, Massachusetts, Michigan, Minnesota, Mississippi, New York, North Carolina, Oklahoma, Rhode Island, South Carolina, Utah, Virginia, and Wisconsin.

4 Colorado, Illinois, Louisiana, Missouri, Nebraska, New Mexico, New York, and Texas.

5 Arizona, California, Delaware, Florida, Idaho, North Dakota, Oregon, Tennessee, Utah, Virginia, Wisconsin, and Wyoming.

6 The states that, as of the writing of this book, recognize an honest and reasonable mistake with respect to the age of the victim are Alaska, Arizona, Arkansas, Indiana, Kentucky, Maine, Missouri, Montana, New York, Pennsylvania, Washington, West Virginia, and Wyoming.

REFERENCES

720 Illinois Compiled Statutes §§ 11–35, 11–45 (2015).

Aggrawal, A. (2009). *Forensic and medico-legal aspects of sexual crimes and unusual sexual practices*. Boca Raton, FL: CRC Press.

Agunbiade, O. M., & Ayotunde, T. (2012). Ageing, sexuality and enhancement among Yoruba people in south western Nigeria. *Culture, Health, & Sexuality: An International Journal for Research, Intervention, and Care*, 14(6), 705–717. doi: 10.1080/13691058. 2012.677861

Alabama Code § 22–11A-21(c) (2015).

Amnesty International (2005). *Stonewalled: Police abuse and misconduct against lesbian, gay, bisexual, and transgender people in the U.S.* Retrieved from http://www.amnesty.org/en/library/asset/AMR51/122/2005/en/2200113d-d4bd-11dd-8a23-d58a49c0d652/amr511222005en.pdf

Animal Legal Defense Fund. (2014). *Animal protection laws of the United States of America and Canada.* Retrieved from http://aldf.org/resources/advocating-for-animals/animal-protection-laws-of-the-united-states-of-america-and-canada/

Annuschat, K. (2010). An affair to remember: The state of the crime of adultery in the military. *San Diego Law Review, 47,* 1161–1204.

Apostolopoulos, Y., Sonmez, S., Shattell, M., Kronenfeld, J., Smith, D., & Stanton, S. (2011). Cruising for truckers on highways and the internet: Sexual networks and infection risk. *AIDS Education and Prevention, 23*(3), 249–266. doi: 10.1521/aeap.2011.23.3.249

ARIZONA REVISED STATUTES §§ 13–1403, 13–1408 (2015).

Ascione, F. R. (2005). Bestiality: Petting, "human rape," sexual assault, and the enigma of sexual interactions between humans and non-human animals. In A. M. Beetz & A. L. Podberscek (Eds.), *Bestiality and zoophilia: Sexual relations with animals* (pp. 120–129). Ashland, OH: Purdue University Press.

Ayikukwei, R. M., Ngare, D., Sidle, J. E., Ayuku, D. O., Baliddawa, J., & Greene, J. Y. (2007). Social and cultural significance of the sexual cleansing ritual and its impact on HIV prevention strategies in western Kenya. *Sexuality & Culture, 11*(3), 32–50. doi: 10.1007/s12119-007-9010-x

Ayres, I., & Baker, K. K. (2005). A separate crime of reckless sex. *University of Chicago Law Review, 72*(2), 599–666.

Ball, C. A. (2008). Privacy, property, and public sex. *Columbia Journal of Gender and Law, 18,* 1–59.

Barnhart, D. M. (1981). *Commonwealth v. Bonadio*: Voluntary deviate sexual intercourse—a comparative analysis. *University of Pittsburgh Law Review, 43,* 253–284.

Beale, J. H. (1895). Consent in the criminal law. *Harvard Law Review, 8,* 317–327.

Berkowitz, E. (2012). *Sex and punishment: Four thousand years of judging desire.* Berkeley, CA: Counterpoint Press.

Berube, A. (2003). The history of gay bathhouses. *Journal of Homosexuality, 44,* 33–53.

Bhugra, D., Popelyuk, D., & McMullen, I. (2010). Paraphilias across cultures: Contexts and controversies. *Journal of Sex Research, 47*(2–3), 242–256.

Blackstone, W. (1979). Of offenses against God and religion. In T. A. Green (Ed.), *Commentaries on the laws of England* (Vol. IV, Ch. IV, pp. 41–65). Chicago,

IL: University of Chicago Press. (Original work published 1765–1769.)

Bohlen, F. H. (1924). Consent as affecting civil liability for breaches of the peace. *Columbia Law Review, 24,* 819–835.

Boswell, J. (1993). On the history of social attitudes toward homosexuality from ancient Greece to the present. In M. Wolinsky & K. Sherrill (Eds.), *Gays and the military: Joseph Steffan versus the United States* (pp. 40–48). Princeton, NJ: Princeton University Press.

Brehm, J. W., & Brehm, S. S. (1981). *Psychological reactance: A theory of freedom and control.* San Diego, CA: Academic Press.

Brooks, A. E. (1985). *Doe* and *Dronenburg*: Sodomy statutes are constitutional. *William and Mary Law Review, 26,* 645–82.

Burris, S., Beletsky, L., Burleson, J., Case, P., & Lazzarini, Z. (2007). Do criminal laws influence HIV risk behavior? An empirical trial. *Arizona State Law Journal, 39,* 467–517.

CALIFORNIA HEALTH & SAFETY CODE § 120291(a) (2014).

Cantor, D. J. (1964). Deviation and the criminal law. *Journal of Criminal Law, Criminology & Police Science, 55*(4), 441–453.

Carpenter, D. (2004). Is *Lawrence* libertarian? *Minnesota Law Review, 88,* 1140–1170.

Chiesa, L. E. (2011). Consent is not a defense to battery: A reply to Professor Bergelson. *Ohio State Journal of Criminal Law, 9*(1), 195–208.

Cocca, C. E. (2004). *Jailbait: The politics of statutory rape laws in the United States.* Albany, NY: State University of New York Press.

Cole, G. W. (2007). Barebacking: Transformations, dissociations, and the theatre of countertransference. *Studies in Gender and Sexuality, 8*(1), 49–68.

Cruz, D. B. (2005). Spinning *Lawrence*, or *Lawrence v. Texas* and the promotion of heterosexuality. *Widener Law Review, 11,* 249–257.

Davis, D. L., & Whitten, R. G. (1987). The cross-cultural study of human sexuality. *Annual Review of Anthropology, 16,* 69–98.

Devlin, P. (1977). Morals and the criminal law. In K. Kipnis (Ed.), *Philosophical issues in law* (pp. 54–65). Englewood Cliffs, NJ: Prentice Hall. (Original work published 1965.)

Dover, J. K. (1978). *Greek homosexuality.* Cambridge, MA: Harvard University Press.

Eidson, R. (1980). The constitutionality of statutory rape laws. *UCLA Law Review, 27,* 757–815.

Ellis, H. (1964). *The psychology of sex: A manual for students.* New York, NY: Emerson Books.

Elstein, S. G., & Davis, N. (1997). Sexual relationships between adult males and young teen girls: Exploring the legal and social responses. Retrieved from http://www.americanbar.org/content/dam/aba/migrated/

child/PublicDocuments/statutory_rape.authcheckdam.pdf

Escoffier, J. (1998). *American homo: Community and perversity*. Berkeley, CA: University of California Press.

Eskridge, W. N. (1997). Law and the construction of the closet: American regulation of same-sex intimacy 1880–1946. *Iowa Law Review, 82*, 1007–1136.

Falco, M. C. (2004). The road not taken: Using the Eighth Amendment to strike down cruel and unusual punishment for engaging in consensual acts. *North Carolina Law Review, 82*, 723–758.

Fan, M. D. (2012a). Decentralizing STD surveillance: Toward better informed sexual consent. *Yale Journal of Health Policy, Law, and Ethics, 12*, 1–38.

Fan, M. D. (2012b). Sex, privacy, and public health in a casual encounters culture. *U.C. Davis Law Review, 45*, 531–596.

Fernández, M. I., Warren, J. C., Varga, L. M., Prado, G., Hernandez, N., & Bowen, G. S. (2007). Cruising in cyber space: Comparing internet chat room versus community venues for recruiting Hispanic men who have sex with men to participate in prevention studies. *Journal of Ethnicity in Substance Abuse, 6*(2), 143–162. doi: 10.1300/J233v06n02_09

Ferzan, K. K. (2006). A reckless response to rape: A reply to Ayres and Baker. *U.C. Davis Law Review, 39*, 637–667.

Findholt, N., & Robrecht, L. C. (2002). Legal and ethical considerations in research with sexually active adolescents: The requirement to report statutory rape. *Perspectives on Sexual and Reproductive Health, 34*(5), 250–264.

Fischer, R. G., Fradella, H. F., & Ireland, C. E. (2009). Sex, violence, and the boundaries of the defense of consent. *Criminal Law Bulletin, 45*(6), 1137–1155.

Font, B. R. S. (2000). *Homophobia: A history*. New York, NY: Picador.

Florida Statutes Annotated §§ 796.01, 800.02 (2014).

Fradella, H. F. (1993). *Is your state a peeping Tom? A historical, constitutional, philosophical, and sociological examination of the outdated regulation of private, sexual acts between consenting adults by the criminal justice system*. Unpublished master's thesis. The George Washington University, Washington, DC.

Fradella, H. F. (2002). Legal, moral, and social reasons for decriminalizing sodomy. *Journal of Contemporary Criminal Justice, 18*(3), 279–301. doi: 10.1177/1043986202018003005

Fradella, H. F. (2003). *Lawrence v. Texas*: Genuine or illusory progress for gay rights in America? *Criminal Law Bulletin, 39*(5), 597–607.

Frank, D. J., Camp, B. J., & Boutcher, S. A. (2010). Worldwide trends in the criminal regulation of sex, 1945 to 2005. *American Sociological Review, 75*(6), 867–893. doi: 10.1177/0003122410388493

Franklin, J. (2012). Where art thou, privacy? Expanding privacy rights of minors in regard to consensual sex: Statutory rape laws and the need for a "Romeo and Juliet" exception in Illinois. *The John Marshall Law Review, 46*, 309–331.

Freeh, Sporkin, & Sullivan LLP, on behalf of the Pennsylvania State University Board of Trustees, Special Investigations Task Force (2012). *Report of the special investigative counsel regarding the actions of the Pennsylvania State University related to the child sexual abuse committed by Gerald A. Sandusky*. Retrieved from http://thefreehreportonpsu.com

Freeman, G. A. (2003). In search of death. *Rolling Stone, 915*, 44–48.

Galletly, C. L., Glasman, L. R., Pinkerton, S. D., & DiFranceisco, W. (2012). New Jersey's HIV exposure law and HIV-related attitudes, beliefs, and sexual and seropositive status disclosure behaviors of persons living with HIV. *American Journal of Public Health, 102*(11), 2135–2140.

Galletly, C. L., & Pinkerton, S. D. (2008). Preventing HIV transmission via HIV exposure laws: Applying logic and mathematical modeling to compare statutory approaches to penalizing undisclosed exposure to HIV. *Journal of Law and Medical Ethics, 36*, 577–584.

Gallo, R. C., & Montagnier, L. (2003). The discovery of HIV as the cause of AIDS. *New England Journal of Medicine, 349*, 2283–2285. doi: 10.1056/NEJMp038194

Gauthier, D. K., & Forsyth, C. J. (1999). Bareback sex, bug chasers, and the gift of death. *Deviant Behavior, 20*, 85–100.

Ginn, D. (2000). Can failure to disclose HIV positivity to sexual partners vitiate consent? *R. v. Cuerrier*. *Case Comments/Chroniques de jurisprudence, 12*, 235–245.

Glazer, E. M. (2008). When obscenity discriminates. *Northwestern University Law Review, 102*, 1379–1439.

Goldstein, A. B. (1988). History, homosexuality, and political values: Searching for the hidden determinants of *Bowers v. Hardwick*. *Yale Law Journal, 97*, 1073–1103.

Grant, I. (2009). Rethinking risk: The relevance of condoms and viral load in HIV nondisclosure prosecutions. *McGill Law Journal, 54*, 389–404.

Gross, B. (2006). The pleasure of pain. *The Forensic Examiner, 15*(1), 57–61.

Grov, C., Parsons, J. T., & Bimbi, D. S. (2007). Sexual risk behavior and venues for meeting sex partners: An intercept survey of gay and bisexual men in LA and NYC. *AIDS Behavior, 11*, 915–926. doi: 10.1007/s10461-006-9199-y

Guterman, J. T., Martin, C. V., & Rudes, J. (2011). A solution-focused approach to frotteurism. *Journal of Systemic Therapies, 30*(1), 59–72.

Harrison, J. V. (2000). Peeping through the closet keyhole: Sodomy, homosexuality, and the amorphous right of privacy. *St. John's Law Review, 74*, 1087–1138.

Hart, H. L. A. (1971). Immorality and treason. In R. A. Wasserstrom (Ed.), *Morality and the law* (pp. 49–54). Belmont, CA: Wadsworth. (Original work published 1959.)

Harvard Law Review. (1986). Right to privacy and consensual sodomy: *Bowers v. Hardwick. Harvard Law Review, 100,* 210–215.

Herdt, G. H. (1984). Semen transactions in Sambia culture. In G. H. Herdt (Ed.), *Ritualized homosexuality in Melanesia* (pp. 167–210). Berkeley, CA: University of California Press.

Herdt, G. H. (1999). *Sambian sexual culture: Essays from the field.* Chicago, IL: University of Chicago Press.

Herdt, G. H. (2000). Why the Sambia initiate boys before age 10. In J. Bancroft (Ed.), *The role of theory in sex research* (pp. 82–109). Bloomington, IN: Indiana University Press.

Herdt, G. H. (Ed.). (2009). *Moral panics, sex panics: Fear and the fight over sexual rights.* New York, NY: New York University Press.

Higdon, M. J. (2008). Queer teens and legislative bullies: The cruel and invidious discrimination behind heterosexist statutory rape laws. *UC Davis Law Review, 42,* 195–253.

Hines, D., & Finkelhor, D. (2007). Statutory sex crime relationships between juveniles and adults: A review of social scientific research. *Aggression & Violent Behavior, 12,* 300–314.

Hogarth, N. (2003). Our motives. Retrieved from http://www.thegiftdocumentary.org/ourmotives.html

Hollister, J. (1999). A highway rest area as a socially reproducible site. In W. L. Leap (Ed.), *Public sex/gay space* (pp. 55–70). New York, NY: Columbia University Press.

Horvath, K. J., Weinmeyer, R., & Rosser, S. (2010). Should it be illegal for HIV-positive persons to have unprotected sex without disclosure? An examination of attitudes among US men who have sex with men and the impact of state law. *AIDS Care, 22*(10), 1221–1228.

Humphreys, L. (1970). *Tearoom trade: Impersonal sex in public places.* Chicago, IL: Aldine.

Huppin, M., & Malamuth, N. (2012). The obscenity conundrum, contingent harms, and constitutional consistency. *Stanford Law & Policy Review, 23,* 31–100.

Jacobs, E. T. (2012). Online sexual solicitation of minors: An analysis of the average predator, his victims, what is being done and can be done to decrease occurrences of victimization. *Cardozo Public Law, Policy and Ethics Journal, 10,* 505–537.

Jerry Sandusky. (2012). *New York Times.* Retrieved from http://topics.nytimes.com/top/reference/timestopics/people/s/jerry_sandusky/index.html?8qa

Joint Service Commission on Military Justice. (2008). *Manual for courts-martial United States.* Retrieved from http://www.loc.gov.ezproxy1.lib.asu.edu/rr/frd/Military_Law/pdf/MCM-2008.pdf

Kane, M. D. (2007). Timing matters: Shifts in the causal determinants of sodomy law decriminalization, 1961–1998. *Social Problems, 54*(2), 211–239.

KANSAS STATUTE ANNOTATED § 21–3508(1) (2014).

Kaplan, M. (2012). Rethinking HIV-exposure crimes. *Indiana Law Journal, 87,* 1517–1569.

Kaplan, M. (2014). Sex-positive law. *New York University Law Review, 89,* 89–164.

Kenworthy, T., & Bloem, F. (2005). Exhibitionism: Development and treatment. In E. W. Hickey (Ed.), *Sex crimes and paraphilia* (pp. 257–265). Upper Saddle River, NJ: Pearson.

Koppelman, A. (2004). *Lawrence*'s penumbra. *Minnesota Law Review, 88,* 1171–1183.

Lehman, J. S., Carr, M. H., Nichol, A. J., Ruisanchez, A., Knight, D. W., Langford, A. E., Gray, S. C., & Mermin, J. H. (2014). Prevalence and public health implications of state laws that criminalize potential HIV exposure in the United States. *AIDS and Behavior.* doi: 10.1007/s10461-014-0724-0. Retrieved from http://link.springer.com/article/10.1007/s10461-014-0724-0/fulltext.html#CR17

Leslie, C. R. (2000). Creating criminals: The injuries inflicted by "unenforced" sodomy laws. *Harvard Civil Rights and Civil Liberties Law Review, 35,* 103–181.

Leveno, E. A. (1994). New hope for the new federalism: State constitutional challenges to sodomy statutes. *University of Cincinnati Law Review, 62,* 1029–1054.

Marshall, D. S. (1971). Sexual behavior in Mangaia. In D. S. Marshall & R. C. Suggs (Eds.), *Human sexual behavior* (pp. 103–162). New York, NY: Basic Books.

Martinson, F. M. (1994). *The sexual life of children.* Westport, CT: Bergin & Garvey/Greenwood Publishing.

MASSACHUSETTS GENERAL LAWS c. 272, § 16 (2014).

McElroy, L. T. (2010). Sex on the brain: Adolescent psychosocial science and sanctions for risky sex. *New York University Review of Law and Social Change, 34,* 708–759.

Meidinger, M. H. (2012). Peeking under the covers: Taking a closer look at prosecutorial decision-making involving queer youth and statutory rape. *Boston College Journal of Law & Social Justice, 32,* 421–451.

MINNESOTA REVISED STATUTES § 609.355 (2014).

Mogul, J. L., Ritchie, A. J., & Whitlock, K. (2011). *Queer (in)justice: The criminalization of LGBT people in the United States.* Boston, MA: Beacon Press.

Moore-Emmett, A. (2004). *God's brothel: The extortion of sex for salvation in contemporary Mormon and Christian fundamentalist polygamy.* San Francisco, CA: Pince-Nez Press.

Moskowitz, D. A., & Roloff, M. E. (2007). The ultimate high: Sexual addiction and the bug-chasing phenomenon. *Sexual Addiction & Compulsivity, 14,* 21–40.

NEBRASKA REVISED STATUTES § 28–934 (2014).

NEW JERSEY STATUTES ANNOTATED §§ 2C:34–1, 34–5 (2014).

Oberman, M. (2004–2005). Turning girls into women: Re-evaluating modern statutory rape law. *DePaul Journal of Health Care Law*, 8(1), 109–177. doi: 0091-4169/94/8501-0015

REVISED CODE OF WASHINGTON § 9A.88.010 (2014).

Rodriguez-Rust, P. C. (2000). *Bisexuality in the United States: A social science reader*. New York, NY: Columbia University Press.

Rosen, S. A. (1981). Police harassment of homosexual women and men in New York City 1960–1980. *Columbia Human Rights Law Review*, 12, 159–190.

Rubenfeld, J. (2013). The riddle of rape-by-deception and the myth of sexual autonomy. *Yale Law Journal*, 122, 1372–1443.

Ryan White Comprehensive AIDS Resources Emergency Act of 1990, Pub. L. No. 101–381, 104 Stat. 576, *codified as amended at* 42 U.S.C. §§ 300ff.

Sandusky Grand Jury Presentment. (2011). Pennsylvania Attorney General. Retrieved from http://www.washingtonpost.com/wp-srv/sports/documents/sandusky-grand-jury-report11052011.html

Schug, R. A., & Fradella, H. F. (2014). *Mental illness and crime*. Thousand Oaks, CA: Sage.

Seto, M. C. (2008). *Pedophilia and sexual offending against children: Theory, assessment, and intervention*. Washington, DC: American Psychological Association.

Sipsma, H. L., Chen, P. G., Ofori-Atta, A., Ilozumba, U. O., Karfo, K., & Bradley, E. H. (2012). Female genital cutting: Current practices and beliefs in western Africa. *Bulletin of the World Health Organization*, 90, 120–127. doi: 10.2471/BLT.11.090886

Sklansky, D. A. (2012). One train may hide another: *Katz*, Stonewall, and the secret subtext of criminal procedure. *U.C. Davis Law Review*, 41, 875–934.

SOUTH CAROLINA CODIFIED LAWS § 16-15-70 (2014).

Strader, K. (2011). *Lawrence*'s criminal law. *Berkeley Journal of Criminal Law*, 16, 41–111.

Streit, Z. D. (2007). Birds of an illegal feather: Prostitution and paid pornography should be criminalized together. *Cardozo Public Law, Policy, & Ethics Journal*, 5, 729–756.

Summers, J. A. (2003). A complication of an unusual sexual practice. *Southern Medical Journal*, 96(7), 716–717.

Sweeny, J. (2014). Undead statutes: The rise, fall, and continuing uses of adultery and fornication criminal laws. *Loyola University Chicago Law Journal*, 46, 127–173.

TENNESSEE CODE ANNOTATED § 39–13–109 (2014).

Tewksbury, R. (1995). Adventures in the erotic oasis: Sex and danger in men's same-sex, public, sexual encounters. *The Journal of Men's Studies*, 4(1), 9–24.

Tewksbury, R. (2008). Finding erotic oases: Locating the sites of men's same-sex anonymous sexual encounters. *Journal of Homosexuality*, 55(1), 1–19. doi: 10.1080/00918360802129253

Tewksbury, R., & Polley, N. (2007). Conversation at the erotic oasis. *Journal of Men's Studies*, 15(2), 147–159. doi: 10.3149/jms.1502.147

TEXAS PENAL. CODE § 205.014 (2014).

Tikkanen, R., & Ross, M. W. (2003). Technological tearoom trade: Characteristics of Swedish men visiting gay internet chat rooms. *AIDS Education and Prevention*, 15(2), 122–132.

Tribe, L. H. (2004). *Lawrence v. Texas*: The "fundamental right" that dare not speak its name. *Harvard Law Review*, 117, 1893–1955.

Troup-Leasure, K., & Snyder, H. (2005). *Statutory rape known to law enforcement* (Juvenile Justice Bulletin No. NCJ 208803). Washington, DC: Office of Juvenile Justice & Delinquency Prevention.

Turcios, M. (2014, February 20). Bestiality laws: Our dirty little secret. *Hastings Women's Law Journal Blog*. Retrieved from http://hastingswomenslj.org/journal/2014/2/20/e3y5p9h4xformoldf658mebzcse7va

U.S. Centers for Disease Control and Prevention. (2001, June 1). HIV and AIDS—United States, 1981–2000. *Morbidity and Mortality Weekly Report*, 50(21), 430–434. Retrieved from http://www.cdc.gov/mmwr/preview/mmwrhtml/mm5021a2.htm

U.S. Centers for Disease Control and Prevention. (2014). HIV-specific criminal law. Retrieved from http://www.cdc.gov/hiv/policies/law/states/exposure.html

UTAH CODE ANNOTATED § 76–7–101 (2013).

Viera, M. (2011, December 7). Sandusky arrested on charges involving two new accusers. *The New York Times*. Retrieved from http://www.nytimes.com/2011/12/08/sports/ncaafootball/sandusky-arrested-on-new-sexual-abuse-charges.html

Waldman, A. E. (2011). Exceptions: The criminal law's illogical approach to HIV-related aggravated assaults. *Virginia Journal of Social Policy & the Law*, 18, 550–605.

Weinstein, J. D. (1986). Adultery, law, and the state: A history. *Hastings Law Journal*, 38, 195–238.

Weiss, A. (2006). Criminalizing consensual transmission of HIV. *The University of Chicago Legal Forum*, 2006, 389–408.

White, J. H. (2007). Evidence of primary, secondary, and collateral paraphilias left at serial murder and sex offender crime scenes. *Journal of Forensic Sciences*, 52(5), 1194–1201.

Williamson, B. J. (1989). The constitutional privacy doctrine after *Bowers v. Hardwick*: Rethinking the second death of substantive due process. *Southern California Law Review*, 62, 1297–1330.

Wolf, L. E., & Vezina, R. (2004). Crime and punishment: Is there a role for criminal law in HIV prevention policy? *Whittier Law Review*, 25, 821–886.

Woods, J. B. (2009). Don't tap, don't stare, and keep your hands to yourself! Critiquing the legality of gay sting operations. *Journal of Gender, Race and Justice, 12*(3), 545–578.

Wright, S. A., & Richardson, J. T. (Eds.). (2011). *Saints under siege: The Texas state raid on the Fundamentalist Latter Day Saints*. New York, NY: New York University Press.

Cases

Baskin v. Bogan, 766 F.3d 648 (7th Cir. 2014).

Berkovsky v. State, 209 S.W.3d 252 (Tex. App. 2006).

Bostic v. Schaefer, 760 F.3d 352 (4th Cir. 2014).

Bowers v. Hardwick, 478 U.S. 186 (1986).

Boyer v. Belleque, 659 F.3d 957 (9th Cir. 2011).

Brown v. Buhman, 947 F. Supp. 2d 1170 (D. Utah 2013).

Commonwealth v. Burke, 457 N.E.2d 622 (Mass. 1983).

Eisenstadt v. Baird, 405 U. S. 438 (1972).

Ferguson v. Skrupa, 372 U.S. 726 (1963).

Griswold v. Connecticut, 381 U. S. 479 (1965).

Hardwick v. Bowers, 760 F.2d 1202 (11th Cir.); rehearing en banc denied, 765 F.2d 1123 (11th Cir. 1985); rev'd, 478 U.S. 186 (1986).

In re J.M., 575 S.E.2d 441 (Ga. 2003).

In re R.L.C., 643 S.E.2d 920 (N.C. 2007).

Kansas v. Limon, 122 P.3d 22 (Kan. 2005).

Kitchen v. Herbert, 755 F.3d 1193 (10th Cir. 2014).

Latta v. Otter, 771 F.3d 456 (2014).

Lawrence v. Texas, 539 U.S. 558 (2003).

Loving v. Virginia, 388 U. S. 1 (1967).

Lowe v. Swanson, 639 F. Supp. 2d 857 (N.D. Ohio 2009), aff'd, 663 F.3d 258 (6th Cir. 2011).

Martin v. Ziherl, 607 S.E.2d 367 (Va. 2005).

McDonald v. Commonwealth, 630 S.E.2d 754 (Va. Ct. App. 2006).

Muth v. Frank, 412 F.3d 808 (7th Cir. 2015).

Obergefell v. Hodges, 135 S. Ct. 2584 (2015).

People v. Haynes, 760 N.W.2d 283 (Mich. App. 2008).

People v. Hollins, 971 N.E.2d 504 (Ill. 2012).

People v. McEvoy, 154 Cal. Rptr. 3d 914 (Cal. Ct. App. 2013).

Reynolds v. United States, 98 U.S. 145 (1879).

Rodgers v. Ohio Dep't of Rehab & Correction, 632 N.E.2d 1355 (Ohio Ct. App 1993).

Roe v. Wade, 410 U. S. 113 (1973).

State v. Bussmann, 741 N.W.2d 79 (Minn. 2007).

State v. Clinkenbeard, 123 P.3d 872 (Wash. Ct. App. 2005).

State v. Coman, 214 P.3d 1198 (Kan. Ct. App. 2009).

State v. Fischer, 199 P.3d 663 (Ariz. Ct. App. 2008).

State v. Freeman, 801 N.E.2d 906 (Ohio 2003).

State v. Freitag, 130 P.3d 544 (Ariz. Ct. App. 2006).

State v. Green, 989 N.E.2d 1088 (Ohio Ct. App. 2013).

State v. Hinkhouse, 912 P.2d 921 (Or. Ct. App. 1996).

State v. Holm, 137 P.3d 726 (Utah 2006), cert. denied, 549 U.S. 1252 (2007).

State v. Hughes, 261 P.3d 1067 (Nev. 2011).

State v. Lowe, 861 N.E.2d 512 (Ohio 2007).

State v. Neatherlin, 154 P.3d 703 (N.M. Ct. App. 2007).

State v. Romano, 155 P.3d 1102 (Haw. 2007).

State v. Senters, 699 N.W.2d 810 (Neb. 2005).

State v. Wesie, 118 N.W. 20 (N.D. 1908).

Talbert v. State, 239 S.W.3d 504 (Ark. 2006).

United States v. Extreme Associates, 352 F. Supp. 2d 578 (W.D. Pa.), rev'd, 431 F.3d 150 (3d Cir. 2005).

United States v. Johnson, 27 M.J. 798 (Air Force Ct. Mil. Rev. 1988).

United States v. Marcum, 60 M.J. 198 (C.A.A.F. 2004).

United States v. McClelland, 2006 WL 228927 (N.M. Ct. Crim. App. Jan. 24, 2006).

United States v. Orellana, 62 M.J. 595 (2005).

United States v. Thompson, 458 F. Supp. 2d 730 (N.D. Ind. 2006).

United States v. Windsor, 133 S. Ct. 2675 (2013).

Washington v. Glucksberg, 521 U.S. 702 (1997).

CHAPTER 7

The Regulation of Sex Work and Sex Workers

Elisabeth Jandro

In 2007, a 20-year-old single mother who was making a living by selling sexual services for money agreed, via Craigslist, to provide one hour of oral and vaginal sex for a payment of $150. She agreed to meet the customer (Gindraw) at a designated address. After she arrived, she realized that the location was not the client's home, as she expected; rather, it was an abandoned building. Her client asked if she would agree to have sex with an additional customer. She agreed under the condition that an extra $100 would be owed and paid. After the friend of the initial client arrived at the scene, it became quickly apparent that no payments would be made. At this point, the sex worker clearly expressed that she did not wish to continue. But the men forced her at gunpoint to provide sexual services. Over the course of time, additional men arrived at the scene and forcefully sexually penetrated her. The last man who arrived at the scene rescued her after asking her why she was crying. He dressed her and removed her from the situation. The sex worker reported the rape to the police and Gindraw was charged with rape and aggravated assault. The other men were not charged.

In October 2007, Philadelphia Municipal Court Judge Teresa Carr Deni dismissed the sexual assault charges and instead allowed the case to proceed as a "theft of services" case. In justifying her ruling, Judge Deni claimed that the sex worker had consented to sexual activity in exchange for money, but "didn't get paid" (Michels, 2007, para. 11).

Judge Deni also stated that prosecuting the perpetrator for the rape of a sex worker in this case "minimizes true rape cases and demeans women who are really raped" (Michels, 2007, para. 3).

After the ruling was publicized, the Philadelphia Bar Association received complaints from people all over the United States (Michels, 2007). The bar publicly criticized Judge Deni's decision. Jane Dalton, Association Chancellor of the Philadelphia Bar Association, stated: "As a chancellor, a lawyer, and a human being, I am personally offended by this unforgivable miscarriage of justice. The victim has been brutalized twice in this case: first by the assailants, and now by the court" (Philadelphia Bar Association, November 1, 2007, para 8).

- Recall from Chapter 5 that rape is defined as any sexual penetration that is accomplished without the consent of the victim. The sex worker in this case consented to sex with one person via Craigslist. To what, if anything, did she subsequently consent? Did she ever withdraw consent? Keeping in mind the case of *In re John Z.* (Chapter 5), do you feel she was the victim of a rape? Why or why not?
- Critique the judge's reasoning in the case. Explain your position.

(Michels, 2007; Philadelphia Bar Association, 2007; Zuzu, 2007)

LEARNING OBJECTIVES

- Describe the terminology used when discussing sex work and prostitution and the implications each term has within a larger political and ideological debate.
- Trace the history of prostitution legislation.
- Explain what effect perceptions of morality and perceived dangers associated with prostitution have on the development of prostitution laws.
- Describe the contours of sex work, including varied settings in which it occurs and the diversity of individuals involved.
- Identify which acts surrounding sex work are regulated by law.
- Discuss the competing ideological and political perspectives surrounding prostitution and its regulation.
- Understand and identify the different kinds of systems of regulation of prostitution in different geographical contexts (legalization, partial legalization, decriminalization, de facto legalization, etc.) and the advantages and disadvantages of each.
- Explain why exclusionary practices are utilized to combat high prostitution activity and evaluate how effective they are at doing so.
- Compare and contrast sex trafficking and prostitution.
- Analyze the secondary consequences of prostitution (beyond legal punishment).

Prostitution is often referred to as "the oldest profession." Technically, **prostitution** refers to the selling of sexual services in exchange for anything of pecuniary value, including money, services, or goods, such as food, shelter, drugs, and other favors. Even though the sale of sex has existed for millennia, such transactions remain illegal in all U.S. states except Nevada, where prostitution is legal in counties with fewer than 400,000 inhabitants.[1] Within the diverse populations and varied contexts in which prostitution occurs (e.g., street versus "indoor" prostitu-tion), a wide range of motivations exist for engaging in sex work, ranging from prostitution as a means of survival to prostitution as a form of sexual and economic empowerment. This chapter critically examines the actors involved in prostitution; the ideological debate around whether prostitution constitutes violence and patriarchy or professional choice; the legal regulations that structure prostitution at the local, state, and federal levels, as well as in international settings; and secondary effects of prostitution (such as drug addiction, sexually transmitted diseases, mental health, and gender differences). The importance of a well-rounded understanding of prostitution is explained by Bernstein (1999) who argues, "We cannot assess what is wrong or right with prostitution without first understanding what it is" (p. 94). This includes considering the varied terminology used when examining the issue.

Many terms are used to refer to those who are involved in prostitution. Because the discourse around prostitution is often contentious, the related terminology also has ideological and political underpinnings (Weitzer, 2005). Although these competing perspectives will be examined more thoroughly later in this chapter, for now, here are the most commonly used terms and their implications:

- *Prostitute*: This term is often perceived as outdated and stigmatizing, containing notions of shame, responsibility, unworthiness, and/or wrongdoing (Bernstein, 1999; Weitzer 2005).
- *Prostituted woman*: The word "prostituted" implies that prostitution is something done to women, rather than something that can be chosen (Weitzer, 2005).
- *Survivor*: This term is commonly used when referring to individuals who were involved in prostitution in the past. This is meant to convey that the individual has escaped from something harmful (Weitzer, 2005).
- *Sex worker*: This is considered a more liberal term for individuals involved in prostitution, often used by socialist feminists. It implies that prostitution should be understood as a choice of occupation, as 'service work' or as a 'caregiving profession' (Bernstein, 1999).
- *Sex slaves and victims*: These terms signal that prostitution constitutes violence, coercion, and exploitation and are primarily used by radical feminists.

MacKenzie, who had been involved in prostitution herself, suggests that we should refrain from trying to fit all those involved in prostitution into one of the above categories arguing that "they are a non-homogeneous group of people doing a job. The same job. And that is about the only common characteristic many prostitutes share" (1992, p. 1). Accordingly, this chapter uses a wide variety of terminology, depending on the context of the issues discussed.

A BRIEF HISTORY OF PROSTITUTION

Like many issues we face in contemporary society, prostitution is a product of its history. Thus, a complete understanding of prostitution and related issues necessarily requires us to "use that history to rethink the present" (Garland, 2001, p. 2). At the outset, however, it should be noted that a comprehensive history of prostitution is beyond the scope of this chapter; indeed, entire books have been written devoted to such a history (see Ringdal, 2004; Sanger, 1858/2013). This section of the chapter presents some of the most important points concerning the history of prostitution in an attempt to contextualize continuing contemporary debates on its legal status.

Early Civilizations

Prostitution has been existent in most parts of the world since the early days of humanity. Some scholars even argue that prostitution predates humanity:

Animal behaviorists have documented high-level primates engaging in prostituting behavior. Primates have been observed offering sexual services in exchange for food or to avoid an attack. There have also been studies of penguins in the Antarctic exchanging sex in return for stones. These findings show that only the female penguins prostitute themselves for stones, even female penguins with partners.

(Carrasquillo, 2014, p. 698–699; see also Bullough & Bullough, 1987)

Prostitution's first appearance in world literature dates back four thousand years (Ringdal, 2004). The Sumerians (circa 2400 B.C.E.) worshiped the goddess Ishtar, "who came to Earth accompanied by courtesans and prostitutes" (Carrasquillo, 2014, p. 699; see also Bullough & Bullough, 1987).

"Egypt was famous for her courtesans before the time of Herodotus ... There is little reason to doubt that the temples, like those of Baal, were houses of prostitution on an extensive scale" (Sanger, 1858/2013, pp. 40–41).

Six sections in the Code of Hammurabi (circa 1780 B.C.E.) mention the rights of prostitutes and their children. The Babylonians viewed different types of prostitution as deserving of different social statuses, ranging from slaves who could be sold for sex to "revered temple prostitutes" (Carrasquillo, 2014, p. 699; see also Bullough & Bullough, 1987). In fact, "Every Babylonian female was obliged by law to prostitute herself once in her life in the temple of the Chaldæan Venus" (Sanger, 1858/2013, p. 41). Similar practices took place in Carthage, Syria, Cyprus, and Persia (Sanger, 1858/2013).

Commercial **brothels** (houses of prostitution) were common in China by the seventh century B.C.E. (Bullough & Bullough, 1987). These establishments were taxed as a means of increasing the income of the state (Bullough & Bullough, 1987).

Prostitution was ubiquitous in Ancient Greece (Sanger, 1858/2013). The Greeks had a hierarchical caste system classifying different types of prostitutes (Bullough & Bullough, 1987). *Dicteriades*—female slaves who were bound by law to work in brothels—lay at the low end of the spectrum (Hough, 2004; Thompson, 2000). Street-walkers ranked only slightly higher on the social scale; they were

required to dress in a manner that made their profession identifiable to all in the community (Bullough & Bullough, 1987; Carrasquillo, 2014; Hough, 2004; Thompson, 2000). *Auletrides*—"dancers, flute players, and acrobats" who sold sexual services for extra money—ranked higher than streetwalkers (Bullough & Bullough, 1987; Carrasquillo, 2014; Sanger, 1858/2013). And the highest class of prostitutes in Greece were called *Hetairæ*, "which literally means 'companion.' The *Hetairæ* were among the most educated women in Greece and would attract the attention of the most prestigious men" (Carrasquillo, 2014, p. 700; see also Bullough & Bullough, 1987; Sanger, 1858/2013).

Prostitution was also omnipresent in Ancient Rome (Sanger, 1858/2013). Although it was considered a "trade that was in great demand," prostitutes were not well respected (Hough, 2004, p. 107). Nonetheless, the Romans viewed them as essential to keeping the social order (read: satisfying the needs of young men). Indeed, the Romans "protected" prostitutes through a system of legal regulation.

Prostitutes were required to be licensed and, once licensed, their names could never be removed from the official list of prostitutes. The *aedile*, or official inspectors, were in charge of making sure that prostitutes followed the regulations, which included wearing the proper clothing and behaving in an acceptable manner. The aedile also ensured that the customers paid the prostitutes, and additionally that the prostitutes were not at risk of physical danger.

(Hough, 2004, p. 107)

The Middle Ages through the Enlightenment

The rise and spread of Christianity shaped views of prostitution that hold to this very day. Although Christianity prohibited all forms of sexual activity outside of marriage—and even then only for procreation, prostitution was tolerated to varying degrees throughout Europe as a "necessary evil to combat rape, sodomy, and masturbation" (Carrasquillo, 2014, p. 701). In fact, St. Augustine proclaimed that the suppression of prostitution would allow "capricious lusts [to] overthrow society" (as quoted in Sanger, 1858/2013, p. 91) "The Bible's portrayal of Mary Magdalene as a prostitute created a new attitude that prostitutes were poor, exploited women who needed to be 'saved' rather than condemned" (Carrasquillo, 2014, pp. 701–702). That view may help to explain why prostitution thrived in some parts of continental Europe in spite of Christianity's influence.

Byzantine Emperor Justinian the Great married Theodora, an alleged former prostitute, in 525 (Ringdal, 2004). They banished brothel-keepers from the capital, freed slaves who had been forced into prostitution, and banned sex in public bathhouses. By 600, King Recared, the Catholic ruler of the Visigoths of Spain, had issued a decree banning prostitution entirely. Violators were flogged and banished from the kingdom (Mizuta & Mulvey-Roberts, 1994). Charlemagne imposed similarly tough punishment on both prostitutes and "all who harbored them, kept houses of debauch, or lent their assistance to prostitutes or debauchees" (Sanger, 1858/2013, p. 94). By 1469, King Henry IV of Castilia instituted similarly harsh punishments for men who acted as procurers of prostitution services for others. These men were referred to as *ruffians* and they were subject to flogging for a first offense, banishment for a second offense, and execution if they returned and committed further acts of procurement (Mizuta & Mulvey-Roberts, 1994).

Holy Roman Emperor Frederick Barbarossa declared similarly harsh penalties for prostitution in 1158 when he required that prostitutes have their noses cut off in order to make them less desirable. Soldiers who hired prostitutes were also physically maimed,

either by cutting off a finger or by gouging out their eyes (Hardaway, 2003). King Louis IX of France similarly banned prostitution in 1254 (Rossiaud, 1988). Of course, none of these legal prohibitions on prostitution actually had the effect of ending the practice.

Not all European countries took such a harsh approach to prostitution. England, for example, instituted a system of regulation. In 1161, King Henry II implemented formal regulations of prostitution in England. He outlawed forced prostitution, but permitted *stew-houses* (brothels) to operate under a set of rules that includes weekly inspections by constables and mandatory closures on holidays (Evans, 1979). Between 1350 and 1450, different Italian city-states institutionalized prostitution by establishing municipal brothels in areas that lacked such establishments (Ringdal, 2004). In 1358, the great Council of Venice ratified a decree stating that prostitution was "absolutely indispensable to the world" (Ringdal, 2004, p. 139).

By that time in Europe, prostitution was subject to regulation through registration and inspections; indoor prostitution in brothels was the standard practice in most places (Ringdal, 2004). Although sex workers enjoyed some popularity in medieval times, they did not benefit from any form of legal or judicial rights. Nonetheless, they often had some protection, mostly through their own guilds and members of the "night watch," who were paid a certain sum on a weekly basis (Ringdal, 2004).

Europe was struck with a wave of syphilis in the late fifteenth century. This epidemic significantly changed the European perspective of prostitution (Ringdal, 2004). A decree issued in 1495 by Emperor Maximilian of Habsburg declared prostitutes as the main source of syphilis and other venereal diseases. As a consequence, brothels were closed down and other forms of prostitution were outlawed throughout Europe (Ringdal, 2004). For example, Henry VIII issued a royal proclamation in 1546 ending England's regulation of prostitution by banning the practice (Kelly, 2000). And in 1586, Pope Sixtus V decreed that prostitution was such a sin against nature that Catholics should impose the death penalty on offenders (Ringdal, 2004).

Europe experienced a time of "religious purification" in the 1600s caused by the rise of Protestantism. Lutherans shaved the hair and cut off the ears of prostitutes; Calvinists branded offenders and forced them to serve time in the stocks in public places where others would see their punishment (Ringdal, 2004). Yet again, however, the institution of prostitution proved impossible to eradicate.

Although prostitution was officially banned in France in 1560, French prostitutes were unofficially licensed by the police (Evans, 1979). France came to dominate the sex industry through the eighteenth and nineteenth centuries. In 1840, prostitution was so widespread in France that it became the first country in the Enlightenment era to reject prohibition and institute a series of legal regulations that included licensing and mandatory health checks for prostitutes. Most European countries followed suit. For example, the Netherlands enacted the Local Government Act of 1851 which instituted a system of regulation that had existed during Napoleon's occupation of the country in 1810 (Boutellier, 1991). By 1870, all European countries and their colonies had implemented systems of regulation of prostitution (Ringdal, 2004). Recall from Chapter 2, however, that these regulations were often very harsh on women. The Contagious Disease Acts of 1868 and 1869 in England, for example, allowed police to arrest women they suspected of being prostitutes and force them to undergo medical examination for venereal diseases. If the tests were positive, the women were hospitalized until they were cured. Notably, though, the men who frequented prostitutes were not subject to arrest, medical examination, and forced hospitalization (Walkowitz, 1992).

Although the Contagious Disease Acts were repealed in 1886, by that time Victorian

morality ushered in an era that ended tolerance toward and legal regulation of prostitution (Ringdal, 2004). And not just in Britain. Alliances between women's rights organizations, workers' associations, and religious groups were formed to combat prostitution and its legality throughout Europe. They advocated against prostitution through public declarations, demonstrations, and petitions directed at government officials. And their efforts were largely successful.

Prostitution in the United States

The first people who settled in the New World were predominantly male; thus, European women were "sent" overseas with the hope that European settlers in the American colonies (Colonial America 1492–1763) would marry them (Grant, 2013). However, many of these women turned to prostitution instead (Grant, 2013; Jackson, 2004). Even though brothels were outlawed in many places (e.g., Boston) in the late 1700s, prostitution legally took place outside of such premises, outdoors or in public spaces (Jackson, 2004).

Over time, prostitution became a major concern within communities—especially from the standpoint of morality and public health. In the late eighteenth and early nineteenth centuries, "gangs and rowdy clubs" took the matter into their own hands acting as a form of "informal police" (Rosen, 1983, p. 4). These unorganized acts of violence, referred to as the "whorehouse riots," occurred in major cities across the United States, including Boston, New York City, St. Louis, Chicago, and Detroit. Even though sex workers were not specifically the targets of the riots, some were injured or even killed; brothels were vandalized; and the property of sex workers was destroyed (Grant, 2013; Jackson, 2004; Smolak, 2013). By the mid-nineteenth century, laws were created that resulted in **de facto criminalization**; although prostitution was not considered illegal, behavior associated with it was: night walking, vagrancy, and a variety of improprieties of conduct, such as cross-dressing. Laws against such actions made prostitution illegal in a practical sense and, as a result, police assumed enforcement of these legal regulations (Grant, 2013; Jackson, 2004; Rosen, 1983). In 1917, for example, a law was enacted in New Orleans that led to a fine of $25 for any woman or girl "notoriously abandoned to lewdness who committed scandal or disturbance of peace" (Grant, 2013, para. 13).

When the women's movement formed in Victorian America (1837–1901), members blamed male customers for prostitution and developed organizations aimed at helping women "escape" from it. Even though sex workers were considered "immoral," they were also perceived as "useful under the 'doctrine of necessity' " (Jackson, 2004, p. 3). During this time, the first legal regulations of sex work were also enacted, including city ordinances regulating mandatory medical examinations, licensing procedures, and taxing of income earned through prostitution (Jackson, 2004). These efforts to regulate prostitution failed, however, due, in large part, to lax enforcement. This led to the establishment of the first **red-light district**—an area in which prostitution is tolerated—in the New World: Storyville, the red-light district of the city of New Orleans was established in 1879 (Grant, 2013).[2]

Smolak (2013) explains that during the Progressive Era (1890–1920), medical professionals argued that prostitution caused the rapid spread of venereal diseases (VD). As a result, VD—later termed sexually transmitted diseases (STDs) and, more recently, sexually-transmitted infections (STIs)—became a focal point in the battle against prostitution. Under this thematic umbrella, the military "joined" the battle against prostitution during World War I and World War II. Soldiers were encouraged to make this fight their own, with slogans such as, "you can't beat the Axis if you have VD" (Jackson, 2004, p. 8).

As the immigration of women from the Old World continued, brides entered the sex trade once their marriage has been consummated. Critics coined the term "White slavery" to describe this practice (Jackson, 2004). This term aimed to signal that no woman would or could willfully choose to engage in prostitution; rather, an element of coercion must be part of one's "decision" to become involved (Jackson, 2004; Smolak, 2013). The idea of White slavery and the continuing immigration of women from the Old World led to the enactment of the White-Slave Traffic Act of 1910, also known as the Mann Act. The Mann Act (1910) addressed, among other issues, prostitution, immorality, and human trafficking, and made it a federal offense to transport women over state lines for "immoral purposes" (36 Stat. 825; see also Johnson, 2014; Smolak, 2013). At roughly the same time, "red-light abatement" laws began to be enacted at the local or state level; these laws made it a crime to own or operate an establishment in which prostitution took place (Johnson, 2014; Smolak, 2013).

Despite federal enactment of the Mann Act, the legal regulation of prostitution remained largely a matter of state law. By 1925, all U.S. states had enacted laws regulating prostitution (Johnson, 2014). Until the latter half of the twentieth century, these laws primarily targeted the individual offering sexual services for sale (Johnson, 2014).

THE CONTOURS OF PROSTITUTION

Prevalence

Individuals involved in prostitution constitute a hidden and, therefore, hard to reach population, which can largely be attributed to their legal status and the severe social stigmatization they face as a consequence of their involvement (Benoit, Jansson, Millar, & Phillips, 2005; Magnani, Sabin, & Heckathorn, 2005; Shaver, 2005; Weitzer, 2005). Thus, prevalence rates should be interpreted with caution, as prostitution may be included among what criminologists refer to as the "dark figure of crime" (see Coleman & Moynihan, 1996). Moreover, arrest rates are likely "the tip of the iceberg," because they reflect only those individuals who have been subject to criminal justice proceedings. Nonetheless, these data do provide an understanding of the extent to which prostitution constitutes a "workload" for the criminal justice system and allow for observation of trends.

According to the Federal Bureau of Investigation's *Uniform Crime Reports* (2014), 45,865 arrests were reported in the United States for prostitution and commercialized vice in 2013. Unsurprisingly, in light of issues of visibility and public concern (see Tsenin, 2000), the majority of documented arrests for prostitution and commercialized vice involve people engaged in street-level prostitution (Weitzer, 2010). As Table 7.1 illustrates, arrest rates decreased substantially between 2008 and 2013. In the absence of comparable data indicating a decrease in individual involvement in prostitution during this time, this suggests a change in official response to the crime.

Places of Conduct

As previously indicated, prostitution occurs in various locations, with a broad distinction between indoor and outdoor prostitution. The main point of departure between indoor and outdoor (or street-level) prostitution is the location of the initial contact between sex worker and client. Sex workers involved in indoor prostitution operate out of brothels, hotels, and massage parlors, or work with escort services as call girls or gigolos. With indoor prostitution, the business transaction (i.e., offer, acceptance, and agreed-upon compensation) takes place indoors and is thus, less visible. In contrast, these business transaction portions of outdoor or street-level prostitution take place in public spaces; the actual sexual acts may occur either in public or private settings (Weitzer, 2010).

Those involved in street-level prostitution tend to be at greater risk of victimization (Bernstein, 1999; Oselin, 2014). They also tend to engage in street-level prostitution as a means of survival (as they largely come from disadvantaged socioeconomic backgrounds) or in order to feed a problematic drug habit (Bernstein, 1999; Dank, et al., 2014; Oselin, 2014; Weitzer, 2010). And, as this chapter will subsequently explore in more detail, because street-level prostitution is more visible than its indoor counterpart, those involved in the former are more likely to be subject to criminal justice system responses such as arrest, prosecution, conviction, incarceration, and related measures (Bernstein, 1999). The combination of all of these factors results in the majority of academic, political, and media attention being directed towards the street-level market, rather than the indoor sector of prostitution (Weitzer, 2005).

Researchers who have examined indoor prostitution have repeatedly found that those working indoors tend to enter the trade at an older age, engage in risky behavior less frequently, and report lower incidence of victimization both during their childhoods and during their involvement in sex work (Weitzer, 2010). Because people working in indoor prostitution are less visible to the public eye, they not only prompt low levels of concern and complaint, but also are at lower risk of arrest (Weitzer, 2007). In addition, those working indoors tend to earn more money and work under safer working conditions (Weitzer, 2007). However, studies also suggest that it is common for individuals involved in prostitution to have worked in varied locations throughout their involvement; thus, some sex workers have experienced both the indoor and outdoor market (Dank et al., 2014).

Involvement in Prostitution

When people engage in sex work voluntarily (as opposed to by force through violence,

Table 7.1 Prostitution arrest statistics 2008–2013 by states

	2008	2009	2010	2011	2012	2013
U.S.A. Total	64,843	61,936	53,329	48,658	48,148	45,865
Alabama	260	296	74	0	0	4
Alaska	159	217	161	69	38	647
Arizona	1,602	1,503	956	777	679	743
Arkansas	316	298	269	166	255	198
California	13,385	12,904	11,344	10,659	10,484	10,260
Colorado	618	651	417	319	307	314
Connecticut	523	346	445	386	371	221
Delaware	132	67	27	29	39	100
District of Columbia	1	0	n/a	0	n/a	3
Florida	6,059	5,296	5,048	4,484	4,753	3,755
Georgia	1,848	1,702	1,414	1,524	1,614	1,176
Hawaii	421	315	296	n/a	15	6
Idaho	21	5	13	18	27	14
Illinois	3,616	3,473	2,525	2,432	2,154	1,424
Indiana	1,256	1,185	203	977	828	725
Iowa	129	141	123	128	189	113
Kansas	227	239	185	213	154	245
Kentucky	539	379	275	196	270	298
Louisiana	412	288	257	351	447	529
Maine	26	27	10	26	56	49
Maryland	1,337	1,322	1,465	1,121	1,116	759
Massachusetts	1,229	836	905	860	941	923
Michigan	761	732	446	320	386	295
Minnesota	1,338	1,087	966	885	297	721
Mississippi	119	225	149	146	193	149
Missouri	635	569	338	306	381	222
Montana	11	1	1	5	4	7
Nebraska	212	180	148	143	198	164
Nevada	4,659	4,561	3,738	3,941	3,620	3,550
New Hampshire	56	46	24	49	103	48
New Jersey	1,453	1,372	1,489	1,086	892	1,147
New Mexico	219	287	347	264	289	265
New York	824	871	783	777	802	1,158
North Carolina	1,408	1,080	1,145	989	808	715
North Dakota	3	4	5	10	34	43
Ohio	1,266	1,891	1,724	1,374	794	1,710
Oklahoma	412	411	247	189	364	320
Oregon	752	660	296	376	431	49
Pennsylvania	2,498	1,871	1,958	1,939	2,139	1,995
Rhode Island	216	97	103	42	74	66
South Carolina	388	642	624	524	528	473
South Dakota	10	14	22	19	49	67
Tennessee	2,111	2,531	2,387	2,390	2,174	1,507
Texas	8,784	8,604	7,554	6,493	7,009	6,597
Utah	463	550	414	64	104	177
Vermont	6	7	5	2	3	9
Virginia	558	848	689	783	829	862
Washington	694	795	836	239	432	399
West Virginia	150	125	114	98	73	117
Wisconsin	687	371	358	457	383	495
Wyoming	34	14	7	13	18	32

Source: Federal Bureau of Investigation (2009–2014).

threat, or deceit), they do so for a wide variety of reasons. Nonetheless, research consistently points to financial earnings as the number one reason for involvement (Benoit & Millar, 2001; Dank et al., 2014; Jeffrey & MacDonald, 2006; Oselin, 2014; Smith, Grov, Seal, & McCall, 2012; Vanwesenbeeck, 2013; Weinberg, Shaver, & Williams, 1999). As individuals involved in prostitution have diverse education backgrounds that range from a lack of a high-school diploma to the holding of graduate degrees (Luckenbill, 1986; Weinberg et al., 1999), not all enter prostitution as a means for survival and due to a lack of alternative options to gain a viable income. Many choose prostitution as a profession even though they possess the education or other professional skills that have prepared them for employment in lawful occupations. Beyond monetary reasons, other commonly mentioned factors leading to engagement in prostitution include childhood victimization (Dalla, 2000; El-Bassel, Witte, Wada, Gilbert, & Wallace, 2001; Widom & Kuhns, 1996), drug addiction (Benoit & Millar, 2001; Erikson, Butters, McGillicuddy, & Hallgren, 2000; Pittman, 1971; Weinberg et al., 1999), sexual empowerment (St. James, 1987), and expression of sexual identity (Logan, 2010; Sausa, Keatley, & Operario, 2007).

Most social, political, and legal debates, as well as scholarly research, focus on female involvement in prostitution. However, male and transgender participation in prostitution comprise a significant segment of the sex trade (Weitzer, 2005). The scholarly literature on male prostitution has been slowly expanding since the second half of the twentieth century (e.g., Caulkins & Coombs, 1976; Coombs, 1974; Craft, 1966; Ginsburg, 1967; MacNamara, 1965; Pittman, 1971; Reiss, 1961), with early studies focusing heavily on homosexuality. Even less research addresses the experiences of transgender individuals engaged in prostitution (Weitzer, 2005). Most existing research on transgender prostitution focuses on the intersection between trans-

gender involvement in the sex trade and HIV risk (e.g., Elifson et al., 1993). To date, only a handful of studies have examined transgender prostitution that move beyond a focus on HIV risk and infection rates (Nadal, Davidoff, & Jujii-Doe, 2014; Nadal, Vargas, Meterko, Hamit, & Mclean, 2012; Sausa, Keatley, & Operario, 2007). Therefore, it is difficult to draw any conclusions about this understudied segment of the sex worker business. Still, some gendered patterns have begun to emerge:

- In contrast to prostitution by women, male sex work is often reported as a profession of choice (Lee-Gonyea et al., 2009; Smith et al., 2012).
- Male sex workers are less often referred to as victims (Vanwesenbeeck, 2013). This may be due, in part, to the fact that in comparison to their female counterparts, male sex workers report fewer incidents of violence by clients and lower levels of sexual abuse during childhood (Luckenbill, 1986; Vanwesenbeeck, 2013; Weitzer, 2005).
- Male prostitution is often linked to homosexuality and bisexuality (Boyer, 1989; Timpson, Ross, Williams, & Atkinson, 2007).
- Male prostitution can be understood as one means to explore, define, and live one's gay sexuality (Logan, 2010; Weitzer, 2005).
- Male sex workers appear to be less commonly targeted and arrested by law enforcement (Luckenbill, 1986; Weinberg et al., 1999; Weitzer, 2005).
- For males, prostitution is often "just" a part-time job (Pittman, 1971; Weitzer, 2005).
- Male and transgender sex workers experience a higher risk of HIV infection than female sex workers (Sausa et al., 2007; Timpson et al., 2007).
- Male sex workers are more likely to experience feelings of enjoyment

and job gratification than their female counterparts (Vanwesenbeeck, 2013; Weinberg et al., 1999; Weitzer, 2005).

- Males tend to exit prostitution in their mid-to-late twenties, comparatively earlier than female sex workers (Pittman, 1971; Weinberg et al., 1999).
- Prostitution by transgender people may be motivated by a general lack of love and social acceptance (Crosby & Pitts, 2007); a need to pay for hormone therapy and surgeries (Crosby & Pitts, 2007); or a lack of legal employment opportunities due to discrimination on the job market (Nadal et al., 2014).
- Transgender sex workers often perceive prostitution as an integral part of their transgender identity and of the transgender culture (Sausa et al., 2007).

Pimps: Facilitators and Promoters of Prostitution

"A **pimp** is one who controls the actions and lives off proceeds of one or more women who work the streets," often referred to as "players" in the "game" (Williamson & Cluse-Tolar, 2002, p. 1074). They promote, facilitate, and advance prostitution for their own financial benefit. **Advancing prostitution** is the initiation or facilitation of engagement in prostitution by a third person, the recruitment of customers for another person, the promotion of locales for prostitution, and the operation of a locale where prostitution takes place. Even though a pimp is neither a provider nor a purchaser of sexual services, such actions are illegal in the United States. The number of pimps is largely unknown. First-hand research in which pimps constitute the study population is scarce (Levitt & Venkatesch, 2007; Raphael & Myers-Powell, 2010). Pimps, therefore, may be the most hidden sub-population of the entire sex work industry (Dank et al., 2014). Nonetheless, research suggests between 40% and 80% of prostitutes are "pimp-controlled" (Kennedy,

Klein, Bristowe, Cooper, & Yuille, 2007; Norton-Hawk, 2004; Williamson & Cluse-Tolar, 2002). The common perception that all pimps are male appears to be erroneous; research suggests that a significant number of pimps are females, the majority of whom were previously prostitutes (e.g., Raphael & Myers-Powell, 2010).

Pimps have been characterized in various ways. *Macks* are said to be the most successful and respected pimps. For this category, the "game" is purely professional and the pimp employs a great number of women (Williamson & Cluse-Tolar, 2002). *Tennis-shoe pimps* most commonly only employ one or two sex workers at a time. The "game" is hardly ever operated as a business. Instead, tennis-shoe pimps often get caught in a cycle of drug abuse with the people working with them. *Gorilla pimps* are known to use the most primitive forms of recruitment strategies and measures to keep individuals engaged in playing their game, which includes brute violence, such as beating, threats, and kidnapping (Kennedy et al., 2007).

Rules

Pimps often perceive their involvement in the "game" as a profession, with certain rules imposed on their "employees" required to qualify the employee as a professional "player" of the "game" (Dank et al., 2014; Williamson & Cluse-Tolar, 2002). Such rules often include the following:

- *Drug/alcohol use*: Although some pimps, especially *tennis-shoe pimps*, choose to use drugs with their employees, more business-oriented pimps see drug abuse as grounds for dismissal of the individual employee (Williamson & Cluse-Tolar, 2002).
- *Limitations on clientele*: A significant portion of pimps in a study conducted by Dank and colleagues (2014) prohibited their employees from "turning

tricks" with young or Black individuals, fearing they could be competing pimps.

- *Restricted communication with other pimps*: In the same study, 19% of participants who operated as pimps did not allow communication by their employees with other pimps in order to protect their own authority and control over their employees. In addition, restricted contact also was a tool to maintain the dependency of prostitutes toward their pimps (Dank et al., 2014).
- *Earning quotas*: A study conducted by Raphael & Myers-Powell (2010) found that 36% of pimps did not allow their employees to keep any of their earnings; the remainder had fee-sharing agreements.

Punishment is a common consequence in cases in which the "employee" violates any of these set rules (Dank et al., 2014; Williamson & Cluse-Tolar, 2002). Even though the portrayal of pimps in contemporary U.S. culture is that of a brutal and violent perpetrator, participants in the study conducted by Dank and colleagues (2014) argue that the media exaggerate the occurrence of violence in a pimp/sex worker relationship. Specifically, they found that only 15% of interviewed pimps (*n* = 73) admitted to the use of physical violence for purposes of control. However, the forms of punishment can vary greatly from pimp to pimp, including physical violence, isolation, confiscation of possessions, emotional abuse, and threats of violence (Dank et al., 2014; Williamson & Cluse-Tolar, 2002). Some respondents even emphasized that violence has the potential to backfire. As one of the pimps explained, "once you get physical with a ho, then that means you ran out of game" (Dank et al., 2014, p. 178).

Recruitment

Recruitment strategies vary greatly. Some employees are recruited through the use of

brute force and threats directed toward the potential employee or his/her family, others through the use of deception or promise of love (Kennedy et al., 2007). At times, recruitment goes hand-in-hand with the development of a drug addiction. Once developed, it is often the individual's only choice to work for the pimp in order to feed her or his habit (Kennedy et al., 2007). Finally, people can be forced into prostitution by authority figures, such as parents, siblings, or other family members (Kennedy et al., 2007). Regardless of how it is accomplished, **pandering**—typically defined as forcing, deceiving, decoying, enticing, or otherwise recruiting someone to become a prostitute—is illegal in all U.S. states.

Although most research on exiting prostitution focuses on factors and processes leading the individual providing sexual services to exit (e.g., Baker, Dalla, & Williamson, 2010; Benoit & Millar, 2001; Cusick & Hickman, 2005; Dalla, 2006; Hedin & Månsson, 2004; Jeffrey & MacDonald, 2006; Norton-Hawk, 2001; Oselin, 2009; 2010; 2014; Saphira & Herbert, 2004; Williamson & Folaron, 2003), Raphael & Myers-Powell (2010) found that it is also difficult for pimps to step away from the "game." As one pimp clarified, "You don't leave pimping, it leaves you" (Raphael & Myers-Powell, 2010, p. 7). The motivations for giving up pimping differ from those for leaving prostitution. Raphael and Myers-Powell (2010) reported that participants rarely "left the game" because they disliked what they were doing; rather, they did so for reasons such as health, age, legal issues (including being on parole, problems with the U.S. Internal Revenue Service, constant involvement with law enforcement), and desire to regain custody of their children.

Johns: Purchasers of Sexual Services

The origin of the term **John**, referring to individuals who patronize sex workers,[3] is not fully certain. However, some argue that the

Law in Action INTERPRETING THE LAW OF PANDERING

According to an undercover police officer, during the summer of 2007, Jomo Zambia drove up to a female police officer working undercover as a street prostitute. He told her several times to get into the truck because he was a pimp. The police officer agreed to talk, but refused to get into Zambia's truck. Zambia asked her how much money she had on her. After she told him, Zambia offered to provide her with housing and clothing and that he would "take care of [her]" in exchange for the $400 she carried in her pocket. After telling Zambia that she felt uncomfortable, he told her that he was a legitimate businessman and that he would not "strong-arm" her. However, the police officer perceived Zambia as a "gorilla-type pimp"—one who utilizes techniques of verbal threats and violence to scare and encourage prostitutes into working with him. After the officer called for backup, she arrested Zambia. He was subsequently charged with one count of pandering under California Penal Code § 266i(a)(2).

While searching Zambia's car, the police found condoms, three cell phones, and business cards on the truck's console. According to the arresting officer, these items are commonly found in the possession of pimps. Zambia invoked his Fifth Amendment privilege against self-incrimination and refused to testify. His mother and his fiancée, however, both testified on his behalf; both denied that they could ever imagine Zambia working as a pimp. Zambia was convicted by a jury and sentenced to four years in prison.

Zambia appealed his conviction, arguing that the statutory definition of pandering in California Penal Code § 266i(a)(2) requires proof that the perpetrator "[b]y promises, threats, violence, or by any device or scheme, causes, induces, persuades, or encourages another person to become a prostitute." Thus, he argued, the statute did not include encouraging a person who was already a prostitute (or, at least, was acting like one during the course of law enforcement vice operations). The appellate court upheld Zambia's conviction. He then appealed to the California Supreme Court.

In line with long-standing case law, the California Supreme Court clarified the purpose of the pandering statute was to prohibit encouraging others to engage in sex work under the control of the person giving the encouragement. The court emphasized that the current status of the individual approached, regardless of whether he or she was a working prostitute, cannot be grounds for acquittal of an individual who committed an act of pandering. The court specifically argued that it is more adequate to interpret the phrase "to become a prostitute" as "to engage in any future acts of prostitution." It is important to note that pandering, as regulated in §266i, constitutes a specific intent crime, which does not need to lead to actual encouragement of an individual to "become a prostitute" within the meaning of the statute. Therefore, the court concluded that the encouragement of someone who is either already a prostitute or, as in this case, an undercover police officer, constituted the crime of pandering.

- Should law be applied as written, or according to its presumed purpose?
- If you had the authority to decide the case, would you have ruled differently? Why or why not?

name John (which is a common name in American culture) is used for those purchasing sexual services due to their desire to remain anonymous. Besides being called John, individuals engaged in prostitution also refer to their clients as "tricks" or "dates." Just as sex workers are considered to be members of a "hidden population," so are the clients of the sex industry. Thus, random sampling for the purposes of generalizable research is a difficult, if not impossible, task. Most research is conducted utilizing convenience samples of either arrested or convicted Johns, or in some rare cases, those who self-reported buying sex for a fee at one point in their life. Therefore, what is known about individuals purchasing sex remains exploratory. Moreover, most research in this area is focused on the street-level market, just as it is for those selling sexual services. Hence, existing literature on Johns largely focuses on those individuals who "shop the streets," rather than on those who seek sex workers in brothels, massage parlors, and through escort services (Bernstein & Schaffner, 2005, p. 117).

Just as the prevalence of prostitution remains largely a best-guess estimate, so are numbers reporting prostitution clients. Nonetheless, research suggests that between 10% and 20% of males in the United States self-report buying sex for money at least once (Shively, Kliorys, Wheeler, & Hunt, 2012). Research to date does not include comparable data for females. Little is known about the characteristics of those who purchase sex. However, according to several studies, male Johns are (as compared with the general male population) more likely to:

- be working full-time (Monto, 1999);
- have viewed X-rated movies within the past year (Monto, 1999);
- be unmarried, separated, or in an "unhappy" relationship/marriage (Monto, 1999, 2004);
- be ethnically representative of the geographic area (Monto, 1999, 2004);[4]

- be older in age (Lever & Dolnick, 2000; Sullivan & Simon, 1998);[5]
- be more sexually active (Sullivan & Simon, 1998); and
- have a higher than average income (Lever & Dolnick, 2000).

Little is known about the characteristics of individuals purchasing sexual services and their motivation around it; thus, more research is needed for a more complete understanding of these interactions. However, as Johns constitute a similarly (and perhaps even more so) hard to reach and invisible population it is uncertain to what extent research will explore this in the future.

IDEOLOGICAL AND POLITICAL CONTEXT

Existing ideological/political views regarding prostitution are predominantly situated within different manifestations of feminism and can be understood as located on the edges of a continuum. Ronald Weitzer (2010) developed a framework accordingly, in which the **oppression paradigm** resides at one end of the ideological spectrum and the **empowerment paradigm** at the other. Weitzer further argues that, due to the complexity of prostitution, it is crucial to leave room for a moderate middle ground, for which he coins the term **polymorphous paradigm**. These categories, as developed by Weitzer (2010), are presented in Figure 7.1.

The Oppression Paradigm

Radical feminism is a branch of feminism that studies patriarchy—in and of itself—as an omnipresent state of oppression to women, rather than as a secondary aspect of a larger system (Willis, 1984/1992). Radical feminists argue that, at its core, prostitution reveals patriarchal gender relations constituted by male domination (see, e.g., Barry, 1995;

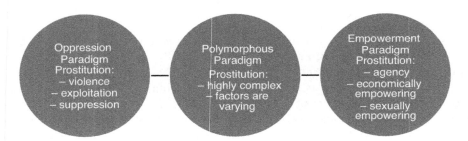

Figure 7.1 Continuum of competing ideological perspectives on prostitution

Dworkin, 1989; Farley, 2004; MacKinnon, 1993; Pateman, 1988). Thus, the oppression paradigm equates prostitution with violence, exploitation, and suppression that constitutes a violation of basic human rights (e.g., Barry, 1995; Dworkin, 1989; Farley, 2004; MacKinnon, 1993; Pateman, 1988). Furthermore, from this perspective, any distinction between "forced" and "voluntary" involvement in prostitution is false. Prostitution by choice, they assert, is a myth; as MacKinnon (1993) states, "If prostitution is a free choice, why are the women with the fewest choices the ones most often found doing it?" (p. 28). From this perspective, prostitution is nothing more than "paid rape" (Farley, 2004, p. 7) or "torture through repeated rape" (MacKinnon, 1993, p. 13). Supporters of this paradigm, primarily radical feminists, dominated the academic discourse around prostitution from approximately 1900 to 1980, but no longer remain the prevailing voice (Jeffreys, 2009).

The Empowerment Paradigm

Socialist feminism rejects radical feminism's premise that patriarchy is the sole or primary source of oppression of women. They view patriarchy as part and parcel of a larger system of inequality rooted in Marxist theory concerning the oppressive nature of capitalism (see Rothstein & Weisstein, 1972). The majority of contemporary scholars who identify with social-

ist feminism support the notion that prostitution can be empowering, especially economically (see, e.g., Almodovar, 2002; Agustin, 2005; Jeffreys, 2009; St. James, 1987). From this point of view, it is not prostitution that constitutes a human rights violation, but rather the criminalization of prostitution since that deprives sex workers of their human agency (Lerum, McCurtis, Saunders & Wahab, 2012). In other words, prostitution is not necessarily oppressive, but can be a form of economic empowerment and expressive freedom in which people should be free to engage without the interference from the law.

The Polymorphous Paradigm

Weitzer (2010) argues that there is a need for a moderate, middle-ground approach to viewing prostitution because the "oppression and empowerment paradigm [are] one-dimensional and essentialist" (p. 6). The core canon of Weitzer's polymorphous paradigm is that constructions such as victimization, exploitation, violence, coercion, choice, job satisfaction, and self-esteem are all dynamic, rather than static (see also Jeffreys, 2009). Differences in victimhood and agency, for example, are revealed when comparing the previously mentioned experiences of those who engage in street versus indoor prostitution (see Monto, 2004).

Debates surrounding the legal status of prostitution, and subsequent structures of regulation (and lack thereof) are closely connected to ideological and political views surrounding prostitution. These are examined in the following section.

THE LEGAL REGULATION OF PROSTITUTION

Debates about the legal status of prostitution primarily revolve around three different approaches, broadly speaking: criminalization, legalization, and decriminalization. **Criminalization** of prostitution in all its forms is the current legal approach in all U.S. states, with the exception of select counties in Nevada. Under this approach, all actors that are involved in some way with prostitution—including the seller, purchaser, pimp, brothel-keeper (an individual who runs a house of prostitution), and even the landlord of houses of prostitution—are subject to prosecution and punishment.

Legalization (which is currently used, for example, in the Netherlands, Germany, and Israel) consists of the removal of some (i.e., *partial legalization*, also found in several counties in Nevada) or all (i.e., *complete legalization*) criminal prohibitions surrounding the purchase of sexual services between consenting adults. But legalization does not mean that the law completely abandons social control of the behavior. Prostitution may become partially or completely legal, but the selling of sexual services is still subject to a system of legal regulations that operate to control one or more aspects of prostitution, such as licensing of businesses, registering of sex workers, zoning, taxes, mandatory health checks, and the provision and availability of health care. Legalization can be intentional—by formal judicial or legislative action. Alternatively, **de facto legalization** may occur when there is a "disjunction between the criminal law and formal policies and practices" (Weitzer, 2012, p. 81). This occurs when prostitution remains illegal, but is tolerated, to varying degrees, by

relevant legal authorities. For example, Western Australia prohibits the operation of brothels. Local law enforcement, however, is fully aware that brothels exist. Rather than close them down, the authorities periodically inspect the brothels and monitor who works there (Weitzer, 2012).

Decriminalization can be partial or complete. **Partial decriminalization** (which is currently used, for example, in Sweden, Norway, and Iceland) can take multiple approaches. Penalties for prostitution could be reduced (e.g., from a felony to a misdemeanor or violation); or, the criminal laws concerning a specific prostitution-related offense could be removed from the criminal code (e.g., for soliciting prostitution), while penalties for procuring and pandering remain on the books. **Complete decriminalization** (which is currently used in New Zealand) means that all laws prohibiting prostitution are removed from criminal codes.[6] When completely decriminalized, prostitution could occur in any setting because the law does not prohibit or regulate any aspect of prostitution between consenting adults.

Debate on Criminalization, Legalization, and Decriminalization

The debate regarding the legalization or decriminalization of prostitution originates in the sex workers' rights movement and, in particular, through an organization called "Call Off Your Old and Tired Ethics" (COYOTE), which has advocated for decriminalization since the 1970s (DeFranco & Stellato, 2013). Some of the central arguments utilized to justify each stance are presented in Table 7.2.

It should be noted that some commentators argue that the legal status of prostitution is relatively inconsequential because prostitution may simply be resistant to laws and policies developed to combat it (Bernstein, 1999; Farley, 2004). In other words, regardless of efforts to prohibit or regulate prostitution, it persists. The following section

Table 7.2 Major arguments for and against the legalization/decriminalization of prostitution

Pro-Legalization/Decriminalization	Anti-Legalization/Decriminalization
• Arrests and fines have no or little deterrent effect. • Arrest and punishment are harmful (stigma of a criminal record). • Criminalization is expensive for the Criminal Justice System. • Sex workers are fearful of reporting victimization to the police due to the illegality of their own actions. • Prostitution is legitimate service work. • It is a civil rights violation to deny women the "right to prostitute." • Legalization of prostitution leads to an improvement of health for those involved in prostitution due to access to health care. • Legalization of prostitution increases economic opportunities for individuals who choose to engage in prostitution. • Prostitution laws are not equally enforced. • Decriminalization potentially facilitates a shift from arrest to protection of sex workers. • Decriminalization has the potential to facilitate enforcement of sex trafficking laws. • Legalization/decriminalization has the potential to facilitate reporting of sex trafficking cases by its victims.	• Male domination is a main reason for legalization. • Promotes the sexual commodification of individuals. • Illegal markets develop even after legalization. For example, many women remain in unregulated street prostitution to avoid registering or undergoing mandatory health checks. • The social stigma for being a sex worker does not vanish with legalization (e.g., registration requirements prevent anonymity). • Legalizing/decriminalizing prostitution normalizes victimization of all women and children under the umbrella of state-sponsored prostitution. • Legalization and decriminalization increase sex trafficking and the sexual exploitation of children.

examines some examples of how select jurisdictions have sought to manage the persistence.

Criminalization of Prostitution in the United States

Few Federal Laws

Federal law in the United States is sparse with regard to prostitution; its legal regulation is largely under state jurisdiction (Weitzer, 2012). However, two federal laws have been enacted that criminalize actions that facilitate prostitution: as previously discussed, the Mann Act (1910) prohibits the transportation of sex workers across state lines; and the Victims of Trafficking and Violence Protection Act of 2000, and its subsequent reauthoriza-

tion laws, target sex trafficking (which will be explored in more detail later in this chapter). Even though the scope of federal jurisdiction is narrow, common confusion between prostitution and sex trafficking often leads to corresponding confusion concerning federal funding and other resources that are intended for anti-trafficking efforts, but may be misused at the local level to combat prostitution (Lerum et al., 2012).

State Law Classifications of the Offense

Prostitution is considered a misdemeanor in all U.S. states except Nevada (see elaboration in greater detail below). A misdemeanor charge can be elevated to a felony if multiple prostitution charges accumulate over time.

State Law Definitions of "What Counts" as Prostitution

Although criminal laws targeting prostitution vary considerably from state to state, there is general agreement that oral sex, vaginal sex, anal sex, and assisted masturbation all fall within the sex acts proscribed by prostitution laws. This, however, was not always the case. Consider that Illinois Revised Statute ch. 38, para. 11–1 (1983) limited the legal definition of prostitution to "penetration of the female sex organ" before it was repealed.

State Laws Targeting Related Offenses

With the exception of Nevada, all U.S. states criminalize the solicitation of prostitution, pimping, procuring a prostitute, and operating a brothel and/or another business that offers or facilitates the trade of sex for a fee. Some jurisdictions go even further, as the "Law in Action" feature explores.

Law in Action "WALKING WHILE TRANS": THE CASE OF MONICA JONES

Section 23–52(A)(3) of the City of Phoenix Municipal Code bars manifesting "an intent to commit or solicit an act of prostitution." Phoenix authorities used this provision controversially in the 2013 prosecution of Monica Jones.

In 2013, Monica Renee Jones was a full-time college student majoring in social work at the Arizona State University. Monica Jones identifies as an African-American transgender woman (assigned male at birth, identifying as female) who serves as an advocate and activist for transgender rights.

According to Monica Jones, she planned to go out the night of her arrest. An undercover police officer approached her and offered her a ride to the neighborhood bar where she intended to go. Monica Jones denies that she had any intentions of selling sexual services to the very "handsome" man who turned out to be an undercover police officer; she simply expected to have drinks with him.

Four minutes after Jones accepted the ride to the bar the car was stopped by another police car for a pre-planned traffic stop. The media (Nichols, 2014) reported that Jones claimed not to have been brought to the police station after her arrest but instead to the basement of a church, which was connected to project ROSE (a religious program run in collaboration with police officers aimed at detaining "community members that are suspected of being sex workers"). This, however, was not mentioned in court documents.

At a bench trial (a nonjury trial before a judge), Jones and the undercover officer were the only two witnesses who testified. The arresting officer corroborated that Monica had not engaged in any behavior suggesting prostitution-related activities other than having accepted a ride from him. Nonetheless, Jones was convicted and sentenced to 30 days in jail and a fine of $150. The ruling judge explained:

I also have to consider factors such as mode of intent by any witnesses testifying. And with respect to this particular proceeding, the Defendant having acknowledged, admitted, a record of not too long ago, less than two years ago, of a prior conviction, the – a motive to avoid a mandatory 30-day sentence would be something that I can't ignore. When evaluating the credibility of witnesses in front of me, I do find that the State has met its burden. I'm going to find the Defendant guilty.

(Appellant Memorandum, August 5, 2014, p. 2)

Jones appealed and argued a variety of constitutional issues regarding Section 23–52(A)(3) of the PHOENIX MUNICIPAL CODE, including violation of the protection of free speech under the First Amendment to the U.S Constitution, as well under the Constitution of Arizona; violation of the due process clause according to the Fourteenth Amendment of the U.S. Constitution and Constitution of Arizona; and select other evidentiary concerning the trial proceedings (e.g., admission of evidence of Jones's prior prostitution conviction, consideration of Jones's potential punishment in the decision of guilt, and denial of a requested jury trial). On January 22, 2015 the Superior Court of Arizona vacated the judgment of guilt and ordered a new trial on the grounds that, "for the trial court to have concluded Defendant was not credible and thus guilty because she was facing conviction and sentence deprived Defendant of a fair trial" (*Arizona v. Jones*, 2015, p. 3).

Select media accounts dubbed Jones's arrest for "manifesting intent to commit acts of prostitution "walking while trans" (Busey, 2014, para 1; see also Nichols, 2014). Jones stated, "If I was a White woman walking down Arcadia [a nice section of Phoenix], I would have never been stopped for manifestation" (Cassidy, 2014, para 4).

- One of Jones's arguments on appeal was that her prior conviction was inappropriately used at trial to show her alleged propensity to engage in prostitution-related activity in violation of relevant rules of evidence. Do you think her past history was relevant to her behavior on the night in question?
- Another of Jones's arguments on appeal concerned the constitutionality of the "manifestation" ordinance under the First Amendment. Given the rights to free speech and expression that Amendment protects, do you think manifestation of an intent to commit an offense should be punishable by law? Do such laws raise any other concerns for you? Might they be unconstitutionally vague or overbroad? Do they raise due process concerns for you about the sufficiency of the evidence necessary for conviction?

(*Arizona v. Jones*, 2015; Appellant's Memorandum, 2014)

Unique Louisiana Law

In 1982, Louisiana expanded its "crime against nature" statute (i.e., sodomy law; see Chapter 6), by criminalizing the intent to offer oral or anal sex in return for compensation (Agathocleous, 2013; DeFranco & Stellato, 2013). Since that time, prosecutors in Louisiana had the discretion to either file a charge under the state's prostitution law or under its "Crime Against Nature by Solicitation" (CANS) statute (LA. REV. STAT. § 14:89.2[A], 1982). The consequences for being convicted either under the prostitution or the CANS statute were shockingly different (Agathocleous, 2013; DeFranco & Stellato, 2013):

- A person, convicted under the prostitution statute, faced a *misdemeanor* conviction with a punishment of no more than $500 and/or a maximum term of imprisonment of six months.
- A conviction under CANS represented a *felony* (subject to imprisonment up to five years and *mandatory* registration as a sex offender upon release).

In order to combat the disparate treatment for those convicted under the CANS statute as compared with those convicted under the prostitution statute, a legal team filed a lawsuit in 2011 seeking to have the sentencing disparity declared unconstitutional on equal protection grounds (see *Doe v. Jindal*, 2012).[7] Louisiana's legislature reacted to the filing of the lawsuit by equalizing existing differences between CANS and Prostitution convictions (Agathocleous, 2013). However, the amendment to the law had no retroactive power, meaning that people who had been convicted prior to the enactment of the amendment remained registered as sex offenders (Agathocleous, 2013; DeFranco & Stellato, 2013). As a result, the legal team in *Doe v. Jindal* focused their equal protection arguments on those who had to remain registered sex offenders even though other, similarly situated, offenders did not—either because they were convicted under the prostitution statute or because they were convicted under the CANS statute after the amendments that harmonized the penalties and removed the sex offender registration requirement. The court sided with the plaintiffs and ordered the removal of the names of the *Doe v. Jindal* plaintiffs from the Louisiana sex offender registry.

Shortly after the *Doe v. Jindal* decision, lawyers for the Center for Constitutional Rights filed *Doe v. Caldwell* as a class action lawsuit seeking to remove all of the names of defendants from the state's sex offender registry who were convicted under the CANS statute prior to its amendment (Agathocleous, 2013). In June 2013, a settlement was finalized that resulted in the removal of all of the people whose names appeared in the Louisiana Sex Offender Registry as a result of a CANS conviction.

Less Common "Prostitution Off-Limit Orders"

Another legal response to prostitution activity, most often imposed post-conviction, is "off-limit orders," intended to eradicate prostitution altogether by motivating sex workers to terminate their involvement utilizing the criminalization of the presence in designated areas of high prostitution activity.

Banishment, or the removal of an individual from certain geographic areas, is not a novel phenomenon; rather these practices have existed globally for centuries and were utilized in colonial America to punish convicts (Borelli, 2003). Historically, they have "served a broader societal role to delineate and segregate those bodies deemed sick, pathological, undesirable, and in some cases disposable" from the healthy community (Edelman, 2011, p. 854). Banishment and similar exclusionary laws require individuals onto whom an exclusionary practice is imposed to leave designated geographic areas without an option to return for a selected period of time (Borelli, 2003). Prostitution "off-limit orders" are a form of limited banishment that requires the individual at whom the order is directed to remain outside designated areas or else face arrest. In Seattle, Washington, such orders are referred to as "Stay Out of Areas of Prostitution" or SOAP orders (Hill, 2004).

Some municipalities create the authority to issue SOAP orders by enacting ordinances (Hill, 2004).[8] "In other municipalities, such as Seattle, SOAP areas are defined by the city attorney's office and imposed by the municipal court" (Hill, 2004, p. 177; see also Seattle Police Department Manual § 15.290, n.d.). SOAP orders are most often imposed by a municipal court judge as a condition of probation or, to a lesser degree, as a condition of deferred prosecution (Beckett & Herbert, 2009; Hill, 2004). As of 2013, six SOAP zones existed in Seattle (making up about 3.5 square miles), which have been identified as areas of high prostitution activity by the City Attorney's Office (Beckett & Herbert, 2009; Hill, 2004). Individuals living under a SOAP order are prohibited from entering the geographic areas specified in the individual order for any reason (including waiting for a bus, shopping, visiting family and friends, soliciting), for a maximum of two years—a time period that corresponds to the maximum period of probation that can be imposed for a prostitution conviction (WASH. REV. CODE

§§ 3.50.330, 35.20.255; see also Beckett & Herbert, 2009; Hill, 2004). The judge has the option to grant certain exceptions if people live or work in these areas, or if they have other "legitimate" reasons to be in these areas. Whenever a person who lives under a SOAP order otherwise enters a SOAP zone, he or she violates the terms of probation or deferred prosecution, which typically then leads to jail time.

Prostitution off-limit orders have been the subject of numerous critiques. The most common criticisms include that these orders:

- violate one's constitutional rights (the right to travel and double jeopardy in cases in which SOAP is used as a tool in deferred prosecution);
- are ineffective in terms of meeting goals of probation (rehabilitation/future offending and the protection of the community from future offenses);
- may lead to relocation, increasing the individual's vulnerability and exposure to violence; and
- lead to criminalization of social status, rather than illegal behavior.

The problems surrounding SOAP and exclusionary practices aside, prostitution off-limit orders represent an "easy" way for legislators, prosecutors, judges, and police officers to respond to public concerns about the crime problem, by "clearing the bums off the street" (Armstrong, 1963, p. 765; see also Beckett & Herbert, 2010).

The most common justification for a policy such as SOAP is rooted in the broken-windows theory of crime prevention (see Wilson & Kelling, 1982). This theory argues that if neighborhoods and communities fail to fix broken windows (a metaphor for less serious criminal and/or deviant behavior), the lack of informal and formal social control will most likely invite higher-level criminal offending. But, like the specific criticisms of prostitution off-limit orders like SOAP, bro-

ken windows theory and practices are not without their critics (see Harcourt & Ludwig, 2006). In the case of SOAP orders, critics argue that these tools merely lead to the relocation of sex workers to areas they do not know or to underground markets. This, in turn, is likely to increase their vulnerability and exposes them to increased levels of violence, harassment, and abuse (Beckett & Herbert, 2009; Hill, 2004; Koyama, 2010).

A System of Partial Legalization in Nevada

As previously mentioned, Nevada is the only state in the United States in which prostitution has been partially legalized (since 1971). However, instead of legalizing all sexual services within its borders, prostitution in Nevada is only legal in counties that have fewer than 400,000 inhabitants (NEV. REV. STAT. § 244.345, 2015). Also, the only form of legalized prostitution in Nevada is the provision of sexual services within licensed brothels. This means that street-level prostitution, as well as prostitution offered through escort services, remains illegal in the entire state of Nevada (Weitzer, 2012). As in other states, pandering is a crime in Nevada, although the statutory definition of the offense in that state includes forcing, deceiving, or enticing someone to work in a brothel (NEV. REV. STAT. §§ 201.300–360, 2015). And, as with other U.S. states, pimping by living off the earnings of a prostitute is illegal throughout the state of Nevada (NEV. REV. STAT. § 201.320, 2015).

According to an online source that locates brothels in Nevada, there were 24 brothels legally operating in nine counties of Nevada as of July 2015 (Las Vegas Escorts and Brothels, n.d.). Counties with fewer than 400,000 have the authority to determine if prostitution should be legalized or not. Thus, legal "prostitution is a privilege not a right, [and the] community can impose any rules it chooses" (Brents & Hausbeck, 2001, p. 311).

Local officials also have the authority to revoke brothel licenses for any reason (Hausbeck & Brents, 2010). Contrary to common understandings, prostitution is *not* legal in Las Vegas and Reno (Weitzer, 2012).

In counties where the operation of brothels is legal, state and local authorities regulate their operation (Brents & Hausbeck, 2005; Weitzer, 2012). Brothels vary greatly in size, with the largest ones employing up to 80 women at any given time, and others only employing two to ten women (Hausbeck & Brents, 2010). In order to be able to own and operate a brothel, a person must be 21 years of age or older and cannot have a previous felony conviction (Weitzer, 2012).

People who want to work in licensed brothels must be 21 or older (except in two counties where the minimum age is 18) and have to acquire a state health card. This card is issued if the applying individual passes a physical exam that includes testing for a range of sexually transmitted infections, such as HIV, syphilis, gonorrhea, and chlamydia (Brents & Hausbeck, 2005, Hausbeck & Brents, 2010; Weitzer, 2012). After being licensed, employees of brothels are mandated to visit a local physician every week for gonorrhea and chlamydia tests. Brothel employees must also undergo monthly tests for HIV and syphilis. In cases in which sex workers test positive for gonorrhea, chlamydia, or syphilis, they are not allowed to work until the disease is cured (Brents & Hausbeck, 2005). In cases in which an individual tests positive for HIV, the sex worker is not permitted to continue working in licensed brothels. It constitutes a felony for any individual to engage in sex work after testing positive for HIV infection; the penalties include a prison sentence of between two and ten years, or a fine in the amount of $10,000 (Nev. Rev. Stat. §§ 201.356, 201.358, 2015).

Statewide, Nevada brothels are required to post visible notices in and around the brothel that condom use is mandatory and non-negotiable (Hausbeck & Brents, 2010). Most counties require brothel employees to reside at the brothel for the time of their contract. Also, in some cities, family members, such as spouses and children, are not allowed to live in the town in which the wife/mother is employed (Weitzer, 2012).

Even in counties in which licensed brothels are legal, they may not be located in any part of the towns or cities. Rather, zoning laws prohibit prostitution in "respectable" areas of the city (Brents & Hausbeck, 2005), keeping them at a "safe distance away from schools, churches, and main streets" (Brents & Hausbeck, 2005, p. 276). This means that brothels may not to be located "within 400 yards of any schoolhouse or schoolroom"; "400 yards of any church, edifice, building or structure erected for and used for devotional services or religious worship in this state"; and may not be on "principal business street[s] or thoroughfare of any of the towns of this state" (Nev. Rev. Stat. §§ 201.380, 201.390, 2015). Additional local restrictions might apply as well.

Advocates of Nevada's state-sanctioned brothels argue that they have resulted in the near-complete eradiation of illegal prostitution in counties that license brothels; even if true, the illegal sex trade flourishes in the rest of the state (Weitzer, 2012), as evidenced by the arrest rates for illegal prostitution and commercialized vice in Nevada (see Table 7.1).

For those working legally in licensed brothels, proponents argue that employees are provided with a safe working environment due to stringent regulations. The majority of licensed brothels have been found to be free of drug use/abuse, violence, underage prostitution, sexually transmitted infections (STIs), and sex trafficking (Weitzer, 2012). In addition, brothels provide employees with built-in safety mechanisms, including surveillance during price negotiation, panic buttons, collaboration with local law-enforcement agencies, "sisterhood" among employees, and strict "in-house" regulations regarding the prevention of STIs (Brents & Hausbeck, 2005).

Owners of brothels in Nevada formed the Nevada Brothel Association in 1984, which unites the owners of the most powerful brothels in the state (Hausbeck & Brents, 2010). However, the association is not particularly active and aims to preserve the status quo rather than try to push changes that would benefit owners, workers, or the prostitution industry (Hausbeck & Brents, 2010).

Since 2009, Nevada has the strictest and most severe regulations regarding underage prostitution in the United States. Those who are found guilty of trafficking individuals younger than 14 years can be sentenced to a fine up to $500,000, and those who have been found guilty of trafficking a person between 14 and 17 can be sentenced to a fine up to $100,000 (NEV. REV. STAT. § 201.352, 2015; see also Pope, 2009).

International Examples of Systems of Regulation

Prostitution is not unique to the United States. Although many countries criminalize prostitution in much the same way the United States does, some nations take very different approaches to the regulation of prostitution and related offenses. Select international examples provide a broader, comparative understanding of legal approaches to prostitution. Consider the varying approach of Sweden, the Netherlands, and New Zealand. As the examples in Table 7.3 demonstrate, it is uncertain which system addresses or eradicates issues that are commonly associated with prostitution.

Legal Responses to Purchasing Sexual Services

As it is in Sweden, the act of purchasing sexual services for a fee is also illegal in all U.S. states except Nevada. Unlike in Sweden, however, both purchasing *and* selling sex for a fee

are considered a misdemeanor in all U.S. states (other than in the specific locations in which legal brothels operate in Nevada). Less attention has been directed toward the customer of sexual services until recently (Monto, 2004; Shively et al., 2012). The newfound interest, both in academic scholarship and the criminal justice system, is in great part due to the argument that "supply and distribution are symptoms; demand is the cause" (Shively et al., 2012, p. 8). Law-enforcement agencies nationwide are increasingly arresting men who seek the services of sex workers, usually by using female police officers as decoys (Monto, 2004). In addition to enforcement of the law, public officials have reacted to the new interest in holding customers of sexual services accountable for their actions by creating new programs and policies. These programs and interventions are designed to deter individuals from seeking prostitutes for sexual services.

John Schools

"John schools" consist of "an education or treatment program for men arrested for soliciting illegal commercial sex" (Shively et al., 2012, p. 1; see also Gurd & O'Brien, 2013; Monto, 2004). Even though there is no uniformity in the organization and regulation of John schools, a general eligibility criterion is a first-time arrest for procuring an adult sex worker (Gurd & O'Brien, 2013; Shively et al., 2012). Thus, individuals who have prior convictions for sexually motivated offenses, or are procuring individuals who are underage, are not eligible to "enroll" in a John school.

Most John schools are implemented as diversion programs, meaning that the prostitution charge will be dropped if the defendant fulfills certain requirements. Most often these requirements include successful completion of the program, payment of fees and fines (usually up to $1,500), and no new arrests within 12 months. If the individual fails to fulfill one of these requirements, his/her case is referred to the court for prosecution (Gurd

Table 7.3 Select international approaches to the regulation of prostitution

Country	The Law	The Aftermath
Sweden Partial Criminalization	No law criminalizes a Swedish citizen for providing sexual services. Thus, being a sex worker is not illegal. However, the law prohibits the purchase of sexual services since 1999 (Violence Against Women Act [Kvinnofrid]). Punishment: Fine or imprisonment for at most 12 months (Swedish Penal Code: Chapter 23).	Governmental evaluation report in 2010 on the effectiveness of the "new regulation" • Street prostitution decreased by 50%. • Demand of sexual services decreased drastically. • Sexual services advertised on the internet increased. Academics call for caution of the interpretation of the results of the evaluation report, indicating that it is largely based on data provided by organizations that have a specific clientele; thus, not representative of the entire population.
The Netherlands Legalization	The provision of sexual services by the individual has never been illegal. Exploitation of others for the purpose of prostitution is illegal under Article 273f of the Dutch Criminal Code with penalties up to 18 years of imprisonment. Employment in prostitution is legal for all citizens of the European Union. The ban of brothels and third-party involvement was lifted in 2000. • Acquisition of a license required (which can be revoked). • Sex workers have to file and pay income tax (Value Added Tax [VAT]).	Many sex workers chose not to utilize labor rights. Change in overall prevalence rate is uncertain even though Dutch authorities claim a decrease of the licensed sector, prevalence of sex trafficking, and underage prostitution.
New Zealand Partial Decriminalization and Partial Legalization	Prior to the Prostitution Reform Act (PRA) of 2003, prostitution was not illegal, but many actions related to prostitution were illegal (such as solicitation, operating a brothel, etc.), making it nearly impossible to engage in prostitution without breaking the law. With the implementation of PRA, several laws were removed from the criminal code, such as the law prohibiting solicitation in public places, the operation of brothels, and living off the proceeds of prostitution. PRA aimed to provide sex workers with the same legal protections (labor rights and human rights) that are available to other workers.	First review of the effectiveness of PRA in 2008 by the Prostitution Law Review Committee. According to the findings the overall goal of PRA had been achieved.

continued . . .

Table 7.3 Continued

Country	The Law	The Aftermath
	Owners of establishments with more than four employees have to obtain an operator's certificate.	
	Individuals can apply if they are 18+, citizens/permanent residents of New Zealand or Australia, and do not have disqualifying convictions (e.g., offenses violating PRA 2003, participation in organized crimes, sexual crimes, murder)	

Sources: Amsterdam.Info (2014); Barnett, Casavant, & Nicol (2011); Dutch Ministry of Foreign Affairs (2012); Ekberg (2004); Ministry of Justice (2010); New Zealand Parliament (2008); Regeringskansliet: Government Offices of Sweden (2012); Skilbrei & Holmström (2013); Warnock & Wheen (2012); Weitzer (2010, 2012)

& O'Brien, 2013; Shively et al., 2012). Less often, the successful completion of a John school is part of post-conviction sentencing requirements (Shively et al., 2012). As of 2012, John schools existed in more than 50 cities and counties all over the United States (Shively et al., 2012).

The purpose of such programs is to deter the individual from purchasing sexual services and, as a natural consequence of that, to reduce the extent of human trafficking and sexual exploitation (Gurd & O'Brien, 2013; Shively et al., 2012). Although the curricula of John schools vary, they most often include educational sessions on health, legal consequences, and the negative impact of prostitution on individuals involved and the communities in which it takes place (Shively et al., 2012).

Shaming Techniques

Shaming of an offender has been practiced since colonial America, often combined with different forms of corporal punishment (Hubacher, 1998). Advocates argue that shaming is a simple and straightforward technique that reduces the demand for purchased sexual services. Today, it is utilized in almost

500 communities all over the United States (Hubacher, 1998; Shively et al., 2012). The majority of the communities that have implemented shaming techniques for the purchasers of sexual services utilize the online and print news media to publicize the names and/or pictures of individuals either arrested or convicted for procuring a sex worker (Shively et al., 2012). Other outlets used to shame Johns are public and private websites, billboards along freeways, and community websites.

"Dear John" letters are another approach used by at least 40 U.S. cities to shame and deter suspected Johns. The purpose of such letters is twofold. First, they aim to warn individuals who are cohabiting with the suspect of the danger of sexually transmitted diseases, including HIV/AIDS. Second, such letters are aimed to shame and pressure the suspect by letting individuals close to him/her know about his/her status as someone suspected to have purchased sexual services (Shively et al., 2012).

Other measures used to combat the demand for prostitution are vehicle seizure and driver's license suspension. In addition, "prostitution off limit orders" (such as Seattle's SOAP) are not only utilized for individuals who sell sex for money but also to reduce the client base of sex workers by excluding Johns from areas of high prostitution activities (Shively et al., 2012).

Although proponents of these techniques argue that this approach constitutes a powerful deterrent, both for the individual offender/suspect (specific deterrence), as well as for the potential future offender (general deterrence), opponents criticize this approach. They draw attention to a potential violation of due process rights, through shaming prior to conviction, and to the potential harmful effects for family and friends of the shamed suspect (Neumeister, 2012; Shively et al., 2012). Hubacher (1998) suggests that while shaming after conviction is unproblematic from a constitutional point of view, shaming prior to conviction may violate the Due Process Clause of Fourteenth Amendment to the U.S. Constitution (see Chapter 3).

In addition, the extent to which such approaches are effective in reducing recidivism warrants consideration. In his work, criminologist John Braithwaite (1989) explores the relationship between shaming techniques in general, and their effects on desistance from crime in particular. He argues that while shaming is essential to the maintenance of social control, the approach used to do so can have different effects. He argues that shaming is most likely to be unsuccessful in an individual's decision to desist from future criminal behavior if the act of shaming is aimed to stigmatize, rather than to reintegrate (Braithwaite, 1989). The stigmatized offender is then further alienated from prosocial peers, which in turn facilitates criminal or deviant behavior.

SEX TRAFFICKING

Although the contours of sex trafficking and best response to address it remain hotly debated in political, academic, and media arenas, opposing sides tend to agree that human trafficking (including trafficking of persons for the purpose of prostitution and/or labor) is a fast-growing business of organized crime, with damaging consequences, and in need of significant attention and resources. Further, it is now acknowledged that trafficking not only occurs across national borders, but also domestically, especially across state lines. According to the federal Victims of Trafficking and Violence Protection Act (VTVPA) passed in 2000, **sex trafficking** is the "recruitment, harboring, transportation, provision, or obtaining of a person for the purpose of a commercial sex act" (22 U.S.C. § 7102[10]). The following discussion not only provides the basic legal framework, it also introduces the surrounding debates, including the extent to which sex trafficking is *not* prostitution. Note that the different ideological views presented in an earlier section of this chapter (e.g., radical feminism and socialist feminism) also underlie the controversial debate on sex trafficking.

It is almost impossible to collect accurate quantitative data documenting the extent of sex trafficking. Still, both governmental agencies and nongovernmental organizations publish statistics on sex trafficking that vary greatly. For example, the U.S. Department of State (2005) reports that between 600,000 and 800,000 people worldwide are trafficked annually (see also O'Connor & Healy, 2006). The Central Intelligence Agency reported that up to 2,000,000 women and children are victims of trafficking on an annual basis (Richard, 2000). These disparate numbers demonstrate how difficult it is to estimate the actual number of sex trafficking victims (Weitzer, 2010).

The Legal Framework

It was not until Congress enacted the Victims of Trafficking and Violence Protection Act (VTVPA) in 2000 that human trafficking became a distinct federal crime in the United States. According to that law, "the term 'severe forms of trafficking in persons' means (A) sex trafficking in which a commercial sex act is induced by force, fraud, or coercion, or in which the person induced to perform such act has not attained 18 years of age" (22 U.S.C. § 7102[9]). The law further indicates that sex trafficking is the "recruitment, harboring, transportation, provision, or obtaining of a person for the purpose of a commercial sex act" (22 U.S.C. § 7102[10]). Not only did this law lead to the creation of the Office to Monitor and Combat Trafficking in Persons, but it also sets forth minimum standards for international efforts combatting sex trafficking (Sonderlund, 2005). In addition, the VTVPA mandates that states create laws to combat sex trafficking. The state of Washington responded to this federal mandate with legislation considered to be a model for other states in that it represents "a comprehensive anti-trafficking legal framework" (Polaris Project, 2013, p. 1).

(1)

(a) A person is guilty of trafficking in the first degree when:

  (i) Such a person:

   (A) Recruits, harbors, transports, transfers, provides, obtains, buys, purchases or receives by any means another person knowing or in reckless disregard of the fact, that force, fraud, or coercion as defined in RCW 9A.36.070 will be used to cause the person to engage in forced labor, involuntary servitude, a sexually explicit act, or a commercial sex act; or that the person has not attained the age of eighteen years and is caused to engage in a sexually explicit act or a commercial sex act;

   (B) Benefits financially or by receiving anything of a value from participating in a venture that has engaged in acts set forth in (a)(i)(A) of this subsection; and

  (ii) The acts or venture set forth in (a)(i) of this subsection:

   (A) Involve committing or attempting to commit kidnapping;

   (B) Involve a finding of sexual motivation under RCW 9.94A.835;

   (C) Involve the illegal harvesting or sale of human organs; or

   (D) Result in a death.

(b) Trafficking in the first degree is a class A felony.

(WASH. REV. CODE § 9A.40.100, 2013)

Another problem addressed by the VTVPA is that most victims of human trafficking faced deportation after their contact with the criminal justice system. To address this concern, the law also introduced the "T" visa (non-immigrant status), which not only improves enforcement and investigation regarding human trafficking, but also strengthens the protection of its victims (U.S. Department of Homeland Security, 2011). In cases in which the individual fulfills the eligibility criteria the individual is permitted to remain in the United States, while facilitating an ongoing or initiated investigation or prosecution against third parties involved in human trafficking (U.S. Department of Homeland Security, 2011).

The Anti-Trafficking Movement

The anti-trafficking movement is largely represented by the "religious right" and anti-prostitution feminists, situated within the oppression paradigm (Weitzer, 2010). Those who advocate this point of view see sex trafficking and prostitution as describing the same issue—regardless of whether the person was forced or deceived—because the oppression paradigm views "women's consent to sex work [as] meaningless" (Gozdziak & Collett, 2005, p. 103; see also Farley, 2004). As a result, sex work can never be understood as a voluntary act. Leidholdt (2004) elaborated this point as follows: "Like prisons or concentration camps, prostitution often does not require overt physical coercion or verbal threat, since the system of domination perpetuated and enforced by sex industry businessmen and buyers is intrinsically coercive" (p. 172). She goes further by stating that "[p]rostitution and trafficking are fundamentally interrelated, to the extent that sex trafficking can accurately be viewed as 'globalized prostitution,' while generic prostitution often is a practice of 'domestic trafficking'" (p. 167). Some even label human trafficking as "modern-day slavery" (Walker-Rodriguez & Hill, 2011).

The Sex Workers' Rights Movement

On the opposite end of the continuum are organizations that advocate for sex worker rights; aim to empower sex workers; and pursue a goal of harm reduction, including the provision of condoms, counseling, and other services (Weitzer, 2010). In addition, these organizations combat police harassment, brutality, and extortion by advocating for the decriminalization of the sex-work industry (Sonderlund, 2005).

Although supporters of the anti-trafficking movement argue that prostitution is inseparable from sex trafficking, critics of this position counter that it is "empirically and conceptually inappropriate to fuse prostitution and trafficking" (Weitzer, 2010, p. 333). They argue that under certain circumstances, prostitution can be understood as a form of legitimate work, while true trafficking involves coerced migration to access a market (Weitzer, 2010). In support of this distinction, scholars who are ideologically situated within the empowerment paradigm point to the lack of empirical support for the proposition that most sex workers are victims of trafficking (Lerum, 2015; Shively et al., 2012; Weitzer, 2010). Oselin (2014), for example, found that none of the 40 participants (former sex

workers) in her research reported to have been a victim of sex trafficking.

The importance of avoiding confusion between trafficking and prostitution is well acknowledged, even beyond supporters of the empowerment paradigm (Weitzer, 2010; Lerum et al., 2012). In 2010, the Obama Administration released a report entitled "Trafficking in Persons Report." The report rejected the approach of the anti-trafficking movement when it stated, "Prostitution by willing adults is not human trafficking regardless of whether it is legalized, decriminalized, or criminalized" (U.S. Department of State, 2012, p. 8).

Although the extent of sex trafficking and how it relates to prostitution remains debated, agreement exists that sex trafficking is real and its consequences are often devastating to those affected by it. Therefore, human trafficking (which includes sex trafficking) is a pressing and important issue worthy of attention. Measures are needed that can raise awareness and create a pool of resources that assist victims. This includes a critical need for legislative and law enforcement attention focused on combatting harmful trafficking. Because of this shared baseline, fighting human trafficking in general—and sex trafficking in particular—has become a common goal reaching across political and religious divides (Sonderlund, 2005). How this is best achieved, however, divides people who subscribe to different ideological perspectives.

THE SECONDARY EFFECTS OF PROSTITUTION

Social Stigma

Stigma, according to Oselin (2014), is a result of different external negative stimuli, such as the experience of being labeled as a deviant individual and the experience of being "treated as deficient" (p. 69). The feeling of being stigmatized is not experienced immediately, but rather develops over time as the individual starts to internalize and identify with the stigma (Oselin, 2014). A stigma reduces the individual "from a whole and usual person to a tainted, discounted one" (Goffman, 1963, p. 3, cited in Sallmann, 2010b, p. 146). Individuals engaged in prostitution are almost always exposed to heavy social stigma. This stigma includes powerful labels that often lead to negative reactions from others, such as shunning, avoidance, restraint, physical abuse, and even assault (Hallgrímsdóttir, Phillips, Benoit, & Walby, 2008; Tomura, 2009). The stigma associated with prostitution does not exist in a social vacuum, but is "firmly rooted in and expressive of specific sociopolitical and cultural environments" (Hallgrímsdóttir et al., 2008, p. 121).

Stigma is often rooted in traditional moral concerns, which are not a product of contemporary society, but have existed for centuries. From this view, prostitution is portrayed and perceived as sinful, evil, and shameful (Weitzer, 2005). Those engaged in prostitution are often interpreted and understood as victims who have to be protected and rescued. Quite apart from whether this is true of them, labeling in this way suggests another origin of social stigma toward sex workers—perceptions of sex workers as lacking rationality, pragmatism, and autonomy (Agustin, 2013). Although supporters of the oppression paradigm argue that stigmatization is a consequence of patriarchy, supporters of the pro-legalization/decriminalization movement argue that stigmatization is a natural consequence of criminalization, as crime (by definition) is prohibited, negative, and unwanted behavior (Agustin, 2013). But even in regions where prostitution is legalized or decriminalized, the stigma associated with prostitution endures over time (Agustin, 2013). In other words, those involved in prostitution hardly ever enjoy "an honorable status in contemporary mainstream societies" (Pheterson, 1993, p. 43).

The Effects of Experiencing Stigma

Stigma has further consequences for those experiencing it. A study conducted by Sallmann (2010b) reveals that the feeling of being stigmatized first most commonly involves living with being labeled or categorized as a "whore" or "hooker" (as the prototype of an individual involved in prostitution). Second, it involves violence, through the internalization of several myths, such as "prostitutes are unrapeable," "prostitutes deserve violence," and "all prostitutes are the same" (p. 151); and discrimination (Sallmann, 2010b). It is also important to acknowledge that stigmatization experienced over lengthy periods of time has the potential to create a persistent and tainted image of the self (Hallgrímsdóttir et al., 2008; Sallmann, 2010b). This internalization can lead to adopting prostitution as an integral part of one's identity, even after stepping away from the "life." As Sanders (2007) explained, "the powerful stigma associated with gendered sexual deviancy is 'lived with' long after the behavior has ceased and conformity adopted" (p. 92). In addition, living with stigma over periods of time potentially impacts future relationships with others. The development of interpersonal relationships is hindered and biased by the belief that no one is to be trusted. As a consequence, the stigmatized sex worker might experience a general lack of informal support services, intimate relationships, healthy family relations, and friendships over time (Sallmann, 2010b).

Stigma and Sexual Orientation

Although involvement in prostitution is accompanied by stigma to varying degrees for all individuals involved, gay males and transgender individuals involved in prostitution often experience double-stigmatization as a result of their sexual and gender identity (e.g., Boyer, 1989). As one male involved in prostitution and sex work explained in Boyer's (1989) research, "I was more worried about being found a homosexual than a prostitute"

(p. 169). This suggests that at the time the study was conducted, his sexual orientation carried a heavier stigma for him than his work in the sex industry. However, consistent with shifts in societal perspectives around sexual orientation more generally, some more recent studies do not support this pattern. In fact, some have found that prostitution among gay males provides a means to further explore, define and live their sexual identity (Logan, 2010; Weitzer, 2005). Still, multiple sources of co-occurring stigmas were identified in studies addressing prostitution among transgender individuals (Nadal et al., 2012; Sausa et al., 2007; Slamah, Winter, & Ordek, 2010), highlighting amplified stigmatization at the intersection of transgender identity, prostitution, and racial/ethnic minority status. In this regard, one participant in Crosby and Pitts's (2007) study explained, "[B]eing African American, trans-sexual, a sex worker, and jobless [is] everything possible to destroy you" (p. 47).

Mental Health Concerns

Although it may be an overgeneralization to claim that prostitution and mental health are characterized by a direct causal relationship, research consistently finds that individuals involved in prostitution are at a higher risk of suffering from mental disorders (Choi, Klein, Shin, & Lee, 2009; Chudakov, Ilan, & Belmaker, 2002; El-Bassel et al., 1997; Roessler et al., 2010; Roxburgh, Degenhardt, & Copeland, 2006)—including substance abuse disorders (Burnette, Schneider, Timko, & Ilgen, 2009; Cusick & Hickman, 2005; Roxburgh et al., 2006; Sallmann, 2010a). It is not entirely clear which factors within prostitution increase the likelihood of developing a mental disorder. Some posit that experiencing frequent violence and trauma (Roessler et al., 2010; Roxburgh et al., 2006) and the perceived burden of prostitution (Roessler et al., 2010) play a role. In addition, many individuals involved in prostitution report a his-

tory of child physical and/or sexual abuse, which can increase one's risk of mental health problems (Roxburgh et al., 2006).

Post-traumatic stress disorder (PTSD) is commonly associated with engagement in prostitution at prevalence rates that generally exceed those found in the general population (Choi et al., 2009; Farley, 2004; Hopper & Hidalgo, 2006; Roessler et al., 2010; Roxburgh et al., 2006; c.f. Chudakov et al., 2002;[9] Romans, Potter, Martin, & Herbison, 2001). Farley, Baral, Kiremire, & Sezgin (1998) suggest that the prevalence and severity of PTSD and violence within sex-worker populations is not culturally specific; rather it exists across time and place as well as individual factors. Yet, PTSD may not only be explained through experiences of violence; increased levels of trauma symptomatology are also evident among individuals engaged in indoor prostitution, even though studies frequently emphasize that individuals engaged in this segment of the sex trade benefit from safer working conditions and lower exposure to violence (Choi et al., 2009; Farley et al., 1998). These findings raise the question of whether psychological distress constitutes a general occupational risk for individuals working in "the game" (Farley et al., 1998).

Other mental health issues experienced (although less often) among those that were involved in prostitution include sexual dysfunction, relational issues, disorder of extreme stress not otherwise specified, depression/sadness (Chudakov et al., 2002; El-Bassel et al., 1997; Hopper & Hidalgo, 2006), guilt and self-blame (Hopper & Hidalgo, 2006), anger and rage (Hopper and Hidalgo, 2006), sleep problems/disturbances (Hopper & Hidalgo, 2006), and psychosis (El-Bassel et al., 1997). In addition, research consistently shows that prostitution and drug use/abuse co-exist (Burnette et al., 2009; Cusick & Hickman, 2005; Roxburgh et al., 2006; Sallmann, 2010a), with studies reporting prevalence rates of drug use/abuse among sex workers between 47.5% and 95% (Sallmann, 2010a). After interviewing 14 women involved in prostitution (currently and previously), Sallmann (2010a) found that drug addiction represented a major part of their lives. As one participant stated, "I talk about drugs a lot, but I also talk about escorting a lot. I talk about 'em both because they go hand-in-hand for me" (p. 123).

Still, the question of temporal order regarding prostitution and substance use/abuse remains unanswered. Is drug addiction a common consequence of involvement in prostitution or is it more likely that a pre-existing drug addiction leads to engagement in prostitution? And related to these questions, how does an existing or newly developed drug addiction progress once involved in prostitution? Most of the studies addressing the connection between prostitution and drug dependency found that the relationship is reciprocal, rather than unidirectional, with prostitution and drug use promoting and facilitating the prevalence, severity, and intensity of each (Burnette et al., 2009; Cusick & Hickman, 2005; Sallmann, 2010a). Once an addiction is developed, prostitution may be perceived as the only means to feed the habit. On the other hand, drug use can facilitate prostitution as it enables sex workers to overcome and cope with many related negative feelings through self-medication for other coexisting conditions, such as pain or other mental health issues (Sallmann, 2010a).

If drug addiction is often a reason for engagement and continuous involvement in prostitution, it may also be considered a factor in exiting. Burnette et al. (2009) found that some participants in their research were only able to reduce their involvement in prostitution after having addressed their substance abuse problem. As indicated above, drug use and prostitution often go "hand-in-hand," creating a cycle of vulnerabilities, which can lead to a more severe and intense involvement in both drug abuse/dependency and sex work (Cusick & Hickman, 2005; Sallmann, 2010a). Cusick and Hickman (2005) investigated the cyclical relationship between drug use and prostitution, finding supportive evidence only within the subsample of individuals who were engaged in street-level prostitution or who were working as drifters.

Societal Consequences of Prostitution

Prostitution not only has potential negative impacts on individuals involved, but it is also often perceived as a neighborhood/community problem by residents and businessowners (Shdaimah, Kaufman, Bright, & Flower, 2014; Weitzer, 2012). No matter the level of tolerance toward prostitution in general, many residents have a "not in my backyard" attitude toward street-prostitution. Still, case studies show wide variation (within the community and across communities) in residents' attitudes, ranging from no tolerance or empathy to high tolerance and empathy on either extreme. The majority of residents in a study by Pitcher, Campbell, Hubbard, O'Neill, and Scoular (2006) were located somewhere in the middle of the continuum. The views and attitudes held by residents in communities with high prostitution activity are not only informed by personal experience but also by moral beliefs/values, the extent to which sex workers are integrated in a community, and by consumption of media coverage on the issue (Pitcher et al., 2006). Even though concerns expressed by residents living in areas of high prostitution activity vary greatly, some themes are evident, keeping in mind that these are based on residents' subjective perceptions of societal consequences of prostitution activity.

Residents often not only fear prostitution in general but also, and sometimes even more so, they fear crime associated with prostitution, such as public drug use/abuse, drug sales, robberies, assaults, and rape (Shdaimah et al., 2014; Shively et al., 2012; Weitzer, 2012). Some residents are also fearful of violence specifically originating from pimps and/or Johns. Another concern mentioned is that prostitution activity in the community is closely linked to a spread of disease, especially STIs (Shdaimah et al., 2014). According to community residents' perception, prostitution is also often connected to increased litter on the streets and in parks (in the form of used condoms, syringes, and broken bottles), as well as human urine and excrement in public spaces (Pitcher et al., 2006; Shively et al., 2012; Weitzer, 2012). Another major concern of residents is the visibility of sex work and its impact on children and families as they are exposed to sexual acts and other disorderly conduct in public spaces, as well as to increased levels of noise (fights, screaming, etc.) at night (O'Neill, Campbell, Hubbard, Pitcher, & Scoular, 2008; Pitcher et al., 2006; Shdaimah et al., 2014; Shively et al., 2012; Weitzer, 2012). In addition, families fear that mothers, daughters, and sisters could eventually be mistaken for sex workers and thus receive propositions from Johns, and/or experience harassment and/or violence by pimps (O'Neill et al., 2008; Pitcher et al., 2006; Shdaimah et al., 2014; Shively et al., 2012). Overall, residents argue that prostitution destroys a community's family character (O'Neill et al., 2008).

Besides concerns about risks and incidents that could occur on a daily basis, residents, as well as business-owners, fear the decline of property values and a decrease in customers, partially due to a declining positive reputation of the community due to prostitution activity (O'Neill et al., 2008; Shdaimah et al., 2014; Weitzer, 2012). As one resident explained, "They work the main-street, are unkempt, high, and more could be done; visitors comment on them and they give a poor impression of our community" (participant in Shdaimah et al., 2014, pp. 283–284).

CONCLUSION

Prostitution is a highly complex phenomenon with differences not only in motivations, but also across places of conduct and individual level factors. In addition, not only is the person who is selling sex for a fee legally responsible, but so are the other actors in the trade, such as the "consumers" of sexual services (Johns) and facilitators (pimps) of prostitution. Despite its status as "the oldest profession," intensive legal, ideological, and academic debates remain inconclusive. To date, the standard legal status of prostitution in the U.S. is one of illegality/criminalization across the entire country, with exception of legalization in select locations within Nevada.

Is prostitution punished in the United States because it is harmful and dangerous to society? Or is it prosecuted in order to "motivate" individuals involved in the trade to disengage from a lifestyle perceived to be morally unacceptable? Regardless, the complexity of the issue warrants programs, policies, and interventions designed not as a one-size-fits all solution but, rather, tailored to an individual's specific needs and challenges. Is such an individualized treatment possible using existing policies, including prostitution off-limit orders, shaming techniques, and John schools? Or is this an opportunity for more innovative approaches that move beyond criminal justice entities to include nongovernmental organizations and individuals actively and/or formerly involved in prostitution?

FURTHER READING

Beckett, K., & Herbert, S. (2009). *Banished: The new social control in urban America*. New York, NY: Oxford University Press.

Bernstein, E. & Schaffner L. (2005). *Regulating sex: The politics of intimacy and identity (Perspectives on gender)*. New York, NY: Routledge.

Dank, M., Khan, B., Downey, P. M., Kotonias, C., Mayer, D., Owens, C., Pacifici, L., & Yu, L. (2014, March). Estimating the size and structure of the underground sex economy in eight major US cities. Research Report for the Urban Institute. Retrieved from http://www.urban.org/UploadedPDF/413047-Underground-Commercial-Sex-Economy.pdf

Rosen, R. (1983). *The lost sisterhood: Prostitution in America, 1900–1918*. Baltimore, MD: The Johns Hopkins University Press.

Shdaimah, C. S., Kaufman, B. R., Bright, C. L., & Flower, S. M. (2014). Neighborhood assessment of prostitution as a pressing social problem and appropriate responses: Results from a community survey. *Criminal Justice Policy Review*, *25*(3), 275–298.

U.S. Department of State (2012). *Trafficking in persons report, 2012.* Retrieved from http://www.state.gov/documents/organization/192587.pdf.

Weitzer, R. (2012). *Legalizing prostitution: From illicit vice to lawful business.* New York, NY: New York University Press.

GLOSSARY

Advancing prostitution: The initiation or facilitation of engagement in prostitution by a third person, the recruitment of customers for another person, the promotion of locales for prostitution, and the operation of a locale where prostitution takes place.

Brothels: houses of prostitution.

Complete decriminalization: All criminal laws prohibiting prostitution are removed from criminal codes; yet other laws might be applicable (e.g., promoting prostitution of an underage individual). Prostitution could occur in any setting, as the law does not regulate any aspect of prostitution.

Criminalization: Criminalization of prostitution (in all its forms) is the current system of legal situation in all U.S. states, with the exception of select counties in Nevada. This means that, when criminalized, all actors that are in some way involved in prostitution, including the seller, purchaser, pimp, brothel-keeper, and even the landlord of houses of prostitution are subject to prosecution and punishment.

De facto criminalization: The situation in which prostitution is not, per se, illegal, but so many behaviors associated with or attendant to prostitution are criminalized (e.g., night walking, vagrancy, and a variety of improprieties of conduct) that it effectively renders prostitution functionally illegal.

De facto legalization: The situation in which prostitution is technically illegal, but is tolerated, to varying degrees, by relevant legal authorities.

Empowerment paradigm: A specific ideological view in which prostitution is understood as empowering—as a form of expressive freedom. The criminalization of prostitution is seen as the main factor leading inevitably to human rights violations.

John: A term commonly used when referring to an individual who purchases sexual services for money or other monetary goods. Johns are also referred to as clients, tricks, and dates.

Legalization: Removal of all or some criminal penalties surrounding prostitution and the introduction of specific regulations regarding prostitution (e.g., licensing of businesses, registering of sex worker, taxes, mandatory health checks).

Oppression paradigm: A specific ideological view regarding prostitution in which prostitution is seen as violence, exploitation, and suppression as well as a violation of basic human rights. From this point of view, a distinction between forced and voluntary involvement in prostitution is not possible.

Pandering: Forcing, deceiving, decoying, enticing, or otherwise recruiting someone to become a prostitute or to work in a brothel.

Partial decriminalization: Can take multiple approaches. Penalties for prostitution could be reduced (e.g., from a felony to a misdemeanor or violation); or, the criminal laws concerning a specific prostitution-related offense could be removed from the criminal code (e.g., for soliciting prostitution) while penalties for procuring and pandering remain on the books.

Patronizing a sex worker: The agreement of a person (i.e., John, client, trick) to provide a monetary or non-monetary payment in exchange for sexual services.

Pimp: An individual who is in control of one or more sex workers' actions and lives and who is generating profit from the incomes of those people.

Polymorphous paradigm: A specific ideological view regarding prostitution that characterizes prostitution as a highly complex phenomenon. From this point of view victimization, exploitation, violence, coercion, choice, self-esteem, empowerment, and other factors are variable, rather than constants.

Prostitution: The provision of sexual intercourse or other sexual services (e.g., oral sex, anal sex, assisted masturbation) in exchange for anything of pecuniary value, including money, services, or goods, such as food, shelter, drugs, and other favors.

Red-light district: An area in which brothels, strip clubs, and other sex businesses are located or prostitution is tolerated.

Sex trafficking: The recruitment, harboring, transportation, provision, or receipt of a person for the purpose of a commercial sex act and sexual exploitation. Any underage individual encouraged (forced or not) to engage in prostitution is considered a victim of sex trafficking (under U.S. federal law).

NOTES

1   Because the population of Clark County, Nevada (the county in which Las Vegas in located) far exceeds the 400,000-person threshold with approximately 2 million inhabitants, contrary to popular believe, prostitution is not legal in Las Vegas.

2   A red-light district can also refer to an area in which brothels, strip clubs, and other sex businesses are located.

3 Patronizing a sex worker refers to an agreement by a person (i.e., John, client, trick) to provide a monetary or non-monetary payment in exchange for sexual services.

4 Other studies, however, report that it is more likely for Johns to be non-White (see Lever & Dolnick, 2000; Sullivan & Simon, 1998).

5 In a review of the literature, Monto (2004) concluded that the average age of Johns clusters around the late 30s.

6 Note that other laws might be applicable, such as promoting prostitution of an underage individual.

7 The Equal Protection Clause of the Fourteenth Amendment requires that states treat similarly situated people in a similar manner. For more information on equal protection, see Chapter 4.

8 See, e.g., EVERETT, WASH., MUN. CODE §10.24.210 (2004); BREMERTON, WASH., MUN. CODE § 9.24.072 (1997); CITY OF SEATAC, WASH., MUN. CODE § 8.05.650 (2004).

9 Findings showed only slightly increased rates of PTSD and depression in a sample of individuals working in brothels compared with the general population.

REFERENCES

Agathocleous, A. (2013). When power yields justice: *Doe v. Jindal* and the campaign to dismantle Louisiana's crime against nature statute. *Loyola Journal of Public Interest Law, 14*(2), 331–354.

Almodovar, N. J. (2002). For their own good: The results of the prostitution laws as enforced by cops, politicians, and judges. In W. McElroy (Ed.), *Liberty for Women* (pp. 71–87). Chicago, IL: The Independent Institute.

Amsterdam.Info. (2014). *Prostitution in Amsterdam.* Retrieved from http://www.amsterdam.info/prostitution/

Agustin, L. M. (2005). Migrants in the mistress's house: Other voices in the "trafficking" debate. *Social Politics: International Studies in Gender, State and Society, 12*(1), 96–117.

Agustin, L. M. (2013, August 17). The sex worker stigma: How the law perpetuates our hatred (and fear) of prostitutes. *Salon.* Retrieved from http://www.salon.com/2013/08/17/the_whore_stigma_how_the_law_perpetuates_our_hatred_and_fear_of_prostitutes_partner/

Armstrong, M. (1963). Banishment: Cruel and unusual punishment. *University of Pennsylvania Law Review, 111*(6), 758–786.

Baker, L. M., Dalla, R. L., & Williamson, C. (2010). Exiting prostitution: An integrated model. *Violence Against Women, 16*(5), 579–600.

Barnett, L., Casavant, L., & Nicol, J. (2011, November 3). Prostitution: A review of legislation in selected countries. Publication No. 2011–115-E. Library of Parliament/Bibliotheque du Parlement. Retrieved from http://www.parl.gc.ca/content/lop/researchpublications/2011-115-e.pdf

Barry, K. (1995). *The prostitution of sexuality: The global exploitation of women.* New York, NY: NYU Press.

Beckett, K., & Herbert, S. (2009). *Banished: The new social control in urban America.* New York, NY: Oxford University Press.

Beckett, K., & Herbert, S. (2010). Penal boundaries: Banishment and the expansion of punishment. *Law and Social Inquiry, 35*(1), 1–38.

Benoit, C., Jansson, M., Millar, A., & Phillips, R. (2005). Community-academic research on hard-to-reach-populations: Benefits and challenges. *Qualitative Health Research, 15*(2), 263–282.

Benoit, C., & Millar, A. (2001). Dispelling myths and understanding realities: Working conditions, health status, and exiting experiences of sex workers. Victoria, British Columbia: Department of Sociology, University of Victoria. Retrieved from http://www.hawaii.edu/hivandaids/Working%20Conditions,%20Health%20Status%20and%20Exiting%20Experience%20of%20Sex%20Workers.pdf

Bernstein, E. (1999). What's wrong with prostitution? What's right with sex work? Comparing markets in female sexual labor. *Hastings Women's Law Journal, 10*(1), 91–117.

Bernstein, E., & Schaffner L. (2005). *Regulating sex: The politics of intimacy and identity.* New York, NY: Routledge.

Borelli, M. (2003). Banishment: The constitutional and public policy arguments against the revived and ancient punishment. *Suffolk University Law Review, 36*(2), 469–486.

Boutellier, J. C. J. (1991). Prostitution, criminal law, and morality in the Netherlands. *Crime, Law, and Social Change, 15*(3), 201–211.

Boyer, D. (1989). Male prostitution and homosexual identity. *Journal of Homosexuality, 17*(1–2), 151–184.

Braithwaite, J. (1989). *Crime, shame and reintegration.* Cambridge, UK: Cambridge University Press.

BREMERTON, WASHINGTON MUNICIPAL CODE § 9.24.072 (1997).

Brents, B. G., & Hausbeck, K. (2001). State-sanctioned sex: Negotiating formal and informal regulatory practices in Nevada brothels. *Sociological Perspectives, 44*(3), 307–332.

Brents, B. G., & Hausbeck, K. (2005). Violence and legalized brothel prostitution in Nevada: Examining safety, risk, and prostitution policy. *Journal of Interpersonal Violence, 20*(3), 270–295.

Bullough, V., & Bullough, B. (1987). *Women and prostitution: A social history.* Buffalo, NY: Prometheus Books.

Burnette, M. L., Schneider, R., Timko, C., & Ilgen, M. A. (2009). Impact of substance-use disorder treatment on women involved in prostitution: Substance use, mental health, and prostitution one year after treatment. *Journal of Studies on Alcohol and Drugs, 70*(1), 32–40.

Busey, K. (2014, March 14). Arizona transgender woman Monica on trial for refusing "Project Rose." *The Transadvocate*. Retrieved from http://www.transadvocate.com/arizona-transgender-woman-monica-jones-on-trial-for-refusing-project-rose_n_13409.htm

Carrasquillo, T. (2014). Understanding prostitution and the need for reform. *Touro Law Review, 30*, 697–721.

Cassidy, M. (2014, August 6). Phoenix transgender activist appeals prostitution-related conviction. *The Arizona Republic*. Retrieved from http://www.azcentral.com/story/news/local/phoenix/2014/08/05/phoenix-transgender-activist-appeals-prostitution-related-conviction/13652561

Caulkins, S. E., & Coombs, N. (1976). The psychodynamics of male prostitution. *American Journal of Psychotherapy, 30*, 441–451.

Choi, H., Klein, C., Shin, M., & Lee, H. (2009). Posttraumatic stress disorder (PTSD) and disorders of extreme stress (DESNOS) symptoms following prostitution and childhood abuse. *Violence Against Women, 15*(8), 933–951.

Chudakov, B., Ilan, K., & Belmaker, R. H. (2002). The motivation and mental health of sex workers. *Journal of Sex & Marital Therapy, 28*, 305–315.

City of SeaTac, Washington Municipal Code § 8.05.650 (2004).

Coleman, C., & Moynihan, J. (1996). *Understanding crime data*. Buckingham: Open University Press.

Coombs, N. (1974). Male prostitution: A psychosocial review of behavior. *American Journal of Psychotherapy, 30*, 441–451.

Craft, M. (1966). Boy prostitutes and their fate. *British Journal of Psychiatry, 112*, 1111–1114.

Crosby, R. A., & Pitts, N. L. (2007). Caught between different worlds: How transgendered women may be "forced" into risky sex. *Journal of Sex Research, 44*(1), 43–48.

Cusick, L., & Hickman, M. (2005). "Trapping" in drug use and sex work careers. *Drugs: education, prevention, and policy, 12*(5), 369–379.

Dalla, R. L. (2000). Exposing the "Pretty Woman" myth: A qualitative examination of the lives of female streetwalking prostitutes. *The Journal of Sex Research, 37*, 344–353.

Dalla, R. L. (2006). "You can't hustle all your life": An exploratory investigation of the exit process among street-level prostituted women. *Psychology of Women Quarterly, 30*, 276–290.

Dank, M., Khan, B., Downey, P. M., Kotonias, C., Mayer, D., Owens, C., Pacifici, L., & Yu, L. (2014, March). Estimating the size and structure of the underground sex economy in eight major US cities. Research Report for the Urban Institute. Retrieved from http://www.urban.org/UploadedPDF/413047-Underground-Commercial-Sex-Economy.pdf

DeFranco, T., & Stellato, R. (2013). Prostitution and sex work. *Georgetown Journal of Gender & the Law, 14*(2), 553–583.

Dutch Ministry of Foreign Affairs (2012). Dutch policy on prostitution: Questions and answers 2012. Retrieved from http://www.minbuza.nl/binaries/content/assets/minbuza/en/import/en/you_and_the_netherlands/about_the_netherlands/ethical_issues/faq-prostitutie-pdf--engels.pdf-2012.pdf

Dworkin, A. (1989). *Pornography: Men possessing women*. New York, NY: Penguin.

Edelman, E. A. (2011). "This area has been declared a prostitution free zone": Discursive formations of space, the state, and trans "sex worker" bodies. *Journal of Homosexuality, 58*(6–7), 848–864.

Ekberg, G. (2004). The Swedish law that prohibits the purchase of sexual services: Best practices for prevention of prostitution and trafficking in human beings. *Violence Against Women, 10*(10), 1187–1218.

El-Bassel, N., Schilling, R. F., Irwin, K. L., Faruque, S., Gilbert, L., Von Bargen, J., Serrano, Y., & Edling, B. R. (1997). Sex trading and psychological distress among women recruited from the streets in Harlem. *American Journal of Public Health, 87*(1), 66–70.

El-Bassel, N., Witte, S., Wada, T., Gilbert, L., & Wallace, J. (2001). Correlates of partner violence among female street-based sex workers: Substance abuse, history of child abuse and HIV risks. *AIDS Patient Care and STDs, 15*, 41–51.

Elifson, K. W., Boles, J., Posey, E., Sweat, M., Darrow, W., & Elsea, W. (1993). Male transvestite prostitutes and HIV risk. *American Journal of Public Health, 83*(2), 260–262.

Erikson, P. G., Butters, J., McGillicuddy, P., & Hallgren, A. (2000). Crack and prostitution: Gender, myths, and experiences. *Journal of Drug Issues, 30*, 767–788.

Evans, H. (1979). *Harlots, whores, and hookers: A history of prostitution*. New York, NY: Taplinger.

Everett, Washington Municipal Code § 10.24.210 (2004).

Farley, M. (2004). "Bad for the body, bad for the heart": Prostitution harms women even if legalized or decriminalized. *Violence Against Women, 10*, 1087–1125.

Farley, M., Baral, I., Kiremire, M., & Sezgin, U. (1998). Prostitution in five countries: Violence and post-traumatic stress disorder. *Feminism & Psychology, 8*(4), 405–426.

Federal Bureau of Investigation. (2009). Table 69: Arrests by State 2008. *Crime in the United States 2008*. Retrieved from http://www.fbi.gov/about-us/cjis/ucr/crime-in-the-u.s/2008

Federal Bureau of Investigation. (2010). Table 69: Arrests by State, 2009. *Crime in the United States 2009*.

Retrieved from http://www.fbi.gov/about-us/cjis/ucr/crime-in-the-u.s/2009

Federal Bureau of Investigation. (2011). Table 69: Arrests by State, 2010. *Crime in the United States 2010*. Retrieved from http://www.fbi.gov/about-us/cjis/ucr/crime-in-the-u.s/2010/crime-in-the-u.s.-2010/tables/10tbl69.xls

Federal Bureau of Investigation. (2012). Table 69: Arrests by State, 2011. *Crime in the United States 2011*. Retrieved from http://www.fbi.gov/about-us/cjis/ucr/crime-in-the-u.s/2011/crime-in-the-u.s.-2011/tables/table_69_arrest_by_state_2011.xls

Federal Bureau of Investigation. (2013). Table 69: Arrests by State, 2012. *Crime in the United States 2012*. Retrieved from http://www.fbi.gov/about-us/cjis/ucr/crime-in-the-u.s/2012/crime-in-the-u.s.-2012/tables/69tabledatadec.pdf

Federal Bureau of Investigation. (2014). Table 69: Arrests by State, 2013. *Crime in the United States, 2013*. Retrieved from http://www.fbi.gov/about-us/cjis/ucr/crime-in-the-u.s/2013/crime-in-the-u.s.-2013/tables/table-69/table_69_arrest_by_state_2013.xls

Garland, D. (2001). *The culture of control: Crime and social order in contemporary society*. Chicago, IL: The University of Chicago Press.

Ginsburg, K. (1967). The meat rack: A study of the male homosexual prostitute. *Journal of Psychotherapy, 21*, 170–185.

Gozdziak, E. M., & Collett, E. A. (2005). Research on human trafficking in North America: A review of literature. *International Migration, 43*(1–2), 99–128.

Grant, M. G. (February 18, 2013). When prostitution wasn't a crime: The fascinating history of sex work in America. *AlterNet*. Retrieved from http://www.alternet.org/news-amp-politics/when-prostitution-wasnt-crime-fascinating-history-sex-work-america

Gurd, A., & O'Brien, E. (2013). Californian "John Schools" and the social construction of prostitution. *Sexuality Research and Social Policy, 10*, 149–158.

Hallgrímsdóttir, H. K., Phillips, R., Benoit, C., & Walby, K. (2008). Sporting girls, streetwalkers, and inmates of houses of ill repute: Media narratives and the historical mutability of prostitution stigmas. *Sociological Perspectives, 51*(1), 119–138.

Harcourt, B. E., & Ludwig, J. (2006). Broken windows: New evidence from New York City and a five-city social experiment. *University of Chicago Law Review, 73*, 271–320.

Hardaway, R. M. (2003). *No price too high: Victimless crimes and the Ninth Amendment*. Westport, CT: Praeger.

Hausbeck, K., & Brents, B. (2010). Nevada's legal brothels. In R. Weitzer (Ed.), *Sex for sale: Prostitution, pornography, and the sex industry* (2nd ed., pp. 255–284). New York, NY: Routledge.

Hedin, U., & Månsson, S. (2004). The importance of supportive relationships among women leaving prostitution. *Journal of Trauma Practice, 2*(3–4), 223–238.

Hill, G. (2004). The use of pre-existing exclusionary zones as probationary conditions for prostitution offenses: A call for the sincere application of heightened scrutiny. *Seattle University Law Review, 28*, 173–208.

Hopper, E. K., & Hidalgo, J. A. (2006). Posttraumatic stress disorder (PTSD). In M. H. Ditmore (Ed.), *Encyclopedia of prostitution and sex work*. Westport, CT: Greenwood.

Hough, N. A. (2004). Sodomy and prostitution: Laws protecting the "fabric of society." *Pierce Law Review, 3*, 101–124.

Hubacher, A. (1998). Every picture tells a story: Is Kansas City's "John TV" constitutional? *University of Kansas Law Review, 46*, 551–591.

Illinois Revised Statute, ch. 38, par. 11–1 (1983), repealed and superseded by 720 Illinois Compiled Statutes § 5/11–14 (2014).

Jackson, A. L. (2004). The history of prostitution reform in the United States. *University of Tennessee Honors Thesis Projects*. Trace: Tennessee Research and Creative Exchange. Retrieved from http://trace.tennessee.edu/cgi/viewcontent.cgi?article=1754&context=utk_chanhonoproj

Jeffrey, L. A., & MacDonald, G. (2006). "It's the money, honey": The economy of sex work in the Maritimes. *Canadian Review of Sociology/Revue Canadienne de Sociologie, 43*(3), 313–327.

Jeffreys, S. (2009). Prostitution, trafficking and feminism: An update on the debate. *Women's Studies International Forum, 32*, 316–320.

Johnson, E. M. (2014). Buyers without remorse: Ending the discriminatory enforcement of prostitution laws. *Texas Law Review, 92*(3), 717–748.

Kelly, H. A. (2000). Bishop, prioress, and bawd in the stews of Southwark. *Speculum: A Journal of Medieval Studies, 75*(2), 342–388.

Kennedy, M. A., Klein, C., Bristowe, J. T. K, Cooper, B. S., & Yuille, J. C. (2007). Routes of recruitment: Pimps' techniques and other circumstances that lead to street prostitution. *Journal of Aggression, Maltreatment & Trauma, 15*(2), 1–19.

Koyama, E. (2010). *Surviving the Witch-hunt: Battle notes from Portland's 82nd Avenue, 2007–2010*. Portland, OR: Confluere Publications. Retrieved from http://eminism.org/store/pdf-zn/witchhunt-web.pdf

Las Vegas Escorts and Brothels (n.d.). Full list and ratings of all Nevada brothels. Retrieved from http://www.nevadabrothelfinder.com/delivery

Lee-Gonyea, J. A., Castle, T., & Gonyea, N. E. (2009). Laid to order: Male escorts advertising on the internet. *Deviant Behavior, 30*, 321–348.

Leidholdt, D. A. (2004). Prostitution and trafficking in women: An intimate relationship. *Journal of Trauma Practice, 2*(2–3), 167–183.

Lerum, K. (2015, April 10). Trafficking policy should focus on empowerment, not coercion. *Ms. Blog Magazine*. Retrieved from http://msmagazine.com/blog/2015/04/10/trafficking-policy-should-focus-on-empowerment-not-coercion

Lerum, K., McCurtis, K., Saunders, P., & Wahab, S. (2012). Using human rights to hold the US accountable for its anti-sex-trafficking agenda: The universal periodic review & new directions for US policy. *Antitrafficking Review*, 1(1), 80–103.

Lever, J., & Dolnick, D. (2000). Clients and call girls: Seeking sex and intimacy. In R. Weitzer (Ed.), *Sex for sale: Prostitution, pornography, and the sex industry* (pp. 85–100). New York, NY: Routledge.

Levitt, S. D., & Venkatesh, A. (2007). An empirical analysis of street-level prostitution. Unpublished paper retrieved from http://economics.uchicago.edu/pdf/Prostitution%205.pdf

Logan, T. D. (2010). Personal characteristics, sexual behavior, and male sex work: a quantitative approach. *American Sociological Review*, 75(5), 679–704.

Louisiana Revised Statutes § 14:89.2(A) (1982), *abrogated by Doe v. Jindal*, 851 F. Supp. 2d 995 (E. D. La. 2012).

Luckenbill, D. F. (1986). Deviant career mobility: The case of male prostitutes. *Social Problems*, 33(4), 283–296.

MacKenzie, S. (1992). *The morality of prostitution*. Libertarian Alliance [Pamphlet No. 19], London, England: Libertarian Alliance & the British Association of Libertarian Feminists. Retrieved from http://www.infotextmanuscripts.org/ncropa/ncropa-lib-6.pdf

MacKinnon, C. A. (1993). Prostitution and civil rights. *Michigan Journal of Gender & Law*, 1, 13–31.

MacNamara, D. E. J. (1965). Male prostitution in an American city: A pathological or socioeconomic phenomenon. *American Journal of Orthopsychiatry*, 35, 204.

Magnani, R., Sabin, K. T., & Heckathorn, D. (2005). Review of sampling hard-to-reach-populations for HIV surveillance. *AIDS*, 19(2), 67–72.

Mann Act, ch. 395, 36 Stat. 825 (June 25, 1910), *codified as amended at* 18 U.S.C. §§ 2421–2424 (2015).

Michels, S. (2007, October 31). Philly judge criticized for rape decision. *ABS News online*. Retrieved from http://abcnews.go.com/TheLaw/story?id=3801167

Ministry of Justice. (2010). *Prohibition of the purchase of sexual services: An evaluation 1999–2008 (English Summary)*. Retrieved from http://www.government.se/content/1/c6/11/98/61/73d97eb9.pdf

Mizuta, T., & Mulvey-Roberts, M. (Eds.). (1994). *Perspectives on the history of British feminism: The rights of married women*. London: Routledge.

Monto, M. A. (1999). *Focusing on the clients of street prostitutes: A creative approach to reducing violence against women*. Washington, DC: National Institute of Justice.

Monto, M. A. (2004). Female prostitution, customers, and violence. *Violence Against Women*, 10(2), 160–188.

Nadal, K. L., Davidoff, K. C., & Jujii-Doe, W. F. (2014). Transgender women and the sex work industry: Roots in systemic, institutional, and interpersonal discrimination. *Journal of Trauma & Dissociation*, 15(2), 169–183.

Nadal, K. L., Vargas, V. H., Meterko, V., Hamit, S., & Mclean, K. (2012). Transgender female sex workers in New York City: Personal perspectives, gender identity development, and psychological processes. In M. A. Paludi (Ed.), *Managing diversity in today's workplace: Strategies for employees and employers, Volume 1: Gender, race, sexual orientation, ethnicity, and power* (pp. 123–153). Santa Barbara, CA: Praeger.

Neumeister, L. (2012, October 14). Public shaming of prostitution clients: A growing trend, can harm families. *Huffington Post Online*. Retrieved from http://www.huffingtonpost.com/2012/10/14/shaming-prostitute-patrons-johns-public_n_1964925.html

Nevada Revised Statutes §§ 201.300–390 (2015).

New Zealand Parliament (2008, May). *Report of the Prostitution Law Review Committee on the operation of the Prostitution Reform Act 2003*. Wellington (New Zealand): Ministry of Justice.

Nichols, J. (2014, April 16). Monica Jones, transgender women, convicted of "manifesting prostitution." The *Huffington Post Online*. Retrieved from http://www.huffingtonpost.com/2014/04/16/monica-jones-transgender_n_5159638.html

Norton-Hawk, M. A., (2001). The counterproductivity of incarcerating female street prostitutes. *Deviant Behavior*, 22, 403–417.

Norton-Hawk, M. (2004). A comparison of pimp- and non-pimp-controlled women. *Violence Against Women*, 10(2), 189–194.

O'Connor, M., & Healy, G. (2006). *The links between prostitution and trafficking: A briefing handbook*. Retrieved from http://www.renate-europe/net/wp-content/uploads/2013/09/CATW_handbook_LinksProstitution_Trafficking2009.pdf

O'Neill, M., Campbell, R., Hubbard, P., Pitcher, J., & Scoular, J. (2008). Living with the other: Street sex work, contingent communities and degrees of tolerance. *Crime, Media, Culture*, 4(1), 73–93.

Oselin, S. S. (2009). Leaving the streets: Transformation of prostitute identity within the prostitution rehabilitation program. *Deviant Behavior*, 30, 379–406.

Oselin, S. S. (2010). Weighing the consequences of a deviant career: Factors leading to an exit of prostitution. *Sociological Perspectives*, 53(4), 527–550.

Oselin, S. (2014). *Leaving prostitution: Getting out and staying out of sex work*. New York, NY: New York University Press.

Pateman, C. (1988). *The sexual contract*. Stanford, CA: Stanford University Press.

Pheterson, G. (1993). The whore stigma: Female dishonor and male unworthiness. *Social text: A special section edition, 37*, 39–64.

Philadelphia Bar Association. (2007, November 1). Association Chancellor Jane Dalton issues statement on judge Deni's recent ruling. Retrieved from http://www.philadelphiabar.org/page/NewsItem?appNum=4&newsItemID=1000699

PHOENIX MUNICIPAL CODE § 23–52 (2015).

Pitcher, J., Campbell, R., Hubbard, P., O'Neill, M., & Scoular, J. (2006). *Living and working in areas of street sex work: From conflict to coexistence.* Bristol: Policy Press. Retrieved from http://www.jrf.org.uk/system/files/9781861348678.pdf

Pittman, D. J. (1971). The male house of prostitution. *Trans-action, 8 (5–6)*, 21–27.

Polaris Project. (2013). *Washington State report: Rate ratings 2013.* Retrieved from http://www.polarisproject.org/storage/documents/Washington_State_Report_2013_08_01_17_29_55_033.pdf

Pope, J. (2009, June 22). New law levies harsher child prostitution punishment: Nevada now has the most stringent punishments nationwide for child prostitution, pandering. *Las Vegas Sun.* Retrieved from http://www.lasvegassun.com/news/2009/jun/22/new-law-levies-harsh-punishments-child-prostitutio/

Raphael, J., & Myers-Powell, B. (2010). *From victims to victimizers: Interviews with 25 ex-pimps in Chicago.* A report from the Schiller DuCanto & Fleck Family Law Center of DePaul University College. Retrieved from http://newsroom.depaul.edu/pdf/family_law_center_report-final.pdf

Regeringskansliet: Government Offices of Sweden (2012). *Legislation on the purchase of sexual services.* Retrieved from http://www.government.se/sb/d/4096/a/119861

Reiss, A. J., Jr. (1961). The social integration of queers and peers. *Social Problems, 9(2)*, 102–120.

Richard, A. O. (2000). *International trafficking in women to the United States: A contemporary manifestation of slavery and organized crime.* Center for the Study of Intelligence. State Department of Intelligence, US State Department. Retrieved from https://www.cia.gov/library/center-for-the-study-of-intelligence/csi-publications/books-and-monographs/trafficking.pdf

Ringdal, N. J. (2004). *Love for sale: A world history of prostitution.* New York, NY: Grove Press.

Roessler, W., Koch, U., Lauber, C., Hass A.-H., Altwegg, M. Ajdacic-Gross, V., & Landolt, K. (2010). The mental health of female sex workers. *Acta Psychiatrica Scandinavica.* Retrieved from https://www.collegium.ethz.ch/fileadmin/autoren/pdf_papers/10_roessler_sex work.pdf

Romans, S. E., Potter, K., Martin, J., & Herbison, P. (2001). The mental and physical health of female sex workers: A comparative study. *Australian & New Zealand Journal of Psychiatry, 35*, 75–80.

Rosen, R. (1983). *The lost sisterhood: Prostitution in America, 1900–1918.* Baltimore, MD: The Johns Hopkins University Press.

Rossiaud, J. (1988). *Medieval prostitution.* Oxford: Blackwell.

Rothstein, V., & Weisstein, N. (1972). Chicago Women's Liberation Union. *Women: A Journal of Liberation, 2(4)*, 4–5.

Roxburgh, A., Degenhardt, L., & Copeland J. (2006). Posttraumatic stress disorder among female street-based sex workers in the greater Sidney area, Australia. *BMC Psychiatry, 6(24)*, 1–12.

Sallmann, J. (2010a). "Going hand-in-hand." Connections between women's prostitution and substance use. *Journal of Social Work Practice in the Addiction, 10*, 115–138.

Sallmann, J. (2010b). Living with stigma: Women's experiences of prostitution and substance use. *Affilia, 25(2)*, 146–159.

Sanders, T. (2007). Becoming an ex-sex worker: Making transitions out of a deviant career. *Feminist Criminology, 2(1)*, 74–95.

Sanger, W. W. (2013). The history of prostitution: Its extent, causes, and effects throughout the world. [Project Gutenberg eBook #41873]. Retrieved from http://www.gutenberg.org/files/41873/41873-h/41873-h.htm (Original work published 1858).

Saphira, M., & Herbert, A. (2004). Exiting commercial sexual activity. ECPAT NZ 2004. Retrieved from http://www.ecpat.org.nz/Other/Researches/Exiting CommercialSexualActivity.aspx

Sausa, L. A., Keatley, J., & Operario, D. (2007). Perceived risks and benefits of sex work among transgender women of color in San Francisco. *Archives of Sexual Behavior, 36*, 768–777.

Seattle Police Department (n.d.) Stay out of areas of prostitution. Retrieved from http://www.seattle.gov/police-manual/title-15---primary-investigation/15290 ---stay-out-of-areas-of-prostitution-%28soap%29

Shaver, F. M. (2005). Sex work research: Methodological and ethical challenges. *Journal of Interpersonal Violence, 20(3)*, 296–319.

Shdaimah, C. S., Kaufman, B. R., Bright, C. L., & Flower, S. M. (2014). Neighborhood assessment of prostitution as a pressing social problem and appropriate responses: Results from a community survey. *Criminal Justice Policy Review, 25(3)*, 275–298.

Shively, M., Kliorys, K., Wheeler, K., & Hunt, D. (2012, April 30). *Prostitution and sex trafficking demand reduction efforts: Final report.* A report for the National Institute of Justice. Retrieved from https://www.ncjrs.gov/pdffiles1/nij/grants/238796.pdf

Skilbrei, M. L., & Holmström, C. (2013, December 16). The 'Nordic model' of prostitution is a myth. *The*

Conversation. Retrieved from http://theconversation.com/the-nordic-model-of-prostitution-law-is-a-myth-21351

Slamah, K., Winter, S., & Ordek, K. (2010). Violence against Trans sex workers: Stigma, exclusion, poverty, and death. *Research for Sex Work*, 12, 30–31.

Smith, M. D., Grov, C., Seal, D. W., & McCall, P. (2012). A social-cognitive of how young men become involved in male escorting. *Journal of Sex Research*, 50(1), 1–10.

Smolak, A. (2013). White slavery, whorehouse riots, venereal disease, and saving women: Historical context of prostitution interventions and harm reduction in New York City during the progressive era. *Social Work in Public Health*, 28, 496–508.

Sonderlund, G. (2005). Running from the rescuers: New U.S. crusades against sex trafficking and the rhetoric of abolition. *The National Women's Studies Association Journal*, 17(3), 64–87.

St. James, M. (1987). The reclamation of whores. In Laurie Bell (Ed.), *Good girls/bad girls: Feminists and sex trade workers face to face* (81–91). Seattle, WA: Seal Press.

Sullivan, E., & Simon, W. (1998). The client: A social, psychological, and behavioral look at the unseen patron of prostitution. In J. E. Elias, V. L. Bullough, V. Elias, & G. Brewer (Eds.), *Prostitution: On whores, hustlers, and johns* (pp. 134–154). Amherst, NY: Prometheus.

Thompson, S. E. (2000). Prostitution – A choice ignored. *Women's Rights Law Reporter*, 21, 217–247.

Timpson, S. C., Ross, M. W., Williams, M. L., & Atkinson, J. (2007). Characteristics, drug use, and sex partners of a sample of sex workers. *The American Journal of Drug and Alcohol Abuse*, 33, 63–69.

Tomura, M. (2009). A prostitute's lived experiences of stigma. *Journal of Phenomenological Psychology*, 40, 51–84.

Tsenin, K. (2000). One judicial perspective on the sex trade. *Research on Women and Girls in the Justice System*, 3, 15–25.

U.S. Department of Homeland Security (2011). *Victims of human trafficking: T nonimmigrant status*. Retrieved from http://www.uscis.gov/humanitarian/victims-human-trafficking-other-crimes/victims-human-trafficking-t-nonimmigrant-status

U.S. Department of State (2008). *Trafficking in persons report, 2008*. Retrieved from http://www.state.gov/documents/organization/105501.pdf

U.S. Department of State (2012). *Trafficking in persons report, 2012*. Retrieved from http://www.state.gov/documents/organization/192587.pdf

Vanwesenbeeck, I. (2013). Prostitution push and pull: Male and female perspectives. *Journal of Sex Research*, 50(1), 11–16.

Victims of Trafficking and Violence Protection Act of 2000, Pub. L. 106–386, 114 Stat. 1464 (2000), *codified as amended in scattered sections of 8 U.S.C., 10 U.S.C., 18 U.S.C., 22 U.S.C., 27 U.S.C., 28 U.S.C., & 42 U.S.C.* (2015).

Walker-Rodriguez, A., & Hill, R. (2011, March). Human sex trafficking. *FBI Law Enforcement Bulletin*. Retrieved from http://www.fbi.gov/stats-services/publications/law-enforcement-bulletin/march_2011/human_sex_trafficking

Walkowitz, J. R. (1992). *City of dreadful delight: Narratives of sexual danger in late Victorian London*. Chicago, IL: University of Chicago Press.

Warnock, C., & Wheen, N. (2012). Sex work in New Zealand: There-importation of moral majoritarianism in regulating a decriminalized industry. *Canadian Journal of Woman and the Law*, 24(2), 414–438.

Washington Revised Code § 9A.88.070 (2015).

Weinberg, M. S., Shaver, F. M., & Williams, C. J. (1999). Gendered sex work in the San Francisco Tenderloin. *Archives of Sexual Behavior*, 28(6), 503–521.

Weitzer, R. (2005). New directions in research on prostitution. *Crime, Law & Social Change*, 43(4–5), 211–235.

Weitzer, R. (2007). Prostitution: Facts and fictions. *Contexts*, 6(4), 28–33.

Weitzer, R. (2010). *Sex for sale: Prostitution, pornography, and the sex industry*. New York, NY: Taylor & Francis.

Weitzer, R. (2012). *Legalizing prostitution: From illicit vice to lawful business*. New York, NY: New York University Press.

Widom, C. S., & Kuhns, J. B. (1996). Childhood victimization and subsequent risk for promiscuity, prostitution, and teenage pregnancy: A prospective study. *American Journal of Public Health*, 86, 1607–1612.

Williamson, C., & Cluse-Tolar, T. (2002). Pimp-controlled prostitution: Still an integral part of the street life. *Violence Against Women*, 8, 1074–1092.

Williamson, C., & Folaron, G. (2003). Understanding the experiences of street level prostitutes. *Qualitative Social Work*, 2(3), 271–287.

Willis, E. (1992). Radical feminism and feminist radicalism. In E. Willis, *No more nice girls: Countercultural essays* (pp. 117–150). Middletown, CT: Wesleyan University Press. (Original work published 1984.)

Wilson, J. Q., & Kelling, G. G. (1982). Broken windows: The police and neighborhood safety. *Atlantic Monthly*, March, 78–78.

Zuzu (2007, October 16). When is rape at gunpoint not rape? When it's "theft of services." *Feministe: In defense of the sanctimonious women's studies set* [Web log]. Retrieved from http://www.feministe.us/blog/archives/2007/10/16/when-is-rape-at-gunpoint-not-rape-when-its-theft-of-services

Cases

Arizona v. Jones, LC2014–000424–001 DT. Appellant's Memorandum. (Ariz. Super. Ct., August 5, 2014). Retrieved from http://www.acluaz.org/sites/default/files/documents/Appellant_s%20Memorandum%20(2)_0.pdf

Arizona v. Jones, LC2014–000424–001 DT (Ariz. Super. Ct, January 22, 2015). Retrieved from https://www.aclu.org/sites/default/files/assets/monica_jones_conviction_reversed.pdf

Doe v. Caldwell, 2:12-cv-01670 (La. E.D. Court, December 20, 2012). Retrieved from http://www.plainsite.org/dockets/n2rc1oou/louisiana-eastern-district-court/doe-et-al-v-caldwell-et-al

Doe v. Jindal, 851 F. Supp. 2d 995 (E. D. La. 2012).

People v. Zambia, 254 P.3d 965 (Cal. 2011).

CHAPTER 8

Obscenity and Pornography

Weston Morrow, Chantal Fahmy, and Henry F. Fradella

In 1988, Larry Flynt of *Hustler* magazine fictitiously portrayed Jerry Falwell, a prominent fundamental Protestant minister, as having an incestuous relationship with his mother in an advertisement. The advertisement featured a picture of Falwell as well as a made-up interview endorsing the products of Campari Liqueur:

FALWELL:	My first time was in an outhouse outside Lynchburg, Virginia.
INTERVIEWER:	Wasn't it a little cramped?
FALWELL:	Not after I kicked the goat out.
INTERVIEWER:	I see. You must tell me all about it.
FALWELL:	I never *really* expected to make it with Mom, but then after she showed all the other guys in town such a good time, I figured, "What the hell!"
INTERVIEWER:	But your mom? Isn't that a bit odd?
FALWELL:	I don't think so. Looks don't mean that much to me in a woman.
INTERVIEWER:	Go on.
FALWELL:	Well, we were drunk off our God-fearing asses on Campari, ginger ale and soda—that's called Fire and Brimstone—at the time. And Mom looked better than a Baptists whore with a $100 donation.
INTERVIEWER:	Campari on the crapper with Mom . . . how interesting. Well, how was it?
FALWELL:	The Campari was great, but Mom passed out before I could come.
INTERVIEWER:	Did you ever try it again?
FALWELL:	Sure . . . lots of times. But not in the outhouse. Between Mom and the shit, the flies were too much to bear.
INTERVIEWER:	We meant the Campari.
FALWELL:	Oh, yeah. I always get sloshed before I go out to the pulpit. You don't think I could lay down all the bullshit *sober*, do you?

(As quoted in Post, 1990, p. 607)

Although the advertisement had a disclaimer stating "Ad Parody—Not to Be Taken Seriously," Falwell sued Flynt and *Hustler* for invasion of privacy, libel, and intentional infliction of emotional distress. The district court ruled for Flynt and *Hustler* on the invasion of privacy claim, finding the parody did not, as a matter of law, invade Falwell's privacy. At trial, Flynt and *Hustler* similarly prevailed on the libel claim because of the disclaimer. Falwell, however, won $150,000 on the intentional infliction of emotional distress claim. Flynt and *Hustler* appealed the emotional distress verdict unsuccessfully to the Fourth Circuit (*Falwell v. Flynt*, 1986). On appeal to the U.S. Supreme Court, however, Flynt and *Hustler* prevailed (*Hustler Magazine, Inc. v. Falwell*, 1988). The Court rejected the claim that the caricature in question was so "outrageous" as to distinguish it from more traditional political cartoons.

> "Outrageousness" in the area of political and social discourse has an inherent subjectiveness about it which would allow a jury to impose liability on the basis of the jurors' tastes or views, or perhaps on the basis of their dislike of a particular expression. An "outrageousness" standard thus runs afoul of our longstanding refusal to allow damages to be awarded because the speech in question may have an adverse emotional impact on the audience. . . . We conclude that public figures and public officials may not recover for the tort of intentional infliction of emotional distress by reason of publications such as the one here at issue without showing, in addition, that the publication contains a false statement of fact which was made with "actual malice," i.e., with knowledge that the statement was false or with reckless disregard as to whether or not it was true.

(pp. 55–56)

- Do you think the made-up interview defamed Reverend Falwell? Explain your reasoning.
- Is intonating that someone committed incest with his mother *obscene*?
- Critique the U.S. Supreme Court's decision in the case. Do you think the actual malice standard is appropriate for public figures, or should some other standard be applied? Why?

LEARNING OBJECTIVES

1. Identify the origins of the First Amendment.
2. Describe the evolution of obscenity law.
3. Define obscenity under past and present case law.
4. Explain the rationale behind child pornography laws in light of the First Amendment.
5. Analyze the First Amendment problems associated with teenagers who engage in "sexting."
6. Evaluate the conservative arguments in support of the legal regulation of non-obscene pornography and the liberal counterarguments in support of First Amendment protection of such materials.
7. Compare and contrast the anti-pornography feminist position with the sex-positive feminist views on the legal regulation of non-obscene pornography.

OVERVIEW OF THE FIRST AMENDMENT AND FREE EXPRESSION

Proposed in 1789 and ratified in 1791, the First Amendment to the U.S. Constitution states that "Congress shall make no law respecting an establishment of religion, or prohibiting the free exercise thereof; or abridging the freedom of speech; or of press; or of the right of the people peaceably to assemble, and to petition the Government for a redress of grievances." The First Amendment received very little U.S. Supreme Court attention until the early twentieth century in the World War I era. Since then, however, the U.S. Supreme Court has been very active in adjudicating First Amendment claims after more than a century of near dormancy.

The Roots of Free Expression in Western Civilization

Modern notions of free expression in the United States can trace their roots back to both Ancient Greece and Rome. In the process of transitioning to a more democratic society between 800 and 600 B.C.E., aristocratic rulers in ancient Greece permitted a limited amount of expressive freedoms from "citizens" of the city-state of Athens. Although these freedoms reached their pinnacle in the mid-400s B.C.E (Radin, 1927; Tedford & Herbeck, 2013), they only applied to adult men because women, juveniles, and resident aliens were not considered citizens (DiStefano, 1991; Jaggar, 1988; Okin, 1979; Phillips, 1991). Thus, the majority of the population enjoyed no rights to free expression. But even the men of age to be deemed citizens had to be careful not to run afoul restrictions on *slander*—false statements damaging to another's reputation, and *sedition*—inciting others to rebel against the authority of a state (Tedford & Herbeck, 2013).

Citizens of the republic of Rome also enjoyed certain limited expressive freedoms, at least until the time of the Roman Empire and the corresponding monarchical rule of the Caesars (Frank, 1927; Momigliano, 1942). Indeed, "republican times displayed a rich vibrant exercise of freedom of speech through the most varied means," including speeches, dramas, poems, satire, and debate (Díaz de Valdés, 2009, p. 133). But these freedoms were significantly curtailed as the Roman government shifted from a form of limited democracy to one-man rule by an emperor. "[D]efamation was criminalized, writings were burned, and authors were condemned for what they wrote" (Díaz de Valdés, 2009, p. 134). And citizens' ability to express political opposition against Roman emperors was limited to nonexistent; indeed, under some emperors, such actions were punished by brutal deaths (Díaz de Valdés, 2009). Notably, this model was adopted by early English monarchs (Cornwell, 2004).

When King John was forced to sign the Magna Carta, a major shift occurred in which England established a new domain of inalienable rights and liberties that abandoned, in part, some of its limitations on the rights of citizens to express themselves. None of the 63 clauses in the Magna Carta referenced any rights to free expression, "but by curbing royal powers and strengthening individual protection, they sought in other ways to extend liberties to the 'freeman of England' " (Roberts, 2011). When the Statute of Treasons was enacted in 1352, it limited prosecutions for treason to "overt acts" in planning the death of the monarch (Roberts, 2011). Thus, speech criticizing the king no longer constituted treason, at least officially; in practice, however, this provision was often ignored such that dissident speech was still punished by death. Indeed, the struggle to balance the power of the monarchy and the rights of English citizens lasted at least 500 years during which individual rights to free expression were often at odds with censorship laws and laws regulating the licensing of written or printed materials (Cornwell, 2004).

The advent of the printing press in the mid-1400s ushered in the ability to circulate thousands of copies of something in print. Early mass-printing suffered from very little "censorship or control from ecclesiastical or secular authority" (Siebert, 1952, p. 24). In fact, once printing was introduced to King Richard III in 1484, he supported the expansion of foreign printing businesses and the importation of foreign materials. Such developments were perceived as enhancing economic prosperity and trade activity. The optimism by King Richard III was short lived, however, when the Church implemented a series of printing restrictions from the early 1500s through the late 1600s. Controlled by the Crown, "[r]egulation of printing was asserted as a royal prerogative" (Cornwell, 2004, p. 20).

English Common Law

English common law came to recognize several exceptions to the principles of free expression, most notably with regard to materials that constituted **criminal libel**, which fell into four primary categories of speech aimed at protecting "established norms of respect and propriety" (Post, 1988, p. 305):

- **defamation**—damaging someone's reputation by making false statements (if the false statements damaging to reputation were spoken, the defamation constituted *slander*; if the false statements damaging to reputation were published, then the defamation constituted *libel*);
- **blasphemy**—disrespect toward God;[1]
- **sedition**—inciting others to rebel against the authority of a state;[2] and
- **obscenity**—profane materials that corrupt public morals that also meet the relevant legal tests for obscene materials (discussed at length later in this chapter).

"Although blasphemy and obscenity originally shared a common concern with regulating the profane, blasphemy was in its early years most closely allied to sedition, since attacks on God and religion were viewed as equivalent to attacks on the social order" (Post, 1988, p. 306). Unsurprisingly, therefore, the legal regulation of criminal libel in England focused on materials that criticized the Church or the Crown, at least until the 1820s.

The Regulation of Heresy and Sedition

Approximately 50 years after printing was introduced to England, King Henry VIII took steps to control the press system by denouncing profane materials and limiting what could be printed. The dissemination of William Tyndale's English translation of the New Testament was one of the first focused efforts to restrict publication of a book since widespread access to the Bible threatened the authority of Church leaders as the sole interpreters and evangelists of the word of God. (Indeed, such access facilitated the spread of the Reformation, see Eisenstein, 1980). The king made a number of provisions to stop its circulation, which included recalling the book, having his bishops' burn as many copies as possible, and enacting anti-press legislation. Parliament's regulatory law of 1542–1543 stated:

> There shall be no annotations or preambles in Bibles or New Testaments in English. The Bible shall not be read in English in any church. No women or artificers, prentices, journeymen, servingmen of the degree of yeomen or under, husbandmen, nor labourers, shall read the New Testament in English . . . anything contrary to the King's instructions . . . shall be thereof convict . . . his first offense recant, for his second abjure and bear a fagot, and for his third shall be adjudged an heretick, and be burned.
>
> (Neal, 1855; as quoted by Cornwell, 2004, p. 21)

Printing restrictions abounded through the reign of Queen Elizabeth. Although she favored criticisms of her predecessor, "Bloody Mary," Queen Elizabeth harshly suppressed opinions that opposed the Crown on the rationalization that such restrictions maintained peace and order (Cornwell, 2004). Because the circulation of derogatory materials was viewed as a threat to the social status quo and government authority, Queen Elizabeth implemented a host of decrees and orders that constrained printing presses, such as the 1586 Star Chamber decree on printing, which limited licenses to certain printers authorized by the Crown and providing for penalties for violating the precursors to modern copyrights (Deazley, 2008). In doing so, Queen Elizabeth sought to insure that no defamatory material about her rule or the Church of England would be published in England. At one point, she even offered compensation to individuals for identifying writers critical of the monarchy (Cornwell, 2004). If an author or writer was caught for promulgating a critical opinion, the English Court of Star Chamber, which was not bound by traditional English law, would prosecute and punish these individuals in a number of ways, including branding, mutilation, flogging, the pillory, imprisonment, unlimited fines, and levying (Scofield, 1900). In 1630, for instance, the Star Chamber sentenced Alexander Leighton for the dissemination of *An Appeal to Parliament*, in which he advocated for scripture over monarchal rule. As a consequence for his actions, Leighton was "whipped, [had] one of his ears cut off, his nose slit, and one side of his face branded" (Siebert, 1952, p. 122). One week later, he was tortured yet again but on the opposite side. Eventually, public outrage over the excessively severe punishments that accompanied seditious libel would contribute to the dismantling of the Star Chamber, along with royal control of printing during the Puritan Revolution (Cornwell, 2004).

As England increasingly shifted from monarchal rule to parliamentary control, the legal restrictions that had been placed on printing became inconsistently enforced. Such inconsistencies were not due to Parliament favoring press freedoms, but rather were a function of the political and religious turmoil that accompanied the transition to parliamentary control of England, especially after the Star Chamber had been abolished. This, in turn, led to a temporary explosion of pamphleteering that disparaged the king and Parliament. Once parliamentary control finally stabilized, Parliament addressed the concern of unrestrained printing through channels aimed at the "elimination of chaos and privacy in printing trade, suppression of sedition, protection for religion, control of news of parliamentary activity, and last, a program of active propaganda in defense of the Parliamentary position" (Siebert, 1952, pp. 179–180). The 1643 Ordinance for the Regulation of Printing, for example, was one of the first laws to combat free press, which "re-created the harsh conditions of suppression that existed under monarchal rule" (Cornwell, 2004, p. 23).

By the mid-1600s, many writers opposed Parliament's new limitations on printing, which inspired them to advocate for the abolition of printing regulations and advocate for a free press. In his polemic literary work entitled *Areopagitica*, John Milton attacked the licensing mechanism that masked the truth from emerging:

> To deliver the press from the restraints with which it was encumbered; that the power of determining what was true and what was false, what ought to be published and what to be suppressed, might no longer be entrusted to a few illiterate and illiberal individuals, who refused their sanction to any work that contained views or sentiments at all above the level of vulgar superstition.
>
> (Milton, 1992/1644, p. 831)

Put simply, Milton believed that licensing undermined the quest for the self-righting principle of truth. Although an advocate for press freedoms, Milton did not think it should be without governance. He maintained the perspective that sanctions should be imposed for the circulation of "mischievous and libelous" materials (Milton, 1957/1653, p. 44).

During the Puritan Revolution, two of Milton's contemporaries also attacked the licensing system from different perspectives. The first contemporary, William Walwyn, approached this endeavor by anonymously publishing the pamphlet entitled *The Compassionate Samaritane* in 1644, in which he argued that not all opposing views should be subject to licensing. Although he believed in a certain degree of restrictions, Walwyn contested the idea of complete regulation because it "stopt the mouthes of good men, who must either not write at all, or no more than is suitable to the judgments or interests of the Licensers" (Walwyn, 1644, A5). Ultimately, Walwyn sought to highlight the impracticality associated with maintaining the licensing system while simultaneously promoting the notion that printing freedoms should encompass materials that were "not highly scandalous or dangerous to the state" (Walwyn, 1644; as quoted in Siebert, 1952, p. 194). The second of Milton's contemporaries, pamphleteer Henry Robinson, advanced the ideology of press freedoms by pointing out how restrictions on free press undermine the values of individualism and a free-market economy, stating "No man can have a natural monopoly of truth, and the more freely each man exercises his own gifts in its pursuit, the more of truth will be discovered and possessed" (as cited in Haller, 1934, p. 69). Despite the published pleas of Milton, Walwyn, Robinson, and other key libertarians, Parliament eventually passed and enacted the Printing Acts of 1649, 1653, and 1662, which marked a brutal shift back to the time of the Star Chamber. In fact, the law of seditious libel, which was founded in the Star Chamber, was re-established with Parliament and now included the death penalty. John Twyn, for instance, published a book that

argued that "the monarchy must be accountable to the people, particularly when the decrees of the king violate the law of God" (as cited in Cornwell, 2004, p. 26). Such an offense was met swiftly and severely with the following sentence:

> [Y]ou shall be hanged by the neck, and being alive, shall be cut down, and. . .shall be cut off, your entrails shall be taken out of your body, and, you living, the same to be burnt before your eyes; your head to be cut off, your body to be divided into four quarters and your head and quarters to be disposed of at the pleasure of the king's majesty. And the Lord have mercy upon your soul.
>
> (*Rex v. Twyn*, 1664, pp. 535–536)

The king later had Twyn's four quarters nailed to various gates throughout the city as a way to deter publishers and writers from disseminating heretical material. Similar trials transpired through much of the 1600s. During the latter half of the seventeenth century, 16 trials for seditious libel occurred over a seven-month span, which successfully worked to control the press (Siebert, 1952). Thus, for 150 years, England was ever present at controlling the press through licensing and various forms of brutal punishment.

Eventually, the brutal licensing system that acted on the impulse of the Church, the Crown, and/or Parliament began to collapse. Its demise was not due to the philosophical commitment to free expression, but rather, the administrative burden associated with overseeing so many printers. Moreover, it also inhibited the benefits related to freedom of trade (Cornwell, 2004). Hence, the Printing Act expired under the reign of William and Mary in 1694 and was free of regulatory **prior restraint**. Although licensing could no longer prevent the press from publishing, there were still rules under common law and parliamentary citation that were used as forms of control, particularly for seditious libel (Siebert, 1952). Blackstone's *Commentaries on the*

Laws of England delineated the then-current status of free expression:

> The liberty of the press is indeed essential to the nature of a free state; but this consists in laying no *previous* restraints upon publications, and not in freedom from censure for criminal matter when published. Every freeman has an undoubted right to lay what sentiments he please before the public: to forbid this is to destroy the freedom of the press: but if he publishes what is improper, mischievous, or illegal, he must take the consequences of his own temerity.
> (Blackstone, 1818/1765–1769, p. 151)

Blackstone's views about free expression embodying little more than freedom from prior restraint on publication—meaning no censorship in advance—shaped both attitudes and laws in the American colonies such that English approaches to restraints on speech were common.

The Regulation of Obscene Materials

As previously addressed, the Star Chamber and, subsequently, the English Parliament were primarily concerned with religious heresy and sedition from the time of the advent of mass printing. But throughout the 1700s, English theater and literature began to incorporate materials of an increasingly sexual nature, some of which was considered immoral. England was largely tolerant of such material throughout much of the eighteenth century. In 1787, however, a royal proclamation by King George III entitled the "Proclamation for the Discouragement of Vice" provided for the criminal prosecution of "excessive drinking, blasphemy, profane swearing and cursing, lewdness, profanation of the Lord's Day, and other dissolute, immoral, or disorderly practices" (Hochschild, 2005, p. 126). The public was largely indifferent to the proclamation, but it nonetheless represented the changing moral standards of the time.

In 1802, William Wilberforce founded the Society for the Suppression of Vice. He sought to increase the impact of the royal proclamation through grassroots moral entrepreneurship. His organization and others like it contributed to Parliament passing the Vagrancy Act of 1824 (Richards, 1974). That law made it an offense to beg or "sleep rough" (homelessness), but also included acts of prostitution at the time. It treated such offenses as a misdemeanor punishable by up to one month at hard labor. In 1838, the Act was significantly broadened by providing for the punishment "of idle and disorderly Persons, Rogues and Vagabonds, incorrigible Rogues and other Vagrants in England" (5 Geo. 4. c. 83, § I, 1838). These amendments included a number of moral welfare offenses, including any form of indecent exposure and the publication of "any obscene Print, Picture, or other indecent Exhibition" (5 Geo. 4. c. 83, § IV, 1838).

The Vagrancy Act of 1838 marked a turning point in English common law for the social control of printed materials by developing a legal mechanism for the suppression of sexual content distinct from the regulation of religious or political sedition and libel. Nineteen years later, growing concern about the proliferation of sexually explicit material led Parliament to enact the Obscene Publications Act 1857 (20 & 21 Vict. c. 83). This Victorian-era law, also known as Lord Campbell's Act, criminalized the sale of obscene material and granted the courts the power to seize and destroy all offending material (Bartee & Bartee, 1992). Notably, the Act did not define the terms "obscene" or "obscenity," leaving it for the courts to interpret. *Regina v. Hicklin* (1868) was arguably the most influential English case to grapple with the meaning of these terms as used in the Obscene Publications Act. Queen's Bench Lord Chief Justice Cockburn ruled that the intention of an author or publisher was immaterial to the question; rather, material could be banned under the Act if it has the "tendency . . . to deprave and corrupt those whose minds are open to such immoral influences, and into whose hands a publication of this sort may fall" (*Regina v. Hicklin*, 1868, p. 371). This formulation of obscenity law more or less remained in force in England until a major reformation of the law in 1957— 100 years after the initial passage of the Obscene Publications Act.

Free Expression in the American Colonies

When the American colonies formed their principles of free expression, they drew heavily from English traditions. Thus, early American law incorporated licensing practices and the doctrine of prior restraint, and punished licentious or scandalous speech (Cornwell, 2004). Moreover, despite being founded as refuge from religious persecution, the American colonies placed restrictions on free expression, especially against those who openly opposed Christianity. Colonies in Virginia, Pennsylvania, and Maryland, for example, all had codes that imposed the death penalty for either speaking poorly about Christianity or not believing in one God.

Outside the sphere of seditious libel and religion, the American colonial presses were regulated in a similar fashion to that of England. The Press Restriction Act, for instance, mandated that printing companies must include their name and publication address on printed documents. Furthermore, in 1662, Massachusetts established a law that required printers to be licensed, which eventually led to the closure of the first colonial newspaper. With the abolition of the English licensing system in the early 1700s, however, the colonies soon abandoned the system and newspapers began appearing throughout the "New World." Some of these new printing shops included John Campbell's *Boston News-Letter*, Andrew Bradford's *American Weekly Mercury*, William

Bradford's *New York Gazette*, and Benjamin Franklin's *Pennsylvania Gazette*. Maintaining these establishments, however, was difficult because literacy rates were low, colonial life was cumbersome, printing logistics were challenging, revenues suffered from the lack of paying subscribers, and the availability of paper was in short supply. Combined, these factors restricted the development of newspapers more than government regulation (Cornwell, 2004).

In the 1730s, libertarians began challenging the practice of seditious libel through published writings under the pseudonym Cato. Prominent writers, such as John Trenchard and Thomas Gordon, advocated for freedom of speech. For these libertarians, the risks associated with libelous statements were worth taking if it meant preserving free press. While Cato writers frowned upon false ranting of the press, they argued that "truthful criticism of government should not be subject to punishment" (Cornwell, 2004, p. 31).

The Cato efforts represented the first organized effort to put forth the notion that the truth should be the defense against libel. But John Peter Zenger put that idea into action. Publishing pamphlets that criticized the administration of New York Royal Governor William Cosby, Zenger was eventually arrested for seditious libel. Zenger's case received wide publicity and attracted an enormous crowd because Andrew Hamilton, one of the most successful and respected lawyers, represented him. In order to have the seditious libel charges dropped, Hamilton had to convince the jury to nullify the judge's guilty ruling. To accomplish such a feat, he argued that it was essential for the press to criticize government truthfully. In his closing argument, Hamilton concluded,

The question before the Court and you, Gentlemen of the jury, is not of small or private concern. It is not the cause of one poor printer, nor of New York alone, which you are now trying. No! It may in its consequence affect every free man that lives under a British government on the main of America. It is the best cause. It is the cause of liberty. And I make no doubt but your upright conduct this day will not only entitle you to the love and esteem of your fellow citizens, but every man who prefers freedom to a life of slavery will bless and honor you as men who have baffled the attempt of tyranny, and by an impartial and uncorrupt verdict have laid a noble foundation for securing to ourselves, our posterity, and our neighbors, that to which nature and the laws of our country have given us a right to liberty of both exposing and opposing arbitrary power (in these parts of the world at least) by speaking and writing truth.

(Linder, 2001)

In one of the most monumental moments for freedom of the press, the jury nullified the judge's guilty finding. Although the trial extended Cato's ideals and is often cited as one of the most significant cases for freedom of the press, it did not change common law (i.e., no precedent was officially established). It would be another 50 years before truth was legally recognized as a defense to charges of libel. In the meantime, however, foundational events unfolded at the end of the Revolutionary War. Although some of the early positions of the states paralleled Blackstone's viewpoints, some states' constitutions incorporated rights to free speech and free press that subsumed the principle Andrew Hamilton articulated in Zenger's trial—that truth should be a legal defense to libel.

As was the case in England, much of colonial American laws targeting free expression concerned sedition or religious libel. Indeed, laws criminalizing blasphemy or heresy first appeared in the early 1700s and were ultimately adopted in all of the American colonies. Obscenity was also proscribed, but there are no reported cases for the crime of obscenity prior to the adoption of the First Amendment.

The First Amendment

During the summer of 1787, delegates to the Constitutional Convention convened to devise a new federal constitution. Whereas federalists supported a centralized federal government, the Anti-Federalists feared it would replicate the oppressive conditions associated with English rule. Specifically, Anti-Federalists advocated for individual rights and limited government involvement, including expressive freedoms. Congress adopted the Bill of Rights on December 15, 1791. In it, the First Amendment provided, "Congress shall make no law respecting an establishment of religion, or prohibiting the free exercise thereof; or abridging the freedom of speech; or of press; or of the right of the people peaceably to assemble, and to petition the Government for a redress of grievances."

During the first seven years of its existence, the First Amendment faced no significant challenges. That changed when Congress enacted the Alien and Sedition Act of 1798. The Sedition Act was largely a political, as well as a security issue, as the United States was very close to being at war with France. The Act enabled President John Adams to sanction Republican dissent for criticizing his administration and government officials; they feared that such rhetoric would change public opinion against the Federalist government. When Thomas Jefferson contested the Sedition Act on First Amendment grounds, Federalists resorted to the Blackstonian interpretation, claiming it only protected against prior restraint of the press (Bergh, 1905). In total, there were approximately ten convictions under the Sedition Act. With the presidential election of Jefferson, however, the Alien and Sedition Act of 1798 expired and he pardoned all those who were found guilty of seditious libel.

Following the expiration of the Alien and Sedition Act of 1798, the First Amendment received very little attention in the federal courts. Consequently, the nineteenth century is often associated with First Amendment dormancy, especially as it related to religious or political expression. State governments, however, continued to regulate expression that the First Amendment did not encompass, namely personal libel and obscenity. Moreover, lingering effects of English common law and the expired Alien and Sedition Act of 1798 perpetuated a prevailing sense in the states that the freedoms of speech and the press were not applicable in cases in which critical expression had been levied against those in power. Thomas Jefferson, for instance, sued Harry Croswell (a Federalist printer) for attacking his administration, claiming the criticisms were licentious (Cornwell, 2004). Advancing Andrew Hamilton's argument in the Zenger case, Crosswell's attorney, Alexander Hamilton, advocated that the truth should be a defense against personal libel. Although Crosswell did not win the case, it eventually resulted in New York passing legislation that made the truth a valid defense against libel. This proposition eventually spread to other states and eventually was recognized by the federal government. In short, speaking or writing about matters that are true, even if such truths damage someone's reputation, eventually came to fall within the protections of the First Amendment.

In the realm of seditious libel, however, suppression of freedom of expression with regard to criticism of the government did not end with the expiration of the Alien and Sedition Act of 1798. In fact, such restrictions on free expression reach their high point during the World War I era (Pember & Calvert, 2011) with the enactment of the Espionage Act of 1917 and the Sedition Act of 1918. The former criminalized a variety of expressive behaviors that interfered with the war effort, ranging from attempting to cause insubordination, disloyalty, or mutiny in the armed forces to obstructing recruitment and enlistment efforts. The latter made it criminal "to utter or print or write or publish disloyal or profane language that was intended to cause contempt of, or scorn for, the federal government, the Constitution, the flag or the uniform of the armed forces" (Pember & Calvert, 2011, p. 28). Given the history of the common law and the lack of First Amendment jurisprudence through the 1800s, these laws resulted in thousands of successful prosecutions. Indeed, the U.S. Supreme Court upheld several convictions under these Acts. For example, the defendant in *Schenck v. United States* (1919) was convicted of violating the Espionage Act of 1917 for preparing and distributing leaflets critical of the war and the draft. The Court reasoned that the First Amendment had no real bearing on the case in light of the defendant's "intent" and the impact of the leaflet. Although a same outcome occurred in the similar case of *Abrams v. United States* (1919), the dissents of Justices Oliver Wendell Holmes and Louis Brandeis passionately argued that the First Amendment should significantly curtail the government from punishing criticisms of it using seditious libel laws unless such expression poses a "a clear and imminent danger that it will bring about forthwith" interference with governmental operations (*Abrams v. United States*, 1919, p. 627, Holmes, J., dissenting).

In 1940, Congress enacted the Smith Act, which made it illegal to advocate for overthrowing the government of the United States or any state by force or violence. A fractured decision of the U.S. Supreme Court in *Dennis v. United States* (1951) upheld the convictions of members of the Community Party of the United States under the Smith Act, reasoning that the gravity of the positions advocated against the government, when weighed against the probability of such advocacy being successful, justified the suppression of communist expression. This reasoning supported the conviction of nearly 100 prosecutions of communists in the 1950s until the Court decided *Yates v. United States* (1957) in which it held that Smith Act prosecutions were justified only when people's expression presented a clear and present danger to incite specific unlawful conduct. Prosecutions under the

Smith Act all but vanished in the wake of the decision in *Yates*. Today, it is clear that the criticism of the government is protected by the First Amendment because of our "profound national commitment to the principle that debate on public issues should be uninhibited, robust, and wide-open" (*New York Times v. Sullivan*, 1964, p. 270). But when a seditious activity takes the form of a *seditious conspiracy*—agreements to take actions designed to overthrow or destroy the government—it may be criminally proscribed because such conspiracies are distinct from mere advocacy of revolution. Hence, the First Amendment did not protect the conspiratorial actions of terrorists who unsuccessfully argued they were fighting a jihad, or holy war, against the United States *United States v. Rahman* (1999).

The First Amendment protection of expression that others find distasteful extends beyond protecting oral or written speech. It includes some forms of conduct that were designed to express an idea or opinion—such as picketing, burning the flag, and wearing armbands or other articles to express protest. Conduct that is designed to communicate such a message is called **symbolic speech**. Although some people undoubtedly find certain types of symbolic speech offensive, such conduct receives significant First Amendment protection even though the "speech" at issue goes beyond oral or written communication (*Texas v. Johnson*, 1989).

The Constitutional Limits of Free Expression

Although the government at federal, state, and local levels may not ban or punish the content of speech it finds objectionable, governmental entities are entitled to regulate the **time, place, and manner** of speech—including picketing and symbolic speech—in a content-neutral way for the good of society. Under the U.S. Supreme Court's decision in *United States v. O'Brien* (1968), governmen-

tal regulation on the time, place, and manner of speech is permissible if:

1. the regulation furthers an important or substantial governmental interest;
2. the governmental interest served by the regulation is unrelated to the suppression of free expression;
3. the regulation is narrowly tailored to serve the government's interest such that the restriction on free speech is not greater than is necessary to achieve the governmental interest; and
4. the regulation still leaves open ample, alternative means for people to communicate their message.

Thus, public authorities may impose limitations on free expression that are reasonably designed to prevent fire, health hazards, obstruction and occupation of public buildings, or traffic obstructions. For example, protesters may want to hold a demonstration in a large city to gain national media attention to their cause. Although they have a First Amendment right to do so, they cannot hold their demonstration whenever and wherever they choose. No one has the right to "insist upon a street meeting in the middle of Times Square at the rush hour as a form of freedom of speech" (*Cox v. Louisiana*, 1965, p. 554). In other words, the time of the demonstration can be prescribed, but the content of it may not. Even groups espousing distasteful, unpopular, or offensive messages still have the right to speak their minds. For instance, a group of neo-Nazis had the right to parade down the streets in a predominantly Jewish neighborhood, but they had to obtain valid permits and conduct their demonstration at a time when authorities could maintain order (*National Socialist Party of America v. Village of Skokie*, 1977).[3]

Beyond valid time, place, and manner restrictions on constitutionally protected forms of free expression, the U.S. Supreme Court has made it clear that some forms of expression offer such little value to the core principles underlying the First Amendment that they receive no constitutional protection. The three leading categories of speech that lie beyond the scope of the First Amendment include defamation, speech that incites immanent lawlessness, and obscenity.

As was the case in English common law, *defamation*—whether spoken (*slander*) or written (*libel*)—may be constitutionally proscribed. No one has the right to lie about someone else and cause damage to that person's reputation. Hence, defamation of character forms a valid civil action in spite of the fact that the action involves speech. Public figures, such as politicians, sports figures, and entertainment stars, must clear a high standard to succeed in a lawsuit for defamation. They need to prove not only that the statement at issue was false, but also that the false statement was not an honest mistake. They must show **actual malice**—either that the person who made the statement actually knew it was false or acted with reckless disregard for the truth (i.e., didn't care whether it was true or not).

By 1974, the U.S. Supreme Court made it clear that "under the First Amendment there is no such thing as a false idea. However pernicious an opinion may seem, we depend for its correction not on the conscience of judges and juries but on the competition of other ideas" (*Gertz v. Robert Welch, Inc.*, 1974, pp. 339–340). Thus, in *Brandenburg v. Ohio* (1969), the Court overturned the conviction of Ku Klux Klan leaders for violating a state sedition law. The Court emphasized that the "constitutional guarantees of free speech and free press do not permit a state to forbid or proscribe advocacy of the use of force or of law violation except where such advocacy is directed to inciting or producing imminent lawless action and is likely to incite or produce such actions" (p. 447; see also Pember & Calvert, 2011). A particular type of such speech that teeters on the brink of First Amendment protection is known as

fighting words—"those which by their very utterance inflict injury or tend to incite an immediate breach of the peace" (*Chaplinsky v. New Hampshire*, 1942, p. 571). But just because insults, epithets, or curse words may offend or anger a listener does not transform the offensive language into fighting words (*South Dakota v. Suhn*, 2008). To fall outside the realm of First Amendment protection, fighting words must be used in a face-to-face encounter that is highly likely to trigger an imminent violent response (*Oregon v. Johnson*, 2008).

Finally, obscenity receives no First Amendment protection. But what is obscene as opposed to merely being indecent or even sexually explicit material? The balance of this chapter is devoted to answering this difficult question.

OBSCENITY

For much of U.S. history, the law of obscenity was considered to regulate sex (Post, 1988).

> Laws prohibiting obscenity were understood to stem from "traditional notions, rooted in this country's religious antecedents, of governmental responsibility for communal and individual "decency" and "morality." They protected our common cultural "environment." The constitutional issue posed by such laws, therefore, was whether the First Amendment permitted expression to be suppressed for the purpose of preserving "the purity of the community and . . . the salvation and welfare of the "consumer."
>
> (Post, 1988, pp. 297–298, internal citations omitted)

But obscenity laws are aimed at more than just sex. "The standard dictionary definition of 'obscene' turns on notions of what is offensive to decency, filthy, or disgusting" (Richards, 1974, p. 48). This understanding of the obscene is quite different from that which is merely sexually explicit. Rather, the obscene incorporates notions of "the improper abuse of a bodily function" (Richards, 1974, p. 56). Such an encompassing definition of the obscene was memorialized by the American Law Institute in Section 521.4(1) of its influential Model Penal Code in 1962: "a shameful or morbid interest in nudity, sex, or excretion."

But might reasonable people differ over what constitutes an artistic interest in nudity or a natural or healthy interest in sex? Such inquiry underlies the difficulty in differentiating truly obscene materials that are not protected by the First Amendment from materials that are merely indecent, ranging from the boldly sexually suggestive to the realm of graphically sexually explicit that is subsumed by the term **pornography**, much of which is protected by the First Amendment.

Early Understandings of Obscenity in the United States

During the nineteenth century, harsh restrictions and punishments were implemented for publishers of sexually explicit material. In 1815, for instance, Jesse Sharpless was sanctioned under Philadelphia common law for displaying "for money, to persons . . . a certain lewd, wicked, scandalous, infamous, and obscene painting, representing a man in an obscene, imprudent, and indecent posture with a woman" (as quoted by Cornwell, 2004, p. 46). Around this time, states began enacting statutes to address obscenity, with Vermont leading the way. It was not until 1842 that Congress passed the first federal obscenity statute in conjunction with the Tariff Act, which prohibited the importation of indecent materials into the United States.

The first real crusade to reshape how the government handled sexually explicit material was prompted by Anthony Comstock. After reading literature that he deemed inappropriate, Comstock found the publisher and had him arrested. Finding reward in his actions, he continued on a mission to eliminate explicit materials and eventually founded New York's YMCA Committee for the Suppression of Vice. Under New York law, this organization was empowered with the rights to search, seize, and arrest. With the financial support of J. P. Morgan and Samuel Colgate, Comstock was able to lobby Congress to enact a statute that prohibited the mailing of obscene materials and anything related to birth control or abortion, which was known as the Anti-Obscenity Act of 1873 or the "Comstock Act."

During the Comstock era, many books by classic authors, such as Geoffrey Chaucer, Ernest Hemingway, John Steinbeck, F. Scott Fitzgerald, Daniel Defoe, Voltaire, James Joyce, Walt Whitman, and D. H. Lawrence, were banned. Soon thereafter, the Comstock Act was amended to prohibit sending of obscene materials through the mail. Even today, the U.S. Criminal Code still provides as follows:

> Whoever knowingly uses the mails for the mailing, carriage in the mails, or delivery of anything declared . . . to be nonmailable [by virtue of being obscene] . . . shall be fined under this title or imprisoned not more than five years, or both, for the first such offence, and shall be fined under this title or imprisoned not more than ten years, or both, for each such offense thereafter.
>
> (18 U.S.C. § 1461, 2014)

In order to determine whether materials were classified as obscene, and therefore prohibited to be published or mailed, law enforcement generally relied upon the precedent established in *Rosen v. United States* (1896). The U.S. Supreme Court decided that indecent materials would be assessed using the test adopted in English in *Regina v. Hinklin* (1868), namely whether the material in question tends "to deprave and corrupt those whose minds are open to such immoral influences, and into whose hands a publication of this sort may fall" (p. 371). As a result, a literary work could be deemed obscene for the *potential effect* of an isolated passage on the most susceptible readers or viewers.

Although the *Hicklin* test became the guiding principle for U.S. courts through the early twentieth century, the judiciary was soon called upon again because of the overly broad language outlined in *Regina v. Hinklin* (1868). The *Hinklin* test was put to rest in *United States v. One Book Called "Ulysses" by James Joyce* (1933). In ruling that James Joyce's book *Ulysses* was not obscene, Judge John Woolsey rejected the "isolated passages" and "susceptible person" doctrines of the *Hinklin* test because literary works must be judged by their dominant effect on people. As Judge Woolsey stated, the book "must be tested by the Court's opinion as to its effect on a person with average sex instincts . . . who plays . . . the same role . . . as does the *reasonable man* in the law of torts" (p. 184). Not only did this landmark case mark one of the first times a federal court recognized that obscenity laws may conflict with the First Amendment, but it was also the first case to establish that the conflicting interests underlying obscenity laws and the First Amendment must be considered by examining the materials in question in their entirety, not just on isolated parts.

Roth and the Mid-Twentieth Century

The period between the late nineteenth century and the mid-twentieth century brought significant changes to how the U.S. population received information. Print journalism, especially in most newspapers, became much more professionalized. Largely in response to the sensationalized style of so-called yellow journalism championed by publishers like William Randolph Hearst, mainstream journalism strove to present an objective and balanced style of reporting (Randle, 2001). Indeed, the investigative journalism of that time ushered in some of the reforms of the Progressive Era. Magazine publishing also changed dramatically as a function of the rise of commercial advertising and the availability of four-color printing, resulting in an explosion of magazine options (Randle, 2001). Starting in the 1920s, other media such as radio and motion pictures also became popular means of communicating news, political analysis, and entertainment. In fact, motion pictures were so embraced by 1922 that "the average weekly movie attendance was 40 million with an average weekly household attendance of 1.56" (Randle, 2001, para. 14). By the 1950s, television emerged as a powerful mode of mass communication. As each of these forms of mass communication developed, they increased the channels through which potentially obscene materials could be disseminated. Concerns over indecent material contributing to social decay were used to justify content-based regulations of free expression which, in turn, prompted the courts—and the U.S. Supreme Court, in particular—to examine restrictions under the First Amendment in ways that were previously unnecessary (see Pember & Calvert, 2011).

Following the demise of the *Hinklin* test, new parameters for obscenity were established by the U.S. Supreme Court's decision in *Roth v. United States* (1957). Rather than specifically addressing whether the material presented in the case was obscene, the Court opted to tackle whether obscenity in general was "within the area of protected speech and press" (p. 481).

Delivering the majority opinion for the Court, Justice Brennan concluded that obscenity was not protected under the First Amendment. In his analysis, Brennan began by asserting that when the First Amendment was ratified, there were forms of speech in various states (such as blasphemy and defamation) that were banned or regulated under state law. Although he believed that "[a]ll ideas having even the slightest redeeming social importance—unorthodox ideas, controversial ideas, [and] even ideas hateful to the prevailing climate of opinion" were protected under the First Amendment, obscenity did not qualify for such protection because it is "without redeeming social importance" (*Roth v. United States*, 1957, p. 484).

In addition to offering a logical explanation for obscenity law, Justice Brennan also sought to delineate the meaning of obscenity because the First Amendment was primarily concerned with non-obscene sexual matters. He did not equate sex to obscenity or vice versa: "[o]bscene material is material which deals with sex in a manner appealing to prurient interest" (p. 487). Outlining the definition of *prurient interest*, Brennan referred to the Model Penal Code's draft definition of obscenity as embodying "a shameful or morbid interest in nudity, sex, or excretion" (p. 488). Using this definition of obscenity, and incorporating Judge Woolsey's position in *United States v. One Book Caled "Ulysses" by James Joyce* (1933), Justice Brennan directed judges to examine "the effect of the book, picture, or publication considered as a whole . . . upon the average person in the community, [asking whether the material offends] the common conscience of the community by present-day standards" (*Roth v. United States*, 1957, p. 490). Thus, a work could be adjudicated obscene under *Roth* if three elements were met: (1) the overall theme of a work appeals to the *prurient interest*, (2) the material is patently offensive under contemporary societal standards, and (3) the material is without redeeming social value. Notably, because obscene materials in the United States are limited to those that appeal to the prurient interest, obscenity laws do not apply to violent stories or images that are otherwise devoid of sexually oriented content.

Although Justice Brennan spoke for five justices, there were nuances among the concurring and dissenting opinions that shaped the subsequent precedent on obscenity. Justice Warren, for instance, argued that there should

be greater emphasis on the defendant's conduct than the specific material because it helped influence whether the reader would perceive the work as pornography or otherwise. Consider, for instance, that even if a work were determined to constitute obscenity under *Roth*, the defendant may not be convicted without some culpable state of mind. *Smith v. California* (1959) is a case in point. The Court ruled that a bookstore owner could only be held legally responsible for selling obscene material without *scienter*—knowledge that contents of the material were obscene.

Since the defendant in *Roth* was in the business of marketing material and "plainly engaged in the commercial exploitation of the morbid and shameful craving for materials with prurient effect," Warren affirmed the convictions of the defendant (*Roth v. United States*, 1957, p. 496). On the other hand, those who dissented with the Court's opinion argued that obscenity laws were not punishing individuals for an overt act but rather for provoking bad thoughts, which was unconstitutional under the First Amendment because there must be a relationship connecting the speech to an undesirable action. In short, "[t]he tests by which these convictions were obtained require only the arousing of sexual thoughts. Yet the arousing of sexual thoughts and desires happens every day in normal life in dozens of ways" (*Roth v. United States*, 1957, p. 509, Douglas, J., dissenting).

Ultimately, the decision in *Roth* prompted 25 years of confusion regarding obscenity law because of the overly broad definition that the majority opinion put forth. As Justice Stewart is oft-quoted in a concurring opinion in which he attempted to define the sort of hardcore pornography that is considered obscene, "I shall not today attempt further to define the kinds of material I understand to be embraced within that shorthand description; and perhaps I could never succeed in intelligibly doing so. But I know it when I see it, and the motion picture involved in this case is not that" (*Jacobellis v. Ohio*, 1964, p. 197).

Even though governmental entities may constitutionally criminalize the production and distribution of obscene materials, the same is not true for possession of obscene materials. In *Stanley v. Georgia* (1969), the U.S. Supreme Court upheld the ability of a person to possess obscene materials in the privacy of one's home, reasoning that "[w]hatever the power of the state to control public dissemination of ideas inimical to the public morality, it cannot constitutionally premise legislation on the desirability of controlling a person's private thoughts" (p. 566).

Miller and Current Obscenity Law

Sex and its relationship to obscenity remained highly controversial during the late 1960s and early 1970s. This was due, in large part, to societal concern over an emerging counter-culture whose members protested the Vietnam War, questioned the legitimacy of police power, and participated in a number of acts then considered to be immoral and, in some cases, illegal, such as fornication, vagrancy, and illicit drug use (Lilly, Cullen, & Ball, 2011). Despite the changing mores during this time period, under the leadership of Chief Justice Burger, the U.S. Supreme Court largely

Box 8.1 THE ASSUMPTIONS OF *ROTH*

Implicit in Justice Brennan's rationale in *Roth* (1957) is the psychological assumption that sexual urges are inherently different from other thoughts and emotions. In his opinion on sex, Brennan states that "[s]ex, a great and mysterious motive force in human life, has indisputably been a subject of absorbing interest to mankind through the ages; it is one of the vital problems of human interest and public concern" (p. 487). If sex, however, is just another human motivation, like curiosity or anger, it is difficult to understand why sex-related speech should be judged by a different standard than other speech. Nevertheless, the Court sought to control depictions of sex because the justices seemingly perceived sex to be an especially dangerous instinct. In other words, the *Roth* framework assumes that obscene material will trigger responses that ordinary, reasonable people cannot control, which, in turn, will undermine their ability to function as responsible citizens. Taking Justice Brennan's assumptions about sex into consideration, critically evaluate and answer the following questions:

- Should sex be considered a motivational force different than other forms of motivation (e.g., curiosity, hunger, anger)?
- Why is obscenity treated differently than other offensive forms of speech?
- There is research that links watching violence in movies and in videogames with aggressive or even violent behaviors, especially, but not exclusively, for adolescents and young adults (e.g., Anderson & Bushman, 2001; Bushman, 1995). In fact, such data caused Huesmann and Taylor (2006) to publish an article in the *Annual Review of Public Health* in which they described violence in media as a "threat to public health" (p. 393). Why, then, does sexually explicit media receive limited First Amendment protection—and none if deemed obscene, whereas media depicting graphic violence receives the full protection of the First Amendment?

supported conservative ideals, as indicated by its leading obscenity decision that largely upheld the decision in *Roth*.

The Miller Test

In *Miller v. California* (1973), the appellant had mailed brochures to advertise his sexually explicit illustrated books. The brochures consisted of pictures and drawings that depicted men and women engaging in a variety of sexual activities. One of the recipients of the mailing complained to the police who subsequently arrested Miller for violating the state's obscenity law. He was convicted and appealed. The Court clarified the holding in *Roth* by setting forth a three-part test for obscenity. Under *Miller*, material is obscene if,

1. the average person, applying contemporary community standards, finds that the work, taken as a whole, appeals to the prurient interest (i.e., a shameful or morbid interest in nudity, sex, or excretion);
2. the work depicts, in a patently offensive way, sexual conduct specifically defined by the applicable state law; and
3. the work, taken as a whole, lacks serious literary, artistic, political, or scientific value.
(*Miller v. California*, 1973, p. 24)

The first prong of the *Miller* test mirrors the test set forth in *Roth* with one notable distinction. Whereas *Roth* referenced broad, amorphous contemporary societal standards, *Miller* clarified that trial courts are supposed "to rely on knowledge of the standards of the residents of the community to decide whether the work appeals to a prurient interest" (Pember & Calvert, 2011, p. 475). Thus, there are no national standards for what constitutes obscenity. Rather, local standards govern obscene material. In other words, material that may not be obscene in New York may be obscene elsewhere.

In an attempt to more clearly clarify the kinds of material that fall under the second part of the *Miller* test, the Court offered a few examples. By "patently offensive," the Court was referring to "the representation or description of ultimate sexual acts, normal or perverted, actual or stimulated ... masturbation, excretory functions, and lewd exhibition of the genitals" (*Miller v. California*, 1973, p. 25). Thus, even though courts in Georgia determined that an R-rated movie starring Jack Nicholson and Candice Bergen was obscene, the U.S. Supreme Court reversed the decision because the film did not include graphic depictions of sexual or excretory functions (see *Jenkins v. Georgia*, 1974).

The third and final prong of the *Miller* test refined the portion of *Roth* that required a determination that obscene material be "utterly without redeeming social value." *Miller* clarified this amorphous standard by specifying that "social value" meant "serious literary, artistic, political, or scientific value." By way of example, the *Miller* Court explained that medical books that depict graphic illustrations and descriptions of human anatomy for the purpose of educating physicians would not be considered obscene. But might determinations of what constitutes serious literature or art lie, like beauty, in the eye of the beholder? Consider, for instance, that the manager of an Abercrombie and Fitch store was arrested on obscenity charges for displaying photos of models that included the upper-buttocks of a shirtless young man and the partially bare breast of a young woman (Pember & Calvert, 2011). Although charges were dropped, the arrest demonstrates the subjective nature of obscenity determinations.

In *Pope v. Illinois* (1987), the U.S. Supreme Court clarified that whether a work possesses "serious literary, artistic, political, or scientific value" is not a question to be decided by contemporary community standards. Community standards only guide the determination of the first prong of the *Miller* test concerning whether the material in question appeals to the prurient interest. Rather, the third prong of *Miller* presents a question that transcends the amount of acceptance a work may have won within a given community. Accordingly, in obscenity cases that go to trial, expert testimony is often necessary to help the trier-of-fact determine if the challenged work has "serious literary, artistic, political, or scientific value." But such testimony is not conclusive, as illustrated by *Luke Records, Inc. v. Navarro* (1992). In this case, the rap group "2 Live Crew" released a recording entitled *As Nasty as They Want to Be*. The recording contained both profane and sexually graphic lyrics. It was declared obscene by a Florida judge. The group appealed and won because the prosecution "submitted no evidence to contradict [2 Live Crew's expert] testimony that the work had artistic value" (p. 138). But, as the Law in Action box below illustrates, even with expert testimony, the third prong of the *Miller* test leaves room for subjective opinions.

The Null Effects of Warnings and Good Faith

In *Paris Adult Theatre v. Slaton* (1975), the U.S. Supreme Court was faced with determining whether the defendants' adult theaters were showcasing obscene material in violation of Georgia law. Initially, a judge in bench (non-jury) trial ruled that the theater acted within the constitutionally permissible scope of the First Amendment because the films were only exhibited to consenting adults; the theater clearly notified its audience of the nature of the films; and the theater took precautionary efforts to ensure that the films would not be exposed to minors. Despite the lower court's conclusion, the Supreme Court of Georgia reversed the ruling because the movies shown at the theater were obscene. The steps the theater owners and management had taken to insure that the movies were shown only to consenting adults were irrelevant to the obscene content of the movies themselves. The U.S. Supreme Court agreed, reasoning that

obscene films pose a significant social detriment. According to the Court, there was "ample basis for legislatures to conclude that a sensitive, key relationship of human existence, central to family life, community welfare, and the development of human personality, can be debased and distorted by crass commercial exploitation of sex" (*Paris Adult Theatre v. Slaton*, 1975, p. 63). Thus, the determinative issue in the case was the obscene nature of the movies themselves. But if the movies had not been found to be legally obscene, then the First Amendment would likely have protected the theater owners and operators from criminal liability. Nonetheless, the First Amendment does not create a right for adult establishments to operate anywhere their owners might desire.

Zoning and Regulating Sexually Oriented Businesses

Zoning ordinances may constitutionally regulate where strip clubs, adult movie theaters, and other sexually oriented business establishments may be located. *Renton v. Playtime Theatres, Inc.* (1986) upheld a municipal ordinance prohibiting adult theaters from within 1,000 feet of any residential zone, family dwelling, church, park or school—even though the ordinance left just 5% of the land in the city of Renton, Washington, available for adult-oriented businesses.

Municipalities may also enact ordinances that limit expressive conduct within adult establishments. Therefore, even though exotic dancing is a form of expression protected by the First Amendment, cities can ban fully nude dancing by requiring dancers to wear thongs, G-strings, or pasties (*City of Erie v. Pap's A.M.*, 2000). Similarly, in order to minimize the potentially negative secondary effects of alcohol being served at strip clubs, municipalities may ban the sale of alcohol in adult-oriented establishments in which nudity is allowed (*J.L. Spoons, Inc. v. Dragani*, 2008).

Law in Action INDECENCY, ART, OR OBSCENITY?

The manager of a comic-book store in Dallas, Texas, was convicted of obscenity for selling a Japanese *manga* comic-book, *Demon Beast Invasion: The Fallen*, to an undercover police officer. The comic-book was in an "adults only" area of the store and was not available for minors to purchase.

> It contained graphic images of sexual intercourse, oral sex, male and female genitals in states of arousal, ejaculation, and violent sexual acts. Of particular note was a series of images in which several women were sexually penetrated by roots and branches of a large tree.
>
> (Greene, 2005, p. 174)

The manager was convicted even though the defense had two expert witnesses testify about the serious literary, artistic, and political value of the comic. One of these experts was a professor of Asian Studies and an expert in Japanese *anime* and *manga*. She testified that the comic was part of a series in which the Earth was invaded by demons who lured humans "into sexual encounters by posing as humans for the purposes of propagating a demon race" (p. 174). She explained that the "demon mother" tree had cultural significance to the Japanese as a symbol of nature. She also explained that, in addition to being "beautifully drawn," the work was a commentary on powerlessness. Another expert who had written two books on the medium testified that the comic was one part of a series that "addressed the themes of alien infiltration of Earth culture highly characteristic of Japanese horror and science fiction." Moreover, the entire series emphasized the centrality of serious social conflict—"the value of personal relationships versus one's duty to save mankind" (p. 175). In spite of the expert testimony in the case, a jury convicted the comic-book store manager. That conviction was upheld on appeal by a court that concluded that the "drawings and comments [were] patently offensive and neither advocate[d] nor communicate[d] any ideas or opinions concerning serious literary, artistic, political or scientific values" (*Castillo v. State*, 2002, p. 826). The Supreme Court declined to review the case on appeal, thereby allowing the defendant's sentence of 180 days in jail, a year of probation, and a $4,000 fine to stand.

- Do you agree with the decision in this case? Why or why not?

Obscenity and the Internet

Just as technological developments like the printing press, radio, motion pictures, and television all significantly changed mass media in the past, the advent and evolution of the internet radically transformed not only the ways in which we communicate with each other, but also the ways in which we obtain information. It should come as no surprise that the internet has made it possible to bring pornographic materials to audiences that previously may not have had access to such adult-oriented materials.

Although polls with nonrandom samples often report wildly varying statistics that between 12% of 80% of the internet is devoted to pornography, scientific estimates concerning the amount of pornography on the internet suggests that only about 4% of all websites contain sexually explicit materials (Ogas & Gaddam, 2011). Still, because this accounts for tens of thousands of websites, the internet has made pornography easily accessible even to those who are too young to access such material legally. A study published in the medical journal *Pediatrics* reported that 42% of a nationally representative sample of 1,500 internet users between the ages 10 to 17 had been exposed to online pornography within a one-year period, two-thirds of whom reported unwanted exposure to such material (Wolak, Mitchell, & Finkelhor, 2007; see also Jones, Mitchell, & Finkelhor, 2012). Such exposure has potentially adverse health risks for adolescents. For example, even exposure to sexual media that is not sexually explicit is related to teenagers' likelihood of engaging in sexual activity, as well as an increased likelihood of coercive sexual victimization, including attempted and completed rape (Ybarra, Strasburger, & Mitchell, 2014).

Undoubtedly, some of the sexually explicit materials available on the internet are obscene under *Miller* even though federal law prohibits the transmission of obscene material over the internet in the same way federal law prohibits obscene materials from being transmitted by any form of interstate commerce, such as trucks, cars, trains, mail, or satellite service (see 18 U.S.C. § 1465). Congress attempted to ban "indecent" and "patently offensive" material from being transmitted over the internet when it enacted the Communications Decency Act of 1996. But the U.S. Supreme Court declared the law unconstitutional under the First Amendment in *Reno v. ACLU* (1997). The Court reasoned that the law was vague because the terms "indecent" and "patently offensive" lacked precise definition. Additionally, the Court found that the Communications Decency Act was overbroad because it attempted "to deny minors access to potentially harmful speech . . . effectively suppresses a large amount of speech that

adults have a constitutional right to receive and to address to one another," including information on birth control practices, human sexuality, sexually transmitted diseases, and the consequences of rape (p. 874).

Perhaps the biggest problem with obscene materials on the internet concerns the availability of child pornography. Because the trafficking of such material encourages and compounds the sexual abuse and exploitation of children (Wolak, Liberatore, & Levine, 2014), a number of laws have been enacted to combat the proliferation of obscene materials involving minors.

CHILD PORNOGRAPHY

Although sexualized drawings, paintings, and stories of children have existed for ages, the invention of the camera in the mid-1800s ushered in a new method of producing and distributing sexualized images of children (Wortley & Smallbone, 2012). Relaxed censorship standards in the 1960s and 1970s increased the availability of child pornography. But "law enforcement agencies had considerable success in stemming the trafficking of these traditional hard-copy forms" (Wortley & Smallbone, 2012, p. 5). Still, it is important to keep in mind that protecting children from sexual exploitation is a relatively modern phenomenon. Consider that the age of consent for sexual activity was set at ten years until the 1880s in several U.S. states (Jenkins, 2001). In 1977, "only two states had legislation specifically outlawing the use of children in obscene material" (Wortley & Smallbone, 2012, p. 6). And, the first federal law prohibiting the production and commercial distribution of obscene materials involving minors under the age of 16 was not enacted until 1978 when Congress passed the Protection of Children Against Sexual Exploitation Act (1978). Soon thereafter, the federal courts began to grapple with the First Amendment implications of these laws.

Per Se Rules on Child Pornography

In *New York v. Ferber* (1982), the defendant sold two films to an undercover police officer that depicted underage boys masturbating. The defendant was charged with and convicted of two counts of violating a state law criminalizing the knowing promotion or distribution of any material depicting sexual performances by children under the age of 16. An intermediate appellate court upheld the convictions, but the highest court in New York reversed this decision on the grounds that the statute was "underinclusive because it discriminated against visual portrayals of children engaged in sexual activity by not also prohibiting the distribution of films of other dangerous activity. It was also overbroad because it prohibited the distribution of materials produced outside the State, as well as materials, such as medical books and educational sources" (*New York v. Ferber*, 1982, p. 752). The U.S. Supreme Court reversed.

Although the Court recognized that laws aimed at curbing child pornography may run the risk of suppressing protected expression, the Court made it clear that child pornography is, per se, obscene and, therefore, is entitled to no First Amendment protection. The conclusion rested on several lines of reasoning. First, the state has a compelling interest in safeguarding children by ensuring that their physiological, physical, cognitive, and emotional well-being are not disrupted as they develop into young adults. Second, "[t]he distribution of photographs and films depicting sexual activity by juveniles is intrinsically related to the sexual abuse of children" (*New York v. Ferber*, 1982, p. 759). Third, the production, distribution, and advertisement of child pornography provide an economic motive for the industry to persist. Conversely, outlawing child pornography helps to prevent future sexual exploitation of children. Fourth, children engaging in lewd sexual conduct via live performances or photographs offer no redeeming literary, artistic, political, or scientific value. Lastly, whether the First Amendment protects speech depends on its content. In the case of child pornography, it lacks this protection because "the evil to be restricted so overwhelmingly outweighs the expressive interests, if any, at stake, that no process of case-by-case adjudication is required" (*New York v. Ferber*, 1982, pp. 763–764).

The Court issued another per se rule concerning child pornography in *Osborne v. Ohio* (1990). Recall that *Stanley v. Georgia* (1969) upheld the right of an individual to possess obscene materials in the privacy of one's own home. *Osborne* rejected applying *Stanley* to the possession of child pornography. The Court reasoned that because "safeguarding the physical and psychological well-being of a minor is compelling," prohibiting the possession of child pornography—even in the privacy of one's own home—"passes muster under the First Amendment" (*Osborne v. Ohio*, 1990, p. 109).

Federal Laws Targeting Child Pornography

Two years after *Ferber* was decided, Congress passed the Child Protection Act of 1984. It criminalized the production, distribution, or possession of child pornography, regardless of whether the material was obscene under *Miller* or *Ferber*. The Child Protection Act, as amended, defines child pornography as the "visual depiction" of anyone under the age of 18 engaging in "sexually explicit conduct," which includes "(i) sexual intercourse, including genital-genital, oral-genital, anal-genital, or oral-anal, whether between persons of the same or opposite sex; (ii) bestiality; (iii) masturbation; (iv) sadistic or masochistic abuse; or (v) lascivious exhibition of the genitals or pubic area of any person" (18 U.S.C. § 2256(2)(A)). In *United States v. Dost* (1986), a federal district court ruled that nude pictures of minors photographed in sexually suggestive poses fell within the "lascivious exhibition" provision and, therefore, constitutes child pornography.

Two years later, the Child Sexual Abuse and Pornography Act of 1986 criminalized all advertisements for child pornography. That same year, the Child Abuse Victims' Rights Act of 1986 imposed civil liability on child pornographers for any injuries, including psychological ones, sustained by children. Two years later, Congress enacted the Child Protection and Obscenity Enforcement Act of 1988 to outlaw the use of computers to traffic child pornography. Furthermore, immediately following the decision in *Osborn v. Ohio* (1990), Congress passed the Child Protection Restoration and Penalties Enhancement Act of 1990, making it a federal crime to possess three or more child pornography items.

In 1996, Congress enacted the Child Pornography Prevention Act (CPPA) of 1996. It was the first law of the modern era targeting child pornography that was subsequently declared unconstitutional. Prior to the passage of this law, child pornography could only be criminalized if it involved the *actual depiction* of children engaging in lewd sexual conduct. The CPPA sought to extend such laws in the Digital Age by making it illegal to produce or distribute computer-generated and computer-altered sexual images of children (see Jasper, 2009). The law attempted to criminalize so-called "virtual kiddie porn" because even though an actual child was not involved in the production of the offending images, distribution of such material nonetheless encouraged pedophilia. In *Ashcroft v. Free Speech Coalition* (2002), the U.S. Supreme Court declared the CPPA unconstitutionally overbroad. As Justice Kennedy stated,

The mere tendency of speech to encourage unlawful acts is not a sufficient reason for banning it . . . The Government has shown no more than a remote connection between speech that might encourage thoughts or impulses and any resulting child abuse. Without a significantly stronger, more direct connection, the Government may not prohibit speech on the ground

that it may encourage pedophiles to engage in illegal conduct.

(pp. 253–254)

In the wake of *Ashcroft v. Free Speech Coalition* (2002), Congress enacted the Prosecutorial Remedies and Other Tools to End the Exploitation of Children Today Act of 2003 (PROTECT Act). The Act prohibits "pandering" (i.e., knowingly advertising, promoting, or soliciting) material "in a manner that reflects the belief, or that is intended to cause another to believe" that the advertised material is child pornography involving real minors, even if the underlying material does not, in fact, include real minors or is otherwise completely innocuous" (Pember & Calvert, 2011, p. 481). The U.S. Supreme Court upheld the constitutionality of the PROTECT Act in *United States v. Williams* (2008). The Court made it clear that it was not overruling *Ashcroft v. Free Speech Coalition* (2002): "Simulated child pornography will be as available as ever, so long as it is offered and sought *as such*, and not as real child pornography" (*United States v. Williams*, 2008, p. 303, italics in original).

Sexting as Child Pornography

In the 1970s, the Polaroid camera delivered self-developing photos, a feat that not only seemed miraculous, but also allowed people to take racy pictures without the need to bring film to a photo processing store. Other technological developments, ranging from the hand-held video camera to modern digital photography and videography, not only represent the continued evolution of media, but also the possibility of increased privacy for amateur sexually oriented materials. But the proliferation of cell phones, especially smart phones with high-quality cameras and video-recorders built into them, appears to have decreased privacy given the ease with which such images are shared.

Mobile devices with built-in cameras have created a "new frontier for the production and or distribution of child pornography, including self-produced images" (Leary, 2007, p. 24). Indeed, for a disturbingly large number of teenagers,

> the combination of technology, hormones, and stupidity has led to a practice called "**sexting**," the cell phone texting of sexually-explicit photos [and videos], often of themselves. What's worse, most of these kids are hitting "send" without realizing that in many states, their actions could violate child pornography laws.
> (O'Brien, 2009, p. 10A; see also Calvert, 2009a, 2009b)

Research suggests that approximately "4% of cell-owning teens ages 12–17 say they have sent sexually suggestive nude or nearly nude images of themselves to someone else via text messaging," whereas "15% of cell-owning teens ages 12–17 say they have received sexually suggestive nude or nearly nude images of someone they know via text messaging on their cell phone" (Lenhart, 2009, p. 3). In a similar national survey, Mitchell, Finkelhor, Jones, and Wolak (2012) found that approximately 2.5% of teens reported creating nude images of themselves and 7.1% receiving such an image. Although these estimates may be somewhat conservative given the sensitive subject matter, the issue has been quite burdensome for the criminal justice system because "hormone-raging teens with image-transmitting technologies . . . together in a sex-saturated society replete with outdated laws . . . [is a] sure fire recipe for legal trouble" (Calvert, 2009a, p. 1).

Most states lack legislation specifically addressing sexting. Some states, however, have used their child pornography laws to prosecute sexting by adolescents (Fradella & Galeste, 2011; Hiffa, 2010). Under such laws, teenagers may be charged with possession and/or distribution of child pornography if they are caught with explicit images on their cell phone. The

irony, of course, is that the same laws that were meant to protect minors from sexual exploitation by adults are now being used to punish adolescents for engaging in what Dr. Peter Cumming asserts is the "modern-day equivalent of playing 'spin the bottle' " (as cited in Fradella & Galeste, 2011, p. 443).

Most instances of teenage sexting are never brought to the attention of legal authorities. When they are, the cases are typically either handled informally or punished minimally (Quinn, 2010). But some cases are prosecuted similarly to other child pornography cases leading some critics to claim that law enforcement is "so determined to save teens from themselves . . . [that] they're willing to brand them for life in the process" (Kalson, 2009).

One of the most renowned sexting cases to receive media attention is that of Philip Alpert. While living in Florida, 18-year-old Alpert was dating his 16-year-old girlfriend. Over the duration of their two-year relationship, she sent him many nude and provocative pictures of herself. Following a fight one night, Alpert made the decision to retaliate by sending the explicit photos of his girlfriend to her friends and family. Unaware of the consequences for this action, Alpert was arrested, charged, and convicted for the distribution of child pornography. As a result, he was mandated to register as a sex offender within the state of Florida and placed on probation for five years. The collateral consequences of his sex-offender status and felony conviction were expulsion from college, harsh living restrictions, and employment tribulations because he was perceived as someone who has committed a sex offense against a child victim. Interestingly, while Alpert was charged with the distribution of child pornography, his girlfriend, who created the images, was not punished for its production.

In 2009, the Iowa Supreme Court upheld a felony conviction for knowingly disseminating obscene material to a minor (*State v. Canal*, 2009). The case involved 18-year-old Jorge Canal, who texted a naked picture of himself to a 14-year-old female friend after numerous requests from her; the picture was captioned "I love you." The girl's mother saw the picture and turned it over to the police. Canal was convicted by a jury. He appealed to the Iowa Supreme Court, arguing that the photo was not obscene because the image only appealed to a natural interest in sex rather than a prurient interest in sex. But the court rejected this argument. Canal, therefore, had to register as a sex offender and was placed on probation.

Although the aftermath of the Canal and Alpert cases may seem somewhat extreme given the circumstances, there are instances when malice or coercion may warrant more severe sanctions. In 2010, for example, 19-year-old Anthony Stancl deceived fellow classmates by fictitiously posing as a girl on Facebook and convincing 31 males to send him nude pictures of themselves. Stancl then used the photos to blackmail at least seven of his classmates—all of whom were between the ages 15 to 17—into performing sexual acts with him. Stancl had threatened that he would widely distribute the nude images of his victims at school. Once law enforcement was notified, Stancl was arrested and charged with two felony counts of sexual abuse of a child. He was convicted and sentenced to 15 years in prison (Johnson & Seibel, 2009). Of course, the Stancl case involved coercive sex, whereas the sexting at issue in the cases of Philip Alpert and Jose Canal did not.

Despite the claim that there is no difference between sexted images and child pornography once such material is made available on the internet, a critical aspect of teen sexting demarcates it from "traditional" child pornography. Sexted images are usually self-created by a minor motivated by normal adolescent curiosity and sexual exploration. The lack of any child abuse or exploitation places sexting by teenagers in a qualitatively different position than "lascivious [images] of the genitals or pubic area" that were taken to exploit an adolescent minor 918 U.S.C. § 2256(2)(A)9.

In light of such a difference, at least 21 states have enacted legislation to address incidents of sexting among minors since 2009.[4] Most of these laws approach the problem in one of two ways, either by explicitly exempting teenagers who sext with each other from being prosecuted under state child pornography laws, or by incorporating so-called "Romeo and Juliet provisions" into their child pornography laws. The latter approach amends pre-existing child pornography laws to include an age gap provision. Minors who sext with other teenagers within the relevant age-range window are either exempt from prosecution or are punished at a much lower level—such as for a misdemeanor offense, rather than a felony—and are usually exempted from having to register as a sex offender (Hinduja & Patchin, 2014; Olszewski, 2005). Some states have supplemented age-gap provisions to add additional legislative deterrents to sexting (Szymialis, 2010). For example, in Arizona, minors are provided a defense if "they did not ask for the image; attempted to destroy or delete it; or reported it to a parent, school official, or law enforcement; and did not further distribute it" (Szymialis, 2010, p. 320; see also ARIZ. REV. STAT. ANN. § 8–309(c), 2015). If, however, there is any type of malicious conduct during the act of sexting (e.g., the image was not taken voluntarily), a harsher statutory punishment is authorized to reflect the increased severity of the offense.

Some states have designed diversion programs for adolescent sexters. New Jersey, for instance, gives minors the opportunity to avoid punishment by attending an educational program, provided that they are first-time offenders who were unaware that their actions constituted a crime (N.J. STAT. ANN. § 2A:4A-71.1, 2012).

PORNOGRAPHY

Pornography is hard to define, although most people "know it when [they] see it (*Jacobellis v. Ohio*, 1964, p. 197, Stewart, J., concurring). Today, most people define pornography as printed or visual materials containing the explicit description or display of sexual organs or sexual activity that are intended to cause sexual arousal. Although pornography that is not obscene is entitled to First Amendment protection as a form of free expression, its constitutionally protected status does not translate into sexually explicit material being noncontroversial. In fact, the terms "obscenity" and "pornography" are often used interchangeably, even though they are discrete concepts (Brest & Vandenberg, 1987; Wilcox, 1987). That conflation of the two terms may be due, in part, to the old Hicklin test for obscenity which caused "governmental censorship of a wide range of materials" (Pember & Calvert, 2011, p. 474). Indeed, until the decision in *Miller v. California* (1973), many jurisdictions had anti-pornography ordinances or laws that were justified under the governing obscenity standards of the time (Downs, 1989). Another contributing fact may be the name of a commission appointed by President Lyndon Johnson in 1967: the U.S. Commission on Obscenity and Pornography.

The U.S. Commission on Obscenity and Pornography

This "blue ribbon panel" conducted a multi-year study on the effects of sexually explicit materials. Part of the motivation for the creation of this Commission stemmed from the growth of the pornography industry during the sexual revolution. Print media had been the primary delivery system for such materials since the invention of the printing press. And although print media continued to be the dominant delivery mechanism for sexually oriented materials through the 1960s and 1970s, improved printing technologies in the 1970s "permitted significant qualitative improvements in the glossy magazines, as well as new entrants to the market like *Hustler*"

and *Penthouse* (Coopersmith, 1998, p. 100).

The U.S. Commission on Obscenity and Pornography found that although pornographic materials were inappropriate for children, viewing of such materials by normal adults was not harmful nor did it play a significant role in contributing to deviant or criminal behavior (President's Commission on Obscenity and Pornography, 1970). Because the Commission concluded that pornography and obscenity were not a major social problem (Brest & Vandenberg, 1987; Wilcox, 1987), it recommended the expansion of sex-education programs and increased funding for research on the effects of pornography.

By the time the Commission delivered its report, Richard Nixon had become the president. He rejected the report and its recommendations to relax efforts to curb obscenity, claiming that it came to morally bankrupt conclusions. However, many liberals—including large groups of women—claimed that the Commission's report represented a much-needed start toward liberating people from the repressive notions of sexuality of the past (Brest & Vandenberg, 1987; Segal, 1998).

As the formerly fringe counter-culture of the 1960s became more mainstream in the 1970s, sexual mores in the United States changed (Borstelmann, 2012).

Sex seemed to be newly ubiquitous in the culture, or at least much less hidden than in the past. Whether denouncing or celebrating the trend, Americans talked about it and, in a common phrase of the era, "did it." Books such as *The Joy of Sex* and *Everything You Always Wanted to Know about Sex* became runaway best sellers and were quite explicit; a decade earlier, they would have been considered pornographic. . . . In no realm was the coarsening—or liberating—quality of America's free-market culture more obvious than the metastasizing pornography industry, particularly films. Pornography involved the portrayal of explicit and graphic sexual behavior, particularly genitalia, separated from emotion and relationships. What was new in the 1970s was not pornographic materials themselves, but rather their introduction into the mainstream of American culture.

The mainstreaming of hard-core pornography reached a new high—or low—with the appearance of *Deep Throat* in 1972. . . . It was the first hard-core film to reach millions of middle-class Americans, women as well as men, and to be reviewed in mainstream newspapers, including the *New York Times*, which labeled it "porno chic."

(Borstelmann, 2012, pp. 163–164)

Although social change ushered in the "porno chic" era, the profitability of X-rated movies is what truly spurred the growth of the adult film industry in the 1970s. "*Deep Throat* cost $25,000 to make, but earned over $50 million" by the mid-1990s (Coopersmith, 1998, pp. 101–102)—a figure that grew to over $100 million once re-released on DVD (Borstelmann, 2012). Although a few other films of the porno chic era netted similarly high profits, such as *Behind the Green Door* (1972) and *The Devil in Miss Jones* (1973), most adult movies cost between $75,000 and $115,000 to make, "but usually earned $300,000 within 18 months" (Coopersmith, 1998, p. 102). As the adult film industry grew, the new social acceptability of pornography led to the expansion of adult-oriented businesses, especially in major metropolitan areas. In Manhattan alone, "the number of pornographic businesses rose from nine in 1965 to 245 in 1977" (Borstelmann, 2012, p. 165). Moreover, sexually explicit scenes that bordered on the pornographic started appearing in mainstream Hollywood movies, such as Marlon Brando's performance in *Last Tango in Paris* (1973). But no single factor was more responsible for the growth of the adult film industry than the technological advancements that led to home videocassette recorders. Videotapes "allowed viewers to watch whatever films they wanted in the privacy of their own households. Viewing pornography no longer required a trip to a public theater. Adult cinemas closed by the hundreds. Pornography came home instead" (Borstelmann, 2012, p. 165). Indeed, by the late 1970s, pornographic movies accounted for more than half of all prerecorded videotape sales (Coopersmith, 1998).

Social conservatives viewed the omnipresence of sex in American culture as a symptom of a larger social problem concerning the erosion of traditional moral values in the United States. Older Americans and evangelical Christian groups lamented the broader social impact of the 1960s counter-culture. They blamed the pornography, abortion, homosexuality, feminism, and affirmative action of the 1960s. Such concerns prompted President Ronald Reagan to form another federal commission to study the effects of pornography in connection with his signing of the Child Protection Act of 1984.

The Meese Commission

The Meese Commission was formally known as the Attorney General's Commission on Pornography. It was commonly referred to as the Meese Commission because President Reagan charged his Attorney General, Edwin Meese, with overseeing it.

The Meese Commission published its nearly 2,000-page report in 1986 revealing troubling aspects of the pornography industry and reporting on the harmful effects of pornography on the citizenry (Paletz, 1988; Wilcox, 1987). The Meese Commission differed from the U.S. Commission on Obscenity and Pornography in two important ways. First and foremost, the U.S. Commission on Obscenity and Pornography comprised a blue-ribbon panel of experts; in contrast, Meese appointed an 11-member panel comprising a majority of anti-pornography crusaders (Wilcox, 1987). Second, for its 1970 report, the U.S. Commission on Obscenity and Pornography funded more than 80 independent studies on the effects of pornography. In contrast, the Meese Commission relied primarily on public hearings and only one piece of original "research" that was performed by the U.S. Surgeon General C. Everett Koop for the Meese Commission. This so-called "research," however, occurred during a closed, weekend workshop of "recognized authorities" in the field. These authorities allegedly reached "consensus" on the following five points:

1. Children and adolescents who participate in the production of pornography experience adverse, enduring effects.
2. Prolonged use of pornography increases beliefs that less common sexual practices are more common.
3. Pornography that portrays sexual aggression as pleasurable for the victim increases the acceptance of the use of coercion in sexual relations.
4. Acceptance of coercive sexuality appears to be related to sexual aggression.
5. In laboratory studies measuring short-term effects, exposure to violent pornography increases punitive behavior toward women.
(Koop, 1987, p. 945)

The report concluded that "[a]lthough the evidence may be slim, we nevertheless know enough to conclude that pornography does present a clear and present danger to American public health" (Koop, 1987, p. 944).

But some workshop participants objected to the wording of the report and reported that the participants had not reached "consensus" on a number of the points. Indeed, writing in the *American Psychologist*, Neil Malamuth stated that although "the Surgeon General is entitled to his own opinions in this matter, . . . it would be wrong to conclude that . . . they were endorsed by all of the workshop's participants" (Malamuth, 1989, p. 580; see also Linz, Donnerstein, & Penrod, 1987).

But criticism of the Meese Commission went beyond the Surgeon General's work-

shop report. Media reports suggested that much of the visual representations of pornography shown during the Commission meetings were exceptionally violent so as to present a distorted view of pornographic materials to Commission members (Wilcox, 1987). But regardless of whether the images shown to members of the Commission were intentionally misrepresentative of mainstream pornography, it is clear that the conclusions in the final report suffered from serious errors in data interpretation, if not purposeful bias. In fact, two of the three female members of the Commission, Dr. Judith Becker (Director of the Sexual Behavior Clinic at the New York State Psychiatric Institute) and Ellen Levine (editor of *Woman's Day*), dissented from the final report because they objected to its mischaracterization of the available research data when the report concluded there was a causal link between pornography and violence.

Externally, the Commission's final report was highly criticized by researchers who argued that the report deliberately distorted survey research to support a political agenda (Bates & Donnerstein, 1990; Wilcox, 1987). Consider, for example, that feminist activist Andrea Dworkin appeared before the Commission and claimed that the vast majority (65 to 70%) of women involved in the pornography industry—from writers to prostitutes—were victims of child abuse or incest, "though she supplied no evidence to support this assertion" (Antoniou, 2012, p. 23). The report was found to be so misrepresentative of research that a handful of scholars including Edward Donnerstein, Daniel Linz, and Neil Malamuth, issued statements claiming the inaccurate portrayal the Meese Report concluded of their work (Bates & Donnerstein, 1990; Linz, Donnerstein, & Penrod, 1987). They claim the report included factual errors and unsupported conclusions, none of which were grounded in empirical evidence.[5] Donnerstein and Linz (1986), for example, suggested that violence, which is not depicted in most pornography nearly as much as the

Meese Commission originally reported, was the real social issue (see also Scott, 1987).

In October of 1986, the nonpartisan Congressional Research Service (a branch of the Library of Congress) released a legal analysis of the Meese Commission's final report. It concluded that, even if all of the controversial assertions contained in the Meese Commission's report were accepted as valid, "they do not appear to approach the *Brandenburg* incitement standard which must currently be met before constitutionally protected materials may be regulated" (Reimer, 1986, p. 12). In other words, the conclusion that pornography presented a "clear and present danger to American public health" (Koop, 1987, p. 944) was not legally justified under the First Amendment. Hence, although laws governing obscenity and child pornography could be strictly enforced, "courts and legislature are limited as to the actions they can take against much pornographic (but non-obscene) material" (Reimer, 1986, p. 13). The legally protected status of such materials notwithstanding, they nonetheless continue to stir political and social controversy.

Contrasting Liberal, Conservative, and Feminist Views on Pornography

Differing views on pornography and its regulation center on three issues: (1) the nature and implications of sex, (2) the function of sexual imagery, and (3) the appropriate role of law in the regulation of sexually explicit materials (Hoffman, 1985, p. 3; Zurcher & Kirkpatrick, 1976).

The conservative approach to pornography aligns with Lord Patrick Devlin's views on legal moralism (see Chapter 3). Consistent with other positions taken by legal moralists concerning the legislation of morality, the conservative approach is rooted in religious beliefs, specifically, with regard to pornography, the viewpoint that sex is morally wrong unless it occurs under prescribed circumstances—namely within the confines of a lawful marriage (Griffin, 1982; Zurcher & Kirkpatrick, 1976). Thus, conservatives often view images of sex that are isolated from love and commitment as corrupting the value of the institution of marriage and contributing to a demise in the quality of community and social life (Zurcher & Kirkpatrick, 1976).[6] Therefore, in the name of protecting the moral decency of the citizenry, conservatives conclude that pornography should not be protected by the First Amendment because it harms the institution of the family as well as escalating social decay.

In contrast, liberal views not only tolerate the expression of self via sexual activity, but also embrace it (Hoffman, 1985). Recall that classical liberalism, rooted in the works of philosophers such as John Stuart Mill and H. L. A. Hart, posits that the law should not be used as a tool to regulate morality, but only to restrict behaviors that cause harm to others (see Chapter 3). Thus, the liberal approach to pornography is not concerned with the potential corrupting effects of sexually explicit materials, but rather emphasizes "the inappropriateness of any government efforts to define corruption in the area of consensual sexual relations" (Hoffman, 1985, p. 508). In other words, just as the law protects consenting adults in their sexual relationships, so too should the production and consumption of sexually explicit materials be protected, especially since religion/religious beliefs should not justify governmental intrusion into the realm of sexual behavior between consenting adults (Ackerman, 1980). The defining question for those who espouse a liberal perspective on pornography involves informed consent. Presuming that sexually explicit materials were created by consenting adults and are viewed by consenting adults, the liberal position espouses that liberty must be defended against moralism and paternalism. In other words, absent coercion, consenting adults should be free to make or view pornography in the same ways that they are free (also absent coercion) to engage in a wide range of sexual behaviors to satisfy their sexual tastes.

As with many other specific applications of the Hart–Devlin debate (see Chapter 3), the liberal and legal moralist/conservative viewpoints leave little room for agreement. "Liberal accusations of paternalism are met with conservative accusations of anarchy and license. Conservatives defend [their] underlying moral position by arguing that liberty divorced from virtue is not worthy of political commitment (Hoffman, 1985, p. 509). The only area for potential agreement between the two positions might be the role that empirical research can play in helping us understand the effects of pornography. Unsurprisingly, as the previously summarized arguments over the conclusions in the Meese Commission report evidence, liberals and conservatives often disagree about the meaning of empirical findings. But feminist discourse has provided another lens through which the debate on pornography may be viewed that goes beyond the traditional liberal/conservative philosophical divide.

> Feminists differ considerably from both conservatives and liberals in their responses to all three of the issues delineating political positions on pornography. These differences are largely attributable to the fact that the focal point of the feminist view is neither virtue nor liberty but, instead, equality. This different focus produces a crucial insight: only from a male perspective, whether liberal or conservative, does pornography seems to be primarily about sex. Feminists emphasize equality in sexual relations and evaluate sexually-oriented materials in that light. Pornography, so viewed, is not so much about sex as it is about power.
>
> (Hoffman, 1985, p. 510)

Interestingly, feminist approaches to pornography share a common goal with the conservative approach—namely the legal regulation of the materials at issue. But they arrive at their conclusions from radically different arguments. Some feminists argue that a subset of pornography can be erotic and promote equality by presenting egalitarian images of sex and sexuality (e.g., Steinem, 1980; Tong, 1982). This perspective, of course, shares little with the conservative viewpoint that pornography material is indecent and lacks virtue, regardless of content, (Faust, 1980) and, therefore, corrupts the already precarious social order (Griffin, 1982). Indeed, the mainstream feminist perspective on **erotica** (the preferred feminist term for sexually explicit materials that is not degrading to women) poses an even stronger challenge to the conservative position than the liberal position on pornography by supporting depictions of human sexuality that show women as equal sexual partners to men.

In contrast, mainstream feminists object to pornography that degrades or objectifies women. In fact, they argue that such images serve to reify male dominance in society which, in turn, causes harm to women. Because this type of pornography causes harm (the *sine qua non* of liberalism's justification for using law as a tool to regulate human behavior), mainstream feminists argue that such pornography should be legally regulated. This argument departs from the liberal perspective's focus on liberty. Specifically, liberals maintain that pornographers have free-expression rights to create sexually explicit materials, even if the images do not fall within the feminist definition of erotica. In contrast, given the harm caused to women when pornography objectifies or degrades women, feminists, in a departure from the liberal view, maintain that censorship on the production and consumption of such pornography is warranted (Steinem, 1980; Rodgerson & Wilson, 1991; Tong, 1982).

Another strand of feminist thought takes the censorship argument to a more extreme level. Recall from Chapter 5 that Susan Brownmiller (1975) argued that sexual assaults of women by men are crimes of violence and power, rather than lust. Building on that logic, some feminists argued that all sexually explicit depictions of women constitute female victimization (e.g., Dworkin, 1979). In other words there is no distinction between erotica and other forms of pornography; the former is merely a subcategory of the latter and the entirety of such sexually explicit materials does not represent a form of sexual expression that should receive First Amendment protection. Rather, pornography is a form of male power in which women are dominated, humiliated, objectified, and abused into positions of sexual subservience to men. This, in turn, legitimates the subjugation of women in ways that perpetuate other forms of harm to women by conflating sex with rape, sexual violence, and sexual harassment (see MacKinnon, 1987).

Feminism and the Anti-Pornography Movement

Feminists began to express their opposition to most pornography in the 1970s (see, e.g., Dworkin, 1979; Griffin, 1982), after the U.S. Supreme Court extended First Amendment protections to a vast array of sexual material (Brest & Vandenberg, 1987). Led by scholar-activists like Andrea Dworkin and Catharine MacKinnon, feminists debated the difference between erotica and pornography and the anti-pornography campaigns that stemmed from their positions (Brest & Vandenberg, 1987; Segal, 1998). For example, in Dworkin's (1979) influential book *Pornography: Men Possessing Women*, she argued that the devaluation of women was inherent in the patriarchal society in which pornography is used as a tool to maintain men's power over women.

Other feminists, however, voiced concern over anti-pornography campaigns. Some argued that anti-pornography feminists were unsympathetic to class privilege and the self-determination of sex workers. Indeed, some feminists levied charges of hypocrisy at anti-pornography feminists because the latter

group displayed sexually explicit images during their anti-porn campaigns (see Hoffman, 1985; Rodgerson & Wilson, 1991).

Most anti-pornography feminists maintain that sexually explicit images represent a unique marketing technique by men for men that serves the purpose of men's sexual pleasure. They argue that such imagery inherently objectifies women by misrepresenting women's bodies and women's subservient sexual desires, and that both are reinforced through pornography's anonymity (Dworkin, 1979; Griffin, 1982). Moreover, they argue that the widespread success of the multibillion dollar pornography industry affirms the sexual rights of males over females in a symbolic way that reinforces sexist attitudes in an already sexist society (Gubar, 1987). Accordingly, they assert that pornography should be regulated in such a way as to equalize women's rights to men in society (see also Itzin, 1992; MacKinnon, 1987). Three key points are central to their argument:

1. Pornography is the theory; rape is the practice. In other words, rapists will adhere to the meanings pornography provides (i.e., by mimicking the sexual violence present in some pornography).
2. Pornography in and of itself is a form of violence against women in that the process of making it and the images it portrays are harmful against all women at all times.
3. Pornography is a stimulus to sexual hatred. This idea posits that if male desire is predicated on the violent images depicted in pornography, then his desires will lead to misogyny, not just lust. Thus, the desire for sex converts to a desire for power or harm in all heterosexual encounters.

Oddly enough, some of these points are part and parcel of the conservative/legal moralist position that pornography causes social harm.

Liberals and feminists opposed to the censorship of pornography take issue with each of the three arguments advocated by anti-pornography feminists. First, they point to the methodological flaws of the research that finds a causal link between pornography and sexual assault. Indeed, such evidence is weak and inconsistent, at best (Dwyer, 2008; Ferguson & Hartley, 2009). In 1993, Ronald Dworkin wrote, "No reputable study has concluded that pornography is a significant cause of sexual crime: many of them conclude, on the contrary, that the causes of violent personality lie mainly in childhood, before exposure to pornography can have had any effect, and that desire for pornography is a symptom rather than a cause of deviance" (Dworkin, 1993, p. 38; see also Feinberg, 1985). Since then, social scientists have argued that "it is time to discard the hypothesis that pornography contributes to increased sexual assault behavior" (Ferguson & Hartley, 2009, p. 323). As previously explained in the context of criticisms to the Meese Commission report, research suggests that violent images —not nonviolent sexually explicit ones— are correlated with rape and other forms of sexual violence against women (see Linz, Donnerstein, & Penrod, 1987).

Second, violence against women in pornography is not portrayed nearly as frequently as is often depicted in the pro-censorship propaganda. "In fact, as noted by Palys (1986), nonviolent pornography tends to depict few acts of sexualized aggression as well as egalitarian sexual relationships between males and females" (Ferguson & Hartley, 2009, p. 324). For instance, the most popular and widely viewed pornographic magazines— *Playboy* and *Penthouse*—rarely, if ever, portray violence against women. Moreover, the argument that making pornography is a violent act against women assumes that all women do not enjoy sex and are forced to engage in sex by men, which is simply not the case (Rodgerson & Wilson, 1991). This argument is undercut by powerful women in pornography who find their roles as models, directors, and producers self-empowering (e.g., Mayhem & Lim, 2010; Small, 2011; Sprinkle, 2001). Self-described *pro-sex feminists* or *sex-positive feminists* (e.g., McElroy, 1995; Rubin, 1984; Strossen, 1993; Willis, 1992) similarly argue that when women take charge of erotica, they can construct female identities that are erotic, egalitarian, and even educational (see Ciclitira, 2004).

The third response to the pro-censorship feminists is that it lacks both empirical and even logical support. If pornography truly were an incitement to sexual hatred, these feminists should be fighting for the use of any language or imagery that represents women in a negative light, not just pornography. In fact, these feminists argue that incitement to sexual hatred is paralleled with racial hatred and this behavior should be dealt with by law in the same way (Rodgerson & Wilson, 1991). However, in order to consider this type of legislation, lawmakers would have to pinpoint particular words of disgrace or disrespect in order for someone to be held liable. With regard to this parallel, those who publish or display racist materials do so with a clear assertion of hate toward that particular race or ethnic makeup. The same cannot be said for men in pornography who appear to enjoy and appreciate the women they engage with sexually. Pro-sex feminists argue that by censoring pornography, attention to reducing discrimination and violence against women in general is diverted, and resources are impeded (Strossen, 1993). Indeed, the Dworkin–MacKinnon focus on pornography's accountability for misogyny in society is narrow-minded and overlooks the many complex factors involved with sexism, violence, and hatred against women.

CONCLUSION

Although the First Amendment provides bedrock protections that are fundamental to our notions of freedom and liberty in a democratic society, there can be no doubt that its contours stir passionate debate with regard to a wide range of controversial issues. For instance, recent news reports have touched on First Amendment cases related to Google's control of search results (Timberg & Kang, 2013), violent rap lyrics on Facebook (Pizzi, 2014), and the restrictive speech policies on college campuses (Masatani, 2014). And in spite of judicial resolutions of numerous controversial disputes regarding the limits of free expression, a range of First Amendment freedoms continue to be divisive. Such controversies including hate speech, especially symbolic hate speech such as burning a cross (*R.A.V. v. City of St. Paul*, 1992; *Virginia v. Black*, 2003) or picketing funerals (*Snyder v. Phelps*, 2011); threatening speech, especially if it leads to violence (*Wisconsin v. Mitchell*, 1993); religious displays, such as those depicting tablets of the Ten Commandments or nativity scenes (*McCreary County v. ACLU of Kentucky*, 2005; *Van Orden v. Perry*, 2005); public prayers in school (compare *Abington Township School District v. Schempp*, 1963, with *Santa Fe Independent School Dist. v. Doe*, 2000), or at town meetings (*Town of Greece v. Galloway*, 2014); and, as this chapter explains, a range of issues regarding the legal regulation of sexually explicit materials.

Terms like *pornography* and *obscenity* are difficult to define. Moreover, what constitutes one or the other is often in the eyes of the beholder. But the distinction is not merely one of semantics; the former receives First Amendment protections while the latter does not. Moreover, because the distinction has such palpable legal consequences, critics of First Amendment jurisprudence on obscenity argue that the *Miller* test is unfair due to its inherent vagueness and its reliance on contemporary community standards that likely vary not only from state to state, but also from person to person, based on subjective taste (e.g., Adams, 2014; Duvall, 1992; Strossen,

2000). Such criticisms led the U.S. Court of Appeals for the Ninth Circuit to hold that a " 'national community standards' " test should apply to obscenity charges arising from internet pornography (Adams, 2014, p. 220, quoting *United States v. Kilbride*, 2009). Whether this approach to obscenity is eventually adopted by the U.S. Supreme Court remains to be seen.

Although morality undoubtedly underpins the legal regulation of sexually explicit materials, there are other reasons why obscene materials fall outside the scope of First Amendment protections for free expression, especially when dealing with child pornography. Thus, courts have routinely held that even when the age of consent for sexual activity is below age 18, any photography, filming, or video-recording of such acts when one of the participants is younger than 18 may be criminally regulated (see *State v. Senters*, 2005; *People v. Hollins*, 2012; *State v. Hughes*, 2011).

Another consideration to keep in mind about obscenity-related crime concerns *Lawrence v. Texas* (2003). As discussed in Chapter 6, at least one court dismissed obscenity charges (not involving child pornography) on the grounds that *Lawrence* barred Congress from using the criminal law to enforce a "moral code" (*United States v. Extreme Associates*, 2005, p. 586), although that decision was overturned on appeal. Some scholars and commentators have argued that current obscenity laws are no longer viable after *Lawrence* (Glazer, 2008; Kaplan, 2014; Tribe, 2004). Others argue that the potential harms related to obscenity justify providing only limited constitutional protections for obscene materials, but allowing for regulations that are akin to those governing commercial speech (Huppin & Malamuth, 2012). As of the writing of this book, however, no federal appellate courts have interpreted *Lawrence* in ways that have undercut the law of obscenity as set forth in this chapter.

As you continue to read the book, think about how your religious, political, and cultural beliefs influence your opinion on what might be considered obscene or otherwise deserving of legal regulation. Is it all sexually explicit expressions or those that are degrading or violent? When is the line crossed? What about nonsexual depictions of violence? Should they be legally regulated?

FURTHER READING

Clark, M. D. (2002). *Obscenity, child pornography and indecency*. Hauppauge, NY: Nova Publishers.

Glass, L., & Williams, C. (2011). *Obscenity and the limits of liberalism*. Columbus, OH: The Ohio State University Press.

Jasper, M. C. (2011). *The law of obscenity and pornography* (2nd ed.). Eagan, MN: Thomson Reuters.

MacKinnon, C. A. (1996). *Only words*. Cambridge, MA: Harvard University Press.

Nowlin, C. J. (2003). *Judging obscenity: A critical history of expert evidence*. Quebec City: McGill-Queen's University Press.

Saunders, K. W. (2011). *Degradation: What the history of obscenity tells us about hate speech*. New York, NY: New York University Press.

Strub, W. (2013). *Obscenity rules: Roth v. United States and the long struggle over sexual expression*. Lawrence, KS: University Press of Kansas.

GLOSSARY

Actual malice: A standard of proof in defamation cases in which the party suing for libel or slander must prove either that the person who made the defamatory statement actually knew it was false or acted with reckless disregard for the truth (i.e., did not care whether it was true or not).

Blasphemy: One of the types of criminal libel at English common law that punished speech because it expressed disrespect toward God.

Criminal libel: A category of criminalized speech at English common law that was aimed at protecting established norms of respect and propriety. Criminal libel included *defamation, blasphemy, sedition,* and *obscenity.*

Defamation: False statements that damage another person's reputation. If the false statements damaging to reputation were spoken, the defamation constituted *slander*; if the false statements damaging to reputation were published, then the defamation constituted *libel.*

Erotica: A term feminists prefer to describe sexually explicit materials that are not degrading to women (in contrast to *pornography* that feminists find objectionable because it is degrading to women).

Fighting words: Words which, by their very utterance, inflict injury or tend to incite an immediate breach of the peace.

Libel: The written or broadcast form of *defamation.*

Obscenity: Materials that (a) taken as a whole, the average person applying contemporary community standards finds to appeal to the prurient interest; (b) depict in a patently offensive way, sexual conduct specifically defined by the applicable state law; and (c) taken as a whole, lack serious literary, artistic, political, or scientific value.

Pornography: Printed or visual materials containing the explicit description or display of sexual organs or sexual activity that are intended to cause sexual arousal.

Prior restraint: Governmental suppression of speech in advance of publication or broadcast on the grounds that it is libelous, seditious, or otherwise so harmful as to require censoring.

Sedition: The crime of inciting people to revolt against the government.

Sexting: The sending of sexually explicit photos or videos via cell phone, email, or other forms of electronic communication.

Slander: The oral/spoken form of *defamation.*

Symbolic speech: Conduct that is designed to communicate an idea or message, such as marching in protest, picketing, wearing certain symbolic items, or even burning a flag.

Time, place, and manner restrictions: The ability of government to regulate when, where, and how certain forms of constitutionally protected speech may be expressed. Such restrictions must be content neutral, narrowly tailored to serve an important or substantial governmental interest, and leave open ample alternative means of expression.

NOTES

1 English law sometimes differentiated between spoken blasphemy and *blasphemous libel*, which was written (see Spencer, 1977).

2 English law sometimes differentiated between spoken sedition or *seditious slander* and *seditious libel*, which was written.

3 The government may also constitutionally regulate forms of expression in venues that are not, by tradition or design, forums for public discourse, such as in airspace, on media airwaves (e.g., radio and television), or near election polling places (Pember & Calvert, 2011).

4 Arizona, Arkansas, Connecticut, Florida, Georgia, Hawaii, Illinois, Louisiana, Missouri, Nebraska, Nevada, New Jersey, New York, North Dakota, Pennsylvania, Rhode Island, South Dakota, Texas, Utah, Vermont, and West Virginia (compiled from Hinduja & Patchin, 2014; MobileMediaGuard.com,

n.d.; National Conference of State Legislatures, 2013).

5   Subsequent research substantiated these critics' claims. For example, a 1990 study found that nonviolent sexual behavior accounts for 41% of behavioral sequences in X-rated movies, whereas sexual violence accounted for 4.73% and nonsexual violence accounted for 4.73% of behavioral sequences in pornographic films. In contrast, nonviolent sexual behavior accounted for 4.59% of behavioral sequences in R-rated movies, whereas sexual violence accounted for 3.27% of behavioral sequences and nonsexual violence account for 35% of behavioral sequences in R-rated movies (Yang & Linz, 1990).

6   Indeed, for many social conservatives, this view of sex extends beyond pornography and is associated with many aspects of human sexuality, including birth control, sex education, and homosexuality (Segal, 1998).

REFERENCES

Ackerman, B. A. (1980). *Social justice in the liberal state*. New Haven, CT: Yale University Press.

Adams, R. J. (2014). An objective approach to obscenity in the digital age. *St. John's Law Review*, 86(1), 211–247.

Anderson, C. A., & Bushman, B. J. (2001). Effects of violent video games on aggressive behavior, aggressive cognition, aggressive affect, physiological arousal, and prosocial behavior: A meta-analytic review of the scientific literature. *Psychological Science*, 12(5), 353–359.

Antoniou, L. (2012). Defending pornography. *The Gay and Lesbian Review*, 19(6), 23–24.

ARIZONA REVISED STATUTES § 8–309 (2015).

Attorney General's Commission on Pornography (1986). *Final report*. Washington, DC: U.S. Government Printing Office.

Bartee, W. C., & Bartee, A. F. (1992). *Litigating morality: American legal thought and its English roots*. Westport, CT: Greenwood.

Bates, B. J., & Donnerstein, E. I. (1990). Public opinion and the two pornography commissions: Comparing the incomparable. *Southwestern Mass Communication Journal*, 6(1), 1–14.

Bergh, A. E. (1905). Resolutions relative to the Alien and Sedition Laws. In A. E. Bergh & A. A. Lipscomb (Eds.), *The writings of Thomas Jefferson* (Vol. 17, pp. 381–382). Washington, DC: Thomas Jefferson Memorial Association.

Blackstone, W. (1818). *Commentaries on the laws of England* (Vol. 4). Boston: T. B. Wait & Sons.

Borstelmann, T. (2012). *The 1970s: A new global history from civil rights to economic inequality*. Princeton, NJ: Princeton University Press.

Brest, P., & Vandenberg, A. (1987). Politics, feminism, and the Constitution: The anti-pornography moment in Minneapolis. *Stanford Law Review*, 39(3), 607–661.

Brownmiller, S. (1975). *Against our will: Men, women, and rape*. New York, NY: Fawcett/Ballantine.

Bushman, B. J. (1995). Moderating role of trait aggressiveness in the effects of violent media on aggression. *Journal of Personality and Social Psychology*, 69(5), 950–960.

Calvert, C. (2009a). Sex, cell phones, privacy, and the first amendment: When children become child pornographers and the Lolita Effect undermines the law. *CommLaw Conspectus*, 18, 1–65.

Calvert, C. (2009b). Qualified immunity and the trials and tribulations of online student speech: A review of cases and controversies from 2009. *First Amendment Law Review*, 8, 86–108.

Child Abuse Victims' Right Act of 1986, Pub. L. No. 99–500, 100 Stat. 1783–74–75 (1986), *codified as amended at* 18 U.S.C. § 2255 (2014).

Child Pornography Prevention Act of 1996, Pub. L. No. 104–208, 110 Stat. 3009–26 to 3009–31 (1996), *codified at* 18 U.S.C. § 2252A (2014).

Child Protection Act of 1984, Pub. L. No. 98–292, 98 Stat. 204 (1984), *codified as amended at* 18 U.S.C. §§ 2251–2255 (2014).

Child Protection and Obscenity Enforcement Act of 1988, Pub. L. No. 100–690, § 7501, 102 Stat. 4485 (1988), *codified as amended at* 18 U.S.C. §§ 2251A-2252 (2014).

Child Protection Restoration and Penalties Enhancement Act of 1990, Pub. L. No. 101–647, §§ 301, 323, 104 Stat. 4816 (1990), *codified as amended at* 18 U.S.C. § 2252(a)(4)(B) (2014).

Child Sexual Abuse and Pornography Act of 1986, Pub. L. No. 99–628, § 2, 100 Stat. 3510 (1986), *codified as amended at* 18 U.S.C. § 2251 (2014).

Ciclitira, K. (2004). Pornography, women, and feminism: Between pleasure and politics. *Sexualities*, 7(3), 281–301.

Communications Decency Act of 1996, Pub. L. No. 104–104 (Tit. V), 110 Stat. 133 (1996), *codified at* 47 U.S.C. §§223, 230 (1996).

Comstock Act of 1873, ch. 258, 17 Stat. 598 (1873), *current version codified as amended at* 18 U.S.C. §§ 1416–62 (2014) and 19 U.S.C. § 1305 (2014).

Coopersmith, J. (1998). Pornography, technology, and progress. *Icon*, 4, 94–125.

Cornwell, N. C. (2004). *Freedom of the press: Rights and liberties under the law*. Santa Barbara, CA: ABC-CLIO.

Deazley, R. (2008). Commentary on Star Chamber Decree 1586. In L. Bently & M. Kretschmer (Eds.), *Primary sources on copyright (1450–1900)*. Retrieved from http://www.copyrighthistory.org

Díaz de Valdés, J. M. (2009). Freedom of speech in Rome. *Revista de Estudios Histórico-Jurídicos*, 31, 125–139.

DiStefano, C. (1991). *Configurations of masculinity: A feminist perspective on modern political theory*. Ithaca, NY: Cornell University Press.

Donnerstein, E. I., & Linz, D. G. (1986, December). The question of pornography. *Psychology Today*, 20(12), 56–59.

Downs, D. A. (1989). *The new politics of pornography*. Chicago, IL: University of Chicago Press.

Duvall, S. A. (1992). A call for obscenity law reform. *William and Mary Bill of Rights Journal*, 1, 75–104.

Dworkin, A. (1979). *Pornography: Men possessing women*. New York, NY: Penguin Books.

Dworkin, R. (1993, October 21). Women and pornography. *New York Review of Books*. Retrieved from http://www.nybooks.com/articles/archives/1993/oct/21/women-and-pornography/

Dwyer, S. (2008). Pornography. In P. Livingstone & C. Plantinga (Eds.), The Routledge *companion to philosophy and film* (pp. 515–526). New York, NY: Routledge.

Eisenstein, E. (1980). *The printing press as an agent of change: Communications and cultural transformations in early-modern Europe*. Cambridge, UK: Cambridge University Press.

Espionage Act of 1917, 40 Stat. 217, 219, *codified at* 18 U.S.C. §§ 793–99 (1917) (repealed, in part, Mar. 3, 1921).

Faust, B. (1980). *Women, sex, and pornography: A controversial and unique study*. New York, NY: Macmillan.

Feinberg, J. (1985). *Offense to others*, Oxford: Oxford University Press.

Ferguson, C. J., & Harley, R. D. (2009). The pleasure is momentary . . . the expense damnable? The influence of pornography on rape and sexual assault. *Aggression and Violent Behavior*, 14, 323–329.

Fradella, H. F., & Galeste, M. A. (2011). Sexting: The misguided penal social control of teenage sexual behavior in the digital age. *Criminal Law Bulletin*, 47(3), 438–473.

Frank, T. (1927). Naevius and free speech. *American Journal of Philology*, 48, 105–110.

Glazer, E. M. (2008). When obscenity discriminates. *Northwestern University Law Review*, 102, 1379–1439.

Greene, D. (2005). The need for expert testimony to prove lack of serious artistic value in obscenity cases. *NEXUS: A Journal of Opinion*, 2005, 171–176.

Griffin, S. (1982). *Pornography and silence: Culture's revenge against nature*. New York, NY: Harper & Row.

Gubar, S. (1987). Representing pornography: Feminism, criticism, and depictions of female violation. *Critical Inquiry*, 13(4), 712–741.

Haller, W. (1934). *Tracts on liberty in the Puritan revolution* (Vol. 1). New York: Columbia University Press.

Hiffa, A. M. (2010). OMG Txt Pix Plz: The phenomenon of sexting and the constitutional battle of protecting minors from their own devices. *Syracuse Law Review*, 61, 499–530.

Hinduja, S., & Patchin, J. W. (2014). *State sexting laws: A brief review of state sexting laws and policies*. Retrieved from http://www.cyberbullying.us/state_sexting_laws.pdf

Hochschild, A. (2005). *Bury the chains: Prophets and rebels in the fight to free an empire's slaves*. Boston, MA: Houghton Mifflin.

Hoffman, E. (1985). Feminism, pornography, and law. *University of Pennsylvania Law Review*, 133, 497–534.

Huesmann, L. R., & Taylor, L. D. (2006). The role of media violence in violent behavior. *Annual Review of Public Health*, 27, 393–415.

Huppin, M., & Malamuth, N. (2012). The obscenity conundrum, contingent harms, and constitutional consistency. *Stanford Law & Policy Review*, 23, 31–100.

Itzin, C. (Ed.). (1992). *Pornography: Women, violence and civil liberties*. Oxford: Oxford University Press.

Jaggar, A. M. (1988). *Feminist politics and human nature*. Totowa, NJ: Rowman & Littlefield.

Jasper, M. C. (2009). *The law of obscenity and pornography* (2nd ed.). New York: Oxford University Press.

Jenkins, P. (2001). *Beyond tolerance: Child pornography on the internet*. New York: New York University Press.

Johnson, M., & Seibel, J. (2009, February 5). New Berlin teen accused of using facebook for sexual blackmail. *Milwaukee Journal Sentinel*. Retrieved from http://www.jsonline.com/news/waukesha/39124037.html

Jones, L. M., Mitchell, K. J., & Finkelhor, D. (2012). Trends in youth internet victimization: Findings from three youth internet safety surveys 2000–2010. *Journal of Adolescent Health*, 50, 179–186.

Kalson, S. (2009, March 29). Sexting . . . and other stupid teen tricks. *Pittsburgh Post-Gazette*. Retrieved from http://www.post-gazette.com

Kaplan, M. (2014). Sex-positive law. *New York University Law Review*, 89, 89–164.

Koop, C. E. (1987). Report of the Surgeon General's Workshop on Pornography and Public Health. *American Psychologist*, 42(10), 944–945.

Leary, M. G. (2007). Self-produced child pornography: The appropriate societal response to juvenile self-sexual exploitation. *Virginia Journal of Social Policy Law*, 15, 1–50.

Lenhart, A. (2009). *Teens and sexting: How and why minor teens are sending sexually suggestive nude or nearly nude images via text messaging*. Pew Internet & American Life Project.

Lilly, J. R., Cullen, F. T., & Ball, R. A. (2011). *Criminological theory: Context and consequences*. Thousand Oaks, CA: Sage.

Linder, D. (2001). *The trial of John Peter Zenger: An account.* Available at http://www.law.umkc.edu/faculty/projects/ftrials/zenger/zengeraccount.html

Linz, D., Donnerstein, E., & Penrod, S. (1987, October). The findings and recommendations of the Attorney General's Commission on Pornography: Do the psychological "facts" fit the political fury? *American Psychologist, 42*(10), 946–953.

MacKinnon, C. A. (1987). *Feminism unmodified: Discourses on life and law.* Cambridge, MA: Harvard University Press.

Malamuth, N. M. (1989, March). Distinguishing between the Surgeon General's personal views and the consensus reached at his workshop on pornography. *American Psychologist, 44*(3), 580.

Masatani, M. (2014, Dec. 4). Citrus College to pay $110,000 to settle student's First Amendment lawsuit. *Pasadena Star-News.* Retrieved from http://www.pasadenastarnews.com/general-news/20141204/citrus-college-to-pay-110000-to-settle-students-first-amendment-lawsuit?source=most_viewed

Mayhem, M., & Lim, G. (2010). *Absolute Mayhem: Secret confessions of a porn star.* New York, NY: Skyhorse Publishing.

McElroy, W. (1995). *XXX: A woman's right to pornography.* New York, NY: St. Martin's Press.

Milton, J. (1957). Second defense of the people of England. In M. Hughes (Eds.), *John Milton: Complete poems and major prose* (pp. 831–837). New Haven, CT: Yale University Press. (Original work published 1653).

Milton, J. (1992). *Areopagitica.* S. Ash (Ed.). Santa Barbara, CA: Bandana Books. (Original work published 1644.)

Mitchell, K., Finkelhor, D., Jones, L., & Wolak, J. (2012). Prevalence and characteristics of youth sexting: A national study. *Pediatrics, 129*(1), 13–20.

MobileMediaGuard.com (n.d.). U.S. sexting laws. Retrieved from http://mobilemediaguard.com/state_main.html

MODEL PENAL CODE § 521.4(1), *Obscenity* (1962). Philadelphia, PA: American Law Institute.

Momigliano, A. (1942). Review of Laura Robinson's Freedom of Speech in the Roman Empire. *Journal of Roman Studies, 32,* 120–124.

National Conference of State Legislatures. (2013). *Sexting legislation, 2013.* Retrieved from http://www.ncsl.org/research/telecommunications-and-information-technology/2013-sexting-legislation.aspx

Neal, D. (1855). *The history of the Puritans* (Vol. 1). New York, NY: Harper.

NEW JERSEY STATUTES ANNOTATED § 2A:4A-71.1 (2014).

O'Brien, B. (2009, May 5). To deal with "sexting," XXXtra discretion is advised. *USA TODAY,* p. 10A. Retrieved from http://usatoday30.usatoday.com/printedition/news/20090505/editorial05_st.art.htm

Ogas, O., & Gaddam, S. (2011). *A billion wicked thoughts: What the world's largest experiment reveals about human desire.* New York, NY: Penguin.

Okin, S. M. (1979). *Women in western political thought.* Princeton, NJ: Princeton University Press.

Olszewski, D. J. (2005). Statutory Rape in Wisconsin: History, rationale, and the need for reform. *Marquette Law Review, 89,* 693–720.

Paletz, D. L. (1988). Pornography, politics, and the press: The U.S. Attorney General's Commission on Pornography. *Journal of Communication, 38*(2), 122–136.

Palys, T. S. (1986). Testing the common wisdom: The social content of video pornography. *Canadian Psychology/Psychologie Canadienne, 27*(1), 22–35.

Pember, D. R., & Calvert, C. (2011). *Mass media law* (17th ed.). New York, NY: McGraw Hill.

Phillips, A. (1991) *Engendering democracy.* University Park, PA: Pennsylvania State University Press.

Pizzi, M. (2014, December 1). Supreme Court to hear First Amendment case on violent Facebook rap lyrics. *Al Jazeera America.* Retrieved from http://america.aljazeera.com/articles/2014/12/1/facebook-threat-supremecourt.html

Post, R. C. (1988). Cultural heterogeneity and law: Pornography, blasphemy, and the First Amendment. *California Law Review, 76,* 297–335.

Post, R. C. (1990). The constitutional concept of public discourse: Outrageous opinion, democratic deliberation, and *Hustler Magazine v. Falwell. Harvard Law Review, 103,* 601–686.

President's Commission on Obscenity and Pornography (1970). *Report of the Commission on Obscenity and Pornography.* Washington, DC: U.S. Government Printing Office.

Prosecutorial Remedies and Other Tools to End the Exploitation of Children Today Act of 2003 (PROTECT Act), Pub. L. 108–21, 117 Stat. 650 (2003), *codified at various sections of the U.S. Code* (2014).

Protection of Children Against Sexual Exploitation Act, Pub. L. No. 95–225, 92 Stat. 7 § 2 (1978), *codified as amended at* 18 U.S.C. §§ 2251–2253 (2014).

Quinn, C. (2010, March 26). Forsyth 7th grade suspended for sexting nude photo of self. *The Atlanta Journal-Constitution Forsyth.* Retrieved from http://www.ajc.com/news

Radin, M. (1927). Freedom of speech in Athens. *American Journal of Philology, 48,* 215–220.

Randle, Q. (2001, September). A historical overview of the effects of new mass media introduction on magazine publishing during the 20th century. *First Monday, 6*(9–3). Retrieved from http://firstmonday.org/ojs/index.php/fm/article/view/885/794

Reimer, R. A. (1986, October). Legal analysis of the pornography commission's July 1986 final report. *Congressional Research Service Review, 7*(9), 11–13. Retrieved from http://hdl.handle.net/2027/umn.31951d00272558a

Richards, D. A. J. (1974). Free speech and obscenity law: Toward a moral theory of the First Amendment. *University of Pennsylvania Law Review, 123*, 45–91.

Roberts, J. (2011). The development of free speech in modern Britain. Retrieved from http://www.speakerscornertrust.org/5064/the-development-of-free-speech-in-modern-britain/

Rodgerson, G., & Wilson, E. (1991). *Pornography and feminism: The case against censorship*. London, UK: Lawrence & Wishart.

Rubin, G. (1984). Thinking sex: Notes for a radical theory of the politics of sexuality. In C. S. Vance (Ed.), *Pleasure and danger: Exploring female sexuality* (pp. 267–319). Boston, MA: Routledge & Kegan Paul.

Scofield, C. L. (1900). *A study of the Court of Star Chamber; Largely based on manuscripts in the British Museum and the Public Record Office*. Chicago: University of Chicago Press.

Scott, J. E. (1987). Book reviews: Attorney General's Commission on Pornography: Final report, July 1986. United States of America vs. sex: How the Meese Commission lied about pornography, polluting the censorship debate. *Journal of Criminal Law & Criminology, 78*, 1145–1165.

Sedition Act of 1918, 40 Stat. 553 (1918) (repealed Mar. 3, 1921).

Segal, L. (1998). Only the literal: The contradictions of anti-pornography feminism. *Sexualities, 1*(1), 43–62.

Siebert, F. S. (1952). *Freedom of the press in England, 1476–1776*. Urbana, IL: University of Illinois Press.

Small, O. (2011). *Girlvert: A porno memoir*. Los Angeles, CA: Barnacle.

Smith Act, 54 Stat. 670, *codified as amended* 18 U.S.C. § 2385 (1940),

Spencer, J. R. (1977). Criminal libel—A skeleton in the cupboard. *Criminal Law Review, 1977*, 383–394, 465–474.

Sprinkle, A. (2001). *Hardcore from the heart—The pleasures, profits and politics of sex in performance*. London: Continuum International.

Steinem, G. (1980). Erotica and pornography: A clear and present difference. In L. Lederer (Ed.), *Take back the night: Women on pornography* (pp. 35–39). New York, NY: William Morrow and Co.

Strossen, N. (1993). A feminist critique of "the" feminist critique of pornography. *Virginia Law Review, 79*(5), 1099–1190.

Strossen, N. (2000). *Defending pornography: Free speech, sex, and the fight for women's rights*. New York, NY: New York University Press.

Szymialis, J. J. (2010). Sexting: A response to prosecuting those growing up with a growing trend. *Indiana Law Review, 44*, 301–340.

Tedford, T. L., & Herbeck, D. A. (2013). *Freedom of speech in the United States* (7th ed.). State College, PA: Strata Publishing Co.

Timberg, C., & Kang, C. (2013, June 18). Google challenges U.S. gag order, citing First Amendment. *The Washington Post*. Retrieved from http://www.washingtonpost.com/business/technology/google-challenges-us-gag-order-citing-first-amendment/2013/06/18/96835c72-d832-11e2-a9f2-42ee3912ae0e_story.html

Tong, R. M. (1982). Feminism, pornography, and censorship. *Social Theory and Practice, 8*(1), 1–17.

Tribe, L. H. (2004). *Lawrence v. Texas*: The "fundamental right" that dare not speak its name. *Harvard Law Review, 117*, 1893–1955.

Walwyn, W. (1989). *The compassionate Samaritane*. In J. R. McMichael & B. Taft (Eds.), *The writings of William Walwyn* (pp. 97–124). Athens, GA: The University of Georgia Press. (Original work published 1644).

Wilcox, B. L. (1987). Pornography, social science, and politics: When research and ideology collide. *American Psychologist, 42*(10), 941–943.

Willis, E. J. (1992). *Beginning to see the light: Sex, hope, and rock-and-roll* (2nd ed.). Hanover, NH: Wesleyan University Press.

Wolak, J., Liberatore, M., & Levine, B. N. (2014). Measuring a year of child pornography trafficking by U.S. computers on a peer-to-peer network. *Child Abuse and Neglect, 38*(2), 347–356.

Wolak, J., Mitchell, K. J., & Finkelhor, D. (2007). Unwanted and wanted exposure to online pornography in a national sample of youth internet users. *Pediatrics, 119*, 247–257.

Wortley, R., & Smallbone, S. (2012). *Child pornography on the internet*. Problem-Oriented Guides for Police Problem-Specific Guides Series No. 41. Washington, DC: Center for Problem-Oriented Policing, Inc.

Yang, N., & Linz, D. (1990). Movie ratings and the content of adult videos: The sex-violence ratio. *Journal of Communication, 40*(2), 28–42.

Ybarra, M. L., Strasburger, V. C., & Mitchell, K. J. (2014). Sexual media exposure, sexual behavior, and sexual violence victimization in adolescence. *Clinical Pediatrics*. Advance online publication. doi: 10.1177/0009922814538700

Zurcher, L. A., & Kirkpatrick, R. G. (1976). *Citizens for decency: Antipornography crusades as status defense*. Austin, TX: University of Texas Press.

Cases

Abington School District v. Schempp, 374 U.S. 203 (1963).

Abrams v. United States, 250 U.S. 616 (1919).

Ashcroft v. Free Speech Coalition, 535 U.S. 234 (2002).

Brandenburg v. Ohio, 395 U.S. 444 (1969).

Castillo v. State, 79 S.W.3d 817, 826 (Tex. Crim. App. 2002), *cert. denied*, 538 U.S. 924 (2003).

Chaplinsky v. New Hampshire, 315 U.S. 568 (1942).

City of Erie v. Pap's A.M., 529 U.S. 277 (2000).

Cox v. Louisiana, 379 U.S. 536 (1965).

Dennis v. United States, 341 U.S. 494 (1951).

Falwell v. Flynt, 797 F.2d 1270 (4th Cir. 1986), *rev'd* 485 U.S. 46 (1988).

Gertz v. Robert Welch, Inc., 418 U.S. 323 (1974).

Hustler Magazine, Inc. v. Falwell, 485 U.S. 46 (1988).

Jacobellis v. Ohio, 378 U.S. 184 (1964).

Jenkins v. Georgia, 418 U.S. 153 (1974).

J.L. Spoons, Inc. v. Dragani, 538 F.3d 379 (6th Cir. 2008).

Lawrence v. Texas, 539 U.S. 558 (2003).

Luke Records, Inc. v. Navarro, 960 F.2d 134 (11th Cir.), *cert. denied*, 506 U.S. 1022 (1992).

McCreary County v. ACLU of Kentucky, 545 U.S. 844 (2005).

Miller v. California, 413 U.S. 15 (1973).

National Socialist Party of America v. Village of Skokie, 432 U.S. 43 (1977).

New York v. Ferber, 458 U.S. 747 (1982).

New York Times Co. v. Sullivan, 376 U.S. 254 (1964).

Oregon v. Johnson, 191 P.3d 665 (Ore. 2008).

Osborne v. Ohio, 495 U.S. 103 (1990).

Paris Adult Theatre v. Slaton, 413 U.S. 49 (1975).

People v. Hollins, 971 N.E.2d 504 (Ill. 2012).

Pope v. Illinois, 481 U.S. 497 (1987).

R.A.V. v. City of St. Paul, 505 U.S. 377 (1992).

Regina v. Hinklin, L.R.3 Q.B. 360 (1868).

Reno v. ACLU, 521 U.S. 844 (1997).

Renton v. Playtime Theatres, Inc., 475 U.S. 41 (1986).

Rex v. Twyn, 6 How. St. Tr. 514 (1664).

Rosen v. United States, 161 U.S. 29 (1896).

Roth v. United States, 354 U.S. 476 (1957).

Santa Fe Independent School Dist. v. Doe, 530 U.S. 290 (2000).

Schenck v. United States, 249 U.S. 47 (1919).

Smith v. California, 361 U.S. 147 (1959).

Snyder v. Phelps, 562 U.S. 443 (2011).

South Dakota v. Suhn, 2008 WL 5413753 (S.D. Dec. 30, 2008).

Stanley v. Georgia, 394 U.S. 557 (1969).

State v. Canal, 773 N.W. 2d 528 (Iowa 2009).

State v. Hughes, 261 P.3d 1067 (Nev. 2011).

State v. Senters, 699 N.W.2d 810 (Neb. 2005).

Texas v. Johnson, 491 U.S. 397 (1989).

Town of Greece v. Galloway, 134 S. Ct. 1811 (2014).

United States v. Dost, 636 F. Supp. 828 (S.D. Cal. 1986).

United States v. Extreme Associates, 352 F. Supp. 2d 578 (W.D. Pa.), *rev'd*, 431 F.3d 150 (3d Cir. 2005).

United States v. Kilbride, 584 F.3d 1240 (9th Cir. 2009).

United States v. O'Brien, 391 U.S. 367 (1968).

United States v. One Book Called "Ulysses" by James Joyce, 5 F. Supp. 182 (S.D.N.Y 1933), *aff'd*, 72 F.2d 705 (2d Cir. 1934).

United States v. Rahman, 189 F.3d 88 (2d Cir. 1999).

United States v. Williams, 553 U.S. 285 (2008).

Van Orden v. Perry, 545 U.S. 677 (2005).

Virginia v. Black, 538 U.S. 343 (2003).

Wisconsin v. Mitchell, 508 U.S. 476 (1993).

Yates v. United States, 354 U.S. 298 (1957).

CHAPTER 9

Marriage, Sexuality, and Gender

Henry F. Fradella, Megan Parry, and Lauren E. Fradella

The word *miscegenation* refers to the interbreeding of people considered to be of different races. The word comes from the Latin *miscere* (to mix) and *genus* (kind). Maryland was the first colony to enact the first **anti-miscegenation law** (barring interracial marriage) in the 1660s (Robinson, 2015). Although these laws were clearly racist, proponents argued "natural law"—emanating from religious beliefs—justified barring the mixing of the races. This belief stems from an interpretation of a biblical passage in Deuteronomy 7:3-4, which states,

> Do not intermarry with them. Do not give your daughters to their sons or take their daughters for your sons, or they will turn your children away from following me to serve other gods, and the Lord's anger will burn against you and will quickly destroy you.

Scholars interpret this provision as a directive for Jews not to marry outside their religion—at least with regard to those who worshiped idols, just as Corinthians 6:14 directs Christians as follows: "Do not be yoked together with unbelievers. For what do righteousness and wickedness have in common? Or what fellowship can light have with darkness?" (see Botham, 2009; Weierman, 2005). Yet, these biblical passages formed the basis of religious arguments against interracial marriage. Consider that in 1869, the Georgia Supreme Court ruled that,

> moral or social equality between the different races . . . does not in fact exist, and never can. The God of nature made it otherwise, and no human law can produce it, and no human tribunal can enforce it. There are gradations and classes throughout the universe. From the tallest archangel in Heaven, down to the meanest reptile on earth, moral and social inequalities exist, and must continue to exist throughout all eternity.
>
> (*Scott v. State*, 1869, p. 326)

Forty-one U.S. states enacted anti-miscegenation laws, meaning that only nine states never had such laws (Robinson, 2015). Eleven states repealed their anti-miscegenation laws before 1887; 14 more states repealed their anti-miscegenation laws between 1948 and 1967. But 16 states continued to prohibit interracial marriages until the landmark U.S. Supreme Court decision of *Loving v. Virginia* declared these laws unconstitutional in 1967.

In 1958, Mildred Jeter, a woman of African-American and Native-American descent, married her childhood sweetheart, Richard Loving, a White man. At the time, they were residents of the Commonwealth of Virginia, which criminalized interracial marriage as a felony punishable by a prison sentence of up to five years. So, Jeter and Loving married in the District of Colombia. Upon their return to Virginia after their wedding, however, police raided their house as they slept and they were taken into custody and charged with violating Virginia's anti-miscegenation law, one provision of which prohibited interracial couples from being married out of state and then returning to Virginia (Sullivan, 2008 see also An Act to Preserve Racial Integrity, 1924).

The Lovings pled guilty and were sentenced to one year in prison, with the sentence suspended on the condition that the couple leave Virginia. The trial judge relied on the centuries-old misinterpretation of biblical passages to justify his ruling:

> Almighty God created the races white, black, yellow, malay and red, and he placed them on separate continents. And but for the interference with his arrangement there would be no cause for such marriages. The fact that he separated the races shows that he did not intend for the races to mix.
>
> (Wallenstein, 1994, p. 424, citing *Loving v. Virginia* 1965; see also *Loving v. Virginia*, 1967, p. 3)

In compliance with the terms of their plea, the Lovings moved to the District of Columbia. However, on a visit to Mildred's mother in Virginia five years later, the couple was arrested for leaving the state to evade the law and violation of the state's anti-miscegenation law. Mildred reached out to then Attorney General Robert F. Kennedy, who in turn referred them to the American Civil Liberties Union (ACLU). The ACLU assisted the Lovings in litigating a series of challenges to their convictions in both state and federal courts. These challenges were unsuccessful until the case reached the U.S. Supreme Court, which considered the questions of whether statutes preventing marriages between persons solely on basis of racial classifications violated the Equal Protection and Due Process Clauses of the Fourteenth Amendment. The Court overturned both of the Lovings' convictions and ruled that the nation's remaining anti-miscegenation laws violated the Due Process and Equal Protection Clauses of the Fourteenth Amendment to the U.S. Constitution (see Chapters 3 and 4).

Chief Justice Warren, writing for the Court stated "The freedom to marry has long been recognized as one of the vital personal rights essential to the orderly pursuit of happiness by free men" (*Loving v. Virginia*, 1967). He went on to further state:

> To deny this fundamental freedom on so unsupportable a basis as the racial classifications embodied in these statutes, classifications so directly subversive of the principle of equality at the heart of the Fourteenth Amendment, is surely to deprive all the State's citizens of liberty without due process of law. The Fourteenth Amendment requires that the freedom of choice to marry not be restricted by invidious racial discriminations. Under our Constitution, the freedom to marry, or not marry, a person of another race resides with the individual and cannot be infringed by the State.
>
> (p. 12)

Despite the ruling in *Loving*, anti-miscegenation laws remained "on the books," although unenforceable, in several states. In 2000, Alabama became the last state to repeal its law against interracial marriage (Sengupta, 2000).

- Regardless of the interpretation that may be given to specific biblical passages, do you feel that it is appropriate for courts in the United States to base decisions on the Bible? Why or why not?
- Because *Loving v. Virginia* declared marriage to be a "fundamental right," laws restricting marriage have traditionally been subjected to strict scrutiny—the highest level of judicial review (see Chapter 3). As a result, states may not restrict the right to marry unless the restriction is narrowly tailored to achieve some compelling governmental interest. Thus, for example, prisons may not prohibit inmates from marrying or require inmates to seek the permission of correctional officials to marry since such restrictions impermissibly burden the right to marry and are "not reasonably related to legitimate penological objectives" (*Turner v. Safley*, 1987, p. 99). Given the reasoning and results in *Loving v. Virginia* and *Turner v. Safley*, explain your own views on whether laws banning marriage between people of same-sex are constitutional. Then compare your thoughts to those expressed in the majority and dissenting opinions in *Obergefell v. Hodges*, 2015).

LEARNING OBJECTIVES

1. Recognize the ways in which the institution of marriage has evolved with changing cultural, political and religious sentiments.
2. Analyze how the interpretation of the Fourteenth Amendment, specifically the Due Process Clause and Equal Protection Clause, of the U.S. Constitution has transformed to grant citizens the right to marry.
3. Relate arguments in opposition to and in favor of legalizing interracial marriage to arguments opposing and supporting legalizing same-sex marriage.
4. Assess how culture, religion, and politics influence the right to marry.

DEFINING "MARRIAGE" THROUGHOUT HISTORY

Societies have defined and redefined marriage since the beginning of civilization. In order to understand the "right to marry," one must first recognize how laws and customs have changed marriage throughout time.

The word *marriage* as we know it actually derives from the Middle English word *mariage*, which is derived from Old French *marier* (to marry), and, ultimately the Latin words *marītāre* (to provide with a husband or wife) and *marītāri* (to get married). *Matrimony* derives from the Old French word *matremoine*, which ultimately derives from Latin *mātrimōnium*, which combines the two concepts *mater* meaning "mother" and the suffix *-monium* signifying "action, state, or condition" (*Oxford Dictionary*, 2012).

The actual institution of marriage as we think of it today has an even more lengthy and complex history than the words and its roots. For the past 5,000 years, different cultures, traditions, political beliefs, religious and legal forces have reinvented marriage time and time again. Over the course of human history, marriage has taken many forms and served varying purposes in society. However, as this chapter will show, marriage is not a "static" institution, nor does our contemporary culture subscribe to anything remotely resembling the "traditional" institution of marriage, at least as understood across the historical record (see, e.g., Eskridge, 1993). Consider, for example, that many cultures have practiced **polygamy** (marriage between one man and multiple women) or **polyandry** (marriage between one woman and multiple men). Indeed, leading religious texts endorse such plural marriage. The Bible, for instance, demonstrates an acceptance of the practice in the Old Testament through the depictions of major figures, the first occurring in Genesis (4:19) where Lamech is said to have married two women. Other major figures in the Bible were depicted in polygamous marriages including Abraham, David, and Solomon. In fact, Solomon was said to have 700 wives and 300 concubines (Kings, 11:3). The Quran goes even further by explicitly endorsing polygamy:

> If you fear that you will not act justly towards the orphans, marry such women as seem good to you, two, three, four; but if you fear you will not be equitable, then only one, or what your right hands own; so it is likelier you will not be partial.
>
> (4:3)

Today, polygamy is illegal in the United States (see Chapter 6). But as this chapter explores, our contemporary distain of polygamy is but one example of the seemingly ever-changing landscape of marriage laws across history.

The Earliest Marriages

Anthropologists posit that prior to the Stone Age (approximately 2.5 million years ago between the Middle and Upper Paleolithic eras), sexual promiscuity was the norm, as Neanderthals were driven by two survival instincts: self-preservation and procreation (Chapais, 2009). By the Stone Age, however, our ancestors could make fire and they began to create tools that not only allowed them to hunt and fish more effectively, but also to defend themselves. It is hypothesized that around this time, Neanderthal males began to stay and bond with a particular female as his primary mate, a process known as **pair-bonding** (Chapais, 2009; see also Allen, Callan, & Dunbar, 2011). This process allowed for a division of labor (one that may have created gender roles that still exist, to some degree) that helped to secure the food supply and protect children.

Separate from pair-bonding, which may have been driven in part by biology and psychology, the earliest form of marriage appears to have occurred between 4,000 and 5,000 years ago in ancient Mesopotamia[1] and was clearly driven by social forces (Gadoua & Larson, 2014; Stol, 1995). Indeed, the development of agriculture in the so-called "Fertile Crescent" prompted economic needs for early societies to develop stable arrangements for the transfer of land and labor support systems to farm those lands. Marriages helped to meet both needs. Agriculture provided its earliest practitioners with immense rewards in terms of reliable food, but there were huge costs. Farming required enormous and almost continuous manual labor, and the process of working land brought forth the issues of ownership and property that have been crucial to all later cultures:

> Labor and property worked together to divide the lives of women from the lives of men as a result of the fundamental ability of women to bear children. Children could perform useful

farm labor from a quite young age, and were perhaps less a burden than they had been in pre-agricultural societies. The need for children as workers, combined with high rates of infant mortality, led women to spend far more time in pregnancy and in rearing children . . .

In a very real sense, agriculture created property. In any agricultural economy, the ownership and transference of real property are always central concerns. Landed property, however, in non-monetary cultures is worth far more than usual exchange methods can manage. It can be transferred by gift, but it was much more commonly passed on via inheritance or wedding gift (bride-price or dowry). Women then, as producers of heirs, and as the means of property transfer through marriage, came to function as economic objects in a way that men did not.

(Halsall, 2004, pp. 286–287)

Notably, ancient records suggest that both polygamy and same-sex marriages were sanctioned in Mesopotamia (Eskridge, 1993; Greenberg, 1988).

Marriage in Ancient Greece and Pre-Christian Rome

Although polygamy may have been an accepted practice in Mesopotamia, the practice was viewed with distain in Ancient Greece and Rome. In fact, plural marriage was considered barbaric and the mark of the uncultured (Scheidel, 2009, p. 6). That is not to say, however, that the ancient Greeks and Romans were monogamous; they were not. In fact, it was a socially accepted practice for married men to have sexual relations with their slaves or with prostitutes (Cowell, 1976; Scheidel, 2009). It was similarly accepted that men in the aristocracy would have concubines (Cowell, 1976). And, as discussed in more detail in Chapter 6, Ancient Greek and Roman culture also sanctioned *pederasty*, which involved both emotional and sexual relationships between men and post-pubescent boys in mentor/mentee relationships (Dover, 1978; Eskridge, 1993).

Laws in ancient Greece and Rome prohibited marriages between commoners and the aristocracy (Zoch, 2000). Although legal marriages were favored, the ancient marriage contract was not necessarily viewed as an enduring one. Divorces were relatively easy to acquire and were viewed as socially acceptable (Scheidel, 2009).

Among the aristocracy, marriages were legal contracts often with little emotional attachment between partners. Marriages were meant to secure holdings, increase capital, and produce heirs (Eskridge, 1993). That is not to say that marriages in ancient Greece or Rome were devoid of emotional attachment; some spouses loved each other. But the social expectation was that marriage would serve its economic and social ends, whereas extramarital affairs were expected to serve the purposes of emotional and sexual fulfillment (Eskridge, 1993; Scheidel, 2009). Despite sexual relations being allowed outside of marriage vows, cohabitation outside of marriage was strictly forbidden socially (Scheidel, 2009). Yet, men and women did not even reside in the same household in some parts of the ancient Western world, such as in Sparta and Crete, where the **agōgē** (or public upbringing), was practiced for all male youth other than the immediate heirs to the kingships (Scanlon, 2002).

In ancient Sparta, for instance, boys entered the agōgē at age seven. They remained in military barracks until the age of 30.

There were three general stages, the *paides*, *paidiskoi*, and *hēbōntes*, probably representing ages 7–17, 18–19, and 20–29; several individual year-classes were separately named The *paides* were trained in austerity, obedience, and mock battles by older youths within companies, subdivided into herds of age-mates with their own internal leadership. At age 12 they entered an institutionalized pederastic relationship with a young adult . . . The *paidiskoi* were army reservists . . . The *hēbōntes* joined the *syssitia*[2] and army, could marry, but remained in barrack life, competing for places among the 300

hippeis, the kings' bodyguard. Separating boys from their families, the agōgē inculcated conformity and the priority of collective interests, but also promoted the emergence of future élites.
(Hornblower & Spawforth, 2005, para. 1)

Because married men in their 20s were not permitted to live independently from the military lifestyle, Spartan marriages were somewhat "one-sided" during the first few years of the marriage. Husbands were only allowed to make nightly visits to their wives for the purpose of having sexual intercourse (Cartledge, 2001). Notably, Spartan brides shaved their heads and wore men's clothing and shoes. "This masculine get-up . . . has been explained as apotropaic cross-dressing. But it is also worth pondering the suggestion that the bride's appearance was designed to ease the transition for the groom from his all-male and actively homosexual agōgē and common mess to full heterosexual intercourse" (Cartledge, 2001, p. 122).

Throughout most city-states in Ancient Greece and Rome, same-sex unions were celebrated (Boswell, 1994). In fact, "many if not most, of the emperors enjoyed well-documented relationships—some of them legally sanctioned marriages with other men" (Eskridge, 1993, p. 1446). In his examination of marriage in the ancient world, Eskridge (1993) noted that same-sex relationships in Greece and Rome followed much the same courtship patterns and rituals as their different-sex counterparts. In fact, same-sex couples risked their social reputations if they deviated from the courtship ritual to engage in relations outside of sanctioned marriage.

Marriage in Pre-Islamic Societies of the Middle East

Pre-Islamic societies of the Middle East largely comprised different nomadic tribes (Abudabbeh, 1996). Mernissi (1987) explained that there was little consensus on what constituted a

marriage in pre-Islamic society. Most tribes had strong traditions of **endogamy**, or marrying within tribal or community groups, often in ways that enhanced the economic stability and position of the tribe (Abudabbeh, 1996). Notably, this created instances in which cousins often married (Abudabbeh, 1996). For inter-tribal marriages, however, the practice took many forms among the nomadic tribes of the region, although four approaches dominated: marriage by capture, marriage by purchase, marriage by inheritance, and marriage by agreement (Mernissi, 1987).

In marriages by capture or purchase, a wife was considered the property of a husband who had either kidnapped her from her tribe or purchased her from her family. Similarly, in marriage by inheritance, the heir of the deceased inherited his wife along with the deceased's other property. In such marriages, the heir could take the deceased's wife as his own or he could choose to barter with others for her hand, keeping her bride-price for himself (Smith, 1903). Finally, marriages by agreement occurred when families agreed upon a union of their children. One member of the putative couple would leave his or her tribe to join the tribe of the intended spouse. Apart from marriages by capture, men were expected to pay a bride-price to the woman's family or tribe before a marriage would be granted (Mernissi, 1987).

There were few limits on men's ability to marry or divorce, whereas women were expected to marry only one man and their options for divorce were extremely limited (Khadduri, 1978). The only exception to this general rule was when a man agreed to join a woman's tribe. In such arrangements, the wife had considerably more freedoms, including the right to divorce her husband if she wished. In cases of divorce, the woman's father or family had to repay the bride-price or else the woman would not be free to remarry (Mernissi, 1987).

Ancient Egyptians practiced both polygamy and endogamy. The latter extended to marriages between full and half siblings—both among the nobility and the commoners alike—although these types of marriages were most likely concentrated among city dwellers and wealthy landowners. Among royalty, the practice even sanctioned marriages between father and daughter (Middleton, 1962). Pharaoh Rameses II, for instance, married two of his sisters and two of his daughters (Middleton, 1962). Scholars believe that these types of close-kin marriages

> served to maintain the property of the family intact and to prevent the splintering of the estate through the operation of the laws of inheritance. Since daughters usually inherited a share of the estate, the device of brother-sister marriage would have served to preserve intact the material resources of the family as a unit.
> (Middleton, 1962, p. 610)

Ancient Egypt accepted both same-sex and different-sex relationships. As with certain Roman emperors, evidence suggests that some pharaohs had same-sex partners. For example, the tomb of Pharaoh Ikhnaton, also known as Akhenaten (1353–1336 B.C.E.) depicts the Pharaoh as having had a male lover (Eskridge, 1993). Although direct evidence of acceptance of same-sex relationships comes from the tombs of the nobility and the Pharaohs, Eskridge (1993) argued that further evidence of Egyptian acceptance of same-sex unions could be found in the writings of other cultures and religions, largely those condemning the practice of homosexuality in Egypt.

Marriage in Pre-modern Europe

Anglo-Saxon England (440–1066 C.E.) refers to the time directly following the abandonment of England by Roman soldiers and the occupation of England by German tribes collectively referred to by historians as Anglo-Saxons (Stafford, 1993). The German invaders brought with them their laws and customs.

As in many ancient societies, Anglo-Saxon marriage was a tool used to develop diplomatic ties, ensure peaceful relations, and create or maintain trading agreements with other families (Coontz, 2005). In other words, marriage was considered something of a business merger between two people for economic purposes. A family would arrange a marriage for their son to share the land and business of the bride's family.

In comparison with those in many ancient civilizations, these customs embodied a more enlightened view of marriage and women's rights (Stafford, 1993). Noble families often arranged marriages—usually without consultation from either party. But once married, women and men were considered equal partners in Anglo-Saxon marriages; both contributed family holdings and both exercised some control over them (Buckstaff, 1893). Upon the death of her husband, a wife was considered relatively autonomous and entitled to half of his holdings (Buckstaff, 1893). That is not to say life was truly egalitarian, as bride-price was still meant to guarantee men access to women. Marriage was still a type of sale, as it had been in Rome and Greece (Buckstaff, 1893). Rules about adultery similarly demonstrate how a woman was considered the property of her husband: If a man committed adultery with another man's wife, the adulterer had to provide the husband with a new wife at his own expense (Buckstaff, 1893).

When the Normans, led by William the Conqueror, invaded England in 1066, they forever changed the legal and social landscape of England. Under the new regime, women lost many of the rights and freedoms afforded them under the Anglo-Saxons (Stafford, 1993). By the reign of Henry II (1154–1189), women's rights of property ownership and inheritance had vanished, along with the notion of a marriage being a partnership (Buckstaff, 1893). Legally, a married couple was considered one entity under the will of the husband. A wife "was not able to contradict [her husband's] will in anything and so was not able against his will to look out for her own rights" (Buckstaff, 1893, p. 53). Although a wife was represented by her husband in all things, she could not be punished for his crimes or held responsible for his debts (Schaus, 2006).

Similar to marriage rites of the past, daughters were expected to marry whomever their fathers had arranged for them. Unsurprisingly, fathers wanted their daughters to marry into a family of equal or greater wealth and social status (Coontz, 2005). Many marriage customs and practices changed dramatically with the Norman Conquest. Notably, bride-price began to be replaced with the Roman custom of a dowry, an amount of wealth or property given to a man by the bride's family (Buckstaff, 1893).

The concept of monogamy was not strictly practiced in England, especially for the poor who did not own any land (Scammell, 1974). This was due, in part, to the fact that those who wished to be legally wed had to pay a marriage fine (similar to a tax). This fine varied depending on the status of the bride. According to Scammell (1974), it would have been highly unusual for a poor couple to be able to afford the expenses associated with legal marriage (bride-prices, wedding feasts, and marriage fines). So, they would simply enter into a relationship that was not sanctioned by the state and lacked any of the official formalities associated with marriage.

During this time, English culture began to emphasize the family line. Because issues of succession and inheritance were attendant to family lineage, legitimacy became a focal point of English law. According to Stefoff (2007),

the concept of legitimacy is central to a theory of marriage that focuses on how marriage relates to inheritance, not just of money and property, but also of status and rank. In this view, marriage is the mechanism by which society passes valuable things from one generation to the next.

(pp. 28–29)

Illegitimate children—those born outside of a legally sanctioned marriage—were common at the time, given the high cost associated with legal marriage. These children possessed less legal standing than those conceived in legal unions—and not just with regard to inheritance (Scammell, 1974). Under King Alfred (871–899), for example, laws governing honor and revenge stated that only legitimate sisters, daughters, and mothers who were legally wed could be "avenged by a blood feud" (Scammell, 1974, p. 532).

Marriage in Non-Western Cultures

Native-American Tribes

Although the current population is greatly diminished from before European colonization, the indigenous people of both North and South America currently account for hundreds of unique tribes. These tribes represent separate cultures, religious practices, languages, and history. Much of their histories are lost as a function of the ravages of war and colonization efforts by the Europeans. What little of this history remains is often contained in the writings of missionaries. Their accounts imply that marriage in many Native-American tribes functioned similarly to the tribal systems seen elsewhere (Newell, 2005). Like the tribes of the Middle East, marriage functioned as a means to create kinship bonds and establish economic and political ties between tribes and families (Newell, 2005). Many tribal marriages were marked by exchanging gifts between families or tribes (Newell, 2005). Some tribes were exclusively monogamous; other tribes practiced polygamy, although "[g]enerally, only the wealthy, high status men such as village headmen and shamans [could] support multiple wives or need[ed] additional help that extra wives could provide" (Newell, 2005, p. 69). The type of polygamous relationships also varied by tribe. In some instances, a man would marry a woman as well as her female relatives such as her sisters or aunts; in other polygamous arrangements, the wives came from different families or tribes (Newell, 2005).

Because each indigenous tribe is unique, it is difficult to make generalizations about the Native-American experiences, let alone their marriage customs. Nonetheless, it appears many tribes accepted same-sex unions (Blackwood, 1984). The term **berdache** is a term dating back to the 1700s and was coined by Europeans to describe "special gender roles in Native-American cultures that anthropologists have interpreted as ceremonial transvestitism, institutionalized homosexuality, and gender variance/multiple genders" (Jacobs, Thomas, & Lang, 1997, p. 4). Berdaches were relatively common throughout the Native-American tribes, although they were known by different names (Newell, 2005). Often, berdaches were males who dressed and behaved as women, taking on the social roles and responsibilities of women including marrying men (Newell, 2005). Less commonly, women berdaches took on male roles (Blackwood, 1984).

Many tribes, most notably the Mohave and Yuma, treated berdaches as members of whatever gender they presented themselves (Blackwood, 1984). Blackwood (1984) explained the reason for the relatively widespread acceptance of berdaches and similarly gender nonconforming people was a general lack of hierarchy among the sexes:

> Egalitarian relations of the sexes were predicated on the cooperation of autonomous individuals who had control of their productive activities. In these tribes women owned and distributed the articles they produced, and they had an equal voice in matters affecting kin and community. Economic strategies were dependent on collective activity. Lineages or individuals have no formal authority; a whole group made decisions by consensus. People of both sexes could achieve positions of leadership through skill, wisdom, and spiritual power. Ultimately, neither women nor men had an inferior role but

rather had power in those spheres of activity specific to their sex.
> (Blackwood, 1984, p. 32)

An example of the gender egalitarianism of some Native-American tribes can be found in the Klamath tribe from present-day Colorado. Klamath women participated in hunting, fishing, and many typically male-dominated activities, such as building canoes (Blackwood, 1984).

African Tribes

The vast continent of Africa contains people from a variety of ethnicities and an even greater number of tribal communities (Sayre, 1999). These communities have historically displayed "a great diversity in traditional marriage practices, both within and between ethnic groups" (Meekers, 1992, p. 62). This diversity is not only reflected in differing practices concerning monogamy, but also in the fact that some tribes sanctioned child marriages, temporary marriages, and visiting marriages (Meekers, 1992).

African culture—both historically and currently—has been dominated by the widespread practice of polygamous unions (Draper, 1989; Guyer, 1986; Stacey, 2011). Along with legally binding polygamous marriages, a man might also be legally wed to only one wife, but have similarly styled unions with other women, a practice known as "outside wives" (Meekers, 1992). Polygamous marriages remain particularly favored in rural areas where the women and children were responsible for maintaining the farms and gardens (Draper, 1989). Traditionally, men in these areas served as protection for the family and community and dealt with local politics (Draper, 1989). In these areas, multiple wives are seen as a status symbol signalling elite status and monogamous marriage seen to signal poverty and an inability to care for and protect (Draper, 1989; Guyer, 1986).

Tribal rituals for marriages also varied significantly. In some areas of Africa, marriage could be a lengthy process—sometimes unfolding over the courses of years—comprising multiple stages and rites that must be completed before a couple is viewed as married by the community (Meekers, 1992). These rites included a payment of a bride-wealth by the man's family to the woman's family and were often accompanied by the man performing services and tasks for the woman's family (Guyer, 1986). The payment of the bride-wealth guaranteed "the husband rights to the sexual and economic services of his wife" (Meekers, 1992, p. 61).

There are documented cases of same-sex marriages in tribal Africa. Like the ancient Greeks, the Azande tribe practiced a form of pederasty in which a warrior would take a young boy as a wife (Eskridge, 1993). A man wishing to marry a young boy went through the same steps and rites that were required when marrying a woman, including paying a bride-price to the family of the boy. The young men and boys in these relationships were considered and referred to as the wife and did many of the duties typical of women (Evans-Pritchard, 1970, as cited Eskridge, 1993). Another example of the practice of same-sex marriage in African cultures comes in the form of female husbands (Eskridge, 1993). Especially prominent in West, South, and East Africa, women assumed the roles of men in private (such as taking a wife) and public spheres (taking part in the political leadership of the community (Eskridge, 1993).

Asian Cultures

Asia, the largest populated continent, is generally considered to include the area from India (in the West) to Japan (in the East), and Russia (in the north) to Indonesia (in the South). The people of Asia follow a range of religious traditions including, but not limited to, Hinduism, Islam, Christianity, Buddhism, Confucianism, Sikhism, Shintoism, and Judaism. As such, the traditions and values that govern marriage in these societies

vastly differ from each other. Some of these traditions included arranged marriages, polygamous marriages, and even ghost marriages (also known as spirit marriages or bride-doll marriages) in which one or both parties to the marriage are deceased (Goody, 1990; Martin, 1991; Schattschneider, 2001).

Most Asian cultures are rooted in strong family ties. Parents often choose marital partners for their children (Thornton & Fricke, 1987). In these arrangements, neither the bride nor groom had any input on whom they would marry. As with arranged marriages in ancient cultures and pre-modern Europe, arranged marriages in most Asian cultures were often aimed at increasing or maintaining a family's wealth, status, or reputation. These arrangements were conducted by parents of every caste, from rural farmers to the nobility (Goody, 1990).

Traditionally, many Asian cultures, most especially in China, were guided by the ideal of "filial piety"—a reverence and respect for one's elders that translates into worship after they have deceased (Martin, 1991). In such cultures, the continuation of the paternal line is of the utmost importance.

The family consists of a father who lives in the paternal home, and a mother, who is completely assimilated to her affinal home and family. They have sons who grow up and marry, stay within the home, and rear their own sons. Daughters, temporary members of the natal family, grow up, marry strangers, and become complete members of their affinal families. . . . If there are only daughters, the parents may attempt to arrange an uxorilocal marriage: a young man will be found who will marry the girl and sign a contract to the effect that some or all of the children will bear their matrilineal grandfather's name.

(Martin, 1991, p. 27)

Some Asian cultures practice ghost and bride-doll marriages (Martin, 1991). These marriages—which are still practiced today in some areas—involve the union of at least one deceased person. Many sprit marriages generally required a living person to serve as the ritual spouse for the deceased; sometimes a doll may stand in for one of the participants, although in some cases the corpses of those who died unmarried were actually placed together in the same tomb (Martin, 1991). These marriages serve many purposes, depending on the regional customs. In some cases, these unions are designed to continue the paternal family line; in other cultures, they are meant to appease a spirit. In China, the practice more frequently involved deceased females, whereas in Japan, it was—and is—used more for dead males (Schattschneider, 2001). In Taiwanese culture, daughters were typically seen as temporary members of the family destined to leave the home upon marriage to join her husband's family. Because unmarried females did not belong to the family, and thus could not be memorialized in the family's altar to the ancestors, the woman's "spiritual identity is excised from her natal line (the line of her father) and subsumed within the lineage of her husband" (Jones, 2010, p. 856). This practice would then allow the woman's spirit to be remembered at the altar of her husband's family.

In contrast with many Asian cultures, the Mosuo[3] people in southwestern China—often referred to as the "Kingdom of Women"—have historically been a matrilineal societies (Shih, 2000). The Mosuo practice *tisese*—a "sexual-reproductive institution . . . which differs from marriage in that it is noncontractual, nonobligatory, and nonexclusive" (Shih, 2000, p. 700; see also Stacey, 2011). In other words, the Mosuo do not practice marriage in any sense known to modern Western societies. Their cohabitation practices are not monogamous nor are they patriarchal. Ethnographic research on the Mosuo (see Shih, 2000; Stacey, 2011) suggest that "the absence of marriage and nuclear parenting have had apparently zero negative effects"—a finding that "offers the coup de grâce to the assumption of monog-

amous marriage's universality" (Richman, 2012, p. 1537).

Procreation and the production of heirs have always been emphasized in Asian cultures. Yet, there are many documented accounts of same-sex relationships and marriages being not only accepted, but celebrated (Eskridge, 1993). For example, in ancient China, several male emperors are recorded as having taken one or multiple male lovers during the Han Dynasty (206 B.C.E.–220 C.E.), while during both the Yuan and Ming Dynasties (1264–1644) there is documented evidence of formalized marriage ceremonies between adult men (Eskridge, 1993). The practice of pederasty—similar to that practiced by the ancient Greeks—was also practiced by Japanese samurai (Eskridge, 1993). In these relationships, the samurai would form bonds similar to marriage with young men (Eskridge, 1993). These relationships represented both a romantic and sexual relationship, but also a mentorship in which the younger male was educated in the expectations of manhood and trained in how to be a samurai (Eskridge, 1993).

The Role of Religion

As previously discussed, many ancient cultures viewed marriage as a transaction. As such, it is not surprising that marriage involved the notion of contract. Even religious marriage included the notion of contract:

> Nearly two millennia ago, Jewish Rabbis created the *ketubah*, the premarital contract in which the husband and the wife spelled out the terms and conditions of their relationship before, during, and after the marriage, and the rights and duties of husband, wife, and child in the event of marital dissolution or death of one of the parties. The Talmudic Rabbis regarded these marriage contracts as essential protections for wives and children who were otherwise subject to the unilateral right of divorce granted to men by the Mosaic law. While the terms of the

ketubah could be privately contracted, both the couple's families and the rabbinic authorities were often actively involved in their formation and enforcement.

More than a millennium and a half ago, Christian theologians adopted the marriage pact or bond. These contracts forged a new relationship between husband and wife and their respective families. They adopted and adapted a number of the marital and familial rights and duties set out in the household codes of the New Testament, in the apostolic church constitutions' canons, as well as in Jewish, Greek, Roman, and Patristic writings. The early rules governing these marriage contracts, as well as related contracts respecting dowries and other marital property, were later systematized and elaborated by Christian jurists and theologians—in the eighth and ninth centuries by Eastern Orthodox, in the twelfth and thirteen centuries by Catholics, and in the sixteenth and seventeenth centuries by Protestants.

More than a millennium ago, Muslim jurists and theologians created the *kitab*, a special form of contract (*'adq*) that a devout Muslim was religiously bound to uphold in imitation and implementation of the Prophet's example and teaching. The *kitab* ideally established a distinctive relationship of "affection, tranquility, and mercy" between husband and wife. It defined their respective rights, duties, and identities vis-à-vis each other, their parents and children, and the broader communities of which they were part. The signing of the *kitab* was a solemn religious event involving a cleric who instructed the couple on their marital rights and duties as set out in the Qur'an. While the Qur'an and Hadith set out basic norms of marriage life and liturgy, it was particularly the Shari'a, the religious laws developed in the centuries after the Prophet, which crystallized much of this tradition of marital contracts, with ample variation among the Islamic schools of jurisprudence.

(Witte & Nichols, 2008, pp. 600–601)

Notably, though, religion did not just view marriage as a mere contract. Each of the three major monotheistic religions viewed marriage as something more—something embodying mutual consent and property rights (Witte & Nichols, 2008). And although each religion developed a liturgical rite that solemnified marriage within religious beliefs, it was the Christian rite of marriage that most significantly influenced the development of law in pre-modern Europe.

The Catholic Sacrament of Marriage

In the fourth century C.E., the writings of St. Augustine (c. 410) greatly influenced European views on marriage—and not just through the Middle Ages. Although St. Augustine asserted that celibacy was superior to marriage, he nonetheless wrote an influential piece, *De Bono Conjugali* ("On the Good of Marriage"). In it,

> St. Augustine argued that there exist three goods in a marriage: procreation (*proles*), chastity (*fides*) and the bond of union (*sacramentum*). For St. Augustine, human beings were created in order to be bound together by some kind of bond of friendship, by which the highest expression of this relationship was marriage. Thus, Augustine felt that marriage and the sexual joining of man and woman was something good because it created a union by which man and women would walk on a similar path planning and cooperating together.
>
> The second good that St. Augustine identified in marriage was *fides* or the loyalty of one spouse toward the other. As St. Augustine reasoned, woman and man do not have power over their bodies individually, but rather each has power over the body of the other. And it was this power that Augustine felt was clear evidence of the extreme loyalty that married individuals must show for each other—a loyalty so strong, that the betrayal of such was considered, by St. Augustine, as the disowning of one's body.
>
> The third good identified by St. Augustine was the bond of union. For St. Augustine,

marriage was a lifelong unity that was not to be undone by the personal judgments of the individual. It was a sacramental bond that represented the source and symbol of a permanent union among Christians. Thus, even if a married couple were unable to procreate, because of sterility, it would be unlawful for them to separate and unite with someone else for the sake of having children. By arguing so, St. Augustine furthered his argument that the purpose of marriage dealt with more than just procreation given that it also represented a natural companionship between the individuals.

(Rosas, 2009, p. 423)

Augustine helped to transform the view of marriage as contract to marriage as sacrament that required that a union be blessed by the clergy in order to be valid in the eyes of God (Reynolds, 1994). As a sacrament, marriage functioned as a way for individuals (converts and believers alike) to reaffirm their commitment to the tenets of the Church, as well as to learn the expectations of the religion (Boswell, 1994).

In 1140, a Benedictine monk named Gratian compiled all canon law in a single text: the *Decretum Gratiani*. The text placed two interesting requirements before a union could be considered a legitimate marital bond. First, is that both individuals were required give their verbal consent during the ceremony. The second was that they must consummate the marriage (through sexual intercourse). Both requirements needed to be met for the Church to consider a marriage legitimate (Hartmann & Pennington, 2008).

St. Thomas Aquinas (1265–1274/1989) expounded upon the work of St. Augustine, not only by elaborating on the three marital goods, but also by clarifying certain points, including an analysis of the virtue of sex within the marital relationship as a central part of God's plan for procreation. Aquinas also incorporated the concept of consent as an explicit and integral part of marriage. But as influential as Augustine, Gratian, and Aquinas

were, it was not until 1563 when the Catholic Church made a religious ceremony—the sacrament of matrimony—a mandatory condition of a legitimate marriage by actions taken at the Council of Trent (Witte & Nichols, 2008).

Notably, there is evidence that the Church did not disapprove of same-sex relationships or even marital unions between same-sex couples (Boswell, 1994; Roden, 2001). In fact, literary records show Catholic monks during the Middle Ages espoused the virtues of same-sex relationships and love with a spiritual, religious framework (Roden, 2001). Boswell (1994) uncovered historical Christian texts that describe in detail wedding ceremonies and rites for same-sex couples and found that they did not differ significantly from different-sex marriages during that time.

The Reformation

The Protestant Reformation profoundly altered the course of Western history, including the institution of marriage. Martin Luther preached that marriage should be based on love and companionship—not just procreative sex—and as such could and should be a social institution as important as religion or the state. Once he "identified scriptural support for treating marriage as a contract rather than a sacrament, support grew for giving secular authorities, rather than the church, control of marriage" (Areen, 2014, p. 33). In the wake of the Reformation, not only did civil marriage grow, but so did divorce. The concept of divorce dates back millennia—indeed, the Torah (Deuteronomy 24:1–4) recognizes a *get*, a document that terminates a marriage according to Jewish law. Civil divorce, however, was quickly created in the wake of civil marriage. Zurich enacted the first modern divorce law in 1525, one that included authorization for the dissolution of a marriage between people "who are not fitted for the partners they have chosen" (Areen, 2014, p. 46). Geneva adopted a civil marriage and divorce ordinance in 1546 that was significantly influenced by John Calvin. Other European cities followed suit. But marriage law evolved different in England than it did on the European continent.

Henry VIII broke England's ties to the Catholic Church in 1534 after the Pope denied Henry an annulment to end his marriage to Catherine of Aragon (Areen, 2014; see Act of Supremacy of 1534, declaring Henry "the only supreme head on earth, under God, of the Church of England"). Upon becoming head of the Church of England, Henry VIII maintained the position of the Catholic Church that marriage was a sacrament and divorce was forbidden.

The first statutory legislation in England and Wales was the Clandestine Marriages Act 1753, popularly known as Lord Hardwicke's Marriage Act (Wilson, 1991). Prior to the Act, marriages were only governed by canon law, although they produced a taxable revenue stream for the Crown. The Clandestine Marriages Act "gave teeth to the requirements of the canon law, which had required marriages to be preceded by the calling of banns or the obtaining of a license, had stipulated where and when marriages should take place, and had directed ministers to keep registers" (Probert, 2009, para. 8). The Act also required that marriages be announced publicly (typically during church services); imposed age restrictions (those under 21 needed parental consent to marry); and required that marriages needed to be officially recorded with the government, with signatures from the couple, witnesses, as well as the clergy who performed the service (Wilson, 1991). Thus, the Act tightened ecclesiastical control of marriage (Leneman, 1999).

It was not until the nineteenth century that English marriage law became a civil entity separate from religious control (Areen, 2014). This shift was prompted, in large part, by the Industrial Revolution, which saw both men and women move from the country into the city seeking work outside of the farm. In the cities, they were able to support themselves financially and "gained a measure of independence from parental control" (Stefoff, 2007, p. 63). Without parental pressure, the need for dowry, or the struggle to survive rural farm life, the primary motivation to marry became love—and not just in Protestant England. The shift from agrarian life even prompted changes among Catholics. A study of Roman Catholic Church records in one French town found that before 1770, about 9% of the couples polled said that emotional attachment must be present for a marriage to be valid. After 1770, that percentage increased to 41% (Stefoff, 2007, p. 63).

Notably, the Puritans, who were strongly influenced by John Calvin, believed in civil marriage and divorce. Most kept these thoughts to themselves since those who challenged the official position of the Church of England found themselves charged with sedition, which was punishable by death (Areen, 2014). Dissatisfaction with life in Great Britain led many Puritans to leave England and settle in North America, Ireland, and northern Europe (Baseler, 1998). Thus, the early settlers in New England brought with them the Calvinist view on marriage as a civil institution, not a sacrament. Once the Puritans secured control of the parliament in the Massachusetts Bay Colony, their marriage and divorce laws mirrored those that had been adopted in Zurich and Geneva. "Weddings were performed at home by a magistrate in a simple ceremony. There were no wedding rings. The parties 'agreed to' or 'executed' the marriage before the magistrate; the marriage was not 'performed' or 'solemnized'" (Areen, 2014, p. 67).

Modern Marriage

Civil marriage is the most common form of marriage throughout the world today (Stefoff, 2007). According to Stefoff (2007), a civil marriage is "recognized by the state as valid under the law, the union must meet the state's requirements for a civil ceremony or formality . . . A civil marriage is secular, with no religious element" (p. 60). However, for those who choose to have a religious ceremony, the clergy who conduct weddings act as representatives of the state. Any religious ceremony that does not abide by the state's requirements is not considered a legal, valid marriage (see Cott, 2002).

Studies suggest that the median age for a first marriage in the United States has increased exponentially since the 1920s (Elliot, Krivickas, Brault, & Kreider, 2012). Between the years of 2009 and 2010, the percentage of new marriages dropped 5% (Cohn, Passel, Wang, & Livingston, 2011). Still, marriage remains an important social institution in which people gather to recognize and validate the choice of two people to share their lives together (Cherlin, 2010; Cott, 2002). Indeed, certain key concepts about marriage have not changed through the ages. Marriage remains a bond between two people that involves formal commitment to each other and formal recognition by the state of the marital union.

For some, marriage is not "official" until performed in a religious ceremony. Certainly, the concept of a marriage often has religious overtones (Marks, 2005). But civil marriage is distinct from religious marriage; civil marriage is a contract, not a sacrament. Moreover, as Martha Nussbaum (2010) pointed out, it is legally insufficient for people to be married by clergy in their religious traditions; the state must authorize the marriage and recognize it under law. "The state's involvement raises fundamental issues about equality of political and civic standing" (Nussbaum, 2010, p. 668). Moreover, the state's involvement is marriage clearly serves a public function—and not just in promoting community life (Cott, 2002).

Nonetheless, it is difficult, if not impossible, to define marriage as constituting just one thing throughout the history of humankind. For example, some assert that marriage has, for time immemorial, been defined as the union of one man and one woman. But, as explained in this chapter, that conceptualization of marriage is historically inaccurate. Even beyond the issue of same-sex marriage, though, marriage is often "a social and political battlefield" in the United States in ways that it is not in other developed countries of the world (Cherlin, 2010, p. 3). In his three-decade-long study of marriage in the United States, Andrew Cherlin concluded the different stems from two treasured, yet contradictory American values: social pressure to marry on the one hand, and individualism on the other. As a result, the United States has "one of the highest levels of both marriage and divorce of most any other Western nation" (p. 4) resulting in what Cherlin calls a marriage "merry-go-round" (p. 5).

Marriage is also an expression. When two people are married, they represent themselves to society as a couple who are committed to each other and who accept "socially imposed obligations to one another" (Hafen, 1983, as cited in Wilson, 1991, p. 543). Some view this expression as the creation point of a family—a mechanism of social control wherein individuals are taught the expectations and rules of society (Abbott, 2011). But, as previously stated, the notion of marriage as an expression of love and commitment is a fairly new one in relation to the long history of marriage (Coontz, 2005). The ancient Greeks thought falling in love a type of insanity, and the premodern French called it a "derangement of the mind" (Coontz, 2005, p. 4). In medieval Europe, where marriages were made for political reasons, adultery—not marriage—was considered the highest form of love among the nobles at court (Ante, 1995; Coontz, 2005). Ultimately, as Ante (1995) posited, marriage is a fluid concept that has changed with cultural social shifts over time.

As the next section of this chapter will make clear, civil marriage is considered a fundamental civil right (Wilson, 1991; see also *Loving v. Virginia*, 1967; *Obergefell v. Hodges*, 2015). When people get married, they are granted certain rights, privileges, and responsibilities by both state and federal governments (Wilson, 1991). Indeed, marriage is "rooted in the necessity of providing an institutional basis for defining the fundamental relational rights and responsibilities of persons and organized society" (*Laws v. Griep* 1983, p. 341). At some points historically, these relational rights and responsibilities have been concerned with the transfer of property and inheritance (Ante, 1995), as well as legitimizing heirs to carry on bloodlines (Martin, 1991; Scammell, 1974). Although modern marriage is more of an expression of love today than at other periods in history, the nature of the marriage contract still concerns a host of attendant relational rights and responsibilities, some of which are solely available under law to those in a legally valid marriage. It should come as no surprise, then, that the right to marry has long been considered an important civil right, the contours of which continue to be defined.

THE U.S. CONSTITUTION AND THE RIGHT TO MARRY

The meaning and scope of the constitutional right to marry has been fiercely contested in both the courtroom and political realms. The earliest case that clearly spoke to the "constitutional right to marry" was a case not about marriage at all, but rather, it concerned vasectomies. In *Skinner v. Oklahoma* (1942), the U.S. Supreme Court addressed Oklahoma's Habitual Criminal Sterilization Act (1935), which allowed for the compulsory sterilization of any "habitual criminal"— a person convicted two or more times for crimes "amounting to felonies involving moral turpitude" (57 OKLA. STAT. §173, 1935). The petitioner in *Skinner* had been convicted of stealing chickens and two instances of robbery with a firearm. A judgment directing that the operation of vasectomy be performed on the petitioner was appealed to the Supreme

Court of Oklahoma, where it was affirmed by a five to four decision. This decision was then appealed to the U.S. Supreme Court, which held the Act unconstitutional under the Equal Protection Clause. However, the Court supported its conclusion with sweeping language regarding marriage as a fundamental right:

> Marriage and procreation are fundamental to the very existence and survival of the race. The power to sterilize, if exercised, may have subtle, far-reaching and devastating effects. In evil or reckless hands it can cause races or types which are inimical to the dominant group to wither and disappear. There is no redemption for the individual whom the law touches. Any experiment which the State conducts is to his irreparable injury. He is forever deprived of a basic liberty.
>
> (*Skinner*, 1942, p. 541)

The *Skinner* decision would become the important precedent in the constitutional right to marriage nearly 20 years later. In *Poe v. Ullman* (1961), the Court found that it did not have authority to determine the constitutionality of Connecticut's birth control law, which prohibited the use of contraceptives even within marriage, because it had never been enforced. More importantly, in his dissent, Justice Harlan argued the Court should have struck down the Connecticut law as unconstitutional under the Fourteenth Amendment since "a statute making it a criminal offense for married couples to use contraceptives is an intolerable and unjustifiable invasion of privacy in the conduct of the most intimate concerns of an individual's personal life" (*Poe v. Ullman*, 1961, p. 539, Harlan, J., dissenting).

According to Dubler (2010), Justice Harlan stated his own clarification of the scope of the liberties protected by the Due Process Clause and "in so doing, Harlan became the first Supreme Court justice to cite *Skinner* as a precedent relevant to defining the reach and scope of substantive due process" (p. 1371). Harlan cited *Skinner* to support his view that the right at stake in *Poe*—the right of a married couple to control their own procreation through the use of contraception—was considered a basic right and one the state legislature could not easily discharge by asserting arguments about morality. Justice Harlan then determined that strict scrutiny is appropriate for legislative classifications that involve such important areas of personal liberty as "the privacy of the home" and the "private realm of family life" (*Poe v. Ullman*, 1961, pp. 548, 552).

Justice Harlan's interpretation of *Skinner* formed the basis of the Court's landmark ruling in *Griswold v. Connecticut* (1965), in which the state's birth control law was challenged again. In striking down the contraceptive ban at issue in *Griswold* (see Chapter 3) as violating the right to privacy, the Court reasoned that "[m]arriage is a coming together for better or for worse, hopefully enduring, and intimate to the degree of being sacred. It is an association that promotes a way of life, not causes; a harmony in living, not political faiths; a bilateral loyalty, not commercial or social projects" (*Griswold*, 1965, p. 486). Perhaps more importantly, the Court rooted this analysis in due process. In other words, "*Griswold* allowed Justice Douglas to transform the equal protection opinion in *Skinner* into a due process case about the right to privacy in the context of marriage" (Dubler, 2010, p. 1372). As a result, just two years later, the decision in *Loving v. Virginia* (discussed previously in the case study opening this chapter) declared anti-miscegenation laws unconstitutional under *both* the Equal Protection and Due Process Clauses of the Fourteenth Amendment. Stated differently, *Skinner* paved the way for *Loving*. And it is now clear that *Loving* serves as the key precedent for subsequent cases involving due process and equal protection challenges to restrictions on the right to marriage (*Obergefell v. Hodges*, 2015).

The Right to Marriage after Loving

Zablocki v. Redhail (1978) involved a class action lawsuit challenging a Wisconsin statute that required judicial approval of any marriage in which the male resident was under obligation to pay child support. Redhail challenged the statute as unconstitutional and charged it violated both the Equal Protection and Due Process Clauses. The state defended the statute by arguing that the permission-to-marry framework served two state interests: (1) it furnished an opportunity to check on whether the applicant was fulfilling his prior child support obligations; and (2) it protected the welfare of the out-of-custody children. The Court ruled in Redhail's favor when it held that the law infringed on the right to marry. The Court reasoned that the state could find other ways of achieving the stated interests without infringing on the right to marry —a right "of fundamental importance for all individuals" (*Zablocki v. Redhail*, 1978, p. 384).

Nine years later, the Court decided another influential case for marriage law in the United States, *Turner v. Safley* (1987). As this chapter's "Law in Action" box below should make clear, *Turner* added to the post-*Loving* cases that held that marriage is a fundamental right protected by the Due Process Clause. However, as will be discussed in the next section of this chapter, judges—including the Justices of the U.S. Supreme Court—are conflicted about the full scope of the constitutional right to marry.

Same-Sex Marriage

As previously discussed, historians report that marriages between people of the same sex existed in antiquity, pre-modern Europe, in certain Asian cultures, and select tribes in Africa and the Americas (Lahey & Alderson, 2004; Blackwood, 1984; Eskridge, 1993; Greenberg, 1988). The historical record even supports the notion that such marriages were socially and religiously sanctioned through

Law in Action DO INMATES RETAIN THE RIGHT TO MARRY WHILE INCARCERATED?

The Missouri Division of Corrections promulgated a prison regulation that permitted an inmate to marry only with the prison superintendent's permission. Such permission was to be granted only for compelling reasons. "The term 'compelling' [was] not defined, but prison officials testified at trial that generally only a pregnancy or the birth of an illegitimate child would be considered a compelling reason" (*Turner v. Safley*, 1987, p. 82). Inmates brought a class action lawsuit challenging the constitutionality of the regulation.

The U.S. Supreme Court began its analysis of the regulation at issue by reiterating holdings from prior cases that collectively stood for the proposition that prison inmates retain many of their constitutional rights while incarcerated:

> Prison walls do not form a barrier separating prison inmates from the protections of the Constitution. Hence, for example, prisoners retain the constitutional right to petition the government for the redress of grievances . . ., they are protected against invidious racial discrimination by the Equal Protection Clause of the Fourteenth Amendment . . .; and they enjoy the protections of due process . . . Because prisoners retain these rights, when a prison regulation or practice offends a fundamental constitutional guarantee, federal courts will discharge their duty to protect constitutional rights.
>
> (*Turner*, 1987, p. 84; internal citations and quotations omitted)

Nonetheless, the Court recognized that judges "are ill equipped to deal with the increasingly urgent problems of prison administration and reform" (p. 84). Accordingly, the courts must accord due deference to prison officials and their judgments about the operations of correctional institutions (see *Procunier v. Martinez*, 1974). As a result, even though the right to marry is a fundamental right that normally requires the application of strict scrutiny as the standard of review to any law or regulation burdening the right to marry (see Chapter 3), the Court declined to apply strict scrutiny in light of the reduced liberty interests and greater security needs in the prison context.

> [W]hen a prison regulation impinges on inmates' constitutional rights, the regulation is valid if it is reasonably related to legitimate penological interests. In our view, such a standard is necessary if prison administrators, and not the courts, are to make the difficult judgments concerning institutional operations. Subjecting the day-to-day judgments of prison officials to an inflexible strict scrutiny analysis would seriously hamper their ability to anticipate security problems and to adopt innovative solutions to the intractable problems of prison administration. The rule would also distort the decision-making process, for every administrative judgment would be subject to the possibility that some court somewhere would conclude that it had a less restrictive way of solving the problem at hand. Courts inevitably would become the primary arbiters of what constitutes the best solution to every administrative problem, thereby unnecessarily perpetuating the involvement of the federal courts in affairs of prison administration.
>
> (*Turner*, 1987, p. 89; internal citations and quotations omitted)

In spite of the Court applying a more deferential standard of review to the regulation at issue in *Turner*, the Court held the regulation was not "reasonably related to legitimate penological objectives" and impermissibly burdened inmates' right to marry (*Turner v. Safley*, 1987, p. 79).

> The right to marry, like many other rights, is subject to substantial restrictions as a result of incarceration. Many important attributes of marriage remain, however, after taking into account the limitations imposed by prison life. First, inmate marriages, like others, are expressions of emotional support and public commitment. These elements are an important and significant aspect of the marital relationship. In addition, many religions recognize marriage as having spiritual significance; for some inmates and their spouses, therefore, the commitment of marriage may be an exercise of religious faith as well as an expression of personal dedication. Third, most inmates eventually will be released by parole or commutation, and therefore most inmate marriages are formed in the expectation that they ultimately will be fully consummated. Finally, marital status often is a precondition to the receipt of government benefits (e.g., Social Security benefits), property rights (e.g., tenancy by the entirety, inheritance rights), and other, less tangible benefits (e.g., legitimation of children born out of wedlock). These incidents of marriage, like the religious and personal aspects of the marriage commitment, are unaffected by the fact of confinement or the pursuit of legitimate corrections goals.
>
> (*Turner*, 1987, pp. 95–96; internal citations and quotations omitted)

- What do you think about the Court employing a lower, more deferential standard of judicial review in cases involving the rights of prisoners? Explain your reasoning.
- The Court concluded that the challenged regulation represented an "exaggerated response to such security objectives" (p. 98). Do you agree? Why or why not?
- The holdings in *Loving v. Virginia* (1967), *Zablocki v. Redhail* (1978), and *Turner v. Safley* (1987) make it clear that the right to marry is a fundamental right. Why, then, do you think that the ability for same-sex couples to marry caused such widespread disagreement about the right applying to them?

medieval times (Boswell, 1994). By the thirteenth century, however, laws were enacted to condemn same-sex relationships as unnatural and immoral. This mindset continued through the nineteenth century even when, with the growing acceptance of the medical model, homosexuality came to be viewed as a psychological illness. This view persists today in some nonscientific circles, even though the American Psychiatric Association removed homosexuality from its *Diagnostic Statistical Manual of Mental Disorders* in 1973. Even with the seeming medical/psychological vindication of homosexuality as a natural variation of human sexuality, homosexual activity remained illegal in some U.S. states until the turn of the twenty-first century (see *Lawrence v. Texas*, 2003). As Lahey and Alderson (2004) pointed out, "[t]he fact that records of same-sex relationships and marriages are found in so many different times and places indicates that even though Euro-American marriage laws and religious beliefs may have presumptively linked the concept of 'marriage' with heterosexuality, the concept and practice of same-sex marriage has never been entirely suppressed" (p. 16).

The Birth of the Modern Gay Rights Movement

During the 1950s and 1960s, criminal laws against sodomy (see Chapter 6) remained viable and were disproportionately enforced against those who engaged in sexual acts with others of the same sex. But gay activism began to take root at this time. By the end of the 1960s, this activism grew to become a social movement in its own right. Most commentators link the birth of the modern gay rights movement to a series of demonstrations in June of 1969 that were prompted by a police raid of the Stonewall Inn in Greenwich Village, New York, immediately after Judy Garland's funeral (Carter, 2005). Garland's untimely death, however, probably did not *cause* the riots because the Stonewall Inn had catered to the most marginalized members of the gay community—drag queens, transgender people, and homeless youths (Eisenbach, 2006). Although violent police raids of gay bars were common in the 1960s, on that night, the primarily young patrons of the Stonewall Inn would not take it anymore; they fought back. The "Stonewall riot" as it would be called "was less of a turning point than a final stimulus in a series of public altercations" (Bronski, 2011, p. 210). "After years of being told by the media that gays were passive, vulnerable . . . [they] were street fighting with the NYPD" (Eisenbach, 2006, p. 94).

Within weeks following the Stonewall riots, residents of Greenwich Village transformed into highly organized activist groups working toward acceptance of gay members of the community and promotion of their civil rights. Notably, the riots did more than spur gays and lesbians to demand their civil rights; they caused the media to begin reporting on the underlying causes of the riots—namely the legal repression of homosexuality (Carter, 2005; Eisenbach, 2006). This media attention brought the matter to the attention of heterosexuals while galvanizing the gay and lesbian community to seek rights under the law that they felt were due all citizens, regardless of sexual orientation. But the right to marry was not at the center or even the periphery of the early gay rights movement. These activists were more concerned with changing an anti-homosexual legal system that, through

the existence of sodomy laws, turned them into de facto criminals. They were similarly concerned with the tactic that police used to harass gays and lesbians, including raids on gay bars. In the decade the followed, gay and lesbian rights made numerous advances. In fact, 23 states decriminalized sodomy between 1970 and 1980—two by judicial decision and 21 through legislative repeal (Fradella, 2002).

The first same-sex marriage to be reported in the United States was *Baker v. Nelson* (1971). Two men sought and were denied a marriage license in Minnesota. The supreme court of that state ruled that the Ninth Amendment did not confer a fundamental right to marry on same-sex couples.[4] The court also ruled that such a right was also not conferred by either the Due Process Clause (see Chapter 3) or the Equal Protection Clause (see Chapter 4) of the Fourteenth Amendment to the U.S. Constitution. The court reasoned that,

> The institution of marriage as a union of a man and a woman, uniquely involving the procreation of children within a family, is as old as the book of Genesis. *Skinner v. Oklahoma ex re I. Williamson* . . . (1942), which invalidated Oklahoma's Habitual Criminal Sterilization Act on equal protection grounds, stated in part: "Marriage and procreation are fundamental to the very existence and survival of the race." This historic institution manifestly is more deeply founded than the asserted contemporary concept of marriage and societal interests for which petitioners contend. The Due Process Clause of the Fourteenth Amendment is not a charter for restructuring it by judicial legislation.
>
> (p. 186)

The men appealed to the U.S. Supreme Court, but their appeal was dismissed for want of a substantial federal question. The following year, an appellate court in Kentucky relied on the decision in *Baker v. Nelson* to uphold the denial of a marriage license to two women *Jones v. Hallahan*, 1973; see also Richman, 2013). These cases, in part, put the quest for marriage equality on hold for a generation. But another factor played an even more important role: Acquired Immune Deficiency Syndrome (AIDS). Indeed, although the push for the legal recognition of a host of LGBT civil rights continued through the 1980s and 1990s, much of the energy of the rights movement during those years was channeled into activism for governmental action fighting HIV/AIDS.

> AIDS, probably more than any other external threat, mobilized huge numbers of formerly apathetic gay men and lesbians. Not everyone became "politically" involved, but many helped to raise money, worked on the AIDS Quilt, or volunteered as "buddies" for homebound people with AIDS. AIDS significantly affected which issues the movement targeted as well as policy outcomes. While lesbians had always been concerned with family policies, particularly child custody, such issues were largely ignored by the movement. With the advent of AIDS, family policies, such as domestic partnership, access to a sick or dying partner, and inheritance became critically important to gay men.
>
> (Bernstein, 2002, p. 559, internal citations omitted)

Seeking Rights Attendant to Marriage

The AIDS crisis prompted gay rights activists to focus their efforts on securing some of the legal rights and privileges attendant to marriage (Bernstein, 2002). In Hawaii, activists won a marriage-equality lawsuit in 1993 in which the Hawaii Supreme Court ruled that the state's refusal to issue marriage licenses to same-sex couples violated the state constitutional guarantee of equal rights (*Baehr v. Lewin*, 1993). This case set off a firestorm of anti-gay activism rooted in the fear that if one state legally recognized marriages between members of the same sex, all states would need

to do so because of the Full Faith and Credit Clause of the U.S. Constitution (Art. IV, § 1), which provides, "Full Faith and Credit shall be given in each state to the public Acts, Records and judicial Proceedings of every other state." This constitutional provision is why a marriage between a man and women legally performed in one U.S. state is recognized in every other U.S. state.

In the wake of *Baehr v. Lewin*, Hawaii and other states amended their state constitutions to bar recognition of same-sex marriages. And Congress enacted the **Defense of Marriage Act (DOMA)**, which became law when President Bill Clinton signed it into effect in 1996. DOMA defined *marriage* as "a legal union between one man and one woman as husband and wife" and defined *spouse* as referring "only to a person of the opposite sex who is a husband or a wife." In doing so, DOMA not only effectively barred the federal government from recognizing same-sex marriages that might be legally recognized by any state, but also prevented same-sex couples who might become legally married from accessing any of the federal rights, benefits, and privileges conferred by marriage, as explained in more detail later in this chapter. Although Section 3 of DOMA—the portion of the law excluding same-sex couples from all federal benefits—was declared unconstitutional on equal protection in *United States v. Windsor* (2013), DOMA's nearly 17 years in full force had far-reaching implications (Barnes, 2013).

Notably, Section 2 of DOMA (which was not challenged in *Windsor*) purported to allow states to refuse to recognize valid civil marriages of same-sex couples. Whether prompted by *Baehr v. Lewin* (1993) or DOMA, the overwhelming majority of U.S. states enacted laws or amendments to their own constitutions defining marriage as a union between one man and one woman. These "mini-DOMAs" barred same-sex marriages from being legally recognized in the states that adopted such laws even if the marriages were legally performed elsewhere. At first blush, this seems to be a blatant violation of the Full Faith and Credit Clause. However, that clause has traditionally been interpreted as allowing a state, under very narrow circumstances, to refuse recognition of a public act, law, or judgment of another other state if the act, law, or judgment in question violates important public policies of the forum state. But whether this so-called public policy exception to the usual rules of the Full Faith and Credit Clause could constitutionally be applied to the denial of recognition of legal marriages is highly questionable in spite of the plain language of Section 2 of DOMA.

According to Section 283(2) of the *Second Restatement of Conflict of Laws*,

A marriage which satisfies the requirements of the state where the marriage was contracted will everywhere be recognized as valid unless it violates the strong public policy of another state which had the most significant relationship to the spouses and the marriage at the time of the marriage.

The public policy exception is so narrow that it has not prevented one state from "recognizing out-of-state marriages even when they violated the forum state's restrictions on incest, age, adultery, and even polygamy" (Sack, 2005, p. 526, n. 93, citing Cox, 2000). Given the strong governmental interests "in promoting stability, protecting children, and protecting the parties' expectations," it seems unlikely that public policy exception would permit one U.S. state to refuse to recognize same-sex marriages that are legally valid in other U.S. states (Sack, 2005, p. 526; see also Koppelman, 2006).[5] Interestingly, when the U.S. Supreme Court decided that the U.S. Constitution guarantees the right of same-sex couples to enter into legally recognized civil marriages in *Obergefell v. Hodges* (2015), the Court did not address the Full Faith and Credit Clause at all. Rather, the majority opinion in the case was based on the Due Process and Equal Protection Clauses of the Fourteenth Amendment to the U.S. Constitution.

In sum, 44 states—all except Connecticut, Massachusetts, New Jersey, New Mexico, New York, and Rhode Island—enacted either a statute or state constitutional amendment prohibiting same-sex marriage (Fair, 2008). Given the hostility to full marriage equality, gay rights activists focused on winning state recognition of most of the rights attendant to marriage through either comprehensive domestic partnerships or civil unions.

Domestic Partnerships and Civil Unions

In 1999, the Vermont Supreme Court unanimously affirmed the rights of same-sex couples to equivalent treatment that law grants to different-sex couples (*Baker v. Vermont*, 1999). But the court did not order a specific remedy. Rather, the court left it to the Vermont state legislature to determine if the state's marriage laws should be rewritten to include same-sex couples or, alternatively, if some other remedy would address the court's concerns. The state responded by creating civil unions as a separate institution similar, but not identical, to marriage.

In some jurisdictions, domestic partnerships provided a handful of rights attendant to marriage. In California, for example, the legislation creating statewide domestic partnership registry (CAL. CIV. CODE, § 51.3, 2000; CAL. FAM. CODE, §§ 297–299.6, 1999; CAL. GOV. CODE, §§ 22867–22877, 1999) afforded

only limited substantive benefits, granting domestic partners specified hospital visitation privileges ... and authorizing the state to provide health benefits to the domestic partners of some state employees. ... The following year, the Legislature included domestic partners within the category of persons granted access to specially designed housing reserved for senior citizens.

(*In re Marriage Cases*, 2008, pp. 413–414)

This legislation was subsequently expanded to provide

> the same rights, protections, and benefits, and . . . the same responsibilities, obligations, and duties under law, whether they derive from statutes, administrative regulations, court rules, government policies, common law, or any other provisions or sources of law, as are granted to and imposed upon spouses.
>
> (CAL. FAM. CODE, §§ 297.5(a), 2005)

Such comprehensive domestic partnership legislation mirrored the rights and responsibilities that civil unions provided in Vermont, and the three other states (New Hampshire, New Jersey, and Connecticut) that had put civil unions in place after Vermont's action in the wake of *Baker v. Vermont* (see Cahill, 2009). These statuses represented "a tremendous advance in the struggle for equal treatment of same-sex couples" (National Center for Lesbian Rights [NCLR], 2015, p. 2).

Nonetheless, it quickly became clear that comprehensive domestic partnerships and civil unions failed to produce full equality under the law for same-sex couples (Dorf, 2011). This inequality manifested itself in three distinct ways:

> First, parties to a civil union or domestic partnership [were] denied most of the federally conferred rights, benefits, and responsibilities of marriage. Second, it [was] uncertain whether other states [would] honor civil unions or domestic partnerships, although a few states have enacted legislation. Third, those separate statuses [did] not provide the same dignity, security, and clarity as marriage, and they perpetuate[d] and encourage[d] discrimination by singling out LGBT people and relegating them to a different legal status based solely on their sexual orientation.
>
> (NCLR, 2015, p. 2)

Each of these points warrants further examination.

Federal Rights Conferred by Marriage

A legal marriage under state law confers more than 1,000 federal rights and benefits on married couples (see *Obergefell v. Hodges*, 2015). These benefits range from the financial (e.g., social security survivor benefits; federal public assistance programs such as those related to food stamps, free school lunches, and low-income housing; veterans' benefits; employment benefits; and nearly 200 different tax benefits), to the ability to be with one's spouse when sick (under Family and Medical Leave Act), or to have one's foreign-citizen spouse immigrate to the United States (see Human Rights Campaign, n.d.). Notably, neither comprehensive domestic partnerships nor civil unions allowed same-sex couples to access these benefits.

An example of the impact of the denial of rights and privileges that same-sex couples faced is illustrated in the story of Kate Fleming and Charlene Strong. When Charlene Strong's partner of ten years, Kate Fleming, was admitted into a Seattle emergency room after being pulled unconscious from their flooded home, a social worker told her that the state could not recognize same-sex partners in emergency situations. Charlene had to get permission from Kate's family member in Virginia to be near her just in time to hold her hand when she passed away (Strong, 2009). Another example of this type of situation is in the recent story of Roger Gorley and Allen Mansell. These men entered in a valid civil union under Missouri law. Mr. Allen became ill in 2013 and had to be hospitalized. The event brought Gorley in conflict with Allen's family who, with the assistance of hospital staff, sought to bar Gorley from his partner's bedside. When Gorley refused to leave his partner of five years, police were called and he was arrested and forcibly removed, despite being in a legally recognized civil union with Allen and holding Allen's medical power of attorney (Sieczkowski, 2013).

Table 9.1 presents an overview of some of the federal rights and benefits to which married couples are entitled.

Recognition of Domestic Partnerships and Civil Unions in Other States

As previously discussed, 44 states adopted mini-DOMA laws or state constitutional amendments barring recognition of same-sex marriages in the wake of *Baehr v. Lewin* (1993) and DOMA. But some states went even further. Consider the constitutional amendment enacted by Nebraska in 2000, which stated, "Only marriage between a man and a woman shall be valid or recognized in Nebraska. The uniting of two persons of the same sex in a civil union, domestic partner-

ship, or other similar same-sex relationship shall not be valid or recognized in Nebraska" (NEB. CONST. art. I, § 29). In other words, Nebraska not only refused to allow its gay and lesbian citizens to enter into marriages, civil unions, and domestic partnerships, pursuant to Section 2 of DOMA, Nebraska also refused to recognize any such relationships that might be legally valid elsewhere. And Nebraska was not alone. Thus, DOMA and its state counterparts created a situation in which similarly situated people—namely same-sex and different-sex couples who entered into a state-sanctioned relationship with legally binding rights and responsibilities—were being treated differently under the law in seeming violation of the Equal Protection Clause of the U.S. Constitution

Table 9.1 Federal rights and benefits for married couples

"Common Sense"	• Legally recognized spouses have hospital visitation rights and can make medical decisions in event of illness or disability of their spouse. • Employers offer spouses sick leave, bereavement leave, access to health insurance and pension. • The law provides certain automatic rights to a person's legally recognized spouse when they pass away, regardless of whether a will exists. • Married couples in elderly care facilities are generally not separated unless one spouse's health dictates hospitalization or special care. • The dissolution of a marriage requires a determination of property distribution, award of child custody, and support as well as spousal support.
Finances	• Married couples are permitted to give an unlimited amount of gifts to each other without being taxed. • Married couples can file joint tax returns. • In the event of the death of one spouse, there is no need to prove ownership in the household and household items for tax purposes. • The law presumes that a married couple with both names on the title to their home owns the property as one legal entity. • A married couple, by statute, has creditor protection of their marital home. • Many married people are entitled to financial benefits relating to their spouses, such as disability, pension, and social security benefits. In many of these programs, legal recognition of the marital relationship is integral to the design of the program. • Married couples can obtain joint health, home, and automobile insurance.
Family and Children	• A child who grows up with married parents benefits from the fact that his or her parents' relationship is recognized by law and receives legal protections. • Legally recognized spouses are generally entitled to joint child custody and visitation upon divorce, and bear an obligation to pay child support. • Second-parent (formerly step-parent) adoptions permit a married partner to adopt the child of his or her new spouse without terminating the rights of the consenting parent. This, in turn, creates and secures a legal parental relationship that is recognized in all states.

and its counterparts in the constitutions of the various states.

Separate, but Unequal

Being "civilly unioned" is not the same as being "married." Having state-sanctioned status that is separate and distinct from "marriage" singles out gay and lesbian couples in a manner that communicates their relationships are less worthy than those of heterosexual couples.

In her groundbreaking ethnography *License to Wed: What Legal Marriage Means to Same-Sex Couples* (2013), Kimberly Richman concludes that this distinction in nomenclature between "marriage" and "civil unions" has real and palpable consequences. These separate, but unequal statuses foster a sense of civic disenfranchisement for lesbians and gays. Moreover, same-sex couples reported to Richman that the latter term presents issues with language accessibility and understanding. Specifically, people's families, friends, co-workers, service providers, and community members simply do not understand what a "civil union" or "domestic partnership" are in practice, nor do they grasp the rights that are routinely denied in spite of these legal statuses that would not be denied to married persons—even at the state level. Moreover, family members do not take civil unions or domestic partnerships as seriously or treat couples as married until they are, in fact, legally *married*—not *civilly unioned* (see Richman, 2013). Consider what Connecticut Supreme Court Justice Richard Palmer wrote in his decision that nothing short of full marriage equality in Connecticut was constitutionally permissible:

[I]n light of the history of pernicious discrimination faced by gay men and lesbians, and because the institution of marriage carries with it a status and significance that the newly created classification of civil unions does not

embody, the segregation of heterosexual and homosexual couples into separate institutions constitutes a cognizable harm.

We do not doubt that the civil union law was designed to benefit same sex couples by providing them with legal rights that they previously did not have. If, however, the intended effect of a law is to treat politically unpopular or historically disfavored minorities differently from persons in the majority or favored class, that law cannot evade constitutional review under the separate but equal doctrine. In such circumstances, the very existence of the classification gives credence to the perception that separate treatment is warranted for the same illegitimate reasons that gave rise to the past discrimination in the first place. Despite the truly laudable effort of the legislature in equalizing the legal rights afforded same sex and opposite sex couples, there is no doubt that civil unions enjoy a lesser status in our society than marriage. We therefore conclude that the plaintiffs have alleged a constitutionally cognizable injury, that is, the denial of the right to marry a same sex partner.

(*Kerrigan v. Commissioner of Public Health*, 2008, pp. 412, 419–420)

The Push for Full Marriage Equality

For all of the reasons set forth earlier, it soon became clear that neither comprehensive domestic partnerships nor civil unions provided gay and lesbian couples with full equality under the law. Hence, and with great trepidation, gay rights activists and their allies launched a series of legal challenges seeking true marriage equality. The first major effort was launched in Massachusetts. The plaintiffs in that litigation received a major boost from the U.S. Supreme Court's landmark ruling in *Lawrence v. Texas* in 2003 (see Chapters 3 and 6). In fact, shortly after the decision in *Lawrence*, the Supreme Judicial Court of Massachusetts issued its ruling in *Goodridge v. Department of Public Health* (2003).

Goodridge was the first decision of any state's highest court to find that same-sex couples have the right to marry.

As part of its rationale, the *Goodridge* court found that civil unions created a separate and unequal recognition. The crux of the decision, however, focused on the notion of liberty:

> We are mindful that our decision marks a change in the history of our marriage law. Many people hold deep-seated religious, moral, and ethical convictions that marriage should be limited to the union of one man and one woman, and that homosexual conduct is immoral. Many hold equally strong religious, moral, and ethical convictions that same-sex couples are entitled to be married, and that homosexual persons should be treated no differently than their heterosexual neighbors. Neither view answers the question before us. Our concern is with the Massachusetts Constitution as a charter of governance for every person properly within its reach. Our obligation is to define the liberty of all, not to mandate our own moral code.
>
> (*Goodridge*, 2003, p. 948)

Goodridge paved the way for the progression of same-sex marriage throughout the United States. Judicial decisions legalizing same-sex marriage followed in Connecticut (*Kerrigan v. Commissioner of Public Health*, 2008) and Iowa (*Varnum v. Brien*, 2009). Legislative action created marriage equality in Vermont (2009), New Hampshire (2010), and New York (2011). And Maine (2012), Washington (2012), and Maryland (2013) created marriage equality by popular vote.

The push toward marriage equality in the United States included executive action. In February 2012, U.S. Attorney General Eric Holder sent a letter to Speaker of the U.S. House of Representatives John Boehner declaring, "President [Obama] and I have concluded that classifications based on sexual orientation warrant heightened scrutiny and that, as applied to same-sex couples legally married under state law, Section 3 of DOMA is unconstitutional" (Holder, 2012, para. 3). This stance meant that the Obama Administration would no longer defend DOMA's constitutionality. Holder noted that the congressional debate during the passage of the DOMA "contains numerous expressions reflecting moral disapproval of gays and lesbians and their intimate and family relationships—precisely the kind of stereotype-based thinking and animus the (Constitution's) Equal Protection Clause is designed to guard against" (Holder, 2012, para. 12).

In June of 2013, two important marriage equality cases were decided by the U.S. Supreme Court: *United States v. Windsor* and *Hollingsworth v. Perry*. The decisions in these two cases started an avalanche of federal court rulings striking down mini-DOMAs across the United States.

United States v. Windsor

A major victory for marriage equality for same-sex couples was struck by a most unassuming champion: Edith Windsor, an 83-year-old woman challenging DOMA in an inheritance tax case. Edith Windsor and Thea Spyer met and fell in love in the 1960s—a time when it was dangerous (and, as explained in Chapter 6, criminal in some states) to be openly gay or lesbian. Spyer was a clinical psychologist while Windsor worked for IBM. At that time, both women needed to hide their sexuality from their employers and colleagues or risked being fired. Despite not being able to legally wed, Spyer proposed to Windsor in 1967. Because of the need to hide their sexuality from her colleagues, Spyer gave Winsdor a diamond brooch to wear instead of an engagement ring (Levy, 2013). The two women lived as a married couple for 40 years. In 2007, while both women were residents of New York state, they were legally married in Canada (Levy, 2013). Two years later, in 2009, after years of battling chronic progressive multiple sclerosis, Thea Spyer died.

She left her entire estate to her spouse—her sole heir. Although their marriage was officially recognized by the state of New York, DOMA prohibited the United States government from recognizing their marriage. Consequently, the federal government sought $600,000 in estate taxes that would not have been charged if Spyer and Windsor had been a heterosexual married couple because different-sex spouses are exempt from estate taxes (Applebome, 2012; Levy, 2013). Windsor challenged this discriminatory treatment of her marriage. As Edith Windsor stated, "If Thea was Theo, I wouldn't have had to pay" (Dwyer, 2012, para. 2).

At first, Windsor sought the assistance of several gay rights organizations to mount her challenge to DOMA. She was turned away. Representatives of these organizations told Windsor that it was not the right time for the gay rights movement to make such a challenge; alternatively, she was told that a wealthy widow's estate tax was not a compelling enough case to mount such a challenge (Levy, 2013). Windsor eventually found legal representation with Roberta Kaplan, who assisted in trying a 2006 marriage equality case, albeit unsuccessfully, in New York (Levy, 2013).

During the time her lawsuit was pending in federal district court, President Obama and U.S. Attorney General Eric Holder announced that the federal government would no longer defend DOMA because the administration concluded the law was unconstitutional (Holder, 2011). In June of 2012, the U.S. District Court for the Southern District of New York ruled in favor of Windsor; that decision was later upheld on appeal (*Windsor v. United States*, 2012). A group of congresspersons from the U.S. House of Representatives intervened in the case, seeking to defend DOMA's constitutionality in the wake of the Obama Administration's refusal to do so. Their appeal to the U.S. Supreme Court was unsuccessful. In June of 2013, the Court declared that

Section 3 of DOMA—the section of the law preventing the federal government from recognizing same-sex marriages legally performed by any state—unconstitutionally deprived Windsor of her Fifth Amendment right to equal protection (*Windsor v. United States*, 2013).

The Court found that Section 3 of DOMA violated the Fifth Amendment to the U.S. Constitution, granting equal protection under the law (Smith, 2014). Justice Kennedy wrote the majority opinion, joined by Justices Ginsburg, Breyer, Sotomayor, and Kagan. For these justices, *Windsor* raised important issues of federalism:

> Here the State's decision to give this class of persons the right to marry conferred upon them a dignity and status of immense import. When the State used its historic and essential authority to define the marital relation in this way, its role and its power in making the decision enhanced the recognition, dignity, and protection of the class in their own community. DOMA, because of its reach and extent, departs from this history and tradition of reliance on state law to define marriage.
>
> (p. 2692)

But beyond questions of federalism, the key issue for the majority in *Windsor* was one of equal protection:

> DOMA singles out a class of persons deemed by a State entitled to recognition and protection to enhance their own liberty. It imposes a disability on the class by refusing to acknowledge a status the State finds to be dignified and proper. DOMA instructs all federal officials, and indeed all persons with whom same-sex couples interact, including their own children, that their marriage is less worthy than the marriages of others. The federal statute is invalid, for no legitimate purpose overcomes the purpose and effect to disparage and to injure those whom the State, by its marriage laws, sought to pro-

tect in personhood and dignity. By seeking to displace this protection and treating those persons as living in marriages less respected than others, the federal statute is in violation of the Fifth Amendment. This opinion and its holding are confined to those lawful marriages.

(*Windsor*, 2013, pp. 2695–2696)

Chief Justice Roberts and Justices Scalia, Thomas, and Alito dissented. In his dissenting opinion, Justice Scalia highlighted the politically polarizing nature of same-sex marriage:

In the majority's telling, this story is black-and-white: Hate your neighbor or come along with us. The truth is more complicated. It is hard to admit that one's political opponents are not monsters, especially in a struggle like this one, and the challenge in the end proves more than today's Court can handle. Too bad. A reminder that disagreement over something so fundamental as marriage can still be politically legitimate would have been a fit task for what in earlier times was called the judicial temperament. We might have covered ourselves with honor today, by promising all sides of this debate that it was theirs to settle and that we would respect their resolution. We might have let the People decide. But that the majority will not do. Some will rejoice in today's decision, and some will despair at it; that is the nature of a controversy that matters so much to so many. But the Court has cheated both sides, robbing the winners of an honest victory, and the losers of the peace that comes from a fair defeat. We owed both of them better.

(p. 2711)

Windsor was confined to the question of the constitutionality of Section 3 of DOMA. The case did not address the issue of whether same-sex couples had a fundamental right to marriage and, if so, if it would be constitutionally permissible for states to limit marriage to different-sex couples. But *Windsor*

certainly had far-reaching consequences. For example, *Windsor* buttressed the end of "Don't Ask, Don't Tell" in the military by helping make sure military same-sex spouses receive benefits, can live on-base, and receive the same benefits that are afforded different-sex spouses of members of the military.

In the aftermath of the *Windsor* decision, lower federal courts have begun to address the constitutionality of state statutory and constitutional bans on same-sex marriage. To date, appellate courts in the Fourth, Seventh, Ninth, and Tenth Circuits have upheld lower courts' decisions striking down such bans. The Fourth and Tenth Circuit Courts have concluded that the bans in three states (Utah, Oklahoma, and Virginia) violate both the equal protection and due process guarantees of the Fourteenth Amendment by impermissibly infringing on the fundamental right to marry. Relying on a series of "marriage" cases, these courts have taken a broad or expansive view of the fundamental right to marry and found that this right encompasses same-sex marriage and the recognition of these unions across state lines. While district courts were split as to the appropriate level of judicial review, both appellate courts concluded that strict scrutiny is appropriate as a fundamental right is implicated."

(Smith, 2014, p. 5)

Hollingsworth v. Perry

The California Supreme Court's *In re Marriage Cases* (2008) decision construed the California state constitution as guaranteeing both different-sex and same-sex couples the right to marry. Thus, in the wake of the decision, same-sex marriage became legal in the State of California. Opponents of same-sex marriage, however, mounted a voter initiative known as Proposition 8 to overturn the *In re Marriage Cases* (2008) decision by amending the California state constitution. Proposition 8 and the campaign to enact it reaped massive funding from conservative backers across the country. Much of it comes from prominent donors like the Utah-based Church of Jesus Christ of Latter-Day Saints and the Catholic conservative group, Knights of Columbus. Prop 8 has also received a boost from Elsa Broekhuizen, the widow of Michigan-based Christian backer Edgard Prince and the mother of Erik Prince, founder of the controversial mercenary firm, Blackwater.

(Blumenthal, 2008, para. 2; see also
McKinley & Johnson, 2008)

On November 4, 2008, California voters narrowly passed Proposition 8. The California state constitution was, therefore, amended to provide that "Only marriage between a man and a woman is valid or recognized in California" (CAL. CONST., Article 1, § 7.5).

Proposition 8 sparked a nationwide debate on marriage equality. Proponents argued that "traditional" (i.e., heterosexual) marriage was an essential institution to our society. Often, the rhetoric focused on the effect legalized same-sex marriage could have on children (California General Election Voter Guide, 2008). Not only did proponents stress their belief that children be raised by different-sex parents, they also asserted that if same-sex marriage were legalized, children would be required to be taught in school that homosexuality was morally equivalent to heterosexuality. Opponents of Proposition 8 countered that marriage was a fundamental right that should extend to all Americans. They also argued that Proposition 8 would create a separate and unequal set of rules for LGBT citizens compared with non-sexual minority citizens (California General Election Voter Guide, 2008).

Hollingsworth v. Perry (formerly *Perry v. Brown* and *Perry v. Schwarzenegger*) brought the Proposition 8 case to the federal court system. Significantly, it was the first U.S. federal court case to recognize a constitutional right to same-sex marriage when it held that Proposition 8 violated the Due Process and Equal Protection Clauses of the Fourteenth

Amendment. According to Anderson (2011), the proceedings in *Perry* were unlike those in the state courts:

At trial, the plaintiffs presented a host of witnesses. Nine expert witnesses—historians, economists, psychologists, a social epidemiologist, and a political scientist—testified on the purpose and meaning of marriage, the effects of same-sex marriage on the institution of marriage, and the effects of bans on same-sex marriage on same-sex couples and their children. They further testified that marriage is founded on the affection of two people—not necessarily one man and one woman, that the state has an interest in marriage because it encourages stable households, and that there are no relevant differences between same-sex and opposite-sex couples that justify the state separating them for purposes of marriage. The expert testimony put marriage in its social context: it sought to show what marriage really is in modern America, challenging the proponents' assertion—prominently relied upon by state courts that have upheld same-sex marriage bans—that marriage serves primarily to regulate natural (meaning, heterosexual) procreation.

(Anderson, 2011, pp. 1446–1447)

Proposition 8 proponents contended that the ban served a legitimate governmental purpose and was not adopted to discriminate against homosexual people. Proponents argued that the purpose of marriage was encouraging responsible procreation, and as such same-sex marriage was in direct opposition to that purpose and threatened the institution of marriage (Anderson, 2011). Although proponents stated their arguments were grounded in scientific evidence, they only presented two witnesses to support their claims (Anderson, 2011). The court was unswayed by the evidence presented.[6] Hence, the court concluded that the fundamental right to marry, properly characterized, must include same-sex couples: "Plaintiffs do not seek recognition of a new right. To character-ize plaintiffs' objective as 'the right to same-sex marriage' would suggest that plaintiffs seek something different from what different-sex couples across the state enjoy—namely, marriage. Rather, plaintiffs ask California to recognize their relationships for what they are: marriages" (*Perry*, 2010, p. 993).

The State of California did not appeal the decision in *Perry*. But backers of Proposition 8 sought and were granted permission to appeal the decision to the Ninth Circuit. The U.S. Court of Appeals for the Ninth Circuit affirmed the decision of the federal district court in a decision that has been characterized as both broad and narrow at the same time:

> It is broad in the sense that it specifically raises the question of whether the Constitution in any way protects gay marriage equality, and that is the most fundamental issue surrounding the spreading movement to extend marriage rights beyond opposite-sex couples. But it is narrow in the sense that the Ninth Circuit ruling would seem to apply, in its full force, only to a state where gay marriage once existed and then was denied."

> (Denniston, 2012, para. 8)

After the Ninth Circuit affirmed the lower court's decision in *Perry*, Proposition 8 proponents then filed a petition for certiorari with the U.S. Supreme Court. The U.S. Supreme Court heard the case, but ruled that proponents of Proposition 8 lacked standing to appeal the district court ruling (*Hollings-worth v. Perry*, 2013). Thus, the Court vacated the Ninth Circuit's decision in *Perry*, leaving the district court ruling that Proposi-tion 8 was unconstitutional as the sole lower court precedent in the case. As a result, same-sex marriage was re-legalized in California in June of 2013. Moreover, the U.S. Supreme Court rulings in *Windsor* and *Perry* prompted lower federal courts to issue an avalanche of rulings on the constitutionality of same-sex marriage bans.

The Firestorm of Cases Decided between June 2013 and June 2015

In spite of clear precedent that should have made legal recognition of same-sex marriage in the United States a simple matter of *stare decisis* under *Loving v. Virginia* (1967), *Zablocki v. Redhail* (1978), and *Turner v. Safley* (1987), prior to June 2015, the U.S. Supreme Court had not recognized the fun-damental right to marry a person of the same sex at the national level. Rather, marriage equality had been litigated primarily on a state-by-state basis. Yet, in the decades since *Loving* was decided, "[c]onvicted felons, divorced parents who fail to pay child sup-port, people with a record of domestic violence or emotional abuse, delinquent taxpayers, drug abusers, rapists, murderers, racists, anti-semites, other bigots—all can marry if they choose, and indeed are held to have a funda-mental constitutional right to do so, so long as they want to marry someone of the oppo-site sex" (Nussbaum, 2010, p. 670).

Internationally, marriage equality is being recognized by a growing number of countries each year. The Netherlands was the first coun-try to legalize same-sex marriages in 2001. According to the Pew Research Center (2015), since then same-sex marriages have been legally recognized by at least 20 countries.[7]

Unlike most other countries, in the United States, the path to marriage equality was fought in nearly every state since each state developed its own laws defining and regulat-ing marriage. Between 2003 and 2015, federal appellate courts have overturned same-sex marriage bans in 26 states; eight states have statutorily recognized same-sex mar-riage, and three states have created marriage equality by popular vote (ProCon.org, 2015). The vast majority of the cases striking down bans on the civil marriage of same-sex cou-ples (indeed, 23 of the 26) were decided in the two-year period following the U.S. Supreme Court decisions in *United States v. Windsor* and *Hollingsworth v. Perry*. By March of 2015, 37 U.S. states and the District of Columbia had legally recognized same-sex marriages (The Pew Research Center, 2015; ProCon.org, 2015). Under the direction of Alabama Supreme Court Justice Roy Moore, however, the State of Alabama defied the federal court ruling invalidating the state ban on same-sex marriages (see Box 9.1). And one U.S. Court of Appeals decision by the Sixth Circuit broke with decisions from four other federal appeals courts when it reversed six lower court rulings in favor of marriage equality from Kentucky, Michigan, Ohio, and Tennessee (*DeBoer v. Snyder*, 2014). This created a split of authority among the U.S. Courts of Appeals since the Fourth (*Bostic v. Schaefer*, 2014), Seventh (*Baskin v. Bogan*, 2014), Ninth (*Latta v. Otter*, 2014), and Tenth Circuit (*Kitchen v. Herbert*, 2014) had all decided cases holding that the Due Process and Equal Protection Clauses of the U.S. Constitution guarantee the right to marriage for same-sex couples. This prompted the U.S. Supreme Court to resolve the split among the Circuit Courts of Appeal.

Obergefell v. Hodges Brings Marriage Equality Nationwide

The Sixth Circuit's decision in *DeBoer v. Snyder* (2014) prompted the U.S. Supreme Court to grant certiorari in four cases appealed by the plaintiffs from Kentucky, Michigan, Ohio, and Tennessee. In a landmark decision issued on June 26, 2015, the U.S. Supreme Court ruled by a vote of 5 to 4 that both the Due Process Clause and the Equal Protection Clause of the Fourteenth Amendment to the U.S. Constitution guarantee the rights of gays and lesbians to enter into legally recognized marriages with members of the same sex.

The majority opinion was written by Justice Anthony Kennedy, the same Justice who wrote the majority opinions in *Romer v. Evans* (1996), *Lawrence v. Texas* (2003), and *Windsor v. United States* (2013). Justice Kennedy began his due process analysis by expressing the institution of marriage has a history of "both continuity and change" (p. 2595). The majority did not explore the history of same-sex unions across cultures and time in the manner explained in this Chapter. Rather, Justice Kennedy focused that the institution of marriage—"even as confined to opposite-sex relations—has evolved over time" (p. 2595).

> For example, marriage was once viewed as an arrangement by the couple's parents based on political, religious, and financial concerns; but by the time of the Nation's founding it was understood to be a voluntary contract between a man and a woman. . . . As the role and status of women changed, the institution further evolved. Under the centuries-old doctrine of coverture, a married man and woman were treated by the State as a single, male-dominated legal entity. . . . As women gained legal, political, and property rights, and as society began to understand that women have their own equal dignity, the law of coverture was abandoned. These and other developments in the institution of marriage over the past centuries were not mere superficial changes.
> (*Obergefell*, 2015, p. 2595)

The majority observed that the above-referenced changes to marriage did not weaken the institution, but rather strengthened it (p. 2596).

The Court then noted that society's understanding of human sexuality also evolved over time, especially with regard to the ways in which gays and lesbians were treated by medical science and under the law. The majority explained the social transformation attendant to the criminalization of gays and lesbians under sodomy laws to the decriminalization of sex acts between members of the same sex under *Lawrence v. Texas* (2003). Against that backdrop, the majority traced the evolution of legal thought with regard to same-sex marriage in state courts and legislatures, including with *Baehr v. Lewin* (1993), *Goodridge v. Department of Public Health* (2003), and

Box 9.1 ALABAMA CHIEF JUSTICE ROY MOORE DEFIES THE FEDERAL COURTS

Not all officials have welcomed the new rulings granting same-sex couples the right to marry in their states, with many states experiencing pushback from appointed and elected officials alike. An example of this pushback lies in the actions of Alabama State Supreme Court Chief Justice Roy S. Moore in response to Federal District Judge Callie V. S. Granade's ruling in *Searcy v. Strange* (2015) overturning the state's constitutional bans on same-sex marriage and adoption. Following Judge Granade's ruling, Justice Moore sent a letter to the Alabama governor speaking out in opposition of the ruling. Moore, quoting both the Bible and Thomas Jefferson, urged Governor Bently to "stop judicial tyranny" and ignore Judge Granade's ruling (Moore, 2015a, p. 3). In response to this letter, the Southern Poverty Law Center ([SPLC], 2015) filed an ethics complaint against Moore. According to the complaint, Moore committed ethical violations by speaking out so publicly about ongoing cases as well as actively encouraging the defiance of the ruling. As Richard Cohen of the SPLC, summarized "As a private citizen, Moore is entitled to his views. But as the chief justice of Alabama, he has a responsibility to recognize the supremacy of federal law and to conform his conduct to the canons of judicial ethics" (SPLC, 2015, para. 3).

Justice Moore's threats were not just hollow rhetoric. On February 8, 2015, hours before Judge Granade's ruling would take effect, Moore issued an order to all Alabama court officials and employees instructing them not to comply with the order (Kirby, 2015b). The order stated, "Effective immediately, no Probate Judge of the State of Alabama nor any agent or employee of any Alabama Probate Judge shall issue or recognize a marriage license that is inconsistent with Article 1, Section 36.03, of the Alabama Constitution or § 30–1-19, ALA. CODE 1975" (Moore, 2015b, p. 5).

Although the majority of Alabama probate judges complied with Judge Granade's order, according to Brauchli (2015) at least 17 probate judges followed Justice Moore's instructions to not grant same-sex marriage licenses. However, Judge Granade ruled that the order applied to all judges in Alabama, and that they must comply and grant same-sex marriages in addition to opposite-sex marriages (Kirby, 2015a). Time will tell what fate awaits Justice Moore. Notably, this is not Moore's first time in the news. He had previously been outspoken on denying LGBT parents' custody of their children—(calling them "an abomination" in a published concurring opinion (*Ex parte H.H.*, 2002, p. 33). And, after he commissioned a monument of the Ten Commandments in the Alabama Supreme Court and subsequently refused to remove it despite a federal court order to do so, Moore was censured by his colleagues on the Alabama Supreme Court and eventually removed from office for judicial misconduct in 2003. Yet, the voters of Alabama returned the errant judge to the state high court in 2012. His actions defying a federal court order concerning same-sex marriage therefore mark the second time Roy Moore has violated his judicial oath of office by defying a federal court order.

the numerous state and federal cases that followed. It then stated, in no uncertain terms, that the central due process premise of *Loving v. Virginia* (1967), *Zablocki v. Redhail* (1978), and *Turner v. Safley* (1987)—that marriage is a fundamental right—governed the Court's consideration of the question of same-sex marriage equality. The majority set forth four reasons in support of this premise:

A first premise of the Court's relevant precedents is that the right to personal choice regarding marriage is inherent in the concept of individual autonomy. This abiding connection between marriage and liberty is why *Loving* invalidated interracial marriage bans under the Due Process Clause . . . Like choices concerning contraception, family relationships, procreation, and childrearing, all of which are protected by the Constitution, decisions concerning marriage are among the most intimate that an individual can make . . . Indeed, the Court has noted it would be contradictory "to recognize a right of privacy with respect to other matters of family life and not with respect to the decision to enter the relationship that is the foundation of the family in our society . . ."

A second principle in this Court's jurisprudence is that the right to marry is fundamental because it supports a two-person union unlike any other in its importance to the committed individuals. This point was central to *Griswold v. Connecticut*, which held the Constitution protects the right of married couples to use contraception . . .

As this Court held in *Lawrence*, same-sex couples have the same right as opposite-sex couples to enjoy intimate association. *Lawrence* invalidated laws that made same-sex intimacy a criminal act. And it acknowledged that "[w]hen sexuality finds overt expression in intimate conduct with another person, the conduct can be but one element in a personal bond that is more enduring." But while *Lawrence* confirmed a dimension of freedom that allows individuals to engage in intimate association without criminal liability, it does not

follow that freedom stops there. Outlaw to outcast may be a step forward, but it does not achieve the full promise of liberty.

A third basis for protecting the right to marry is that it safeguards children and families and thus draws meaning from related rights of childrearing, procreation, and education. . . . Under the laws of the several States, some of marriage's protections for children and families are material. But marriage also confers more profound benefits. By giving recognition and legal structure to their parents' relationship, marriage allows children "to understand the integrity and closeness of their own family and its concord with other families in their community and in their daily lives . . ." Marriage also affords the permanency and stability important to children's best interests . . .

As all parties agree, many same-sex couples provide loving and nurturing homes to their children, whether biological or adopted. And hundreds of thousands of children are presently being raised by such couples. Most States have allowed gays and lesbians to adopt, either as individuals or as couples, and many adopted and foster children have same-sex parents . . . This provides powerful confirmation from the law itself that gays and lesbians can create loving, supportive families.

Excluding same-sex couples from marriage thus conflicts with a central premise of the right to marry. Without the recognition, stability, and predictability marriage offers, their children suffer the stigma of knowing their families are somehow lesser. They also suffer the significant material costs of being raised by unmarried parents, relegated through no fault of their own to a more difficult and uncertain family life. The marriage laws at issue here thus harm and humiliate the children of same-sex couples.

That is not to say the right to marry is less meaningful for those who do not or cannot have children. An ability, desire, or promise to procreate is not and has not been a prerequisite for a valid marriage in any State . . .

Fourth and finally, this Court's cases and the Nation's traditions make clear that marriage is a keystone of our social order . . . For that reason, just as a couple vows to support each other, so does society pledge to support the couple, offering symbolic recognition and material benefits to protect and nourish the union. Indeed, while the States are in general free to vary the benefits they confer on all married couples, they have throughout our history made marriage the basis for an expanding list of governmental rights, benefits, and responsibilities. These aspects of marital status include: taxation; inheritance and property rights; rules of intestate succession; spousal privilege in the law of evidence; hospital access; medical decision-making authority; adoption rights; the rights and benefits of survivors; birth and death certificates; professional ethics rules; campaign finance restrictions; workers' compensation benefits; health insurance; and child custody, support, and visitation rules . . . Valid marriage under state law is also a significant status for over a thousand provisions of federal law . . . The States have contributed to the fundamental character of the marriage right by placing that institution at the center of so many facets of the legal and social order.

There is no difference between same- and opposite-sex couples with respect to this principle. Yet by virtue of their exclusion from that institution, same-sex couples are denied the constellation of benefits that the States have linked to marriage. This harm results in more than just material burdens. Same-sex couples are consigned to an instability many opposite-sex couples would deem intolerable in their own lives. As the State itself makes marriage all the more precious by the significance it attaches to it, exclusion from that status has the effect of teaching that gays and lesbians are unequal in important respects. It demeans gays and lesbians for the State to lock them out of a central institution of the Nation's society. Same-sex couples, too, may aspire to the transcendent purposes of marriage and seek fulfillment in its highest meaning.

The limitation of marriage to opposite-sex couples may long have seemed natural and just,

but its inconsistency with the central meaning of the fundamental right to marry is now manifest. With that knowledge must come the recognition that laws excluding same-sex couples from the marriage right impose stigma and injury of the kind prohibited by our basic charter.

(*Obergefell*, 2015, pp. 2599–2603, internal citations omitted)

Justice Kennedy's opinion in *Obergefell* then turned equal protection as a secondary reason for marriage equality. First, Justice Kennedy explained that that "liberty" protected by the Due Process Clause is intertwined with "equality" protected by the Equal Protection Clause. Hence, decisions like *Loving v. Virginia*, *Zablocki v. Redhail*, *Turner v. Safley*, and *Lawrence v. Texas* all relied on both Clauses of the Fourteenth Amendment to support their respective holdings.

This dynamic also applies to same-sex marriage. It is now clear that the challenged laws burden the liberty of same-sex couples, and it must be further acknowledged that they abridge central precepts of equality. Here the marriage laws enforced by the respondents are in essence unequal: same-sex couples are denied all the benefits afforded to opposite-sex couples and are barred from exercising a fundamental right. Especially against a long history of disapproval of their relationships, this denial to same-sex couples of the right to marry works a grave and continuing harm. The imposition of this disability on gays and lesbians serves to disrespect and subordinate them. And the Equal Protection Clause, like the Due Process Clause, prohibits this unjustified infringement of the fundamental right to marry.

(*Obergefell*, 2015, pp. 2604, internal citations omitted)

The majority in *Obergefell* then explained why a judicial decision, rather than the usual democratic process, was the appropriate resolution of the question of marriage equality for same-sex couples.

> The dynamic of our constitutional system is that individuals need not await legislative action before asserting a fundamental right. The Nation's courts are open to injured individuals who come to them to vindicate their own direct, personal stake in our basic charter. An individual can invoke a right to constitutional protection when he or she is harmed, even if the broader public disagrees and even if the legislature refuses to act. The idea of the Constitution "was to withdraw certain subjects from the vicissitudes of political controversy, to place them beyond the reach of majorities and officials and to establish them as legal principles to be applied by the courts." This is why "fundamental rights may not be submitted to a vote; they depend on the outcome of no elections."
>
> (*Obergefell*, 2015, pp. 2605–2606, internal citations omitted)

Justice Kennedy then addressed the concerns of those who oppose legal recognition of same-sex marriages on the basis of their religious beliefs:

> Finally, it must be emphasized that religions, and those who adhere to religious doctrines, may continue to advocate with utmost, sincere conviction that, by divine precepts, same-sex marriage should not be condoned. The First Amendment ensures that religious organizations and persons are given proper protection as they seek to teach the principles that are so fulfilling and so central to their lives and faiths, and to their own deep aspirations to continue the family structure they have long revered. The same is true of those who oppose same-sex marriage for other reasons. In turn, those who believe allowing same-sex marriage is proper or indeed essential, whether as a matter of religious conviction or secular belief, may engage those who disagree with their view in an open and searching debate. The Constitution, however, does not permit the State to bar same-sex

couples from marriage on the same terms as accorded to couples of the opposite sex.

> (*Obergefell*, 2015, p. 2507, internal citations omitted)

Justice Kennedy concluded the majority opinion in *Obergefell* by stating "that there is no lawful basis for a State to refuse to recognize a lawful same-sex marriage performed in another State on the ground of its same-sex character" (p. 2608). He did not, however, support this conclusion with any analysis under the Full Faith and Credit Clause. Rather, he relied on his due process and equal protection analyses as compelling the same treatment of all marriages—whether involving members of different sexes or the same sex—across the entirety of the United States:

> No union is more profound than marriage, for it embodies the highest ideals of love, fidelity, devotion, sacrifice, and family. In forming a marital union, two people become something greater than once they were. As some of the petitioners in these cases demonstrate, marriage embodies a love that may endure even past death. It would misunderstand these men and women to say they disrespect the idea of marriage. Their plea is that they do respect it, respect it so deeply that they seek to find its fulfillment for themselves. Their hope is not to be condemned to live in loneliness, excluded from one of civilization's oldest institutions. They ask for equal dignity in the eyes of the law. The Constitution grants them that right.
>
> (*Obergefell*, 2015, p. 2608)

Transgender Marriage

Thomas Beatie made headlines in March 2007 when he told *The Advocate* that he was pregnant. Born Tracy Lagondino, Thomas is a transgender person that began his transition into a man when he was 24 years old. Although Beatie was assigned female at birth, he always felt that he was male. As an adult,

Box 9.2 FRIED CHICKEN AND SAME-SEX MARRIAGE

Prior to the summer of 2012, Chick-fil-A was mostly known for its fried chicken. However, the opinion of Chick-fil-A's Chief Operating Officer Dan Cathy on same-sex marriage would spark an intense national controversy.

On July 2, 2012, *Biblical Reporter* reported an interview with Dan Cathy who, when asked about opposition to his company's "support of the traditional family," replied: "We are very much supportive of the family—the biblical definition of the family unit. We are a family-owned business, a family-led business, and we are married to our first wives. We give God thanks for that. . . . We want to do anything we possibly can to strengthen families. We are very much committed to that," Cathy emphasized. "We intend to stay the course," he said. "We know that it might not be popular with everyone, but thank the Lord, we live in a country where we can share our values and operate on biblical principles" (Blume, 2012, para. 7).

Same-sex marriage proponents called for boycotts and staged "kiss-ins" at restaurants. Several politicians announced plans to block Chick-fil-A's applications to open new restaurants in their jurisdictions. Boston Mayor Thomas Menino told the *Boston Herald* that the restaurant did not belong in Boston: "We're an open city, we're a city that's at the forefront of inclusion" (Turner, 2012, para. 2). The Jim Henson Company released a statement on its Facebook page that it had "notified Chick-fil-A that we do not wish to partner with them on any future endeavors" (Burra, 2012).

Boycotts, however, can go both ways. Companies on both sides of the issue have been targeted for boycotts by those who do not agree with their positions. For example, in 2004, Procter and Gamble (P&G) infuriated conservative groups by opposing an anti-gay rights statute that would exempt gays and lesbians from so-called "special civil rights" protection in Cincinnati. In response, the American Family Association issued a boycott of some of P&G's most popular products and collected petition signatures from almost 365,000 families requesting that the company change its policy (Wing, 2012).

In January 2012, the National Organization for Marriage launched a website urging people to boycott Starbucks after the coffee chain released a press release in support of marriage equality. In June 2012, Oreo posted a photograph of a rainbow-stacked Oreo cookie to its Facebook page in commemoration of Pride Month. Commentators were outraged and even called for a boycott of Oreo cookies as well as its parent company, Kraft Foods (Bingham, 2012). J.C. Penney likewise came under fire in 2012 when One Million Moms boycotted the department store after it chose Ellen DeGeneres as its spokesperson. And the American Family Association boycotted J.C. Penney when its June 2012 catalog featured a homosexual couple playing with their children (Wing, 2012).

Given the rapid developments on the same-sex marriage front between 2012 and 2015, it is worth noting that threats of boycotts have also occurred in the face of potentially discriminatory actions against LGBT people. For example, several states considered enacting religious freedom laws that were so broad, they could be used to allow a service provider to deny service to LGBT people on the basis of their religious beliefs. The Arizona state legislature passed such a law, but multiple threats of boycotts against the state led then-governor Jan Brewer to veto the bill. Indiana enacted such a law, but fierce public outcry against it and threats of boycotts from SalesForce.com (which announced its intention to halt expansion in the state), the NCAA (headquartered in Indiana), leaders of 70 tech-industry firms, and others collective led the state to amend the law to include anti-discrimination provisions within days of the initial enactment of the law (see Savage, 2015). The backlash against Indiana's law led the governor of Arkansas to veto similar legislation in that state.

1. How does individual morality impact law and politics? To what extent and in what cases should "morality" have any effect on civil law?
2. Offer arguments in favor and against the argument that certain moral and religious viewpoints should be excluded from the same-sex marriage debate. Take into consideration everything you have read and learned regarding the history of marriage and the history of case law addressing the right to marry.
3. Proponents of religious freedom laws argue they protect the rights of religious people from taking actions that violate their religious beliefs, such as delivering flowers and making cakes for weddings between members of the same sex, or even refusing to serve gay or lesbian people in a restaurant. Opponents of such laws argue they provide legal shelter for discrimination, often pointing out that similar religious-based arguments were used to justify a refusal to provide services to African-Americans prior to laws prohibiting such discrimination. Where do you stand on this issue? Why?

Beatie had his breasts removed and underwent male hormone therapy, but maintained his female reproductive organs. In 2003, Beatie married a woman named Nancy Gillespie in Hawaii. The couple wanted to start a family. Nancy, however, could not conceive children, so the couple decided that Thomas would be artificially inseminated with donor sperm. Thereafter, Beatie was branded as the "World's First Pregnant Man." Beatie would go on to give birth to the couple's three children during their nine-year marriage (*Huffington Post*, 2012). Beatie, however, filed for divorce from his wife. In August 2012, an Arizona judge refused to hear the case until it could be determined whether the marriage was valid, reasoning that since the couple both had female sex organs, their union amounted to an invalid same-sex marriage that was not legally recognized in Arizona at the time (Brocklebank, 2012). Indeed, the judge claimed that if the Beaties' marriage were void *ab initio* (i.e., to be treated as invalid from the outset), no court would have the authority to grant a divorce (*Huffington Post*, 2012).

The couple was able to present themselves as a heterosexual couple for a marriage in Hawaii because Thomas had "state-authorized" sex reassignment surgery before the wedding. Beatie provided all the documents that designated him as a male, including his Hawaii birth certificate, which had been changed to identify him as male. Nonetheless, the Arizona judge ultimately decided there was insufficient evidence to prove that Beatie was officially a man in 2003 when the couple married. Additionally, the judge used the fact that Thomas had carried and given birth to children as proof that he was not male. This ruling effectively invalidated the Beaties' marriage not by granting a divorce, but rather by declaring the Beaties had never been legally married (Ring, 2013). Thomas Beatie appealed the ruling. In 2014, an Arizona appellate court overturned the trial court's decision, recognized Thomas Beatie's sex as male, re-validated the Beaties' marriage, and granted the Beaties a legal divorce:

The question before this Court is . . . whether the laws of the State of Arizona allow a marriage, lawfully entered into in another state, between two persons the foreign state formally recognized at the time of the marriage as male and female, to be dissolved. At the time of the Beaties' marriage in Hawaii, that state only allowed marriages between a man and a woman, and Hawaii's legislature, like Arizona's, had established statutory authority allowing persons who had undergone a sex change operation to apply for and obtain an amended birth certificate reflecting the appropriate gender.

(*Beatie v. Arizona*, 2014, p. 757)

Moreover, at the time Thomas and Nancy married, Thomas possessed dispositive, state-issued credentials reflecting his "male" status, and Nancy held similar credentials that dispositively reflected her "female" status. Their marriage, therefore, was "valid by the law of the place where contracted," as reflected by the issuance of the marriage license by the State of Hawaii. Consequently, Thomas and Nancy's marriage is also valid in this state . . ., as their marriage is between a man and a woman, . . . not a "[m]arriage between persons of the same sex" (*Beatie v. Arizona*, 2014, pp. 757, 760).

Thomas Beatie's case brings up many of the important issues surrounding a transgender person's life. Transgender individuals fall in love, get married, and start families. Transgender people fall out of love and get divorced. As Strasser (2010) explained, although they share the same dreams and desires, transgender individuals face legal risks unlike other families, because State laws are extremely unclear in addressing the rights of transgender persons, particularly with the right to marriage.

According to Boso (2009), the complexities surrounding gender are seldom considered when lawmakers draft laws typically written using a strict male/female binary. This is particularly true of marriage laws. Under the binary mentality, a man and woman equate to legal marriage, whereas a man and man or a woman and a woman equate to same-sex marriage which, until very recently, was prohibited throughout most the United States.

The first case to consider the validity of transgender marriage was *Anonymous v. Anonymous* decided in 1971. This short case paid little attention to the complex interplay between sex and gender. It merely stated "mere removal of the male organs would not, in and of itself, change a person into a true female" (*Anonymous*, 1971, p. 984). The marriage in that case was claimed to have never existed because the wife had actually been born biologically male. Strasser (2010) asserted that "a person's biological sex is not merely a reflection of genitalia . . . [it includes] genetics/chromosomes, gonads, internal reproductive morphology, external reproductive morphology, hormones, and phenology/secondary sex features" (p. 158).

Clearly, transgender people face unique legal issues with regard to marriage. In some states, transgender individuals are able to enter into a heterosexual marriage after a sex-reassignment surgery (see, e.g., *M.T. v. J.T.*, 1976). In other states, transgender people may be married to a person of the same sex in cases where the couple was married as a different-sex couple before one of the pair came out as transgender and transitioned. Consider the case of *Roach v. Roach n.k.a. Silverwolf* (2007) in which an individual who was assigned female at birth transitioned to male after 18 years of marriage. When the couple was divorcing, the husband argued that he should not have to pay alimony because his wife was "legally dead" as a result of her transition and because Florida did not recognize same-sex marriages at the time. A Florida appellate court rejected that argument and upheld the alimony award because the marriage was valid at the time the parties had entered into it.

Most states permit an individual to change his or her sex on a birth certificate so long as certain requirements are met. However, even where a person is considered a certain sex on his or her birth certificate or driver's license, some states only recognize that change in sex for limited legal purposes, and not for purposes of marriage (Lambda Legal, 2015). Current law in many states is unclear with respect to whether, or under what conditions, a transgender person can marry someone of his or her assigned sex at birth. As Strasser (2010) argued,

> This is not simply a matter of determining the conditions under which a modification to a birth certificate will be permitted, because in some states an individual can be of one sex for certain purposes and a different sex for other purposes. Matters become even more complicated when families travel through or move to other states with differing rules regarding marriage or birth certificate modifications.
>
> (pp. 81–82)

By the start of 2015, only three states—Idaho, Ohio, and Tennessee—did not authorize transgender individuals to change their birth certificates to reflect their self-identified sex. But the variability in the other 47 states is dauntingly complicated. For example, some states, like New York, place the responsibility for the procedures and records affecting transgender individuals with local authorities. In other words, the city or county in which someone resides may determine what requirements must be met before birth certificates and other official documents might be legally modified (Strasser, 2010).

In Texas, birth certificates can be changed under certain conditions. In *Littleton v. Prange* (1999), a Texas appellate court rejected that an amended birth certificate represented Christie Lee Littleton's true sex, despite the fact that she had undergone sex-reassignment surgery. The case arose when Ms. Littleton brought a wrongful death suit seeking damages for her husband's death as a result of alleged medical malpractice. The court ruled that Littleton could not bring the lawsuit; the court maintains that because she was transgender, she and her husband were the same biological sex and, therefore, their marriage was an invalid one between two males:

> At the time of birth, Christie was a male, both anatomically and genetically. The facts contained in the original birth certificate were true and accurate, and the words contained in the amended certificate are not binding on this court. There are some things we cannot will into being. They just are.
>
> (*Littleton v. Prange*, 1999, p. 231)

As a result of that decision, Ms. Littleton was denied all of the rights afforded to a surviving spouse in a legally recognized marriage, including the right to bring a wrongful death suit, the right to insurance, and the right to her husband's social security (Strasser, 2010).

In addition, there is a common misconception that all transgender people undergo sex-reassignment surgery. However, for a multitude of reasons including the high expense and the nonexistence of a foolproof, safe procedure, many transgender individuals elect not to undergo surgery (Strasser, 2010). This circumstance in and of itself creates tension between the identities that fall under the "transgender umbrella." For example, transgender people that can afford the procedure (phalloplasty or vaginoplasty, the creation of a penis or vagina, respectively) are likely to be more concerned with establishing an enduring legal status as to their gender. Further, new identities have recently been drawn out from the notion of "transgender" with the increase in those youths that consider themselves "genderqueer." Luke Boso (2009) suggested that courts in recent cases continue to cling to the traditional gender binary: "[T]he courts have employed a new justification for their narrow construction of sex: the legislature, not the judiciary, must defined the words of its law" (p. 158 see also Steasser, 2010). Boso (2009) noted, "This stronghold on binary sex jurisprudence comes in light of the increasingly evident reality that real change is forth-coming in the way society thinks about sex" (p. 159). Courts, however, seemingly remain hesitant to embrace more diverse definitions of gender and sex.

CONCLUSION

As this chapter should make clear, what constitutes marriage has varied significantly over time and across cultures: "Throughout its history, marriage has been viewed in varying ways, early on as a mere property arrangement, a form of extending inheritance and dynastic rights, in which love was incidental. Later on, marriage became viewed as a passionate friendship and romantic relationship between two people, regardless of gender" (Ante, 1995, p. 426). Some places in the pre-modern world recognized same-sex marriages, although the passage of time all but eliminated the legal recognition of such unions until recently, when the pendulum of social favor began to swing back toward acceptance of marriage equality.

Until her death in 2008, Mildred Loving supported every person's right to marry. In 1965, while her case was pending before the courts, Loving told the *Washington Evening Star*, "We loved each other and got married. We are not marrying the state. The law should allow a person to marry anyone he wants" (as cited in Abbott, 2011, p. 330). On June 12, 2007, Mildred Loving issued a statement on the 40th anniversary of the *Loving v. Virginia* decision:

My generation was bitterly divided over something that should have been so clear and right . . . But I have lived long enough now to see big changes. The older generation's fears and prejudices have given way, and today's young people realize that if someone loves someone they have a right to marry . . . I am still not a political person, but I am proud that Richard's and my name is on a court case that can help rein-

force the love, the commitment, the fairness, and the family that so many people, black or white, young or old, gay or straight seek in life. I support the freedom to marry for all. That's what *Loving*, and loving, are all about.

(Loving, 2007, p. 2)

With the U.S. Supreme Court's decision in *Obergefell v. Hodges* (2015), Mildred Loving's vision of *Loving*—and loving—appear to have come to full fruition.

FURTHER READING

Cahill, S. (2004). *Same-sex marriage in the United States: Focus on the facts*. Lanham, MD: Lexington Books.

Carpenter, T., & Yeatts, E. H. (1996). *Stars without garters! The memoirs of two gay GIs in WWII*. San Francisco, CA: Alamo Square Distributors.

Currah, P., Juang, R. M., & Minter, S. (Eds.). (2006). *Transgender rights*. Minneapolis, MN: University of Minnesota Press.

Frank, N. (2009). *Unfriendly fire: How the gay ban undermines the military and weakens America*. New York, NY: St. Martin's Press.

Newbeck, P. (2008). *Virginia hasn't always been for lovers: Interracial marriage bans and the case of Richard and Mildred Loving*. Carbondale, IL: Southern Illinois University Press.

GLOSSARY

Agōgē: The rigorous education and training regimen mandated for all male Spartan citizens, except for the firstborn son in the ruling houses, Eurypontid and Agiad. The training involved learning stealth, cultivating loyalty to one's group, military training (e.g., pain tolerance), hunting, dancing, singing, and social preparation.

Anti-miscegenation laws: Laws barring interracial marriage.

Berdache: A term coined by Europeans in the 1700s to refer to Native Americans who did not fit into traditional gender roles.

DOMA: Formally known as the Defense of Marriage Act signed into law by President Bill Clinton.

Endogamy: Marrying within tribal or community groups, often in ways that enhanced economic stability.

Miscegenation: The mixing of different racial groups through marriage, cohabitation, sexual relations and procreation.

Pair-bonding: The exclusive pairing between two individuals, typically for the purposes of mating.

Polyandry: Marriage between one woman and multiple men.

Polygamy: Marriage between one man and multiple women.

NOTES

1 Mesopotamia is used here as a "catch-all" term for the ancient civilizations of Sumer, Babylonia, and Assyria from roughly 3000 to 331 B.C.E.

2 "Common messes" housing 15 males.

3 This culture has also been called the Moso, the Naze, and the Na (Shih, 2000).

4 The Ninth Amendment played a key role six years earlier in the U.S. Supreme Court's 1965 decision in *Griswold v. Connecticut* (see Chapter 3).

5 Koppelman's book *Same Sex, Different States: When Same-Sex Marriages Cross State Lines* (2006) examines how the U.S. Constitution

> forbids states from nullifying family relationships based in other states, or from making themselves havens for people who are trying to escape obligations to their spouses and children . . . [He] offers workable legal solutions to the problems that arise when gay couples cross state borders. Drawing on historical precedents in which states held radically different moral views about marriage (for example, between kin, very young individuals, and interracial couples), Koppelman shows which state laws should govern in specific situations as gay couples travel or move from place to place.
>
> (Yale University Press, 2012)

6 In fact, one of the expert witnesses called to testify about the validity of Prop 8, David Blankenhorn of the Institute for American Values, actually admitted—while testifying on the witness stand—that same-sex marriage benefits couples and the country because it is "more American" not to discriminate against gay people. As a result, he is now an advocate for marriage equality, representing a radical switch in his position (see Blankenhorn, 2012).

7 Belgium (2003), Canada (2005), Spain (2005), South Africa (2006), Norway (2009), Sweden (2009), Argentina (2010), Iceland (2010), Portugal (2010), Denmark (2012), Brazil (2013), France (2013), New Zealand (2013), Uruguay (2013), the United Kingdom (2013), Luxembourg (2014), Finland (2015), Ireland (2015), Greenland (2015), and Mexico (2015). The United States of America joined these countries in June 2015 as a result of the U.S. Supreme Court's decision in *Obergefell v. Hodges*.

REFERENCES

Abbott, E. (2011). *A history of marriage*. New York, NY: Seven Stories Press.

Abudabbeh, N. (1996). Arab families. *Ethnicity and family therapy*, 2, 423–436.

Act of Supremacy of 1534, 26 Hen. 8, c.1

Allen, N. J., Callan, H., & Dunbar, R. (2011). *Early human kinship: From sex to social reproduction*. Malden, MA: John Wiley & Sons.

American Law Institute. (1967). *Restatement of the law (second) of conflict of laws*. Philadelphia, PA: Author.

An Act to Preserve Racial Integrity ("Virginia's Racial Integrity Act of 1924"), VA. CODE ANN. § 20–50 (1924).

Anderson, C. D. (2011). A quest for fair and balanced: The Supreme Court, state courts, and the future of same-sex marriage review after *Perry*. *Duke Law Journal*, 60(6), 1413–1459.

Ante, R. (1995). Same-sex marriage and the construction of family: An historical perspective. *Boston College Third World Law Journal*, 15(2), 421–441.

Applebome, P. (2012, December 10). Reveling in her Supreme Court moment. *New York Times*. Retrieved from http://www.nytimes.com/2012/12/11/nyregion/edith-windsor-gay-widow-revels-in-supreme-court-fight.html?pagewanted=all

Aquinas, T. (1989). *Summa theologiae: A concise translation* (T. McDermott, Ed.). Notre Dame, IN: Ave Maria Press. (Original work published 1265–1274.)

Areen, J. (2014). Uncovering the Reformation roots of American marriage and divorce law. *Yale Journal of Law and Feminism*, 26, 29–90.

Augustine of Hippo. (1887). De bono conjugali (On the good of marriage). In P. Schaff (Ed.) & C. L. Cornish (Trans.), *From Nicene and Post-Nicene Fathers* (1st series, vol. 3). Buffalo, NY: Christian Literature Publishing Co. (Original work published circa 410.)

Barnes R. (2013, June 26). Supreme Court strikes down key part of Defense of Marriage Act. *Washington Post*. Retrieved from http://www.washingtonpost.com/politics/supreme-court/2013/06/26/f0039814-d9ab-11e2-a016–92547bf094cc_story.html

Baseler, M. C. (1998). *Asylum for mankind: America, 1607–1800*. Ithaca, NY: Cornell University Press.

Bernstein, M. (2002). Identities and politics: Toward a historical understanding of the lesbian and gay movement. *Social Science History*, 26(3), 531–581.

Bingham, A. (2012, June 26). Oreo pride: Rainbow-stuffed cookie sparks threats of boycott. *ABC News*. Retrieved from http://abcnews.go.com/blogs/politics/2012/06/oreo-pride-rainbow-stuffed-cookie-sparks-boycott/

Blackwood, E. (1984). Sexuality and gender in certain Native American tribes: The case of cross-gender females. *Signs*, 10(1), 27–42.

Blankenhorn, D. (2012, June 22). How my view on gay marriage changed [op-ed]. *The New York Times*. Retrieved from http://www.nytimes.com/2012/06/23/opinion/how-my-view-on-gay-marriage-changed.html?_r=0

Blume, K. (2012, July 2). Guilty as charged, Dan Cathy says of Chick-fil-A's stand on faith. *Biblical Reporter*. Retrieved from http://www.brnow.org/News/July-2012/%E2%80%98Guilty-as-charged,%E2%80%99-Dan-Cathy-says-of-Chick-fil-A

Blumenthal, M. (2008, November 3). The man behind Proposition 8. *The Daily Beast*. Retrieved from http://www.thedailybeast.com/articles/2008/11/03/the-man-behind-proposition-8.html

Boso, L. (2009). A (trans)gender-inclusive equal protection analysis of public female toplessness. *Law and Sexuality: A Review of Lesbian, Gay, Bisexual and Transgender Legal Issues, 18*, 155–160.

Boswell, J. (1994). *Same-sex unions in pre-modern Europe*. New York, NY: Villard Books.

Botham, F. (2009). *Almighty God created the races: Christianity, interracial marriage, and American law*. Chapel Hill, NC: University of North Carolina Press.

Brauchli, C. (2015, March 21). More Moore. *The Huffington Post*. Retrieved from http://www.huffingtonpost.com/christopher-brauchli/more-moore_b_6715216.html

Brocklebank, C. (2012, August 13). Arizona judge questions validity of trans marriage in divorce case. *Pink News*. Retrieved from http://www.pinknews.co.uk/2012/08/13/arizona-judge-questions-validity-of-trans-marriage-in-divorce-case/

Bronski, M. (2011). *A queer history of the United States*. Boston, MA: Beacon Press.

Buckstaff, F. G. (1893). Married women's property in Anglo-Saxon and Anglo-Norman law and the origin of the common-law dower. *Annals of the American Academy of Political and Social Science, 4*(4), 33–64.

Burra, K. (2012, July 23). Jim Henson Company and Chick-Fil-A: Muppets' makers sever ties with anti-gay fast food chain. *The Huffington Post*. Retrieved from http://www.huffingtonpost.com/2012/07/23/jim-henson-company-chick-fil-a-anti-gay_n_1694809.html

Cahill, M. (2009). (Still) not fit to be named: Moving beyond race to explain why "separate" nomenclature for gay and straight relationships will never be "equal." *Georgetown Law Journal, 97*, 1158–1205.

California Civil Code § 51.3 (2000).

California Family Code §§ 297–299.6 (1999).

California General Election Official Voter Information Guide. (2008, November 4). *Proposition 8: Arguments and rebuttals*. Retrieved from http://www.voterguide.sos.ca.gov/past/2008/general/argu-rebut/argu-rebutt8.htm

California Government Code §§ 22867–22877 (1999).

Carter, D. (2005). *Stonewall: The riots that sparked the gay revolution*. New York, NY: St. Martin's Press.

Cartledge, P. (2001). *Spartan reflections*. Berkeley, CA: University of California Press.

Chapais, B. (2009). *Primeval kinship: How pair-bonding gave birth to human society*. Cambridge, MA: Harvard University Press.

Cherlin, A. J. (2010). *The marriage-go-round: The state of marriage and the family in America today*. New York, NY: Vintage.

Clandestine Marriage Act 1753, 26 Geo. III, c. 32–33 (England and Wales, 1753).

Cohn, D., Passel, J. S., Wang, W., & Livingston, G. (2011, December 14). Barely half of US adults are married—a record low. *Pew Research Social & Demographic Trends*. Retrieved from http://www.pewsocialtrends.org/2011/12/14/barely-half-of-u-s-adults-are-married-a-record-low/

Coontz, S. (2005). *Marriage, a history: From obedience to intimacy, or how love conquered marriage*. New York, NY: Viking.

Cott, N. F. (2002). *Public vows: A history of marriage and the nation*. Cambridge, MA: Harvard University Press.

Cowell, F. R. (1976). *Life in ancient Rome* (Vol. 421). New York, NY: Penguin.

Cox, B. J. (2000). But why not marriage: An essay on Vermont's civil unions law, same-sex marriage, and separate but (un)equal. *Vermont Law Review, 25*, 113–147.

Denniston, L. (2012, July 31). "Proposition 8" defenders appeal filed (final update). *SCOTUSblog, Supreme Court of the United States blog*. Retrieved from http://www.scotusblog.com/2012/07/proposition-8-appeal-filed/

Defense of Marriage Act, Pub. L. 104–199, 110 Stat. 2419 (1996), *codified at* 1 U.S.C. § 7 (2014), abrogated by *Obergefell v. Hodges*, 135 S. Ct. 2584 (2015).

Dorf, M. C. (2011). Same-sex marriage, second-class citizenship, and law's social meanings. *Virginia Law Review, 97*, 1267–1346.

Dover, J. K. (1978). *Greek homosexuality*. Cambridge, MA: Harvard University Press.

Draper, P. (1989). African marriage systems: Perspectives from evolutionary ecology. *Ethology and Sociobiology, 10*(1), 145–169.

Dubler, A. R. (2010). Sexing *Skinner*: History and the politics of the right to marry, *Columbia Law Review, 110*, 1371–1376.

Dwyer, J. (2012, June 7). She waited 40 years to marry, then when her wife died, the tax bill came. *The New York Times*. Retrieved from http://www.nytimes.com/2012/06/08/nyregion/woman-says-same-sex-marriage-bias-cost-her-over-500000.html?_r=0

Eisenbach, D. (2006). *Gay power: An American revolution*. New York, NY: Carroll & Graf Publishers.

Elliott, D. B., Krivickas, K., Brault, M. W., & Kreider, R. M. (2012, May). Historical marriage trends from 1890–2010: A focus on race differences. Paper presented at the annual meeting of the Population Association of America, San Francisco, CA. Retrieved from https://www.census.gov/hhes/socdemo/marriage/data/acs/ElliottetalPAA2012paper.pdf

Eskridge, Jr., W. N. (1993). A history of same-sex marriage. *Virginia Law Review, 79,* 1419–1513.

Fair, B. K. (2008). The ultimate association: Same-sex marriage and the battle against Jim Crow's other cousin. *University of Miami Law Review, 63,* 269–299.

Fradella, H. F. (2002). Legal, moral, and social reasons for decriminalizing sodomy. *Journal of Contemporary Criminal Justice, 18*(3), 279–301. doi: 10.1177/1043 986202018003005

Gadoua, S. P., & Larson, V. (2014). *The new I do: Reshaping marriage for skeptics, realists, and rebels.* Berkeley, CA: Seal Press.

Goody, J. (1990). *The oriental, the ancient and the primitive: Systems of marriage and the family in the pre-industrial societies of Eurasia.* New York, NY: Cambridge University Press.

Greenberg, D. F. (1988). *The construction of homosexuality.* Chicago, IL: University of Chicago Press.

Guyer, J. I. (1986). Indigenous currencies and the history of marriage payments: A case study from Cameroon (*Monnaies indigènes et histoire de la dot au Cameroun*). *Cahiers d'études Africaines, 26*(104), 577–610.

Halsall, P. (2004). Early western civilization under the sign of gender: Europe and the Mediterranean. In T. A. Meade & M. E. Wiesner-Hanks (Eds.), *A companion to gendered history* (pp. 285–304). Malden, MA: Blackwell.

Hartmann, W., & Pennington, K. (Eds.). (2008). *The history of medieval canon law in the classical period, 1140–1234: From Gratian to the decretals of Pope Gregory IX* (Vol. 6). Washington, DC: CUA Press.

Holder, E. (2011, February 23). Statement of the Attorney General on litigation involving the Defense of Marriage Act. *Press Release.* Retrieved from http://www.justice.gov/opa/pr/statement-attorney-general-litigation-involving-defense-marriage-act

Holder, E. (2012, February 17). Letter to House Speaker Boehner regarding *McLaughlin v. Panetta.* Retrieved from http://sldn.3cdn.net/b43c938d6601df41b9_26 m6bu2hc.pdf

Hornblower, S., & Spawforth, A. (Eds.). (2005). *The Oxford classical dictionary* (3rd rev. ed.). New York, NY: Oxford University Press.

Huffington Post. (2012, August 13). "Pregnant man" Thomas Beatie's divorce proceedings delayed as judge questions union's legality. *Huffington Post.* Retrieved from http://www.huffingtonpost.com/2012/08/13/preg nant-man-thomas-beatie-divorce-delayed-same-sex-marriage_n_1772566.html

Human Rights Campaign. (n.d.) *Overview of federal benefits granted to married couples.* Retrieved from http://www.hrc.org/resources/entry/an-overview-of-federal-rights-and-protections-granted-to-married-couples

Jacobs, S. E., Thomas, W., & Lang, S. (Eds.). (1997). *Two-spirit people: Native American gender identity, sexuality, and spirituality.* Champaign, IL: University of Illinois Press.

Jones, G. (2010). Changing marriage patterns in Asia. *Asia Research Institute Working Paper Series No. 131.* Retrieved from http://ssrn.com/abstract=1716533

Khadduri, M. (1978). Marriage in Islamic law: The modernist viewpoints. *The American Journal of Comparative Law, 26*(2) 213–218.

Kirby, B. (2015a). Federal judge clears the way for gay marriage to start in Mobile. *AL.Com.* Retrieved from http://www.al.com/news/index.ssf/2015/02/lawyers_ask_for_broad_order_ma.html

Kirby, B. (2015b). Roy Moore asks judge to dismiss suit accusing him of violating her gay marriage order. *AL.Com.* Retrieved from http://www.al.com/news/mobile/index.ssf/2015/03/roy_moore_asks_judge_to_dismis.html

Koppelman, A. (2006). *Same sex, different states: When same-sex marriages cross state lines.* New Haven, CT: Yale University Press.

Lahey, K. A., & Alderson, K. (2004). *Same-sex marriage: The personal and the political.* Ontario, Canada: Insomniac Press.

Lambda Legal. (2015). Changing birth certificate sex designations: State-by-state guidelines. Retrieved from http://www.lambdalegal.org/know-your-rights/transgender/changing-birth-certificate-sex-designations

Leneman, L. (1999). The Scottish case that led to Hardwicke's Marriage Act. *Law and History Review, 17*(1), 161–169.

Levy, A. (2013, September 30). The perfect wife. *The New Yorker.* Retrieved from http://www.newyorker.com/magazine/2013/09/30/the-perfect-wife

Loving, M. (2007, June 12). Loving for all [speech prepared for delivery on June 12, 2007, the 40th Anniversary of the *Loving vs. Virginia* Announcement]. Text retrieved from http://www.freedomto marry.org/page/-/files/pdfs/mildred_loving-statement.pdf

Marks, L. D. (2005). How does religion influence marriage? Christian, Jewish, Mormon, and Muslim perspectives. *Marriage and Family Review, 38,* 85–111.

"Marriage." (2012). *Oxford Dictionary Online.* Retrieved from http://oxforddictionaries.com/definition/ameri can_english/marriage?region=us&q=marriage

Martin, D. (1991). Chinese ghost marriage. In H. D. R. Baker & S. Feuchtwang (Eds.), *An old state in new settings: Studies in the social anthropology of China in memory of Maurice Freedman* (pp. 25–43). Oxford: Journal of the Anthropological Society of Oxford.

McKinley, J., & Johnson, K. (2008, November 14). Mormons tipped scale in ban on gay marriage. *The New York Times.* Retrieved from http://www.nytimes.com/2008/11/15/us/politics/15marriage.html?page wanted=all&_r=0

Meekers, D. (1992). The process of marriage in African societies: A multiple indicator approach. *Population and development review, 18*(1), 61–78.

Mernissi, F. (1987). *Beyond the veil: Male–female dynamics in modern Muslim society.* Bloomington, IN: Indiana University Press.

Middleton, R. (1962) Brother–sister and father–daughter marriage in Ancient Egypt. *American Sociological Review, 27*(5), 603–611.

Moore, R. S. (2015a). Letter to Governor Bentley dated January 27, 2015. Retrieved from http://www.splcenter.org/sites/default/files/ex-a_moore_letter_to_bentley_jan._27_2015.pdf

Moore, R. S. (2015b). State of Alabama: Judicial system. Administrative Order of the Chief Justice of the Supreme Court. Retrieved from http://ftpcontent4.worldnow.com/waff/moore-order-samesex.pdf

National Center for Lesbian Rights. (2015). Marriage, domestic partnership, and civil unions: Same-sex couples within the United States. Retrieved from http://www.nclrights.org/wp-content/uploads/2013/07/Relationship_Recognition.pdf

Nebraska Constitution, article I, § 29 (2002).

Newell, Q. (2005). "The Indians generally love their wives and children": Native American marriage and sexual practices in missions San Francisco, Santa Clara, and San Jose. *The Catholic Historical Review, 91*(1), 60–82.

Nussbaum, M. C. (2010). A right to marry? *California Law Review, 98*(3), 667–679.

Oklahoma's Habitual Criminal Sterilization Act, 57 Okla. Stat. §§ 171–195 (1935).

Pew Research Center (2015, January, 6) Gay marriage around the world. Retrieved from http://www.pewforum.org/2013/12/19/gay-marriage-around-the-world-2013/

ProCon.org. (2015). Gay marriage pros and cons. *37 States with legal gay marriage and 13 states with same-sex marriage bans.* Retrieved from http://gaymarriage.procon.org/view.resource.php?resourceID=004857

Probert, R. (2009). Control over marriage in England and Wales, 1753–1823: The Clandestine Marriages Act of 1753 in context. *Law and History Review, 27*(2), 413–450.

Proposition 8, Cal. Constitution, Article 1, § 7.5 (2008).

Reynolds, P. L. (1994). *Marriage in the western church: The Christianization of marriage during the patristic and early medieval periods* (Supplements to *Vigiliae Christianae*, Vol. 24). Boston, MA: Brill Academic.

Richman, K. D. (2012). Unhitched: Love, marriage, and family values from West Hollywood to Western China [Review of the book by J. Stacey]. *American Journal of Sociology, 117*(5), 1536–1538.

Richman, K. D. (2013). *License to wed: What legal marriage means to same-sex couples.* New York, NY: New York University Press.

Ring, T. (2013, May 31). Validity question looms for some trans people who marry. *Advocate.* Retrieved from http://www.advocate.com/print-issue/current-issue/2013/05/31/validity-question-looms-some-trans-people-who-marry

Robinson, B. A. (2015). *Conflict over inter-racial marriage in the U.S. Anti-miscegenation laws. The Supreme Court ruling of 1967 in* Loving v. Virginia. Retrieved from http://www.religioustolerance.org/hom_mar14.htm

Roden, F. S. (2001). Queer Christian: The Catholic homosexual apologia and lesbian/gay practice. *International Journal of Sexuality and Gender Studies, 6*(4), 251–265.

Rosas, R. (2009). Matrimonial consent in canon law juridical aspects. *Revista Juridica Universidad Interamericana De Puerto Rico Facultad De Derecho, 43,* 419–472.

Sack, E. J. (2005). The public policy of same-sex marriage and a theory of congressional power under the Full Faith and Credit Clause. *Creighton Law Review, 38,* 507–532.

Savage, D. G. (2015, April 4). Backlash against religious freedom laws helps gay rights in Indiana, Arkansas. *Los Angeles Times.* Retrieved from http://www.latimes.com/nation/la-na-religious-rights-analysis-20150404-story.html#page=1

Sayre, A. P. (1999). *Africa.* Brookfield, CT: Twenty-First Century Books.

Scammell, J. (1974). Freedom and marriage in medieval England. *The Economic History Review, 27*(4), 523–537.

Scanlon, T. F. (2002). *Eros and Greek athletics.* New York, NY: Oxford University Press.

Schattschneider, E. (2001). "Buy me a bride": Death and exchange in Northern Japanese bride-doll marriage. *American Ethnologist, 28*(4), 854–880.

Schaus, M. C. (Ed.). (2006). *Women and gender in medieval Europe: An encyclopedia.* New York, NY: Routledge.

Scheidel, W. (2009). A peculiar institution? Greco-Roman monogamy in global context. *The History of the Family, 14*(3), 280–291.

Sengupta, S. (2000, November 12). Marry at will. *New York Times.* Retrieved from http://www.nytimes.com/2000/11/12/weekinreview/november-5–11-marry-at-will.html

Shih, C. K. (2000). Tisese and its anthropological significance: Issues around the visiting sexual system among the Moso. *L'Homme, 154/155,* 697–712.

Sieczkowski, C. (2013, April 5). Family of Roger Gorley, gay man denied hospital visitation rights, set up legal defense fund. *Huffington Post.* Retrieved from http://www.huffingtonpost.com/2013/04/15/roger-gorley-gay-man-denied-hospital-visitation-legal-defense_n_3086977.html

Smith, A. M. (2014). Same-sex marriage: A legal background after *United States v. Windsor*. Congressional Research Service. Retrieved from https://fas.org/sgp/crs/misc/R43481.pdf

Smith, W. R. (1903). *Kinship & marriage in early Arabia*. London: Adam and Charles Black.

Southern Poverty Law Center. (2015, January 27). SPLC files ethics complaint against Alabama Chief Justice Roy Moore over pledge to defy federal law and enforce same-sex marriage ban. Retrieved from https://www.splcenter.org/news/2015/01/28/splc-files-ethics-complaint-against-alabama-chief-justice-roy-moore-over-pledge-defy

Stacey, J. (2011). *Unhitched: Love, marriage, and family values from West Hollywood to Western China*. New York, NY: New York University Press.

Stafford, P. (1993). Kinship and women in the world of Maldon: Byrhtnoth and his family. In Janet Cooper (Ed.) *The battle of Maldon: fiction and fact* (225–235). Rio Grande, OH: Hambledon Press.

Stefoff, R. (2007). *Marriage*. Tarrytown, NY: Marshall Cavendish Benchmark.

Stol, M. (1995). Women in Mesopotamia. *Journal of the Economic and Social History of the Orient*, 38(2), 123–144.

Strasser, M. (2010). Defining sex: On marriage, family, and good public policy. *Michigan Journal of Gender & Law*, 17(1), 57–82.

Strong, C. (2009, October 23). Charlene Strong calls for equality and dignity. *Seattle Gay News*. Retrieved from http://www.sgn.org/sgnnews37_43/page3.cfm

Sullivan, P. (2008, May 6). Quiet Va. wife ended interracial marriage ban. *Washington Post*. Retrieved from http://www.washingtonpost.com/wp-dyn/content/article/2008/05/05/AR2008050502439.html

Thornton, A., & Fricke, T. E. (1987). Social change and the family: Comparative perspectives from the West, China, and South Asia. *Sociological Forum*, 2(4), 746–779.

Turner, G. (2012, July 20). Menino on Chick-fil-A: Stuff it. *Boston Herald*. Retrieved from http://www.bostonherald.com/business/business_markets/2012/07/mayor_menino_chick_fil_a_stuff_it

U.S. CONST., Full Faith and Credit Clause, Article IV, § 1.

U.S. General Accounting Office, (1997, January 31). Defense of Marriage Act, GAO/OGC-97–16. Retrieved from http://www.gao.gov/assets/230/223674.pdf

U.S. General Accounting Office. (2004, February 24) Defense of Marriage Act: Update to prior report, GAO-04-353R. Retrieved from http://www.gao.gov/new.items/d04353r.pdf

Wallenstein, P. (1994). Freedom: Personal liberty and private law: Race, marriage, and the law of freedom: Alabama and Virginia, 1860s–1960s. *Chicago-Kent Law Review*, 70(2), 371–438.

Weierman, K. W. (2005). *One nation, one blood: Interracial marriage in American fiction, scandal, and law, 1820–1870*. Amherst, MA: University of Massachusetts Press.

Wilson, A. K. (1991). Same-sex marriage: A review. *William Mitchell Law Review*, 17(2), 539–562.

Wing, N. (2012, August 1). Sarah Palin: Chick-Fil-A president getting "crucified," boycott has "chilling effect" on First Amendment. *The Huffington Post*. Retrieved from http://www.huffingtonpost.com/2012/08/01/sarah-palin-chick-fil-a-boycott_n_1727965.html?utm_hp_ref=politics#slide=1154550

Witte, J., Jr., & Nichols, J. A. (2008). Marriage, religion, and the role of the civil state: More than a mere contract: Marriage as contract and covenant in law and theology. *University of St. Thomas Law Journal*, 5, 595–615.

Yale University Press. (2012). Same sex, different states: When same-sex marriages cross state lines [marketing summary of the book by A. Koppelman]. Retrieved from http://yalepress.yale.edu/book.asp?isbn=9780300113402

Zoch, P. A. (2000). *Ancient Rome: An introductory history*. Norman, OK: University of Oklahoma Press.

Cases

Anonymous v. Anonymous, 67 Misc. 2d 982 (N.Y. Sup. Ct. 1971).

Baehr v. Lewin, 852 P.2d 44 (Haw. 1993).

Baker v. Nelson, 191 N.W.2d 185 (Minn. 1971), *cert. denied*, 409 U.S. 810 (1972).

Baker v. Vermont, 744 A.2d 864 (Vt. 1999).

Baskin v. Bogan, 766 F.3d 648 (7th Cir. 2014).

Beatie v. Arizona, 333 P.3d 754 (Ariz. Ct. App. 2014).

Bostic v. Schaefer, 760 F.3d 352 (4th Cir. 2014).

DeBoer v. Snyder, 772 F.3d 388 (6th Cir. 2014).

Ex Parte H.H., 830 So. 2d 21 (Ala. 2002).

Gill v. Office of Personnel Management, 699 F. Supp. 2d 374 (D. Mass. 2010).

Goodridge v. Dep't of Public Health, 798 N.E.2d 941 (Mass. 2003).

Griswold v. Connecticut, 381 U.S. 479 (1965).

Hollingsworth v. Perry, 133 S. Ct. 2652 (2013).

In re Marriage Cases, 183 P.3d 384 (Cal. 2008).

Jones v. Hallahan, 501 S.W.2d 588 (Ken. Ct. App. 1973).

Kerrigan v. Comm'r of Pub. Health, 957 A.2d 407 (Conn. 2008).

Kirby v. Kirby, 206 P. 405 (Ariz. 1922).

Kitchen v. Herbert, 755 F.3d 1193 (10th Cir. 2014).

Latta v. Otter, 771 F.3d 456 (9th Cir. 2014).

Lawrence v. Texas, 539 U.S. 558 (2003).

Laws v. Griep, 332 N.W.2d 339 (Iowa 1983).

Littleton v. Prange, 9 S.W.3d 223 (Tex. App. 1999).

Loving v. Commonwealth, 147 S.E.2d 78 (Va. 1966), *rev'd*, *Loving v. Virginia*, 388 U.S. 1 (1967).

M.T. v. J.T., 140 N.J. Super. 77 (App. Div. 1976).

Obergefell v. Hodges, 135 S. Ct. 2584 (2015).

Perry v. Brown, 671 F.3d 1052 (9th Cir. 2012).

Perry v. Schwarzenegger, 704 F. Supp. 2d 921 (N.D. Cal. 2010).

Poe v. Ullman, 367 U.S. 497 (1961).

Procunier v. Martinez, 416 U.S. 396 (1974).

Roach v. Roach n/k/a Silverwolf, 959 So. 2d 733 (Fla. Ct. App. 2007).

Romer v. Evans, 517 U.S. 620 (1996).

Scott v. State, 39 Ga. 321 (Ga. 1869).

Searcy v. Strange, 2015 U.S. Dist. LEXIS 7776 (S.D. Ala. Jan. 23, 2015).

Skinner v. Oklahoma, 316 U.S. 535 (1942).

Turner v. Safley, 482 U.S. 78 (1987).

United States v. Windsor, 133 S. Ct. 2675 (2013).

Varnum v. Brien, 763 N.W.2d 862 (Iowa 2009).

Windsor v. United States, 833 F. Supp. 2d 394 (S.D.N.Y.), *aff'd* 699 F. 3d 169 (2nd Cir. 2012), *aff'd*, 133 S. Ct. 2675 (2013).

Zablocki v. Redhail, 434 U.S. 374 (1978).

CHAPTER 10

Rare Acts, Sympathetic Victims, and the Emergence of Laws to Regulate Sex Offenders

David Patrick Connor

In August 2013, 18-year-old Kaitlyn Hunt's sexual relationship with another adolescent female became public. Hunt was charged with two counts of lewd and lascivious battery on a child, after being romantically involved with a 14-year-old girl who she met at Sebastian River High School. Hunt and her underage girlfriend were students at the Florida school. Many social commentators expressed disgust with Hunt's arrest, alleging that the criminal charges were only filed because the complaint involved a same-sex relationship. Other observers conveyed their sense of disenchantment toward a criminal justice system that could apprehend, confine, and punish a teenager simply for dating a fellow high school student. In spite of these public sentiments, legal analysts were quick to point out that the Sunshine State's statutes regarding sexual misconduct were straightforward. In Florida, they noted, individuals who were under 16 years of age could not legally give consent to participate in sexual activities.

Shortly after their daughter's arrest, Hunt's parents went to the news media, openly talking about how their child was not a sexual predator. In their minds, Hunt was involved in a normal, consensual relationship and did not resemble monsters who lurked in playgrounds and victimized children. Consequently, Hunt's mother and father felt that she should not be subjected to harsh punishments often designated for convicted sex offenders. In particular, Hunt's supporters wanted to make certain that she was not publicly labeled as a sex offender.

After a few court appearances, prosecutors offered Hunt a plea agreement, which appeared to be relatively lenient. Unlike many convicted sex offenders, Hunt would serve no jail time and, perhaps most significantly, not be obligated to register as a sex offender. The fact that Hunt would not be listed on a publicly accessible sex-offender registry certainly would minimize her public identity as a sex offender. However, the plea deal was soon revoked and an additional criminal charge of transmitting pornography was added to the case, as Hunt continued to contact her girlfriend following the arrest, sending numerous text messages and nude pictures.

Nonetheless, a new plea agreement was ultimately reached between prosecutors and Hunt, which was subsequently approved by a judge in October 2013. Hunt served four months inside a county jail and continues to serve a three-year term under probation supervision, which includes two years of house arrest. Although these consequences are more severe than those spelled out in the original plea deal, Hunt is still not required to register as a sex offender, provided that she stays out of trouble for the next ten years. Throughout the case, Hunt and her supporters acknowledged society's punitive approach toward sex offenders and understood the importance of avoiding the sanction of registration.

LEARNING OBJECTIVES

1. Differentiate between the major forms of sex-offender registration and notification (SORN) legislation.
2. Evaluate the efficacy of SORN laws.
3. Assess public attitudes and beliefs toward SORN in light of sex-offender experiences.
4. Compare and contrast early and contemporary civil commitment statutes as they relate to sexually violent offenders.
5. Describe the controversies related to castration mandates.
6. Distinguish between passive, active, and hybrid electronic monitoring of sex offenders through Global Positioning System (GPS) technology.

Perhaps more than any other type of criminal offender, individuals who have participated in illegal sexual activities have been and continue to be viewed as extreme threats to public safety. Society, as a whole, has consistently looked upon such offenders with disgust and disdain (Quinn, Forsyth, & Mullen-Quinn, 2004). By the same token, sex crimes have reliably evoked the strongest, deep-seated reactions among community members when compared with other forms of criminal behavior (Jenkins, 1998; Meloy, 2006). For these reasons, distinct criminal justice policies and laws have been exclusively reserved throughout history for convicted sex offenders (Leon, 2011; Petrunik, 2003; Terry, 2013). However, over the past several years, societal responses aimed at sexual lawbreakers have increased in severity. In particular, legal efforts have materialized to enhance the supervision of these criminals and decrease their opportunities to further perpetrate sex crimes once they are living in the community (Simon, 1998; Tewksbury & Connor, 2014a).

This chapter focuses on legal responses to convicted sex offenders, with a specific focus on sex-offender registration and notification (SORN) laws as the most widespread and empirically examined sanction. Explanations for punitive sex-offender legislation may be found in the high-profile sexual attacks on children in the 1990s. As a result, the discussion includes descriptions of child victims whose names saturated media headlines and paved the way for castigating sex-offender laws. Other criminal justice policies aimed at sex offenders are subsequently highlighted, including civil commitment statutes, castration mandates, and Global Positioning System (GPS) monitoring policies.

SEX-OFFENDER REGISTRATION AND NOTIFICATION (SORN)

Spotlighting society's harsh treatment of sex offenders, one of the most recent developments has been the creation of **sex-offender registries**. Although it is not a new concept, criminal registration is experiencing a revival (Logan, 2009). Sex-offender registries are utilized in every jurisdiction in the United States, and these repositories of information provide online access to a wide array of facts about convicted sex offenders and their sex offenses (Mustaine & Tewksbury, 2013; Tewksbury & Higgins, 2005). Upon conviction of sex offenses, individuals are typically required to provide local law enforcement and correctional authorities with name, photograph, address, birth date, social security number, fingerprints, offense history, date of convictions, and other information. In addition, sex offenders must verify the accuracy of this information on a routine basis for the duration of their registration, which may range from ten years to life (Tewksbury & Connor, 2014a).

Jacob Wetterling and Resulting Legislation

In 1989, 11-year-old Jacob Wetterling, who was riding his bicycle outside his Minnesota home with his 10-year-old brother and 11-year-old friend, was kidnapped by a masked man. According to police reports, Jacob's brother and friend were instructed by the perpetrator to run away, while the perpetrator forced Jacob into his car (Terry & Ackerman, 2009). The perpetrator was never apprehended; however, a significant amount of media speculation at the time focused on the possibility that a sex offender living in a nearby halfway house was responsible for Jacob's disappearance (Zilney & Zilney, 2009). Five years later, the Jacob Wetterling Crimes Against Children and Sexually Violent Offender Registration Act (1994) was enacted. Patty Wetterling, Jacob's mother, became a

visible participant in setting the agenda as an activist for sex-offender registration requirements (Terry, 2013).

California was the first state to apply registration laws strictly to sex offenders in 1947 (La Fond, 2005). However, the Wetterling Act was the first federal law that mandated registration of sex offenders in state-wide databases, although several jurisdictions already maintained such registries. The statute was largely based on a similar law passed in Minnesota (Zilney & Zilney, 2009). The Wetterling Act's major contribution was to require all states to establish a system that allowed law enforcement to track the residency of adults convicted of violent sex offenses or sex offenses against children (Zgoba, Veysey, & Dalessandro, 2010). Generally speaking, the Wetterling Act, as amended over time, requires convicted sex offenders to keep certain information up-to-date with their local police department, such as their home address, telephone number, social security number, and employment information (Tewksbury & Lees, 2006b).

Megan Kanka and Resulting Legislation

In 1994, at the age of seven, Megan Kanka was kidnapped, raped, and murdered by a 33-year-old sex offender in New Jersey. The perpetrator, Jesse Timmendequas, was on parole supervision and lived in Megan's neighborhood with several other convicted sex offenders. According to police reports, Timmendequas lured Megan to his house by promising to show her a puppy, and Megan's body was later discovered in a nearby park (Tofte & Fellner, 2007). This was particularly shocking to the public, because Timmendequas was previously convicted of sexually assaulting a five-year-old girl in 1979 and a seven-year-old girl in 1981 (Zilney & Zilney, 2009). After Megan's murder, her parents openly stated that they would have been able to protect their daughter if the community was cognizant of the presence of such a dangerous pedophile (Tofte & Fellner, 2007). In other words, Megan's parents, as visible participants in setting the agenda, expressed that it was insufficient to require sex offender registration without public notification (as was then required by the Wetterling Act). Other community members were similarly outraged that such purportedly dangerous child predators were living in their neighborhoods without their knowledge (Terry & Ackerman, 2009). Similar to the disappearance of Jacob Wetterling, Megan's murder received much media attention locally and nationally (Leon, 2011).

Less than one month after Megan's murder, New Jersey passed legislation, known as "Megan's Law" (1994), which mandated the dissemination of sex-offender information to the public. One year following Megan's death, an additional 16 states had passed similar legislation (Zilney & Zilney, 2009). In 1996, the federal government proposed an amendment to the Wetterling Act, which was also named "Megan's Law," and it passed unanimously in both the U.S. House and the U.S. Senate (Tofte & Fellner, 2007). Responsible for transforming sex-offender registries into publicly available online domains, the federal version of Megan's Law (1996) requires state police agencies to make public information about sex offenders. Thus, the federal version of Megan's Law represented a national policy choice to provide information about known sex offenders to the public, rather than only to law enforcement.

Community Notification Laws

Some states went beyond the creation of sex-offender registries by enacting notification laws designed to warn community members when sex offenders live nearby (Farkas & Stichman, 2002). Notification laws assume that community members will not only use this information to protect their children, but that they will also report risky behaviors of convicted sex offenders (that could lead to sex-

ual offending) to their local police department (Galeste, Fradella, & Vogel, 2012; La Fond, 2005). Many states that use **community notification** have a three-tiered system based on the purported dangerousness of sex offenders that determines the degree of notification that will take place (Finn, 1997; Goodman, 1996). When sex offenders are categorized as the lowest risk to public safety, notification is typically reserved for law-enforcement officials only. Schools, daycares, and other neighborhood organizations are notified of the presence of sex offenders posing a medium risk to public safety. Those sex offenders considered the most dangerous, designated at high risk, will generate the most widespread notification, as the general public is notified. However, some jurisdictions subject all convicted sex offenders to community notification.

Residency Restrictions

Like community notification mandates, restrictions on where one may establish a residence may be an accompanying reality that registered sex offenders must face. Well over one-half of all states and numerous municipalities have sex-offender **residency restriction laws**. In 1995, Delaware and Florida were the first jurisdictions to enact legislation that limited where sex offenders could reside (Galeste et al., 2012). In some cases, these policies determine where sex offenders are allowed to work, travel, and be in public (Meloy, Miller, & Curtis, 2008). Today, the most common residency restriction laws feature nebulous language to restrict registered sex offenders from living near locations described as "child congregation" areas (Tewksbury & Connor, 2014a). Such places are typically defined to include schools, parks, playgrounds, daycare centers, bus stops, and recreational facilities. Fluctuating between 500 feet and 2,500 feet, residency restriction laws assert that specific distances must be preserved between a sex offender's residence and various landmarks in the community (see Meloy et al., 2008; Nieto & Jung, 2006). Registered sex offenders in Kentucky, for instance, who were convicted in July 2006 or after, cannot live within 1,000 feet of a school, park, or playground.

Campus and National Registries

On October 28, 2000, the Campus Sex Crimes Prevention Act further amended the original Wetterling Act, requiring registered sex offenders studying and working at colleges and universities to provide notice of their status as sex offenders to these institutions of higher learning. College and university officials are required to inform the campus community where information regarding registered sex offenders may be obtained. As a result, many colleges and universities consequently maintain their own distinctive online sex-offender registries (Tewksbury & Lees, 2006a; Tewksbury, 2013). Exposing convicted sex offenders to further public scrutiny, a nationwide databank of registered sex offenders was created in 2005. The Dru Sjodin National Sex Offender Public Registry, as it was named in 2006, was designed by the Department of Justice to provide more efficient access to individual state sex-offender registries (Tewksbury & Connor, 2014a).

Adam Walsh and SORNA

The notification approach was adopted nationally in 2006 when Congress passed the Adam Walsh Act—also known as the Sex Offender Registration and Notification Act (SORNA). Strikingly, this legislation made failing to register as a sex offender a federal felony offense. The law was named after Adam Walsh, who in 1981, while six years of age, was abducted from a Florida shopping mall. Two weeks later, Adam was found murdered (Leon, 2011). Although the alleged perpetrator was not identified until 2008, this piece of legislation was widely advocated from its inception by John Walsh, Adam's father, who hosted *America's Most Wanted* (Terry, 2013).

SORNA created a comprehensive and national system for sex-offender registration (McPherson, 2007) and mandated that each state collect a wide variety of information about sex offenders that could be used to identify and locate them. Specifically, the legislation puts sex offenders into three tiers of risk. Sex offenders who are tier three are considered to be the most serious and must verify their location with law enforcement every three months for the rest of their lives. Sex offenders defined as tier two must update their whereabouts every six months for 25 years, and sex offenders described as tier one must verify their location annually for 15 years (Terry, 2013). At the same time, the Office of Sex Offender Sentencing, Monitoring, Apprehending, Registering, and Tracking (SMART) was authorized by the Walsh Act to ensure that jurisdictions comply with SORNA (U.S. Department of Justice, 2014). Like the earlier federal statutes concerning the public disclosure of sex offenders, all jurisdictions must adhere to the provisions of the Walsh Act or face reduced federal grant funding.

Under the Walsh Act, all states were obligated to establish SORN statutes in compliance with SORNA guidelines by July 2009. The penalty for not adhering to these requirements is the loss of 10% of federal funding from the Byrne program law-enforcement assistance funds (Zilney & Zilney, 2009). And yet, no states were compliant with the Walsh Act requirements by July 2009, prompting the SMART Office to extend the deadline for compliance to July 27, 2011 (Terry, 2013). At present, however, only 16 states, three territories, and 36 tribes have successfully implemented SORNA guidelines.[1] (SORNA extended the registration requirement to include federally recognized Indian tribes.) When implementing SORNA, some states required sex offenders to provide local law enforcement with a recent picture of themselves, their fingerprints, and documentation of any treatment they may have received for mental disorders. By 2010, all 50 states required that convicted sex offenders provide a DNA sample to the state's database (National Conference of State Legislatures, 2010).

The fact that the majority of jurisdictions in the United States have not implemented the Walsh Act indicates that doing so may be problematic for individual states, territories, and tribes. The primary obstacle to implementing the Walsh Act appears to be financial cost. A national survey of states (Harris & Lobanov-Rostovsky, 2010) identified a wide variety of costs associated with SORNA execution, including system development, reclassification, expanded enforcement personnel, judicial and correctional expenses, and legal expenses related to prosecution, defense, and litigation. Jurisdictions may cover some of these initial costs through Department of Justice programs authorized by the Walsh Act; however, state fiscal analyses revealed significant operational costs that would be necessary to maintain SORNA requirements (Harris & Lobanov-Rostovsky, 2010). For instance, Virginia does not seem willing to implement the Walsh Act, as it determined that the first year of compliance with SORNA would cost more than $12,000,000. The subsequent cost of maintaining SORNA requirements would be approximately $8,887,000 annually (Justice Policy Institute, 2008; Virginia Department of Planning and Budget, 2008).

ASSESSING THE EFFECTS OF SORN ON PUBLIC SAFETY AND RECIDIVISM

Beyond the previously mentioned financial burdens, efforts to publicly identify and announce the whereabouts of convicted sex offenders through SORN have been empirically denounced at the more fundamental levels of public safety and **recidivism**. Most arguments supporting the public monitoring of sex offenders emphasize the welfare of society, particularly the protection of children. The expressed goals of SORN are to promote public safety and reduce recidivism through the pursuit of deterrence (Tewksbury, Jennings, & Zgoba, 2012). By informing the public about the identity and whereabouts of convicted sex offenders, SORN laws purportedly increase awareness of potential danger among community members. This knowledge afforded to the public allegedly allows community members to be better prepared to avoid situations in which sex offenders, who are residing, studying, working, and otherwise engaging in daily life among them, may have opportunities to repeat criminal behavior. At the same time, the possibilities for participating in criminal activity again are believed to be restricted, as public identification and exposure of previous sexual misconduct supposedly make sex offenders feel more susceptible to the risks associated with repeating criminal behavior. Further, proponents contend that registration will permit law-enforcement officials to quickly and easily ascertain the locations of sex offenders in their communities, facilitating sex crime investigations (Powell, Day, Benson, Vess, & Graffam, 2014).

Making the Public Aware of Sex Offenders

Despite the assumption that such laws increase awareness of the presence of sex offenders, a large majority of the public does not actively utilize available information that is disseminated through SORN, potentially limiting its ability to protect community members from sex offenders in their neighborhoods. Although residents commonly know that resources about sex offenders exist (Anderson & Sample, 2008; Burchfield, 2012), they often do not use sex-offender registries (Anderson & Sample, 2008; Kernsmith, Comartin,

Craun, & Kernsmith, 2009). This limited use of publicly available information about sex offenders through SORN may subsequently reduce community members' awareness of sex offenders. Indeed, most residents are ignorant of the presence of sex offenders in their communities (Burchfield, 2012), even when they access sex-offender registries (Kernsmith et al., 2009) or live directly adjacent to registered sex offenders (Craun, 2010). Thus, while community members are largely aware of SORN, such policies do not appear to raise actual public awareness of the presence of local sex offenders.

Alternatively, when the public does utilize SORN to become informed about local sex offenders, this strategy often leads to excessive, and perhaps harmful, precautionary behavior and fear of crime (Beck & Travis, 2004; Caputo & Brodsky, 2004). For instance, Caputo and Brodsky (2004) found that Alabama residents who interpreted SORN as important reported greater fear of general victimization, personal victimization, and sexual victimization than those who did not interpret SORN as important. This increased fear of being victimized by sex offenders produced by SORN may unnecessarily make community members uneasy, as being afraid of already convicted sex offenders (i.e., registered sex offenders) may be irrational. Sex offenders, on the whole, have relatively low rates of recidivism (Furby, Weinrott, & Blackshaw, 1989; Sample & Bray, 2006), especially in comparison to other criminal offenders (Langan & Levin, 2002; Sample & Bray, 2003).

Reducing Sex-Offender Recidivism

Regardless of whether the public uses information available to them or knows about sex offenders through SORN, the impact of SORN is limited, at best, with respect to reducing future sex crimes by convicted sex offenders. There is substantial evidence across numerous jurisdictions that SORN does not prevent convicted sex offenders from continuing to participate in sexual misconduct in the community (Agan, 2007). Whether or not sex offenders were subjected to SORN failed to predict which sex offenders would sexually recidivate in Arkansas (Maddan, 2008), Iowa (Adkins, Huff & Stageberg, 2000; Tewksbury & Jennings, 2010), Massachusetts (Petrosino & Petrosino, 1999), New Jersey (Tewksbury et al., 2012; Zgoba, Witt, Dalessandro, & Veysey, 2008), and Washington (Schram & Milloy, 1995). Similar results were found in New York, where Sandler, Freeman, and Socia (2008) showed no support for the effectiveness of SORN in reducing sex offenses by previously convicted rapists, child molesters, or sexual recidivists. The lack of significant influence of SORN on recidivism remained, even when these rates were considered as a whole.

Thus, based on these studies, it becomes clear that SORN does not effectively deter convicted sex offenders from sexually re-offending. The number of victims involved in sex offenses was also not reduced by SORN laws (Zgoba et al., 2008). If anything, there is some evidence to the contrary. For example, in their analysis of National Incident-Based Reporting System data in 15 different states, Prescott and Rockoff (2011) found that SORN *increased* recidivism rates among sex offenders (see also Drake & Aos, 2009; Letourneau, Levenson, Bandyopadhyay, Sinha, & Armstrong, 2010). In short, it is fair to say that research across two decades and several U.S. jurisdictions indicates that SORN fails to improve public safety.

Additional Concerns

Beyond its inability to make the public aware of the presence of sex offenders and reduce recidivism rates, there are other unflattering realities about SORN laws. In theory, such policies are supposed to help prevent sexual victimizations by strangers (Meloy, Saleh, & Wolff, 2007) through the release of their identities and whereabouts, but strangers are the least common perpetrators of sex offenses. Individuals known to victims are most likely to commit sex crimes against them (Simon, 2000; Vanzile-Tamsen, Testa, & Livingston, 2005). As a result, community members may have a false sense of confidence regarding their safety (La Fond, 2005; Sandler et al., 2008), thinking that their children are more likely to be sexually battered by the bogey-man than a family member or friend (Craun & Theriot, 2009).

Also, sex-offender registries may contain inaccurate or misleading information, due to errors, incomplete data, outdated records, or other mishaps (Salmon, 2010). For instance, Tewksbury (2002) found that 43% of sex-offender profiles on the Kentucky Sex Offender Registry were missing a photograph. Levenson and Cotter (2005a) reported that more than one-half of their sample of 183 registered sex offenders had profiles on the Florida Sexual Offenders and Predators Registry that contained misinformation. Such incomplete or invalid information makes the identification of convicted sex offenders and their where-abouts extremely difficult, if not impossible.

Even if sex-offender registries always provided their consumers with up-to-the-minute, straightforward, and flawless information, it is important to note that they are not comprehensive lists of sex offenders (Meloy et al., 2007). Many perpetrators of sex offenses are neither detected nor successfully prosecuted, some may avoid SORN through plea agreements or because their criminal offenses do not obligate them to register, and others may fail to adhere to SORN requirements. What is more, SORN laws are focused on the control and surveillance of sex offenders, rather than their treatment (Zevitz & Farkas, 2000a), despite the fact that sex-offender treatment programs appear to be a promising means for managing sex offenders in the community. Treated sex offenders are often less likely to recidivate in comparison to untreated sex offenders (Hall, 1995; Hanson et al., 2002; Losel & Schmucker, 2005).

Further, SORN laws may negatively impact individuals who are not convicted sex offenders. (The consequences that sex offenders who are subjected to SORN face are discussed later.) SORN is responsible for decreasing home values of residents in neighborhoods where registered sex offenders live (Linden & Rockoff, 2008; Pope, 2008). Time, money, energy, and other resources are significantly depleted from police departments (Zgoba et al., 2008) and probation and parole agencies (Zevitz & Farkas, 2000a) who are responsible for implementing and maintaining SORN. Moreover, family members of sex offenders subjected to SORN are likely to experience negative repercussions, including chronic hopelessness, depression, frustration, stress, shame, and embarrassment that prevent them from participating in community activities, and deterioration and loss of social relationships (Comartin, Kernsmith, & Miles, 2010; Farkas & Miller, 2007; Levenson & Tewksbury, 2009; Tewksbury & Levenson, 2009). Children of registered sex offenders are often treated differently by teachers and other children at school (Levenson & Tewksbury, 2009) and cannot have their sex-offender parent attend school events (Tewksbury & Humkey, 2010).

So, in light of their numerous drawbacks, why do SORN laws persist? Why are SORN policies expanding and becoming more inclusive? The answer may lie with a moral panic surrounding sex crimes and resulting public expectations.

Moral Panic and the Public

Despite evidence suggesting little or no effect of SORN on public awareness and sex-offender recidivism rates, as well as its other criticisms, general public approval of such sanctions to control convicted sex offenders in the community remains (Brannon, Levenson, Fortney, & Baker, 2007; Brown, Deakin, & Spencer, 2008; Comartin, Kern-smith, & Kernsmith, 2009; Kernsmith, Craun,

& Foster, 2009; Levenson, Brannon, Fortney, & Baker, 2007; Lieb & Nunlist, 2008; Mears, Mancini, Gertz, & Bratton, 2008; Phillips, 1998; Salerno et al., 2010; Schiavone & Jeglic, 2009; Zevitz & Farkas, 2000a). Among 194 Florida residents, for instance, Levenson and colleagues (2007) found that community notification (83%) and residency restrictions (58%) were considered to be effective strategies for the reduction of sex offenses. About 73% of residents indicated that they would support such sanctions even without scientific evidence of their effectiveness with respect to preventing sex offenses (Levenson et al., 2007).

Such endorsement of SORN and its accompanying mandates, especially without scientific evidence, is likely the result of a national **moral panic** (Horowitz, 2007; Jenkins, 1998). Crime that involves sexual behavior often generates community trepidation and uniquely frightens the public. Fear of sex offenders appears to be so pervasive among the public that they are willing to subject all individuals convicted of sex offenses to castigating SORN policies. In Kernsmith, Craun, and Foster's study (2009), 733 Michigan residents were asked questions about their fear of sex offenders and whether or not they agreed with SORN focused on specific types of sex offenders. Most residents reported that they were afraid of pedophiles (80%), incest offenders (78%), and juvenile sex offenders (70%). A majority reported that they were afraid of date-rape offenders (66%), sex offenders with a sex offense that was ten years old (62%), and spousal rapists (59%). A significant minority (45%) reported that they were fearful of statutory rapists. All types of sex offenders, pedophiles (97%), incest offenders (96%), juvenile sex offenders (86%), date-rape offenders (84%), sex offenders with a sex offense more than ten years old (86%), spousal rapists (71%), and statutory rapists (65%), were seen by a majority of residents as appropriately subjected to SORN. Correspondingly, after surveying 115 community members from 15 different states, Schiavone and Jeglic (2009) found that high-risk sex offenders (89%), moderate-risk sex offenders (82%), and low-risk sex offenders were seen as appropriately subjected to SORN.

It is clear that the public largely fears all sex offenders—especially those who victimize children—and expresses the most desire for such offenders to become subjected to SORN. With this in mind, it is important to note that members of the general public, who already largely support punitive sanctions for sex offenders in the community, may be more likely to endorse these policies if they have children. In fact, those with more children are more likely to see community-based strategies aimed at sex offenders as appropriate restrictions. Using data from a telephone survey with 1,308 Florida residents, Mancini, Shields, Mears, and Beaver (2010) found that residents with children were significantly more likely than residents without children to endorse sex-offender residency restrictions. The odds of residents with children supporting these laws rather than not supporting them were 58% greater than the odds among residents without children. They also found that even greater support for sex-offender residency restrictions existed among residents with three or more children. The odds of residents with three or more children supporting these laws, in comparison with residents without children, increased to 70%. "Having multiple children (not just one child)," they concluded, "significantly increases support for laws that prohibit where sex offenders can live, and this effect appears to be greater among parents with more children" (p. 1026). Similarly, in another study, residents who were parents were more likely to value information received about sex offenders living in their community through SORN than residents who were not parents (Caputo & Brodsky, 2004).

The overwhelming fear of sex offenders reported by Americans and the supportive attitudes and beliefs of residents with children toward SORN laws should not be surprising, as the media has made a habit of sensationalizing heinous sex crimes throughout the United States, particularly acts perpetrated against children. Such media exposure subsequently intensifies the public's apprehension and fear about sexual violence and sex offenders who live among them. Media coverage of children who were sexually (and sometimes mortally) assaulted, including Jacob Wetterling, Megan Kanka, and Adam Walsh, continues to facilitate a societal focus on sex offenders and produce a moral panic regarding the safety of children (Galeste et al., 2012), which seems unlikely to diminish or regress in intensity (Burchfield, Sample, & Lytle, 2014).

The media are largely responsible for how community members understand criminal behavior and societal responses to it, as the internet, newspapers, and television are the most common sources of knowledge about the American criminal justice system (Dowler, 2006; Weitzer & Kubrin, 2004). However, the media often unnecessarily heighten public fears of victimization, particularly with respect to sexual attacks, as constant coverage of violent and extraordinary sex crimes makes such acts appear to be more prevalent than in reality (Quinn et al., 2004). Indeed, outrage and intense fear that stem from media reports of sex offenders assaulting helpless children, which tend to saturate news outlets for extended periods of time, personalize the reality of criminal behavior, and embellish the likelihood of reoccurrence, pave the way for perpetrators of sex crimes to be seen as a societal threat (Maguire & Singer, 2011; Palermo & Farkas, 2001; Zgoba, 2004). In providing conditions necessary for alarm, the media depict an inaccurate view of sex offenders and sex offenses, which shape public attitudes and beliefs and lead to distorted impressions (Soothill, 2010).

The most common myths that the media perpetuate, which the public tend to accept as conventional wisdom, include sex offend-ers as unfamiliar to victims (Berliner, Schram, Miller, & Milloy, 1995; Craun & Theriot, 2009; Fortney, Levenson, Brannon, & Baker, 2007; Fuselier, Durham, & Wurtele, 2002; Levenson et al., 2007), highly recidivistic (Fortney et al., 2007; Katz-Schiavone et al., 2008; Levenson et al., 2007; Levenson & D'Amora, 2007; Quinn et al., 2004), specialists (Magers, Jennings, Tewksbury, & Miller, 2009; Miethe, Olson, & Mitchell, 2006), homogeneous (Sample & Bray, 2006), and unable to be rehabilitated (Levenson et al., 2007; Katz-Schiavone et al., 2008). Galeste and colleagues (2012) explored the prevalence of four of these myths (i.e., sex offenders have high recidivism rates, specialize in sex offenses, represent a homogeneous group, and cannot be rehabilitated), finding that one or more of these myths showed up in more than one-third of the 334 newspaper articles in their sample. Indeed, sex offenders with these alleged characteristics (i.e., myths) have been and continue to be constructed as a social problem by the media, especially when they are living in communities, and lawmakers have subsequently exploited and continue to exploit public sentiment (Burchfield et al., 2014) by responding with legislative efforts to assuage unfounded fears and project an image of control over such offenders. Widespread myths about sex offenders and sex offenses, then, that stem from the media and the perspectives of the public (Quinn et al., 2004; Sample & Kadleck, 2008) prompt lawmakers to act to combat the socially constructed problem of sex offending (Galeste et al., 2012).

The fact that residents who have been convicted of a crime may be less likely to endorse criminal registries for lawbreakers besides sex offenders (see Box 10.1) may be telling. This not only suggests that criminal offenders may have a unique vantage point with respect to criminal sanctions, but they may also have important reasons for failing to endorse such policies that are not immediately apparent to the rest of society. Thus, it may be valuable to examine the perspectives of sex offenders themselves about returning to communities under SORN.

Sex-Offender Experiences

Some research has considered the lived experiences of sex offenders with regard to SORN. Studies soliciting the attitudes and beliefs of sex offenders suggest that such offenders occasionally recognize the potential value in community-based sanctions. However, more often than not, sex offenders do not support the distinct criminal justice policies to which they are exposed. A large majority report negative, **collateral consequences** associated with SORN, which may undermine its potential

effectiveness, beyond the financial obstacles of implementation and inability to increase awareness and reduce recidivism. In fact, the unpleasant reality of having to register under SORN laws has prompted numerous legal challenges by convicted sex offenders, and to date, the U.S. Supreme Court has considered two cases (see "Law in Action" box below).

Numerous collateral consequences are directly associated with criminal convictions. These collateral consequences are the unfavorable experiences that may exist in association with criminal penalties (Buckler & Travis, 2003; Wheelock, 2005). Most studies have approached collateral consequences from the perspective of general felony convictions. Social consequences are largely apparent in the

Box 10.1 SHOULD REGISTRIES BE USED FOR OTHER CRIMINALS?

Craun, Kernsmith, and Butler (2011) utilized telephone surveys with 728 Michigan residents to determine whether or not members of the general public supported extending criminal registries beyond sex offenders, and if so, to which types of offenders. Generally, findings revealed a split among respondents. Fifty-three percent reported that they supported additional, publicly available registries, nearly 43% reported that they did not want such registries, and 4% reported that they were undecided.

Several indicators positively predicted community support for any type of additional registry. Residents who reported higher average scores on support for the requirement of registration for various types of sex offenders, those who reported that they had accessed the state's sex-offender registry, those who reported that they were a victim of a sex offender, and those who reported that they knew of someone who had been a victim of a sex offender were more likely to support the creation of additional criminal registries. Conversely, residents who reported that they had been convicted of a criminal offense, in comparison with those who did not report that they had been convicted of a criminal offense, were less likely to endorse additional criminal registries.

- Do these results surprise you? Why or why not?
- Do the indicators that predicted support for additional registries make sense to you? Why? Are there some indicators not discussed that you believe may play a role in whether or not someone supports the establishment of additional registries? If so, what are they?
- Do you believe other types of criminals should be placed on a publicly available registry? If so, what types of criminals? Why? What factors influenced your decision?

Law in Action CONSTITUTIONALITY OF SORN

The constitutionality of SORN laws has been challenged in two U.S. Supreme Court cases. *Smith v. Doe* (2003) considered the Fifth Amendment double-jeopardy clause and whether or not SORN laws amount to further punishment of sex offenders. Can jurisdictions obligate convicted sex offenders, who were sentenced prior to the passage of SORN, to comply with SORN requirements, after the fact? Two defendants, John Doe I and John Doe II, were convicted of aggravated sex offenses, served prison time, and completed sex-offender treatment before the passage of the Alaska Sex Offender Registration Act. In spite of this, the Act required them to become registered sex offenders in Alaska, where their identities, workplaces, crimes, and whereabouts were announced to the world through the state's publicly available, online registry. John Doe I and John Doe II, along with John Doe II's wife, challenged the constitutionality of the retroactive requirement. In their minds, the obligation to register as a sex offender after the fact was unfair.

Although the District Court ruled against the three individuals and the Ninth Circuit Court of Appeals ruled in favor of them, the Supreme Court decided to entertain the matter and had the final say. The Supreme Court found in *Smith v. Doe* (2003) that SORN is regulatory and consequently is not additional punishment. Moreover, the Court ruled in the 6 to 3 decision that individuals convicted of sex crimes prior to the establishment of SORN can still be obligated to comply with these laws, since SORN policies are not punishment. John Doe I, John Doe II, and John Doe II's wife were out of luck.

The second Supreme Court case regarding SORN, *Connecticut Department of Public Safety v. John Doe* (2003), examined the issue of cruel and unusual punishment. The Supreme Court was tasked with deciding whether or not Connecticut was in violation of the U.S. Constitution by posting sex-offender information on the internet. John Doe, a convicted sex offender, was listed on the state's publicly available, online registry. He felt that the SORN law, which tarnished his reputation by exposing his status as a sex offender, unfairly took away his sense of liberty and therefore violated the Fourteenth Amendment's Due Process Clause.

After Doe's challenge to Connecticut's SORN policy, the District Court temporarily stopped the law's public disclosure requirement, and the Second Circuit Court of Appeals subsequently affirmed this decision, acknowledging that the widespread revelation of one's sex-offender status proved to be detrimental to a person's well-being. The Supreme Court in *Connecticut Department of Public Safety v. John Doe* (2003), however, in a united opinion, ruled that the posting of sex-offender photographs online is constitutional. Injury to reputation is not a deprivation of liberty, the Court said, so the due process rights of registered sex offenders are not violated.

Taken together, the Supreme Court does not view SORN policies as obstacles to personal freedom, but sees them as appropriate mechanisms for promoting public safety.

- Do you believe that SORN laws are intended to be a form of punishment aimed at convicted sex offenders? Why? After reading the section in this chapter entitled "Sex Offender Experiences," do you feel the same way? Why?
- Is it fair to make individuals adhere to SORN policies, if they were sentenced before such laws were in place? Why?

additional, supposedly unintended, outcomes resulting from felony convictions. These issues include stigmatization, employment difficulties, relationship problems, and negative feelings regarding self-image (Dodge & Pogrebin, 2001; Pogrebin, Dodge, & Katsampes, 2001). For instance, Harding (2003) found that social consequences, particularly stigmatization of convicted felons, make societal reintegration extremely difficult. Academic works concerning felony convictions have also pinpointed numerous legal repercussions, which include employment restrictions, loss of voting rights, and other civil limitations (Burton, Cullen, & Travis, 1987; Olivares, Burton, & Cullen, 1996).

The nature and degree of collateral consequences for sex offenders may be greater than for other convicted felons (Tewksbury & Connor, 2014b). Sex offenders have reported significant obstacles resulting from SORN that have prevented them from easily reintegrating into society. The social damage caused by SORN laws are often insurmountable, as the social stigmatization (Robbers, 2009; Tewksbury, 2005, 2012; Tewksbury & Lees, 2006b) experienced by registered sex offenders leads to their ostracism by community members (Zevitz & Farkas, 2000b) in the forms of harassment (Levenson & Cotter, 2005a; Tewksbury, 2004, 2005; Tewksbury & Lees, 2006b; Zevitz & Farkas, 2000b), threats (Zevitz & Farkas, 2000b), and vigilante attacks (Tewksbury & Lees, 2006b; Zevitz & Farkas, 2000b). These active demonstrations of contempt aimed at registered sex offenders cause them to have persistent feelings of vulnerability (Tewksbury & Lees, 2006b), undergo heightened levels of stress (Robbers, 2009), and witness emotional harm to their family members (Zevitz & Farkas, 2000b). Individuals who are publicly identified as sex offenders through SORN struggle with maintaining relationships and developing new associations (Tewksbury & Lees, 2006b), even with family members (Tewksbury & Connor, 2012a). Once individuals

are subjected to SORN, most of their friendships are lost altogether and the quality of the few relationships that persist is greatly diminished (Tewksbury, 2004, 2005). As a result of their social exclusion, registered sex offenders tend to internalize their spoiled identity (Tewksbury, 2012) and intentionally withdraw from community involvement, which further reduces their social support (Robbers, 2009).

Beyond social impacts, sex offenders frequently lose their jobs (Tewksbury, 2004, 2005; Zevitz & Farkas, 2000b) when coworkers and employers discover their status through SORN. Unemployed registered sex offenders appear to have particularly onerous and unsuccessful experiences with finding work (Levenson & Cotter, 2005a; Tewksbury, 2004, 2005; Tewksbury & Lees, 2006b). The loss of housing (Tewksbury, 2004, 2005; Zevitz & Farkas, 2000b) and need to locate to a new residence (Levenson & Cotter, 2005a) are more common experiences for sex offenders subjected to SORN. In many cases, the challenges associated with housing are connected to SORN's accompanying residency restriction laws.

Residency Restrictions

After being subjected to the state's residency restriction law, 135 registered sex offenders in Florida were asked about how such a policy impacted their lives (Levenson & Cotter, 2005b). Fifty-seven percent found it difficult to locate affordable housing, 44% were unable to live with family members, and approximately 25% reported that they had to relocate to a new residence. Sixty percent of the registered sex offenders in the study also expressed emotional distress as a direct outcome of the residency restriction law. In spite of making it difficult for sex offenders to find housing and otherwise move on with their lives, lawmakers often believe that residency restrictions, which limit where such offenders can live, help to reduce access to children

Box 10.2 CAMPUS SEX-OFFENDER REGISTRIES

Tewksbury and Lees (2006a) examined the experiences of an important subset of registered sex offenders—those listed on university-maintained sex-offender registries (see the section in this chapter entitled "Campus and National Registries"). Through surveys of such registrants, they found high levels of collateral consequences. Specifically, they reported that 65% of these sex offenders were not hired or lost a job, 42% lost or were denied a place to live, and 42% lost a friend as a result of their registration status.

In a qualitative investigation of this population, Tewksbury (2013) discovered that registered sex offenders on university campuses commonly experienced social isolation, as well as intense and unrelenting feelings of vulnerability. The fact that these sex offenders could be found on a university registry, in addition to a state registry, seemed to heighten these undesirable ramifications. As Connor and Tewksbury (2012) explained, when academic institutions maintain campus-based registries, the results may be particularly damaging, as students and employees subjected to campus-based registration and notification may find it especially challenging to avoid the stigma that is associated with public identification as sex offenders. This is because, with college and university registries, more specificity is provided, where "the number of potential registrants per registry decreases and the more identifiable [listed] registrants ultimately become" (Connor & Tewksbury, 2012, p. 337).

- Do you agree with Connor and Tewksbury's (2013) contention that campus-based registries may increase the likelihood of certain sex offenders being identified?
- Find out if your college or university has a sex-offender registry. If your school has a sex-offender registry, will you use it? Why? Does it make you feel safer to know that your school has a sex-offender registry? Why? If your school does not have a sex-offender registry, would you use it, if it were available to you? Why? Does it make you feel less safe to know that your school does not have a sex-offender registry? Why?

(Sample & Kadleck, 2008). In other words, by ensuring that sex offenders establish a residence a certain distance away from areas where children commonly frequent, opportunities for future sex offenses are reduced, because instances of being in close proximity to children are minimized.

And yet, in reality, residency restrictions for sex offenders do not facilitate public safety. When compared with sex offenders who do not repeat sex offenses, child sex offenders who recidivate do not live closer to schools, parks, and other child congregation landmarks (Colorado Department of Public Safety, 2004). In fact, only one in five registered sex

offenders live in close proximity to such locations (Tewksbury & Mustaine, 2006). If sex offenders do repeat their crimes, they are more likely to seek victims in neighborhoods other than their own to avoid detection (Minnesota Department of Corrections, 2003).

However, residency restriction laws for sex offenders certainly exacerbate the limited choices for home placement already facing many ex-offenders (Tewksbury & Connor, 2012b). Policies that limit where registered sex offenders live may restrict their possible housing options to as little as 2% of all housing stock (Zandbergen & Hart, 2006, 2009). As a result of residency restrictions, registered sex offenders are also likely to be concentrated in very dense, socially disorganized communities or in rural locations with limited employment, treatment, and transportation opportunities (Minnesota Department of Corrections, 2003; Tewksbury & Mustaine, 2006, 2008; Zandbergen & Hart, 2006, 2009).

Brannon, Levenson, Fortney, and Baker (2007) showed that, when comparing perceptions and experiences of sex offenders and community residents, sex offenders reported far more negative experiences arising from SORN than was realized by the public. Almost one-half of sex offenders reported experiencing threats, property damage, and physical assault, while only 10% of residents were aware of such vigilantism resulting from public disclosure. Correspondingly, Schiavone and Jeglic (2009) noted that only 17% of the public believed that SORN made sex offenders' reintegration more stressful.

When these studies are taken together, the contention that a significant number of sex offenders, who are almost invariably exposed to SORN and accompanying residency restrictions in communities, will experience associated negative, unintended consequences that make societal reintegration more challenging is difficult to contest. Think back to the beginning of this chapter and consider Kaitlyn Hunt's case. Do you think the removal of SORN as a sanction in the plea agreement likely saved Hunt from a lifetime of stigma and suffering?

OTHER SEX-OFFENDER LAWS

Civil Commitment Statutes for Sexually Violent Predators

Although the Wetterling Act initially helped to increase awareness of sex offenders across the United States, several years earlier, Washington state became the first jurisdiction to provide neighborhood residents with information about sex offenders living among them

(see La Fond, 2005). As with the earlier laws concerning sex offenders, heinous acts against children spurred the legislation. In 1989, after returning to society from incarceration, Earl Shriner sexually assaulted and tortured a seven-year-old boy. Strikingly, this was not an isolated episode of violence, as Shriner had previously been confined for murder and three separate instances of child molestation. This, as well as a series of other, publicly known violent offenses against children, prompted Washington state to pass the Community Protection Act (1990), which was the first American notification statute that allowed law enforcement to notify the public about released sex offenders in their communities. Among the 14 sections related to the punishment and management of sex offenders, the Community Protection Act (1990) established the first contemporary provision for the **civil commitment** of sexual predators.

Early Versions

In response to high-profile sex crimes, the first American sexual psychopath laws were passed in the 1930s (Ewing, 2011). Community protection, as well as treatment and incapacitation of sex offenders, were the explicit goals of these laws. Often calling for the civil commitment of so-called mentally disordered sex offenders to public mental hospitals, these statutes rested on the assumption that mental health professionals were capable of identifying, confining, and treating sexual psychopaths (Leon, 2011). Those offenders determined to be sexual psychopaths were often committed to mental institutions indefinitely with few procedural safeguards. These laws may have also been aimed at sex offenders other than violent recidivists, including exhibitionists, voyeurs, and gays (Zilney & Zilney, 2009). Moreover, public disenchantment with rehabilitation and uncertainty regarding effective treatment methods for sexual psychopaths eventually dissuaded efforts to utilize these policies. By the late 1960s, many states started to repeal, intentionally disregard, and seldom use sexual psychopath legislation (Ewing, 2011; Leon, 2011; Terry, 2013).

Contemporary Strategies

The premise of sexually violent offender civil commitment statutes is that many sex offenders cannot be rehabilitated; consequently, such criminals must be incapacitated to the greatest extent possible. Under civil law, sex offenders may be committed to institutions. Modern civil commitment statutes for sexually violent predators allow governments to confine particular sex offenders to secure mental health facilities upon their release from prisons or a judicial finding of incompetency to stand trial (Terry, 2013). Upon the decision of a court, sex offenders considered to have mental abnormalities or other psychological disorders that may prompt harmful sexual conduct in the future may be subjected to civil commitment. Today, 20 states and the federal government have civil commitment laws aimed at sex offenders (Tewksbury & Connor, 2014a).

Following the placement of committed sex offenders to secure institutions, mental health clinicians and other professionals are assigned the responsibility of evaluating offenders at regular intervals. During periods of civil commitment, medical and psychological assessments of sex offenders are performed to assess improvements in mental status (Zilney & Zilney, 2009). Examinations and subsequent reports prepared for the court concerning the mental conditions of committed sex offenders are typically completed on an annual basis. After these examinations by medical and mental health officials, sex offenders civilly committed to institutions may petition for release, appear before a judge, and ask the court to determine whether their commitments continue to be necessary to protect the public (Leon, 2011). In order to be released, psychologists and the court must agree that mental abnormalities or personality disorders once exhibited by sex offenders no longer pose a threat to society.

Whereas earlier sexual psychopath laws may have centered on rehabilitation, current civil commitment laws focus on the social control and incapacitation of sex offenders (Ewing, 2011). Depicting the social control function of civil commitment laws, the U.S. Supreme Court in *Kansas v. Hendricks* (1997) upheld a sexually violent predator statute, which sent sex offenders determined to be violent predators likely to recidivate to state mental hospitals. Although Hendricks challenged the civil commitment law as a violation of due process and prohibitions against double jeopardy and *ex post facto* laws, the Court found such to be constitutional as the civil commitment statute was not deemed to be punishment. In 2002, the U.S. Supreme Court ruled in *Kansas v. Crane* that mental abnormalities displayed by sex offenders must differentiate committed individuals from ordinary recidivists. Moreover, besides showing the likelihood that offenders will commit sex crimes upon release, it must be shown that offenders have a serious inability to control their behaviors.

Controversies

Many disputes surround the civil commitment of sex offenders. Critics assert that in reality sex offenders committed to mental facilities are almost never released. Only about 10% of sexually violent predators who were civilly committed in the United States since 1990 have been released (Gookin, 2007). In Minnesota, not a single civilly committed sex offender has been liberated (Terry, 2013). This is particularly alarming, because the North Star State contains the highest rate of committed sex offenders per capita of jurisdictions with civil commitment legislation. Others oppose civil commitment for sex offenders because such laws apparently punish individuals who have already paid their debt to society. Despite the Supreme Court decision in *Kansas v. Hendricks* (1997), civil confinement seems to hinge on the desire to continue punishment and incapacitation (Friedland, 1999). It may be that civil commitment is a mechanism to permanently remove sex offenders from society.

Civil commitment statutes raise issues concerning mental health professionals and money. Such legislation targeting sex offenders may inappropriately utilize experts in the mental health field (Wettstein, 1992). Although many sex offenders are committed due to their mental deficiencies or personality disorders, this does not necessarily mean that civilly committed sex offenders are genuinely mentally ill. In addition, the increasing number of sex offenders and the need to commit them may exhaust government money allotted for the entire mental health field, which may not be the most effective use of mental health resources already in short supply (Zilney & Zilney, 2009). Because civil commitment entails confinement, clinical treatment, and legal assistance, expenditures related to these functions must be considered. It costs nearly $100,000 to civilly commit one sex offender for a one-year period of time (Terry, 2013). This is an enormous annual cost for which states are responsible. If mental health professionals are trusted to confine sex offenders, funding for treatment and other mental health services may become even scarcer. When appropriate mental health treatment is absent, many mental health patients may be more likely to participate in criminal activities.

Castration Mandates

For many centuries, convicted sex offenders were punished through **physical castration**. In the United States, castration was first popularly used for slaves suspected of having sex with White women. The eugenics movement (1905–1935) supported castration and sterilization of criminals and the mentally ill.

Currently, voluntary **chemical castration** has largely replaced physical castration, as medical doctors believe that similarly effective results can be reached through treatment with medication. Concerns over body mutilation, intrusiveness, and the lasting results of surgery have rendered physical castration of sex offenders in the United States as a less common practice (Tewksbury & Connor, 2014a). The widespread availability of medications as an alternative to physical castration may also explain this change. Although some laws concerning sex offenders allow physical and chemical castration as a substitute or adjunct to other forms of punishment, chemical castration seems to be the more socially acceptable solution.

Chemical castration commonly consists of injecting Depo-Provera, the synthetic hormone medroxyprogesterone acetate, to reduce the blood serum testosterone levels in males. Taken on a regular basis, Depo-Provera is supposed to reduce sexual impulses, erections, and ejaculations. Presently, many chemical castration laws call for the forced dispensing of medication to control the behavior of recidivist sex offenders. In 1997, California was the first jurisdiction to require chemical castration for repeat sex offenders (with victims under the age of 13). Under California Penal Code § 645 (2003), repeat sex offenders are obligated to receive chemical injections prior to their release on parole. These injections persist until offenders complete their criminal sentences. Although sex offenders may refuse chemical castration, parole will be immediately denied to those deciding not to participate. Following California's example, other states—including Colorado, Florida, Georgia, Iowa, Louisiana, Montana, Oregon, Texas, and Wisconsin—enacted similar sex-offender castration laws (Scott & del Busto, 2009; Tewksbury & Connor, 2014a).

Controversies

Debates continue over the utility of sex-offender castration laws. "What should be

Box 10.3 COMPARING CASTRATION LAWS

There are many similarities and differences with respect to castration laws for convicted sex offenders. In Louisiana, a conviction for aggravated rape, simple rape, forcible rape, aggravated sexual battery, sexual battery, aggravated oral sexual battery, oral sexual battery, aggravated incest, incest, and aggravated crimes against nature qualifies an individual as suitable for physical or chemical castration, when the victim is less than 13 years of age, or if the individual is a repeat sex offender. However, in Oregon, where only chemical castration is used, any individual convicted of a sex offense, when the victim is of any age, is eligible.

And yet, Louisiana and Oregon are similar in that they are the only jurisdictions in which chemical castration is mandatory for certain first-time sex offenders. In Texas, where only physical castration is used, all convicted sex offenders must voluntarily consent before they participate in the procedure. This is distinct from Florida, for instance, where certain first-time sex offenders undergo castration at the discretion of a judge, but castration for certain repeat sex offenders is mandatory.

- What types of sexual behavior do you believe warrant castration? Why?
- Does the age of the victim matter in terms of whether or not a sex offender is castrated? Why?
- Should castration be voluntary, discretionary, or mandatory? Why is your choice the best? Why are the other two options less desirable?
- If castration is discretionary, who should decide whether or not sex offenders are to be castrated? Prosecutors? Judges? Lawmakers? Physicians? Victims?

done with sex offenders?" you ask. A common response may be, "Castrate them!" However, castration mandates have many downsides. Whether sex offenders voluntarily or forcibly have their testicles removed from their bodies (i.e., physical castration) or ingest drugs on a routine basis (i.e., chemical castration), the attitudes, behaviors, and circumstances that led them to initially engage in sexual misconduct are not addressed during these processes (Fitzgerald, 1990; Zilney & Zilney, 2009). As a result, subsequent participation in sex offenses is still a possibility for castrated sex offenders, and the enhancement of public safety is not immediately obvious. Having genitalia that fails to properly function or a reduced sex drive does not mean that the motivation to continue unlawful sexual activities has dissipated, but the

public may believe otherwise. Consequently, a false sense of security may stem from castration mandates.

What is more, informed consent is deemed necessary for medical treatment in America. And yet, sex offenders are sometimes forced to undergo castration, and other sex offenders who agree to be castrated are commonly offered incentives to do so, such as release from prisons or community-based sentences, which calls into question whether or not their consent is really voluntary at all (Scott & del Busto, 2009). In addition, the practice of sterilizing habitual offenders who are viewed as unsuitable for procreation was declared unconstitutional in *Skinner v. Oklahoma* (1942). Physical castration certainly seems to violate this Supreme Court ruling, but supporters of castration mandates note that chemically castrating sex offenders does not violate their fundamental rights to procreate, because the effects of Depo-Provera and other similar drugs are temporary and completely revocable upon termination of the injections (Melella, Travin, & Cullen, 1989). However, despite Depo-Provera's allegedly temporary obstruction to sexual activity, the ability to procreate is still infringed upon during the period of treatment, which may last for years or even one's entire life (Spalding, 1998). Some chemical castration laws, such as Florida's statute, permit the courts to order injections of Depo-Provera for the remainder of a sex offender's life. In this way, sex offenders sentenced to lifetime chemical castration may have their right to procreate removed permanently.

There are specific problems with physical castration. Physical castration may not reduce sexual functioning. Many individuals who are physically castrated are still able to sustain a full erection three to five years after their procedures (Wille & Beier, 1989), and some sex offenders who are physically castrated continue to have sexual intercourse three to seven years after their procedures (Sheldon, Bluestone, Coleman, Cullen, & Melella, 1985). At the same time, the effects of physical castration on sex offenders are completely reversible, if they intravenously or orally receive testosterone (Zilney & Zilney, 2009). Moreover, the removal of body parts (i.e., testicles), even if they belong to "despicable" and "nasty" sex offenders, as a form of punishment may be regarded as draconian.

The use of chemical castration, too, is problematic. Common medications used to chemically castrate sex offenders do not always have an impact on sexual fantasy, erectile responses, or sexual aggression outside experimental situations (Terry, 2013). Also, in order for chemical castration of sex offenders to continue, they often must have a lifelong dependence on drugs. This commitment (as well as the financial cost of medications) may be too burdensome for some individuals, and

lapses in treatment should be expected. Have you ever forgotten to take your medicine? Have you ever intentionally decided that it was in your best interest not to take a specific medication? It is very likely that you have, and it is very likely that at least some sex offenders will do the same. When sex offenders who are prescribed drugs for purposes of chemical castration stop taking these medications, they are immediately at an increased risk for re-offending (Berlin & Meinecke, 1981). Further, the side effects of the drugs used for purposes of chemical castration and their lasting impacts should be considered. At present, no longitudinal studies have assessed the risks associated with drugs used for castration. However, in the short term, such medications may cause adverse outcomes, including Cushing's Syndrome, depression, and osteoporosis (Terry, 2013).

Global Positioning System (GPS) Monitoring Policies

Perhaps the most innovative category of laws designed to regulate sex offenders concerns electronic monitoring through GPS technology. Under such arrangements, sex offenders living outside of the direct supervision of correctional officials and inside communities are required to wear a transmitter, often in the form of a bracelet, which tracks their movements and geographic locations. In theory, GPS monitoring is supposed to reduce the likelihood of recidivism, because sex offenders should be deterred from future criminal behavior while knowingly being monitored (Levenson & D'Amora, 2007). In 1984, New Mexico was the first jurisdiction to track sex offenders with GPS technology (Levenson & D'Amora, 2007). Sex offenders are commonly monitored through GPS technology while on probation or parole; however, some states require sex offenders who have completed their criminal sentences to be electronically supervised. Strikingly, Florida requires sex offenders who are convicted of child sexual assault and living outside of correctional institutions to wear a GPS device for the rest of their lives (Padgett, Bales, & Blomberg, 2006). The Sunshine State is not alone, as Colorado, Missouri, Ohio, Oklahoma, and Wisconsin also electronically watch the activities of convicted sex offenders in the community until they die (IACP, 2008). Today, more than one-half of states utilize GPS technology to electronically track sex offenders in communities, and the number of jurisdictions doing so is likely to increase, as the Walsh Act endorses pilot projects to implement such policies (Terry, 2013).

Electronic monitoring of sex offenders through GPS technology may be passive, active, or hybrid. When sex offenders are monitored through *passive GPS technology*, probation and parole officials select specific periods of time in which to upload information about them, and continuous, real-time surveillance is not utilized. A probation officer, for instance, may decide that she wants to verify whether or not her client is attending his sex-offender treatment program. Through a computer, she inquires about the monitored sex offender's exact location at 2:15 p.m. last Thursday, because she knows that his treatment sessions are scheduled on Thursdays from 2:00 p.m. to 3:00 p.m. The transmitter sends a report to the probation officer's computer, providing information about her client's whereabouts at 2:15 p.m. last Thursday. If her client was located elsewhere without a plausible explanation, he likely will face the real possibility of having his probation revoked and may be incarcerated.

Alternatively, *active GPS technology* provides uninterrupted information about where monitored sex offenders are located, and such feedback about their movements and positions are available as they happen. The same probation officer, for example, may observe her client's locations and travel patterns during the actual time in which they occur through a computer that displays these movements. Rather than requesting a report for a certain time/date interval, she is able to know exactly where her client is, without interruption, at all times.

Hybrid approaches to electronic monitoring through GPS, which represent a combination of the active and passive systems, are emerging as popular alternatives, whereby information is transmitted following longer time frames than would be the case with active systems, while the ability to immediately notify supervising officials of problems remains (IACP, 2008).

There is a belief that the use of GPS technology for the purposes of monitoring and tracking sex offenders in communities is valuable (Delson, 2006). For instance, assistance with investigations, court hearings, case management, and overall control of sex offenders living in communities without constant supervision are said to be important functions of electronic monitoring through GPS technology (IACP, 2008). Nonetheless, the disadvantages of these policies are difficult to overlook. It costs a significant amount of money to track sex offenders, as the daily cost of tracking devices may be up to $15 per offender, which does not include the resources needed for supervising officers (Meloy & Coleman, 2009). What is more, attention by probation and parole officers may be diverted away from their surveillance functions, as they may be consumed by responding to faulty GPS alerts and maintenance of equipment (Armstrong & Freeman, 2011), rather than checking in with sex offenders face-to-face. Further, electronic monitoring of sex offenders through GPS technology is really only an additional source of information, potentially allowing criminal justice officials to respond to offenders after something occurs. Simply put, GPS tracking cannot stop criminal behavior or other misconduct from happening (Meloy & Coleman, 2009). There were no significant differences with respect to recidivism or technical violations between sex offenders who were tracked through GPS and sex offenders who were not tracked through GPS in California and Tennessee (Tennessee Board of Probation and Parole, 2007; Turner et al., 2007). Moreover, even when probation and parole officers and other supervising officials know where sex offenders are, this knowledge does not shed light on all forms of misconduct. Individuals who are tracked through GPS may be engaged in illegal sexual activities while at their homes, including assaulting another person or viewing child pornography (Terry, 2013). Thus, sex offenders may be positioned at approved locations, but involved in criminal behavior.

CONCLUSION

Over the past three decades, individuals convicted of sex offenses in the United States have faced increasingly extreme forms of punishment. A number of legal responses have emerged to specifically satisfy the public's perception that sexual lawbreakers are an objectionable group of individuals who present a tremendous risk to communities and are almost certain to repeat their criminal acts without proper management and surveillance. SORN laws likely constitute the most widespread of these criminal justice policies aimed at sexual perpetrators, as they arguably impact the majority of convicted sex offenders in America. Although less common, sex-offender civil commitment statutes, castration mandates, and GPS monitoring policies are growing in number and impact the lives of numerous sex offenders.

The sanctions outlined in this chapter have largely stemmed from a national moral panic that focused on rare (albeit heinous) acts and sympathetic (child) victims. As a result, SORN, civil commitment, castration, and GPS monitoring were hasty, ill-conceived strategies that were largely untested prior to their full-scale implementation. Debates, as well as empirical evidence, about the efficacy of these

specialized regulations that target sex offenders are beginning to take shape (and become widely established and recognized, in the case of SORN). In spite of the challenges and controversies associated with sex-offender laws, the development of new strategies and expansion of existing approaches do not appear to be slowing down. Be that as it may, policymakers, practitioners, and the public should consult scientific evidence before determining appropriate responses to sex offenders.

FURTHER READING

Leon, C. S. (2011). *Sex fiends, perverts, and pedophiles: Understanding sex crime policy in America.* New York, NY: New York University Press.
Terry, K. J. (2013). *Sexual offenses and offenders.* Belmont, CA: Wadsworth.
Tewksbury, R., & Connor, D. P. (2014). Sex offenders and criminal policy. In G. Bruinsma & D. Weisburd (Eds.), *Encyclopedia of criminology and criminal justice* (pp. 4782–4791). New York, NY: Springer.
Zilney, L. J., & Zilney, L. A. (2009). *Perverts and predators: The making of sexual offending laws.* Lanham, MA: Rowman & Littlefield.

GLOSSARY

Chemical castration: An act by which pharmaceutical drugs are used to temporarily facilitate an individual's sterilization and decreased sexual drive.

Civil commitment: An act by which a government confines a sex offender to a secure mental health facility for an indefinite period of time upon his or her release from a prison or a judicial finding of incompetency to stand trial.

Collateral consequences: The unfavorable and often unintended experiences that may exist in association with criminal penalties.

Community notification: A method of disseminating information about registered sex offenders to a community in which they reside, work, or attend school.

Moral panic: A set of events, such as sex crimes, or a group of individuals, such as sex offenders, which become known as a threat to society through the media and social commentators.

Physical castration: An act by which a biological male's testes or a biological female's ovaries are removed from his or her body to facilitate sterilization and decreased sexual drive.

Recidivism: The repeated or habitual relapse into criminal behavior; the act of re-offending or participating in crime again, despite earlier police detections, court convictions, and possible correctional punishments.

Residency restriction laws: Policies that obligate registered sex offenders to live a specific distance, usually between 500 feet and 2,500 feet, from "child congregation" areas, such as schools, parks, playgrounds, daycare centers, bus stops, and recreational facilities.

Sex-offender registries: Repositories of information usually maintained by governmental agencies that provide the public with online access to a wide array of facts about many convicted sex offenders, including their identities, residential locations, and sex offenses.

NOTE

1   According to the National Conference of State Legislatures (2014), Alabama, Delaware, Florida, Kansas, Louisiana, Maryland, Michigan, Mississippi, Missouri, Nevada, Ohio, Pennsylvania, South Carolina, South Dakota, Tennessee, and Wyoming are considered to be in compliance with the Walsh Act.

REFERENCES

Adam Walsh Act, Pub. L. 109–248, 120 Stat. 587 (2006), *codified as amended at* 42 U.S.C. §§ 16901–91 (2014).

Adkins, G., Huff, D., & Stageborg, P. (2000). *The Iowa Sex Offender Registry and recidivism*. Des Moines, IA: Iowa Department of Human Rights.

Agan, A. Y. (2007). *Sex offender registries: Fear without function?* Unpublished manuscript, University of Chicago.

Anderson, A. L., & Sample, L. L. (2008). Public awareness and action resulting from sex offender community notification laws. *Criminal Justice Policy Review, 19*(4), 371–396.

Armstrong, G. S., & Freeman, B. C. (2011). Examining GPS monitoring alerts triggered by sex offenders: The divergence of legislative goals and practical application in community corrections. *Journal of Criminal Justice, 39*(2), 175–182.

Beck, V. S., & Travis, L. F. (2004). Sex offender notification and protective behavior. *Violence and Victims, 19*(3), 289–302.

Berlin, F. S., & Meinecke, C. F. (1981). Treatment of sex offenders with antiandrogen medication: Conceptualization, review of treatment modalities, and preliminary findings. *American Journal of Psychiatry, 138*(5), 601–607.

Berliner, L., Schram, D., Miller, L., & Milloy, C. D. (1995). A sentencing alternative for sex offenders: A study of decision making and recidivism. *Journal of Interpersonal Violence, 10*(4), 487–502.

Brannon, Y. N., Levenson, J. S., Fortney, T., & Baker, J. N. (2007). Attitudes about community notification: A comparison of sexual offenders and the non-offending public. *Sexual Abuse: A Journal of Research and Treatment, 19*(4), 369–379.

Brown, S., Deakin, J., & Spencer, J. (2008). What people think about the management of sex offenders in the community. *The Howard Journal of Criminal Justice, 47*(3), 259–274.

Buckler, K. G., & Travis, L. F. (2003). Reanalyzing the prevalence and social context of collateral consequence statutes. *Journal of Criminal Justice, 31*(5), 435–453.

Burchfield, K. B. (2012). Assessing community residents' perceptions of local registered sex offenders: Results from a pilot survey. *Deviant Behavior, 33*(4), 241–259.

Burchfield, K., Sample, L. L., & Lytle, R. (2014). Public interest in sex offenders: A perpetual panic? *Criminology, Criminal Justice, Law & Society, 15*(3), 96–117.

Burton, V. S., Cullen, F. T., & Travis, L. F. (1987). The collateral consequences of a felony conviction: A national study of state statutes. *Federal Probation, 51*(3), 52–60.

California Penal Code § 645 (2003).

Campus Sex Crimes Prevention Act, Pub. L. No. 106–386, div. B, § 1601, 114 Stat. 1464, 1537 (2000), *codified as amended at* 42 U.S.C. § 14071; 20 U.S.C. § 1092(f)(1)(I); and 20 U.S.C. § 1232g(b)(7)(A).

Caputo, A. A., & Brodsky, S. L. (2004). Citizen coping with community notification of released sex offenders. *Behavioral Sciences and the Law, 22*(2), 239–252.

Colorado Department of Public Safety (2004). *Report on safety issues raised by living arrangements for and location of sex offenders in the community*. Denver, CO: Sex Offender Management Board.

Comartin, E. B., Kernsmith, P. D., & Kernsmith, R. M. (2009). Sanctions for sex offenders: Fear and public policy. *Journal of Offender Rehabilitation, 48*(7), 605–619.

Comartin, E. B., Kernsmith, P. D., & Miles, B. W. (2010). Family experiences of young adult sex offender registration. *Journal of Child Sexual Abuse, 19*(2), 204–225.

Community Protection Act, REVISED CODE OF WASHINGTON §71.09 (1990).

Connor, D. P., & Tewksbury, R. (2012). Ex-offenders and educational equal access: Doctoral programs in criminology and criminal justice. *Critical Criminology, 20*(3), 327–340.

Craun, S. W. (2010). Evaluating awareness of registered sex offenders in the neighborhood. *Crime and Delinquency, 56*(3), 414–435.

Craun, S. W., Kernsmith, P. D., & Butler, N. K. (2011). Anything that can be a danger to the public: Desire to extend registries beyond sex offenses. *Criminal Justice Policy Review, 22*(3), 375–391.

Craun, S. W., & Theriot, M. T. (2009). Misperceptions of sex offender perpetration: Considering the impact of sex offender registration. *Journal of Interpersonal Violence*, 24(12), 2057–2072.

Delson, N. (2006). Using Global Positioning Systems (GPS) for sex offender management. *ATSA Forum*, 18(3), 24–30.

Dodge, M., & Pogrebin, M. R. (2001). Collateral costs of imprisonment for women: Complications of reintegration. *The Prison Journal*, 81(1), 42–54.

Dowler, K. (2006). Sex, lies, and videotape: The presentation of sex crime in local television news. *Journal of Criminal Justice*, 34(4), 383–392.

Drake, E. K., & Aos, S. (2009). *Does sex offender registration and notification reduce crime? A systematic review of the research literature.* Olympia, WA: Washington State Institute for Public Policy.

Ewing, C. P. (2011). *Justice perverted: Sex offense law, psychology, and public policy.* New York, NY: Oxford.

Farkas, M. A., & Miller, G. (2007). Reentry and reintegration: Challenges faced by the families of known sex offenders. *Federal Sentencing Reporter*, 20(2), 88–92.

Farkas, M. A., & Stichman, A. (2002). Sex offender laws: Can treatment, punishment, incapacitation, and public safety be reconciled? *Criminal Justice Review*, 27(2), 256–283.

Finn, P. (1997). *Sex offender community notification.* Washington, DC: National Institute of Justice.

Fitzgerald, E. A. (1990). Chemical castration: MPA treatment of the sexual offender. *American Journal of Criminal Law*, 18(1), 1–60.

Fortney, T., Levenson, J. S., Brannon, Y., & Baker, J. (2007). Myths and facts about sex offenders: Implications for practice and public policy. *Sex Offender Treatment*, 2(1), 1–17.

Friedland, S. (1999). On treatment, punishment, and the civil commitment of sex offenders. *University of Colorado Law Review*, 70(1), 73–154.

Furby, L., Weinrott, M., & Blackshaw, L. (1989). Sex offender recidivism: A review. *Psychological Bulletin*, 105(1), 3–30.

Fuselier, D. A., Durham, R. L., & Wurtele, S. K. (2002). The child sexual abuser: Perceptions of college students and professionals. *Sexual Abuse*, 14(3), 267–276.

Galeste, M. A., Fradella, H. F., & Vogel, B. (2012). Sex offender myths in print media: Separating fact from fiction in U.S. newspapers. *Western Criminology Review*, 13(2), 4–24. Retrieved from http://www.westerncriminology.org/documents/WCR/v13n2/Galeste.pdf

Goodman, E. A. (1996). Megan's Law: The New Jersey Supreme Court navigates uncharted waters. *Seton Hall Law Review*, 26, 764–802.

Gookin, K. (2007). *Comparison of state laws authorizing involuntary commitment of sexually violent predators: 2006 updated, revised.* Olympia, WA: Washington State Institute for Public Policy.

Hall, G. C. N. (1995). Sex offender recidivism revisited: A meta-analysis of recent treatment studies. *Journal of Consulting and Clinical Psychology*, 63(5), 802–809.

Hanson, R. K., Gordon, A., Harris, A. J., Marques, J. K., Murphy, W., Quinsey, V. L., & Seto, M. C. (2002). First report of the collaborative outcome data project on the effectiveness of psychological treatment for sex offenders. *Sexual Abuse*, 14(2), 169–194.

Harding, D. J. (2003). Jean Valjean's dilemma: The management of ex-convict identity in the search for employment. *Deviant Behavior*, 24(6), 571–595.

Harris, A., & Lobanov-Rostovsky, C. (2010). Implementing the Adam Walsh Act's Sex Offender Registration and Notification Provisions: A survey of the states. *Criminal Justice Policy Review*, 21(2), 202–222.

Horowitz, E. (2007). Growing media and legal attention to sex offenders: More safety or more injustice? *The Journal of the Institute of Justice and International Studies*, 7, 143–158.

International Association of Chiefs of Police. (2008). *Tracking sex offenders with electronic technology: Implications and practical uses for law enforcement.* Washington, DC: U.S. Department of Justice.

Jacob Wetterling Crimes Against Children and Sexually Violent Offender Registration Act, Pub. L. No., 103–322, 108 Stat. 2038, 2042 (1994), *codified as amended at 42 U.S.C. § 14071 (2014).*

Jenkins, P. (1998). *Moral panic: Changing concepts of the child molester in modern America.* New Haven, CT: Yale University Press.

Justice Policy Institute. (2008). *What will it cost states to comply with the Sex Offender Registration and Notification Act?* Retrieved from http://www.justicepolicy.org/images/upload/08–08_FAC_SORNACosts_JJ.pdf

Katz-Schiavone, S., Levenson, J. S., & Ackerman, A. R. (2008). Myths and facts about sexual violence: Public perceptions and implications for prevention. *Journal of Criminal Justice and Popular Culture*, 15(3), 291–311.

Kernsmith, P. D., Comartin, E., Craun, S. W., & Kernsmith, R. M. (2009). The relationship between sex offender registry utilization and awareness. *Sexual Abuse: A Journal of Research and Treatment*, 21(2), 181–193.

Kernsmith, P. D., Craun, S. W., & Foster, J. (2009). Public attitudes toward sexual offenders and sex offender registration. *Journal of Child Sexual Abuse*, 18(3), 290–301.

La Fond, J. Q. (2005). *Preventing sexual violence: How society should cope with sex offenders.* Washington, DC: American Psychological Association.

Langan, P. A., & Levin, D. J. (2002). *Recidivism of prisoners released in 1994*. Washington, DC: U.S. Department of Justice.

Leon, C. S. (2011). *Sex fiends, perverts, and pedophiles: Understanding sex crime policy in America*. New York, NY: New York University Press.

Letourneau, E. J., Levenson, J. S., Bandyopadhyay, D., Sinha, D., & Armstrong, K. S. (2010). Effects of South Carolina's sex offender registration and notification policy on deterrence of adult sex crimes. *Criminal Justice and Behavior*, 37(5), 537–552.

Levenson, J. S., Brannon, Y. N., Fortney, T., & Baker, J. N. (2007). Public perceptions about sex offenders and community protection policies. *Analyses of Social Issues and Public Policy*, 7(1), 137–161.

Levenson, J. S., & Cotter, L. P. (2005a). The effect of Megan's Law on sex offender reintegration. *Journal of Contemporary Criminal Justice*, 21(1), 49–66.

Levenson, J. S., & Cotter, L. P. (2005b). The impact of sex offender residence restrictions: 1,000 feet from danger or one step from absurd? *International Journal of Offender Therapy and Comparative Criminology*, 49(2), 168–178.

Levenson, J. S., & D'Amora, D. A. (2007). Social policies designed to prevent sexual violence: The Emperor's New Clothes? *Criminal Justice Policy Review*, 18(2), 168–199.

Levenson, J. S., & Tewksbury, R. (2009). Collateral damage: Family members of registered sex offenders. *American Journal of Criminal Justice*, 34(1), 54–68.

Lieb, R., & Nunlist, C. (2008). *Community notification as viewed by Washington's citizens: A ten-year follow-up*. Olympia, WA: Washington State Institute for Public Policy.

Linden, L. L., & Rockoff, J. E. (2008). There goes the neighborhood? Estimates of the impact of crime risk on property values from Megan's Laws. *American Economic Review*, 98(3), 1103–1127.

Logan, W. A. (2009). *Knowledge as power: Criminal registration and community notification laws in America*. Stanford, CA: Stanford University Press.

Losel, F., & Schmucker, M. (2005). The effectiveness of treatment for sexual offenders: A comprehensive meta-analysis. *Journal of Experimental Criminology*, 1(1), 117–146.

Maddan, S. (2008). *The labeling of sex offenders*. Lanham, MD: University Press of America.

Magers, M., Jennings, W. G., Tewksbury, R., & Miller, J. M. (2009). An exploration of the sex offender specialization and violence nexus. *Southwest Journal of Criminal Justice*, 6(2), 133–144.

Maguire, M., & Singer, J. K. (2011). A false sense of security: Moral panic driven sex offender legislation. *Critical Criminology*, 19(4), 301–312.

Mancini, C., Shields, R. T., Mears, D. P., & Beaver, K. M. (2010). Sex offender residence restriction laws: Parental perceptions and public policy. *Journal of Criminal Justice*, 38(5), 1022–1030.

McPherson, L. (2007). Update: Practitioner's guide to the Adam Walsh Act. *American Prosecutors Research Institute*, 20(9&10), 1–8. Retrieved from http://www.ojp.usdoj.gov/smart/pdfs/practitioner_guide_awa.pdf

Mears, D. P., Mancini, C., Gertz, M., & Bratton, J. (2008). Sex crimes, children, and pornography: Public views and public policy. *Crime and Delinquency*, 54(4), 532–559.

Megan's Law, N.J. Stat. Ann. §§ 2C:7–1– 2C:7–11 (1994).

Megan's Law, Pub. L. 104–145, 110 Stat. 1345 (1996), *codified as amended at* 42 U.S.C. § 13701 (2014).

Melella, J. T., Travin, S., & Cullen, K. (1989). Legal and ethical issues in the use of antiandrogens in treating sex offenders. *Bulletin of the American Academy of Psychiatry and Law*, 17(3), 223–232.

Meloy, M. L. (2006). *Sex offenses and the men who commit them*. Boston, MA: Northeastern University Press.

Meloy, M. L., & Coleman, S. (2009). GPS monitoring of sex offenders. In R. G. Wright (Ed.), *Sex offender laws: Failed policies, new directions* (pp. 243–266). New York: Springer.

Meloy, M. L., Miller, S. L., & Curtis, K. M. (2008). Making sense out of nonsense: The deconstruction of state-level sex offender residence restrictions. *American Journal of Criminal Justice*, 33(2), 209–222.

Meloy, M. L., Saleh, Y., & Wolff, N. (2007). Sex offender laws in America: Can panic-driven legislation ever create safe societies? *Criminal Justice Studies*, 20(4), 423–443.

Miethe, T. D., Olson, J., & Mitchell, O. (2006). Specialization and persistence in the arrest histories of sex offenders: A comparative analysis of alternative measures and offense types. *Journal of Research in Crime and Delinquency*, 43(3), 204–229.

Minnesota Department of Corrections (2003). *Level three sex offenders' residential placement issues*. St. Paul, MN: Author.

Mustaine, E. E., & Tewksbury, R. (2013). What can be learned from an online sex offender registry site? An 8 year follow-up. *Journal of Community Corrections*, 23(1), 5–10.

National Conference of State Legislatures. (2010). State laws on DNA data banks: Qualifying offenses, others who must provide sample. Washington, DC: Author. Retrieved from http://www.ncsl.org/issues-research/justice/dna-laws-database.aspx

National Conference of State Legislatures. (2014). *Adam Walsh Child Protection and Safety Act*. Retrieved from http://www.ncsl.org/research/civil-and-criminal-justice/adam-walsh-child-protection-and-safety-act.aspx

Nieto, M., & Jung, D. (2006). The impact of residency restrictions on sex offenders and correctional management practices: A literature review. (CRB # 06–008). Sacramento, CA: California Research Bureau. Retrieved from http://www.library.ca.gov/crb/06/08/06-008.pdf

Olivares, K. M., Burton, V. S., & Cullen, F. T. (1996). The collateral consequences of a felony conviction: A national study of state legal codes 10 years later. *Federal Probation*, 60(3), 10–17.

Padgett, K. G., Bales, W. D., & Blomberg, T. G. (2006). Under surveillance: An empirical test of the effectiveness and consequences of electronic monitoring. *Criminology and Public Policy*, 5(1), 61–91.

Palermo, G. B., & Farkas, M. A. (2001). *The dilemma of the sexual offender*. Springfield, IL: Charles C. Thomas.

Petrosino, A. J., & Petrosino, C. (1999). The public safety potential of Megan's Law in Massachusetts: An assessment from a sample of criminal sexual psychopaths. *Crime and Delinquency*, 45(1), 140–158.

Petrunik, M. (2003). The hare and the tortoise: Dangerousness and sex offender policy in the United States and Canada. *Canadian Journal of Criminology and Criminal Justice*, 45(1), 43–72.

Phillips, D. M. (1998). *Community notification as viewed by Washington's citizens*. Olympia, WA: Washington State Institute for Public Policy.

Pogrebin, M. R., Dodge, M., & Katsampes, P. (2001). The collateral costs of short-term jail incarceration: The long-term social and economic disruptions. *Corrections Management Quarterly*, 5(4), 64–69.

Pope, J. C. (2008). Fear of crime and housing prices: Household reactions to sex offender registries. *Journal of Urban Economics*, 64(3), 601–614.

Powell, M., Day, A., Benson, M., Vess, J., & Graffam, J. (2014). Police officers' perceptions of interviewing offenders on sex offender registries. *International Journal of Police Science and Management*, 16(4), 255–266.

Prescott, J. J., & Rockoff, J. E. (2011). Do sex offender registration and notification laws affect criminal behavior? *Journal of Law and Economics*, 54(1), 161–206.

Quinn, J., Forsyth, C., & Mullen-Quinn, C. (2004). Societal reaction to sex offenders: A review of the origins and results of the myths surrounding their crimes and treatment amenability. *Deviant Behavior*, 25(3), 215–233.

Robbers, M. L. P. (2009). Lifers on the outside: Sex offenders and disintegrative shaming. *International Journal of Offender Therapy and Comparative Criminology*, 53(1), 5–28.

Salerno, J. M., Najdowski, C. J., Stevenson, M. C., Wiley, T. R. A., Bottoms, B. L., Vaca, R., & Pimentel, P. S. (2010). Psychological mechanisms underlying support for juvenile sex offender registry laws: Prototypes, moral outrage, and perceived threat. *Behavioral Sciences and the Law*, 28(1), 58–83.

Salmon, T. M. (2010). *Sex offender registry: Report of the Vermont State Auditor*. Montpelier, VT: Office of the State Auditor.

Sample, L. L., & Bray, T. M. (2003). Are sex offenders dangerous? *Journal of Criminology and Public Policy*, 3(1), 59–82.

Sample, L. L., & Bray, T. M. (2006). Are sex offenders different? An examination of rearrest patterns. *Criminal Justice Policy Review*, 17(1), 83–102.

Sample, L. L., & Kadleck, C. (2008). Sex offender laws: Legislators' accounts of the need for policy. *Criminal Justice Policy Review*, 19(1), 40–62.

Sandler, J. C., Freeman, N. J., & Socia, K. M. (2008). Does a watched pot boil? A time-series analysis of New York State's sex offender registration and notification law. *Psychology, Public Policy, and Law*, 14(4), 284–302.

Schiavone, S. K., & Jeglic, E. L. (2009). Public perceptions of sex offender social policies and the impact on sex offenders. *International Journal of Offender Therapy and Comparative Criminology*, 35(6), 679–695.

Schram, D. D., & Milloy, C. D. (1995). *Community notification: A study of offender characteristics and recidivism*. Olympia, WA: Washington Institute for Public Policy.

Scott, C., & del Busto, E. (2009). Chemical and surgical castration. In R. G. Wright (Ed.), *Sex offender laws: Failed policies, new directions* (pp. 291–338). New York, NY: Springer.

Sheldon, T., Bluestone, H., Coleman, E., Cullen, K., & Melella, J. (1985). Pedophilia: An update on theory and practice. *Psychiatric Quarterly*, 57(2), 89–103.

Simon, J. (1998). Managing the monstrous: Sex offenders and the new penology. *Psychology, Public Policy, and the Law*, 4(1/2), 452–467.

Simon, J. (2000). Megan's Law: Crime and democracy in late modern America. *Law and Social Inquiry*, 25(4), 1111–1150.

Soothill, K. (2010). Sex offender recidivism. *Crime and Justice*, 39, 145–211.

Spalding, L. H. (1998). Florida's 1997 chemical castration law: A return to the dark ages. *Florida State University Law Review*, 25, 117–139.

Tennessee Board of Probation and Parole. (2007). Monitoring Tennessee's sex offenders using global positioning systems: A project evaluation. Nashville, TN: Tennessee Board of Probation and Parole.

Terry, K. J. (2013). *Sexual offenses and offenders*. Belmont, CA: Wadsworth.

Terry, K. J., & Ackerman, A. R. (2009). A brief history of major sex offender laws. In R. G. Wright (Ed.), *Sex offender laws: Failed policies, new directions* (pp. 65–98). New York, NY: Springer.

Tewksbury, R. (2002). Validity and utility of the Kentucky Sex Offender Registry. *Federal Probation*, 66(1), 21–26.

Tewksbury, R. (2004). Experiences and attitudes of registered female sex offenders. *Federal Probation*, 68(3), 30–33.

Tewksbury, R. (2005). Collateral consequences of sex offender registration. *Journal of Contemporary Criminal Justice*, 21(1), 67–81.

Tewksbury, R. (2012). Stigmatization of sex offenders. *Deviant Behavior*, 33(8), 606–623.

Tewksbury, R. (2013). Sex offenders and campus-based sex offender registration: Stigma, vulnerability, isolation, and the classroom as refuge. *Journal of Qualitative Criminology and Criminal Justice*, 1(2), 221–242.

Tewksbury, R., & Connor, D. P. (2012a). Incarcerated sex offenders' perceptions of family relationships: Previous experiences and future expectations. *Western Criminology Review*, 13(2), 25–35.

Tewksbury, R., & Connor, D. P. (2012b). Inmate reentry. In D. McDonald & A. Miller (Eds.), *Race, gender, and criminal justice: Equality and justice for all?* (pp. 141–157). San Diego, CA: Cognella Academic Publishing.

Tewksbury, R., & Connor, D. P. (2014a). Sex offenders and criminal policy. In G. Bruinsma & D. Weisburd (Eds.), *Encyclopedia of criminology and criminal justice* (pp. 4782–4791). New York, NY: Springer.

Tewksbury, R., & Connor, D. P. (2014b). From troubling actions to troubled lives: Sex offender registration and notification. In J. F. Gubrium & M. Jarvinen (Eds.), *Turning troubles into problems: Clientization in human services* (pp. 211–227). London: Routledge.

Tewksbury, R., & Higgins, G. E. (2005). What can be learned from an online sex offender registry site? *Journal of Community Corrections*, 14(3), 9–11, 15–16.

Tewksbury, R., & Humkey, T. (2010). Prohibiting registered sex offenders from being at school: Assessing the collateral consequences of a public policy. *Justice Policy Journal*, 7(2). Retrieved from http://www.cjcj.org/uploads/cjcj/documents/Prohibiting_Registered.pdf

Tewksbury, R., & Jennings, W. G. (2010). Assessing the impact of sex offender registration and community notification on sex offending trajectories. *Criminal Justice and Behavior*, 37(5), 570–582.

Tewksbury, R., Jennings, W. G., & Zgoba, K. M. (2012). A longitudinal examination of sex offender recidivism prior to and following the implementation of SORN. *Behavioral Sciences and the Law*, 30(3), 308–328.

Tewksbury, R., & Lees, M. B. (2006a). Sex offenders on campus: University-based sex offender registries and collateral consequences of registration. *Federal Probation*, 70(3), 50–56.

Tewksbury, R., & Lees, M. B. (2006b). Perceptions of sex offender registration: Collateral consequences and community experiences. *Sociological Spectrum*, 26(3), 309–334.

Tewksbury, R., & Levenson, J. S. (2009). Stress experiences of family members of registered sex offenders. *Behavioral Sciences and the Law*, 27(4), 611–626.

Tewksbury, R., & Mustaine, E. E. (2006). Where to find sex offenders: An examination of residential locations and neighborhood conditions. *Criminal Justice Studies*, 19(1), 61–75.

Tewksbury, R., & Mustaine, E. E. (2008). Where registered sex offenders live: Community characteristics and proximity to possible victims. *Victims & Offenders*, 3(1), 86–98.

Tofte, S., & Fellner, J. (2007). *No easy answers: Sex offender laws in the U.S.* New York, NY: Human Rights Watch.

Turner, S., Hess, J., Myers, R., Shah, R., Werth, R., & Whitby, A. (2007). *Implementation and early outcomes for the San Diego High Risk Sex Offender GPS Pilot Program*. Irvine, CA: Center for Evidence-Based Correction.

United States Department of Justice. (2014). *About SMART*. Retrieved from http://www.smart.gov/about.htm

Vanzile-Tamsen, C., Testa, M., & Livingston, J. A. (2005). The impact of sexual assault history and relationship context on appraisal and responses to acquaintance sexual assault risk. *Journal of Interpersonal Violence*, 20(7), 813–832.

Virginia Department of Planning and Budget. (2008). *Fiscal impact statement*. Richmond, VA: Author.

Weitzer, R., & Kubrin, C. E. (2004). Breaking news: How Local TV News and Real-World Conditions Affect Fear of Crime. *Justice Quarterly*, 21(3), 497–520.

Wettstein, W. M. (1992). A psychiatric perspective of Washington's sexually violent predator statute. *University of Puget Sound Law Review*, 15, 597–633.

Wheelock, D. (2005). Collateral consequences and racial inequality: Felon status restrictions as a system of disadvantage. *Journal of Contemporary Criminal Justice*, 21(1), 82–90.

Wille, R., & Beier, K. M. (1989). Castration in Germany. *Sexual Abuse*, 2(2), 103–133.

Zandbergen, P. A., & Hart, T. C. (2006). Reducing housing options for convicted sex offenders: Investigating the impact of residency restrictions laws using GIS. *Justice Research and Policy*, 8(2), 1–24.

Zandbergen, P. A., & Hart, T. C. (2009). Availability and spatial distribution of affordable housing in Miami–Dade County and implications of residency restriction zones for registered sex offenders. Miami: American Civil Liberties Union of Florida.

Zevitz, R. G., & Farkas, M. A. (2000a). The impact of sex-offender community notification on probation/parole in Wisconsin. *International Journal of Offender Therapy and Comparative Criminology*, 44(1), 8–21.

Zevitz, R. G., & Farkas, M. A. (2000b). Sex offender community notification: Managing high risk criminals or exacting further vengeance? *Behavioral Sciences and the Law, 18*(2–3), 375–391.

Zgoba, K. M. (2004). Spin doctors and moral crusaders: The moral panic behind child safety legislation. *Criminal Justice Studies, 17*(4), 385–404.

Zgoba, K. M., Vesey, B. M., & Dalessandro, M. (2010). An analysis of the effectiveness of community notification and registration: Do the best intentions predict the best practices? *Justice Quarterly, 27*(5), 667–691.

Zgoba, K. M., Witt, P., Dalessandro, M., & Veysey, B. (2008). *Megan's Law: Assessing the practical and monetary efficacy.* Washington, DC: National Institute of Justice.

Zilney, L. J., & Zilney, L. A. (2009). *Perverts and predators: The making of sexual offending laws.* Lanham, MA: Rowman & Littlefield.

Cases

Connecticut Department of Public Safety v. John Doe, 538 U.S. 1 (2003).
Kansas v. Crane, 534 U.S. 407 (2002).
Kansas v. Hendricks, 521 U.S. 346 (1997).
Skinner v. Oklahoma, 316 U.S. 535 (1942).
Smith v. Doe, 538 U.S. 84 (2003).

CHAPTER 11

Sex in Jails and Prisons

James E. Robertson

In one day—the very first day—of his confinement in a Texas prison, Roderick Keith Johnson experienced prison for what it is: a site that privileges masculinity. Parole violations following a burglary conviction had sent Johnson to one of Texas's biggest and meanest prisons (Liptak, 2004; Solis, 2005). Because inmates readily conflate sex with **gender**, as an openly gay man, Johnson was given a woman's name, "Coco" (Solis, 2005, para. 1). In short order, an inmate claimed him as "sort of a wife" and raped him (Liptak, 2004, para. 1). He was then sold and resold, becoming a commodity in the prison's underground economy. "Once, a bidding war broke out. He was told he was worth $100 in the open market" (Liptak, 2004, para. 4). Although his sex had not changed, he was performing as a woman—a performance that lasted 18 months, during which he was raped daily.

In becoming "sort of a wife" (Liptak, 2004, para. 4), Johnson was performing as a wife. Moreover, his performance as a wife effectively transformed his gender from that of a gay man to a heterosexual woman in the eyes of other inmates.

To escape his tormentors, Johnson requested that prison staff place him in solitary confinement, where he would be segregated from other inmates. Prison officials refused even though, as one inmate would testify, "they knew" of his fate (Solis, 2005, para. 6).

Following his repeated sexual assaults at the hands of inmates, Johnson later brought a civil rights lawsuit, naming as defendants the several prison officers who had failed to protect him. For Johnson to secure damages for his injuries, he had to convince the jury that the defendant officers, by virtue of their failure to protect him, violated his right under the Eighth Amendment to the U.S. Constitution be free of "cruel and unusual punishment." The defendant officers' attorney countered that, as the *Dallas Morning News* reported, "He had willingly adapted to his role as a sexual subservient to other inmates" (Solis, 2005, para. 5). The jury found in favor of all the defendant officers.

The jury's verdict was neither surprising nor correct. Victims of prison rape face strong and volatile headwinds in the courtroom. As in Johnson's trial, victims of prison rape are readily cast by defense attorneys as untruthful by virtue of their criminal histories. In turn, juries such as Johnson's fail to grasp how inmates are pressured into sexual relationships. As one commentator wrote of the Johnson verdict, "It appears that jurors expected Johnson to demonstrate that he physically resisted his rapists and that he had not previously engaged in consensual homosexual sex" (Capers, 2011, p. 1271).

- Does the failure of prison staff to segregate Johnson suggest that they did not perceive him as a legitimate victim?
- Should prison sex be presumed to be involuntary? Would such a presumption result in false claims of rape by inmates seeking generous jury awards?

LEARNING OBJECTIVES

1. Describe "doing" gender.
2. Explain the process by which cultural beliefs about gender are replicated and exaggerated by the prison experience.
3. Compare and contrast the gender roles found in prison.
4. Analyze how the Prison Rape Elimination Act proposes to achieve "zero-tolerance" of prison rape.
5. Evaluate Ristroph's (2006) critique of the Prison Rape Elimination Act.
6. Explain "benign variation" and how it finds expression in the Prison Rape Elimination Act.
7. Compare and contrast self-reported sexual victimization by inmates-on-inmates with staff-on-inmates according to Bureau of Justice Statistics (Beck, Harrison, Berzofsky, & Caspar, 2013).
8. Explain the controversial debate around the placement of gay, bisexual, and transgender inmates in protective custody.
9. Present the pros and cons of permitting "shielding relationships" between inmates.
10. Analyze the concept of "deliberate indifference" as set forth in *Farmer v. Brennan* (1994).
11. Present the constitutional arguments for and against permitting same-sex marriage between an inmate and a non-inmate.

It is said that sexuality does not necessarily reveal "the hidden truth of self" (Seidman, 1997, p. 229). In perhaps no other social institution is this more true than the American prison. Make no mistake, the prisoner is no less a sexual being than his or her counterpart on the other side of prison walls. Yet, inside those walls, the coercive power of social life can often require an inmate to hide or repudiate the truth of one's sexual self.

Roderick Keith Johnson can bear witness: a gay man when he entered prison, his assailants coerced him into performing as a heterosexual woman. Indeed, Johnson's victimization and his subsequent civil rights lawsuit provide a template for this chapter. This chapter will first examine how men and women in prison perform gender through several socially constructed gender roles. Cruelly, as Johnson learned, performing gender in prison leads to sexual victimization at alarming rates, which is explored next. The chapter then will introduce and critique the Prison Rape Elimination Act, a federal statute that rhetorically proclaims "zero tolerance" of sexual victimization while, according to its critics, lacking meaningful enforcement tools. Finally, the chapter will examine how courts have responded to prisoner lawsuits arguing that nonconforming expressions of gender merit constitutional protection. In presenting these topics, the chapter challenges the reader to think critically why the world's largest correctional population (Beckett & Evans, 2015) is housed under intended and unintended conditions that readily disparage and frequently injure one's sexual self.

GENDER BEHIND BARS

"Doing" gender, a sociological concept developed by West and Zimmerman (1987), "is an ongoing activity embedded in daily action" that both creates and revises gender (p. 130). As West and Zimmerman (1987) further explained, "Doing gender means creating differences between girls and boys and women and men, differences that are not natural, essential, or biological" (p. 137). These "differences" are the product of social and institutional practices (Vojdik, 2002). Thus, doing gender is a social process conducted by individuals acting within a social order, the outcome of which is the construction, reinforcement, or transformation of gender roles (West & Zimmerman, 2009). For West and Zimmerman (1987), "ladylike behavior" (p. 139) exemplified doing gender.

Doing gender involves varying degrees of individual agency, but it is primarily guided by "the arrangements that privilege membership in a sex category" (West & Zimmerman, 1987, p. 126). In prison, the privileged category is an extreme form of masculinity: hypermasculinity—"a masculinity in which the strictures against femininity and homosexu-

ality are especially intense and in which physical strength and aggressiveness are paramount" (Harris, 2000, p. 793). Consider Roderick Keith Johnson's case; hypermasculinity dictated the impaired choice given to him by his keepers—you can either "fight or fuck" (Weill-Greenberg, 2005, para. 8). But LGBTQIA inmates are not alone in doing gender. Every inmate partakes of doing gender because, as West and Zimmerman (1987) posited, "doing gender is unavoidable" in that gender is always relevant in the allocation of power, resources, and status (p. 145). Thus, heterosexual male inmates are part of the inclusive list of inmates doing gender. If heterosexual imprisoned males are to maintain their privileged status, they must perform an exaggerated masculinity in their words and deeds (Dolovich, 2012). As Robinson (2011) noted, "Masculinity is a complex set of social regulations that determine what 'real men' can and cannot do" (p. 1331).

"Doing" Gender in Men's Correctional Facilities

"Prison sexuality," wrote Pardue, Arrigo, and Murphy (2011), "is shaped by multiple levels of social life that . . . are amplified by the idiosyncratic subculture of correctional confinement" (p. 280). Concrete walls and iron bars do not strip inmates of the "behavioral baggage" that they bring into the prison (Cressey, 1980, p. ix). This baggage carries the norms, roles, needs, and the cultural, racial, and ethnic identities that inmates acquired through their lives before going to prison (Irwin & Cressey, 1962).

As to the gendered content of this baggage, we find two mutually reinforcing systems of belief about gender: "a hierarchical system in which men dominate women . . . and a hierarchical process of inter-male dominance in which groups of elite males subjugate and dominate groups of lesser-status males" (Sabo, Kupers, & London, 2001, p. 5). Nowhere is this more evident than in Anderson's (2000) hypermasculine code of the street, a normative system he attributed to a culture of inner city poverty. Its nexus with men's prisons is illustrated in Dolovich's (2012) study of hypermasculinity in the Los Angeles County Central Jail, where this street code "no doubt governs life for many men in custody when they are free. This makes the transition from hypermasculine performance on the streets to hypermasculine performance in prison a seamless one" (p. 1008).

Thus, imprisonment does not dismantle these beliefs about gender. Quite the opposite, it functions to replicate these beliefs (Dolovich, 2012). It does so primarily by imposing a host of deprivation (Haney, 2011), which Sykes (1971/1958) famously called the "pains of imprisonment" (p. 65). Sykes, in his groundbreaking study of a New Jersey prison, identified the pains of imprisonment as deprivations of liberty, autonomy, goods and services, personal safety, and sexual relationship with women. Sykes contended that these deprivations collectively presented a "set of threats or attacks which are directed against the very foundations of the prisoner's being" (p. 79). For Sykes and many other penologists, a male prisoner's primary identity is his masculinity, including the status and power bestowed by society upon his sex—an identity that is undermined by the pains of imprisonment. Take, for example, the loss of companionship with the other sex:

> A society composed exclusively of men tends to generate anxieties in its members concerning their masculinity ... The inmate is shut off from the world of women which by its very polarity gives the male world much of its meaning. Like most men, the inmate must search for his identity not simply within himself but also in the picture of himself which he finds reflected in the eyes of others; and since a significant half of his audience is denied him, the inmate's self-image is in danger of becoming half complete, fractured, a monochrome without the hues of reality.
>
> (Sykes, 1971/1958, pp. 71–72)

Sykes and many other observers have concluded that prison experience is emasculating, with prisoners feeling "dishonored" (Ignatieff, 1986, p. 13) or "fallen" (Haney, 2011, p. 134). Inmates respond by seeking refuge in their own subculture, which includes a hierarchy of gender roles that are exaggerated replications of gender roles in society (Rideau & Wikberg, 1992). This prison gender hierarchy awards dominance and punishes submission (Donaldson, 2001). In such a world, doing gender functions as zero-sum game in which one inmate's affirmation of his masculinity frequently entails the degradation of another inmate. And there is no greater degradation than being raped by another inmate.

These two dynamic forces—(1) the prison's organizational structure as a single-sex institution that denies inmates most of the attributes associated with manhood; and, arguably of greater importance, (2) the understandings of masculinity culturally acquired prior to incarceration—make gender a *verb*: "a process, a practice, a tool for marking and enforcing the bounds of gender" (Vojdick, 2002, p. 90). As a verb, gender is expressed through a hierarchy of gender roles that privilege hypermasculinity and reproduce the gender inequality found outside prison (Ridgeway, 2011).

The Real Man

If there is an ideal-type of gender role for men in prison, it is the *real man* (Rideau & Sinclair, 1982, p. 5). He is the personification of hypermasculinity (Holmberg, 2001; Lockwood, 1980). He is tough, resilient, and desirous of dominating and exploiting his fellow prisoners. Some real men limit their sexual activity to masturbation. Inmates of this ilk have been called the "true straight" (Fleisher & Krienert, 2009, p. 69). Their refusal to engage in sex with a fellow inmate symbolizes mental strength. The longer his incarceration, however, the more likely an inmate will engage in same-sex relationships (Fleisher & Krienert, 2009).

The sexually active real men are *wolves* (Hensley, 2001). Wolves, in turn, can be subdivided as follows: The *pitcher* secures his sexual partners (a *catcher*) through overt aggression. By contrast, the "*daddy* . . . courts, befriends, or patronizes weaker, inexperienced inmates into sexual relations" (Dumond, 1992, p. 139). Pitchers come to own their catchers and will sometimes prostitute them. The daddy, however, may have an emotional attachment to the catcher. For example, "Donny the Punk" (aka Stephen Donaldson) wrote of the sexual abuse he encountered in prison at the hands of pitchers and daddies, yet he acknowledged "a wide range of relationships, ranging from ruthless exploitation to romantic love" (Donaldson, 2001, p. 121).

To retain his real man status while anticipating same-sex relationships, a prisoner must be the dominant sexual actor (i.e., the "inserter"). As Donaldson (2001), himself a victim of prison rape (and thus a "catcher"), observed, "The sexual penetration of another male prisoner by a man is sanctioned by the subculture, is considered a male rather than a homosexual activity, and is considered to validate the penetrator's masculinity" (p. 119). Consequently, the prison society views the real man "as the model of heterosexual masculinity" (Ristroph, 2006, p. 152).

Fags and Closet Gays

Fags are perceived as the "true" homosexuals. They entered prison as gay and did not hide their sexual orientation while imprisoned. A subcategory of fags are the *closet gays*, the sexually active, nonaggressive inmates who entered prison with a "hidden homosexual identity" (Castle, Hensley, & Tewksbury, 2002, p. 19). This transformation was observed by Fleisher and Krienert (2009), who wrote of the "fluidity of sex roles . . . as indicated by the expression 'gay for the stay'" (pp. 71–72). Wooden and Parker (1982)

reported that gay inmates as a whole were pressured to adopt feminine names and display feminine characteristics.

Queens/Sissies

Queens, who are also known as *sissies*, are male inmates who voluntarily pursue a female persona (Wooden & Parker, 1982, p. 3). They dress and act the part by wearing makeup and women's clothing (Ross & Richards, 2002). Queens play the passive role in sexual encounters. Staff and inmates treat them as women. Queens have a slightly higher status than openly gay inmates (Sexton, Jenness, & Sumner, 2010). They are a desirable, yet scarce, sexual partner. Their scarcity requires that wolves look for sexual partners among the vulnerable heterosexual men who can be transformed into punks.

Ladies

Ladies are transgender women confined in men's prison. They identify as female and are thus committed to "act like a lady" so that they are seen as "authentically female" (Jenness & Fenstermaker, 2014, p. 14). In the correctional setting, where prisoners are either male or female for institutional purposes, ladies aspire to what Jenness and Fenstermaker (2014) described as a "feminine ideal" rooted in "Victorian-era notions of womanhood" (p. 18).

Punks

As the old saw goes, "Fags are born, punks are made." The *punk* usually enters prison as a heterosexual, but through intimidation and rape is "turned" into a socially constructed woman by being coerced into assuming a female persona. Punks are often young, first-time offenders, who are inexperienced in combat (Donaldson, 2001; Robertson, 2003a, 2012b). A survey of correctional officers in

California conducted in the early 1980s revealed that they strongly agreed that "it is a very common occurrence for young straight boys to be turned out, or forced into being punks" (Wooden & Parker, 1982, p. 204.) Later, in 2000, the U.S. Court of Appeals for the Ninth Circuit concluded, "It is well-documented in both scholarly literature and reported judicial opinions that young, slight, physically weak male inmates, particularly those with 'feminine' physical characteristics, are routinely raped"—and thus likely to be "turned" (*Schwan v. Hartford*, 2000, p. 1203, n. 14). The inmate society, as well as the correctional officer subculture, views the punk as weak, unmanly, and thus disdainful, assigning him to the bottom of a hierarchical system of gender roles (Robertson, 2004a). Punks represent "the fragility of masculinity . . ., signify[ing] that a single sexual act may strip a person of his manhood and 'make him gay'" (Robinson, 2011, p. 1352). The punk may question his own heterosexual identification in that staff and fellow inmates will often assert that he invited the encounter (Scarce, 1997).

"Doing" Gender in Women's Correctional Facilities

Two prominent students of the gendering effects of prison wrote that "[t]he sexual activity of incarcerated women has been and continues to be a major characterization of the female prison setting" (Koscheski & Hensley, 2001, p. 272). In this setting, women do gender just as surely as they do time. As is true of their male counterparts, the gender roles of female inmates are contingent upon a host of factors, which, in turn, dispel the notion that sex and gender are one and the same (Kunzel, 2008).

How women do gender has been primarily attributed to the importation of pre-imprisonment gender norms and their responses to the hardships of confinement (Giallombardo, 1966; Koscheski & Hensley, 2001; Owen, 1998). Thus, the scholarly literature attributes women prisoners' gender roles to the "affectional starvation" of daily life in confinement (Ward & Kassebaum, 2007, p. 73); the desire for "romantic love" in a single-sex institution (Giallombardo,

Box 11.1 THE PUNK AS SEX SLAVE

Jack Henry Abbott (2002) gained literary notice for his book *In the Belly of the Beast*, an autobiographical account of his life in juvenile institutions and prisons, which Abbott characterized as brutal, dehumanizing, and ultimately unjust. In it, Abbott describes a punk, apparently his punk:

> He is like a slave, a chattel love. It is the custom that no one addresses her directly. He cleans my cell, my clothing and runs errands for me. Anything I tell him to do, he must do—exactly the way a wife is perceived in some marriages even today. But I can sell her or lend her out or give her away at any time. Another prisoner can take her from me if he can dominate me.
>
> (p. 80)

- Why would Abbott refer to his punk using the feminine pronoun "her" as well as the masculine pronoun "him?"

1966, p. 141); and a longing for the pre-imprisonment roles of father, mother, and daughter (Owen, 1998). Although women prisoners' gender roles diverge sometimes dramatically from their counterparts in men's prisons, they do include sexually dominant masculine roles. And, as in men's prisons, these roles enjoy the highest status (Owen, 1998; Waterson, 1996).

The *play family* is the most prominent and enduring gender role in women's prisons (Owen, 1998). The members of the prison play family do gender through traditional gender roles (i.e., the sexually dominant father, sexually passive mother, and sexually inactive children). In the federal women's prison she studied, Giallombardo (1966) observed that the "vast majority of inmates adjust to the prison world by establishing a homosexual alliance with a compatible partner as a marriage partner" (p. 136). More recent research indicates that sexual alliances are less stable and subject to various motivations by the parties (Jones, 1993), including economic gain (Greer, 2000). Presently, the tendency to form play families may well be influenced by ethnicity, with Chicanas more inclined to form play families than other ethnic groups (Diaz-Cotto, 2006). What appears to remain constant, though, is that female inmates "play the part of husband, lover, and protector" or "wife, mother, [and] comforter" (Waterson, 1996, p. 293).

Stud Broad

The *stud broad*, who is also known as "the "husband, butch, and little boy" (Owen, 1998, p. 143), assumes the male role in the play family. Accordingly, the stud broad displays aggression, strength, and dominance over the family (Ward & Kassebaum, 1964). The male persona of the stud broad finds expression in attire, hairstyle, and walk (Owen, 1998; Waterson, 1996). As Diaz-Cotto (2006) observed, "[Stud broads] cut their hair short and dressed like working-class

men of their own ethnic group" (p. 138). Stud broads are often situational rather than "true" lesbians (Giallombardo, 1966; Waterson, 1996). The former comprise the *players* or *turnouts*, given their heterosexual orientation before imprisonment. Some stray from their family ties by "sleeping around" or become "commissary hustlers" who benefit from the generosity of the women who seek them out.

Are transgender inmates in a women's prison distinct from stud broads? Sumner and Sexton (2014) concluded that "transgender is simply not as apt a term in women's prisons as it is in men's prisons" in regards to prison culture and prisoner identities (p. 8). The female inmates they interviewed preferred to use the term *aggressor*—a "masculine role in heteronormative relationships" (p. 11). A variant of the stud broad, the aggressor role is synonymous with " 'controlling,' 'dominating,' and 'intimidating' . . . vulnerable femmes" (p. 13).

Femmes

Femmes occupy traditional female roles. Accordingly, they defer to stud broads and assume a passive role in same-sex relationships. Most femmes see themselves as heterosexual and resume such relationships when they leave prison. One inmate wrote,

> The majority of girls who come here, they are not gay. They see these girls that look like men, and they are going to say, well, I am going to try it with her because she looks like a man. She will do it until she gets home and get [sic] a real man. That's how a majority of these women see it.
>
> (Quoted in Owen, 1998, p. 146)

Greer (2000) subdivided these play male–female partnerships into those who are sincere versus those engaged in "dibbling" and "dabbling" (p. 457). "True" lesbians were more likely to engage in sincere relationships (p. 454). By contrast, some femmes sought economic gain by exploiting their stud broad lovers, thus becoming "canteen whores," with the highest status bestowed to inmates with the biggest balance in their prison accounts (p. 454).

Problems Attendant to "Doing" Gender in Correctional Facilities

"Doing" gender in correctional settings can present a host of problems for inmates, correctional officials, and the judicial system alike when it also constitutes violence and coercion. Perhaps the most vexing of these problems concerns the need to protect prisoners from sexual assaults, sexual abuse, and sexual harassment by both other incarcerated people and correctional staff (National Prison Rape Elimination Commission Report, 2009). Accordingly, this chapter focuses on these concerns and the related issues attendant to providing medical care to victims of sex crimes while incarcerated. At the outset, though, it is important to understand that the Eighth Amendment to the U.S. Constitution unpins the need to address all of these problems attendant to doing gender in the correctional setting.

The Eighth Amendment

The **Eighth Amendment** of the U.S. Constitution consists of a single sentence: "Excessive bail shall not be required, nor excessive fines imposed, nor cruel and unusual punishments inflicted." The first clause concerns bail—an attempt to secure a defendant's appearance in court during the pendency of a criminal case (Neubauer & Fradella, 2016). Typically, in exchange for being released from pretrial custody, a defendant who is released on bail is required to post some form of collateral—cash, a bond, or some other form a surety—that is subject to forfeiture if he or she fails to appear in court for all subsequent pretrial and trial proceedings in a criminal case (Neubauer & Fradella, 2016). The second clause of the Eighth Amendment concerns a specific type of criminal sanction. If a court

imposes a fine on a defendant as part of a criminal sentence, the fine must not be "grossly disproportional to the gravity of the offense" it is designed to punish (*United States v. Bajakajian*, 1988, p. 324). The third clause prohibits the imposition of "cruel and unusual punishments." As such, it forms the backbone of all correctional law, including the law that governs the range of issues attendant to doing gender in the correctional setting.

The Cruel and Unusual Punishments Clause was historically interpreted as a bar against torture and barbaric forms of execution that involved lingering deaths, such as "burying alive, drawing and quartering, tearing asunder, or breaking on the wheel" (Gilreath, 2003, p. 572). For nearly 185 years, the U.S. Supreme Court did not interpret the Eighth Amendment as regulating any aspects of conditions of confinement. An appellate court decision from 1951 summed up the then-prevailing judicial view on the Eighth Amendment's inapplicability to regulating prison life as follows: "It is not the function of the courts to superintend the treatment and discipline of prisoners in penitentiaries, but only to deliver from imprisonment those who are illegally confined" (*Stroud v. Swope*, 1951, pp. 851–852). But that changed with the landmark decision in *Estelle v. Gamble* (1976).

The plaintiff in *Gamble* was an inmate in the custody of Texas when he was injured when a bale of cotton fell on him while he was unloading a truck as part of his prison work assignment duties. He received pain killers and muscle relaxers to treat the pain associated with the back injuries caused by the accident. In spite of ongoing pain, prison officials insisted that Gamble rejoin his work detail or face disciplinary action. Gamble filed a lawsuit alleging that the inadequate treatment he received after the injury violated his Eighth Amendment right to be free from cruel and unusual punishment. The Court held that "deliberate indifference to serious medical needs of prisoners" constituted the "unnecessary and wanton infliction of pain" of the type that the Eighth Amendment prohibited (*Gamble*, 1976, p. 104). The Court, however, did not rule in Gamble's favor. The Court concluded that because Gamble had been examined by prison doctors on several occasions and given medication to treat his symptoms, correctional officials had not been deliberately indifferent to his serious medical needs.

Since the decision in *Estelle v. Gamble* (1976), it has been clear that the Eighth Amendment bars the "unnecessary and wanton infliction of pain" in correctional settings. That standard is a high one; it goes beyond mere negligence or medical malpractice. It requires proof that correctional officials were "deliberately indifferent" to prisoners' serious medical needs. But the U.S. Supreme Court did not explain that standard for 18 years until the decision in *Farmer v. Brennan* (1994).

When Douglas Coleman Farmer was sentenced to a men's prison, "he" entered an institution that had historically practiced binary sexual classifications; in other words, prisoners were classified as being either male or female. Farmer, however, did not fit into that binary. Farmer had been born a biological male. When Farmer entered the federal prison system on credit card fraud charges, however, Farmer identified as Dee Farmer, a transgender woman. She had taken hormones since her teen years (Flowers, 2014) and, at the time of incarceration, had silicone breast implants (Flowers, 2014). "She'd undergone an unsuccessful black-market operation to remove her testicles—a botched job she attempted to complete while behind bars, with a razor blade" (Flowers, 2014, para. 13). Yet, she was left to fend for herself in the general prison population while sharing a cell with the male inmate who eventually beat her and raped her at knifepoint.

Farmer sued various prison officials, alleging that their failure to protect her from sexual violence amounted to a violation of Farmer's right not to be subjected to cruel and unusual punishment under the Eighth Amendment to the U.S. Constitution. After losing at the federal district court level and on her first appeal,

the U.S. Supreme Court agreed to hear the case. During oral arguments, the American Civil Liberties Union (ACLU) lawyers who represented Farmer referred to her using the feminine pronouns "she" and "her"; attorneys for the government used masculine pronouns. In writing the Court's majority decision, Justice David H. Souter "performed grammatical gymnastics and avoided using either pronoun in referring to Farmer" (Flowers, 2014, para. 28).

The Court held that an inmate's rape does not violate the Eighth Amendment unless the correctional staff were "deliberately indifferent" to the threat facing the victim (*Farmer v. Brennan*, 1994, p. 834). The Court operationalized the **deliberate indifference** standard as being akin to criminal recklessness—a *mens rea* standard that has both objective and subjective components. Regarding the objective component, the Court stated that a risk of harm "must be, objectively, sufficiently 'serious' . . ." (*Farmer v. Brennan*, 1994, p. 834). The subjective component requires proof that the defendant officer(s) subjectively knew that the inmate faced a "substantial risk of serious harm" and, with such knowledge, nonetheless disregarded "that risk by failing to take reasonable measures to abate it" (*Farmer v. Brennan*, 1994, p. 847).

[A] prison official cannot be found liable under the Eighth Amendment for denying an inmate humane conditions of confinement unless the official knows of and disregards an excessive risk to inmate health or safety; the official must both be aware of facts from which the inference could be drawn that a substantial risk of serious harm exists, and he must also draw the inference. This approach comports best with the text of the Amendment as our cases have interpreted it. The Eighth Amendment does not outlaw cruel and unusual "conditions"; it outlaws cruel and unusual "punishments." An act or omission unaccompanied by knowledge of a significant risk of harm might well be something society wishes to discourage, and if harm does result society might well wish to assure compensation. The common law reflects such concerns when it imposes tort liability on a purely objective basis. But an official's failure to alleviate a significant risk that he should have perceived but did not, while no cause for commendation, cannot under our cases be condemned as the infliction of punishment.

(*Farmer v. Brennan*, 1994, pp. 837–838)

The lower courts had ruled against Farmer, finding that correctional officials had not been deliberately indifferent to her plight because she had "never expressed any concern for his safety to any of [the defendants]. Since [the correctional officials] had no knowledge of any potential danger to [Farmer], they were not deliberately indifferent" to her safety (*Farmer v. Brennan*, 1994, p. 832). But the U.S. Supreme Court disagreed, finding that the lower courts had overlooked some key evidence in the case, including an admission by correctional officers that Farmer was "a nonviolent transsexual who, because of [Farmer's] 'youth and feminine appearance' [was] 'likely to experience a great deal of sexual pressure' in prison" (*Farmer v. Brennan*, 1994, p. 848). In fact, the warden of a federal penitentiary at which Farmer had been previously housed had stated that there was "a high probability" that Farmer could not safely function in general population (*Farmer v. Brennan*, 1994, p. 848). So, the Court remanded the case for a determination as to whether correctional officials knew of risks to Farmer, but disregarded those risks and exposed Farmer to sexual victimization. A jury subsequently ruled in favor of the correctional officials. In the end, the jury did not believe that Farmer had been raped (Flowers, 2014).

Farmer Facilitates Enactment of the Prison Rape Elimination Act

Dee Farmer's case helped to bring the problem into the national spotlight. In the years following the Supreme Court's decision in the case, a diverse coalition of moral entrepreneurs on both political right and left—including Charles Colson's Prison Fellowship Ministries and human rights organizations, such as Human Rights Watch and Stop Prisoner Rape (now Just Detention International)—lobbied Congress to combat what they characterized as a harrowing epidemic of prison rape (Robertson, 2004b, 2004c). The most influential actors, corrections organizations, however, came late to the cause yet played an oversized role in framing the legislation (Jenness & Smyth, 2011). The fruit of their labors, the Prison Rape Elimination Act of 2003 (PREA) received unanimous support in Congress.

In pronouncing a zero-tolerance policy toward prison rape, the PREA provides for the following:

- the study of sexual victimization in prison and the issuance of national standards to guide staff in their response to this phenomenon;
- the collection of statistical data about sexual victimization in prison;
- money to educate and train staff to recognize and prevent sexual victimization; and
- a federal panel to review the response of correctional agencies to prison rape (see Just Detention International, 2009).

As the chapter will explore, however, the PREA suffers from numerous shortcomings. Before critiquing that law and its effects thus far, this chapter explores the nature of sexual victimization in American corrections.

INMATE-ON-INMATE SEXUAL ASSAULT

In writing about the normalcy of rape in men's prisons, Ristroph (2006) suggested that part of "doing" gender in a male prison involves doing rape. Prior to their confinement, most males have embraced Western gender norms, including the "code of the street" notion that masculinity must be aggressively acquired by controlling people and resources (Anderson, 2000). As previously explained, imprisonment only intensifies these norms in response to conditions of confinement that strip inmates of nearly all control over their lives, which further threatens their masculinity. Rather than accept their official identity as state-owned bodies, inmates will desperately attempt to maintain their status as hyper-masculine men of agency. And at the apex of those strategies of agency resides prison rape. By raping a fellow inmate, the rapist stakes his claim to being a *real man* by virtue of an act that symbolizes his capacity to dominate another fellow prison, forcing of him to assume the role of "a woman" (Rideau & Wikberg, 1992, p. 75).

Controversially, there is a case to be made that prison staff are co-conspirators in the rape of prisoners. Robertson (2003a) marshaled anecdotal accounts of staff voicing homophobic attitudes that delegitimize victims of prison rape, such as "that plaintiff 'must be gay' for 'letting them make you suck dick," (p. 446). Eigenberg (2000a) charged that prison staff use prison rape to control inmates in a host of ways:

[s]ome officers may manipulate housing assignments to intimidate inmates by threatening to assign more vulnerable inmates to bunk with known sexual predators. Or, perhaps officers may tolerate coercive acts because they facilitate divisions among inmates, making them, as a group, more manageable.

(p. 436)

In a similar vein, Wacquant (2001) wrote that under-resourced prison staff welcome a sexual hierarchy based on rape because it is a means by which inmates control other inmates, leaving staff to control those at the top of the hierarchy.

Defining Prison Rape

The PREA is the first federal statute that speaks to "the rape of an inmate in the actual or constructive control of prison officials" (42 U.S.C.A. § 15609[8]). It defines rape as follows:

(A) the carnal knowledge, oral sodomy, sexual assault with an object, or sexual fondling of a person, forcibly or against that person's will;

(B) the carnal knowledge, oral sodomy, sexual assault with an object, or sexual fondling of a person not forcibly or against the person's will, where the victim is incapable of giving consent because of his or her youth or his or her temporary or permanent mental or physical incapacity; or

(C) the carnal knowledge, oral sodomy, sexual assault with an object, or sexual fondling of a person achieved through the exploitation of the fear or threat of physical violence or bodily injury.

(42 U.S.C.A. § 15609[9])

In implementing the PREA, the U.S. Department of Justice (2012) concluded that "sexual abuse is a more accurate term to describe the behaviors that Congress aimed to eliminate" than prison rape (28 C.F.R. § 115.6, 2012). The PREA's definition of sexual abuse is broader than the definition of rape, as illustrated by the language in Section 115.6 of the Act:

Sexual abuse of an inmate, detainee, or resident by another inmate, detainee, or resident includes any of the following acts, if the victim does not consent, is coerced into such act by overt or implied threats of violence, or is unable to consent or refuse:

(1) Contact between the penis and the vulva or the penis and the anus, including penetration, however slight;

(2) Contact between the mouth and the penis, vulva, or anus;

(3) Penetration of the anal or genital opening of another person, however slight, by a hand, finger, object, or other instrument; and

(4) Any other intentional touching, either directly or through the clothing, of the genitalia, anus, groin, breast, inner thigh, or the buttocks of another person, excluding contact incidental to a physical altercation.

Prison Rape as Global Harm

Testifying before the National Prison Rape Elimination Commission, a sexual assault nurse examiner, Jennifer Pierce-Weeks, stated that prison rape has global consequences for its victim, potentially inflicting harm in "every dimension of life: psychological, physical, spiritual, and social" (National Prison Rape Elimination Commission Report, 2009, p. 126). Her observations are consistent with the findings of the National Former Prisoner Survey (Beck & Johnson, 2012). Following their release from prison, 72% of the victims of inmate-on-inmate sexual victimization indicated that they felt shame or humiliation, and 56% said they felt guilt" (p. 6). The Commission's Report concluded that prison sexual assault victims often experience post-traumatic stress disorder, the symptoms of which include "sadness, explosive anger, feelings of hopelessness, changes in memory or thinking, feeling marked or changed in a permanent way, obsessing about the event or persons involved, relating to others differently, losing trust in others, and other detrimental reactions" (National Prison Rape Elimination Commission Report, 2009, p. 127).

Penile penetration also brings the risk of transmitted HIV/AIDS and other sexually transmitted diseases acquired through the exchange of bodily fluids (Robertson, 2003b). The National Former Prisoner Survey, 2008 (Beck & Johnson, 2012) found that men reporting sexual abuse during confinement were much more likely to be diagnosed with a sexually transmitted disease (6.5%) than the former inmates who reported otherwise (2.6%).

Comparatively few sexually victimized inmates report their assault to prison medical staff. One survey pegged the number at 14% (Beck & Harrison, 2007). Even when they sustained physical injury, two of every three victims failed to notify medical personnel (Beck & Harrison, 2007). "Due to fear of reprisal from perpetrators, a code of silence among inmates, personal embarrassment, and lack of trust in staff, victims are often reluctant to report incidents to correctional authorities" (Beck & Hughes, 2005, p. 2). Inmates who do report their sexual victimization have historically received little to no medical care (see 42 U.S.C. § 15601[8], [11], 2003).

Male prison rape has long been marginalized as being less than "real" rape. In their controversial, "bitterly disputed" study of prison rape (Curtis, 2006, para. 1), Fleisher and Krienert (2009) concluded that the inmate culture contains a "sexual world view" that "allows for a wide berth of sexual freedom," with "rape on the margin of what otherwise would be culturally permissible sexual behavior" (p. 78). Deciding whether a "real" rape occurred largely rests on the degree of blame assigned the victim—in other words, the greater the blame, the less likely it is a rape. Blame accrues through exhibiting weakness, accruing debts that cannot be paid, and other shortfalls that reveal a lack of manliness. Fowler (2007) reached a similar conclusion. After randomly surveying inmates in six Texas prisons, she found that "rape-supportive beliefs led inmates to excuse perpetrators, blame victims, and prevent inmates from accepting legally defined incidents of sexual assaults" (p. 4870).

Moreover, a sizeable proportion of correctional staff appear to embrace a similar perspective. Moster and Jeglic (2009) reported that one-third of the responding wardens did not characterize a sex-for-protection transaction as a sexual assault. Earlier, Eigenberg's

Box 11.2 "REAL" RAPE OR LEGITIMATE SEXUAL EXPRESSION?[1]

In a letter to Human Rights Watch, Colorado inmate J.D. wrote:

I came into prison in April, 1991. I'd never been to prison before. I basically feared for my life. . . . Eventually, I ended up with a roommate who took advantage of my situation. He made me feel "protected" somewhat. But, at the same time, he let me know he could quite capably beat me up, if he wanted. One night, after we were all locked down for the night, he told me he could help me overcome my sexual inhibitions, if I would let him. He told me he was bisexual. I knew he was quite sexually active, so to speak, as he had female pornography in the room as well as masturbating frequently to it. But, I was surprised he would come on to me. However, I felt very much in danger if I did not give in to him. I was very scared. I ended up letting him penetrate me anally.

(Human Rights Watch, 2001, p. 87)

J.D. clearly feared his cellmate and in no manner perceived his penetration as consensual despite his failure to object to his cellmate's conduct. While the purported assailant (inmate "X") let it be known that he could beat him up, his aim may have been defensive; if you received a new cell partner, wouldn't you put him on notice that you were capable of assault? More importantly, J.D. himself describes X as "coming on" to him, offering ("if I would let him") to "help [him] overcome [his] sexual inhibitions." Did J.D.'s failure to object amount to implied consent for the sex act that followed?

(2000b) survey of correctional officers in a Midwestern state found that 36% of the responding officers also refused to characterize sex for protection as prison rape. Still, a substantial portion of officers faulted the victims of a prison rape based on their homosexuality (12%), feminine dress and speech (17%), earlier consensual sex (23%), and, prior to their rape, exchanging money or cigarettes for sex (24%). By contrast, when force or the threat of force was used, 95% of the officers agreed that rape occurred.

The "Bad Man" Myth and the Tactics of Prison Rapists

The **"bad man" myth** represents the popularly held, but false, belief that prison rapists are exclusively men who employ physical force to subdue their victims (Ristroph, 2006). Indeed, violent prison rape, much like the rape

described below, has dominated the cultural imagination around the issue (Caster, 2008).

"Holler, whore, and you die," a hoarse voice warned, the threat emphasized by the knife point at his throat . . . He was thrown on the floor, his pants pulled off him. As a hand profanely squeezed his buttocks, he felt a flush of embarrassment and anger, more because of his basic weakness—which prevented him from doing anything to stop what was happening—than because of what was actually going on. His throat grunted painful noises, an awful pleading whine that went ignored as he felt his buttocks spread roughly apart. A searing pain raced through his body as the hardness of one of his attackers tore roughly into his rectum.

(Rideau & Wikberg, 1992, p. 73)

This depiction of the prison rape suggests that inmates are the "other"—a breed apart, who have created a patriarchal society enclosed by iron bars, where evil choices are commonplace. The "bad man" perception of inmates as the "other" carries racial baggage. Born of the Jim Crow era, the cultural image of the Black man as "the beast rapist" (Hale, 1998, p. 41) persists in the contemporary prison (Robertson, 2006). And flawed studies showing that the prototypic aggressor is Black and his victim is White (Carroll, 1974; Lockwood, 1980) have created what Buchanan (2010) calls "the specter (or fantasy) of Black-on-White prison rape" (p. 64).

Importantly, much of prison sexual victimization is non-violent yet coercive, where gay and bisexual inmates and the mentally ill are far more likely to be victims than those who are heterosexual, and women disproportionately outnumber men in self-reporting sexual victimization (Ristroph, 2006). The National Former Prisoner Survey, 2008 (Beck & Johnson, 2012) found that over half of sexually abused inmates (51.7%) attributed their victimization to "coercion other than force/threat," with the most frequent non-violent scenario being "[I was] persuaded or being talked into it" (34.3%), followed by the following scenarios: bribery and/or blackmail (25.6%); exchanging sexual acts for protection from fellow inmates (24%); under the influence of alcohol or other drugs (9%); and settling debts through a sex act (8%). Moreover, of the inmates reporting sexual victimization by force or the threat thereof, only a quarter (24.8%) were physically harmed—the sine qua non of a "real" rape in the minds of many prisoners and a sizeable minority of correctional officers and wardens. The survey also reveals that sexual orientation is the greatest risk factor for male inmates but not female inmates. Among male inmates, 3.5% of self-identified heterosexual inmates reported sexual victimization, as did 33.7% of bisexual and 38% of gay inmates. By contrast, lesbian prisoners self-reported sexual victimization by other inmates at the same rate as their heterosexual counterparts (13%).

Box 11.3 PRISON RAPE SCENARIOS

In the writings of Victor Hassine (2009) a "lifer" himself, one finds a sharply drawn, harrowing description of prison life, including a nuanced typology of inmate-on-inmate rape.

Strong Arm Rape: A violent sexual predator targets a young, attractive, physically weak inmate, who is either a loner or a "fish" (new inmate).

Extortion Rape: A jailhouse hustler, such as drug dealer or loan shark, rapes his deeply indebted mark, punishing him for failure to pay his debts.

Date Rape: A con-artist targets a physically and psychologically weak inmate (who is often gay) by being in his constant presence, which identifies them as a "couple" to the inmate population and prison staff.

Confidence Rape: A con-artist targets a young, weak, frightened (and often heterosexual) inmate, convincing his mark that he is his only true friend and protector.

Drug Rape: In a variation of confidence rape, the assailant targets a fellow drug user by developing a drug relationship with target, striking when the target is drug impaired.

(pp. 159–162)

The Frequency of Prison Rape

Throughout the history of the penitentiary, commentators have identified rape as an expected condition of confinement. For example, in the 1830s, Louis Dwight discerned "one general fact" from his extensive prison visits: "Boys are prostituted to the behest of old convicts" (quoted in Heilpern, 1998, p. 63). However, no major study of male prison rape occurred until 1968 when Davis (1968) interviewed 3,304 male inmates housed in Philadelphia's jails, concluding that 3% had been raped.

A host of subsequent studies conducted in the closing decades of the twentieth century yielded disparate findings. Struckman-Johnson, Struckman-Johnson, Rucker, Bumby, and Donaldson (1996) undertook the most noteworthy and reliable survey of prisoners. Published in 1996, their first survey was of prisoners confined in one minimum and two maximum-security prisons in Nebraska. They found that 22% of the male prisoners and 7.7% of the female prisoners reported "coerced sexual contact" (p. 74). In 1998, Struckman-Johnson & Struckman-Johnson (2000) surveyed some 7,000 men confined in seven Midwestern states. Twenty-one percent of the respondents reported coerced sexual contact during confinement in a state prison system. The likelihood of sexual abuse varied greatly from one prison to another, with the incidence of coerced oral or anal sex and coerced sexual contact ranging from 0% to 11% and 4% to 21%, respectively.

Nonetheless, Buchanan (2012) observed that "[u]ntil about 2007, empirical evidence of the prevalence and dynamics of prison rape was relatively scanty, and methodologically unreliable" (p. 1645). In 2007, as statutorily mandated by the PREA, the Bureau of Justice Statistics released its much anticipated findings on the sexual violence (i.e., "either non-consensual sexual acts or abusive sexual contacts") based on the self-reporting sample of 23,398 state and federal prisoners (Beck & Harrison, 2007, p. 2). An estimated 4.5% —or about 60,500—of the nation's prisoners experienced sexual violence at the hands of inmates and/or prison staff during the 12 months prior to the self-interviewing date or, for inmates who had yet to serve 12 months at the facility, since their arrival.

The Bureau of Justice Statistics survey, *Sexual Victimization in Prisons and Jails Reported by Inmates, 2011–12* (Beck, Harrison, Berzofsky & Caspar, 2013), established the following baselines:

- Among all state and federal prisoners, during an average exposure period of 8 months, 2% reported one or more sexual victimizations by inmates and 4% by staff.
- Among all jail inmates, during an average exposure period of 3.7 months, 1.6% reported one or more sexual victimizations by inmates and 1.8% by staff.

However, these baselines alone do not describe the great statistical divide based on sex and sexual orientation that this survey found.

- Among male prisoners and jail inmates, 1.7% and 1.4%, respectively, reported sexual victimization by another inmate. By contrast, among female prisoners and jail inmates, 6.9% and 3.6%, respectively, reported sexual victimization by another inmate.
- Among heterosexual prisoners and jail inmates, 1.2% and 1.2%, respectively, reported sexual victimization by another inmate. By contrast, among non-heterosexual ("including gay, lesbian, bisexual, and other sexual orientations") prisoners and jail inmates, 12.2% and 8.5%, respectively, reported sexual victimization by another inmate (Beck, et al., 2013, p. 18).

In addition to inmate-on-inmate sexual victimization, the sad reality is that inmates are also victimized by personnel who work in correctional institutions—a problem to which we now turn our attention.

CORRECTIONAL STAFF PERPETRATORS OF SEXUAL MISCONDUCT[2]

One member of the National Prison Rape Commission observed that the "sexual exploitation [of women by male staff] has been a subtext of imprisonment since its inception" (Smith, 2006, p. 197). Women were first confined in the attics, kitchens, and backrooms of men's penitentiaries where, left unattended, they fell victim to male guards. Accounts of the resulting sexual abuse spurred the women's reformatory movement of 1860–1935. Its legacy was the imprisonment of women in cottage-style, sex-specific prisons overseen exclusively by female matrons (Johnson, 1997). However, the enactment of the Civil Rights Act of 1964—which included under Title VII the prohibition of employment discrimination based on race, color, religion, sex, and national origin—opened men's prisons to female officers and returned male officers to women's prisons in such numbers as to outnumber their female counterparts (Moss, 2009). In one women's prison in Massachusetts, the arrival of male officers led to

> a building full of constitutionally disempowered women being ruled over by uniformed male guards, in which [t]here were officers who liked to be touched and officers who like to touch; officers who dared only to kiss and officers who liked to go the whole way. There were a couple who liked to watch girls together, and one whose preference it was to get blow jobs by thrusting his penis through the food slots [in the cells housing the residents].
>
> (Rathbone, 2005, p. 45)

Even the most routine invasions of a prisoner's privacy, pat-down searches, left inmates, particularly women, vulnerable to sexual abuse. *Orange is the New Black* author Piper Kerman (2011), housed in a federal women's prison, described how

> [m]ost of the male guards made a show of performing the absolute minimal frisk necessary, skimming their fingertips along your arms, legs, and waist in such a way that said, "Not touching! Not touching! Not really touching!" They didn't want any suggestion of impropriety raised against them. But a handful of the male guards apparently felt no such fear about grabbing whatever they wanted. They were allowed to touch the lower edge of our bras, to make sure we weren't smuggling goodies in there—but were they really allowed to squeeze our breasts?
>
> (p. 235)

Defining Staff Sexual Misconduct

Section 115.6 of the Prison Rape Elimination Act of 2003 states:

> [S]exual abuse of an inmate, detainee, or resident by a staff member, contractor, or volunteer includes any of the following acts, with or without consent of the inmate, detainee, or resident:
>
> (1) Contact between the penis and the vulva or the penis and the anus, including penetration, however slight;
> (2) Contact between the mouth and the penis, vulva, or anus;
> (3) Contact between the mouth and any body part where the staff member, contractor, or volunteer has the intent to abuse, arouse, or gratify sexual desire;
> (4) Penetration of the anal or genital opening, however slight, by a hand, finger, object, or other instrument, that is unrelated to official duties or where the staff member, contractor, or volunteer has the intent to abuse, arouse, or gratify sexual desire;

(5) Any other intentional contact, either directly or through the clothing, of or with the genitalia, anus, groin, breast, inner thigh, or the buttocks, that is unrelated to official duties or 196 where the staff member, contractor, or volunteer has the intent to abuse, arouse, or gratify sexual desire;

(6) Any attempt, threat, or request by a staff member, contractor, or volunteer to engage in the activities described in paragraphs (1)–(5) of this section;

(7) Any display by a staff member, contractor, or volunteer of his or her uncovered genitalia, buttocks, or breast in the presence of an inmate, detainee, or resident, and

(8) Voyeurism by a staff member, contractor, or volunteer.

The Frequency of Staff Sexual Misconduct

In 2012, the National Former Prisoner Survey, 2008 (Beck & Johnson, 2012) reported the results of a survey of more than 17,000 former state prisoners, with an average imprisonment period of some 39 months. Nearly 10% reported at least one sexual victimization (i.e., "all types of unwanted [or abusive] sexual activity with other inmates . . . and both willing and unwilling sexual activity with staff") during their last imprisonment (p. 13). The survey also found that a higher percentage of males (5.4%) than females (4.4%) reported staff sexual misconduct. About 9 of 10 (87%) of the males reporting staff sexual misconduct identified the perpetrators as female. The rates of sexual abuse varied greatly by the sexual orientation of the former prisoners. Among males, 5.2% of heterosexuals, 18% of bisexuals, and 12% of gays reported sexual victimization by staff. Among the women, 3.7% of heterosexuals, 7.5% of the bisexuals, and 18% of the lesbians reported sexual victimization by staff. Buchanan (2012) argued that these findings run counter to conventional gender expectations that the typical victim of inmate-on-

inmate sexual victimization is female, revealing the "selective blindness of prison rape discourse to counter-stereotypical forms of abuse" (p. 1630).

The Criminalization of Staff Sexual Misconduct

Any sexual contact between an inmate and a staff person is prohibited by state and federal law (see Just Detention International, 2015). Moreover, the inmate's consent is not a defense. Illustrative is the federal law applicable to persons working in the Federal Bureau of Prisons, which reads:

(b) Of a ward. Whoever, in the special maritime and territorial jurisdiction of the United States or in a Federal prison, or in any prison, institution, or facility in which persons are held in custody by direction of or pursuant to a contract or agreement with the head of any Federal department or agency, knowingly engages in a sexual act with another person who is—

(1) in official detention; and
(2) under the custodial, supervisory, or disciplinary authority of the person so engaging; or attempts to do so, shall be . . . imprisoned not more than 15 years, or both.

(918 U.S.C. § 2243)

Statutes such as the one above are based on the rationale that the power imbalance between officer and inmates "vitiates the possibility of meaningful consent" (National Prison Rape Elimination Commission Report, 2009, p. 13). Piper Kerman (2011), a former inmate herself, agrees:

It is hard to conceive of any relationship between two adults in America being less equal than that of prisoner and prison guard. The formal relationship, enforced by the institution, is that one person's word means everything and the other's means almost nothing; one person can command the other to do just about anything, and refusal can result in total physical restraint.

(p. 129)

The Bureau of Justice Statistics' Special Report, *Sexual Violence Reported by Correctional Authorities 2006* (Beck, Harrison, & Adams, 2007) revealed that 56% of substantiated instances of staff sexual misconduct led to legal sanctions and three of every four accused officers lost their jobs. Does gender influence the sanctions imposed on staff who have sexual relationships with inmates? There is anecdotal evidence that female staff perpetrators are treated more leniently than their male officer counterparts. Teichner (2008) juxtaposed the prosecution of a Wisconsin female officer sentenced in 2006 to two years of probation and a $100 fine for sexual misconduct involving a male prisoner, with prison sentences of 10 years and 10–20 years imposed on two male officers in New York and Tennessee, respectively, for similar behavior.

However, the tough sanctions meted out to male officers in New York and Tennessee are not the rule. Cogan (2012) found that "staff sexual abuse is rarely prosecuted" (p. 196). She looked to the Bureau of Justice Statistics' Special Report, *Sexual Violence Reported by Correctional Authorities, 2006* (Beck, Harrison, & Adams, 2007), which reported that 34% of substantiated sexual misconduct cases were referred for prosecution in 2005 and 45% in 2006. Why so few prosecutions? Cogan (2012) identified four reasons. First, prison staff do not do a good job in preserving crime scenes, collecting evidence, and interviewing victims, suspects, and witnesses. Second, there is a long-standing perception of prosecutors that the deck is stacked against a conviction because juries view the inmate-victim as unsympathetic and untruthful. Third, prosecutors often define a sexual assault committed by staff as less than serious crime (e.g., a "stupid sex case") and thus, worthy of administrative penalties at best.

Law in Action CAN INMATES CONSENT TO SEX WITH CORRECTIONAL STAFF?

Officer Forbes first met inmate McGregor when he was detained at the county jail where Forbes worked. When McGregor was transferred to a state prison, they exchanged letters. After parole violations returned McGregor to county jail, "their relationship morphed from friendly to flirtatious, until their relationship became intimately physical" (p.1). Soon she was bringing him contraband, which included cigarettes and marijuana. Their relationship initially went undetected by Forbes's superiors because McGregor performed janitorial duties, giving him access to areas otherwise off limits to inmates and thus unsupervised by staff, and, in particular, the couple sought out rooms that did not have security camera coverage. Some five months after their sexual relationship commenced, another officer discovered them, which led to her resignation and conviction under New York law for third-degree sexual assault. Was their relationship consensual? Not according to McGregor. He claimed that their sexual encounters occurred amid "a veiled threat of violence . . ." and she "implicitly threatened him with some unspecified retaliation if he stopped their sexual relationship" (p. 2).

- Do you think a relationship of this kind can be consensual?
- What specific aspects of this example lead you to conclude that this was or was not consensual? Why?

Box 11.4 *WOOD V. BEAUCLAIR (2012) AND "WILLING" RELATIONSHIPS*[3]

Eighty-six percent of male inmates reporting involvement with female officers characterized their participation as "willing," as juxtaposed to 5.5% of the female inmates reporting willing involvement with male officers (Beck & Johnson, 2012). Of the inmates characterizing their sexual involvement with staff as willing, 62% also said that they experienced coercion or offers of special treatment from the involved staff members.

Can a "willing" relationship with a staff member be a consensual one? Prosecutions of staff for sexual misconduct are rare partly because of their assertion of consent (Cogan, 2012). Yet some courts deem all sexual relationships between inmates and officers as inherently nonconsensual for Eighth Amendment purposes. The plaintiff in *Wood v. Beauclair* (2012) urged the federal court system to embrace this position. Because this issue was "a matter of first impression" (p. 1046) and involved contested case law, the court's analysis merits scrutiny.

The plaintiff and a female officer began what was initially a romantic relationship. When he heard rumors that she was married, he questioned her. Eventually, he told her to "back off" (p. 1044). Nonetheless, she pursued him, entering the plaintiff's cell and placing her hand on his groin. He sued her. Before the U.S. District Court, the officer successfully argued that the relationship had started as a consensual one and continued as such during this incident. Still, the court found no constitutional violation because "welcome and voluntary sexual interactions, no matter how inappropriate, cannot as a matter of law constitute 'pain' as contemplated by the Eighth Amendment" (*Wood v. Idaho Department of Correction*, 2009, p. 3, quoting *Freitas v. Ault*, 1997, p. 1339).

On appeal to the U.S. Court of Appeals for the Ninth Circuit, the three-judge panel stated that it was unsure if any sexual relationships between an officer and an inmate could be truly consensual. On the one hand, the Ninth Circuit expressed "concern about the implications of removing consent as a defense in Eighth Amendment claims" (*Wood v. Beauclair*, 2012, p. 1048). On the other hand, it agreed with the following rationale for regarding all relationships between inmates and staff as inherently coercive:

> Prisoners have no control over most aspects of their daily lives. They cannot choose what or when to eat, whether to turn the lights on or off, where to go, and what to do. They depend on prison employees for basic necessities, contact with their children, health care, and protection from other inmates. The power disparity between prisoners and prison guards is similar to that of an adult over a child or a teacher over a student. . . . Just as power inequities between adults and minors, teachers and students, and owners and slaves foster opportunities for sexual abuse, so too does the prisoner–guard relationship.
>
> (p. 1047)

The Ninth Circuit "split the difference" by presuming that any sexual contact between an inmate and an officer is not consensual, thus allowing the officer the opportunity to rebut the presumption by demonstrating that their relationship was free of (a) "explicit assertions or manifestations of non-consent"; and (b) "favors, privileges, or any type of exchange for sex" (p. 1049). As to the facts of this case, while implying that the relationship started as a consensual one, the Ninth Circuit ruled that the plaintiff's telling the defendant to "back off" ended the consensual relationship from that point forward—including the first claimed instance of sexual harassment.

- Explain whether you think relationships between correctional officers and the inmates they supervise can ever been truly consensual. Do the sex and gender identity of the officers and the prisoners affect your views? Why or why not?

Last, although consent is not a defense, prosecutors nonetheless decline to prosecute those cases they define as consensual.

THE PRISON RAPE ELIMINATION ACT OF 2003

As previously mentioned, the Prison Rape Elimination Act (PREA) was enacted in 2003 with the goal—as the title of the legislation states—of eliminating sexual victimization in prisons. As is often the case with major pieces of legislation, the PREA itself did not address the minutiae of implementing the law. Rather, the legislation "created the National Prison Rape Elimination Commission and charged it with developing draft standards for the elimination of prison rape. Those standards were published in June 2009, and were turned over to the Department of Justice for review and passage as a final rule" (National PREA Resource Center, 2015a, para. 2).

The *National Standards to Prevent, Detect, and Respond to Prison Rape* ("PREA Standards") were published in the *Federal Register* on June 20, 2012. The PREA Standards set forth rules for correctional agencies concerning the need to assess their current policies, practices, and facilities against those set forth in the PREA Standards; to plan for addressing gaps in compliance; and to implement their strategic plans (National PREA Resource Center, 2015b).

The PREA Standards and Benign Variation[4]

Robertson (2012–2013) argued that the PREA Standards represented a significant break from a binary classification system that purported to identify inmates as either male or female. The PREA Standards instead embrace what Eskridge (2010) called the "liberal norm of **benign variation**" (i.e., the recognition of "a wide range of gender and sexual variation as tolerable or (more ambitiously) as benign" (p. 1341). Eskridge (2010) further stated that "[b]enign variation suggests that no gender role is inevitably 'best' for every woman or every man, and no sexual practice or orientation is inevitably 'best' for every person" (p. 1341).

The PREA Standards implicitly distinguish between assigned sex at birth and gender identity. Moreover, the PREA Standards expressly state that "[t]he standards account in various ways for the particular vulnerabilities of inmates who are LGBTQIA or whose appearance or manner does not conform to traditional gender expectations" (U.S. Department of Justice, 2012, pp. 8–9).

With regard to these several non-normative gender and sexual identities, the PREA Standards provide for a host of affirmative duties:

- "training in effective and professional communication with [LGBTQIA] and gender nonconforming inmates";
- screening to consider "whether the inmate is, or is perceived to be, [LGBTQIA] or gender nonconforming";
- post-incident reviews "to consider whether the (sexual) incident was motivated by [LGBTQIA] identification, status, or perceived status";
- "training security staff in conducting professional and respectful cross-gender pat-down searches and searches of transgender and intersex inmates"; and

- providing "transgender and intersex inmates . . . the opportunity to shower separately from other inmates."

  (U.S. Department of Justice, 2012, pp. 8–9)

The PREA Standards also bar some long-standing, offensive practices, including:

- placing "[LGBTQIA] inmates in dedicated facilities, units, or wings in adult prisons, jails, or community confinement facilities solely on the basis of such identification or status, unless such placement is in a dedicated facility, unit, or wing established in connection with a consent decree, legal settlement, or legal judgment for the purpose of protecting such inmates";
- "searching or physically examining a transgender or intersex inmate for the sole purpose of determining the inmate's genital status"; and
- assigning "transgendered or intersex inmates to a facility based on genital status."

  (U.S. Department of Justice, 2012, p. 9)

A Critique of the PREA

Robertson (2012b) contended that the PREA Standards are hobbled by two statutory limitations. First, the PREA dictates that the standards cannot "impose substantial additional costs compared to the costs presently expended by Federal, State, and local prison authorities" (42 U.S.C. § 15607[a][3]). Second, while the PREA Standards are binding on federal detention facilities, they lack a formal enforcement mechanism at the state level other than the loss of 5% of federal correctional funding for states that fail to implement them.

In addition, the PREA may be flawed conceptually. Ristroph (2006) characterized the PREA as "a mostly hortatory statute, seemingly intended primarily to express condemnation of physically violent sexual aggression" (p. 175). She described the Act's perspective

as one that built on the "bad man" myth by perpetuating "a very, very bad man account of prison rape," involving a "clear aggressor and a clear victim" (p. 182). Yet, according to Ristroph, much of sexual abuse is nonviolent, but "deeply coercive" (p. 175), born of a prison environment that strips inmates of almost all control over their lives while leaving them wanting "money, drugs, food, comfort, physical gratification, and love" (p. 156). Ristroph also faulted the PREA for its emphasis on surveillance and policing of inmates to counter prison rape. Such measures, she contended, deprive inmates of "sexual autonomy," the need for which, she asserts, is a driver of sexual relationships between inmates (p. 179).

Complementing Ristroph's critique, Jenness and Smyth (2011) asserted that the drafting of the Act was hijacked by correctional officials. They exercised great control over the lawmaking process, thereby allowing them to frame the proposed law in terms of safety and security, which the authors equate with the "new managerialism" (i.e., "that social, economic, and political problems can be solved through effective and efficient management"), thus redefining prison rape as a problem based on "statistically grounded risk assessment" rather than human rights violations (p. 514).

The PREA and LGBTQIA Inmates[5]

Jenness, Maxon, Matsuda, and Sumner's (2007) survey of inmates housed in seven men's prisons in California indicated that transgender inmates receive a hostile reception from their fellow inmates and their keepers. For instance, the authors recounted their interview with

a transgender inmate who identifies as straight (i.e., a straight female attracted to men) and lives in an HIV unit . . . [who] explained it this way: "We transgender inmates get harassed all the time by both inmates and officers. When you move to a new housing unit, everyone is like bees. We need crisis cells." When asked if she had ever had to do anything sexual against her will, she replied, "A lot—so many times I can't count." When pushed for an estimate, she said "50."

(p. 43)

Alarmingly, this research suggests an indifference by prison staff to the sexual victimization of transgender inmates. Whereas inmates in a representative sample of the overall inmate population reported receiving needed medical attention in 70% of the sexual victimization incidents, their counterparts in the transgender sample reported that they *did not* receive needed medical attention in 64.3% of the sexual victimization incidents.

What is the likely fate of all gender noncomforming inmates when left to their own devices in the general population? The National Prison Rape Elimination Commission Report (2009) warned that "[r]esearch on sexual abuse in correctional facilities consistently documents the vulnerability of men and women with non-heterosexual orientations" (p. 73). Indeed, it has long been open season on them. In one of the earliest and most widely cited studies, Wooden and Parker (1982) reported that 41% of gay prisoners had been sexually victimized as compared with 9% of all male inmates in a medium security California prison. In 2012, the Bureau of Justice Statistics, in reporting the finding of its large-scale national study of recently released inmates, confirmed that the risk of sexual victimization is strongly correlated with non-heterosexual orientation in that one of three bisexuals and nearly four of ten gays reported their sexual victimization, as compared to 3.5% of heterosexuals, during their last period of confinement (which was, on average, 34.9 months; see Beck & Johnson, 2012). Are gay inmates also the perpetrators? Hardly ever, according to Human Rights Watch (2001): "The myth of the homosexual predator is groundless. Perpetrators of

rape typically view themselves as heterosexual and, outside of the prison environment, prefer to engage in heterosexual activity" (p. 52).

To lessen the vulnerability of gay, bisexual, and transgender inmates confined to men's prisons, staff have frequently confined them in **solitary confinement** upon admission to prison (Arkles, 2009) or after their victimization (Beck & Johnson, 2012). Yet the segregation of gender noncomforming inmates is controversial. On the one hand, the PREA's goal of "zero tolerance" of prison rape invites the segregation of this group as a safety measure. On the other hand, as the National Prison Rape Elimination Commission Report stated, conditions in solitary confinement "may be as restrictive as those imposed to punish prisoners" (p. 79), which would include exclusion from prison programs. Moreover, a 2005 study found that "[i]n some cases, the isolation is difficult to endure and may constitute a de facto punishment for a gender identity that does not conform to societal norms" (Stop Prisoner Rape & the National Prison Project of the American Civil Liberties Union, 2005, p. 9). Also, Suk (2011) contended that their placement in protective custody redistributes rape across the prison hierarchy because inmates who would otherwise be the next best targets of rape are now at the head of the line.

The PREA Standards provide conflicting advice on this matter. On the one hand, they call for "individualized determination about how to ensure the safety of each inmate" (U.S. Department of Justice, 2012, p. 204). Elsewhere, the PREA National Standards recommend "keeping separate those inmates at high risk of being sexually victimized from those at high risk of being sexually abusive" (p. 204).

Dolovich (2012), while sympathetic to the plight of all vulnerable inmates, has favored separate housing for transgender and gay inmates held in men's prisoners. She has argued that confining them with other vulnerable men will result in an influx of so-called "**situational homosexuals**" (p. 1070), some of whom will practice the hypermasculine imperative of raping inmates perceived as weak (e.g., transgender and gay prisoners). Consequently, Dolovich advances an alternative—a two-track strategy: one unit for transgender and gay inmates and a catch-all unit for the remaining vulnerable men.

The PREA and Consensual Sex

Smith (2006), a member of the National Prison Rape Elimination Commission, asserted that male and female inmates should be permitted a degree of "sexual expression," including sexual activity. Because Smith viewed sexual expression as "a core feature of any social environment" (p. 225), she advocates recognition of consensual sexual relationships amongst inmates. Indeed, Smith posited that inmates possess several constitutionally protected interests in sexual expression:

- Sex as pleasure: "From my perspective, the state has little interest in regulating inmates' sexual expression for pleasure, except to the extent that it compromises safety and security or other legitimate penological goals."
- Sex as trade: "In some institutions, there is a menu of sexual practices that are bartered for common items like cigarettes, candy, chips, or a phone call."
- Sex as freedom: "For many prisoners sexual expression is a corollary of freedom."
- Sex as transgression: Sex "as freedom of expression . . . is closely associated with transgression—breaking the rules and going against the normative structures imposed by society, the state, and other institutions."
- Sex as procreation: "[B]oth male and female prisoners desperately want to become parents."
- Sex as love: "Even in the prison setting, where individuals are legally stripped of their autonomy and dignity and face violence from other prisoners and staff, prisoners manage

to establish meaningful and sometimes loving relationships."

(Smith, 2006, pp. 204–226)

Yet prisons have historically prohibited all sexual activity, including masturbation. For instance, Chapter XI of the Mississippi Department of Corrections Inmate Handbook (2011) provides that "[i]nappropriate sexual behavior with another person or indecent exposure" are serious rule violations (Section III, Rule B-25). "An underlying assumption of these provisions is heterosexuality is normative, and any deviation from heterosexuality merits sanction because it will threaten the safety of staff and inmates" (Cohen, 2010, p. 529).

The propensity of consensual sexual activity between inmates remains elusive, with estimates ranging from 2% to 65% of male prisoners (Hensley, 2001). The wide variance arises from methodological issues such as the underreporting of homosexual activity by inmates (Hensley, 2001). Historically, research on this subject has taken a back seat to the study of sexual abuse because, as Saum, Surratt, Inciardi, and Bennett (1995) found, "consensual sex is seen as less of a threat to inmate or institutional security than is rape and thus does not demand the attention of more violent behavior" (p. 415).

The U.S. Department of Justice's proposed PREA National Standards (U.S. Department of Justice, 2012) would have required prison staff to give explicit recognition to consensual sex by directing that "an agency must not consider consensual sexual contact between inmates to constitute sexual abuse" (p. 140). The National Prison Rape Elimination Commission Report (2009) likely contains the rationale for the standard's demarcation of consensual sex:

In situations where one prisoner has allegedly abused another prisoner, the question of consent goes to the heart of the matter . . . because investigators are going to have to find ways to interpret and understand the relationship that took place. And that's going to be a particular challenge for the profession.

(p. 113)

Would prison staff be up to this task? Eigenberg (2000a) found that 96% of surveyed correctional officers reported great difficulty in distinguishing between consensual sex and sexual assault in the prison environment. There may be no more challenging a case than a **"shielding relationship"** in which sexual acts are exchanged for protection from predators. A survey of prison staff found that they "did agree that much sexual activity is in the form of a shielding relationship between two inmates" (National Institute of Corrections & The Moss Group, 2006, p. 8). This perception finds empirical support in a recent Bureau of Justice Statistics' report on *Sexual Victimization by Former State Prisoners, 2008* (Beck & Johnson, 2012). Of those self-reporting sexual victimization through coercion other than force, 24% indicated that they were "offered or given protection from other inmates" (p. 12). Yet, in her interviews of 40 male parolees regarding their perceptions of a shielding relationship, Trammell (2011) found that they do not regard it as sexual abuse. For example, one of the parolees, Robert, responded as follows:

Robert: I knew men that got raped in prison and I know of men that, what's a good word for it? Volunteered, that's not the right word but I guess they volunteered to fuck guys in prison because they thought they'd get taken care of. Does that make sense? I don't know if these guys were really homos or not, I just know that they didn't care about fucking these guys since they get something out of it. If I told you [speaking to me] that you had to fuck me or I'll let another guy stab you, you'd call it rape right? In prison, it's just business.

Question: You think people volunteer for this?

Robert: More like accepting. Some men accept their place in prison, trust me, it's not a lot of guys, most get with the program, toughen up, take no shit, demand respect all that stuff. But you come across some of these guys that put up with being someone's "punk" for protection.

(p. 14)

A shielding relationship is hardly consensual and is better understood as illustrative of Buchhandler-Raphael's (2011) concept of **impaired choices.** She characterized impaired choices as "conduct amount[ing] to impermissible interference with free will" (p. 211). Whereas the inmate identified above as Robert believes that "punks" are not raped, but rather "accept their place in prison," they are actually choosing between two evils, a choice that is impaired because of the failure of prison staff to create a civil society inside prison walls. One inmate, in a letter to Human Rights Watch (2001), put it best: "A prisoner that is engaging in sexual acts, not by force, is still a victim of rape because I know that deep inside this prisoner does not want to do the things that he is doing but he thinks that it is the only way that he can survive" (p. 7).

The U.S. Department of Justice's (2012) proposed recognition of consensual sex between inmates did not survive the comment stage. The PREA National Standards admonish critics who reject the possibility of a consensual relationship among inmates, stressing that "it is essential that staff make individualized assessments regarding each inmate's behavior, and not simply label as an abuser every inmate caught having sex with another inmate" (p. 140). The Standards fail to define consent but do indicate that consent is absent when an inmate is "coerced by overt or implied threats of violence, or is unable to consent or refuse" (p. 197).

JUDICIAL OVERSIGHT OF "DOING" GENDER IN PRISON[6]

Until the 1960s courts adhered to their self-declared and self-imposed "hands-off" doctrine, which decreed that courts had no business in the declaration and enforcement of prisoners' rights (e.g., *Douglas v. Sigler*, 1967; *Garcia v. Steele*, 1951; *United States ex rel. Atterbury v. Ragen*, 1956). By 1974, however, the U.S. Supreme Court declared that "[t]here is no iron curtain drawn between the Constitution and the prisons of this country" and, as a consequence, courts must ensure **"mutual accommodation"** between inmate rights and the administration of jails and prisons (*Wolff v. McDonnell*, 1974, pp. 555–556). In practice, courts appear more inclined to an accommodation of a different sort—that of deferring to prison administrators' routine assertion that inmates' rights must be of the narrowest sort (e.g., *Bell v. Wolfish*, 1979, *Rhodes v. Chapman*, 1981; *Turner v. Safley*, 1987).

The judicial pronouncement of prisoners' rights has implicitly been influenced by gender norms—and none more so than that of the hypermasculine, violence-prone, heterosexual male. For instance, in ruling that inmates' living quarters lack Fourth Amendment protection, the U.S. Supreme Court unhesitantly portrayed inmates largely as "antisocial . . . and often violent" (*Hudson v. Palmer*, 1984, p. 526). The Court thereby ignored the large majority (presently 63%) of female inmates "doing time" for non-violent offenses (Carson & Golinelli, 2013). Similarly, in *Thornburgh v. Abbott* (1989), where the Court applied the rational basis test (see Chapter 3) to prisoners' access to subscription publications, the Court all but invoked the image of the inmate as gladiator, who is responsible for the "Herculean obstacles blocking . . . efforts to maintain security and prevent escapes or other criminal conduct" (p. 429). And yet the staff of Minnesota's women's prison see no need for even a perimeter fence.

Protection from Sexual Assault

In 2001, Human Rights Watch faulted prison staff for doing little to prevent sexual assault in prison. Indeed, Eigenberg (1994) had earlier concluded that correctional officers, "[i]n the prison vernacular, . . . [officers offer] little assurance to inmates except the age-old advice of 'fight or fuck" (p. 159). Courts, however, have long read the Eighth Amendment prohibition of "cruel and unusual punishment" as imposing affirmative duty on prison staff to protect inmates from the abuses of their fellow inmates, as well as their keepers (Feeley & Rubin, 1998). The U.S. Supreme Court defined the parameters of that duty when prison rape occurs in *Farmer v. Brennan* (1994). As previously explained, the Court held in *Farmer* that correctional officials could be subject to liability for being deliberately indifferent to the safety needs of inmates at risk for sexual victimization. That standard, however, requires an objectively serious risk that is consciously ignored or disregarded.

The decision in *Farmer v. Brennan* (1994) has not made imprisonment safe for transgender prisoners. A 2007 study of California prisoners found that 50% of transgender inmates reported "oral or anal penetration by force or threat of force" on one or more occasions (Jenness, Maxon, Matsuda & Sumner, 2007, p. 3). Indeed, sexual victimization in the correctional setting remains a vexing problem. Time will tell if implementation of PREA Standards facilitates the desired goal of curbing such victimization.

Protection from Sexual Harassment[7]

When asked if "staff had hassled or harassed them in a sexual way," 8.9% of the responding 18,526 prisoners said "yes" (Beck & Johnson, 2012, p. 10). Examples of alleged sexual harassment abound in case law (e.g., *Abney v. Thompson*, 2013; *Green v. Thompson*, 2013). Consider *Smith v. Potter* (2013), in which a Tennessee inmate alleged that a jailer repeatedly made homosexual references to the plaintiff in front of other inmates, grabbed himself and made vulgar comments, and told other inmates and jail officials that the plaintiff was homosexual and that the plaintiff was in jail for beating and choking his girlfriend (which was not true).

(p. *1)

Nonetheless, the court dismissed his suit for want of a sufficient painful physical injury.

On the other side of the ledger, female officers have frequently brought suit alleging that their superiors failed to protect them from the sexual harassment of male inmates (e.g., *Freitag v. Ayers*, 2006; *Hicks v. Alabama*, 1998). For instance, in *Garrett v. Department of Corrections* (2007), the court found that "masturbating in the presence of female nurses, occurred at almost every prison facility" within the Florida Department of Corrections (DOC) and was "so commonplace that it became known within the DOC as 'gunning'" (*Garrett*, 2007, p. 1292). The court concluded that the Florida DOC could be liable for "gunning" if it led to a "discriminatorily abusive working environment" (p. 1297).

The Role of the PREA

As the U.S. Department of Justice (2012) noted, "the PREA does not reference sexual harassment" (p. 21). However, the Justice Department found that sexual harassment was "a precursor to sexual abuse" and thus fell within the purview of a section of the PREA that "authorized the Attorney General to draft standards relating to 'such other matters as may reasonably be related to the detection, prevention, reduction, and punishment of prison rape'" (U.S. Department of Justice, 2012, p. 79). Subsequently, Section 115.6 of the PREA National Standards provides that "[s]exual harassment includes:

(1) Repeated and unwelcome sexual advances, requests for sexual favors, or verbal comments, gestures, or actions of a derogatory or offensive sexual nature by one inmate, detainee, or resident directed toward another; and

(2) Repeated verbal comments or gestures of a sexual nature to an inmate, detainee, or resident by a staff member, contractor, or volunteer, including demeaning references to gender, sexually suggestive or derogatory comments about body or clothing, or obscene language or gestures.

(U.S. Department of Justice, 2012, p. 198)

The Role of the Eighth Amendment

Sexual harassment can inflict cruel and unusual punishment. The rationale for such is set forth in *Freitas v. Ault* (1997), a ruling described as a "gate keeper" of prisoners' sexual harassment claims brought under the Eighth Amendment (Rich, 2009, p. 22). In *Freitas*, an inmate sued an officer after their consensual relationship, which had been limited to kissing and hugging, turned sour. The penultimate language of *Freitas* reads as follows:

Because the sexual harassment or abuse of an inmate by a corrections officer can never serve a legitimate penological purpose and may well result in severe physical and psychological harm, such abuse can, in certain circumstances, constitute the unnecessary and wanton infliction of pain forbidden by the Eighth Amendment.

(p. 1338)

Yet, few allegations of sexual harassment are found to inflict cruel and unusual punishment because most courts have ruled that words alone are insufficient; there must be physical contact (Robertson, 1999). Illustrative is *Jones v. Heyns* (2013).

The plaintiff in *Jones* had sued over the remarks made by an officer as he was leaving the prison cafeteria with another prisoner, Walker: "Jones, I always see you and Walker, walking together. I wonder know [sic] which one of you are [sic] the boy, and who's the girl" (p. *1). He then asked the officer not to refer to him as a boy, which, in the prison context, is an epithet that identifies an inmate as weak and thus effeminate—an affront to one's manhood in the hypermasculine inmate social world. The officer responded unrepentantly: "I'm just saying. It look like it to me" (p. *1). Despite this affront to the inmate's manhood, one that would constitute "fighting words" in the prison's sexual subculture (Robertson, 1995), the plaintiff's case collapsed for want of alleging any physical contact by his tormentor.

Medical Care

For Victims of Sexual Assault

Do the victims of staff sexual abuse receive appropriate care? The Bureau of Justice Statistics reported that among the victims of staff sexual assault only 6% received a medical exam and a mere 12% received counseling or mental health treatment (Beck, Harrison, & Adams, 2007). Robertson (2009) asserted that "[o]n its face, this finding suggests that correctional authorities view the victims of staff sexual abuse—regardless of their sex—as less than legitimate victims" (p. 9).

Other Forms of Gender-Related Medical Care

Correctional institutions are on the front lines of a public health crisis. Cohen (2008), one of the foremost authorities on correctional health care, elaborated:

> Our jails and prisons have increasingly become the *de facto* clinical depositories for hundreds of thousands of inmates who are very sick and who require all manner of specialty medical, dental, and mental health care. Prisons are not only the new mental asylums; they are the new community hospitals and emergency wards for certain segments of the poor.
>
> (p. 5)

Yet, correctional facilities face an acute shortage of well-qualified physicians, especially in those specialties addressing psychiatry, infectious diseases, and substance abuse (Westoff, 2008). Among correctional medical doctors, 48% lack specialty training and 22% lack board certification (Westoff, 2008). Prison overcrowding exacerbates these deficiencies.

Prisoners have a limited constitutional right to health care. Recall that in *Estelle v. Gamble* (1976), the U.S. Supreme Court ruled that deliberate indifference to an inmate's serious medical needs inflicted cruel and unusual punishment in violation of the Eighth Amendment to the U.S. Constitution. The Court, however, failed to define the key term "deliberate indifference" other than to say that allegations of mere negligence would not state a valid claim. Eighteen years later, in *Farmer v. Brennan* (1994), the Court decided that deliberate indifference in the Eighth Amendment context required something akin criminal recklessness. This standard, which basically requires conscious disregard of a known risk, presents a high hurdle to state a valid claim. Consequently, when a prisoner gets some medical treatment, courts are quite hesitant to find constitutional fault (Thompson, 2010). Indeed, negligence acts of medical malpractice do not rise to the level of an Eighth Amendment violation; "a prisoner must allege acts or omissions sufficiently harmful to evidence deliberate indifference to serious medical needs" (*Estelle*, 1976, p. 106; see also *Hudson v. McMillian*, 1992).

In 2005 the Wisconsin state legislature passed the Inmate Sex Change Prevention Act. It prohibited "the payment of any funds or the use of any resources of this state or the payment of any federal funds passing through the state treasury to provide or to facilitate the provision of hormonal therapy or sexual assignment surgery." The statute epitomized what Thompson (2010), a staff attorney with Massachusetts' Prisoners' Legal Services, describes as the dominant theme in contemporary prison health care: attention to an inmate's medical complaint, but no treatment. In *Fields v. Smith* (2011), however, "attention without treatment" did not fare well in court. Three transgender inmates who had been receiving hormonal therapy in Wisconsin while incarcerated argued that they would find themselves in a bind if the statute took effect. They filed a lawsuit seeking an injunction and prevailed in U.S. District Court. The U.S. Court of Appeals for the Seventh Circuit heard the defendant's appeal. Stated broadly, the issue before the appellate court was whether inmates lack a right to a specific treatment. There had been **dicta** to that effect in two Seventh Circuit cases, *Meriwether v. Faulkner* (1987) and *Maggert v. Hanks* (1997). However, in distinguishing these cases, the *Field* court held that disallowing the only effective treatment in this instance (sexual assignment surgery) inflicted torture and thus worked cruel and unusual punishment.

Subsequently, in *Kosilek v. Spencer* (2012), the U.S. District Court for Massachusetts characterized the plaintiff's lawsuit as seeking an unprecedented court order requiring that the state department of corrections provide "him" (the court used the masculine pronoun) with sexual assignment surgery. Because Kosilek was serving a life sentence, waiting out the sentence to secure the surgery was not an option. Nor would an alternative treatment be efficacious; the parties agreed that sexual reassignment surgery was necessary and nothing less would be minimally adequate. The commissioner of corrections agreed with this medical assessment, but still forbade the surgery claiming that "providing such treatment would create insurmountable security problems" (p. 195). The court, however, refused to defer to the commissioner's professional judgment in light of the plaintiff's convincing response that Kosilek was already a tempting target. Citing and quoting the *Fields* opinion for the proposition that "[refusing to provide effective treatment for a serious medical condition serves no valid penological purpose and amounts to torture," the

Kosilek court ordered the surgery (p. 199). An appeal followed to the U.S. Court of Appeals for the First Circuit. It reversed the ruling (*Kosilek v. Spencer*, 2014). The court reasoned that the treatment provided by prison authorities—"hormones, facial hair removal, feminine clothing and accessories, and access to regular mental health"—was constitutionally adequate (p. 90). The appellate court also reasoned that the district court had failed to give proper weight to the prison staff's fears about housing post-operative, male-to-female transgendered prisoners with either male prisoners or female prisoners.

Marriage, Visitation, and Conjugal Visits[8]

Recall from Chapter 9 that inmates have a right to marry (*Turner v. Safley*, 1987). That right, however, is a qualified one: "The right to marry, like many other rights, is subject to substantial restrictions as a result of incarceration" (p. 94). Do these restrictions preclude marrying someone of the same sex? The language of the *Turner* decision and the context of the times make it clear that the Court considered the question of inmates marrying with the assumption that the marriage would be between a man and a woman. But, as Chapter 9 makes clear, times have changed. In 2015, the U.S. Supreme Court held in *Obergefell v. Hodges* that marriage is a constitutional right that extends to same-sex couples. Although the Court did not expressly address in *Obergefell* whether prisoners of the same sex also possess this right, same-sex marriage is not inconsistent with any of the attributes of marriage the *Turner* Court found compatible with prison life: "expressions of emotional support and public commitment"; "an exercise of religious faith as well as an expression of personal dedication"; "the expectation that they ultimately will be fully consummated; and "marital status . . . as a precondition to the receipt of government benefits" (*Turner v. Safley*, 1987, p. 94).

Notably, the *Turner* Court omitted reference to conjugal visits and procreation—a clear indication that it implicitly deemed these attributes incompatible with inmate marriages be they of the same sex or the opposite sex.

Courts have long entertained litigation over prison rules that bar visitation by persons who are romantically involved with inmates of the same sex. Two cases merit attention. In *Doe v. Sparks* (1990), the plaintiff, an adult female serving a jail sentence, alleged "that the institution's visitation policy unconstitutionally discriminates against her because she is a lesbian and is denied any visit from the woman with whom she is romantically involved. Routine visits are permitted between heterosexual prisoners and members of the opposite sex with whom they are romantically involved" (p. 228). The defendant warden advanced two justifications:

> the protection of the homosexual inmate (typically the male homosexual prisoner), who if identified as homosexual might be targeted for assaults and abuse by other prisoners, and for the prevention of the discipline and health problems that official approval of homosexual relationships between inmates and visitors would create by implicitly condoning consensual homosexual relationships between inmates.
> (pp. 232–233)

The court rejected the warden's justifications. First, existing practices already had created a "multiplicity of permissible sources" for identifying a prisoner's sexual orientation (p. 233). Moreover, the prison's liberal correspondence policy, which permitted "love letters containing sexual themes and pornographic materials," showed that the warden already condoned the "[lesbian] activity" in question (p. 233). Thus, the court ruled for the plaintiff, finding that the sexual discrimination on the basis of sexual orientation lacked a rational basis.

In *Whitmire v. Arizona* (2002), the lover of a gay male prisoner was informed that there could no same-sex kissing and hugging during visitation, "with the exception of immediate relatives and family" (p. 1135). Opposite-sex lovers, however, encountered a far different policy: "Kissing and embracing shall be permitted only at the beginning and end of each visit and shall not be prolonged" (p. 1135). After losing in U.S. district court, Whitmire appealed to the U.S. Court of Appeals for the Ninth Circuit. Applying rational basis review (see Chapter 4), the court examined whether there was a common-sense connection between the restrictions complained of by the plaintiff and the safety and security of the prison.

The *Whitmire* court ruled in favor of the plaintiff, explaining that the Arizona Department of Corrections (ADOC) had asserted "that its visitation policy protects inmates from being labeled as homosexuals and from being targeted for physical, sexual, or verbal abuse on account of such labeling. The ADOC's visitation policy, however, does not possess a common-sense connection to the concern against homosexual labeling" (p. 1136). The court reiterated this point: "Common sense indicates that an inmate who intends to hide his homosexual sexual orientation from other inmates would not openly display affection with his homosexual partner during a prison visit. Rather, prisoners who are willing to display affection toward their same-sex partner during a prison visit likely are already open about their sexual orientation" (p. 1136).

CONCLUSION

Male prisoners come to occupy a host of hierarchical gender roles, with the *real man*—the embodiment of hypermasculinity—at its summit. Who performs these roles can be the outcome of impaired choices. Roderick Keith Johnson, for instance, was forced to perform as a woman. Women in prison also "do" gender, but not in manner identical to their male counterparts. Patriarchy privileges some women's roles over others. The "play family" remains the most prominent and enduring of women prisoners' gender roles.

Congress enacted the Prison Rape Elimination Act of 2003 to study the incidence of prison rape, to train staff and inmates alike to counter prison rape and other forms of sexual victimization, and to create standards to guide staff in detecting and responding to sexual victimization, including sexual harassment, by inmates as well as staff. The PREA, however, may be largely hortatory because of its hobbled enforcement capability. However, the PREA does acknowledge a wide range of gender and sexual identities.

The PREA's provisions for gathering and analyzing data about incidence of sexual victimization have illuminated the identity of victims and victimizers. Historically, the portrait of victimizers is that of a "bad man"—often African-American—who engages in violent, brutal rapes. Although many inmates do attribute their sexual victimization to coercion, a minority or prison rapists fall into the "bad man" category. Among inmates in men's prisons, those with non-normative sexual and gender identities are at the highest risk-level for inmate-on-inmate sexual victimization. Not so for female inmates, whose overall rates of inmate-on-inmate sexual victimization are nearly three times greater than men in prison.

In *Farmer v. Brennan* (1994), the U.S. Supreme Court ruled that deliberate indifference to a significant risk of sexual victimization violated the constitutional prohibition of cruel and unusual punishment. Most courts do not find sexual harassment, absent offensive physical contact, to inflict constitutionally prohibited punishment. Recently, courts have addressed lawsuits brought by LGBTQIA inmates with regard to a host of gender-related issues, including sexual reassignment surgery. Generally, courts have embraced a policy of deference to the decisions of correctional staff except when faced with irrational distinctions based on gender.

FURTHER READING

Capers, B. (2011). Real rape too. *California Law Review*, 99, 1259–1308.

Curtis, K. (2006, January 17). Disputed study: Rape rare in prisons. Associated Press. Retrieved from http://www.justdetention.org/en/jdinews/2006/0117.aspx

Fleisher, M. S., & Krienert, J. L. (2009). *The myth of prison rape: Sexual culture in American prisons.* Lanham, MD: Rowman & Littlefield.

Human Rights Watch. (2001). *No escape: Male rape in U.S. prisons.* New York, NY: Human Rights Watch.

Jenness, V., & Smyth, M. (2011). The passage and implementation of the Prison Rape Elimination Act: Legal endogeneity and the uncertain road from symbolic law to instrumental effects. *Stanford Law & Policy Review*, 22, 489–528.

Kunzel, R. (2008). *Criminal intimacy: Prison and the uneven history of modern American sexuality.* Chicago, IL: University of Chicago Press.

National Prison Rape Elimination Commission (2009). *National prison rape elimination commission report.* Retrieved from https://www.gov/pdffiles1/226680.pdf

Ristroph, A. (2006). Sexual punishments. *Columbia Journal of Gender and Law*, 15, 139–184.

Robertson, J. E. (2004a). A punk's song about prison reform. *Pace University Law Review*, 24, 527–562.

Robinson, R. K. (2011). Masculinity as prison: Sexual identity, race, and incarceration. *California Law Review*, 90, 1309–1408.

Sabo, D., Kupers, T. A., & London, W. (Eds.). *Prison masculinities.* Philadelphia, PA: Temple University Press.

Scacco, A. M. (Ed.) (1982). *Male rape: A casebook of sexual aggression* (pp. 3–29). New York, NY: AMS Press.

Seidmen, S. (1997). *Difference troubles: Queering social theory and sexual politics.* Cambridge, UK: Cambridge University Press.

Vojdik, V. K. (2002). Gender outlaws: Challenging masculinity in traditionally male institutions. *Berkeley Women's Law Journal*, 17, 68–121.

GLOSSARY

"Bad man" myth: The widely held but false belief that prison rapists are exclusively men who employ physical force to subdue their victims.

Benign variation: A norm that signifies gender variation as harmless and thus socially acceptable.

Deliberate indifference: A legal standard under the Eighth Amendment that imposes liability on prison staff when they have actual knowledge of a high risk of sexual victimization or other injury and fail to take reasonable preventive measures.

Dicta: Any part of a court's written decision that is not part of its holding (i.e., the rationale for the decision, and, therefore, does not carry the full force of precedent).

"Doing" gender: A sociological concept initially formulated by West and Zimmerman (1987) that conceives of gender as the social product of daily social interaction.

Eighth Amendment: An amendment to the U.S. Constitution that prohibits the imposition of excessive bail, grossly disproportionate fines, or the infliction of cruel and unusual punishment, which courts interpret as imposing a duty on prison staff to protect inmates from assault as well as providing adequate medical care and other basic human needs.

Gender: Socially constructed characteristics for identifying sexual behavior as either masculine, feminine, or intersex.

Hypermasculinity: An exaggerated form of masculinity that emphasizes physical strength and aggressiveness.

Impaired choices: When consent to sexual acts is compromised by coercion.

Mutual accommodation: A legal concept developed by the U.S. Supreme Court to reconcile the rights of prisoners with the security needs and objectives of prisons.

Shielding relationship: A relationship between inmates based upon one party protecting another party from predators in exchange for sexual acts.

Situational homosexuals: Persons who participate in homosexual behaviors because of a social or institutional environment that precludes heterosexual behaviors.

Solitary confinement: A form of correctional housing in which a prisoner is confined alone in a cell 24 hours per day with the exception of limited opportunities for exercise and bathing.

NOTES

1   Portions of this section of the chapter are taken from Robertson, J. E. (2010). Was it a "real" rape? *Correctional Law Reporter*, 22(2), 25–26. Used with the gracious permission of Civic Research Institute.

2   Portions of this section of the chapter are taken from Robertson, J. E. (2013). The "bad women" guarding male inmates. *Correctional Law Reporter*, 24(5), 75–76. Used with the gracious permission of Civic Research Institute.

3   Portions of this section of the chapter are taken from Robertson, J. E. (2013). Recent legal developments: Correctional case law, 2012. *Criminal Justice Review*, 38(2), 256–270. Used with the gracious permission of SAGE Publications, Inc.

4   Portions of this section of the chapter are taken from Robertson, J. E. (2012–2013). Transgendered prisoners and the PREA standards: What will be the legacy of Dee Farmer? *Correctional Law Reporter*, 24(4), 59–61. Used with the gracious permission of Civic Research Institute.

5   Portions of this section of the chapter are taken from Robertson, J. E. (2012). If they ask, should you tell? *Correctional Law Reporter*, 3(5), 71–72. Used with the gracious permission of Civic Research Institute.

6   Portions of this section of the chapter are taken from Robertson, J. E. (2015). Prisoners' right to gender identity. *Correctional Law Reporter*, 27(1), 9–10, 12. Used with the gracious permission of Civic Research Institute.

7   Portions of this section of the chapter are taken from Robertson, J. E. (2013). Sexual harassment that the Eighth Amendment tolerates. *Correctional Law Reporter*, 25(1), 7–8, 13. Used with the gracious permission of Civic Research Institute.

8   Portions of this section of the chapter are taken from Robertson, J. E. (2013). Same-sex "makin' out": Prison visitation and gender/sexual orientation discrimination. *Correctional Law Reporter*, 24(6), 91–92, 97. Used with the gracious permission of Civic Research Institute.

REFERENCES

Abbott, J. H. (1982). *In the belly of the beast: Letters from prison*. New York, NY: Vintage Books.

Anderson, E. (2000). *Code of the street: Decency, violence, and the moral life of the inner city*. New York, NY: W.W. Norton.

Arkles, G. (2009). Safety and solidarity across gender lines: Rethinking segregation of transgender people in detention. *Temple Political & Civil Rights Law Review*, 18, 515–560.

Beck, A. J., Harrison, P. M., Berzofsky, M., & Caspar, R. (2013). *Sexual victimization in prisons and jails reported by inmates, 2011–12*. Washington, DC: Bureau of Justice Statistics.

Beck, A. J., & Johnson, C. (2012). *Sexual victimization by former state prisoners, 2008*. Washington, DC: Bureau of Justice Statistics.

Beck, A. J., & Harrison, P. M. (2007). *Sexual victimization in state and federal prisons reported by inmates*. Washington, DC: Bureau of Justice Statistics.

Beck, A. J., Harrison, P. M., & Adams, D. B. (2007). *Sexual violence reported by correctional authorities, 2006*. Washington, DC: Bureau of Justice Statistics.

Beck A. J., & Hughes, T. A. (2005). Sexual *violence reported by correctional authorities, 2004*. Washington, DC: Bureau of Justice Statistics.

Beckett, K., & Evans, H. (2015). Crimmigration at the local level: Criminal justice processes in the shadow of deportation. *Law and Society Review*, 49, 241–277.

Buchanan, K. S. (2012). Engendering rape. *UCLA Law Review*, 9, 1630–1688.

Buchanan, K. S. (2010). Our prisons, ourselves: Race, gender and the rule of law. *Yale Law and Policy Review*, 29, 1–82.

Buchhandler-Raphael, M. (2011). Failure of consent: Reconceptualizing rape as sexual abuse of power. *Michigan Journal of Gender & the Law*, 18, 147–228.

Capers, B. (2011). Real rape too. *California Law Review*, 99, 1259–1308.

Carroll, L. (1974). Hacks, Blacks, and cons: Race relations in a maximum security prison. Prospect Heights, Ill: Waveland Press.

Carson, A. A., & Golinelli, D. (2013). *Prisoners in 2012 – Advance counts*. Washington, DC: Bureau of Justice Statistics.

Caster, P. (2008). *Prisons, race, and masculinity in twentieth century U.S. literature and film*. Columbus, OH: Ohio State University Press.

Castle, T., Hensley, C., & Tewksbury, R. (2002). Argot roles and prison sexual hierarchy. In C. Hensley (Ed.), *Prison sex: Practice and policy* (pp. 13–26). Boulder, CO: Lynne Rienner Publishers.

Civil Rights Act of 1964, Pub. L. No. 88–352, 78 Stat. 241 (July 2, 1964), *codified as amended at 42 U.S.C. § 2000e et seq.*

Cogan, B. A. (2012). Public health consequences of denying access to justice for victims of prison staff sexual misconduct. *UCLA Women's Law Journal*, 18, 195–237.

Cohen, D. S. (2010). Keeping men and women down: Sex segregation, anti-essentialism, and masculinity. *Harvard Journal of Law and Gender*, 33, 509–553.

Cohen, F. (2008). Correctional health care: A retrospective. *Correctional Law Reporter*, 20, 5–6, 9, 12.

Cressey, D. (1980). Foreword. In J. Irwin (Ed.), *Prisons in turmoil* (pp. vii–xi). Chicago, IL: Little, Brown.

Curtis, K. (2006, January 17). Disputed study: Rape rare in prisons. *Associated Press*. Retrieved from http://www.justdetention.org/en/jdinews/2006/0117.aspx

Davis, A. J. (1968). Sexual assaults in the Philadelphia prison system and sheriff's vans. *Trans Action*, 6(2), 8–16.

Diaz-Cotto, J. (2006). Gender, sexuality and family kinship networks. In R. Solinger, P. C. Johnson, M. L. Raimon, T. Reynolds, & R. C. Tapia (Eds.), *Interrupted life: Experiences of incarcerated women in the United States* (pp. 131–144). Berkeley, CA: University of California Press.

Dolovich S. (2012). Two models of the prison: Accidental humanity and hypermasculinity in the L.A. County Jail. *Journal of Criminal Law and Criminology*, 102, 965–1117.

Donaldson, S. (2001). A million jockers, punks, and queens. In D. Sabo, T. A. Kupers, & W. London (Eds.), *Prison masculinities* (pp. 118–126). Philadelphia, PA: Temple University Press.

Dumond, R. W. (1992). The sexual assault of male inmates in incarcerated settings. *International Journal of the Sociology of Law*, 20, 135–157.

Eigenberg, H. M. (2000a). Correctional officers' definitions of rape in male prisons. *Journal of Criminal Justice*, 28, 435–449.

Eigenberg, H. M. (2000b). Correctional officers and their perceptions of homosexuality, rape, and prostitution in male prisons. *Prison Journal*, 80, 415–433.

Eigenberg, H. (1994). Rape in male prisons: Examining the relationship between correctional officers' attitudes toward male rape and their willingness to respond to acts of rape. In M. Braswell, R. Montgomery, & L. Lombardo (Eds.), *Prison violence in America* (2nd ed., pp. 145–166). Cincinnati, OH: Anderson.

Eskridge, W. N., Jr. (2010). Sexual and gender variation in American public law: From malignant to benign to productive. *UCLA Law Review*, 57, 1333–1373.

Feeley, M. M., & Rubin, E. L. (1998). *Judicial policy making and the modern state: How the courts reformed America's prisons*. New York, NY: Cambridge University Press.

Fleisher, M. S., & Krienert, J. L. (2009). *The myth of prison rape: Sexual culture in American prisons*. Lanham, MD: Rowman & Littlefield Publishers.

Flowers, A. (2014, January 29). Dee Farmer won a landmark Supreme Court case on inmates' rights. But that's not the half of it. *The Village Voice*. Retrieved from http://www.villagevoice.com/2014-01-29/news/dee-farmer-v-brennan-prison-rape-elimination-act-transgender-lgbt-inmate-rights/full/

Fowler, S. K. (2007). *Prison rape-supportive cultural beliefs and inmate perceptions of sexual assault: A Texas inmate sample*. ProQuest Digital Dissertations (AAT 3288391).

Giallombardo, R. (1966). *Society of women: A study of a women's prison*. New York, NY: John Wiley.

Gilreath, S. D. (2003). Cruel and unusual punishment and the Eighth Amendment as a mandate for human dignity: Another look at original intent. *Thomas Jefferson Law Review*, 25, 559–592.

Greer, K. (2000). The changing nature of interpersonal relationships in a women's prison. *Prison Journal*, 80, 442–468.

Hale, G. (1998). *Making whiteness: The culture of degradation in the South, 1890–1940*. New York, NY: Pantheon Books.

Haney, C. (2011). The perversions of prison: On the origins of hypermasculinity and sexual violence in confinement. *American Criminal Law Review*, 48, 121–141.

Harris, A. P. (2000). Gender, violence, race, and criminal justice. *Stanford Law Review*, 52, 777–806.

Hassine, V. (2009). *Life without parole* (4th ed.). Los Angeles, CA: Roxbury Publishing.

Heilpern, D. M. (1998). *Fear or favour: Sexual assault of young prisoners.* Lismore, NSW: Southern Cross University Press.

Hensley, C. (2001). Consensual homosexual activity in male prisons. *Corrections Compendium, 26,* 1–4.

Holmberg, C. B. (2001). The culture of transgression: Initiations in the homosociality of a Midwestern state prison. In D. Sabo, T. A. Kupers, & W. London (Eds.), *Prison masculinities* (pp. 78–92). Philadelphia, PA: Temple University Press.

Human Rights Watch (2001). *No escape: Male rape in U.S. prisons.* New York, NY: Human Rights Watch.

Ignatieff, M. (1986). *The needs of strangers: An essay on privacy, solidarity and the politics of being human.* New York, NY: Penguin Books.

Inmate Sex Change Prevention Act, 2005 Wis. Act 105, codified at Wis. Stat. § 302.3865(m) (2010).

Irwin, J., & Cressey, D. (1962). Thieves, convicts and the inmate culture. *Social Problems, 10,* 145–155.

Jenness, V., & Fenstermaker, S. (2014). Agnes goes to prison: Gender authenticity, transgender inmates in prisons for men, and pursuit of "the real deal." *Gender & Society, 28,* 5–31.

Jenness, V., Maxon, C. L., Matsuda, K. N., & Sumner, J. M. (2007). *Violence in California correctional facilities: An empirical examination of sexual assault.* Irvine, CA: University of California, Center for Evidence-Based Corrections.

Jenness, V., & Smyth, M. (2011). The passage and implementation of the Prison Rape Elimination Act: Legal endogeneity and the uncertain road from symbolic law to instrumental effects. *Stanford Law & Policy Review, 22,* 489–528.

Johnson, R. (1997). Race, gender, and the American prison: Historical observations. In J. M. Pollock (Ed.), *Prisons: Today and tomorrow* (pp. 26–51). Gaithersburg, MD: Aspen Publishers.

Jones, R. S. (1993). Coping with separation: Adaptive responses of women prisoners. *Women & Criminal Justice, 5,* 71–96.

Just Detention International. (2009). *Fact sheet: Prison Rape Elimination Act.* Retrieved from http://www.justdetention.org/en/factsheets/Prison_Rape_Elimination_Act.pdf

Just Detention International. (2015). *Review of applicable federal and state sex offense laws.* Retrieved from http://www.justdetention.org/en/state_by_state_laws.aspx

Kerman, P. (2011). *Orange is the new black.* New York, NY: Spiegel & Grau.

Koscheski, M., & Hensley, C. (2001). Inmate homosexual behavior in a southern female correctional facility. *American Journal of Criminal Justice, 25,* 269–277.

Kunzel, R. (2008). *Criminal intimacy: Prison and the uneven history of modern American sexuality.* Chicago, IL: University of Chicago Press.

Liptak, A. (2004, October 16). Ex-inmate's suit offers view into sexual slavery in prisons. *New York Times.* Retrieved from http://www.nytimes.com/2004/10/16/national/16rape.html?_r=0

Lockwood, D. (1980). *Prison sexual violence.* New York, NY: Elsevier North-Holland.

Mississippi Department of Corrections. (2011). *Mississippi Department of Corrections inmate handbook.* Retrieved from http://www.mdoc.state.ms.us/Inmate%20Handbook.htm

Moss, H. (2009). Invisible aggression, impossible abuse: Female inmate-on-inmate sexual assault. *Georgetown Journal of Gender and the Law, 20,* 979–997.

Moster, A., & Jeglic, E. L. (2009). Prison warden attitudes toward prison rape and sexual assault: Findings since the Prison Rape Elimination Act (PREA). *Prison Journal, 89,* 65–78.

National Institute of Corrections & The Moss Group. (2006). *Staff perspectives: Sexual violence in adult prisons and jails, trends from focus group interviews.* Washington, DC: U.S. Department of Justice.

National PREA Resource Center. (2015a). *Prison Rape Elimination Act.* Retrieved from http://www.prearesourcecenter.org/about/prison-rape-elimination-act-prea

National PREA Resource Center. (2015b). *Embracing the standards.* Retrieved from http://www.prearesourcecenter.org/training-technical-assistance/prea-in-action/embracing-the-standards

National Prison Rape Elimination Commission (2009). *National prison rape elimination commission report.* Retrieved from https://www.ncjrs.gov/pdffiles1/226680.pdf

Neubauer, D. W., & Fradella, H. F. (2016). *America's courts and the criminal justice system* (12th ed.). Belmont, CA: Cengage.

Owen, B. (1998). *In the mix: Struggle and survival in a women's prison.* Albany, NY: State University of New York Press.

Pardue, A., Arrigo, B. A., & Murphy, D. S. (2011). Sex and sexuality in women's prisons: A preliminary typological investigation. *Prison Journal, 91,* 279–304.

Rathbone, C. (2005). *A world apart: Women, prison, and life behind bars.* New York, NY: Random House.

Rich, C. G. (2009). What dignity demands: The challenges of creating sexual harassment protections for prisons and other nonworkplace settings. *Southern California Law Review, 83,* 1–80.

Rideau, W., & Sinclair B. (1982). The sexual jungle. In A. M. Scacco (Ed.), *Male rape: A casebook of sexual aggression* (pp. 3–29). New York, NY: AMS Press.

Rideau, W., & Wikberg, R. (1992). *Life sentences: Rage and survival behind bars.* New York, NY: Random House.

Ridgeway, C. L. (2011). *Framed by gender: How gender inequality persists in the modern world.* New York, NY: Oxford University Press.

Ristroph, A. (2006). Sexual punishments. *Columbia Journal of Gender and Law*, 15, 139–184.

Robertson, J. E. (2012–2013). Transgendered prisoners and the PREA Standards: What will be the legacy of Dee Farmer? *Correctional Law Reporter*, 24, 59–61.

Robertson, J. E. (2012b). The "turning-out" of boys in a man's prison: Why and how we need to amendment the Prison Litigation Reform Act. *Indiana Law Review*, 44, 819–851.

Robertson, J. E. (2010). Was it a "real" rape? *Correctional Law Reporter*, 22(2), 25–26.

Robertson, J. E. (2009). "Donny's law": Assessments of the Prison Rape Elimination Act. *Correctional Law Reporter*, 20, 89–91.

Robertson, J. E. (2006). Foreword: "Separate but equal" in prison: *Johnson v. California* and common sense racism. *Journal of Criminal Law and Criminology*, 96, 795–848.

Robertson, J. E. (2004a). A punk's song about prison reform. *Pace University Law Review*, 24, 527–562.

Robertson, J. E. (2004b), The Prison Rape Elimination Act of 2003: A primer. *Criminal Law Bulletin*, 40, 270–279.

Robertson, J. E. (2004c). Compassionate conservatism and prison rape: The Prison Rape Elimination Act of 2003. *New England Journal on Criminal & Civil Confinement*, 30, 1–18.

Robertson, J. E. (2003a). A clean heart and an empty head: The Supreme Court and sexual terrorism in prison. *North Carolina Law Review*, 81, 434–482.

Robertson, J. E. (2003b). Rape among incarcerated men: Sex, coercion STDs. *AIDS Patient Care*, 17, 423–430.

Robertson, J. E. (1999). Cruel and unusual punishment in United Stated prisons: Sexual harassment among male inmates. *American Criminal Law Review*, 36, 1–51.

Robertson, J. E. (1995). "Fight or F . . ." and constitutional liberty: An inmate's right to self-defense when targeted by aggressors. *Indiana Law Review*, 29, 339–363.

Robinson, R. K. (2011). Masculinity as prison: Sexual identity, race, and incarceration. *California Law Review*, 90, 1309–1408.

Ross, J. I., & Richards, S. C. (2002). *Behind bars: Surviving prison*. New York, NY: Alpha/Penguin Group.

Sabo, D., Kupers, T. A., & London, W. (2001). Gender and the politics of punishment. In D. Sabo, T. A. Kupers, & W. London (Eds.), *Prison masculinities* (pp. 3–18) Philadelphia, PA: Temple University Press.

Saum, C., Surratt, H., Inciardi, J., & Bennett, R. (1995). Sex in prison: Exploring the myths and realities. *Prison Journal*, 75, 413–430.

Scarce, M. (1997). *Male on male rape: The hidden toll of stigma and shame*. New York, NY: Insight Books.

Seidman, D. (1997). *Difference troubles: Queering social theory and sexual politics*. Cambridge, UK: Cambridge University Press.

Sexton, L., Jenness, V., & Sumner, J. M. (2010). Where the margins meet: A demographic assessment of transgender inmates in men's prisons. *Justice Quarterly*, 27, 835–860.

Smith, B. V. (2006). Rethinking prison sex: Self-expression and safety. *Columbia Journal of Gender and Law*, 15, 185–236.

Solis, D. (2005, October 17). Suit underscores state's prison rape problem. *Dallas Morning News*. Retrieved from http://www.november.org/stayinfo/breaking3/Texasrape.html

Stop Prisoner Rape & the National Prison Project of the American Civil Liberties Union. (2005). *Still in danger: The ongoing threat of sexual violence against transgender prisoners*. Retrieved from http://www.justdetention.org/pdf/stillindanger.pdf

Struckman-Johnson, C. J., & Struckman-Johnson, D. L. (2000). Sexual coercion rates in seven midwestern prison facilities for men. *Prison Journal*, 80, 379–390.

Struckman-Johnson, C. J., Struckman-Johnson, D. L., Rucker, L., Bumby, K., & Donaldson, S. (1996). Sexual coercion reported by men and women in prison. *Journal of Sex Research*, 33, 67–76.

Suk, J. (2011). Redistributing rape. *American Criminal Law Review*, 48, 111–119.

Sumner, J., & Sexton, L. (2014). Lost in translation: Looking for transgender identity in women's prisons and locating aggressors in prisoner culture. *Critical Criminology*, 23, 1–20.

Sykes, G. M. (1971). *The society of captives: The study of a maximum security prison*. Princeton, NJ: Princeton University Press. (Original work published 1958.)

Teichner, L. A. (2008). Unusual suspects: Recognizing and responding to female staff perpetrators of sexual misconduct in U.S. prisons. *Michigan Journal of Gender and Law*, 14, 259–298.

The Prison Rape Elimination Act of 2003, Pub. L. No. 108–79, 117 Stat. 972 (September 4, 2003), *codified as amended at* 42 U.S.C. §§ 15601–15609 (2015).

Thompson, J. H. (2010). Today's deliberate indifference: Providing attention without providing treatment to prisoners with serious medical needs. *Harvard Civil Rights–Civil Liberties Law Review*, 45, 635–654.

Trammell, R. (2011). Symbolic violence and prison wives: Protective pairing in men's prisons. *Prison Journal*, 91, 305–324.

U.S. Department of Justice. (2012, May 16). National standards to prevent, detect, and respond to prison rape, *codified at* 28 C.F.R. § 115. Retrieved from http://www.gpo.gov/fdsys/pkg/FR-2012-06-20/html/2012-12427.htm

Vojdik, V. K. (2002). Gender outlaws: Challenging masculinity in traditionally male institutions. *Berkeley Women's Law Journal*, 17, 68–121.

Wacquant, L. (2001). Deadly symbiosis: When ghetto and prison meet and mesh. *Punishment & Society, 3,* 95–133.

Ward, D. A., & Kassenbaum, G. G. (1964). Homosexuality: A mode of adaptation in a prison for women. *Social Problems, 12*(2), 159–177.

Ward, D. A., & Kassebaum, G. G. (2007). *Women's prison: Sex and social structure.* Piscataway, NJ: Aldine Transaction.

Waterson, K. (1996). *Prison: Inside the concrete womb.* Boston, MA: Northeastern University Press.

Weill-Greenberg, E. (2005, October 7). Gay man sues over Texas prison rapes. *Washington Blade.* Retrieved from http://www.justdetention.org/en/jdinews/2005/1007.aspx

West, C., & Zimmerman, D. H. (2009). Accounting for doing gender. *Gender & Society, 23,* 112–122.

West, C., & Zimmerman, D. H. (1987). Doing gender. *Gender & Society, 1,* 125–151.

Westoff, M. (2008). An examination of prisoners' constitutional right to health care: Theory and practice. *Health Lawyer, 20,* 1–12.

Wooden, W. S., & Parker, J. (1982). *Men behind bars: Sexual exploitation in prison.* New York, NY: Plenum.

Cases

Abney v. Thompson, 2013 WL 752170 (W.D. Ky. Feb. 27, 2013).

Bell v. Wolfish, 441 U.S. 520 (1979).

Doe v. Sparks, 733 F. Supp. 227 (W.D. Pa. 1990).

Douglas v. Sigler, 386 F.2d 684 (8th Cir. 1967).

Estelle v. Gamble, 429 U.S. 97 (1976).

Farmer v. Brennan, 511 U.S. 825 (1994).

Fields v. Smith, 653 F.3d 550 (7th Cir. 2011).

Freitag v. Ayers, 463 F.3d 838 (9th Cir. 2006).

Freitas v. Ault, 109 F.3d 1335 (8th Cir. 1997).

Garcia v. Steele, 193 F.2d 276 (8th Cir. 1951).

Garrett v. Department of Corrections, 589 F. Supp. 2d 1289 (M.D. Fla. 2007).

Green v. Thompson, 2013 WL 550621 (N.D. Cal. Feb. 12, 2013).

Hicks v. Alabama, 45 F. Supp. 2d 921 (S.D. Ala. 1998).

Hudson v. McMillian, 503 U.S. 1 (1992).

Hudson v. Palmer, 468 U.S. 517 (1984).

Johnson v. Wood, 2013 WL 373578 (W.D. Mich. Jan. 30, 2013).

Jones v. Heyns, 2013 WL 353762 (W.D. Mich. Jan. 29, 2013).

Kosilek v. Spencer, 774 F.3d 63 (1st Cir. 2014).

Kosilek v. Spencer, 889 F. Supp. 2d 190 (D. Mass. 2012), *rev'd, Kosilek v. Spencer,* 774 F.3d 63 (1st Cir. 2014).

Maggert v. Hanks, 131 F.3d 670 (7th Cir. 1997).

McGregor v. Forbes, 2010 WL 3724133 (N.D.N.Y. Aug. 20, 2010).

Meriwether v. Faulkner, 821 F.2d 408 (7th Cir. 1987).

Obergefell v. Hodges, 135 S. Ct. 2584 (2015).

Rhodes v. Chapman, 452 U.S. 337 (1981).

Schwan v. Hartford, 204 F.3d 1187 (9th Cir. 2000).

Smith v. Potter, 2013 WL 393447 (M.D. Tenn. Jan. 30, 2013).

Stroud v. Swope, 187 F.2d 850 (9th Cir.), *cert. denied,* 342 U.S. 829 (1951).

Turner v. Safley, 482 U.S. 78 (1987).

United States ex rel. Atterbury v. Ragen, 237 F.2d 953 (8th Cir. 1956).

United States v. Bajakajian, 524 U.S. 321 (1988).

Whitmire v. Arizona, 298 F.3d 1134 (9th Cir. 2002).

Wolff v. McDonnell, 418 U.S. 539 (1974).

Wood v. Beauclair, 692 F.3d 1041 (9th Cir. 2012).

Wood v. Idaho Department of Corrections, 2009 WL 3104036 (D. Idaho Sept. 22, 2009).

CHAPTER 12

Sex Offenders and their Treatment

Thomas Nolan and Mary Maguire

Campbell-Fuller and Craig (2009) conducted a case study in which they examined "the use of olfactory aversion and directed masturbation in modifying deviant sexual interest" (p. 179). They conducted a 26-week intervention with a 33-year-old man, "A.W.," who had been convicted of possessing and distributing child pornography through the Internet:

> He was found with a total of 699 pornographic images of children depicting involvement in oral and anal sex, masturbation with adults, urination, homosexual and group acts. He also had possession of 15 images included in the total of 699 indecent images which comprised: four indecent movie clips, eight indecent email messages and three compressed archive files containing pornographic images of children. A.W. reported committing a sexual contact offense against his nephew prior to his current conviction.
>
> (2009, p. 182)

A.W. began having sexual fantasies toward males at about age 14. A.W. reported that, prior to the intervention conducted in the research study, he engaged in fantasy and masturbatory activity for up to five hours per day. When A.W. observed children on a street corner, at a shopping mall, or on television, he would often engage in impulsive masturbatory activity. A.W. volunteered to participate in the study using the olfactory aversion (OA) and directed masturbation (DM) techniques and he "engaged in a total of 26 sessions (once per week) aimed at modifying his sexual interests and behaviors" (p. 183). A.W. was directed at keeping a "fantasy diary" as part of the study, in which he was to record the date, time, and nature of his sexual fantasies (whether they were abusive or non-abusive), as well as the fantasy "trigger." The olfactory aversion (OA) device consisted of a small, portable bottle of ammonia (smelling salts):

> It was explained that the use of the smelling salts provided an interruption to thought processes, allowing him to appraise the situation, respond to and replace the deviant sexual fantasies. A.W. was also instructed to reinforce non-deviant fantasies only through directed masturbation and complete the fantasy diary in the same process.
>
> (p. 184)

Campbell-Fuller and Craig found that the OA and DM techniques used in this single-subject case study did result in a significant reduction of deviant fantasy and masturbatory practices, but that it did not succeed in promoting a corresponding increase in non-deviant sexual fantasies. The authors conclude that OA and DM techniques are successful strategies for reducing deviant fantasies "over a limited period of time" (p. 186).

1. What issues do you see in the design of this research study that might affect the generalizability of the results reported by the researchers?
2. The authors suggest that A.W.'s engaging in masturbatory activity as a result of experiencing non-deviant fantasies is a desirable result of the intervention. Do you agree that this is desirable outcome? How and why do you believe this to be true?
3. Do you have any ethical concerns with the ways that these researchers conducted this particular research study?

LEARNING OBJECTIVES

1. To articulate different feminist perspectives on female sex offending and how "doing gender" may inform these understandings.
2. To demonstrate a competent level of understanding of the manner in which sex offenses and offenders are defined, categorized, and classified by the American criminal justice system.
3. To survey and assess the historical and contemporary trends in sex-offender treatment.
4. To analyze contemporary understandings of mental health and mental disorder and the ways that these perspectives inform the treatment of various types of sex offenders, as well as the public's sentiment regarding sex-offender treatment.
5. To identify sex-offender typologies and paraphilic disorders and to understand the ways that classifications, typologies, and diagnoses of mental disorder inform treatment paradigms.
6. To examine similarities and differences in the offense typologies of child molesters who are adult males, female sex offenders, juvenile sex offenders, cyber-offenders and rapists who sexually assault adult victims.
7. To explore the various strategies of sex-offender treatment in an effort to identify treatments that have had minimal success in reducing risk for re-offending as well as those treatments that show promise in reducing recidivism.

Attempts to assess the frequency and prevalence of instances of sexual offenses in official crime reports in the United States have, by all accounts, proven elusive and the numbers largely inaccurate and underreported. Sexual assaults have been among the lowest in numbers of crimes reported to police and this is in evidence, at least in part, by the continued disparity in the numbers of sexual assaults reported to the police and the Federal Bureau of Investigation (FBI) through the Uniform Crime Reports (UCR) and the numbers of sexual assaults reported through a different reporting mechanism compiled by the Bureau of Justice Statistics (BJS), the National Crime Victimization Survey (NCVS).

This has owed, at least in part, to the different operational definitions of sexual assault necessary for official recording by the UCR and the NCVS. Since 1927, the UCR program has defined rape as "the carnal knowledge of a female, forcibly and against her will"—mirroring the common-law definition of the crime as discussed in Chapter 5. Other sexual assaults that did not meet this criterion were not reported to or recorded by the UCR. In January of 2013, Attorney General Eric Holder announced a change in the definition of rape to: "The penetration, no matter how slight, of the vagina or anus with any body part or object, or oral penetration by a sex organ of another person, without the consent of the victim" (U.S. Department of Justice, 2013). Even given this newly expanded definition of rape, it continues to be the case that sexual assault is among the crimes least often reported to the authorities. For example, a 2014 BJS report on the incidence of rape and sexual assault among college-age women who were ages 18–24 found that "rape and sexual assault victimizations of students (80%) were more likely than nonstudent victimizations (67%) to go unreported to police" (Sinozich & Langton, 2014).

Even with that caveat and qualification, incidents of rape reported to the police in the United States, as reflected in the UCR statistics and the common-law legacy definition, have fallen gradually in the last two decades. In 1994, there were 102,216 rapes reported to the police in the United States, the highest number of rapes in the last 20 years. In every year since 1994 up until 2008 (except 1999), there were over 90,000 rapes per year reported to the police. In 2009, the annual reports of rapes as reflected in the UCR saw the numbers fall below 90,000, and in 2013 the number of rapes reported to the police, still using the old "legacy definition," fell to 79,770—the lowest number of rapes according to the UCR in 20 years (FBI, 2013).

Recall from Chapter 5 that the legal definitions of the crimes *sexual assault* and *sexual battery* differ by state. The description expresses that it is a statutory offense that happens when a person causes another person to participate in any sexual act by utilizing force or threat. This often takes place when Person A touches Person B in a sexual manner. However, mere touching does not have to transpire for an act to be considered a sex crime. Even offending or disturbing someone sexually is considered a sexual offense. Exhibitionism is an example of a sex crime that lacks physical contact; it is simply an act where an individual exposes themselves in a sexual manner to a nonconsenting person or persons.

Although there are anticipated characteristics, there is no exclusive profile for sexual perpetrators. Numerous researchers have constructed typologies of sex crimes and offenders (Groth, 1979; Hale, 1997; Knight & Prentky, 1990). Offenders are principally classified as (1) rapists, (2) child molesters, (3) female offenders, (4) juvenile offenders, and (5) cyber offenders. This chapter focuses largely on rapists and child molesters.

PREVALENCE AND INCIDENCE OF "SEX OFFENDING"

A study by Grattet, Petersilia, Lin, and Beckman (2009) showed that a fear of recidivism among sexual offenders enticed by media, compared with other types of criminals, may very well be groundless. The national rate of recidivism is approximately 40% for all crimes, California being a significantly large portion at 66%. However, during the study that spanned from 2003 to 2005, merely 1.5% of sex offenders were convicted of a new sexual offense. Grattet and colleagues (2009) discovered that parolees who had a history of previous sex-related offenses perpetrated 25% of sexual crimes. The other 75% of sexual offenses were committed by parolees convicted of crimes of a non-sexual nature.

Additional studies have approximated sex-offender recidivism rates to range broadly from 2.43% to 22%. This is contingent on factors such as whether or not arrests and convictions are the measure for re-offense and the amount of years offenders were tracked for criminal activity after their release. The California Department of Corrections and Rehabilitation (CDCR) found that sexual offenders who were paroled and followed for three years were reconvicted for a new sexual offense at a rate of 2.43% after their first year to a cumulative rate of 3.55% by the conclusion of their third year (California Sex Offender Management Board (CASOMB) Initial Report, 2008).

Furthermore, Arizona statistics showed that 5.5% of 3,205 sex offenders released and tracked for 6.85 years were reconvicted for a new sexual offense (CASOMB Initial Report, 2008). Hanson and Morton-Bourgon (2009) utilized a meta-analysis that examined 100 samples and included 28,757 sex offenders. They identified that the recognized recidivism rate for new sexual offense convictions was approximately 11.5%.

Although the official recidivism rates for sex offenders were low, many researchers found issues pertaining to the actual numbers of sex offense recidivists due to the fact that several crimes of sexual nature go unreported and therefore undetected. Of those that are reported, prosecution and conviction are unlikely (Friendship & Beech, 2005; Prentky, Lee, Knight & Cerce, 1997; Harris & Rice, 2006). However, due to the limited official rates of sexual recidivism, it is arduous to determine the precise differences between a conglomerate of sex offenders who will commit a new sex crime during their parole and sex offenders who will forgo committing any type of offense or violation of parole.

PARAPHILIAS IN SEX OFFENDERS

When considering types of sex crimes and the behaviors of those who commit sexual-related crimes, it is relevant to consider *paraphilias* and *paraphilic disorders*, since individuals afflicted with these types of disorders or who manifest paraphilias may engage in criminogenic behavior in seeking to satisfy their paraphilic need or disorder. Paraphilias embody some of the most legally controversial sexual practices (Saleh, Malin, Grudzinskas, & Vitacco, 2010). Categorized as sexual disorders in the DSM-IV-TR (American Psychiatric Association, 2000), **paraphilias** are "recurrent, intense sexually arousing fantasies, sexual urges, or behaviors generally involving 1) nonhuman objects, 2) the suffering or humiliation of oneself or one's partner, or 3) children or other nonconsenting persons that occur over a period of at least six months" (p. 566; see also DSM-5, 2013).

The DSM-5 (American Psychiatric Association, 2013) distinguished between *paraphilias* and *paraphilic disorders* to reflect that many people may practice atypical sexual behaviors without meriting a diagnosis of mental illness. The DSM-5 lists eight "relatively common" paraphilic disorders (although there are many more paraphilias that are less commonly encountered), since "some of them entail actions for their satisfaction that, because of their noxiousness or potential harm to others, are classified as criminal offenses" (p. 685). Closely resembling the definition of paraphilias in the DSM-IV-TR (2002), the DSM-5 defines paraphilia as "intense and persistent sexual interest other than sexual interest in genital stimulation or preparatory fondling with phenotypically normal, physically mature, consenting human partners" (p. 685). The *paraphilia* becomes a *paraphilic disorder* when it causes severe levels of harm to oneself or to others, e.g., physical harm to a nonconsenting other person, or such marked levels of distress, preoccupation, anxiety, and fixation in the individual to cause significant impairment in normal functioning—in the workplace, at school, in the family or in the community, or to socially interact with other people in anything resembling normal social activity.

It is beyond the scope of this book to detail the many paraphilias in existence. Some paraphilias are intertwined with specific criminal offenses (e.g., pedophilia and child molestation), while other paraphilias lead people to commit crimes that are encompassed by laws prohibiting trespass, indecent exposure, assault, rape, or even homicides (Fischer, Fradella, & Ireland, 2009; Neumann, et. al., 2006; Paclebar, Furtado, & McDonald-Witt, 2006). The paraphilias that cause recurrent problems for the criminal justice system are outlined in this section.

Voyeurism

A *voyeur*, sometimes called a "Peeping Tom," derives sexual gratification through nonconsensual observation of an "individual who is naked, disrobing, or engaging in sexual activity" (Neumann, 2006). It has been proposed that individuals are afflicted with this paraphilia along a continuum, ranging in severity from mild "pseudo-voyeurs," who only fantasize about committing the act, to "criminal voyeurs," whose propensity for observation can escalate into physically aggressive behavior (Aggrawal, 2009).

Persons with "**voyeuristic disorder**" may engage in criminal activity to satisfy their urges and in this sense voyeurism may be considered a type of sex crime. Voyeurs, if not sex offenders in the legal sense, "engage in law-breaking sexual behaviors" (DSM-5, p. 687). Voyeurs typically spy on unsuspecting individuals in some form of undress and/or engaging in sexual activity in a setting where the victims have an expectation of privacy. Oftentimes the voyeur will commit a criminal trespass or even a burglary to facilitate the viewing of the nonconsenting victim engaging in private activities.

The voyeur meets the criteria for a mental disorder (voyeuristic disorder) when he (the disorder is rarely observed in females), experiences "fantasies, urges, or behaviors, (and) over a period of at least six months, (that result in) recurrent and intense sexual arousal from observing an unsuspecting person who is naked, in the process of disrobing, or engaging in sexual activity" (DSM-5, p. 685). The individual must be at least 18 years old to meet the diagnostic criteria and must have either acted on his fantasies or urges or have experienced significant impairment in normal functioning as a result of his fantasies and urges.

Aggrawal (2009) explained that "video voyeurism" is a serious concern that has prompted a wave of new legislation. This disturbingly popular trend is a form of voyeurism involving electronic surveillance equipment (such as a digital camera or camera-equipped cell phone). It is comprised primarily of "upskirting" and "downblousing," in which pictures are taken either up women's skirts or down their blouses, respectively. The highest court in Massachusetts (*Commonwealth v. Robertson*, 2014) ruled that upskirting was not covered by a law that stipulates:

> Whoever willfully photographs, videotapes or electronically surveils another person who is nude or partially nude, with the intent to secretly conduct or hide such activity, when the other person in such place and circumstance would have a reasonable expectation of privacy in not being so photographed, videotaped or electronically surveilled, and without that person's knowledge and consent, shall be [guilty and punished].
>
> (MASS. GEN. LAWS c. 272, § 105[b])

Although the court condemned the practice of upskirting, the voyeuristic practice in the case had taken place when the defendant secretly photographed his victim under her skirt on the subway. The justices reasoned that the female passenger was not "nude or partially nude" nor was she in a place where she had a reasonable expectation of privacy. The very next day, the Massachusetts state legislature amended the above-referenced law to include secretly photographing, videotaping, or electronically surveilling another person's sexual or other intimate parts, "whether under or around a person's clothing" under circumstances when a reasonable person would believe that his or her intimate parts would not be visible to the public (MASS. GEN. LAWS c. 272, § 105[b]).

In *Ex parte Thompson* (2014), the highest criminal court in Texas invalidated the convictions of a man who took 26 pictures of women and children in bikinis at a water park. The court found that such photos, taken in public, are "inherently expressive" and are therefore protected by the First Amendment. The court left intact the portion of the law that makes it illegal to photograph or record a visual image of someone without the other person's consent and "with intent to arouse or gratify the sexual desire of any person" (TEX. PENAL CODE § 21.15(b)(1), 2014).

Voyeurism is a perfect example of the law's struggle to keep pace with technology. There are a number of laws in many states that condemn voyeurism specifically; Neumann (2006) estimates that as many as 25 of the 50 states directly criminalize it. Many of the existing states also indirectly do so by looping the act of voyeurism into trespassing laws. Additionally, the Video Voyeurism Prevention Act of 2004 was enacted by Congress, significantly reducing the difficulty in securing federal prosecutions for acts of video voyeurism. Nearly every jurisdiction in the country has followed suit.

(Aggrawal, 2009)

Exhibitionism

Exhibitionists and those with "**exhibitionistic disorder**" derive sexual satisfaction from exposing one's genitals to nonconsenting and unsuspecting persons (Schug & Fradella, 2014). Exhibitionism involves an array of behaviors. *Mooning*, for instance, involves "baring one's buttocks by removing clothing" (Aggrawal, 2009, p. 88). *Streaking* requires removing all of one's clothes and running around in a public area. And *flashing* involves a man exposing his penis or, less commonly (except in New Orleans during Mardi Gras) a female exposing her breasts or genitals. These activities are commonly encompassed in "indecent exposure" laws, though there is some debate as to the divide between exhibitionism and indecent exposure.

Activities like strip shows, mothers feeding their children in public … nude sunbathing on beaches and swimming … have been termed as both acts of exhibitionism and indecent exposure in the lay media. It is important to appreciate that an important difference exists between the two. While exhibitionism is pathological, indecent exposure is not. … Instances of mothers nursing babies in public may not even be termed as acts of indecent exposure, as many jurisdictions now allow mothers to do so publicly.

(Aggrawal, 2009, p. 90)

While not all exhibitionists are mentally disordered, those who experience "[o]ver a period of at least six months, recurrent and intense sexual arousal from the exposure of one's genitals to an unsuspecting person, as manifested by fantasies, urges, and behaviors" and who act "on these sexual urges with a nonconsenting person, or the sexual urges or fantasies cause significant distress or impairment … in functioning" will meet the criteria for exhibitionistic disorder (DSM-5, p. 698). Some exhibitionists seek sexual gratification by exposing themselves to prepubescent children, while others confine themselves to exposing their genitals to physically mature women. Some have no "specialty" and will expose themselves to both women and children.

Frotteurism

Another sexually focused criminal behavior that is not typically considered when discussing "sex crimes" or "sex offenders" is the paraphilia *frotteurism* and the associated mental disorder "**frotteuristic disorder.**" Frotteurs seek and derive sexual gratification from touching or rubbing against an unsuspecting and nonconsenting person (Schug & Fradella, 2014). This is, again, an almost exclusively male domain, and the victims are almost always females. According to the DSM-5, up to 30% of the adult male population may have engaged in frotteuristic acts (2013, p. 692). Males meeting the criteria for frotteuristic disorder generally exhibit behavior for at least six months (although shorter time periods apply in certain cases), that includes "recurrent and intense sexual arousal from touching or rubbing against a nonconsenting person as manifested by fantasies, urges or behaviors" and who act "on these sexual urges with a nonconsenting person, or the urges and fantasies cause significant distress or impairment . . . in functioning" (DSM-5, 2013, p. 691).

While not all men who "grope" women are mentally disordered, frotteurism is nonetheless a sex crime, in fact a felony in most jurisdictions. Some states have designated variations of frotteuristic acts as their own crimes. For example, New York has a crime called "forcible touching" (N.Y. PENAL CODE § 130.52, 2014). In other states, sexually motivated, nonconsensual groping, grinding, pinching, grabbing, or rubbing falls within the statutory definition of *sexual abuse* or *sexual contact* laws. Victims of such acts rarely report the offense, so arrests for the violation of these laws are relatively uncommon (Guterman, Martin, & Rudes, 2011).

Sexual Sadism and Sexual Masochism

Strictly speaking, sexual sadism and sexual masochism are unique paraphilic disorders, though are often found comorbidly (Aggrawal, 2009). **Sexual sadism** involves deriving pleasure from the infliction of pain, humiliation, or suffering on another, whereas **sexual masochism** is the enjoyment of the receipt of such pain, humiliation, or suffering (Paclebar, Furtado, & McDonald-Witt, 2006). As Gross (2006) noted, the term *sadomasochism* has also entered the public lexicon, and is what most people think of when referring to sex that is "kinky" or "rough," despite there being no clear formula for acts that fall into this category of sexual activity (see also Fischer, Fradella, & Ireland, 2009 Newmahr, 2010).

Pain, suffering, and humiliation serve as sexual stimulants for many people as evidenced by the widespread success of novels like the *Fifty Shades of Grey* trilogy (James, 2011–2012). Statistics vary on how many people engage in this sort of behavior, though it is estimated that of those involved, between 5 and 20% are women (Aggrawal, 2009). Among those who participate, common practices include flagellation (whipping), spanking, domination, and submission (i.e., giving or obeying commands), and the use of various forms of restraints (Williams, 2006). Some behaviors are more extreme, including piercing, branding, flesh ingestion, and various types of asphyxiation (Paclebar, et. al., 2006).

The Boundaries of Consent

Mild to moderate sadomasochism between consenting adults is rarely of concern to criminal justice system actors (Fischer, et al., 2009), even though criminal laws have historically been hostile toward these behaviors or of the individuals who engage in them (Yost, 2010). The law's primary concern is the ability of individuals to give valid consent. Fischer and colleagues (2009) compared the law's sanctioning of consent to assault and battery in sports with consent to assault and battery of a sexual nature. They noted, as did Houlihan (2011), that the "criminal law mostly speaks about sexuality as aberrance, through interpretations and translations of a moralistic jurisprudential model of socio-sexuality which is heteronormative and procreative" (Houlihan, 2011, p. 2).

Courts in the United States have been inconsistent in their reasoning in cases involving consensual sadomasochism gone awry. The dividing line appears to be the seriousness of the injuries inflicted. Fischer and colleagues assert that after the U.S. Supreme Court's decision in *Lawrence v. Texas* (2003), it is likely that consenting adults may give valid consent to minor forms of bodily harm—acts that would otherwise constitute simple assault, simple battery, or false imprisonment but for the consent (e.g., spanking, tying someone up)—presuming that such activities occur in private and the harms caused are reasonably foreseeable in light of the joint participation in concerted activity of a kind not otherwise forbidden by the law (see, e.g., 11 DEL. LAWS c. 4, § 452, 2015; N.J. REV. STAT. § 2C:2–10, 2014). In contrast, consent is not a valid defense to any serious form of bodily harm, such as aggravated assaults that require hospitalization to treat the injuries (Fischer, et al., 2009). But, as Bergelson (2007) pointed out, this rule is of "limited use . . . for offenses involving bodily harm" since what constitutes a "serious" injury is ill-defined and open to debate (p. 174; see also this chapter's "Law in Action" box).

Courts consistently find "serious harm" in cases even when the injuries are not permanent, seriously debilitating, or harmful enough that they cause a risk of death. For example, criminal liability has been upheld for injuries S&M participants received from being hit with a belt or a riding crop (*Commonwealth v. Appleby*, 1980; *State v. Collier*, 1985). In critiquing such an approach, Professor Vera Bergelson (2007) wrote,

[In a case in which the] defendant was convicted of inflicting "serious physical injury" in the course of a sexual encounter, there was no evidence that the victim "ever required any medical attention or suffered any wounds of any sort." Yet the appellate court sustained the assault conviction, reasoning that the sadomasochistic paraphernalia the defendant used must have caused serious physical pain (candle wax was "hot and it stung" and nipple clamps were "tight and cutting") and "serious physical pain" satisfied the definition of "physical injury" [under the applicable statute]. Naturally, under a statute of this type, practically any sadomasochistic activity automatically qualifies as criminal.

(pp. 178–179)

Nonconsensual Conduct

Of perhaps more serious concern to law-enforcement officers and investigators are sexual sadists, as these are men (and some women) who derive intense sexual satisfaction from inflicting physical or psychological suffering on another, nonconsenting person. How prevalent are those with **sexual sadism disorder** in the general population? According to the DSM-5: "Among civilly committed sexual offenders in the United States, less than 10% have sexual sadism. Among individuals who have committed sexually motivated homicides, rates of sexual sadism range from 37% to 75%" (p. 698).

There are sexual sadists who will not meet the criteria for sexual sadism disorder, due largely to the fact that they report no psychological difficulties or impairment in functioning in their infliction of pain and suffering on nonconsenting individuals (although these individuals may meet the criteria for other mental disorders). To meet the criteria for a diagnosis of sexual sadism disorder, an individual must experience "[o]ver a period of at least six months, recurrent and intense sexual arousal from the physical or psychological

Law in Action THE CRIMINAL LAW'S LIMITS ON CONSENT IN SEXUAL VIOLENCE

Edward Collier was a paroled felon living in Iowa. After his release from prison, he met a woman named Leanne Steele, with whom he entered into business. According to court documents Steele was employed as a model by Collier who, after returning without payment from a day-long "appointment," was then tied to a bed and beaten. The court records provide the following description:

> Collier forced Steele to remove her clothing and tied her spread-eagle face up on the bed. He then blindfolded her and proceeded to whip her with a belt. Steele testified that she was struck on the thighs, legs, and chest. When she began crying and begging him to stop, he slapped her across the face and gagged her. Defendant then performed sexual acts with her using various types of paraphernalia. He eventually untied her, beat her on her back side and proceeded to have intercourse with her anally. As a result of the beating and sexual acts, Steele suffered a swollen lip, large welts on her ankles, wrists, hips, buttocks, and severe bruises on her thighs.
>
> (State v. Collier, 1985, p. 304)

Collier then untied her and went to the bathroom, at which time Steele grabbed a gun from Collier's bedside cabinet and fired, missing him.

At trial, Collier claimed that he and Steele had arranged for the two to engage in sado-masochism for her birthday. Collier went on to say that Steele even researched specific acts she wanted him to perform. If true, Steele clearly did not know what she was in for. Collier was tried and convicted for unlawfully possessing two firearms (due to his status as a parolee), and for further committing assault resulting in serious injury to Steele.

The court struggled to determine whether the violent sexual behavior between Collier and Steele violated a criminal statute, or if her desire to engage in "rough sex" gave rise to a valid defense of consent to the assault charges.

> We are hesitant to give a precise definition of [sadomasochism] and believe it is more appropriate that its meaning be interpreted on a case by case basis. However, it is obvious to this court that the legislature did not intend the term to include an activity which has been repeatedly disapproved by other jurisdictions and considered to be in conflict with the general moral principles of our society. In fact, the statutory provision in question specifically excludes activities which would "create an unreasonable risk of serious injury." There can be little doubt that the sadomasochistic activities involved in this case expose persons to the very type of injury deemed unacceptable by the legislature. . . . Whatever rights the defendant may enjoy regarding private sexual activity, when such activity results in the whipping or beating of another resulting in bodily injury, such rights are outweighed by the State's interest in protecting its citizens' health, safety, and moral welfare.
>
> (p. 307)

Collier was decided 18 years before the U.S. Supreme Court's decision in *Lawrence v. Texas* (2003), a case that makes it clear morality cannot support the criminal prosecution of private intimate conduct by consenting adults. Yet, in the wake of *Lawrence*, courts have refused to extend its holding to provide constitutional protection for sadomasochistic activities. For example, in *State v. Van* (2004), the Nebraska Supreme Court stated, as a matter of public policy, a person cannot avoid criminal responsibility for an assault that causes injury or carries a risk of serious harm, even if the victim asked for or consented to the act. . . . [A]ny right to sexual privacy held by a citizen would be outweighed in the constitutional balancing scheme by the State's interest in preventing violence by the use of dangerous weapons upon its citizens under the claimed cloak of privacy in sexual relations. . . . The *Lawrence* Court did not extend constitutional protection to any conduct which occurs in the context of a consensual sexual relationship. Rather, the Court indicated that State regulation of such conduct was inappropriate "absent injury to a person or abuse of an institution the law protects" . . . We therefore conclude that [criminal assaults statutes] are not unconstitutional as applied to [sadomasochistic acts that result in severe injuries].

(pp. 825–826)

1. Supporters of the approach taken in the *Collier* case argue that the consent given by S&M participants is irrational and, therefore, legally defective. For example, in upholding a conviction for aggravated assault for whipping an apparently willing victim, a California court said that it was a matter of "common knowledge that a normal person in full possession of his mental faculties does not freely consent to the use, upon himself, of force likely to produce great bodily injury" (*People v. Samuels*, 1967, p. 447). Do you agree? Why or why not? What would this approach to consent mean if it were applied to boxers, mixed-martial artists, and so-called "extreme fighters"?
2. Several scholars (Baker, 2009; Bergelson, 2007; Egan, 2007; Fischer, Fradella, & Ireland, 2009) proposed that the law should recognize consent misdemeanor assaults (i.e., assaults that do not involve serious injury or risks of either serious bodily harm or death). In contrast, the defense of consent should continue to be unavailable in cases of aggravated assault—those assaults which create a substantial risk of death, or which cause death or serious and protracted disfigurement, protracted impairment of health or protracted loss or impairment of the function of any bodily organ. Critique this approach by comparing and contrasting its advantages and drawbacks, paying particular attention to its ambiguities, if any.

suffering of another person, as manifested by fantasies, urges, or behaviors" and who act "on these sexual urges with a nonconsenting person, or the sexual urges or fantasies cause significant distress or impairment in . . . functioning" (DSM-5, p. 695). In the clinical sense "recurrent" refers to the sexual sadist having at least three or more victims, or having inflicted pain and suffering on the same nonconsenting victim multiple times.

Paraphilias and Rape

Although an understanding of legal definitions is essential, a comprehension of the distinctions between offenders is crucial for determining future risks. The Massachusetts Treatment Center (MTC) at Bridgewater has developed and seen empirical validation, by both internal and external researchers, of a model that identifies and classifies typologies of rapists. The typologies are based on their decades-long extensive examination of individuals who have been civilly committed by the court to the MTC, after being adjudicated "sexually dangerous," as well as examinations of inmates incarcerated in prisons in Massachusetts for sex-related crimes. (Knight & Prentky, 1990) (Barbaree, Seto, Serin, Amos, & Preston, 1994; Harris, Rice, & Quinsey, 1994).

The model, entitled the Massachusetts Treatment Center Rapist Typology – Version 3 (MTC: R3), classifies rapists into four distinct categories based on motives: pervasively angry, vindictive, sexual, and opportunistic. Furthermore, it groups these four categories into nine subtypes that are classified by six temperamental or cognitive dimensions: aggression, sadism, sexual fantasies, impulsivity, social competence, and naïve cognitions or beliefs. These classifications supply basic profiles and insight into sex-offender motivations.

The malicious rapist directs his anger to a target that does not deserve such treatment. His motivation consists solely of anger and is not driven by sexual desire thus his attack is violent and aggressive. Void of sexual feelings, the offender rapes in order to harm, humiliate, and degrade his victim. This rapist usually targets strangers; nevertheless, his victims may have certain characteristics that act as "triggers," such as hair color, race, or aspects of physical appearance. In addition, this type of offender is more likely to be violent to others in general, outside of the context of sexual assaults.

This type of rapist is consumed in pervasive anger by temperament that is not gender-specific. These individuals have often experienced a history of antisocial behavior throughout childhood and into adolescence and adulthood; violence has likely been a pervasive, life-course persistent aspect of their lived experience. Their offenses are frequently unplanned and lack premeditation. These assaults are usually characterized by intense violence and may cause serious injury to the victims.

Unlike the vengeful and pervasively angry rapist, the non-sadistic and sexually motivated rapist is not compelled by anger, but rather by feelings of insufficiency and inadequacy. Their capability to overpower and control a victim aids them in compensating for a sense of impotence. Sexually motivated rapists are typically shy and lack adequate social skills. The sexual assault enhances their self-esteem increases their sense of sexual adequacy and competence. The sexually motivated rapist often fantasizes and is preoccupied with visions of the enactment of sexual assaults that he acts out in the commission of the rape.

Sexually motivated rapists are inclined to fantasize that their victim will enjoy the experience and return to them for more, even if they resisted the first time.

Sadistic rapists with sexual motives combine arousal with pain and violence to commit their offense. This male offender believes that the potential victim enjoys being controlled and dominated. The sadistic rapist is more likely to seriously injure and in extreme situations even murder their victim. They are also more inclined to be involved in intimate partner violence and pathological dysfunction in intimate partner relationships.

Lastly, the opportunistic rapist commits a sexual assault impulsively, when the opportunity arises. These rapists have poor impulse control and act in self-gratification. They view their victims strictly as sexual objects and may engage in instrumental violence to complete their assault. These rapists are unconcerned with their victim's pain or trauma. Opportunistic rapes are frequently secondary (and opportunistic) assaults that co-occur with the commission of another crime, such as burglary or robbery.

Contemporary Rapist Typologies[1]

The growing emphasis on empiricism during the 1970s contributed to the rise of **diagnostic psychiatry** (see Houts, 2000; Mayes & Horwitz, 2005). Until the 1970s, psychology and psychiatry did not concern themselves too much with specific diagnoses.

Dynamic explanations posited that symptoms were symbolic manifestations that only became meaningful through exploring the personal history of each individual. The focus of analytic explanations and treatment, therefore, was the total personality and life experiences of the person that provided the context for the interpretation of symptoms. . . . [Diagnostic manuals, therefore,] made little effort to provide elaborate classification schemes, because overt symptoms did not reveal disease entities but disguised underlying conflicts that could not be expressed directly.

(Mayes & Horwitz, 2005, pp. 249–250)

Psychology's evolution as an empirical science and the corresponding rise of diagnostic psychiatry led to a system for classifying mental disorders not on etiology, but rather on observable symptoms that could be used to promote reliable clinical diagnoses (Fradella, 2008). Even some Neo-Freudians conceded that sex offenders rarely exhibited classic symptoms of severe mental illness, but rather evidenced a wide range of "character neuroses, character disorders, and more severe borderline and psychotic states" (Cohen, Garofalo, Boucher, & Seghorn, 1971, as cited in Albin, 1977, p. 430). Nonetheless, they developed their own classification system for rapists, albeit one rooted in psychodynamics: "those with aggressive aims, sexual aims, and sex-aggression diffusion" (Albin, 1977, p. 430). But as classification systems grew in popularity (and as psychoanalytic theory continued its decline), social psychology and its focus on empirical methods grew to be the dominant lens through which rapists, motivations were analyzed. This led to the development of various typologies of rapists that merely describe common motivational traits among an otherwise heterogeneous group of offenders.

As previously mentioned, Neo-Freudians Cohen and colleagues (1971) were among the first social scientists to conduct empirical research on the motivational factors contributing to the crime of rape. Groth (1979) expanded upon their work by developing a three-part typology of rape offenders that included the anger rapist, the power rapist, and the sadistic rapist. Groth became one of (and arguably the only), clinician whose views on motivation for rape were still influential in the post-Freudian era. His analyses were based on clinical observations. Groth blended psychoanalytic and feminist perspectives insofar as including sexual gratification motives in his typology, but emphasizing that power and domination motives were the most common causes of rape. By emphasizing power, Groth (1979) was able to delineate a hypothesis about acceptance into the peer group, as well as the desire to confirm or prove masculinity by the rapist.

Groth's concepts were subsequently refined by Knight and Prentky (1991), who also added a fourth primary typology, the opportunistic rapist. Before exploring this typology, it is important to note that rapist typologies have been criticized both on validity grounds and conceptually for conflating "behaviors, motives, and cognitions without differentiating among them" (McCabe & Wauchope, 2005, p. 241). Still, the refinements made by Knight and Prentky (1990) to the earlier work of Cohen et al. (1971) and Groth (1979) appear to have significant empirical support. In fact, McCabe and Wauchope (2005) validated the primary types of rapists as previously described in the literature by Knight and Prentky, finding that "characteristics associated with each of [the major rapist] types were generally consistent with those proposed by other researchers" (p. 250). Accordingly, we explore the four primary types of rapists as set forth by Groth and refined by Knight and Prentky.

Anger Rapists

The anger rape occurs when the offender attacks his victim, pushes her to the ground, beats her, physically removes her clothing, and rapes her (Knight, Warren, Reboussin, & Soley, 1998). Anger rapists are typically men who have long histories of antisocial behavior of which rape is just another form (Knight, et al., 1998). The anger rapist usually uses one of two methods of attack: the blitz style or the confidence-approach technique (Groth, 1979). The blitz style typically plays out with "the use of weapons, physical harm to victims, and a lot of physical and verbal resistance by victims" (Bondurant, 2001, p. 296; see also McCabe & Wauchope, 2005). The confidence style, on the other hand, is characterized by the rapist gaining access by "falsely stating the reason for his presence" (Burgess & Holmstrom, 1974, p. 22). This scenario is typically associated with rapes that take place within a woman's home.

The primary motivator for the anger rapist's behavior appears to be the release of anger and rage (Douglas & Olshaker, 1988). "His aim is to hurt and debase his victim, and he expresses his contempt for her through abusive and profane language" (Groth, 1979, p. 14). The reason an offender who is extremely angry will not merely beat the victim is because rape is considered the "ultimate offense he can commit against another person" (p. 14). Perhaps surprisingly to some, the "anger rapists typically finds little or no sexual gratification in the rape—in fact, his subjective reaction to the sexual act itself is frequently one of revulsion and disgust" (p. 15). This differentiates him from the sadistic rapist because their aggression is eroticized (see Knight & Prentky, 1990). The anger rapist is extremely likely to psychologically detach himself from the rape situation, often rationalizing it as if he were an observer and not a participant (Groth, 1979).

The leading theory seeking to explain the source of the anger rapist's rage hypothesizes that the offender's "relationships to important persons in his life are frequently fraught with conflict, irritation, and aggravation" (Groth, 1979, p. 16). The anger with these relationships is then taken out on others, often complete strangers. The stranger usually is in the offender's presence when he "snaps" and

rapes as an immediate outlet for his anger (pp. 16–17). This can lead to horribly gruesome rapes. The anger rapist is a psychologically disturbed individual who has avoided dealing with his own problems. He is unhappy with his family and friends, but he does not convey these disappointments. He bundles up his hostility and rage and unleashes it on an unsuspecting victim (pp. 16–17).

Power Rapists

The primary aim of power rapists is control their victims (McCabe & Wauchope, 2005). "Power can be conceptualized on the basis of inadequacy and a corresponding need to compensate" (sometimes referred to as the *power reassurance rapist*), "on the basis of hostility and a corresponding need to dominate" (sometimes referred to as the *power assertive/power exploitive rapist*), or on the basis of a socialized macho-dominant image and a corresponding need to use and conquer women (McCabe & Wauchope, 2005, p. 251; see also Burgess & Holmstrom, 1974; Douglas & Olshaker, 1988). Thus, while there may be several subtypes of power rapists depending on their motivation to rape, they share in common a goal for sexual conquest as evidence of their power. Accordingly, the power rapist tends to rely on threats and intimidation as his primary weapon, using "only the amount of force necessary to accomplish this objective" (Groth, 1979, p. 25).

The power rapist often uses fantasies about having sex to fuel his behavior (Groth, 1979). The rapes become repetitive and compulsive because the perpetrator continues to see victims as means to fulfill his fantasies (Groth, 1979). The power rapist is typically insecure about his masculinity and feels the need to reaffirm it by raping women (Groth, 1979). "Although such an offender may exude a sense of confidence and self-assurance on a superficial level, internally his feelings about himself are much different" (Graney & Arrigo, 2002, p. 128). This insecurity sometimes further manifests itself by the power rapist's need to be complimented by the victim during the sexual encounter (Groth, 1979). "In addition, as if he were attempting to maintain some sort of relationship with them, he may at times contact his victims after the assault to inquire about them or express the satisfaction he gained from the assault" (Graney & Arrigo, 2002, p. 130). This is due, in part, to the fact that power rapists usually do not consider their behavior to be rape (Groth, 1979). They tend to view women as objects to be taken and used at their convenience (Graney & Arrigo, 2002). Moreover, they see these women not as victims, but as willing participants who wanted to have sex with them (Groth, 1979).

Sadistic Rapists

"This offender finds the intentional mal-treatment of his victim intensely gratifying" (Groth, 1979, p. 30). Sex and aggression are intertwined in the mind of sadistic rapists. They are quite similar to anger rapists except that they are preoccupied with sex in a man-ner that melds it with aggression, dominance, coercion, and feelings of inadequacy, leading to a morbid fascination with sadistic sex, caus-ing them to live out sexual fantasies on their victims in a manner that causes the three Ds: dread, dependency, and degradation (McCabe & Wauchope, 2005). The more pain that is inflicted on the victim, the greater the amount of pleasure for the offender. The "sexual areas of the victim's body (her breasts, genitals, and buttocks) become a specific focus of injury and abuse" (Groth, 1979, p. 44). The rape is so much about abusing the victim that the sadistic rapist often does not ejaculate during the crime (Keppell, 1997). Instead, he will wait until he is in a safe location with "sou-venirs" from the victim with him, (e.g., panties) and then masturbates, while eroti-cizing the pain and degradation he inflicted on his victim, thereby increasing his sexual pleasure. Additionally, sadistic rapists tend to plan their sexual assaults with much greater

deliberation than other types of rapists (Knight & Prentky, 1990). This is partly due to the enjoyment they receive from fantasizing about the rape they plan to commit, and it is also due, in part, to the fact that sadistic rapists go to great lengths to hide sexual sadism from friends and family. While many such rapists are married or in a relationship, physical abuse of his partner as a sign of his dominance is typical (Douglas & Olshaker, 1988).

Opportunistic Rapists

Knight and Prentky (1990) added to Groth's typology of sexual assaults by creating a cat-egory they termed opportunistic rapists. A sexual assault for this type of rapist appears to be "an impulsive, typically unplanned predatory act, controlled more by contextual and immediately antecedent factors than by any obvious protracted or stylized sexual fan-tasy" (Knight & Prentky, 1990, p. 44). An example is a burglar who breaks into a house with the intent to steal, but, upon entering, finds a potential victim; he sees the opportu-nity to exploit her, and does so (Burgess & Holmstrom, 1974). The sexual assaults com-mitted by opportunistic rapists are more a result of poor impulse control, which is evi-denced by their extensive history of unso-cialized behavior in multiple domains (Knight & Prentky, 1990). Opportunistic rapists are indifferent to the comfort and welfare of their victims, but are not usually physically abu-sive or degrading towards them; they will only use as much force as is necessary to achieve immediate sexual gratification, exhibiting lit-tle or no evidence of unnecessary force or anger (Knight & Prentky, 1990). Their goal is immediate sexual gratification from a sex act, not through the use of power, intimida-tion, or sadism. Accordingly, since the fac-tors motivating an impulse rapist lie beyond aggressive psychodynamics, many researchers have paid little attention to them (Burgess & Holmstrom, 1974).

Pedophilia

Of obvious concern to criminal justice professionals are individuals who have sexual contact with children. Most of these sex offenders are mentally disordered. While the diagnosis of a mental disorder (as with all sex crimes) is not in any way intended to mitigate the circumstances of sexual assault or to diminish in any way the criminal responsibility that inheres in the commission of sexual assaults, students of criminology and criminal justice (future practitioners) will no doubt find an understanding of the etiology of certain types of sexual assaults on children to be helpful. While not all sex offenders whose victims are children would meet the diagnostic criteria for what the DSM-5 now refers to as **"pedophilic disorder,"** a consideration of the criteria used to diagnose mentally disordered pedophiles is instructive. There are some individuals (the vast majority of whom are men) who may self-report a sexual attraction to children but who have never acted on their attractions or urges and these individuals have a *pedophilic sexual orientation*, although they may not meet the criteria for a diagnosis of pedophilic disorder.

According to the DSM-5, those who experience "[o]ver a period of at least six months, recurrent, intense sexually arousing fantasies, sexual urges, or behaviors involving sexual activity with a prepubescent child (generally age 13 years or younger)" and that "the individual has acted on these sexual urges, or the sexual urges or fantasies cause marked distress or interpersonal difficulty" would meet the diagnostic criteria for pedophilic disorder if, in addition, "the individual is at least age 16 years and at least five years older than the child or children" who are the intended targets of the fantasies, urges, or activities (2013, p. 697). It is estimated that anywhere from 3% to 5% of the adult male population may meet the criteria for the diagnosis of pedophilic disorder, and the disorder is seen infrequently in females. Men with pedophilic disorder often make extensive use of pornography depicting prepubescent children (DSM-5, 2013), and these individuals may come to the attention of law enforcement while engaging in these activities.

Of the eight paraphilias listed in the DSM-5, individuals who meet the diagnostic criteria for the five examined above—voyeuristic disorder, exhibitionistic disorder, frotteuristic disorder, sexual sadism disorder, and pedophilic disorder—are those who are most likely to commit sexual assaults or to engage in law-breaking sexual behavior (and certainly the argument could be made that any law-breaking sexual behavior, even voyeurism, is in fact an assault). These men (and even occasionally some women) will be of interest to, and come to the attention of criminal justice professionals. There are three other paraphilias listed in the DSM-5—"sexual masochism disorder," "fetishistic disorder," and "transvestic disorder"—and individuals diagnosed with these paraphilic disorders will not usually engage in criminal activity and come to the attention of law enforcement for reasons directly related to their disorder.

The best contrast between a rapist and a pedophile is the kind of victim. Pedophiles are attracted to and/or assault children whereas rapists target adults as their victims. *Pedophilia* is a term used to cover the acts of child molestation and sexual abuse. The American Psychiatric Association defines pedophilia as possessing frequent and acute sexual urges toward children or experiencing sexual fantasies about them that cause distress or interpersonal issues (2000). The MTC has classified pedophiles into four categories based on their typical behavioral patterns: fixated, regressed, exploitative, and aggressive.

Fixated pedophiles are exclusively attracted to children; hence the Freudian terminology of being *fixated* on a certain developmental stage. In most cases, victims are between the ages of 1 to 13, while being at least five years younger than the offender. Pedophiles are more likely to be socially awkward, shy, and timid toward adults. They usually feel more comfortable when consorting with children and prefer them as both social and sexual objects. Sexual contact does not transpire until the pedophile and the child become familiarized with one another. Fixated pedophiles do not utilize aggression in order to manipulate their victims and largely focus on caressing and fondling in comparison to actual sexual intercourse.

Regressed pedophiles may not be mainly interested in children whatsoever. This type of offender's interest in children is often triggered by rejection or humiliation by a peer. Their sense of inadequacy concerning finding a partner psychosexually equal to their caliber leads them to target children as a sexual partner. They regress to an earlier developmental stage to feel sexually comfortable with the child victim. They usually prefer female targets who live a lengthy distance from them to pursue intercourse with.

Exploitative pedophiles take advantage of a child's developmental vulnerabilities to receive sexual pleasure. They are less worried about the child as an individual and are wholly motivated by a craving for sexual dominance. This type of pedophile is more likely to molest strangers and is willing to utilize physical aggression and force. Due to their deep-seated impulsive nature, they are more likely to have a prior criminal record.

The infliction of pain and application of violence in order to become sexually aroused is a staple of the *sadistic pedophile*. They usually have an extensive history of violence that began in their early adolescent years. They may prefer same-sex relationships and are largely responsible for abductions and murders of children.

Hickey (2006) has provided a helpful analysis of the work of Cohen, Seghorn, and Calmas, (1969) in describing and classifying child molesters and pedophiles. According to these researchers, child molesters exist in three subtypes: fixated, regressed, and aggressive. Groth (1979) also described child sexual abusers as "fixated" and "regressed." Fixated

offenders prefer the company of children and seek them out. They often assault children they know. Regressed molesters have some adult sexual interest, but because of feelings of inadequacy, they resort to children. "The aggressive type of molester is sadistic and prefers children they do not know, especially boys" (Hickey, 2006, p. 6). Some pedophiles and child molesters are fixated on children as their sole sexual interest, and some prefer boy victims, others prefer girl victims, and some sex offenders will assault both boys and girls (and often within certain specific age ranges). Other child molesters are "opportunistic" in that they prefer adult sexual relationships, but will sexually assault children if adults are unavailable, or if the opportunity presents itself. Men who are opportunistic child molesters will sexually assault children often when they are under the influence of some substance (alcohol or other drugs), and experiencing stress.

Other researchers suggest that, while no single child molester "profile" exists, and that sex offenders take many "pathways" toward sexually offending with children, there are certain characteristics common in certain groups of offenders that are helpful in understanding the underlying causes, characteristics, and circumstances of offenders and the offences that they commit. Prentky, Knight, and Lee (2012) consider six characteristics of child molesters. The first characteristic considers how sexually focused the child molester is on children in "two separate components. The first is the intensity of pedophilic interest, i.e. the degree to which offenders are focused or 'fixated' on children as sexual objects. The second component involves the exclusivity of their preference for children as sex objects" (Prentky, et al., 2012, p. 107).

The second characteristic concerns the "varying degrees of physiological arousal" to children that the child molester experiences. "Offenders with strong pedophilic interest show more sexual arousal to depictions of children than their low-fixated counterparts (Prentky, et al., 2012, p. 108). Opportunistic and incest offenders would fall into the latter category, while fixated pedophiles would fall into the former.

Prentky, Knight, and Lee's third characteristic of child molesters refers to the "victimization of offenders as children." And they suggest, "some support exists for the notion that child molestation may be related to an offender's restaging or recapitulation of his own sexual victimization" (Prentky, et al., 2012, p. 108). Although not all victims of childhood sexual abuse will go on to molest children in adolescence and adulthood, children who come from homes where other forms of abuse are present (physical and emotional abuse and neglect), and an absence of prosocial adult nurturance and care, as well as other risks for family dysfunction, may see a degree of positive correlation to sexually offending with children when these victims reach adolescence and adulthood.

The fourth characteristic of child molesters refers to their social competence. "A variety of studies have documented the inadequate social and interpersonal skills, under-assertiveness, and poor self-esteem that, in varying degrees, characterize individual offenders" (p. 108). While social competence deficits alone will not be predictive of an offender's likelihood of sexually molesting children, this variable should be considered within the spectrum of other criteria commonly observed in child molesters.

These authors describe a fifth characteristic that research has shown is common in the behavioral history of child molesters is their impulsive, antisocial personality. For example, children with serious, protracted, and pronounced behavioral control issues at home or in school who might be diagnosed with conduct disorder and later, as adults, with antisocial personality disorder, exhibit the types of impulsive, antisocial, harmful, narcissistic, and aggressive behaviors that many child molesters engage in while assaulting their victims. "A history of impulsive, antisocial behavior is a well-documented risk factor

associated with some child molesters" (Prentky, et al., 2012, p. 108).

The sixth and final set of characteristics that Prentky, Knight, and Lee consider consists of developmental influences. One developmental factor in particular according to these authors is *caregiver inconstancy*. "Caregiver inconstancy, a powerful predictor of the degree of sexual violence expressed in adulthood, interferes with the development of long-term supportive relationships, increasing the likelihood of an attachment disorder" (Prentky, et al., 2012, p. 109). Thus children who are shuffled from one adult caregiver to another "may lead to interpersonal deficits that severely undermine development of secure adult relationships" (Prentky, et al., 2012, p. 109). For some of these children, their adolescence and adulthood may see them prefer the company of children to adults, with the concomitant danger of sexual contact.

Finkelhor's (1979) classic analysis of sexually victimized children provides a description of the diversity of child molesters that has currency in the second decade of the twenty-first century. He does urge caution and characterizes his descriptions as "generalizations," but they are nonetheless illustrative and useful. He observed that "[o]nly a minority of incarcerated child molesters (25 to 33 percent) have a primary and relatively permanent interest in children...The rest become involved for what seem more transient reasons: an unusual opportunity, stress, the frustration of other sexual outlets" (Finkelhor, 2005, p. 44). This is consistent with the observations of Groth (1979), Prentky, Knight, and Lee (2012), Hickey (2006), and others have reported regarding pedophiles and child molesters.

Finkelhor further suggested that "sexual involvement with children has very different motivational roots in different men." For some offenders the assault constitutes an act of sexual gratification; for others it satisfies the need for closeness; for other men it satisfies an aggressive urge or impulse (Finkelhor, 2005,

p. 44). Finkelhor also viewed "sexual interest in children, particularly on an enduring basis, (as) connected to a fear of adults and adult sexuality. Children are often attractive to such men because they are naïve, undemanding, and do not have adult physical characteristics" (2005, p. 44). He further describes the motivations of different men seeking sexual contact with children that "depend a great deal on the age of the offender, the age of the child, and the activity involved. Men who are sexually interested in very young children differ from those interested in older ones" (Finkelhor, 2005, p. 44). That "alcohol shows a consistent connection with patterns of sexual abuse of children" does not, according to Finkelhor, mean that alcohol "causes or releases a sexual interest in children," but that its use is often present during acts of child sexual abuse.

FEMALE SEX OFFENDERS

Although a considerable body of empirical research has been conducted on the various typologies of male sex offenders, the research conducted on the typologies and etiology of female sex offenders is relatively scant. Vandiver and Kircher (2004) studied 471 female sex offenders in Texas who they examined through a mandatory sex-registration database. Thus their research overcame limitations to earlier research of female sex

---

Box 12.1 SHOULD JUVENILES HAVE TO REGISTER AS SEX OFFENDERS? *CONNECTICUT DEPARTMENT OF PUBLIC SAFETY V. DOE,* 538 U.S. 1 (2003)

The Sex Offender Act of 1994 requires those convicted of sex crimes to register their address with local law enforcement. Locally, sex-offender registration, informally known as Megan's Law, serves to notify the community of sex offenders living nearby and provides a tracking mechanism for law enforcement. Studies of Megan's Law have found no effect on community safety, or rearrest rates for offenders.

In 2003, John Doe, a sex offender having served his prison term, challenged the Connecticut version of Megan's Law. Doe argued that since the site did not communicate that he was a low-risk offender, publicly posting his photo and address would violate his Fourteenth Amendment right to due process. The Connecticut District Court agreed with him, as did the Court of Appeals, stating that Doe was not provided with a hearing prior to the public disclosure of his status. In a unanimous opinion, the U.S. Supreme Court reversed the lower court's decision, ruling that the law served to protect the public. They found that even if the person's reputation is harmed, defamation in itself is not a violation of liberty.

1. Should juveniles be required to register as sex offenders even though court proceedings against them are typically not open to the public?
2. Should individuals convicted of non-contact sex crimes like indecent exposure and stalking be required to register as sex offenders?
3. Should individuals convicted in "enticement sting" operations (where police pose as underage minors on the internet) be required to register as sex offenders?

offenders that suffered from low sample size (usually fewer than 20 subjects) and being restricted to prison inmates (where only the most egregious and atypical offenders are likely to be studied). Vandiver and Kircher's analysis led to their identification of six different "clusters" of sex offenders: "Heterosexual nurturers" comprised the majority of the offenders studied (n = 146). "This group victimized only male victims. The average age was 12. This type of sexual offender is comparable to many of the female sexual offenders who have caught the attention of the media" (Vandiver & Kircher, 2004, p. 130). The "nurturer" group are teachers and "other females who are in a mentorship or care taking role" with their victims (Vandiver & Kircher, 2004, p. 131). Box 12.2 summarizes some high-profile cases involving "nurturer" female sex offenders.

Vandiver and Kircher's second cluster of female sex offenders were "noncriminal homosexual offenders" whose "average age was 32 at the time of arrest for the offense that led to their registration. Most (96%) of the victims were female, with an average age of 13, the second highest average victim age" (Vandiver & Kircher, 2004, p. 131). The offenders in this group (n = 114) "were the least likely to have subsequent arrests after their target offense, the lowest average number of arrests, and were the least likely to commit sexual assault" (Vandiver & Kircher, 2004, p. 131).

The third cluster of female sex offenders was called "female sexual predators" (n = 112) whose "average age was 29. Most (60%) of the victims were male and had an average age of 11. This offender has similar characteristics to other female criminals and her sexual offending may be part of her criminal disposition" (Vandiver & Kircher, 2004, p. 131). These offenders were more likely than other offenders to have a lengthy and

---

BOX 12.2 FEMALE SEX OFFENDERS: TEACHERS HAVING SEXUAL RELATIONSHIPS WITH UNDERAGE STUDENTS

- 2014: Kathryn Murray, 30, middle-school teacher in Houston, TX, had sex with 15-year-old male student, one year in jail, register as sex offender
- 2011: Brittni Colleps, 28, married with three children, high-school teacher near Forth Worth, TX, had group sex with four male students, as well as a fifth, five years in prison
- 2011: Stacy Schuler, 33, high-school teacher in Ohio, had sex with five students, four years in prison, not guilty by reason of insanity defense
- 2004: Debra LaFave, 25, Tampa, FL, middle-school teacher, had sex with 14-year-old student, bipolar disorder, three years house arrest and required to register as sex offender
- 2005: Pamela Rogers, 28, McMinnville, TN, elementary-school teacher, had sex with teenage boy, seven years in prison, claimed "sex addiction"
- 2008: Stephanie Ragusa, 31, Tampa, FL, middle-school teacher, had sex with 14- and 16-year-old boys, ten years in prison
- 2010: Kristen Sullivan, 25, Lauderhill, FL, middle-school teacher, had sex with 14-year-old boy, three years in prison but does not have to register as sex offender
- 1996: Mary Kay Letourneau, 34, Burien, WA, elementary-school teacher, had sex with 12-year-old who she married when he turned 21 and had two daughters with, eight years in prison

varied criminal history and to be rearrested again after their sexual assault arrest.

Vandiver and Kircher's fourth cluster were called "young adult child exploiters" (*n* = 50). These were the youngest group on average at the time of their offense and had the fewest number of overall arrests compared to the other groups. "Their victims were also likely to be young, with an average age of 7. One-half of the victims were related to the offender. Thus, this group is made up of young adult offenders who prey on young (male or female) victims" (Vandiver & Kircher, 2004, p. 132). Mothers who molest their own children would be appropriately classified in this cluster.

A fifth cluster of female sex offenders identified by Vandiver and Kircher (2004) was "homosexual criminals" (*n* = 22) and these offenders had, at ten, the highest average number of arrests. Most of their victims were

> female adults with an average age of 32. None of the offenders in this category were arrested for sexual assault; instead, their crimes included indecency with a child and a high proportion of "forcing behavior" including sexual performance of a child and compelling prostitution. For at least a portion of these offenders, the motivation appears to be more economical than sexual based.
>
> (Vandiver & Kircher, 2004, p. 132)

Vandiver and Kircher's sixth cluster they called "aggressive homosexual offenders" and these offenders comprised the smallest group in the study (*n* = 17). Offenders in this group committed sexual assaults upon adult victims who were usually female.

Earlier researchers established female sex-offender typologies that were based on the relationship between victim and offender. Faller, in a 1987 Michigan study, identified "poly-incestuous abuse," "single-parent abuse," "psychotic abusers," "adolescent perpetrators," and "noncustodial abusers" as typologies of female sex offenders based on their custodial relationships with their victims (Faller, 1987,

p. 266–268). Noncustodial abusers were mothers who did not have custody of their children but who sexually abused them during unsupervised visits. Polyincestuous abuse exists in families with multiple victims and multiple perpetrators, both male and female, such as mothers who sexually abuse their children with stepfathers and boyfriends.

According to Faller, female sex offenders engage in the following types of sexual abuse with their victims: "fondling, oral sex, digital (penetration), intercourse, group sex, exploitation (women allowing others to use the victim sexually), pictures (taking pornographic pictures of children or causing them to be taken), made kids watch sex, made kids have sex" (Faller, 1987, p. 268).

Vandiver's later (2006) research on the presence of co-offenders during females' commission of sexual assaults provides further insight into the nature of female sex offending. She found that while over 91% of female sex offenders used no weapon during the commission of their crimes (Vandiver, 2006, p. 346), almost "half (46%) of female sex offenders arrested in 2001 for a sex offense had co-offenders; thus, a substantial portion of female sex offenders are not acting alone (Vandiver, 2006, p. 350).

Cyber Offenders

Sex offenders who use the internet to facilitate the commission of sex-related crimes are becoming more commonly referred to as *cyber offenders*, a specific type of cyber-criminal who uses technology, social networking, and the anonymity of the Internet in the furtherance of the identification, solicitation, surveillance, targeting, and exploitation of victims. Babchishin, Hanson and Hermann (2015) identified a typology of online sex offenders according to how these offenders use the Internet to commit sex offenses. They include

> those who (a) access child pornography out of curiosity or impulse, without specific sexual

interest in children; (b) access child pornography to satisfy sexual fantasies, but do not commit contact offenses; (c) create and distribute child pornography solely for financial gain; and, lastly (d) use the Internet to facilitate contact offenses.

(2015, p. 171)

Babchishin and colleagues' (2015) meta-analysis on cyber offenders found that, compared with "offline" sex offenders, online offenders were likely to be younger, more likely to be Caucasian, less likely to report having a history of physical abuse, more likely to have empathy for victims, more likely to be sexually deviant, and less likely to be emotionally identified with children (pp. 172–175). Compared with normative groups (non sex offenders), these authors found that cyber offenders "reported significantly more physical and sexual abuse than males in the general population [and] . . . were more likely to have never been married and to be unmarried at the time of assessment" (p. 176). The meta-analysis also demonstrated that cyber offenders had no significant differences in level of education than the general male population, but "they were twice as likely to be unemployed" (p. 176). Finally, "the rate of criminal involvement was low among online sexual offenders . . . only 12% of the online offenders had prior offenses for nonsexual crimes" (p. 179).

Tomak, Weschler, Ghahramanlou-Holloway, Virden, and Nademin's (2009) study on the personality characteristics of cyber offenders found that "individuals arrested for internet sexual offenses appear to be different from other offenders who have been incarcerated for a contact sexual offense, in that they appear less deviant, less physically aggressive and less impulsive" (p. 145). These researchers observed that:

the internet has become another mechanism for the commitment of sexual crimes, allowing offenders to build networks and resources to promote victimization, the exchange of child pornography and instruction on how to lure victims, all masked by anonymity. In essence, the internet allows a way for predators to perfect their craft and test personal skills while avoiding detection. The abundance of child pornography on the internet is of particular concern due to its likelihood to fuel fantasy, which could in effect exacerbate offending behaviour and accelerate the offence cycle.

(Tomak, et al., 2009, p. 146)

Juvenile Sex Offenders

According to the U.S. Department of Justice's Office of Juvenile Justice and Delinquency Prevention (U.S. Department of Justice, 2009), juveniles account for 35.6% of sexual assaults committed against children. These juveniles are more likely to offend in schools (11.9%) than adult sex offenders (1.6%), and are likely to have more male victims (24.7%) than their adult counterparts (13.4%). Sexual assaults committed by juveniles usually occur in the home (68.8%) or at school (11.9%). Sixty-three percent of their victims are acquaintances and 25% are family members. Female juveniles account for 7.3% of all juvenile sex offenders. The OJJDP also reported that 49.4% of juvenile sex offenses involved fondling and that 24% involved a rape. Other sex offenses committed by juveniles were: sex assaults using an object (4.7%), sodomy (12.5%), and other nonforcible sex offenses (9.5%). Sexual assaults reported to authorities involving juvenile offenders resulted in arrest 30.5% of the time as opposed to 34.1% for adult sex offenders (U.S. Department of Justice, 2009).

Bartol and Bartol (2015) have observed that juvenile sex offenders have social deficits that include "inadequate interpersonal skills, poor peer relationships, and social isolation" (p. 315). Juvenile sex offenders also "engage in a wide range of nonsexual criminal and antisocial behavior. They tend to shoplift, steal, set fires, bully, assault others (including adults), and are often cruel to animals" (p. 315).

In research on juvenile sex offenders whose victims are prepubescent children (as opposed to pubescent females), Hunter, Figuerdo, Malamuth, and Becker (2003) established a dichotomy in offender typology and found that these offenders

> were less aggressive in their sexual offending, and more likely to offend against victims to whom they were related. This group of juvenile sex offenders was also less likely to be under the influence of drugs or alcohol at the time of the sexual offense or to use a weapon.
>
> (p. 43)

These authors also report deficits in social and psychological functioning in juvenile sex offenders who offend with young children. They suggest that these juvenile sex offenders have needs for intimacy that are not being fulfilled and suffer from "a lack of social confidence, and concomitant depression, anxiety, and pessimism. Associated with a sense of social isolation are feelings of sadness and loneliness, an acknowledged dependency on adults, and a preference for the company of younger children" (Hunter, et al., 2003, p. 42).

TREATMENT OF SEX OFFENDERS

Recall from Chapter 10 that President George W. Bush signed the Adam Walsh Child Protection and Safety Act in 2006. This Act devised three levels of sex offenders who represent the increasing risk of dangerousness and re-offense:

- Level 1 offenders must annually update their address during their first 15 years of registration.
- Level 2 offenders are required to update their address every six months of their 25 years of registration.

- Level 3 offenders update their address every 90 days during their lifetime registration.

Thus, the Adam Walsh Act provides the country with a national registry requirement with a felony charge upon failure to register.

Risk-Need-Responsivity (RNR)

One of the more widespread treatment paradigms for sex offenders, developed in 1990 by Andrews, Bonta, and Hoge, is called the "**risk-need-responsivity**" (RNR) model. RNR treatment is based on an articulation of three criteria:

1. Risk principle—match level of program intensity to offender risk level; intensive levels of treatment for higher-risk offenders and minimal intervention for low-risk offenders.
2. Need principle—target criminogenic needs or those offender needs that are functionally related to criminal behavior.
3. Responsivity principle—match the style and mode of intervention to the offender's learning style and abilities.

(Andrews, Bonta, & Wormith, 2011, p. 735)

A more expanded version of RNR emphasized "overarching principles" governing the delivery of treatment in a human service framework that demonstrated respect for the dignity of the individual, using an established theoretical framework, in strategies that sought a reduction in criminogenic behavior and recidivism. This later version also endorsed more specifically the means for conducting assessments and delivering treatment in a community-based setting that would lead to more successful interventions and fewer treatment failures (Andrews, et al., 2011, p. 738).

In targeting high-risk and moderate-risk offenders, RNR proposes that treatment provide prosocial alternatives to criminogenic behavior, such as sexual offending, that are more rewarding for the offender than the commission of crime. RNR treatment sees that criminal activity will decrease "with (a) the density of the rewards for noncriminal alternatives, (b) the density of the costs for crime, (c) decreases in the density of costs for noncriminal alternatives, (d) decreases in the density of the rewards for crime" (Andrews, et al., 2011, p. 744). RNR strategies tailor treatment to the individual offender's personality, history, and abilities using a "general personality and cognitive social learning (GPCSL) theoretical perspective" (Andrews, et al., 2011, p. 739). The ultimate goal of RNR treatment is desistance from criminogenic behavior through individualized therapeutic care that recognizes the offender's needs; these are needs that have been met through and are related to sex offending. Desistance will occur when the offender learns to privilege, endorse, and act upon a prosocial worldview and prosocial behaviors in ways that had, in his prior criminogenic life, supported a procriminal worldview and procriminal behaviors.

Relapse Prevention (RP)

Relapse prevention (RP) is a cognitive behavioral model for the treatment of sex offenders that is based on a treatment strategy for substance abuse. While RP used in the treatment of substance addiction defines "lapse" and "relapse" in terms of an occurrence of the reuse of a substance, such as smoking a cigarette or a taking a drink of alcohol, that may lead to a full-blown return to the addictive behavior ("relapse"), in using RP as a treatment model for sex offenders "the terms 'lapse' and 'relapse' have been re-defined to account for the differences between addictive behaviors and sexual offending; specifically, to account for the more harmful and victimizing nature of sexual offenses" (Wheeler, George, & Marlatt, 2006, p. 245).

Consider that sexual offending is a "cycle" that begins with "an offenders' progression

from a triggering event (typically a negative affective state), to engaging in deviant sexual fantasies (as a maladaptive coping response), to committing a sexual offense" (Wheeler, et al., 2006). In the treatment of sex offenders using RP, the goal is to prevent harm to potential victims, so the term "lapse" must refer to an event for the sex offender that occurs prior to an offense that harms a victim, and something from which the sex offender learns effective coping strategies in order to avoid a "relapse," that is, a new sex offense that harms yet another victim. According to Wheeler and colleagues: "Within the RP model, when an individual experiences a lapse, this lapse could be used as a constructive learning experience to help the individual develop better techniques for preventing future lapses" (2006, p. 239).

Since the mid-1980s, relapse prevention has been a widely used strategy for the treatment of sex offenders in North America and it embraces a "harm reduction" strategy toward potential victims. Lapses in RP are events that may have led the sex offender in the past to commit a sexual offense, "such as having a willful deviant sexual fantasy or "cruising" for victims" (Wheeler, et al., 2006, p. 239). Within the RP treatment model, a new sexual offense is a relapse.

RP is predicated on an understanding of the "abstinence violation effect" (AVE), "a key cognitive/emotional event in the relapse cycle; it is hypothesized to occur following a relapse" (Wheeler, et al., 2006, p. 235). This is the individual's reaction to the realization that he has violated a rule that he set for himself and the accompanying response to the rule breaking. The AVE can determine whether a full relapse will occur or whether the lapse can be seen as a learning experience and the redoubling of positive efforts to avoid future lapses.

As regards to the efficacy of the RP treatment model, Wheeler and colleagues suggest that: "Further analysis and additional research must be conducted on the sexual offense cycle and the particular role of the Abstinence Violation Effect, in order to accurately understand the experiences of sexual offenders and to develop more accurate approaches to their treatment" (2006, p. 245).

Strength-Based Therapy

Marshall and Marshall (2012) are roundly critical of the relapse prevention model of treatment and its emphasis on avoidance and on the negative aspects of the behavior of those with a history demonstrative of an inability to "avoid" criminal behavior. They cite the scant evidence of empirical support in the literature for RP and instead advocate for "strength-based" models of sex-offender treatment. Marshall and Marshall are supportive of the RNR treatment articulated by Andrews and colleagues as well as the **"Good Lives Model"** (GLM) proposed by Ward (2002) and the "positive psychology" approach suggested by Seligman (2002).

GLM

The GLM is based on identifying the need for human fulfillment "in several domains of functioning." Ward identifies nine such domains: "(1) optimal mental, physical, and sexual health; (2) knowledge; (3) mastery in work and play; (4) autonomy; (5) inner peace; (6) relatedness; (7) creativity; (8) spirituality; and (9) happiness" (Marshall & Marshall, 2012, p. 55). Sex offenders possess maladaptive strategies for meeting their needs for human fulfillment, and "[p]roviding them with sensible goals (i.e., the issues involved in the nine domains identified above) and the skills and plans necessary to meet these goals, will, therefore, constitute effective treatment" (p. 55). The GLM treatment model "encourages a more optimistic and positive therapeutic approach that emphasizes the development of strengths rather than focusing on deficits as do programs based on the Relapse Prevention model" (p. 55).

Positive Psychology

Positive psychology is another "strength-based" model of sex-offender treatment and this approach emphasizes building upon the strengths that the client possesses and in developing the positive skills necessary to confront problems and deficits that have caused the offender to engage in criminogenic behaviors. While not ignoring past problems or justifying sexual offending, positive psychology "equips clients with the skills necessary to fulfill their potential while at the same time not neglecting efforts to ameliorate the problems they have" (Marshall & Marshall, 2012, p. 55). Positive psychology stresses "building the skills, self-confidence, and attitudes essential to functioning effectively in relationships, necessarily allows the sexual offender to overcome deficiencies in intimacy and thereby reduce loneliness; both of which are criminogenic factors" (p. 55).

Biologically Based Treatments

Biologically or organically based treatments for sex offenders fall into two main categories: surgical and pharmacological. Surgical treatment for sex offenders include surgical castration, brain surgery, and estrogen implants. Of these three surgical approaches, only castration, "bilateral scrotal orchiectomy," is practiced in the United States (Greenfield, 2006, p. 437). The practice of surgical castration as part of the adjudication process for male sex offenders is extremely rare, however, and is typically considered by a court as part of a plea agreement where a defendant convicted of a sex crime agrees to the procedure in order for a reduction in his prison sentence. There are obvious ethical considerations with surgical castration procedures that may violate the Eighth Amendment as well as medical concerns implicated in irreversible and medically unnecessary surgeries. There are also concerns with the inherently coercive nature in which these juridical "agreements" take place.

Greenfield describes three different pharmacological approaches to the treatment of sex offenders: the two primary means utilize hormonal agents and psychotropic agents. A third option utilizes anti-epileptic drugs that are anti-seizure and anti-convulsant medications in an experimental treatment not in widespread practice. Hormonal agents are anti-androgenic drugs that act to reduce male hormone production, such as testosterone. Psychotropic agents treat male aggressive hypersexuality through the use of selective serotonin reuptake inhibitors (SSRIs) that are often used to treat depression. Medications that are anti-anxiety, anti-psychotic, and mood stabilizing are also used to treat sex offenders. Sex offenders who have diagnosed mental disorders such as pedophilic disorder often have anxiety, mood, and substance abuse disorders, so psychotropic medications, in combination with other therapeutic treatments, may be indicated for those sex offenders with co-occurring conditions (Greenfield, 2006).

As for the overall efficacy of this treatment approach, Greenfield (2006) argues

> that organic treatment alone for paraphilics and sex offenders is not enough. Such treatment should be combined with psychotherapeutic/behavioral approaches as well, in a comprehensive model addressing individual, victim, societal, legal, and other needs in a multidisciplinary context, including individual, group, family, and community venues, with both psychotherapeutic/behavioral and organic components.
>
> (p. 450)

Cognitive Behavioral Therapy (CBT)

Cognitive behavioral therapy (CBT) is one treatment paradigm that has shown promise over the last 30 or so years as an effective means of treating sex offenders and those diagnosed with paraphilic disorders. CBT interrogates offenders' interpretations of benign social cues as having sexual overtones and invitations and re-educates offenders in appropriate understandings of and expectations in socially acceptable behaviors. "The principle treatment approach of behavior therapy for paraphilias is to eliminate the pattern of sexual arousal to deviant fantasy by assisting the patient with decreasing inappropriate sexual arousal" (Kaplan & Krueger, 2012, p. 292).

Therapeutic techniques such as *covert sensitization*, *satiation*, and *systematic desensitization* are used to decrease inappropriate sexual arousal in sex offenders and paraphilics (Kaplan & Krueger, 2012). *Covert sensitization* "pairs urges and feelings that lead an individual to engage in a deviant act with aversive images which reflect the adverse consequences of continuing with the deviant behavior" (p. 292). *Satiation* is another therapeutic strategy that aims to make deviant sexual fantasies uninteresting and non-arousing for the sex offender: "Masturbatory satiation is a technique that is effective in decreasing deviant sexual arousal by making the deviant fantasy boring" (p. 292). *Systematic desensitization* "is a technique that aims at the decrease of maladaptive anxiety by pairing relaxation with imagined scenes depicting anxiety-producing situations" (p. 292).

These techniques, coupled with strategies designed "to assist the patient with enhancing sexual interest in and arousal to adult partners" (Kaplan & Krueger, 2012, p. 292) attempt to divert the paraphiliac or sex offender away from atypical and inappropriate sexual fantasies and toward more typical sexual fantasies and activities involving adults.

Kaplan and Kreuger (2012) describe some of the most commonly used cognitive-behavioral treatment strategies thus:

1. Cognitive Restructuring: Most individuals who engage in atypical sexual behaviors have developed permission-giving statements or rationalizations and hold irrational beliefs regarding their fantasies and behaviors. An example of such a distortion is "Having sex

with a child is a good way for an adult to teach the child about sex."

2. Assertive Skills Training: Some paraphiliacs are unable to express positive or negative feelings, state what they want, or ask others to change their behavior. Some are passive or aggressive. Techniques used include: modeling, rehearsal, and social feedback.

3. Social Skills Training/Intimacy Deficits: Some paraphiliacs have deficits in establishing effective communication with adult partners. An example would be inappropriate questions of others in initiating conversations. Role rehearsal is used to model appropriate interactions.

4. Sexual Education/Sexual Dysfunction Treatment: Some paraphiliacs lack knowledge of what is considered appropriate sexual behavior. Others have sexual problems that are in need of treatment, such as premature ejaculation or erectile dysfunction.

5. Empathy: Often sexual offenders have deficits in empathy for their victims and little sensitivity to what their victims have experienced. One component of therapy is enhancement of empathy.

(Kaplan & Krueger, 2012, p. 292)

Although one of the most commonly used treatment strategies for sex offenders, the effectiveness of CBT, like many of the sex-offender treatment therapies and approaches previously discussed, suffers from challenges and shortcomings in research conducted to evaluate their effectiveness in reducing recidivism, relapse, and harm to victims. Kaplan and Krueger's (2012) review of the literature and their meta-analysis revealed largely positive outcomes with result to research on the effectiveness of CBT, the data were far from being unequivocal. They report that, ultimately, "the evidence base for cognitive-behavioral treatment is extremely limited and empirical research focusing on effective treatment for this population is critically needed" (Kaplan & Krueger, 2012, p. 295).

Cognitive-behavioral treatment remains the model of sex-offender treatment most commonly utilized in the second decade of the twenty-first century. According to Yates (2013) and other researchers, CBT is "the most widely accepted and empirically supported model of sex offender treatment with respect to the reduction of recidivism" (p. 90). The success of CBT in reducing risk for re-offense lies in targeting "dynamic risk factors known to be linked to risk for re-offending" where "sexual offending is conceptualized as behavioral and cognitive patterns that are developed and maintained as a result of modeling, observational learning, and reinforcement of behavior, attitudes, and cognition" (Yates, 2013, p. 90).

Yates observed that components of CBT that target empathy for victims and taking responsibility for behavior have received scant empirical validation and should be questioned as targets for treatment. She suggests that CBT treatment that targets identification and alteration of an offender's *schema* shows promise in improving CBT. Schemas are based on an offender's "previous experiences, contain attitudes, beliefs, assumptions about self, the world, and others, and provoke affective and behavioral responses" (Yates, 2013, p. 91). Yates contends that "among sexual offenders, specific schema, such as sexual entitlement, a general view that the world is a hostile place, or the belief that children can consent to sexual activity, have been found to have been implicated in sexual offending" (p. 91). CBT treatments that endorse and support the rehearsal and practice of behavioral and affective responses to relearned and newly acquired schema show the most promise in continuing to reduce risk for a sexual re-offense.

Jennings and Deming (2013) offer specific enhancements to CBT to enhance treatment success and effectiveness in reducing risk for re-offense and recidivism. They suggest that the group sessions that form the core of CBT be conducted in ways that facilitate behavior change through "focusing greater attention on directly observable behaviors [through] expanding empirical awareness of events occurring in the group; streamlining interventions with non-verbal signals; [and] targeted reinforcement of social interaction and bonding" (Jennings & Deming, 2013, p. 7). Jennings and Deming believed that CBT strategies that privileged verbal communication at the expense of nonverbal communication and group and individual behavior limited the potential for CBT to achieve significant changes in behavior.

Heaton and Murphy (2013) reported that CBT was an effective long-term treatment for men with intellectual disabilities who were also sex offenders. Their research showed that men with autism spectrum disorders were more likely to engage in sexually abusive behaviors after undergoing CBT, and that many of these behaviors were not necessarily criminal, but worrisome nonetheless. Of the 34 men with intellectual disabilities who participated in the study, 11 engaged in sexually abusing behavior ranging from actual victim penetration to non-contact abuse such as verbal sexual harassment or indecent exposure. Only two of the men in the study went to court and received a conviction. Heaton and Murphy concluded that CBT, while not without certain limitations, was a viable treatment for men with intellectual disabilities who had a history of sexually offending.

Apsche, Evile, and Murphy (2004) conducted a study of male juvenile sex offenders in a residential treatment center and found that CBT was an effective treatment strategy for this population of sex offenders. The subjects of the study were adolescent males with diagnosed personality disorders and a history of failed treatment in prior settings. Through CBT treatment, subjects in the study "developed a sense of empathic responses to understand how their dysfunctional cognition is related to their sexual offending behavior" (Apsche, et al., 2004, p. 106).

In sum, CBT remains the most effective and viable means for treating sex offenders, although the treatment continues to require refinement, modification, and improvement, and the research supporting its efficacy is ongoing.

Prevalence of Mental Illness in Sex-Offender Populations

A small number of studies have investigated large-scale conglomerations of sex offenders for serious mental illnesses with Axis I characteristics as defined by the DSM-IV-TR (2002), such as psychotic and major mood disorders.[2] The majority of these studies (Becker, Stinson, Tromp, & Messer, 2003; Jackson & Richards, 2007; Lieb & Nelson, 2001; Vess, Murphy, & Arkowitz, 2004) have focused largely on sexually violent predator populations (SVPs). They identified mental illnesses such as high levels of pathology that may be characterized as substance abuse disorders, personality disorders (usually antisocial personality disorder), paraphilia, and dysthymia.

However, the prevalence of mental disorder in sex offenders also reaches even civilly committed offenders. Jackson and Richards (2007) discovered that almost one-quarter of their sample suffered from a serious mental illness, such as schizoaffective disorder or schizophrenia. Most of their subjects (civilly committed offenders in Washington) were diagnosed with both a paraphilia and a personality disorder. Vess and colleagues (2004) identified approximately 10% of their SVP sample had been diagnosed with schizoaffective disorder, schizophrenia, major depression, or bipolar disorder. A study by Lieb and Nelson (2001) found that about 20% of their sample of 42 SVPs had a major mood or psychotic disorder.

Multiple samples of sex offenders receiving residential or inpatient treatment were identified as having moderate to high levels of major mental disorders. Alish and colleagues (2007) detected a relatively low rate of sex crimes among individuals with schizophrenia in particular. Those with severe mental illnesses who committed sexual offenses were usually higher functioning than a regular population of mentally ill individuals. Kafka and Hennen (2002) found that 72% of their 120 subjects (sex offenders referred for outpatient treatment for a paraphilia) were diagnosed with mood disorders and 4% had psychotic disorders.

Records of 245 sex offenders undergoing inpatient psychiatric care were examined by Stinson and Becker (2011). The findings concluded that 67% suffered from psychotic disorders, 60% from mood disorders, 14% from anxiety disorders, and 14% from attention deficit hyperactivity disorder (ADHD) or impulse regulation disorders. It is important to note that some inpatients had multiple diagnoses. The researchers also discovered that their participants were likely to be low functioning due to their higher rate of unemployment, never being married, and of having prior offenses.

A 1991 Bureau of Justice survey of 1,273 sex offenders incarcerated in state institutions, representing 9% of overall incarcerated offenders, was assessed by Peugh and Belenko (2001). The participants engaged in confidential interviews concerning demographic and behavioral characteristics. Fifteen percent of sex offenders self-reported prior treatment for mental health complications.

Långström, Sjöstedt, and Grann (2004) conducted a large study in Sweden that analyzed the prevalence of neurological and psychiatric disorders and their correlation with re-offense. They found that approximately 14% of the 1,215 sexual offenders who were released from prison between 1993 and 1997 had been diagnosed with a psychiatric disorder up to ten years before committing their index offense. These results are similar to that of Peugh and Belenko's (2001) study. However, Långström and colleagues (2004) com-

mented that their percentage is low most likely because of the fact that sex offenders who suffer from mental illnesses are usually hospitalized instead of imprisoned for their crimes.

Fazel, Sjöstedt, Långström, and Grann (2007) compared the total number of sexual offenders in Sweden (8,495) to a randomly selected sample of males from a control population (19,935). Their findings stated that sex offenders were six times more likely to have a history of hospitalization due to psychiatric issues than the general population. Furthermore, they concluded that people with an extensive history of psychiatric hospitalization committed 20% of all sexual offenses in Sweden.

Mental Illness and Possible Predisposition of Offenders

A national survey of inmates in state and federal correctional facilities in 1997 (a total of 17,248) was utilized by Silver, Felson, and Vaneseltine (2008) in order to evaluate the possibly causal effect mental illness had on violence or type of offense. They hypothesized that the offenders with mental illnesses and disordered thought processes would be more likely to commit a deviant crime. It was expected that sex offenders would be more likely to suffer from a mental health complication than other offenders because sex crimes are viewed as more socially deviant than physical assault. These researchers also had to control for gender, race, and socioeconomic status (SES) due to the fact that men, minorities, and those with lower SES are less likely to receive treatment for mental health issues than women, yet are more likely to commit violent offenses.

While controlling for a vast range of factors (i.e., prior aggressive violence and sexual offenses), Silver and colleagues (2008) found that offenders with mental disorders are more likely to commit sexual offenses rather than other sorts of crimes, such as property or drug offenses. Silver and colleagues deduced that the evidence they collected suggests that mental illness is a causal component of deviant behavior. The more deviant the behavior is, the greater the effect of the offender's mental illness.

Långström and colleagues (2004) identified a longitudinal association between suffering from a psychiatric disorder and sexual re-offending, all the while controlling for potentially discomfiting factors, that is, age, being single, and minority race/ethnicity. Stinson, Robbins, and Crow (2011) assessed a sex-offender population in a forensic psychiatric hospital. They examined self-control deficiencies and their relationship to sexual offending. The state of extreme moods, such as depression and bipolar disorder, was defined as *emotional dysregulation*.

The distorted beliefs, disorganized thought processes, and deficits in problem solving in abstract thinking are defined as *cognitive dysregulation*. This is often found in psychotic disorders such as schizoaffective disorder and schizophrenia. Stinson, Robbins, and Crow (2011) concluded that both emotional and cognitive dysregulations predict criminal behavior, although solely cognitive dysregulation predicted sexual behavior.

Risk Assessment

Hanson and Morton-Bourgon's 2009 study comparing the accuracy of the various means of predicting sex-offender recidivism rates observed that "no single measure has yet to establish itself as clearly more accurate than other, similar measures" (p. 10), yet nonetheless did offer support for the following instruments in evaluating risk for sex-offender recidivism as well as risk for re-offense with a crime of violence:

Static-99: Is a ten-item actuarial instrument used to assess risk for adult male sex offenders who are 18 years of age and older. It asks information regarding age, whether ever lived with a lover,

convictions for a sex offense, number of prior sex offenses, non-contact sex offenses, unrelated victims, stranger victims, and male victims. Assigning a numerical code to each variable leads to a calculation of risk for re-offense.

Static-2002/R: This is an expanded version of the Static—99 that asks 14 questions similar to those asked on the Static—99 but includes questions regarding deviant sexual interests, juvenile arrests for sex offending and general criminal activity.

MnSOST-3: The Minnesota Sex Offender Screening Tool Version 3 measures risk for sexual recidivism with a Microsoft Excel application using a predictive logistic regression model.

Risk Matrix 2000 Sex: This is an actuarial instrument used to assess risk for recidivism with a sexual offense asking questions regarding age, number of court appearances for sex crimes, for other crimes, sexual offenses against a male, against a stranger, whether single or married, any non-contact sex offenses, crimes of violence and burglaries.

SVR-20: The Sexual Violence Risk 20 is an instrument designed to assess an individual's risk for committing a crime of sexual violence.

Violence Risk Appraisal Guide (VRAG): This is an actuarial instrument designed to predict risk for violence and uses a 12-item scale that records demographic information as well as information on history of violence, alcohol use, and diagnosis of mental disorder.

SORAG: The Sex Offender Risk Appraisal Guide is a 14-item questionnaire and actuarial instrument that is substantively similar to the VRAG.

LSI-R: The Level of Service Inventory—Revised was developed by Andrews and Bonta and is a quantitative device measuring ten "scales" consisting of resources available to an offender that, when enumerated, assess the offender's likely success or failure in community re-entry and likelihood of recidivating.

CONCLUSION

Sex offenders and sexual assault remain an understandable and justifiable concern and a priority for criminal justice policymakers, practitioners, criminologists, legal and victim advocates, and the public at large. In the second decade of the twenty-first century, increased attention and concern has focused on the widespread incidence of sexual assault on college campuses as well as sexual assaults facilitated through the use of substances, licit and illicit, and through technology, particularly the Internet. Of cross-national urgency is the issue of human trafficking of women and girls, particularly for coerced work in the sex industry. Criminal justice advocates, researchers, students, and those working in the criminal justice professions will need to maintain vigilance, diligence, and awareness of sexual assault dynamics in order to minimize harm to victims while seeking effective sanction and treatment strategies for offenders.

FURTHER READING

Flora, R., & Keohane, M. L. (2013). *How to work with sex offenders: A handbook for criminal justice, human service, and mental health professionals.* New York, NY: Routledge.

National Criminal Justice Reference Service. (n.d.). *Special feature: Sex offenders—sex offense statistics.* Retrieved from https://www.ncjrs.gov/sexoffenders/statistics.html

Seto, M. C. (2013). *Internet sex offenders.* Washington, DC: American Psychological Association.

Stinson, J. D., & Becker, J. V. (2012). *Treating sex offenders: An evidence-based manual.* New York, NY: The Guilford Press.

Terry, K. J. (2012). *Sexual offenses and offenders: Theory, practice, and policy.* Belmont, CA: Cengage.

Wilcox, D. T., Garrett, T., & Harkins, L. (Eds.). (2014). *Sex offender treatment: A case study approach to issues and interventions.* Hoboken, NJ: Wiley-Blackwell.

GLOSSARY

Biologically or organically based treatments: Treatments for sex offenders that fall into two main categories: surgical and pharmacological. Surgical treatment for sex offenders include surgical castration, brain surgery, and estrogen implants. Pharmacological treatments are drug protocols that purport to inhibit deviant sexual fantasies and behaviors.

Cognitive behavioral therapy: A treatment and therapy strategy for sex offenders and paraphiliacs that uses techniques to de-emphasize atypical and deviant sexual arousal patterns and to emphasize normal adult sexual arousal patterns and adult sexual activity.

Exhibitionistic disorder: One of eight paraphilic disorders listed in the DSM-5. Exhibitionists and those with "Exhibitionistic Disorder" derive sexual satisfaction from exposing one's genitals to nonconsenting and unsuspecting persons (this is most often a male exposing his genitals to a female).

Frotteuristic disorder: One of eight paraphilic disorders listed in the DSM-5. Frotteurs seek and derive sexual gratification from touching or rubbing against an unsuspecting and nonconsenting person.

Good Lives Model: A treatment and therapy strategy for sex offenders. The GLM treatment model "encourages a more optimistic and positive therapeutic approach that emphasizes the development of strengths rather than focusing on deficits as do programs based on the Relapse Prevention model" (Marshall & Marshall, 2012, p. 55).

Paraphilia: The DSM-5 defines paraphilia as "intense and persistent sexual interest other than sexual interest in genital stimulation or preparatory fondling with phenotypically normal, physically mature, consenting human partners" (p. 685). The paraphilia becomes a paraphilic disorder when it causes severe levels of harm to oneself or to others, e.g., physical harm to a nonconsenting other person, or such marked levels of distress, preoccupation, anxiety, and fixation in the individual to cause significant impairment in normal functioning.

Pedophilic disorder: One of eight paraphilic disorders listed in the DSM-5. According to the DSM-5, those who experience "[o]ver a period of at least six months, recurrent, intense sexually arousing fantasies, sexual urges, or behaviors involving sexual activity with a prepubescent child (generally age 13 years or younger)" and that "the individual has acted on these sexual urges, or the sexual urges or fantasies cause marked distress or interpersonal difficulty" would meet the diagnostic criteria for pedophilic disorder if, in addition, "the individual is at least age 16 years and at least five years older than the child or children" who are the intended targets of the fantasies, urges, or activities (p. 697).

Relapse prevention (RP): A treatment and therapy strategy for sex offenders. In the treatment of sex offenders using RP, the goal is to prevent harm to potential victims, so the term "lapse" must refer to an event for the sex offender that occurs prior to an offense that harms a victim, and something from which the sex offender learns effective coping strategies in order to avoid a "relapse," i.e., a new sex offense that harms yet another victim.

Risk-need-responsivity (RNR): A treatment and therapy strategy for sex offenders. The ultimate goal of RNR treatment is desistance from criminogenic behavior through individualized therapeutic care that recognizes the offender's needs; these are needs that have been met through and are related to sex offending. RNR, in targeting high-risk and moderate-risk offenders, proposes that treatment provides prosocial alternatives to criminogenic behavior, such as sexual offending.

Sexual masochism: Sexual masochists are people who derive intense sexual satisfaction from the receipt of pain, humiliation, or suffering.

Sexual sadism disorder: One of eight paraphilic disorders listed in the DSM-5. Sexual sadists are men (and some women) who derive intense sexual satisfaction from inflicting physical or psychological suffering on another, nonconsenting person.

Voyeuristic disorder: One of eight paraphilic disorders listed in the DSM-5. Voyeurs typically spy on unsuspecting individuals in some form of undress and/or engaging in sexual activity in a setting where the victims have an expectation of privacy.

NOTES

1   Portions of this section of the chapter are taken from Fradella, H. F., & Brown, K. (2007). The effects of using social scientific rape typologies on juror decisions to convict. *Law and Psychology Review*, *31*, 1–19. Used with the gracious permission of *Law and Psychology Review*.

2   Because the DSM-5 is so new, there are few, if any, studies to report that use its revised diagnostic criteria. Thus, studies applying DSM-IV-TR criteria are reported here. Since the two editions of the DSM differ only slightly with regard to most major mental disorders previously classified on Axis I, studies of sex offenders that employed DSM-IV-TR criteria should still be valid and reliable guides to offenders under the newer edition of the DSM.

REFERENCES

11 DEL. LAWS c. 4, § 452 (2015).

Aggrawal, A. (2009). *Forensic and medico-legal aspects of sexual crimes and unusual sexual practices*. Boca Raton, FL: CRC Press.

Albin, R. S. (1977). Psychological studies of rape. *Signs*, *3*(2), 423–435.

Alish, Y., Birger, M., Manor, N., Kertzman, S., Zerzion, M., Kotler, M., & Strous, R. D. (2007). Schizophrenia sex offenders: A clinical and epidemiological comparison study. *International Journal of Law and Psychiatry*, *30*(6), 459–466.

American Psychiatric Association. (2000). *Diagnostic and statistical manual of mental disorders* (4th ed., text rev.). Washington, DC: American Psychiatric Publishing.

American Psychiatric Association. (2013). *Diagnostic and statistical manual of mental disorders* (5th ed.). Washington, DC: American Psychiatric Publishing.

Anderson, A. L., & Sample, L. L. (2008). Public awareness and action resulting from sex offender community notification laws. *Criminal Justice Policy Review*, *19*(4), 371–396.

Andrews, D. A., Bonta, J., & Hoge, R. D. (1990). Classification for effective rehabilitation: Rediscovering psychology. *Criminal Justice and Behavior*, *17*, 19–52.

Andrews, D., Bonta, J., & Wormith, J. (2011). The risk-need-responsivity (RNR) model: Does adding the good lives model contribute to effective crime prevention? *Criminal Justice and Behavior*, *38*, 735–755.

Apsche, J., Evile, M., & Murphy, C. (2004). The thought change system: An empirically based cognitive behavioral therapy for male juvenile sex offenders. *The Behavior Analyst Today*, *5*(1), 101–107.

Babchishin, K., Hanson, R., & Hermann, C. (2015). The characteristics of online sex offenders. In C. Bartol & A. Bartol (Eds.), *Current perspectives in forensic psychology and criminal behavior* (4th ed., pp. 171–186). Thousand Oaks, CA: Sage Publications.

Baker, D. J. (2009). The moral limits of consent as a defense in the criminal law. *New Criminal Law Review*, *12*, 93–121.

Barbaree, H. E., Seto, M. C., Serin, R. C., Amos, N. L., & Preston, D. L. (1994). Comparisons between sexual and nonsexual rapist subtypes sexual arousal to rape, offense precursors, and offense characteristics. *Criminal Justice and Behavior*, *21*(1), 95–114.

Bartol, C., & Bartol, A. (2015). *Introduction to forensic psychology: Research and application* (4th ed.). Thousand Oaks, CA: Sage Publications.

Becker, J. V., Stinson, J., Tromp, S., & Messer, G. (2003). Characteristics of individuals petitioned for civil commitment. *International Journal of Offender Therapy and Comparative Criminology*, *47*(2), 185–195.

Bergelson, V. (2007). The right to be hurt: Testing the boundaries of consent. *George Washington University Law Review*, *75*, 165–236.

Bondurant, B. (2001). University women's acknowledgment of rape: Individual, situational, and social factors. *Violence Against Women*, *7*(3), 294–314.

Burgess, A. W., & Holmstrom, L. L. (1974). *Rape: Victims of crisis*. Upper Saddle River, NJ: Prentice Hall.

California Sex Offender Management Board. (2008). *An assessment of current management practices of adult sex offenders in California*. Report to the Legislature and Governor's Office. Retrieved from http://www.casomb.org/docs/sombreport1.pdf

Campbell-Fuller, N., & Craig, L. A. (2009). The use of olfactory aversion and directed masturbation in modifying deviant sexual interest: A case study. *Journal of Sexual Aggression: An International, Interdisciplinary Forum for Research, Theory, and Practice, 15*(2), 179–191.

Cohen, M. L., Garofalo, R., Boucher, R., & Seghorn, T. (1971). The psychology of rapists. *Seminars in Psychiatry, 3*, 307–327.

Cohen, M. L., Seghorn, T., & Calmas, W. (1969). Sociometric study of the sex offender. *Journal of Abnormal Psychology, 74*, 749–755.

Douglas, J. E., & Olshaker, M. (1988). *Obsession*. Sydney, Australia: Pocket Books.

Egan, K. (2007). Morality-based legislation is alive and well: Why the law permits consent to body modification but not sadomasochistic sex. *Albany Law Review, 70*, 1615–1642.

Faller, K. (1987). Women who sexually abuse children. *Violence and Victims, 2*, 263–276.

Fazel, S., Sjöstedt, G., Långström, N., & Grann, M. (2007). Severe mental illness and risk of sexual offending in men: A case-control study based on Swedish national registers. *The Journal of Clinical Psychiatry, 68*(4), 588–596.

Federal Bureau of Investigation. (2013). *Uniform crime reports: Crime in the United States*. Retrieved from: http://www.fbi.gov/about-us/cjis/ucr/crime-in-the-u.s/2013/crime-in-the-u.s.-2013/tables/1tabledatadecoverviewpdf/table_1_crime_in_the_united_states_by_volume_and_rate_per_100000_inhabitants_1994-2013.xls

Finkelhor, D. (1979). *Sexually victimized children*. New York, NY: The Free Press.

Finkelhor, D. (2005). Sexually victimized children. In R. K. Bergen, J. L. Edleson, & C. M. Renzetti (Eds.), *Violence against women: Classic papers* (pp. 42–55). Boston, MA: Pearson Publications.

Fischer, R. G., Fradella, H. F., & Ireland, C. E. (2009). Sex, violence, and the boundaries of the defense of consent. *Criminal Law Bulletin, 45*(6), 1137–1155.

Fradella, H. F. (2008). *Forensic psychology: The use of behavioral sciences in civil and criminal justice* (2nd ed.). Belmont, CA: Wadsworth/Cengage.

Friendship, C., & Beech, A. R. (2005). Reconviction of sexual offenders in England and Wales: An overview of research. *Journal of Sexual Aggression, 11*(2), 209–223.

Graney, D. J., & Arrigo, B. A. (2002). *The power serial rapist: A criminology-victimology typology of female victim selection*. Springfield, IL: Charles C. Thomas.

Grattet, R., Petersilia, J., Lin, J., & Beckman, M. (2009). Parole violations and revocations in California: Analysis and suggestions for action. *Federal Probation, 73*(1), 2–11.

Greenfield, D. (2006). Organic approaches to the treatment of paraphilics and sex offenders. *The Journal of Psychiatry & Law, 34*, 437–454.

Gross, B. (2006). The pleasure of pain. *The Forensic Examiner, 15*(1), 57–61.

Groth, A. N. (1979). *Men who rape: The psychology of the offender*. New York, NY: Plenum Press.

Guterman, J. T., Martin, C. V., & Rudes, J. (2011). A solution-focused approach to frotteurism. *Journal of Systemic Therapies, 30*(1), 59–72.

Hale, R. (1997). Motives of reward among men who rape. *American Journal of Criminal Justice, 22*(1), 101–119.

Hanson, R. K., & Morton-Bourgon, K. E. (2009). The accuracy of recidivism risk assessments for sexual offenders: A meta-analysis of 118 prediction studies. *Psychological Assessment, 21*(1), 1–21.

Harris, G. T., & Rice, M. E. (2006). Treatment of psychopathy. In C. Patrick (Ed.), *Handbook of Psychopathy* (pp. 555–572). New York, NY: The Guilford Press.

Harris, G. T., Rice, M. E., & Quinsey, V. L. (1994). Psychopathy as a taxon: Evidence that psychopaths are a discrete class. *Journal of Consulting and Clinical Psychology, 62*(2), 387–397.

Heaton, K., & Murphy, G. (2013). Men with intellectual disabilities who have attended sex offender treatment groups: A follow-up. *Journal of Applied Research in Intellectual Disabilities, 26*, 489–500.

Hickey, E. (2006). *Sex crimes and paraphilia*. Upper Saddle River, NJ: Prentice Hall.

Houlihan, A. (2011). When "no" means "yes" and "yes" means harm: HIV risk, consent, and sadomasochism case law. *Law and Sexuality: A Review of Lesbian, Gay, Bisexual, and Transgender Legal Issues, 20*, 31–59.

Houts, A. C. (2000). Fifty years of psychiatric nomenclature: Reflections on the 1943 War Department Technical Bulletin, Medical 203. *Journal of Clinical Psychology, 56*(7), 935–967.

Hunter, J., Figuerdo, A., Malamuth, N., & Becker, J. (2003). Juvenile sex offenders: Toward the development of a typology. *Sexual Abuse: A Journal of Research and Treatment, 15*(1), 27–48.

Jackson, R. L., & Richards, H. J. (2007). Diagnostic and risk profiles among civilly committed sex offenders in Washington State. *International Journal of Offender Therapy and Comparative Criminology, 51*(3), 313–323.

James, E. L. (2011–2012). *Fifty shades trilogy: Fifty shades of grey, fifty shades darker, and fifty shades of freed*. New York, NY: Vintage/Random House.

Jennings, J., & Deming, A. (2013). Effectively utilizing the "behavioral" in cognitive-behavioral group therapy of sex offenders. *International Journal of Behavioral Consultation and Therapy, 9*(2), 7–13.

Kafka, M. P., & Hennen, J. (2002). A DSM-IV Axis I comorbidity study of males (*n*=120) with paraphilias and paraphilia-related disorders. *Sexual Abuse: A Journal of Research and Treatment, 14*(4), 349–366.

Kaplan, M. S., & Krueger, R. B. (2012). Cognitive-behavioral treatment of the paraphilias. *Israel Journal of Psychiatry and Related Sciences, 49*(4), 291–296.

Keppel, R. D. (1997). *Signature killers: Interpreting the calling cards of serial murderers.* New York, NY: Pocket.

Knight, R. A., & Prentky, R. A. (1990). Classifying sexual offenders: The development and corroboration of taxonomic models. In W. L. Marshall, D. R. Laws, & H. E. Barbaree (Eds.), *Handbook of sexual assault: Issues, theories, and treatment of the offender* (pp. 23–52). New York, NY: Springer/Plenum.

Knight, R. A., Warren, J. I., Reboussin, R., & Soley, B. J. (1998). Predicting rapist type from crime-scene variables. *Criminal Justice and Behavior, 25*(1), 46–80.

Långström, N., Sjöstedt, G., & Grann, M. (2004). Psychiatric disorders and recidivism in sexual offenders. *Sexual Abuse: A Journal of Research and Treatment, 16*(2), 139–150.

Levenson, J. S., & Cotter, L. P. (2005). The effect of Megan's Law on sex offender reintegration. *Journal of Contemporary Criminal Justice, 21*(1), 49–66.

Lieb, R., & Nelson, C. (2001). Treatment programs for sexually violent predators: A review of states. In A. Schlank (Ed.), *The sexual predator: Volume II: Legal issues, clinical issues, special populations* (pp. 5-2-5-22). Kingston, NJ: Civic Research Institute.

Lovell, D., Johnson, L. C., & Cain, K. C. (2007). Recidivism of supermax prisoners in Washington State. *Crime & Delinquency, 53*(4), 633–656.

Marshall, W., & Marshall, L. (2012). Integrating strength-based models in the psychological treatment of sex offenders. *Sex Abuse in Australia and New Zealand, 4*(1), 53–58.

MASSACHUSETTS GENERAL LAWS c. 272, § 105 (2014).

Mayes, R., & Horwitz, A. V. (2005). DSM-III and the revolution in the classification of mental illness. *Journal of the History of the Behavioral Sciences, 41*(3), 249–267.

McCabe, M. P., & Wauchope, M. (2005). Behavioral characteristics of men accused of rape: Evidence for different types of rapists. *Archives of Sexual Behavior, 34*(2), 241–253.

Neumann, S. (2006). Voyeurism. In E. W. Hickey (Ed.), *Sex crimes and paraphilia* (pp. 231–236). Upper Saddle River, NJ: Pearson-Prentice Hall.

NEW JERSEY REVISED STATUTES § 2C:2–10 (2014).

Newmahr, S. (2010). Rethinking kink: Sadomasochism as serious leisure. *Journal of Qualitative Sociology, 33*, 313–331. doi: 10.1007/s11133–010–9158–9

NEW YORK PENAL CODE § 130.52 (2014).

Paclebar, A. M., Furtado, C., & McDonald-Witt, M. (2006). Sadomasochism: Practices, cultures, and behaviors in American society. In E. W. Hickey (Ed.), *Sex crimes and paraphilia* (pp. 215–227). Upper Saddle River, NJ: Pearson-Prentice Hall.

Peugh, J., & Belenko, S. (2001). Examining the substance use patterns and treatment needs of incarcerated sex offenders. *Sexual Abuse: A Journal of Research and Treatment, 13*(3), 179–195.

Prentky, R., Knight, R., & Lee, S. (2012). Child sexual molestation: Research issues. In C. Bartol & A. Bartol (Eds.), *Current perspectives in forensic psychology and criminal behavior* (pp. 106–117). Thousand Oaks, CA: Sage Publications.

Prentky, R. A., Lee, A. F., Knight, R. A., & Cerce, D. (1997). Recidivism rates among child molesters and rapists: A methodological analysis. *Law and Human Behavior, 21*(6), 635–659.

Saleh, F. M., Malin, H. M., Grudzinskas Jr., A. J., & Vitacco, M. J. (2010). Paraphilias with co-morbid psychopathy: The clinical and legal significance to sex offender assessments. *Behavioral Sciences & the Law, 28*(2), 211–223.

Schug, R. A., & Fradella, H. F. (2014). *Mental illness and crime.* Thousand Oaks, CA: Sage.

Seligman, M. (2002). *Authentic happiness: Using the new positive psychology to realize your potential for lasting fulfillment.* New York, NY: Free Press.

Silver, E., Felson, R. B., & Vaneseltine, M. (2008). The relationship between mental health problems and violence among criminal offenders. *Criminal Justice and Behavior, 35*(4), 405–426.

Sinozich, S., & Langton, L. (2014). *Rape and sexual assault among college-age females, 1995–2013.* Retrieved from http://www.bjs.gov/content/pub/pdf/rsavcaf9513.pdf

Stinson, J. D., & Becker, J. V. (2011). Sexual offenders with serious mental illness: Prevention, risk, and clinical concerns. *International Journal of Law and Psychiatry, 34*(3), 239–245.

Stinson, J. D., Robbins, S. B., & Crow, C. W. (2011). Self-regulatory deficits as predictors of sexual, aggressive, and self-harm behaviors in a psychiatric sex offender population. *Criminal Justice and Behavior, 38*(9), 885–895. doi: 10.1177/0093854811409872

TEXAS PENAL CODE § 21.15(b)(1) (2014).

Tomak, S., Weschler, F., Ghahramanlou-Holloway, M., Virden, T., & Nademin, M. (2009). An empirical study of the personality characteristics of internet sex offenders. *Journal of Sexual Aggression, 15*(2), 139–148.

U.S. Department of Justice. (2009, December). *Juveniles who commit sex offenses against minors.* Retrieved from: https://www.ncjrs.gov/pdffiles1/ojjdp/227763.pdf

U.S. Department of Justice. (2013, January). Attorney General Eric Holder announces revisions to the Uniform Crime Report's definition of rape. Retrieved from http://www.justice.gov/opa/pr/attorney-general-eric-holder-announces-revisions-uniform-crime-report-s-definition-rape

Vandiver, K. (2006). Female sex offenders: A comparison of solo offenders and co-offenders. *Violence and Victims, 21*, 339–354.

Vandiver, D., & Kircher, G. (2004). Offender and victim characteristics of female sexual offenders in Texas: A proposed typology of female sexual offenders. *Sexual Abuse: A Journal of Research and Treatment, 16*, 121–137.

Vess, J., Murphy, C., & Arkowitz, S. (2004). Clinical and demographic differences between sexually violent predators and other commitment types in a state forensic hospital. *Journal of Forensic Psychiatry & Psychology, 15*(4), 669–681.

Ward, T. (2002). Good lives and the rehabilitation of offenders: Promises and problems. *Aggression and Violent Behavior, 7*, 513–528.

Wheeler, J. G., George, W. H., & Marlatt, G. A. (2006). Relapse prevention for sexual offenders: Considerations for the "abstinence violation effect." *Sexual Abuse: Journal of Research and Treatment, 18*, 233–248.

Williams, D. (2006). Different (painful!) strokes for different folks: A general overview of sexual sado-masochism and its diversity. *Sexual Addiction & Compulsivity, 13*, 333–346. doi: 10.1080/10720160 601011240

Yates, P. (2013). Treatment of sexual offenders: Research, best practices, and emerging models. *International Journal of Behavioral Consultation and Therapy, 8*(3–4), 89–95.

Yost, M. R. (2010). Development and validation of the attitudes and sadomasochism scale. *Journal of Sex Research, 47*(1), 79–91. doi: 10.1080/0022449090 2999286

Cases

Commonwealth v. Appleby, 402 N.E.2d 1051 (Mass. 1980).

Commonwealth v. Robertson, 5 N.E.3d 522 (Mass. 2014).

Connecticut Department of Public Safety v. Doe, 538 U.S. 1 (2003).

Ex parte Thompson, No. PD-1371–13 (Tex. Ct. Crim. App. 2014).

Lawrence v. Texas, 539 U.S. 558 (2003).

People v. Samuels, 58 Cal. Rptr. 439 (Cal. Ct. App. 1967).

State v. Collier, 372 N.W.2d 303 (Iowa Ct. App. 1985).

State v. Van, 688 N.W.2d 600 (Neb. 2004).

CHAPTER 13

Sex, Gender, Sexuality, and Victimology

Jayn von Delden

Justin Zapata was born a biological male in 1990. One of six children, Zapata was raised in the rural community Fort Lupton, Colorado. Early in life, Zapata identified as female. By the age of 12, Zapata had begun living her life as a girl and, by age 16, identified as Angie Zapata (Frosch, 2008). According to her sister, Angie was "a teenage girl in every sense but the biological one" (Tilleman, 2010, p. 1660).

When Angie was 18 years old in 2008, she met 32-year-old Allen Ray Andrade online on a social networking site. Eventually, she agreed to meet Andrade in person. After their initial date, Angie spent three days with Andrade before leaving him alone in her Greeley, Colorado, apartment while she left to watch over her sister's children. Andrade would later tell police that he spent that day alone in Angie's apartment becoming increasingly suspicious about her.

When Angie returned to the apartment, Andrade confronted her about being transgender. When Andrade reached for Angie's crotch, he felt a penis. Andrade began punching Angie with his fists until she fell to the floor and then he hit her head with a fire extinguisher. Andrade testified that he covered Angie's body with a blanket, but when he heard gurgling sounds coming from under the blanket, he hit her again with the fire extinguisher. Angie's sister, Monica, found Angie's body in the apartment where she had been beaten to death. Andrade was arrested less than a week later. Police found him using Angie's car and credit card.

Andrade's defense lawyers argued that he had been deceived about something so substantial that he reacted in a heat of uncontrollable passion that happened so fast that he couldn't stop himself from beating Angie to death. Prosecutors asserted that Andrade was a cold-hearted killer motivated by hatred and bigotry. After hearing both sides of the story, a jury took less than two hours to find Andrade guilty of first-degree murder. He was sentenced to life in prison (Spellman, 2009).

At the time of Andrade's trial, Colorado was one of 11 states with hate-crime laws that protect transgender people (as of the writing of this book, 14 states and the District of Columbia have such laws according to the Movement Advance Project, 2015). LGBTQIA-rights advocates believe that Andrade was the first person in the United States convicted of a hate crime for murdering a transgender person (Spellman, 2009). Many transgender victims are unknown to our criminal justice system and their killers are neither found nor brought to justice (see Tilleman, 2010).

- Andrade's trans-panic defense rested upon the notion that a reasonable person could snap into a violent rage upon discovering the person's biological sex to whom one is romantically or sexually linked does not align with the person's gender identity and expression. What do you make of this argument? Do reasonable people go into homicidal rages upon learning of such information? Explain your reasoning.
- A similar trans-panic defense also proved unsuccessful in the 2002 murder of Gwen Araujo by four men. She had allegedly been sexually intimate with two of the men who, after discovering Gwen was transgender, beat and strangled her to death. Although the defendants in that case were convicted of second-degree murder and voluntary manslaughter, their defense helped those defendants avoid the hate-crime sentencing enhancement. What do you think about hate-crime laws? Why?

LEARNING OBJECTIVES

1. Distinguish between criminology and victimology.
2. Identify the characteristics of a victim of crime.
3. Describe the four major theories of victimology.
4. Explain the two divergent approaches to "restorative justice."
5. Define the differences between private and public justice.
6. Analyze the need for victims' services in a public justice system.
7. Consider other ways to envision victims' services and rights.

A HISTORY OF VICTIMS IN THE WORLD OF CRIMINAL JUSTICE

The history of law, crime, and punishment does not neatly align with the history of victims and victimization. Victims and their issues have moved back and forth from the forefront of our concerns with crime. In other words, the degrees to which our notions of justice have focused on victims has varied significantly across cultures and time. Victimology, like any other academic field, is best understood via its historical development. That is where we now begin.

Early Human Civilization

Early human civilizations viewed wrongful acts as actions taken against individuals, not against society as a whole. Human emotions of grief and loss are easily interpreted as anger and/or fear, which can result in lethal retaliatory conduct (Boehm, 2011). Perhaps unsurprisingly, then, victims determined the nature and degree of punishment deserved if the perpetrator was caught. This has been described as a "victim justice system" because justice was sought and achieved by the victim, or other individuals, on behalf of the victim

(Doerner & Lab, 2014, p. 4). Such conduct today is called vigilantism, but, at that time, there was no formal justice system—no law enforcement agencies, no courts, and in most early societies, no written laws with set punishments. Rather, this way of life was often based on the notion of lex talionis, later codified in the Old Testament of the Bible and better known to us today as "an eye for an eye, a tooth for a tooth" (Doerner & Lab, 2014, p. 5). This is not to say that there were no rules of engagement.

Often, such personally vengeful conduct was controlled by a powerful individual or group within the community who tolerated only one revenge killing in response to a homicide. It was incumbent upon the entrusted leader to prevent a single revenge killing from escalating into a series of vengeful violence that would harm the community through a significant loss of healthy providers, those tasked with caring for others. Unstoppable violence could entail significant losses of those members resulting in further strain on the social structure to provide for the survivors. This concern was so great that members of one's own family or clan may even have carried out the vengeful act on behalf of the victim in order to abate cycles of retaliatory violence (Boehm, 2011). Over time, social customs that made up this private, victim-based justice were codified into written laws. One of the earliest, the Code of Hammurabi (a King in early Mesopotamia at about 2000 B.C.E.), included specific provisions that provided for retribution to the victim in the form of restitution (Doerner & Lab, 2014).

Early English Common Law

Justice remained private and victim based through the Middle Ages. Small villages scattered throughout the countryside were controlled internally. Neighbors were held responsible to, and for, each other. Justice was still sought by or on behalf of the victim and was motivated primarily by vengeance and compensation. The earliest known written code of laws in England is that of Ethelbert, King of Kent, at about 600 C.E. It included specific financial remedies for specific harms done to a person. For instance, if an ear was cut off the fine was 12 shillings; but if the ear was only pierced the fine was 3 shillings, unless the damage included a loss of hearing, in which case the fine was 25 shillings and it was paid to the victim (Attenborough, 1963, pp. 2–17).

Then, in 1066, the Normans, led by William the Conqueror, successfully invaded England and set about regulating social customs a different way. They created a feudal system of landowners and their serfs, or servants, who were secured to the landlord along with the land. Landlords began taking for themselves the 12 shillings that would have been paid to a victim who was relieved of an ear if the victim was a serf under their dominion. This marks the beginning of the idea that wrongful acts may be committed against someone other than the victim (Hudson, 2014). The wrongful act against a person was redefined as a wrongful act against the king's and his lords' holdings, including people. Henry II, third in succession after William the Conqueror and crowned King of England in 1154, established the Royal Magistrate Courts to sort out with greater efficiency who was due what remedy for which harm to whom. In other words, the government took over the task of determining if a crime was committed and who was entitled to a remedy because of it. The Royal Magistrate Courts became the foundation of the English Common Law that was transported to the American colonies and became the basis for modern American law (Hudson, 2014).

Post-Industrialism

The Industrial Revolution, as its name suggests, changed our social structures again as well as our needs for justice. The implementation of mass manufacturing required a large labor force. Vast numbers of people relocated from rural towns and villages into tightly packed and fast-growing cities leaving behind their agrarian subsistence way of life to seek wealth in a larger economy. However, as people were crowded into cramped living quarters in close proximity of one another, crime rates rose dramatically, threatening the fledgling public justice system that now held society together (Hudson, 2014). Essentially, as society became centralized in cities, the justice system necessarily became more public and less private.

Rising crime rates in the eighteenth century paved the way for paid thief takers, who were private citizens who took compensation to apprehend alleged criminals (McLynn, 1989). They often exacted payment from both sides of the law and their use of violence in doing so was notorious. Henry Fielding sought to clean up the thief-taker system in London and began operating an organized group of paid agents from an address on Bow Street. They came to be known as the Bow Street Runners (Roth, 2011, p. 41). Not long afterward, England's home secretary, Sir Robert Peel, organized London's first official police force (Roth, 2011, p. 105). They became, and still are, known as "bobbies," offering homage to their founder. The most significant improvements to the justice system made by Fielding and Peel were a centralized command and administration structure that survives today in our modern policing agencies.

Just as American legal history emanates from English legal history, so does our history of policing and law enforcement. Our police departments came about as a response to the rampant urban gang violence associated with our early American cities[1] (Spillane & Wolcott, 2013). Their salient purpose was to maintain order and the earliest police officers also were tasked with unrelated duties, such as cleaning the streets (Siegel, 2011). Most of these early police officers lacked formal training and legal education. They operated with minimal supervision; yet, as the instruments of the law in the streets and neighborhoods of our cities, they exercised tremendous, if not exclusive, discretion to determine who was a criminal and who was a victim of crime (Siegel, 2011).

Industrialization and urbanization brought with them centralized fully professional law-enforcement agencies. Police officers today are required to achieve at least minimum educational standards, undergo legal training at our various police academies, and continue to be certified to serve. They are even divided into multiple agencies exercising authority in overlapping jurisdictions at federal, state, and local levels.

Along with a public system of criminal justice came the idea that crimes are committed against society as a whole, rather than individuals. Emile Durkheim, notable French philosopher and a founder of the field of sociology, emphasized that industrialization and urbanization brought new goals for criminal justice (Clarke, 1976). Post-industrialization society experiences a severe division of labor among competing members and a system of criminal justice is needed to maintain order and "harmony" more so than to enforce "increasingly impossible conformity" (Clarke, 1976, p. 251). Government authorities, in the form of official action by state or federal law enforcement agencies, are tasked with stemming crime in order to maintain the existing social order. Individuals may still initiate the process by making reports or engaging in other communications with the police, but it is the system of legal professionals (i.e., police officers, criminal attorneys, and judges) that determines if a crime was committed and thereby identifies the victim(s). This makes the system fully public.

Private actions taken by private parties toward revenge or other individual justice goals outside of the public justice system are called vigilantism. A public justice system's intolerance for vigilantism is an important aspect of such a system because it entails the public, or institutional, identification of victims. In other words, we depend on the same government apparatus to recognize and treat both criminals and victims. This can sometimes blur the lines of demarcation between victim and aggressor, adding strain to the system depended upon to maintain order.

Long-standing, private, and unofficial patterns of justice still may not be completely excised from our culture. In 1983, Donald Black discovered a strong undercurrent in the American justice system that seems to condone a private killing that can easily be viewed as retaliation for a heinous wrong that was perpetrated against the killer. He suggests an enduring yet unspoken common understanding of morality that can prevent some officials from bringing the public justice system to bear in certain cases. For instance, in a small town, a son who waits with a shotgun until his father gets home and then kills the father may not be charged with homicide if the local sheriff is well aware of, and objects to, the fact that the father regularly subjects the son and his mother to brutal beatings (Black, 1983). Sometimes, such incidents go down in history as tragic accidents and are not deposited into our crime or victim statistics. In such cases too, the line between victim and aggressor can be blurred almost beyond recognition.

Another important aspect of our public criminal justice system is the obligation to attend to and honor the constitutional civil rights of the accused in a system predicated on the promises of the Due Process and Equal Protection Clauses of the U.S. Constitution (see Chapters 3 and 4). Police and prosecutors decide whom to charge and with which crime(s). Professional defense counsel is available for the accused. Prosecutors, defenders, and judges make decisions about any plea-bargaining that might occur. In the public justice system, the victim is relegated to the role of a witness to the crime, maybe even just one among many (Cassell & Joffee, 2011). As our focus turned to the just treatment of the crim-

inal by the state, the role of the victim was further diminished.

Complaints arose from both ends of the political spectrum, lamenting the absence of the victim from the public justice system (see Beloof, Cassell, & Twist, 2010; Cassell, 2005, 2007; Joffee, 2009; Ready, Weisburd, & Farrell, 2002; Smith, Sloan, & Ward, 1990; Stark & Goldstein, 1985; Underwood & Edmunds, 2003; Wallin, 2010). The call, on behalf of victims, to restore some of the mechanisms of private justice, was two-sided. Political conservatives raised concerns about taking a tougher stance against a perceived "crime problem"; political liberals raised concerns about the need to advocate for a "voiceless victim" (Levine, 2010).

Those concerned about getting tough on crime sought the inclusion of victims as a means to securing more criminal convictions. This aspect of the call for the inclusion of victims can be seen as largely retributive in nature (Beckett & Sasson, 2004). In 1982, President Ronald Reagan created the President's Task Force on Victims of Crime with a goal that the victim's role in the criminal justice process be restored. The final report of the Task Force (Herrington, et al., 1982) demonstrated that assisting and including victims in the criminal justice process increases conviction rates: "We're showing people that we really care about them . . . I think more people will be reporting crime and will be willing to testify" (p. 6). In this context, victim's rights advocates have come to understand "the right not to be a victim of crime" as an individual right to involvement in the punishment of the criminal as a "victim's right" (Beckett & Sasson, 2004, p. 160). The rehabilitative arm of the collective call, from those who advocate for a voice in the justice system for a voiceless victim, has been embraced and forwarded by the restorative justice movement. The salient distinction between these two very different agendas of the collective call to restore private mechanisms of justice is the former's focus on

Box 13.1 WHEN DOES SELF-DEFENSE TURN INTO VIGILANTISM?

Most of our criminal laws discourage vigilantism. Barring emergency situations in which one must defend oneself or others from imminent, unlawful force, private citizens are expected to rely on the public justice system rather than employing self-help strategies. But how self-defense laws operate in reality may be at odds with broader notions of justice.

Bernard Goetz: "The Subway Vigilante"

Mr. Goetz was an electronics engineer from Queens, NY, who had been mugged repeatedly. He therefore decided to carry a gun for personal protection, even though he was not licensed to do so. On December 22, 1984 in Manhattan, Mr. Goetz entered a subway car that was empty save for four male African-American teenagers. When they approached him and one of the teens said, "Give me $5.00," Goetz perceived them as attacking him and he shot and wounded all four leaving one permanently paralyzed. Although he was found not guilty of attempted murder, he was convicted on an illegal weapon charge and spent nearly a year in jail. He also lost a civil suit brought by the paralyzed teen and was ordered to pay $43 million dollars in damages. Goetz filed bankruptcy and, because the judgment was a civil award and not criminal restitution, the victim has not received any compensation. The victim remains confined to a wheelchair.

George Zimmerman: Neighborhood Watch Gone Bad

On February 26, 2012, 17-year-old Trayvon Martin was walking back to a house at which he was a guest after purchasing Skittles and a fruit drink from a local 7-Eleven. George Zimmerman, a 28-year-old, mixed-race Hispanic male, was patrolling the neighborhood as a member of his local Neighborhood Watch program. Zimmerman called 911 and reported Martin, an African-American teenager wearing a gray hoodie, as a "suspicious person." Although police instructed Zimmerman not to get out of his vehicle or otherwise engage the person he called to report, Zimmerman ignored these instructions. Armed with a 9-millimeter pistol, Zimmerman pursued Martin on foot. Within minutes, Zimmerman shot and killed Martin, who was unarmed. Zimmerman claimed he did so in self-defense after the unarmed teenager "knocked him to the ground, punched him, and slammed his head repeatedly against the sidewalk" (Alvarez & Buckley, 2013, p. A1). Zimmerman was eventually charged with second-degree murder and the lesser offense of manslaughter. The events following Martin's death and Zimmerman's acquittal set off a national debate on racial profiling, the scope of self-defense laws, and even gun rights.

   The law in Florida (which governed Zimmerman's trial) permits the use of deadly force to thwart an unlawful attack that one reasonably believes poses a risk of death or serious injury to oneself, even if the person who uses deadly force could have retreated from the encounter in complete safety. Some states have laws that are even more permissive than Florida's when it comes to the use of deadly force. Consider, for example, that Arizona allows citizens to carry a gun, concealed or not, with or without a permit or any licensing or training. Moreover, Arizona law permits the use of lethal force to thwart the commission of a felony against oneself or another.

- Do you think that social attitudes toward crime victims swing like a pendulum between cries for public or private measures as we wrestle with our changing social culture? Explain your reasoning.
- With geographically and culturally diverse populations crowded together into large urban areas, do race relations play a significant role in our notions of justice? Do you think Goetz or Zimmerman would have resorted to the same self-help measures if their alleged attackers had been White, or female, or dressed differently?
- What race, gender, or class issues may be involved in our own perceptions and subsequent sense of who is an aggressor and who is a victim?

retribution and the latter's focus on rehabilitation and healing, or restorative justice.

Restorative justice is a relatively new term that refers to restoring the aggressor to an acceptable member of the community, restoring the victim by making him as whole again as possible, and restoring the community peace and stability that was broken by the crime (Barnett, 1977; Levad, 2011; Zernova, 2007). Advocates of this model assert that justice is best defined and achieved not by the state, but by individual stakeholders, including victims and aggressors, and those directly and personally involved in the crime. They suggest that doing so will better restore the stakeholders' happiness, thereby better protecting and ensuring stability in society and in our social structures overall. Taken together, the pressures from both ends of the political spectrum seeking to increase private mechanisms in the public criminal justice system took root and have flourished (Levine, 2010).

The Modern Victims' Rights Movement

The Victims' Rights Movement began in the 1960s and 1970s and was nurtured by, and alongside, the Civil Rights Movement and the Feminist Movement (Beckett & Sasson, 2004). In America and elsewhere, the 1950s and 1960s was a tumultuous era that can be characterized as a time when many things changed quickly in society and in our needs from the justice system. The 1960s were marked with riots and civil protests against U.S. military action in Vietnam, race relations, and gender biases (Farber & Bailey, 2001). Men burned their draft cards and women burned their bras in public demonstrations of dissatisfaction with society, government, and the legal system (Farber & Bailey, 2001). Our justice system responded by expanding its attention to the individual liberties and protections promised in the Bill of Rights and the U.S. Supreme Court undertook and decided landmark civil rights cases.

During the 1950s and 1960s, the U.S. Supreme Court decided numerous cases that increased procedural due process protections for state criminal defendants (see Chapter 3). Collectively, these cases—and others like them that were decided under the leadership of Chief Justice Earl Warren—are referred to as the **due process revolution**. For example, *Mapp v. Ohio* (1961) extended the exclusionary rule (a rule barring the admission at trial of evidence seized in violation of the defendant's constitutional rights) to state trials as a remedy for violations of constitutional rights by state actors. *Gideon v. Wainwright* (1963) held that indigent felony defendants in state court proceedings had the right to have an attorney appointed to represent them at no cost to defendants who cannot afford to hire their own lawyers. To preserve the privilege against self-incrimination (a right that protects suspects from being compelled from saying anything that might implicate themselves in criminal activity), *Miranda v. Arizona* (1966) required police to inform suspects of the rights to remain silent and have legal representation, even if the person could not afford an attorney, before subjecting a suspect to custodial interrogation. And *Katz v. United States* (1967) extended search and seizure protections to people in situations in which they reasonably expected privacy, even in the absence of any property rights.

A backlash to the enhanced consideration of defendants' civil and constitutional rights fueled arguments that the courts and criminal justice system were too lenient. The constitutional provisions that safeguard our civil rights came to be seen as "loopholes" that allowed criminals—even violent ones—to escape prosecution and punishment. The perceived leniency of the justice system at the height of the due process revolution was viewed as causing further harm to victims who were dependent upon the system to see that justice was done. This led to the creation of public victim-assistance programs that include funding for compensating victims of crime (see Neubauer & Fradella, 2016).

Public Assistance

Federal legislation creating public victim-assistance programs can be traced to the conservative, retributivist arm of the call for victims' rights. The primary goals of these programs are to increase conviction rates by facilitating victim participation in the criminal justice system (Beckett & Sasson, 2004). Their history begins with the passage of the Victims of Crime Act of 1984 (VOCA). It was the result of a compromise in the unsuccessful push for a constitutional amendment intended to balance the rights of criminal defendants and victims (Roberts, 1990).

VOCA provides funding for public **victim-assistance programs**. The money comes from fines and forfeitures by federal offenders and is distributed through the Office for Victims of Crime (OVC) in the form of grants to all 50 states, the District of Columbia, and the U.S. Virgin Islands (Fritsch, Caeti, Tobolowsky, & Taylor, 2004).

VOCA has been amended multiple times and used as a model for subsequent legislation including the Crime Victims' Rights Act of 2004 (CVRA). CVRA authorizes public monies to assist victims in asserting and encouraging enforcement of victims' rights and promoting compliance with victims' rights laws. It also delineates specific victims' rights and provides mechanisms for their enforcement. Victims in all federal criminal cases have the right to timely proceedings, to discuss the case with the prosecution, to be reasonably protected, notified, present, heard, and to be treated with fairness and respect for privacy concerns.

Another important addition to federal victims' rights legislation is the Violence Against Women Act of 1994 (VAWA), enacted in recognition of the severity of crimes associated with sexual assault, domestic violence, and stalking. It was reauthorized in 2000, 2006, and again in 2013. The 2013 reauthorization closed some critical gaps in the availability of victims' services that had not been addressed in prior versions of the VAWA. The National Network to End Domestic Violence (2013, paras. 8–12) summarized these important changes as follows:

- Justice and safety for Native American women: Native American victims of domestic violence often cannot seek justice because their courts are not allowed to prosecute non-Native offenders—even for crimes committed on Tribal land. This major gap in justice, safety, and violence prevention must be addressed. VAWA 2013 includes a solution that would give Tribal courts the authority they need to hold offenders in their communities accountable.
- Justice and safety for LGBT survivors: Lesbian, gay, bisexual, and transgender

survivors of violence experience the same rates of violence as straight individuals. However, LGBT survivors sometimes face discrimination when seeking help and protection. VAWA 2013 prohibits such discrimination to ensure that all victims of violence have access to the same services and protection to overcome trauma and find safety.

- Safe housing for survivors: Landmark VAWA housing protections that were passed in 2005 have helped prevent discrimination against and unjust evictions of survivors of domestic violence in public and assisted housing. The law, however, did not cover all federally subsidized housing programs. VAWA 2013 expands these protections to individuals in all federally subsidized housing programs, explicitly protects victims of sexual assault and creates emergency housing transfer options.
- Protections for immigrant survivors: VAWA 2013 maintains important protections for immigrant survivors of abuse, while also making key improvements to existing provisions including by strengthening the International Marriage Broker Regulation Act and the provisions around self-petitions and U visas.
- Justice on campuses: College students are among those most vulnerable to dating violence. Provisions in VAWA 2013 add additional protections for students by requiring schools to implement a recording process for incidences of dating violence, as well as report the findings. In addition, schools would be required to create plans to prevent this violence and educate victims on their rights and resources.

The enactment and reauthorizations of this legislation mark a shift toward a finer focus on victims. It resulted in significant changes in the ways we respond to victims. The funding made available through this legislation made it possible to bring together diverse members of the justice system, health care professionals, and victims' advocates into a "coordinated community response" (The Increased Importance of the Violence Against Women Act in Times of Economic Crisis, 2010, p. 4). In other words, it created a new political framework and community network within which victims could be better recognized and their needs better served.

The federal legislative scheme results in local public victim-assistance programs housed typically in local prosecutors' offices (Neubauer & Fradella, 2016). In general, these programs provide victim notification services that afford the victim access to the workings of the public justice system through notice of hearings and other court proceedings along with updates regarding postponements, continuances, and outcomes. They also provide private waiting areas for victims and other witnesses that are more comfortable than courtrooms or courthouse hallways, official escorts within the courthouse, and representatives to explain and interpret court orders and processes in laymen's terms. Information is provided about other resources, including programs specifically for victims of sex crimes that include carefully tailored psychological assistance.

The Sexual Assault Nurse Examiner (SANE) and Sexual Assault Response Team (SART) programs are examples of publicly funded victim-assistance units specialized in responding to victims of sex crimes. SANEs are forensic registered nurses with advanced training in examining victims of sex crimes, collecting evidence, and acting as expert witnesses (if needed) in criminal trials (Ledray, 1997). SARTs are groups composed of law enforcement officers, victim advocates, forensic nurse examiners, and sometimes even prosecutors with advanced training related to victims of sex crimes (Howton, 2010). SANEs and SARTs intervene as quickly as possible to ensure that victims receive the treatment, services, and respect needed to reduce or eliminate the negative experiences that often prevent victims' cooperation with the public justice system. In many places, SANEs and SARTs work in conjunction with private community-based victim advocates (Littel, 2001).

Private Assistance

The 1970s and 1980s saw the emergence of private victims' advocacy organizations (Karmen, 2013). Many of these private organizations were intended to garner attention for specific types of crime victims, such as Mothers Against Drunk Drivers (MADD) and Parents of Murdered Children (POMC). These groups have flourished and now exert significant influence in our justice system (Beckett & Sasson, 2004). For instance, some states permit—and some even require—judges to sentence those convicted of driving under the influence offenses to participate in educational programs (see, e.g., ARIZONA REVISED STATUTES § 28–1381, 2015). One of the more prominent programs to which offenders may be sentenced are "impact panels" run by MADD. Offenders sentenced to attend such programs must do so as a prerequisite to the return of driving privileges (Nesci, 2009).

Recognition of the special concerns and needs of victims of sex crimes in the early 1970s led to the creation of rape crisis centers (RCCs). In fact, in the early 1970s a significant aspect of the feminist wave of the times was an anti-rape movement (Corrigan, 2013). The earliest RCCs were set up in 1972 in Berkeley, California, and Washington, DC. They provided comfort, security, and practical resources for rape victims and functioned as social and political gathering and rallying points for consciousness-raising and legal reform efforts (Largen, 1981; Rose, 1977; Schechter, 1982). Still, in 2012, a national study of such centers by the National Alliance to End Sexual Violence (NAESV) found that most had waiting lists for services such as counseling and support groups.

In the 1980s, feminist and other activists intent on eradicating rape utilized these centers to rally and unite behind the slogan "take back the night" (Lederer, 1980). The effort drew national attention and participation. The push to prevent rape has resulted in some success insofar as there are now more and more stringent laws on the books defining and criminalizing sexual conduct (see Chapters 5 and 6). However, Corrigan (2013) argues that these laws serve a mostly symbolic purpose because "law on the books" does not necessarily translate into fewer instances of sexual victimization nor does it stem patriarchal and misogynistic attitudes that sometimes subjectively prevent their application.

Pressure from both public and private victims' assistance and advocacy organizations has helped to broaden the justice system's focus from victims' needs for compensation, rehabilitation, and healing to a more comprehensive set of rights that includes an individual victim's right to be involved in the punishment of the aggressor. The rhetoric of this transition helped fuel legal reforms that now afford victims specific individual rights in the public criminal justice process.

VICTIMOLOGY

"The sword does not feel the pain that it inflicts. Do not ask it about suffering."
(Hallie, 2013, p. 9)

Victimology is the study of victimization, or the study of victims and their relationships to criminal offenders, society and social institutions, and criminal court processes. It is the study of the connections and interactions between victims and their offenders and seeks to understand crime as an interactive social process. One central reason for studying crime is to learn to prevent it, or at least to curb it, because it causes suffering to its victims and arguably to society as a whole.

Generally, a **crime victim** is an identifiable person or persons who have been harmed individually and directly by a perpetrator or perpetrators, but not by society, social institutions, or our social structure as a whole. This may seem a simple concept, but it can be complicated. For instance, is the deceased the only victim of a murder, or might others whom the killing harms indirectly also be identified in this way? What about the fear of also becoming a murderer's victim that is instilled in others who learn of the crime? Of course, the victim's loved ones are harmed by the loss, and society is harmed by the fear created, but, for the immediate purpose of defining of a victim in our public justice system, only the deceased is identified as the victim of a homicide. Likewise, only the person who was sexually assaulted is seen as the victim of rape and appears in our victimization statistics.

Victimization can be episodic and/or institutional. An **episodic victimization** is an instance of crime recognized as such by the justice system and recorded. In an episodic victimization, both the perpetrator and the victim are usually immediately aware of the wrongful act, although the victims of some crimes (e.g., some forms of theft) may not be aware of their victimization until it is discovered sometime in the future. An assault, for instance, is easily recognized as an episodic crime, or episodic victimization, regardless of whether it is reported to or handled by the criminal justice system. These events are recognized as crimes and appear in our statistics about victimization. Table 13.1 presents data from the National Crime Victimization Survey (Truman & Langton, 2014) to illustrate the types and numbers of victimization that occurred in the United States in 2013 and reports the official number of arrests made for each type of crime according to the Federal Bureau of Investigation (2014). As a review of the statistics in Table 13.1 should make clear, many victims never report the crime committed against them to the police.

Institutional victimization is the harm done by social institutions rather than by individual actors. It results from persistent and enduring cultural patterns that are believed to be and continue to be justified by language, customs, and social structures that maintain oppressive power imbalances (Hallie, 2013).

Table 13.1 Victimization in 2013

Type of Crime	Victimizations Reported to NCVS	Rate per 100,000 Persons Age 12 & Over	Percent Reported to Police	Arrests Made
Violent Crime				
Murder & Non-negligent Manslaughter	N/A*	N/A*	N/A*	10,231
Rape/Sexual Assault	300,170	1.1	34.80%	16,863
Robbery	645,650	2.4	68.00%	94,406
Aggravated Assault	994,220	3.8	64.30%	358,860
Other Assaults	4,186,390	18.2	38.50%	1,097,741
Property Crimes				
Burglary	3,286,210	25.7	57.30%	252,629
Larceny	12,826,620	100.5	28.60%	1,231,580
Motor Vehicle Theft	661,250	5.2	75.50%	64,566

*NCVS is based on interviews with victims and, therefore, does not measure homicides.

In other words, social power imbalances that are recreated and maintained in our social institutions can cause those institutions to fail to recognize some episodic victims. Although this kind of victimization is not as readily or widely identified and does not appear in our crime and victimization statistics, it nevertheless creates victims because it causes harm and suffering.

For instance, rape and its victims may be understood differently when the wrong is viewed as episodic versus institutional. As explained in Chapter 5, the same conduct (i.e., forcible sexual intercourse) that constitutes the crime of rape between strangers is not always punishable by the criminal justice system if it occurs between a man and his wife. In other words, the status of being married to the aggressor obfuscates the crime—even if sexual intercourse was accomplished by force. Why would rape laws in some U.S. states treat spouses differently from other victims of forcible rape? It could be an institutionalized biased belief that it is a wife's duty to be sexually available to her husband; therefore, only unmarried women are extended the protection of rape statutes. When rape is not recognized as rape because the victim is married to the attacker, the victim can be viewed as an institutional victim even though she is not recognized as an episodic victim. She is harmed by the institutions that deny her both status as a victim and a legal remedy. When only some victims are recognized and protected while others similarly in need of protection are not, those who are not protected are victims of the social institutions that fail to recognize their episodic victimization.

Hate-crime legislation is focused on episodic victimizations that emanate from biases or hatred. A hate crime is a violent criminal offense, "committed against a person or property that is motivated in whole, or in part, by bias or prejudice (Bell & Perry, 2015). Hate crimes are subjected to heightened attention because when a victim is targeted because of a status—or perceived status—as a member of an oppressed community, a powerful and nefarious message is delivered to that entire community (Iganski, 2001; Levin, 1999; Weinstein, 1992) that tends to recreate and reaffirm existing hegemonic social hierarchies (Perry, 2001). In other words, the result of a hate crime is continued, and maybe even exacerbated, by intimidation and oppression (Bell & Perry, 2015). Table 13.2 reports hate-crime data in the United States as reported by the Bureau of Justice Statistics' National Crime Victimization Survey (Wilson, 2014). Figure 13.1 breaks down the motivations for hate crimes reported to police in 2013 based on the victims' perceived motivations for the offenses.

Initially, federal law protected only a very narrow class of victims of hate crimes via the Civil Rights Act of 1968. It protected only those who were engaged in a federally protected activity, such as voting, when they were victimized (Levin & McDevitt, 1993). It was used to protect African-Americans who were denied full access to democratic society and social structures by violent intimidation and oppression. Still, although it addressed institutionalized racism, the law did not protect victims of violence motivated by bias related to sex, sexual orientation, gender, or gender identity and it could be applied only in the federal criminal courts.

The Matthew Shepard and James Byrd, Jr. Hate Crimes Prevention Act of 2009 (Shepard–Byrd Act) changed that when it finally became settled law in 2012. The Shepard–Byrd Act expanded federal hate-crime legislation to protect victims of violence motivated by bias related to sex, sexual orientation and gender identity (Lee & Kwan, 2013). This law, and many of the state laws that now replicate it in part or in whole, not only provide for enhanced punishments for hate crimes, but also allocate resources for data gathering and analyses. Some state laws (e.g., Indiana, Michigan, and Rhode Island), however, only require data collection and

Table 13.2 Hate crime victimizations, 2004–2012

Year	Total Hate Crimes[a]		Violent Hate Crimes[b]			Property Hate Crimes[c]		
	Number	Percent of Total Victimizations	Number	Rate[d]	Percent of Total Violent Victimizations	Number	Rate[e]	Percent of Total Property Victimizations
2004	281,670	1.0%	220,060	0.9	3.1%	61,610	0.5	0.3%
2005	223,060	0.9	198,400	0.8	2.9	21,740	0.2	0.1
2006	230,490	0.8	211,730	0.9	2.8	15,830	0.1	0.1
2007	263,440	1.0	236,860	1.0	3.1	24,640	0.2	0.1
2008	266,640	1.1	241,800	1.0	3.7	22,890	0.2	0.1
2009	284,620	1.2	267,170	1.1	4.4	17,450	0.1	0.1
2010	273,100	1.3	255,810	1.0	4.8	17,290	0.1	0.1
2011	217,640	1.0	195,500	0.8	3.6	22,140	0.2	0.1
2012	273,790	1.2	263,540	1.0	4.2	30,250	0.2	0.2

[a] Includes violent crimes, personal larceny, and household property crimes.
[b] Includes rape and sexual assault, robbery, aggravated assault, and simple assault.
[c] Includes household burglary, motor vehicle theft, and other theft.
[d] Per 1,000 persons age 12 or older.
[e] Per 1,000 households

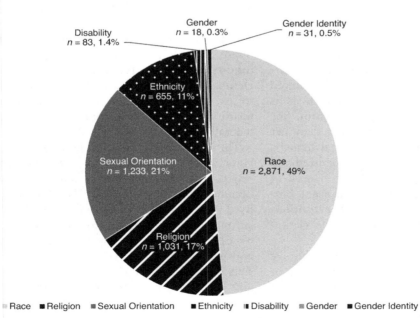

Figure 13.1 Bias motivation of 5,922 single bias hate-crime incidents, 2013

do not provide for additional penalties (Movement Advance Project, 2015). Four states— Arkansas, Georgia, South Carolina, and Wyoming—have not yet enacted any form of hate-crime legislation (Movement Advance Project, 2015).

The attempts to address institutional victimization by enhancing punishments for episodic crimes motivated by hate are countered with criticism that doing so unconstitutionally restrains the freedom of speech and expression guaranteed by the First Amendment of the U.S. Constitution (Gellman, 1991; Gey, 1997; Jacobs & Potter, 1997). This argument posits that hate is a feeling, thought, or a belief that is not punishable pursuant to the First Amendment. The U.S. Supreme Court upheld a hate-crime conviction in *Wisconsin v. Mitchell* (1993) stating clearly its justifications for upholding the constitutionality of hate-crime legislation. The Court decided that although the First Amendment forbids the punishment of thoughts, feelings, or beliefs, it allows enhanced punishment based on the motives for a crime. Hate-crime laws do not punish thoughts, ideas, or beliefs; they enhance the punishment for criminal conduct that is a manifestation of a social bias (read here: institutionalized cruelty). The Court reasoned that hate-crime laws, "address the greater individual and *societal harms* caused by bias-related offenses in that they are more likely to provoke retaliatory crimes, *inflict distinct emotional harms on their victims*, and *incite community unrest*" (*Wisconsin v. Mitchell*, 1993, p. 488, italics added for emphasis). Put simply, enhanced sentences for hate crimes are justified by the enhanced harm done to both the individual victim and to society in general (Iganski, 2001; Levin, 1999; Weinstein, 1992).

MAJOR THEORIES OF VICTIMOLOGY

Several theories have been developed in an attempt to explain criminal victimization. Each of the leading theories offers insights that help to explain why some people are victimized and others are not, although no theory completely explains the full continuum of criminal victimization.

Precipitation Theory

The **precipitation theory of victimization** suggests that victims of crime may create opportunities for, or precipitate, their victimization. The precipitation can be *passive* or *direct*. A person who is loud and outspoken to the point of being obnoxious and offensive to others and actively draws the attention of others, including potential combatants, is more likely to be a victim of assault because they may offend or provoke an attacker. Also, a person may unintentionally attract the attention of an assailant by her or his physical appearance, manner of dress, mannerisms, or even mere presence. The arrival of a well-known progressive social activist in a small, tight-knit, conservative religious community may be perceived by some members of that community as a threat and may passively precipitate violence by her or his mere presence. Alternatively, the person might precipitate violence by speaking out about beliefs that community members find objectionable. In contrast, another newcomer whose attitudes more closely match those of the new community is unlikely to precipitate violence by his or her presence or by voicing opinions with which most members of the community agree. In other words, some behaviors and appearances may attract a potential attacker who, without it, may not have attacked or may have chosen a different victim. From this theoretical perspective who we are, what we do, and where we do it may increase our chances of becoming a victim of crime. To be clear, although this theory may ring of blaming the victim, value judgments should not be part of the analysis. The theory does not suggest that victimization is warranted or deserved, only that certain behavior or appearances may render a person more likely to be a victim of certain crimes.

This theory was initially conceived in the context of the crime of homicide (Wolfgang, 1967) where it may be somewhat easier to imagine how a victim might have provoked an attacker. Especially after a physical altercation has occurred and one party is deceased, it can be difficult to distinguish the victim and attacker. The phenomenon in which victims become offenders and vice versa is referred to as **victim–offender overlap** (Jennings, Piquero, & Reingle, 2012). Recently, precipitation theory has been applied to explain aspects of the phenomenon of intimate partner violence (Durfee, 2012) wherein victims also are sometimes offenders. The notions of victim–offender overlap and victim-precipitation theory illustrate various connections between victims and their offenders.

An important twist to this theory relates to its application to the crime of sexual assault and the controversial suggestion that female rape victims may contribute to their victimization by dressing or acting provocatively in public (Amir, 1971). The suggestion was dubbed a thinly veiled attempt at victim blaming (Clark & Lewis, 1977) and the controversy that arose from that debate resulted in "a virtual halt on victim precipitation research for nearly three decades" (Muftić & Hunt, 2013, p. 241).

The suggestion that women precipitate their sexual victimization is referred to as a "rape myth" (Cowan, 2000, p. 808). Rape and rape myths, addressed in greater detail in Chapter 5, generally encourage victim blaming and, correspondingly, fail to hold assailants responsible for the crime. Unfortunately, rape myths continue to influence commonly held beliefs about the causes of rape (Muftić & Hunt, 2013) and our understanding of the causes of rape is critically important to victims because how victims are treated is determined by beliefs about the causes of their victimization. Strategies for rape prevention that focus on the victim and the tendency of rape victims to blame themselves rather than the attacker are some of the remaining manifestations of such myths (Lottes, 1988).

Lifestyle Theory

The **lifestyle theory** of victimization argues that a person's lifestyle is a good predictor of potential criminal victimization. It indicates the likelihood of victimization increases as a function of engaging in a deviant lifestyle. A deviant lifestyle is, "characterized by situations with high victimization risk and associations with deviant individuals" (Corkin, Wiesner, Reyna & Shukla, 2015, p. 409). More specifically, two mechanisms within that framework connect lifestyle to victimization: exposure to deviants and association with deviance (Hindelang, Gottfredson, & Garofalo, 1978). Either or both may indicate a deviant lifestyle (Jensen & Brownfield, 1986; Sampson & Lauritsen, 1990; Schreck, et al., 2002; Schreck, Fisher, & Miller, 2004).

Importantly, a deviant lifestyle may not be strictly a matter of choices made, but also a result of the choices available. Victimization is related to life activities such as school and education, income and financial means, and leisure activity options (Hindelang, Gottfredson, & Garofalo, 1978). Life activities are a product of demographics and other social circumstances including age, gender, race, socioeconomic status and familial associations and obligations (Corkin, et al., 2015). Put simply, social circumstances constrain lifestyle choices. For example, those who reside in economically disadvantaged neighborhoods are more likely to be victimized than those who live in affluent ones (Lauritsen, 2001; Rountree, et al., 1994). A person may experience a deviant lifestyle by residing in a neighborhood that necessitates association with and exposure to deviants.

The Rape, Abuse, and Incest National Network (RAINN) is the largest anti-sexual assault organization in the United States. Drawing on data obtained from the National Crime Victimization Survey, RAINN (n.d.) reports that of all rape/sexual assault incidents,

- 7% take place in a school.
- 13% take place at the home of a friend, neighbor, or relative.
- 18% take place in a public area, such as a commercial venue, parking lot, or park.
- 43% of rapes occur between 6:00 p.m. and midnight; 24% occur between midnight and 6:00 a.m.; and the other 33% take place between 6:00 a.m. and 6:00 p.m.

According to the Bureau of Justice Statistics (Planty, Langton, Krebs, Berzofsky, & Smiley-McDonald, 2013), since 2005, the rate of sexual violence for females in rural areas (3.0 per 1,000) has been higher than the rate of sexual violence for females in urban (2.2 per 1,000) and suburban (1.8 per 1,000) areas. Alcohol consumption is involved in approximately four out of 10 sexual assaults (Planty, et al., 2013). Applying the lifestyle theory of victimization, it can be hypothesized that a female who spends time at a rural bar frequented by men consuming alcohol is more likely to be a victim of crime than someone who does not. Likewise, women who consume alcohol to the point of inebriation in such surroundings are more likely to be a victim of rape or sexual assault (Bromley, 1995; Fischer, Cullen, & Turner, 2001). Recent research suggests that residing in or near a college campus community may be a risky lifestyle for women (Sinozich & Langton, 2014). Other "risky" lifestyles may include homelessness (Kushel, Evans, Perry, Robertson, & Moss (2003) or drug addiction (Armstrong & Griffin, 2007).

Deviant Place Theory

Deviant place theory is closely related to lifestyle theory and holds that the more frequently a person is exposed to deviant or dangerous places the more likely it is that the person will be victimized by crime. Deviant places are places typically characterized as economically depressed, densely populated, and highly transient (Stark, 1987). Often, both commercial and residential properties are found in close proximity to each other in these areas. Nearby commercial properties offer lucrative targets for crime for a concentration of motivated offenders. When some people move to another, safer area to decrease their chances of victimization, those left behind may be victimized in greater numbers (Wilson, 2012). This theory also encompasses the notion of victim–offender overlap in that criminals may also become victims, and vice versa, due to their presence in the same deviant places. In this model, it is the amount of time spent in the deviant place that predicts victimization.

Routine Activities Theory

As the name suggests, **routine activities theory** relates to the relationship between the activities of our daily lives and our potential for victimization. This theory requires an examination of the intersections of the routine activities of both victims and offenders. "[E]veryday life tempts and impairs potential offenders, influencing their decisions about crime" (Felson, 2002, p. 35). The primary focus of the theory concerns the temporal and physical intersection of three variables: the presence of suitable targets, the absence of capable guardians for those targets, and the presence of motivated offenders (Cohen & Felson, 1979). If the number of suitable targets and/or motivated offenders increases, yet the number of suitable guardians in a particular time and place does not similarly increase, increased victimization can be anticipated. This theory has been used to explain sexual harassment (Clodfelter, Turner, Hartman, & Kuhns, 2010), habitual sex offending (Sasse, 2005), and the sexual assault of men (Tewksbury & Mustaine, 2001). A target-rich environment with a lack of suitable guardians may generate motivated offenders.

Summary

Several theories of victimization may be used simultaneously to explain victimization. A common theoretical combination is referred to as lifestyle-routine activity theory (LRAT). Utilizing the premises of both lifestyle theory and routine activity theory, LRAT posits that victimization is an operation of both deviance *and* the number of targets, suitable guardians, and motivated offenders. It has been used to explain the increasing prevalence of cyber-crimes, such as cyberstalking of women by men (Holt & Bossler, 2009). Women who are interested in and engage in technology experience higher rates of online victimization than do their male counterparts perhaps because women are easily singled out as such if they do not exhibit the dominant masculine styles of online communication and because they lack adequate guardians and are exposed to motivated offenders in an online environment (Herring, 1999; Taylor, 2003).

Even when considered separately, though, these theories reasonably predict that a number of factors increase the likelihood of criminal victimization, including how people behave, how and where people live, the activities and social customs in which people routinely engage, and even how individuals present themselves publicly.

SEXUAL MINORITIES AS BOTH OFFENDERS AND VICTIM

Up to this point in the chapter, we have examined crime victimization, broadly speaking, as well as the theories associated with victimology, in general. With these principles and theories in mind, the chapter now turns to examining victimization as it specifically relates to issues of sex, gender, and sexuality.

The Criminalization of Sexual Conduct

The criminalization of sexual conduct has its underpinnings in religion and religious beliefs (Crompton, 1976). Condemnation and the criminalization of sex acts between members of the same sex is a prime example. As explained in Chapter 2, a religion-based condemnation of sexual activity outside of marriage and of non-procreative sexual activity (which, of course, includes oral and anal sex) was welded into our law when canon law merged with English common law centuries ago and formed the foundation for American colonial law[2] which, in turn, has evolved into our modern bodies of law today. Contempt for those who live their lives outside of these social norms has long since been institutionalized in our legal and social culture.

As explored in several chapters of this book, homosexual sexual activity came to be classified as a crime; as a result, homosexuals came to be viewed not just as sexual deviants, but also as criminals (Fradella, 2002). Commenting on the social construction of bias against sexual minorities from 1890 through 1946, William N. Eskridge, Jr., detailed,

> Fairies had cavorted in New York City long before 1890, and women passed as men throughout the modern era. What was new was the publicness of their self-conscious deviation from traditional male and female roles, and society's anxious perception that a good many people shared their inclinations. That perception propelled a social discourse about same-sex intimacy that evolved from a focus on theology-based unnatural acts to medically-based gender inversion and, ultimately, deviant sexual orientation. The discourse created specific categories of disapproved people—the sodomite, the sexual invert, and the homosexual—who fit into yet broader stigmatized groups—the heretic, the degenerate, and the psychopath.
>
> (Eskridge, 1997, p. 1009)

The criminalization of homosexual sexual conduct was forced into the American public eye in 1987 in the U.S. Supreme Court case *Bowers v. Hardwick* (1986) (addressed in more detail in Chapter 6 of this book). The Court determined that the U.S. Constitution did not prohibit the continued criminalization of homosexual sexual conduct, even when consensual and in complete privacy—a position from which they retreated 17 years later in *Lawrence v. Texas* (2003). Although homosexual sexual conduct remained illegal in about half of U.S. states at the time *Bowers* was decided (see Fradella, 2002), sexual minorities continued to be victimized by crime. Based on the institutionalized social bias and legal stigma attendant to *Bowers*, however, they were not viewed as sympathetic victims deserving of protection. Similarly, social stigma and irrational fear surrounding homosexual sexual conduct, both as a crime and as a social menace, underpinned some notable criminal convictions (as illustrated by Box 13.2), as well as some dubious criminal defenses as explained in the next section.

The Treatment of Victims of Sex/Sexuality-Based Crime

Although members of the LGBT communities historically have been treated as deviants at best and criminals at worst, they also commonly are victims of sex/sexuality-based violence. The history of violence against sexual minorities is well documented. The experience of victimization in such victims is exacerbated when institutionalized bias and hatred are allowed to creep into our public justice system. In other words, their episodic victimization is exacerbated by institutionalized victimization that blurs the lines of demarcation between victim and attacker. The creation of the so-called gay panic defenses illustrates the disparate treatment of these victims.

The Gay Panic Defense

The term *homosexual panic* was first introduced as a medical/psychiatric theory for otherwise unexplainable violent eruptions (Kempf, 1920). The theory suggests that an internal fear of being, or being perceived as, homosexual could create a severe psychological conflict in an individual who also experiences homoerotic desires. That conflict could lead to panic in severe cases resulting in personality dissociation that provokes aggressive automatic responses similar to those provoked by a sense of impending violent aggression or death (Kempf, 1920). After some refinement and redefinition, the theory was repurposed as a criminal defense strategy. Importantly, it was not a recognized affirmative defense in and of itself; it was a strategy to invoke the already established defenses of insanity/diminished capacity and provocation.

The so-called **gay panic defense** is the assertion that a heterosexual person (who in gay panic cases are almost always males) can become so distraught over sexual advances from someone of the same sex that he or she can succumb temporarily to an uncontrollable violent rage sufficient to kill. In other words, the defendant argues that he was subjected to unwanted sexual advances from the victim, which he found so frightening and offensive that he suffered a temporary psychotic episode characterized by unusual and uncontrollable violence (Lee, 2008). In legal terms, the alleged unwanted homosexual advances triggered such distress in the defendant that he was either temporarily legally insane or was reasonably provoked to action in self-defense.

The defense emerged first as a version of the insanity defense to homicide (*Commonwealth v. Shelley*, 1978; *People v. Parisie*, 1972; *State v. Thornton*, 1975). Legal insanity, pursuant to the M'Naghten Rules, is a diminished mental capacity in which the defendant was unable to determine "whether the act was right or wrong" (*Black's Law Dictionary*, 1999, p. 894; see Fradella, 2007). Underlying this concept is the notion that a defendant who did not understand the wrongfulness of his conduct should not be held accountable for it. It is analogous to the proposition that a very young child should not be

Box 13.2 THE GAY NINETIES

"The Gay Nineties" is an American nostalgic reference to the 1890s. The moniker first appeared in the 1920s and is attributed to artist Richard Culter who released a wildly popular series of drawings in *Life* magazine entitled "the Gay Nineties" depicting the happy and carefree social life of wealthy Americans prior to the serious economic downturn and federal income tax tensions of the 1920s. He later published a book of those collected drawings (Culter, 1928). The phrase should not be confused with the modern use of "gay" to refer to homosexuality. In an interesting contrast, in the United Kingdom, the same decade is referred to as "the Naughty Nineties." The 1890s in the UK have been characterized by the licentious art of Aubrey Beardsley, the enormously popular plays and public trials of Oscar Wilde, and the social upset of the Cleveland Street Scandal (Wilson, 1976).

Oscar Wilde, one of the greatest literary talents of the nineteenth century, was living in London in 1895 when he was convicted of the crime of "gross indecency." He spent the next two years incarcerated and subjected to hard labor. When he was released, he moved to Paris where he died, destitute, in 1900. The "gross indecency" conviction stemmed from allegations that Wilde enjoyed sexual relationships with men. It was quite an historical scandal.

First, Wilde charged the Marquess of Queensbury with libel for accusing him of "posing as a sodomite." Because the truth always has been an absolute defense to libel, Queensbury set about proving that his statement was true. Although much of the evidence introduced was related to Wilde's writings and what they meant (or could mean) about his personal proclivities, Queensbury also introduced private letters written by Wilde to Queensbury's son. Wilde admitted to a relationship with Queensbury's son, but denied any indecency. Wilde was able to abate the concerns about his writings by painting himself as a whimsical artist; but when Queensbury announced the presence in the courthouse of several young men whose testimony would contradict Wilde's protestations of innocence, Wilde suddenly abandoned the case. Shortly thereafter, Wilde was charged with the crime of "gross indecency" and was ultimately convicted (Foldy, 1997).

The 1889 "Cleveland Street Scandal" may have impacted Wilde's conviction. A male brothel was discovered at 19 Cleveland Street in London. The investigation began when a 15-year-old telegraph messenger boy, Charles Swinscow, suspected of stealing, was asked to explain why he had 18 shillings in his pocket. He told police that he earned the money "going to bed with a gentleman at 19 Cleveland Street" (Hyde, 1976, p. 21; see also Foldy, 1997). The police subsequently determined that several local telegraph messenger boys were acting as courtesans for wealthy older men at that location. A report of the clients of the brothel included Lord Arthur Somerset, Henry FitzRoy the Earl of Euston, and Prince Albert Victor—oldest son of the Prince of Wales and second in line, at the time, to the British throne. None of the aristocrats were arrested, although some were charged and left England before they could be arrested. A warrant was issued for the arrest of Lord Somerset, also on charges of gross indecency, but he fled to France where, at the time, he could not be extradited. The owner of the brothel went to Belgium and then to the United States. The Earl of Euston went to Peru. The lawyer who represented Lord Somerset, solicitor Newton, was charged and convicted of the equivalent of obstruction of justice for helping several of the messenger boys relocate to Australia. He served six weeks of incarceration; but, interestingly, he was not disbarred and five years later represented Oscar Wilde when he was charged and convicted of gross indecency (Foldy, 1997).

As a result of the lack of convictions related to the scandal, the government was perceived as protecting the aristocratic clients of the brothel and that fueled the notion that homosexuality was an aristocratic vice that corrupted lower-class youths (Foldy, 1997). Such perceptions were still prevalent a few years later when the Marquess of Queensberry accused Oscar Wilde of being a sodomite. At the time of his conviction, Oscar Wilde was a celebrated playwright in his 40s and his accusers were much younger men, in their early 20s, who made their livings as servants, stable boys, messengers or the like (Foldy, 1997).

- Can Oscar Wilde be viewed as victim of institutionalized bias or hatred?
- If so, was Wilde's victimization related more closely to issues of gender or sexuality? In other words, do you think he and his accusers would have been treated differently if Wilde had been female and the accusers were male? What if Wilde was female and so were his courtesans? Why?
- Do you think the Cleveland Street Scandal might have played out differently if the messenger boys had been messenger girls? What if the aristocrats had been women? How significant was the age difference between the aristocrats and their consorts compared with the gender and sexuality issues? Who do you think was most protected by the law in this fiasco?

held criminally accountable for his or her conduct due to his or her incapacity to understand right from wrong in the ways adults are presumed capable of doing. Defendants who used the gay panic defense hoped to be exonerated, or at least have their punishment mitigated, because the non-violent homosexual advance by the victim triggered a panic in the defendant sufficiently severe to cause the defendant to temporarily lose his capacity to distinguish between right and wrong, the requisite mental state for legal insanity.

Essentially, the legal theory underlying the defense strategy arises from the defendant's internal struggle with his latent, highly repressed homosexuality and/or fear of it. It was legally tenable at that time because homosexuality still was viewed as a mental illness, or defect, with which the defendant was burdened. However, once the American Psychiatric Association officially changed its position and removed homosexuality from its com-

pendium of mental defects, the defense strategy was divested of its medical and scientific underpinnings because homosexuality, even latent, highly repressed homosexuality, no longer was considered a mental disorder (Pei-Lin Chen, 2000). Put simply, the defendant could no longer be viewed as struggling under a mental defect that could give rise to a diminished capacity, or temporary insanity, induced by homosexual panic. However, rather than leave it behind, the criminal defense bar reincarnated it as a provocation defense.

Defenses of provocation are sometimes referred to as "heat of passion" defenses. They differ from insanity as a criminal defense in that insanity requires a showing that a mental illness or defect rendered the defendant unable to appreciate the wrongfulness of his or her acts (Fradella, 2007). In contrast, provocation defenses are based on the comparative "normalcy" of a particular person having "snapped" under circumstances in which any similarly situated reasonable person, similarly provoked, would have also reacted violently (Tilleman, 2010). To be successful, the defendant must show that his or her conduct was adequately provoked, creating a sudden heat of passion, and there is a causal connection between the provocation and the killing. A causal connection between the provocation and the killing is established if the heat of passion created by the provocation did not dissipate prior to the killing. This version of the strategy is also known as the non-violent homosexual advance (NHA) defense and has been used to mitigate killings of gays from murder to the lesser crime of manslaughter (Pei-Lin Chen, 2000).

The Trans Panic Defense

A similar version of the gay panic defense strategy has been deployed against transgender victims (Tilleman, 2010). In presenting the **trans panic defense** strategy, the defendant argues that he or she (again, almost invariably the defendant is male) engaged in sexual relations with the victim but believed her to be a woman and was provoked to an uncontrollable heat of passion and the point of killing upon discovering that she possessed the genitalia of a man (Lee & Kwan, 2013). An important distinction here is the supposition that the discovery of having been a victim of "sexual misrepresentation" should be considered legally adequate provocation (Bigler, 2006). Note, however, that the criminal law does not condone violent retribution for misrepresentations or deceits of any other kind (Lee & Kwan, 2013).

The Problem with Panic Defenses

Panic defenses beg the question: "Do 'reasonable people' really fly into violent rages under such circumstances?" Or might a reasonable person simply terminate the encounter if they do not desire to move forward with sexual contact with a member of that biological sex? Some scholars have suggested that the answer to these questions is "no" and, therefore, rather than calling them "panic" defenses, the more appropriate label is one of "rage" (e.g., Lee & Kwan, 2013). The difference arises out of the construction of the legal notion of provocation. What might cause an uncontrollable panic and how one then responds in a state of panic are far more subjective determinations than the more objective consideration of whether a reasonable person should have been able to control his rage if such a situation were to arise. Today, though, such distinctions raise more academic questions than practical ones because most gay panic defenses (and trans variations on them) are all but defunct due to the passage of federal and state hate-crime legislation. Recall that hate-crime laws can enhance penalties for crimes motivated by hatred or bias and that a goal of these defense strategies is to mitigate murder to a lesser crime. Evidence presented by the defense of uncontrollable panic, or rage, required to make out the defense is the same evidence that would be used by the prosecution to enhance the defendant's sentence if he is convicted of a lesser crime than murder, which is a goal of the defense.

The panic, or rage, defense strategies invoke the legal elements of insanity/diminished capacity and provocation in an attempt to justify or excuse violence and victimization based on sex, gender, or sexuality. They exemplify the institutional nature of victimization based on sex, gender, or sexuality. In each instance, the defendants attempt to characterize the victim as deviant and attempt to elicit notions of empathy or sympathy at having been subjected to the deviance. The defendants attempt to blame the victim for the violence in an appeal to socialized, or institutionalized, biases condoning their conduct. This is a common tactic in the defense of those accused of rape as well.

Law in Action SOME HIGH-PROFILE CASES FEATURING VARIATIONS ON THE GAY PANIC DEFENSE

Teena Brandon (December 12, 1972–December 31, 1993) was a trans man who became the victim of a brutal assault, rape, and subsequent murder. Hollywood highlighted Brandon's death in a movie entitled *Boys Don't Cry* (Hart, Kolodner, Sharp, Vachon, & Peirce, 1999). Brandon was arrested for writing a bad check and because he still was anatomically female he was held in the female section of the jail. News of his anatomical sex spread quickly across the small community of Humboldt, Nebraska. When Brandon's associates, John Lotter and Tom Nissen, learned about Brandon's anatomical sex, they brutally raped him. After much urging from Lisa Lambert, Brandon grudgingly reported the horrific assault to the local police; but, before the wheels of justice began turning, Lotter and Nissen went to Brandon's residence and killed him. They also killed Lisa Lambert and Phillip DeVine, who were with Brandon at the time of the murder, to eliminate the witnesses. They claimed they were outraged at being duped by Brandon (see *State v. Lotter*, 2003; *State v. Nissen*, 1997).

Scott Amedure (January 26, 1963–March 9, 1995) was the victim in another high-profile case of this nature that began with an appearance on *The Jenny Jones Show* (1995) that was never broadcast. In an episode devoted to "same-sex crushes," Amedure was encouraged by the producers of the show to create and divulge a sexual fantasy about his friend, Jonathon Schmitz. Schmitz was informed of Amedure's feelings on the show and did not appear to be outraged or even insulted. Three days later, Amedure left an amorous note for Schmitz. After receiving the note, Schmitz purchased a shotgun, went to Amedure's residence, and shot Amedure twice in the chest killing him. Schmitz claimed he was so angered and humiliated by Amedure's advances that he was reduced to a panic-induced, violent, psychotic state. A jury rejected his defense and convicted Schmitz of second-degree murder. He was sentenced to 25 to 50 years in prison (see *People v. Schmitz*, 1998).

Matthew Shepard (December 1, 1976–October 12, 1998) was the victim in another widely publicized case in 1998. Shepard was a 21-year-old college student in Wyoming. Shepard was drinking in a bar and allegedly solicited a ride home from Aaron McKinney and Russell Henderson, also both 21 years old. A passerby found him 18 hours after he had been pistol-whipped and tied to a rural fence post. He died five days later. McKinney claimed that Shepard made sexual advances toward him that triggered an episode of psychotic violence that resulted in the killing. The trial court judge, however, ruled that the defendants would not be permitted to assert the gay panic defense at trial because Wyoming does not recognize temporary insanity or diminished capacity as criminal defenses (Janofsky, 1999). Both Henderson and McKinney received double life sentences for kidnapping and for murder (*State v. McKinney*, 1999). Shepard's death brought national attention to anti-gay hate crime which, in turn, prompted the legislation that bears his name.

Gwen Araujo (February 24, 1985–October 3, 2002) was a trans woman in California killed by three defendants convicted in 2004. She had previously engaged in sexual acts with two of her killers. The killers claimed they were enraged to violence upon learning afterward that Araujo had male genitalia and she was beaten and strangled to death. Two of the defendants were convicted of second-degree murder and the third pled guilty to voluntary manslaughter (Tilleman, 2010).

Sex, Rape, and the Evolution of Rape Shield Laws

A good portion of the research conducted regarding the victims of sex crimes involves the victims of rape. More specifically, it involves female victims of male rapists (Cahill, 2001; Dahl, 1993; Estrich, 1987; Fisher, Daigle, & Cullen, 2010; Gordon, & Riger, 1989; Jordan, 2004; Konradi, 2007; Koss, Harvey, & Butcher 1987; Lees, 2002; Madigan, & Gamble, 1991; Underwood & Edmunds, 2003). This is not surprising given that the early feminist movement declared rape to be a crime against all women and set about the creation of rape crisis centers to aid those victims.

At common law, the chastity, or the lack thereof, of the victim was admissible as evidence for the defense. Prevailing attitudes about women had much to do with this. In *State v. Sibley* (1895), the Missouri Supreme Court explained the institutional understanding that "[i]t is a matter of common knowledge that the bad character of a man for chastity does not even in the remotest degree affect his character for truth, when based upon that alone, while it does that of a woman" (p. 171). In other words, promiscuous men were not necessarily liars, but promiscuous women were. The assumption made was that an unchaste woman was likely to have consented regardless of any subsequent representations. Overzealous defenders learned to use this to their advantage and embarked on cross-examinations bent on painting the victim as an unchaste woman whose denial of consent could not be trusted. Rape trials were turned upside down with the defense accusing the victim of either leading on or wrongfully rejecting her attacker, a strategy that led to acquittal (Berger, 1977). Yet, the victim's cooperation and testimony are still indispensable in the prospect of a rape conviction. Rape shield laws were developed in light of this; and, from a victim's perspective, the development of rape shield laws is a story of protection.

Protecting Some Victims

In defending against an allegation of rape, the defendant must show either that the alleged conduct did not occur or, alternatively, that the alleged victim consented to the conduct. Proving the alleged victim was unchaste was a boon for the defense because prevailing attitudes about women at the time suggested that unchaste women were unlikely to tell the truth about such things so the unchaste woman was hard-pressed to prove she did not consent. This made for a simple defense theory: unchaste women lie about sex and, therefore, if this woman is unchaste, she is lying about sex with the accused (Berger, 1977). Such notions still held sway as late as the 1970s when famed defense attorney F. Lee Bailey suggested that a rape victim be subjected to "attack" by defense attorneys in order to "totally destroy her character or reputation" (Bailey & Rothblatt, 1973, p. 212).

Rape shield laws were introduced to protect victims from the defense technique of maligning the victim's character. Such protection increases conviction rates by increasing victim participation in the criminal justice system (Hazelton, 1992). Toward that end, **rape shield laws** restrict the use of evidence regarding the victim's past sexual experiences or conduct (see Chapter 5). Unfortunately, rape shield laws sometimes miss the mark because they are based on prevailing attitudes about women and take for granted a female victim of a male attacker. Although they offer some protection for some victims, they do not account for the experiences of all rape victims.

Male Victims

Recall from Chapters 5 and 6 that not all rape or sexual assault statutes are gender neutral. Typically, in jurisdictions where those statutes are not gender neutral, neither is the application of a rape shield statute. Additionally, even where such statutes are gender neutral, they may not equally address the concerns of a male victim of a male attacker or a male victim of a female attacker. This is a grave concern because recent statistics show that sexual victimization—other than for the crime of rape—is experienced at almost equal levels by women and men (Stemple & Meyer, 2014).[3] Also, evidence shows that men experience the harm of sexual victimization in much the same ways as women: depression, suicidal ideation, anxiety, sexual dysfunction, loss of self-esteem, and long-term relationship difficulties are some consequences (Struckman-Johnson & Struckman-Johnson, 1992). Treating male sexual victimization as an exception to, or aberration from, the problem of sexual victimization further stigmatizes and harms those men who are so victimized (Scarce, 1997). This helps to explain why male rape victims are even less likely to report their victimization than female victims.

Alongside the numerous reasons that a female victim may not report an attack, or be unwilling to cooperate fully with a public prosecution, a male victim may have additional concerns. Social constructions of masculinity may be significant to an analysis of the sexual victimization of men (Dunn, 2012). Traditional masculinity has been described as hegemonic; meaning it is anti-feminine, aggressive, stoic, and encompasses a sense of power that includes a willingness, and ability, to do violence, if it is needed, to maintain masculinity (Cheng, 1999; Connell & Messerschmidt, 2005; Donaldson, 1993; Kimmel, 1994).[4] Notably, as it is used here, violence can encompass non-physical acts as well. For instance, a bookish man might maintain hegemonic masculinity through his capacity for cyber violence. The salient aspect of this conception of masculinity is power. "The hegemonic definition of manhood is a man in power, a man with power, and a man of power" (Kimmel, 1994, p. 125). This keen definition of masculinity requires a man to maintain a powerful identity and that entails he be "tough" (Cheng, 1999). A male rape

victim may be concerned with being perceived as unmanly for not being able to successfully defend such an attack. In other words, acknowledging sexual victimization might be perceived as equivalent to acknowledging weakness, which would create severe dissonance in a traditional masculine identity (Kimmel, 1997). Additionally, it may create fear of a perception in others that the sexual contact was not actually forced, thereby invoking the host of homophobic demons that also underlie this conception of masculinity (Kimmel, 1997). A gay male victim may share these concerns and be troubled further by the prospect of having his sexual proclivities judged publicly, or being forced out of the closet into a public courtroom (Kramer, 1998).

Another possible explanation is that the feminist-led anti-rape movement produced a social discourse about sexual victimization that is devoted almost exclusively to women (Stemple & Meyer, 2014). That feminist discourse led to the practical determination that "the victimization of a woman is not her fault, that it is not caused by her prior sexual history or her choice of attire, and that for survivors of rape and other sexual abuse, speaking out against victimization can be politically important and personally redemptive" (Stemple & Meyer, 2014, p. e20). A similar discourse about male victims was all but absent from that early feminist agenda. Moreover, the extant social discourse about men as victims of sex crimes is very different. It includes jokes about prison rape (Stemple & Qutb, 2002), the notions that men ought to be able to protect themselves from such attacks (Scarce, 1997), and those who do not or who are not able to protect themselves harbor latent homosexual tendencies and "asked for it," even if subtly or unconsciously (Wakelin & Long, 2003).[5] Put simply, our social discourse regarding male victims of sex crimes does not assist and empower individual men who are victimized in the ways the feminist discourse assists and empowers individual women who are similarly victimized. This also is an instance of institutionalized victimization because some victims (women) are afforded legal protection while others (men) are not.

This female-victim-dominant paradigm of sexual victimization that obfuscates male victims of male attackers also obfuscates male victims of female attackers. Perhaps surprisingly, the numbers of men and women who are victims of nonconsensual sex acts other than rape are almost equivalent when the tools used to measure such acts are more carefully calibrated (Stemple & Meyer, 2014, p. e21). A significant aspect of the newly calibrated survey is the use of new terminology. The term "made to penetrate" was crafted to refer specifically to male victimization in which a male, without his consent, penetrates another. Although it may seem counterintuitive in our culture, the biological operation of the male genitalia makes it possible, and not even uncommon, for a male to experience an erection and even ejaculation in response to a sexual assault (Fuchs, 2004). When a man is sexually assaulted, either by a woman or by another man, his "erection and any subsequent ejaculation is a physical response rooted in biology, not in implied consent" (Widor, 1996). Although use of the "made to penetrate" language highlights men and boys as previously unseen victims and paints a fuller picture of sexual victimization, the new terminology also creates new challenges.

Since the creation of the female-victim-centered paradigm of sexual victimization, statistics-gathering strategies have routinely categorized sexual victimization as either "rape" or "other sexual violence" (Stemple & Meyer, 2014, p. e22). Unfortunately, "made to penetrate" is categorized as a subset of "other sexual violence." This means that at least some male victimization still is not accurately captured and reflected in our statistics. For instance, based on the new distinction, in the case of forcible oral sex acts, an assault on a female would be recorded as an instance of rape yet an assault on a male

would be recorded in the lesser category of "other sexual violence" (Stemple & Meyer, 2014). Research suggests that a better strategy might be to employ broader, gender-neutral terms, such as "sexual assault" or, "sexual victimization," without regard for which party is penetrated (Stemple & Meyer, 2014, p. e23). At least 37 states now have codified "sexual assault" in place of "rape" and its use continues to gain favor (Stemple & Meyer, 2014).

Additional Unrecognized and Unprotected Victims

Other victims remain invisible for different reasons. For example, significant portions of our population are simply not counted because they are excluded from the major victimization surveys. Those surveys are conducted exclusively in American households. This results in the homeless, incarcerated, institutionalized, or otherwise non-household persons being completely excluded. Moreover, the flawed accuracy of our knowledge in this area is exacerbated by the explosion of the American prison population in the past several decades, and the expanding homeless population (Walmsley, 2012). Given that our rape shield laws are a product of the female victim/male perpetrator paradigm of sexual violence, can they be made to include all victims in their protection? Some scholars have already suggested the need for a "gay shield law" to help prevent victim-blaming strategies deployed against gay victims (Strader, Selvin, & Hay, 2015).

VICTIM PERSPECTIVES OF JUSTICE PROCESSES AND ACTORS

So far, this chapter has examined victimology with a focus on sexual victimization from a systemic viewpoint. The remainder of the chapter will focus directly on victims' perspectives of the edifices of that system. In other words, so far this examination has focused on how the justice system sees and responds to victims; the following section explores how victims see and respond to the system. For purposes of this discussion, the criminal justice system consists of three parts: police/law enforcement, courts and legal processing, and victims' services.

Over the past several decades, many researchers have examined crime victims and their perspectives of the public justice system. On the whole, these researchers found that a victim's satisfaction largely depends on his or her perception of **procedural justice**, a measure of the fairness of the system's procedures for achieving an outcome (Casper, Tyler, & Fisher, 1988; Laxminarayan, 2012; Thibaut & Walker, 1975; Tyler, 2006). More specifically, victim assessments of procedural justice depend on perceptions of the efforts made by authorities to act fairly and ethically, as well as the degree of politeness accorded and the amount of respect extended to individual rights (Tyler, 1988). It also has been shown that perceptions of procedural justice are more important than actual outcomes (Tyler, Boeckmann, Smith, & Huo, 1997) and that notions of procedural justice can directly affect victim satisfaction with the system as a whole (Laxminarayan, 2012). Indeed, actual outcomes may have the least impact on determinations about procedural justice because such determinations are made, in part, depending on whether the interaction with the system was voluntary or not (Tyler, 1988).

Secondary victimization is also an important concept in understanding victim perspectives of the justice system. **Secondary victimization** describes a victim's negative interactions with others, including courts, police and other legal actors, causing the victim to feel victimized again (Berrill & Herek, 1990; Montada, 1994; Koss, 2000; Orth, 2002). In this model, the **primary victimization** is the initial episodic victimization. The phenomenon of secondary victimization was first described as a "second assault" experienced by a crime victim (Symonds, 1980). Importantly, secondary victimization is not the result of a second crime per se; rather, it is the potentially harmful psychological impact caused by certain types of interactions with justice system actors—some of which may even be actively or tacitly condoned. For instance, a lesbian or gay man may be treated negatively as a result of his or her sexual orientation being exposed by the victimization in that he or she loses employment or housing at the hands of a bigoted boss or landlord. Also, a victim subjected to one of the victim-blaming defense strategies experiences secondary victimization in the form of "negative influences" to a victim's "self-esteem, faith in the future, trust in the legal system, and faith in a just world" (Laxminarayan, 2012, p. 391). In other words, the lack of systematic protection of certain crime victims can cause secondary institutional victimization.

Victim Perspectives of Police/Law Enforcement

The criminal justice system is usually triggered when a crime is discovered by or reported to the police. The officers who arrive at the scene of a crime, or receive a report of a crime, are the first representatives of the justice system to interact with crime victims. Unfortunately, they may not always act as emissaries of justice. Victims typically expect that police will respond quickly to calls for service. Moreover, victims expect that police will demonstrate understanding and concern for the victim's plight. And victims anticipate that police will conduct comprehensive investigations that will result in the apprehension and punishment of perpetrators. But law-enforcement personnel may not always be able to meet all of these victim needs, which can lead to tension or even direct conflict between victims and law-enforcement officers (see Elliott, Thomas, & Ogloff, 2012).

Logically, police response times depend on a variety of circumstances, including geography and departmental capacity. Applying the major theories of victimology, we should expect victimization rates to be higher during large public gatherings, such as parades or political rallies, making it difficult for police to locate and reach victims. Even in the ordinary course of daily events, traffic emergencies or congestion may delay police progress to the location of the victim. Communication challenges also may make it difficult for police to locate or reach a victim. Finally, as with other emergency responses, there may be a need to prioritize efforts to ensure that those victims with the perceived greatest needs are reached first (Karmen, 2013). Conduct that may seem terrifying and immediately threatening and dangerous to one person (e.g., a young or elderly victim, a member of a sexual minority, someone with a history of domestic abuse) may be discounted by a police dispatcher as little more than a shouting match. This can leave a victim, or potential victim, feeling unprotected.

Another contributing factor to the tension or conflict between the needs of victims and law enforcement is the police officers' need to remain emotionally detached in order to do their jobs as effectively and objectively as possible (Karmen, 2013). Additionally, unlike the victim, a well-seasoned officer is likely to have witnessed similar victimization experiences in the past and is somewhat desensitized to it (Ready, Weisburd, & Farrell, 2002). This can cause a responding officer's demeanor to be interpreted by the victim as cold, distant, or disinterested; such reaction can cause a victim to feel unprotected and even experience secondary victimization.

In addition, physical evidence needed to advance the investigation and potentially convict the perpetrator(s) may be scarce or difficult to locate. Sometimes, officers feel the need to challenge the victim's story of the events in order to identify pertinent facts and/or secure a usable statement for conviction. A victim may be in shock, pain, or otherwise disoriented, thereby limiting his or her abilities to communicate effectively what

happened resulting in disbelief or disregard by the investigating officers.

Finally, and unfortunately, the criminal justice system is troubled by the phenomenon of false reports. Estimates of the frequency of false claims of sexual assault vary but are generally understood to be rare (see Spohn, White, & Tellis, 2014). Yet, some criminal justice system personnel routinely approach reports of sexual assault with suspicion of the victim even though such a mindset is unwarranted (see Maier, 2014). Cases like the one presented in Box 13.3 may help to explain why.

Victim Perspectives of the Courts and Judicial Processes

Victims of sex crimes, like most other crime victims, continue to interact with criminal justice system actors after a law-enforcement investigation ends. In fact, for most crimes, victim cooperation and participation are needed throughout various stages of the adjudication process. Although this can be traumatic for many types of victims, it is especially the case for victims of sex crimes, many of whom re-experience their victimization each time they need to retell the events in excruciating detail—first to a prosecutor and, perhaps, subsequently in a public courtroom that may be filled with spectators. If so, the victim is likely to be questioned and challenged by the defense attorney. Often, defense strategies involve challenging the victim's credibility, shaming the victim, or even blaming the victim. The so-called panic defenses, addressed earlier, are examples of this. Others include ruthless attacks on a rape victim's appearance, style of dress, alcohol consumption, or other indicators of perceived deviance that are not restricted by rape shield laws.

The challenging nature of court appearances for victims of crime is not limited to testifying in open court. The nature of pretrial and trial processes is a focus on the constitutional rights of the criminally accused

Box 13.3 THE DUKE LACROSSE DEBACLE

Duke University is one of America's most prestigious institutions of higher learning. It also is the site of a series of scandalous events that forced the nation to consider more carefully our attitudes and assumptions about sex, class, race, and victimization. Three of the young men on the Duke lacrosse team, Dave Evans, Collin Finnerty, and Reade Seligmann, were charged with first-degree rape, first-degree kidnapping, first-degree sexual offense, common-law robbery, felonious strangulation, and conspiracy to commit murder following allegations made by an exotic dancer hired to entertain them at a lacrosse house party during spring break of 2006. Interestingly, none of the players spent any time incarcerated; however, their prosecutor did. Some background about the university and its community may help to explain how this happened.

In 2006, U.S. News and World Report ranked Duke as the fifth-best university in the country. Duke, in Durham, North Carolina, had positioned itself as the Stanford of the East and the Harvard of the South. Unfortunately, and as is the case in some major universities even today, athletic endeavors seemed to overshadow academics. "[T]he tail of athletics wagged the dog of the university itself" and its "athletes were pashas" (Miller, 2014). Not only did they engage in "repeated incidents of drunk and disorderly behavior, but they so dominated the university's social life that, as one Durham journalist memorably put it, parents were shelling out 'close to a quarter of a million dollars, no bargain, for a jock-dominated sex zoo where Junior can play Hugh Hefner to a hutchful of willing bunnies with high SATs'" (Miller, 2014, p. 2).

Kim Roberts and Crystal Mangum were the two African-American women hired to entertain the lacrosse athletes on March 13, 2006. Crystal had passed out and had to be carried to Kim's car when they left. The players insisted that Crystal had arrived at the party under the influence of some unknown substance and Crystal claimed she was drugged while there. Kim summoned the police because she did not know where the unconscious woman lived, or where to take her. Cohan (2014) suggests that Crystal told the police a story about rape and robbery to distract them from the fact that she was severely intoxicated at a party while her two small children were left at home alone. We would find out later that she suffered from serious mental health challenges.

Although Crystal's story changed dramatically several times, Mike Nifong, the local prosecutor, pursued charges against the Duke lacrosse players. The case bore on for 13 months before it was dismissed and announced that the players would not be prosecuted for any crimes. During those months, the remainder of the 2006 lacrosse season was cancelled, the coach was fired, and a scathing indictment of the players by a contingent of 88 Duke professors was published in the school newspaper. The young men were all but convicted until the prosecutor's nefarious conduct was exposed. Nifong was found to have made untruthful statements to the public and to the court regarding the DNA evidence in the case. He also was found to have withheld that exculpatory DNA evidence from the defense. The evidence showed, clearly and early on, that the lacrosse players were not guilty of the charges against them. Nifong was disbarred and spent a day in jail for contempt of court. He also filed for bankruptcy protection in light of the very real prospect of personal civil liability to the lacrosse players.

The three players that were charged have since recovered an undisclosed number of millions of dollars from civil suits against the university and the prosecutors' office (Dent, 2014).

However, 41 players on the team were subjected to the intensive investigation. They were interrogated, requested to give DNA samples, and herded to police headquarters where they were stripped of their clothing and photographed naked for evidence. Those that remained in school suffered seemingly endless taunting from classmates, failing grades from professors, and spent employment and social opportunities (Miller, 2014).

Ryan McFadyen was a sophomore on the team at the time. After leaving the party, at about 2:00 a.m., he drafted a satiric email to his teammates invoking horrific themes from the movie *American Psycho* (Solomon, et al., 2000). He was not charged with any crimes but was suspended from Duke University. He was later readmitted and has since earned a Duke diploma, but, rather than landing a posh position on Wall Street like many other players had done in the past, Ryan has changed his name and is working as an associate at a real estate development firm owned by the father of a teammate (Cohan, 2014). Crystal has had several more encounters with the law since then and currently is serving a sentence of at least 14 years for second-degree murder. She was found to have stabbed her boyfriend to death and was unable to convince a jury that she was a victim of domestic abuse and had acted in self-defense.

(see Neubauer & Fradella, 2016). Moreover, the processing of cases through the bureaucracy of the court system lends itself to delays (Neubauer & Fradella, 2016). Thus, victims may be asked or even summoned to court numerous times for grand jury proceedings, pretrial hearings, and trials. Sometimes such proceedings are postponed, which can inconvenience victim-witnesses who took time off from work or spent money traveling to the courthouse. Even when the proceedings occur on the date scheduled, victims usually must wait outside the courtroom until they are called to give testimony. Waits sometimes last for intolerably long periods of time, often in corridors or small office spaces of the courthouse to avert the possibility of witnesses interacting with each other (and thereby potentially tainting each other's testimony).

Financial costs, or losses, involved in participating in our criminal courts and legal processes are another direct concern for victims in the justice system. Additional financial costs, even beyond those necessitated by the episodic victimization (such as medical treatment or loss of property), are associated with cooperating with courts and legal processes. Victims are not compensated for

the considerable amount of time that may be spent cooperating with the system. Some victims may have to traverse long and/or inconvenient routes in order to appear personally at county, state, or federal courthouses as required by the system (Neubauer & Fradella, 2016). If witness fees are available, the meager amounts offered do not compensate victims for such things as lost wages from missed work or travel expenses. To help address these problems, some jurisdictions have established victim-compensation programs to help victims offset some of these costs. But, as will be addressed in more detail later in this chapter, such victims' services rarely fully compensate victims of crime.

Even a judge's actions can be viewed by victims as causing additional harm or exacerbating suffering. Painted in very broad strokes, in the adversarial justice system employed in the United States, the prosecutor is pitted against the defender and the judge is the referee in a high-stakes, winner-takes-all gamble for the defendants', and in some important ways, the victims' futures. A judge has many tasks that may affect the victim. A judge must decide whether to hold the accused in custody or release him back into society on bail prior to a final hearing of the case. A pretrial release may leave a victim feeling unprotected and vulnerable. A judge may be asked to accept a plea bargain agreed upon by the prosecutor and defender without the victim's input. Without input, the victim may not feel satisfaction with the bargain struck. Even where a jury determines a guilty or not guilty verdict, a judge alone may determine a sentence of punishment and the severity or leniency of the sentence may affect the victim's satisfaction with the criminal justice process. In many U.S. jurisdictions, a judge may only sentence a convicted defendant after hearing from the victim (or a deceased victim's survivors).

Victim-Impact Statements

One of the changes implemented as a result of the victims' rights movement requires judges (and, in some cases, sentencing juries), to listen to victim-impact statements prior to pronouncing punishment (Gordon & Brodsky, 2007). A **victim-impact statement** is an oral or written statement "read into the record during sentencing to inform the judge or jury of the financial, physical, and psychological impact of the crime on the victim and the victim's family" (*Black's Law Dictionary*, 1999, p. 1561). "These emotion-filled statements are usually offered in an attempt to sway the sentencing court to impose a severe sentence on the convicted offender, although pleas for leniency do occur from time to time" (Neubauer & Fradella, 2016, p. 259; see also Miller, 2013). Every U.S. state permits victim-impact statements (VISs) as part of the sentencing process (Neubauer & Fradella, 2016). Some jurisdictions even allow victim input as early as charging and/or bail decisions (NCVC, 2013). VISs may also be considered at hearings concerning the potential revocation of probation or the possible grant of parole (see Morgan & Smith, 2005). Regardless of the nature of the proceeding, the delivery of a VIS is usually an efficient way of including the often overlooked or even ignored victim in the public justice system (Cassell & Joffee, 2011).

Actual and Perceived Effects

Much empirical work is left to be done regarding the full potential of a VIS in terms of both benefits and detriments not only for victims, but also for the criminal justice system as a whole. For instance, offering a VIS encourages victims to personally implore the judge to mete out a punishment that will satisfy an internal notion of justice (Alexander & Lord, 1994; Hoyle, 2011; Kirchengast, 2013); thus, the practice may be therapeutic (Cassell & Joffee, 2011). However, it can also cause the victim or survivors to relive the trauma of the victimization (Bandes, 1999). An early study found that offering a VIS does not necessarily generate in victims a greater sense of satisfaction with the outcome or necessarily a sense of meaningful involvement (Davis & Smith, 1994). Moreover, if the punishment handed down does not comport with the victim's personal sense of justice, he or she may feel slighted by what is often perceived as the minimization of the primary victimization. This can result in a feeling by the victim of being revictimized by the system (Kilpatrick & Otto, 1989). In other words, making a victim-impact statement may create false hopes and expectations leaving some victims with an even greater sense of disappointment, disinterest, or even betrayal (Frey, 2009; Villmoore, & Neto, 1987).

VISs can have a very emotional impact on jurors, especially in death-penalty cases where victim-impact evidence typically stirs jurors' punitive impulses (Miller, Greene, Dietrich, Chamberlain, & Singer, 2008; Salerno, & Bottoms, 2009). In noncapital cases, however, it is usually judges, not juries, to whom victim-impact evidence is offered. The effect of such evidence on judges appears to be minimal, as VISs do not appear to materially affect sentence length (Davis & Smith, 1994; Erez & Rogers, 1999; Villmoare &

Neto, 1987). However, it may affect judicial imposition of special conditions of probation, "causing the judge to order anger-management treatment, drug and alcohol supervision, domestic violence counseling, or such" (Propen & Schuster, 2008, p. 315). That may be a function of the fact that there is some evidence indicating that victim-impact evidence may not be commonly offered. Consider that one study in Texas found that only 22% of the VIS applications distributed by a district attorney's office were returned (Yun, Johnson, & Kercher, 2005). But one should not assume that this low rate is a function of victim apathy. Some victims do not understand that they have the right to give a VIS. Others are illiterate and cannot easily compose a VIS. Language barriers, fear, trauma, and reluctance to speak in front of the offender also influence why a victim might elect not to prepare a VIS (see Sanders & Jones, 2007).

Constitutionality

The constitutionality of victim-impact information has been tested in the context of death-penalty cases. Logically, those cases represent the highest stakes at risk in a criminal action. The jurisprudence regarding victim information emanates from three major cases that were decided over just four years. See Box 13.4 for details of those cases.

Some scholars view the decision to allow victim-impact information as a major victory for the victims' rights movement—one in which the U.S. Supreme Court attempted to balance the rights of victims with those of defendants in a meaningful way (e.g., Mandery, 2004; Nadler & Rose, 2003). Others, however, maintain that couching the issue as a contest of sorts between victim and defendant ignores the vast power of the state to prosecute criminals (Harris, 1992). Indeed, some victims' rights advocates suggest that the overwhelming power of the state even contravenes the procedural advances that support

victims and their input to the system, such as victim-impact information (Erez & Laster, 1999). Still others claim that the use of VIS creates an unjustified inequality in sentencing because some victims may appear more sympathetic than others or are better able than others to articulate their harms resulting in disparate punishments (e.g., Hoffman, 2003; McCampbell, 2006; Philips, 1997).

This debate notwithstanding, the Supreme Court of the United States decided that the Eighth Amendment is "not a per se bar to victim impact evidence during sentencing, even in death penalty cases" (Neubauer & Fradella, 2016, p. 260). Still, due process can serve as the basis of a challenge to victim-impact evidence in a particular case if the evidence is inflammatory and unduly prejudicial (see *Salazar v. State*, 2002).

Balancing the Rights of Criminal Defendants and Victim Protection

Recall the earlier discussion regarding why a victim may not feel satisfaction with a judge's decisions in the criminal justice process. This is because judges have a legal duty to safeguard the constitutional rights of defendants. That duty impacts a judge's decisional authority regarding bail, plea bargaining, and sentencing and creates tension between the rights of criminal defendants and the needs of victims.

Bail

There are constitutional standards and statutory requirements to be met in determining whether release on bail is appropriate for each defendant and at what price (see Neubauer & Fradella, 2016). The defendant's release on bail also is governed by the Eighth Amendment, which prohibits both "excessive bail" and "cruel and unusual punishment." However, the Eighth Amendment does not provide a right to bail at all; it only prohibits "excessive" bail amounts if bail is granted.

BOX 13.4 THE CONSTITUTIONALITY OF VICTIM-IMPACT INFORMATION

The first case to address victim-impact evidence was John Booth's 1987 appeal of a death sentence meted out for murdering Rose and Irvin Bronstein during a robbery of their home. At the sentencing hearing, an agent of the state read a report into the record. The report noted that the Bronsteins "were loving parents and grandparents"; that their funeral was "the largest in the history of the Levinson Funeral Home"; and that they both were "extremely good people who wouldn't hurt a fly" (*Booth v. Maryland*, 1987, pp. 414–415). Booth argued that the Eighth Amendment right against cruel and unusual punishment was violated because the jury was prejudiced by facts that were not known to the defendant when he committed the murder (Wood, 2005). The U.S. Supreme Court agreed and overturned Booth's death sentence accordingly.

The second case concerned Demetrius Gathers's confession to murdering Richard Haynes. Gathers was convicted and sentenced to death. He appealed his sentence on the grounds that the prosecutor made impermissible statements to the jury extolling the victim's character, much like those made in the *Booth* case. The Court overturned his death sentence as well: "While in this case it was the prosecutor rather than the victim's survivors who characterized the victim's personal qualities, the statement is indistinguishable in any relevant respect from that in *Booth*" (*South Carolina v. Gathers*, 1989, p. 811).

Two years later, however, the Court decided *Payne v. Tennessee* (1991). Payne was convicted of attacking a woman and her two young children. The mother and daughter were killed but, the younger child, 4-year-old Nicholas, survived. At Payne's sentencing hearing, Nicholas's grandmother, who was raising him since his mother's death, was allowed to talk to the jury about how distraught Nicholas was and that he still asks about his mother and sister and cries for them at night (*Payne*, 1991, pp. 814–815). The prosecutor subsequently implored the jury to render a verdict "for Nicholas," so that when he grows up he will know that "justice was done" (*Payne*, 1991, p. 815). The Tennessee Supreme Court upheld the sentence, deciding that the grandmother's and the prosecutor's statements were "'relevant to [the defendant's] personal responsibility and moral guilt'" (*Payne*, 1991, pp. 816–817). When Payne appealed his case to the U.S. Supreme Court, the Court upheld the use of victim information, reasoning that there was nothing unfair about "allowing the jury to bear in mind that harm at the same time that it considers the mitigating evidence introduced by the defendant" (*Payne*, 1991, p. 826). *Payne* effectively overruled *Booth* and *Gathers*.

The prohibition of excessive bail means the cost of bail must be aligned with the seriousness of the crime, not the accused's ability to pay. The legal purpose of bail is to incentivize the defendant's return to court and future cooperation with further proceedings against him. Bail is routinely denied if the defendant is deemed to be a flight-risk. Bail also is denied if the defendant presents a verifiable risk to the victim(s) or community (Karmen, 2013). Neubauer and Fradella (2016) offer a detailed

analysis of bail decisions and identify the uncertainty of the data available, the perception of risk to the victim and community, and jail overcrowding as the three main contexts within which such decisions are made (Neubauer & Fradella, 2016).

From a victim's perspective, releasing the accused back into society under any terms may be unsatisfactory. Victims may fear additional violence to themselves or others in the form of retaliation for invoking and cooperating with the justice system (Herman, 2005). Perpetrators of sexual violence typically have intimate information about their victims that make those victims particularly vulnerable to such intimidation (Herman, 2005). Granting bail and releasing the defendant, even with a condition of no-contact with the victim, can be seen as a slight or even an outright betrayal from a judge who is perceived as unconcerned with the victim's needs. Victims left less than satisfied with their experiences in the justice system are less likely to participate further, a situation that is problematic because victim cooperation is usually necessary to solve and close cases (Worrall, 2008).

Orders of Protection

An **order of protection**, also called a *protective order* or a *restraining order*, is a civil court order specifically prohibiting contact with the protected person by the person named in the order (*Black's Law Dictionary*, 1999, p. 1315). They typically are sought by victims who petition the court for an emergency order of limited duration in an *ex parte* evidentiary hearing (meaning that the person the order restrains does not need to be present, only the person seeking the order of protection) that does not require proof that a crime has been committed (Logan & Walker, 2009). Then, after the person the order restrains has been served with the order, a full hearing is usually held after a relatively short period of time at which all parties may present evidence. If, at the end of such a hearing, a judge or other judicial officer feels an order for a longer period of time is warranted, a typical order "will either fully or partially restrict the contact the parties may have" and likely remain "in effect for one to two years and can be enforced even in jurisdictions outside of the issuing jurisdiction (Friedman, 2010, p. 245).

Once issued, a civil order of protection is enforced by the criminal law. That is to say that a violation of an order of protection constitutes a criminal offense warranting immediate arrest. If an order of protection is violated and an arrest is made, the accused may remain in custody. Alternatively, if bail is granted, criminal court judges routinely require, as a condition of release, that the accused have no contact with the victim (Pierce & Quillen, 2013).

Pierce and Quillen (2013) suggest that orders of protection will better serve victims than bail because they "address the victim–abuser power dynamic" by providing for the immediate rearrest of the defendant, unlike a forfeiture of bail (Pierce & Quillen, 2013, p. 287). If the accused defendant threatens the victim holding an order of protection, the police can immediately arrest him or her for violating the order. If the accused defendant threatens the victim in violation of the conditions of his or her release, the victim must contact the prosecuting attorney who must file a motion with the court, allowing time for notice and response from the defense attorney, requesting the court to revoke the release and order the accused defendant be found and rearrested. In other words, the violation of an order of protection will immediately mobilize law enforcement in ways that a defendant's failure to adhere to release conditions will not because it creates a new crime to be addressed.

On the other hand, orders of protection are just pieces of paper. Even though they are backed by a threat of arrest, they are not a guarantee that a motivated offender, such as a stalker or an abusive partner, will obey the court order. In fact, one study reported that as many as 40% of orders of protection are violated (Spitzberg, 2002). When orders of protection are honored, most women report lower levels of violence for up to two years after obtaining the orders (Gist, et al., 2002; McFarlane, et al., 2003). But when the orders are violated, there can be profound consequences. Women whose abusers violate the terms of an order of protection have "significantly higher severities of abuse" (Maddox,

McFarlane, & Liu, 2015, p. 36; see also Connelly & Cavanagh, 2007; McFarlane, et al., 2003, 2004).

Plea Bargaining

Recall that plea bargains are deals that exchange trials and trial rights for a guaranteed lesser punishment for the defendant. They are negotiated between the prosecutor and the defense attorney, or between the prosecutor and the defendant if an attorney does not represent him or her. Also, the judge must consent to the agreement before it can be culminated (see Neubauer & Fradella, 2016). Although such agreements are expedient for the criminal justice system—indeed, upwards of 90% of all criminal cases are resolved by plea bargain (Neubauer & Fradella, 2016)—they may result in a compromise that is unacceptable to a victim who has had no part in the negotiations. Negotiations between the prosecution and defense treat the victim as a third party at best, if at all. Such relegation to a comparatively unimportant position rarely, if ever, serves the victim's interests (Cullen & Jonson, 2012). And given the frequency of plea bargaining, this translates into the practical exclusion of meaningful victim input in the vast majority of criminal cases.

Various approaches have been proposed to remedy this challenge. The proposals range from granting the victim veto power over any such plea agreement (Kennard, 1989) to imposing on the prosecutor a duty to consult or confer with the victim and report to the court regarding such. Even where prosecutors are required to consult or confer with victims, there are no consequences for not doing so. Moreover, in some jurisdictions, the obligation to consult or confer has been interpreted as a requirement of notification to the victim that a plea agreement has been reached prior to seeking approval from the judge (Crime Victims Institute, 2005). Of course, this means the victim, yet again, is left out of any plea negotiation until the process has already

moved so far that the victim's input has little or no effect.

Perhaps the greatest frustration for victims in the plea-bargaining process is the degree of secrecy and discretion afforded prosecutors in the criminal justice system (O'Hear, 1991). The plea negotiation is not a public proceeding. It is carried out informally and often behind doors closed not only to the public, but also to other officials concerned with the case, such as social workers or probation officers, and most importantly, the victim. Moreover, the prosecutor is not pressed to explain such decisions to others, including the victim (O'Hear, 1991). This can leave the victim without an understanding or appreciation for the process and feeling slighted by it.

Sentencing

Criminal sentences are largely set by sentencing guidelines or statutes that restrict judicial discretion. All punishments meted out must fall within such dictates. A sentence that falls outside of the mandated or standardized sentencing guidelines is vulnerable to appeal by the accused (see Neubauer & Fradella, 2016). Victims may be disappointed by any particular criminal sentence, believing it to be unsatisfactory punishment in comparison with the harms they feel were inflicted (Davis & Smith, 1994). Moreover, if a victim has proffered an impact statement that includes a sentencing recommendation and that recommendation was not followed, the victim is likely to feel wronged and betrayed, or experience secondary victimization, at the hands of the justice system (Erez & Tontodonato, 1992). Generally, research shows that the perception of a negative trial outcome is associated with negative psychological effects for the victim (Laxminarayan, 2013). Because many procedural aspects of the criminal justice system precede the sentencing outcome, those earlier activities significantly influence a victim's perception of the overall fairness of the system (Wemmers & Cyr, 2006). The frustrations of lack of victim input or control in plea bargaining are mirrored in a victim perspective of sentencing. Nonetheless, as with other aspects of the justice system, increased input and control from victims with regard to sentencing could likely threaten the due process rights of the defendant (Ruddy, 2014).

Summary

From a victim's perspective, the pains of victimization do not end with the cessation of the episodic or primary victimization. In addition to the social and financial costs of victimization, victims must also grapple with police policies and the performances of individual officers with whom they interact. Then, victims must navigate the gauntlet of the criminal courts and its processes that may appear to thwart their needs at every turn.

VICTIMS' SERVICES

Some victims—and sometimes their families—need help coping with and recovering from their criminal victimization. Both public agencies and private organizations provide a range of aid to victims of crime in the form of compensation and assistance that are collectively known as **victims' services**. *Victim-compensation programs* address the financial needs victims experience for crime-related expenses, such as medical costs, mental health counseling, funeral and burial costs, lost wages, or loss of support. *Victim-assistance programs* provide a range of services, including crisis intervention, counseling, emergency shelter, criminal justice advocacy, emergency transportation, and job training and placement. The nature of services offered is as wide and diverse as the foci and agendas of the agencies and organizations that offer them (Sims, Yost & Abbott, 2005). Yet, a recent study indicates that less than 10% of violent crime victims (the majority of which involved sexual assaults) seek such assistance and, of those who do, more than half of the services were

received from public agencies (Langton, 2011). Notably, the low utilization rate of victim services corresponds to the high rate of underreporting of sexual victimizations. This is a salient point for several reasons. First, in many jurisdictions, victims are eligible to receive services only if they do specific things, such as report the crime to the police, cooperate with the investigation, and testify in court proceedings. Thus, victim services are inaccessible to those victims who are unwilling to take all of the required steps. Second, even in jurisdictions where victim services are not tied to reporting and subsequent cooperation with the criminal justice system, it may be that victims are unaware of the services available to them if police or court personnel do not refer victims to the agencies or organizations that can help crime victims. Third, there may be a self-selection bias insofar as victims who are more likely to access such services are more willing to report their victimizations to the police. Or finally, it may be that police are more likely to inform some types of victims about services available to them than they are other types of victims. As Zaykowski (2014) stated, "exploratory work is needed in uncovering the mechanism of police involvement in linking victims to services" (p. 365; see also Langton, 2011).

Public Victim Services

Public victim services can be traced to the enactment of the 1984 Victims of Crime Act (VOCA), which established a federal fund for victim assistance. The VOCA Fund is composed of fines paid by federal offenders, special assessments (taxes) and forfeited bonds, property or other collateral (Fritsch, et al., 2004). It provides grants to all 50 states, the District of Columbia, and the U.S. Virgin Islands (OVC, n.d.). Typically, the funds and programs are administered statewide and are meant to be accessible to all victims.

Typically, a victim's first (and sometimes only) contact with the criminal justice system is the responding police officers. Naturally, victims depend on police for information regarding victim services. However, philosophical views of the goals of victims' services vary among referring officers. Public services for victims may be viewed by police officers as government entitlements for disadvantaged victims, as due compensation only for completely innocent victims, or as a method of enhancing victim cooperation only when it is needed. Research has suggested that police officers' individual perceptions and decisions about the appropriateness of victim services for each victim helps determine what information (if any) is disseminated (Sims, Yost, & Abbott, 2005). Police officers also may refer some victims to private sources providing victim services.

Private Victim Services

Recall the discussion earlier in this chapter regarding the development of private victim-assistance organizations. These are organizations created by victims, survivors, and their advocates and supporters that often specialize in particular types of victims or victimizations and offer specifically tailored assistance. They may receive government funding in the form of grants or other sources, but they are nongovernmental organizations and are privately directed. Though they remain privately controlled, often they must act in conjunction with public actors including law-enforcement officers and SARTs, SANEs or other medical personnel, and even prosecutors (Zweig & Yahner, 2013).

The sensitive nature of providing victim assistance services in the wake of sexual or related victimizations necessitates the collaboration of private and public agencies and must be achieved through a coordinated response (Zweig & Yahner, 2013). Campbell (2006) compared sexual-assault victims who had been connected to victim advocates with victims who had not been so linked before being discharged from the hospital and found

that those who had received the services of a victim advocate were less likely to report feeling bad about themselves (60% compared to 83%), feeling guilty (59% compared to 81%), or feeling depressed (53% compared to 88%).

Even with the continued and growing coordination of public and private resources for crime victims, some victims remain underserved, including those residing in rural areas, those from racial and ethnic minority groups, those with language and other barriers to receiving services including mental health and substance abuse challenges, and elderly victims (Zweig & Yahner, 2013). Sexual minorities are among them. As much as 25% of the LGBTQ community has been victimized by an attempted or completed act of violence based in sexual orientation (Herek, 2009). Moreover, although the LGBTQ population is estimated at about 3.5% of the total population, as much as 30% of reported hate crimes are based in sexual orientation (Stotzer, 2012). Yet, the National Center for Victims of Crime surveyed 10,000 public and private agencies about services for the LGBTQ community and found that, "LGBTQ-relevant victim assistance is generally lacking in every area included in the survey" (National Center for Victims of Crime & National Coalition of Anti-Violence Programs, 2013). The history of prejudice against this community and the remaining social stigma are identified as reasons why the general victims' services community is unable to meet the unique needs of these victims.

CONCLUSION

Victims have played varied roles in our notions of justice. Historically, victims were the focus of the earliest and private mechanisms of justice and then faded to the background of a modern, post-industrial public justice system wherein crime is construed as perpetrated against society as a whole and the protective focus is on the due process rights of the criminal defendant. The victims' rights movement, as an attempt to restore notions of private justice that focus on the victim, brought us recognition that victims continue to experience their victimization individually in ways that society, as a whole, does not and that victims remain in need of our attention. There are two approaches to the restoration of victims' perspectives. One seeks the reintroduction of the retributivist aspects of private justice and the other seeks reintroduction of the rehabilitative aspects of private justice. The prospect of restoring private mechanisms of justice to our public justice system also raises a concern that rights for victims may only be secured at the cost of rights for defendants in a public justice system predicated on objective concerns of the state and of society generally.

Finding ways to reincorporate victims into the public justice system may help to ensure a more just society, especially if an appropriate balance between the rights of victims and criminals can be achieved. Institutionalized biases and prejudices that may have crept into our justice system can be challenged allowing for an expanded view of victims that includes non-traditional or non-paradigmatic victims. Individual biases affecting data collection and analyses regarding victims can be further examined and reduced. These and other victimology insights should prove beneficial in responding to and better serving the needs of victims generally, and of victims of crimes involving sex, gender, or sexuality especially because an imbalance of power is at the crux of the sex-crime enigma.

FURTHER READING

Catalano, S. (2013). *Intimate partner violence: Attributes of victimization, 1993–2011.* Washington, DC: U.S. Department of Justice, Office of Justice Programs, Bureau of Justice Statistics.

Durfee, A. (2012). Situational ambiguity and gendered patterns of arrest in intimate partner violence. *Violence Against Women, 18*(1), 64–84.

Meadows, R. J. (2013). *Understanding violence and victimization* (6th ed.). Upper Saddle River, NJ: Prentice Hall.

Paludi, M. A. (1999). *The psychology of sexual victimization: A handbook.* Westport, CT: Greenwood Press.

Paludi, M. A., & Denmark, F. L. (2010). *Victims of sexual assault and abuse: Resources and responses for individuals and families.* Santa Barbara, CA: Praeger.

Quinn, E., & Brightman, S. (2015). *Crime victimization: A comprehensive overview.* Durham, NC: Carolina Academic Press.

Richards, T. N., & Marcum, C. D. (2014). *Sexual victimization: Then and now.* Thousand Oaks, CA: Sage.

Shichor, D., & Tibbetts, S. G. (2002). *Victims and victimization: Essential readings.* Long Grove, IL: Waveland Press.

Stemple, L., & Meyer, I. H. (2014). The sexual victimization of men in America: New data challenge old assumptions. *American Journal of Public Health, 104*(6), e19–e26. doi: 10.2105/AJPH.2014.301946.

Wallace, H., & Roberson, C. (2014). *Victimology: Legal, psychological, and social perspectives* (4th ed.). Upper Saddle River, NJ: Prentice Hall.

GLOSSARY

Crime victim(s): An identifiable person or persons who has/have been harmed individually and directly by a perpetrator or perpetrators, but not by society, social institutions, or our social structure as a whole.

Deviant place theory: The theory that victimization can be predicted based on a victim's presence in certain places or areas.

Due process revolution: The shift in the U.S. Supreme Court's focus from economic rights to civil rights, particularly the due process rights of criminal defendants.

Episodic victimization or **episodic crime:** An event that temporally links specific victims to specific crimes, or victimizations.

Gay panic defense: A criminal defense rooted in temporary insanity or provocation theories in which a defendant proffers that he perceived himself to be the object of sexual advances by the victim that he found so frightening and offensive that he suffered a psychotic episode characterized by unusual violence.

Institutional victimization or **institutional crime:** Harms done to victims by social institutions rather than other individuals.

Lifestyle theory of victimization: The theory that victims' lifestyles are a good measure of their potential victimization.

Order of protection: Sometimes referred to as a "restraining order," an order of protection is an official court order, issued by a judge or other qualified judicial officer, that directs someone to keep a certain distance from another person and otherwise refrain from any and all abusive or threatening behaviors. If the person who is the target of the order fails to comply, he or she is subject to arrest and criminal prosecution for violating the court order.

Precipitation theory of victimization: The theory that victims of crime may actually precipitate their victimization. Such precipitation may be passive or direct.

Primary victimization: The harm resulting from an episodic instance of crime or a specifically identifiable episode of criminal conduct.

Procedural justice: A determination regarding the fairness of a system of justice based on its processes and procedures.

Rape shield laws: Laws that restrict or prohibit the use of evidence regarding a rape victim's past sexual experiences or conduct to discredit the victim's testimony regarding a lack of consent.

Restorative justice: A movement to restore private rehabilitative mechanisms of justice to our public criminal justice system.

Routine activities theory: The theory that the activities we engage in routinely relate to our potential for victimization.

Secondary victimization: A victim's negative interactions with others, including police and other legal actors, after a primary victimization has been reported, that cause the victim to feel victimized again on the basis of his or her sexuality or sexual orientation.

Trans panic defense: A criminal defense strategy in which the defendant admits to having sexual relations with the victim but believed her to be female and was provoked to an uncontrollable heat of passion that resulting in the killing upon discovering that she possessed the genitalia of a male.

Victim-assistance programs: Programs that provide information and aid to people who have suffered direct physical, emotional, or pecuniary harm as a result of the commission of a crime.

Victim-impact statement: A statement read into the court record during a criminal sentencing to inform the judge or jury of the financial, physical, and psychological impact of the crime on the victim and the victim's family.

Victim–offender overlap: Victims may become offenders and vice versa.

Victimology: The study of crime victimization including the relationships between victims and offenders and the interactions between victims and the criminal justice system.

Victims' services: Any organization or agency that exists for the purpose of aiding victims of crime whether public or private.

Vigilantism: Private action by individuals or groups taken outside an existing public system of criminal justice to secure private, or individual, justice goals.

NOTES

1   The website found at http://www.history.com/news/history-lists/7-infamous-gangs-of-new-york offers a list of New York City's seven most notorious gangs and descriptions of them.

2   Bear in mind, though, that the legal systems of the American colonies did not spring forth fully formed with the landing of the boats. They developed over more than a century from the founding of Jamestown in 1607, through the settlement of Georgia in the 1730s, until the American Revolution and independence from Britain in 1776. This poses a challenge in treating colonial America as a single historical or legal entity. Still, the most researched American Colonial legal systems are those of New York and Massachusetts Bay and references to American Colonial Law, generally, are references to those systems.

3   Stemple and Meyer (2014) used five data sets that had been collected independently by the Bureau of Justice Statistics, the Centers for Disease Control and Prevention, and the Federal Bureau of Investigation between 2010 and 2012. Other than for the crime of rape, they found a "high prevalence of sexual victimization among men—in many circumstances similar to the prevalence found among women" in that approximately 1 in 20 women (5.6%) and men (5.3%) reported having experienced some form of sexual victimization—other than rape—in the 12 months prior to taking the survey (p. e19). This encompasses the notion that "made to penetrate" and "penetrated" without consent both constitute sexual victimization though only the latter is defined as rape. They "identified factors that perpetuate misperceptions about men's sexual victimization: reliance on traditional gender stereotypes, outdated and inconsistent definitions, and methodological sampling biases that exclude inmates" (p. e19).

4   In examining the "seamless" association between rape and war, Zurbriggen noted that hegemonic masculinity "is a causal antecedent of both rape and war" (2010, p. 538). Zurbriggen goes on to suggest that rape will not be eradicated, "as long as there continues to be a need (real or perceived) for soldiers and war" (2010, p. 545) because military training values and reinforces hegemonic masculinity. In other words, until we are able to resolve conflicts without violence at a macro level to prevent war, we will not be able to avoid violence at a micro level to prevent rape.

5   It should be noted that the same misconception underlies a common rape myth for female victims as well, without the assumption of latent homosexual tendencies—e.g., "she didn't resist enough, so she must have wanted it" (see Berger, 1977).

REFERENCES

Alexander, E., & Lord, J. H. (1994). *Impact statements—A victim's right to speak . . . A nation's responsibility to listen.* Arlington, VA: National Center for Victims.

Alvarez, L., & Buckley, C. (2013, July 13). Zimmerman is acquitted in Trayvon Martin killing. Retrieved from http://www.nytimes.com/2013/07/14/us/george-zimmerman-verdict-trayvon-martin.html?_r=0

Amir, M. (1971). *Patterns in forcible rape.* Chicago, IL: University of Chicago Press.

ARIZONA REVISED STATUTES § 28–1381 (2015).

Armstrong G. S., & Griffin, M. L. (2007). The effect of local life circumstances on victimization of drug-involved women. *Justice Quarterly, 24*(1), 80–105.

Attenborough, F. (1963). *The laws of the earliest English kings.* New York: Russell & Russell.

Bailey, F. L., & Rothblatt, H. (1973). *Crimes of violence: Rape and other sex crimes.* Rochester, NY: Lawyers Co-operative Publishing Company.

Bandes, S. (1999). Victim standing. *Utah Law Review, 2,* 331–348.

Barnett, R. E. (1977). Restitution: A new paradigm of criminal justice. *Ethics, 87*(4), 279–301.

Beckett, K., & Sasson, T. (2004). *The politics of injustice: Crime and punishment in America* (2nd ed.). Thousand Oaks, CA: Sage Publications.

Bell, J. G., & Perry, B. (2015). Outside looking in: The community impacts of anti-lesbian, gay, and bisexual hate crime. *Journal of Homosexuality, 62*(1), 98–120.

Beloof, D., Cassell, P., & Twist, S. (2010). *Victims in criminal procedure* (3d ed.). Durham, NC: Carolina Academic Press.

Berger, V. (1977). Man's trial, woman's tribulation: Rape cases in the courtroom. *Columbia Law Review, 77*(1), 1–103.

Berrill, K. T., & Herek, G. M. (1990). Primary and secondary victimization in anti-gay hate crimes; *Journal of Interpersonal Violence, 5*(3), 401–413.

Bigler, B. (2006). Sexually provoked: Recognizing sexual misrepresentation as adequate provocation, *UCLA Law Review, 53,* 783–831.

Black, D. (1983). Crime as social control. *American Sociological Review, 48,* 34–45.

Black's Law Dictionary. (1999). 7th ed. Bryan A. Garner, Ed. in Chief. St. Paul, MN: West Group Pub.

Boehm, C. (2011). Retaliatory violence in human prehistory. *British Journal of Criminology, 51,* 518–534.

Bromley, M. L. (1995). Comparing campus and city crime rates: A descriptive study. *American Journal of Police, 14*(1), 131–148.

Cahill, A. J. (2001). *Rethinking rape.* Ithaca, NY: Cornell University Press.

Campbell, R. (2006). Rape survivors' experiences with the legal and medical systems: Do rape victim advocates make a difference? *Violence Against Women, 12,* 30–45.

Casper, J. D., Tyler, T. R., & Fisher, B. (1988). Procedural justice in felony cases. *Law & Society Review, 22,* 483–507.

Cassell, P. (2005). Recognizing victims in the federal rules of criminal procedure: Proposed amendments in light of the Crime Victims' Rights Act. *Brigham Young University Law Review, 4,* 835–926.

Cassell, P. (2007). Treating crime victims fairly: Integrating victims into the Federal Rules of Criminal Procedure. *Utah Law Review, 4,* 861–970.

Cassell, P., & Joffee, S. (2011). The crime victim's expanding role in a system of public prosecution: A response to the critics of the Crime Victims' Rights Act. *Northwestern University Law Review Colloquy, 105,* 164–183.

Cheng, C. (1999). Marginalized masculinities and hegemonic masculinity: An introduction. *Journal of Men's Studies, 7,* 295–315.

Civil Rights Act of 1968, Pub. L. 90–284, 82 Stat. 73 (April 11, 1968) *codified as amended at* scattered sections of 42 U.S.C. (2015).

Clarke, L., & Lewis, D. (1977). *Rape: The price of coercive sexuality.* Toronto: Women's Press.

Clark, M. (1976). Durkheim's sociology of law. *British Journal of Law and Society, 3*(2), 246–255.

Clodfelter, T. A., Turner, M. G., Hartman, J. L., & Kuhns, J. B. (2010). Sexual harassment victimization during emerging adulthood: A test of routine activities theory and a general theory of crime. *Crime & Delinquency, 56*(3), 455–481.

Cohan, W. D. (2014). *The price of silence: The Duke lacrosse scandal, the power of the elite, and the corruption of our great universities.* New York, NY: Scribner, Simon & Schuster.

Cohen, L., & Felson, M. (1979). Social change and crime rate trends: A routine activities approach. *American Sociological Review, 44,* 588–608.

Connell, R. W., & Messerschmidt, J. W. (2005). Hegemonic masculinity: Rethinking the concept. *Gender and Society, 19,* 829–859.

Connelly, C. & Cavanagh, K. (2007). Domestic abuse, civil protection orders and the 'new criminologist': Is there any value in engaging with this law? *Feminist Legal Studies, 15,* 259–287.

Corkin, D., Wiesner, M., Reyna, R. S., & Shukla, K. (2015). The role of deviant lifestyles on violent victimization in multiple contexts. *Deviant Behavior, 36*(5), 405–428. doi: 10.1080/01639625.2014.9356 90.

Corrigan, R. (2013). *Up against a wall: Rape reform and the failure of success.* New York, NY: New York University Press.

Cowan, G. (2000). Beliefs about the causes of four types of rape. *Sex Roles, 42*(9/10), 807–823. doi: 10.1023/A:1007042215614.

Crime Victims Institute. (2005). Inviting victim participation in plea agreements. *Legislative Brief, 2,*

1–4. Retrieved from http://dev.cjcenter.org/_files/cvi/no22005.pdf

Crime Victims' Rights Act of 2004, Pub. L. No. 108–405, 118 Stat. 2260 (2004), *codified as amended at 18 U.S.C. § 3771 (2014)*.

Crompton, L. (1976). Homosexuals and the death penalty in Colonial America. *Journal of Homosexuality, 1*(3), 277–293.

Cullen, F. T., & Jonson, C. L. (2012). *Correctional theory: context and consequences*. Thousand Oaks, CA: Sage Publications.

Culter, R. (1928). *The Gay Nineties, an album of reminiscent drawings*. New York, NY: Doubleday, Doran & Company, Inc.

Dahl, S. (1993). *Rape—A hazard to health*. Oslo, Norway: Scandinavian University Press.

Davis, R. C., & Smith, B. E. (1994). The effects of victim impact statements on sentencing decisions: A test in an urban setting. *Justice Quarterly, 11*, 453–469.

Davis, R. C., & Smith, B. E. (2002). Victim impact statements and victim satisfaction: An unfulfilled promise? *Journal of Criminal Justice, 22*(1), 1–12. doi: 10.1016/0047–2352(94)90044–2.

Dent, M. (2014). The price of silence: The Duke lacrosse scandal and the games people play. *McClatchy Tribune Business News*, April 27. Retrieved from http://login.ezproxy1.lib.asu.edu/login?url=http://search.proquest.com/docview/1519287437?accountid=4485

Doerner, W., & Lab, S. (2014). *Victimology* (7th ed.). New York, NY: Routledge.

Donaldson, M. (1993). What is hegemonic masculinity? *Theory & Society, 22*, 643–657.

Dunn, P. (2012). Men as victims: "Victim" identities, gay identities, and masculinities. *Journal of Interpersonal Violence, 27*(17), 3442–3467.

Durfee, A. (2012). Situational ambiguity and gendered patterns of arrest in intimate partner violence. *Violence Against Women, 18*(1), 64–84. doi: 10.1177/107780 1212437017.

Elliott, I., Thomas, S. D., & Ogloff, J. R. (2012). Procedural justice in contacts with the police: The perspective of victims of crime. *Police Practice & Research, 13*(5), 437–449. doi: 10.1080/15614263. 2011.607659.

Erez, E., & Laster, K. (1999). Neutralizing victim reform: Legal professionals' perspectives on victims and impact statements. *Crime & Delinquency, 45*, 530–553.

Erez, E., & Rogers, L. (1999). Victim impact statements and sentencing outcomes and processes: The perspectives of legal professionals. *British Journal of Criminology, 39*(2), 216–239.

Erez, E., & Tontodonato, P. (1992). Victim participation in sentencing and satisfaction with justice. *Justice Quarterly, 9*, 393–415.

Eskridge, W. N., Jr. (1997). Law and the construction of the closet: American regulation of same-sex intimacy, 1880–1946. *Iowa Law Review, 82*, 1007–1136.

Estrich, S. (1987). *Real rape*. Cambridge, MA: Harvard Press.

Farber, D., & Bailey, B. (2001). *The Columbia guide to America in the 1960s*. New York, NY: Columbia University Press.

Federal Bureau of Investigation. (2014). *Uniform crime reports: Crime in the United States, 2013*. [Table 29: Estimated number of arrests]. Retrieved from https://www.fbi.gov/about-us/cjis/ucr/crime-in-the-u.s/2013/crime-in-the-u.s.-2013/tables/table-29/table_29_estimated_number_of_arrests_united_states_2013.xls

Felson, M. (2002). *Crime and everyday life* (3rd ed.). Thousand Oaks, CA: Sage Publications.

Fischer, B., Cullen, F., & Turner, M. (2001). *The sexual victimization of college women*. Washington, DC: National Institute of Justice.

Fisher, B., Daigle, L. E., & Cullen, F. T. (2010). *Unsafe in the ivory tower: The sexual victimization of college women*. Los Angeles, CA: Sage Publications.

Foldy, M. S. (1997). *The trials of Oscar Wilde: Deviance, morality, and late-Victorian society*. New Haven, CT: Yale University Press.

Fradella, H. F. (2002). Legal, moral, and social reasons for decriminalizing sodomy. *Journal of Contemporary Criminal Justice, 18*(3), 279–301. doi: 10.1177/1043 986202018003005

Fradella, H. F. (2007). *From insanity to diminished capacity: Mental illness and criminal excuse in contemporary American law*. Bethesda, MD: Academica Press.

Frey, C. (2009). Allocution. In J. Wilson (Ed.), *The Praeger handbook of victimology* (pp. 11–12). Santa Barbara, CA: Praeger.

Friedman, R. F. (2010). Protecting victims from themselves, but not necessarily from abusers: Issuing no-contact order over the objection of the victim-spouse. *William & Mary Bill of Rights Journal, 19*(1), 235–261.

Fritsch, E. J., Caeti, T. J., Tobolowsky, P. M., & Taylor, R. W. (2004). Police referrals of crime victims to compensation sources: An empirical analysis of attitudinal and structural impediments. *Police Quarterly, 7*(3), 372–393.

Frosch, D. (2008). Death of a transgender woman is called a hate crime. *The New York Times*, August 2. Retrieved from http://www.nytimes.com/2008/08/02/us/02murder.html

Fuchs, S. F. (2004). Male sexual assault: Issues of arousal and consent. *Cleveland State Law Review, 51*, 93–121.

Gellman, S. (1991). Sticks and stones can put you in jail, but can words increase your sentence? Constitutional and policy dilemmas of ethnic intimidation laws. *UCLA Law Review, 39*, 333–396.

Gey, S. G. (1997). What if *Wisconsin v. Mitchell* had involved Martin Luther King, Jr.? The constitutional flaws of hate crime enhancement statutes. *George Washington Law Review, 65,* 1014–1070.

Gist, J. H., McFarlane, J., Malecha, A., Wilson, P., Watson, K., Fredland, N., & Smith, S. (2002). Protection orders and assault charges: Do justice interventions reduce violence against women? *American Journal of Family Law, 15,* 59–69.

Gordon, T. M., & Brodsky, S. L. (2007). The influence of victim impact statements on sentencing in capital cases. *Journal of Forensic Psychology Practice, 7*(2), 45–52. doi: 10.1300/J158v07n02–03.

Gordon, M. T., & Riger, S. (1989). *The female fear.* New York, NY: Free Press.

Hallie, P. (2013). From cruelty to goodness. In C. H. Sommers & F. Sommers (Eds.), *Virtue and vice in everyday life: Introductory readings in ethics* (9th ed., pp. 4–14). Boston, MA: Wadsworth.

Harris, A. P. (1992). The jurisprudence of victimhood. *Supreme Court Review, 3,* 77–102.

Hart, J. (Producer), Kolodner, E. (Producer), Sharp, J. (Producer), Vachon, C. (Producer), & Peirce, K. (Director). (1999). *Boys don't cry.* USA: Fox Searchlight Pictures.

Hazelton, P. M. (1992). Rape shield laws: Limits on zealous advocacy. *American Journal of Criminal Law, 19,* 35–56.

Herek, G. M. (2009). Hate crimes and stigma-related experiences among sexual minority adults in the United States: Prevalence estimates from a national probability sample. *Journal of Interpersonal Violence, 24*(1), 54–74. doi: 10.1177/0886260508316477.

Herman, J. L. (2005). Justice from the victim's perspective. *Violence Against Women, 11*(5), 571–602. doi: 10.1177/1077801205274450.

Herring, S. C. (1999). The rhetorical dynamics of gender harassment online. *The Information Society, 15,* 151–167.

Herrington, L. H., Bobo, G., Carrington, F., Damos, J. P., Dolan, D. L., Eikenberry, K. O., Miller, R. J., Robertson, P., & Samenow, S. E. (1982). *Final report of the President's Task Force on Victims of Crime.* Retrieved from http://ojp.gov/ovc/publications/presdntstskforcrprt/87299.pdf

Hindelang, M., Gottfredson, M., & Garofalo, J. (1978). *Victims of personal crime.* Cambridge, MA: Ballinger.

Hoffman, J. L. (2003). Revenge or mercy? Some thoughts about survivor opinion evidence in death penalty cases. *Cornell Law Review, 88,* 530–542.

Holt, T. J., & Bossler, A. M. (2009). Examining the applicability of lifestyle-routine activities theory for cybercrime victimization. *Deviant Behavior, 30,* 1–25. doi: 10.1080/01639620701876577.

Howton, A. J. (2010). Sexual assault response team (SART). In B. S. Fisher & S. P. Lab (Eds.), *Encyclopedia of victimology and crime prevention* (Vol. 2, pp. 855–856). Los Angeles, CA: Sage.

Hoyle, C. (2011). Empowerment through emotion: The use and abuse of victim impact evidence. In E. Erez, M. Kilching, & J. Wemmers (Eds.), *Therapeutic jurisprudence and victim participation in justice: International Perspectives* (pp. 249–283). Durham, NC: Carolina Academic Press.

Hudson, J. (2014). *The formation of the English common law: Law and society in England from the Norman Conquest to Magna Carta.* New York, NY: Routledge.

Hyde, H. M. (1976). *The Cleveland Street scandal.* New York, NY: Coward, McCann, & Geoghegan.

Iganski, P. (2001). Hate crimes hurt more. *American Behavioral Scientist, 45*(4), 627–638.

Jacobs, J. B., & Potter, K. A. (1997). Hate crimes: A critical perspective. *Crime and Justice, 22*(1), 1–50.

Janofsky, M. (1999, November 2). Judge rejects gay panic as defense in murder case. *The New York Times.* Retrieved from http://www.nytimes.com/1999/11/02/us/judge-rejects-gay-panic-as-defense-in-murder-case.html

Jennings, W. G., Piquero, A. R., & Reingle, J. M. (2012). On the overlap between victimization and offending: A review of literature. *Aggression and Violent Behavior, 17*(1), 16–26.

Jenny Jones Show, The. (1995). Same-sex secret crushes [Television series episode]. In *The Jenny Jones show,* March 6. Burbank, CA: Warner Brothers Television.

Jensen, G. F., & Brownfield, D. (1986). Gender, lifestyles, and victimization: Beyond routine activity. *Violence and Victims, 1,* 85–99.

Joffee, S. (2009). Validating victims: Enforcing victims' rights through mandatory mandamus. *Utah Law Review, 1,* 241–255.

Jordan, J. (2004). *The word of a woman? Police, rape, and belief.* Basingstoke: Palgrave Macmillan.

Karmen, A. (2013). *Crime victims: An introduction to victimology* (8th ed.), Belmont, CA: Wadsworth/Cengage Learning.

Kempf, E. J. (1920). *Psychopathology.* St. Louis, MO: C. V. Mosby Co.

Kennard, K. (1989). The victim's veto: A way to increase victim impact on criminal case dispositions. *California Law Review, 77*(2), 417–453.

Kilpatrick, D., & Otto, R. K. (1989). Constitutionally guaranteed participation in criminal proceedings for victims: Potential effects on psychological functioning. *Wayne State Law Review, 34,* 7–28.

Kimmel, M. S. (1994). Masculinities as homophobia: Fear, shame, and silence in the construction of gender identity. In H. Brod & M. Kaufman (Eds.), *Theorizing masculinities* (pp. 119–141). Newbury Park, CA: Sage.

Kirchengast, T. (2013). Victim lawyers, victim advocates, and the adversarial criminal trial. *New Criminal Law Review, 16*(4), 568–594.

Konradi, A. (2007). *Taking the stand: Rape survivors and the prosecution of rapists*. Westport, CT: Praeger.

Koss, M. P. (2000). Blame, shame, and community: Justice responses to violence against women. *American Psychology, 55,* 1332–1343.

Koss, M. P., Harvey, M. R., & Butcher, J. N. (1987). *The rape victim: Clinical and community approaches to treatment*. Lexington, MA: S. Greene Press.

Kramer, E. J. (1998). When men are victims: Applying rape shield laws to male same-sex rape. *New York University Law Review, 73,* 293–332.

Kushel, M. B., Evans, J. L., Perry, S., Robertson, M. J., & Moss, A. R. (2003). No door to lock: Victimization among homeless and marginally housed persons. *Archives of Internal Medicine, 163*(20), 2492–2499.

Langton, L. (2011). *Use of victim service agencies by victims of serious violence crime 1993–2009*. Washington, DC: U.S. Department of Justice, Bureau of Justice Statistics.

Largen, M. A. (1981). Grassroots centers and national task forces; A history of the anti-rape movement. *Aegis,* Summer, 46–52.

Lauritsen, J. L. (2001). The social ecology of violent victimization: Individual and contextual effects in the NCVS. *Journal of Quantitative Criminology, 17*(1), 3–32.

Lauritsen, J. L., Laub, J. H., & Sampson, R. J. (1992). Conventional and delinquent activities: Implications for the prevention of violent victimization among adolescents. *Violence and Victims, 7,* 91–108.

Laxminarayan, M. (2012). Procedural justice and psychological effects of criminal proceedings: The moderating effect of offense type. *Social Justice Research, 25*(4), 390–405. doi: 10.1007/s11211-012-0167-6.

Lederer, L. (1980). *Take back the night*. New York, NY: Morrow.

Ledray, L. E. (1997). SANE program locations: Pros and cons; Sexual Assault Nurse Examiner. *Journal of Emergency Nursing, 23*(2), 182–186.

Lee, C. (2008). The gay panic defense. *University of California Davis Law Review, 471,* 1–72.

Lee, C., and Kwan, P. (2013). The trans panic defense: Masculinity, heteronormativity, and the murder of transgender women. *Hastings Law Journal, 66,* 77–132.

Lees, S. (2002). *Carnal knowledge: Rape on trial*. London: Women's Press.

Levad, A. (2011). *Restorative justice: Theories and practices of moral imagination*. El Paso, TX: LFB Scholarly Publishing.

Levin, B. (1999). Hate crimes: Worse by definition. *Journal of Contemporary Criminal Justice, 15*(1), 6–21.

Levin, J., & McDevitt, J. (1993). *Hate crimes: The rising tide of bigotry & bloodshed*. Boulder, CO: Westview Press.

Levine, D. (2010). Public wrongs and private rights: Limiting the victim's role in a system of public prosecution. *Northwestern University Law Review, 104,* 335–362.

Littel, K. (2001). *Sexual Assault Nurse Examiners (SANE) programs: Improving the community response to sexual assault victims*. Washington, DC: U.S. Department of Justice, Office for Victims of Crime.

Logan, T. K., & Walker, R. (2009). Civil protective order outcomes: Violations and perceptions of effectiveness. *Journal of Interpersonal Violence, 24*(4), 675–692.

Lottes, I. L. (1988). Sexual socialization and attitudes toward rape. In A. W. Burgess (Ed.), *Rape and sexual assault II* (pp. 194–220). New York, NY: Garland.

Maddox, J., McFarlane, J., & Liu, F. A. F. (2015). Risks for women from abusers violating protection orders. *American Journal of Family Law, 29*(1), 32–40.

Madigan, L., & Gamble, N. C. (1991). *The second rape: Society's continued betrayal of the victim*. New York, NY: Lexington Books.

Maier, S. L. (2014). *Rape, victims, and investigations: Experiences and perceptions of law enforcement officers responding to reported rapes*. New York, NY: Routledge.

Mandery, E. J. (2004). Notions of symmetry and self in death penalty jurisprudence (with implications for the admissibility of victim impact evidence). *Stanford Law and Policy Review, 15*(2), 471–518.

Matthew Shepard and James Byrd, Jr. Hate Crimes Prevention Act of 2009, Pub. L. No. 111–84, 123 Stat. 2835, *codified as amended at* 18 U.S.C. § 249 (2015).

McCampbell, E. (2006). Tipping the scales: Seeking death through comparative value arguments. *Washington & Lee Law Review, 63,* 379–420.

McFarlane, J., Malecha, A., Gist, J., Watson, K., Batten, E., Hall, I., & Smith, S. (2003). Intimate partner violence against women: Measuring the effectiveness of protection orders. *Family Law Research, 16,* 244–252.

McFarlane, J., Malecha, A., Gist, J., Watson, K., Batten, E., Hall, I., & Smith, S. (2004). Protection orders and intimate partner violence: An 18-month study of 15 Black, Hispanic, and White women. *American Journal of Public Health, 94,* 613–618.

McLynn, F. (1989). *Crime and punishment in eighteenth-century England*. London: Routledge.

Miller, K. (2013). Purposing and repurposing harms: The victim impact statement and sexual assault. *Qualitative Health Research, 23*(11), 1445–1458. doi: 10.1177/1049732313507753.

Miller, L. (2014). The Duke lacrosse rape scandal: The definitive account. *Salon,* April 6. Retrieved from http://www.salon.com/2014/04/06/the_duke_lacrosse_rape_scandal_the_definitive_account/

Miller, M. K., Greene, E., Dietrich, H., Chamberlain, J., and Singer, J. A. (2008). How emotion affects the trial process. *Judicature, 92,* 56–64.

Montada, L. (1994). Injustice in harm and loss. *Social Justice Research*, 7, 5–28.

Morgan, K., & Smith, B. (2005). Victims, punishment, and parole: The effect of victim participation on parole hearings. *Criminology & Public Policy*, 4(2), 333–361.

Movement Advance Project. (2015). *Hate crime laws.* Retrieved from http://www.lgbtmap.org/equality-maps/hate_crime_laws

Muftić L. R., & Hunt, D. E. (2013). Victim precipitation: Further understanding the linkage between victimization and offending in homicide. *Homicide Studies*, 17(3), 239–254. doi: 10.1177/1088767912 461785.

Nadler, J., & Rose, M. R. (2003). Victim impact testimony and the psychology of punishment. *Cornell Law Review*, 88, 419–546.

National Alliance to End Sexual Violence (NAESV). (2012). 2012 rape crisis center survey. Retrieved from http://endsexualviolence.org/files/2012RCCFundingSurveyResults.pdfhttp://endsexualviolence.org/files/2012RCCFundingSurveyResults.pdf

National Center for Victims of Crime & National Coalition of Anti-violence Programs. (2013). *Why it matters: Rethinking victim assistance for lesbian, gay, bisexual, transgender, and queer victims of hate violence & intimate partner violence.* Washington, DC, and New York, NY: National Center for Victims of Crime & National Coalition of Anti-violence Programs.

National Network to End Domestic Violence (2013). *Violence Against Women Act.* Retrieved from http://nnedv.org/policy/issues/vawa.html?highlight=WyJ2YXdhIiwidmF3YSJdIl0=

Nesci, J. (2009). *Arizona DUI defense: The law and practice* (2nd ed.). Tucson, AZ: Lawyers & Judges Publishing Company, Inc.

Neubauer, D., & Fradella, H. F. (2016). *America's courts and the criminal justice system* (12th ed.). Belmont, CA: Cengage Learning.

Office for Victims of Crime (OVC). (n.d.). http://ojp.gov/ovc/

O'Hear, M. M. (1991). Plea-bargaining and victims: From consultation to guidelines. *Marquette Law Review*, 91, 323–347.

Orth, U. (2002). Secondary victimization of crime victims by criminal proceedings. *Social Justice Research*, 15(4), 313–325.

Pei-Lin Chen, C. (2000). Provocation doctrine and homosexual defense. *Cornell Journal of Law & Public Policy*, 10, 195–235.

Perry, B. (2001). *In the name of hate: Understanding hate crimes.* New York, NY: Routledge.

Philips, A. K. (1997). Thou shalt not kill any nice people: The problem of victim impact statements in capital sentencing. *American Criminal Law Review*, 35, 93–118.

Pierce, P., & Quillen, B. (2013). No contest: Why protective orders provide victims superior protection to bond conditions. *American Journal of Criminal Law*, 40(3), 227–254.

Planty, M., Langton, L., Krebs, C., Berzofsky, M., & Smiley-McDonald, H. (2013). *Female victims of sexual violence, 1994–2010.* Washington, DC: U.S. Department of Justice, Office of Justice Programs, Bureau of Justice Statistics. Retrieved from http://www.bjs.gov/content/pub/pdf/fvsv9410.pdf

Propen, A., & Schuster, M. L. (2008). Making academic work advocacy work: Technologies of power in the public arena. *Journal of Business and Technical Communications*, 22, 299–329.

RAINN. (n.d.). *The offenders.* https://www.rainn.org/get-information/statistics/sexual-assault-offenders

Ready, J., Weisburd, D., & Farrell, G. (2002). The role of crime victims in American policing, *International Review of Victimology*, 9, 175–195.

Roberts, A. R. (1990). *Helping crime victims: Research, policy, and practice.* Thousand Oaks, CA: Sage.

Rose, V. M. (1977). Rape as a social problem: A byproduct of the feminist movement. *Social Problems*, 25, 75–89.

Roth, M. P. (2011). *Crime and punishment: A history of the criminal justice system* (2nd ed.). Belmont, CA: Wadsworth Publishing Co.

Rountree, P., Land, K. C., & Miethe, T. D. (1994). Macro-micro integration in the study of victimization: A hierarchical logistic model analysis across Seattle neighborhoods. *Criminology*, 32, 387–414.

Ruddy, R. (2014). Victim's role in the justice process. *Internet Journal of Criminology*, 2014, 1–22. Retrieved from http://www.internetjournalofcriminology.com/Ruddy_The_Victim's_Role_in_the_Justice_Process_IJC_Jan_2014.pdf

Salerno, J. M., & Bottoms, B. L. (2009). Emotional evidence and jurors' judgments: The promise of neuroscience for informing psychology and law. *Behavioral Sciences & The Law*, 27(2), 273–296. doi: 10.1002/bsl.86.

Sampson, R. J., & Lauritsen, J. L. (1990). Deviant lifestyles, proximity to crime, and the offender–victim link in personal violence. *Journal of Research in Crime and Delinquency*, 27, 110–139.

Sanders, A., & Jones, I. (2007). The victim in court. In S. Walklate (Ed.), *Handbook of victims and victimology.* Portland, OR: Willan Publishing.

Sasse, S. (2005). Motivation and routine activities theory. *Deviant Behavior*, 26, 547–570.

Scarce, M. (1997). *Male on male rape: The hidden toll of stigma and shame.* New York, NY: Insight Books.

Schechter, S. (1982). *Women and male violence: The visions and struggles of the battered women's movement.* Cambridge, MA: South End Press.

Schreck, C. J., Fisher, B. S., & Miller, J M. (2004). The social context of violent victimization: A study of the delinquent peer effect. *Justice Quarterly*, 21(1), 23–47.

Schreck, C. J., Wright, R. A., & Miller, J. M. (2002). A study of individual and situational antecedents of violent victimization. *Justice Quarterly*, 19, 159–180.

Siegel, L. J. (2011). *Essentials of criminal justice* (7th ed.). Belmont, CA: Wadsworth.

Sims, B., Yost, B., & Abbott, C. (2005). Use and nonuse of victim service programs: Implications from a statewide survey of crime victims, *Criminology and Public Policy*, 4(2), 361–384.

Sinozich, S., & Langton, L. (2014). *Rape and sexual assault victimization among college-age females, 1995–2013*. Washington, DC: U.S. Department of Justice, Office of Justice Programs, Bureau of Justice Statistics. Retrieved from http://www.bjs.gov/content/pub/pdf/rsavcaf9513.pdf

Smith, B., Sloan, J., & Ward, R. (1990). Public support for the victims' rights movement: Results of a statewide survey. *Crime and Delinquency*, 36(4), 488–502.

Solomon, C. H. (Producer), Hanley, C. (Producer), Pressman, E. R. (Producer), & Harron, M. (Director). (2000). *American psycho*. USA: Lions Gate Films.

Spellman, J. (2009). Transgender murder, hate crime conviction a first. CNN.com, April 23. Retrieved from http://edition.cnn.com/2009/CRIME/04/22/transgender.slaying.trial/index.html

Spillane, J. F., & Wolcott, D. B. (2013). *A history of modern American criminal justice*. Thousand Oaks, CA: Sage Publications.

Spitzberg, B. (2002). The tactical topography of stalking victimization and management. *Trauma, Violence, & Abuse*, 3(4), 261–288.

Spohn, C. C., White, C., & Tellis, K. (2014). Unfounding sexual assault: Examining the decision to unfound and identifying false reports, *Law and Society Review*, 48, 161–192.

Stark, J., & Goldstein, H. (1985). *The rights of crime victims*. Toronto: Bantam Books.

Stark, R. (1987). Deviant places: A theory of the ecology of crime, *Criminology*, 25(4), 893–910.

Stemple, L., & Meyer, I. H. (2014). The sexual victimization of men in America: New data challenge old assumptions. *American Journal of Public Health*, 104(6), e19–e26. doi: 10.2105/AJPH.2014.301946.

Stemple, L., & Qutb, S. (2002). Just what part of prison rape do you find amusing? *San Francisco Chronicle*. Retrieved from http://www.sfgate.com/opinion/article/PRISONS-Selling-a-Soft-Drink-Surviving-Hard-2811952.php

Stotzer, R. L. (2012). *Comparison of hate crime rates across protected and unprotected groups: An update*. Los Angeles, CA: The Williams Institute. Retrieved from http://williamsinstitute.law.ucla.edu/research/violence-crime/comparison-of-hate-crime-rates-across-protected-and-unprotected-groups/

Strader, J. K., Selvin, M., & Hay, L. (2015). Gay panic, gay victims, and the case for gay shield laws. *Cardozo Law Review*, 36, 1473–1531.

Struckman-Johnson, C., & Struckman-Johnson, D. (1992). Acceptance of male rape myths among college men and women. *Sex Roles*, 7(3/4), 85–100.

Symonds, M. (1980). The "second injury" to victims. In L. Kivens (Ed.), *Evaluation and change: Services for survivors* (pp. 36–38). Minneapolis, MN: Minneapolis Medical Research Foundation.

Taylor, P. A. (2003). Maestros or misogynists? Gender and the social construction of hacking. In Y. Jewkes (Ed.), *Dot.cons: Crime, deviance and identity on the internet* (pp. 126–146). Portland, OR: Willan Publishing.

Tewksbury, R., & Mustaine, E. E. (2001). Lifestyle factors associated with the sexual assault of men: A routine activity theory analysis. *Journal of Men's Studies*, 9(2), 153–182.

The Increased Importance of the Violence Against Women Act in Times of Economic Crisis: Hearings Before the Committee on the Judiciary of the U.S. Senate, 112th Cong. 4 (2010, May 5) (testimony of Susan Carbon). Retrieved from http://www.justice.gov/sites/default/files/ovw/legacy/2010/05/21/statement-impt-economic-crisis.pdf

Thibaut, J., & Walker, L. (1975). *Procedural justice: A psychological analysis*. Hillsdale, NJ: Erlbaum.

Tilleman, M. (2010). (Trans)forming the provocation defense. *Journal of Criminal Law & Criminology*, 100(4), 1659–1688.

Truman, J. L., & Langton, L. (2014). Criminal victimization, 2013. Washington, DC: U.S. Department of Justice, Office of Justice Programs, Bureau of Justice Statistics. Retrieved from http://www.bjs.gov/content/pub/pdf/cv13.pdf

Tyler, T. R. (1988). What is procedural justice? Criteria used by citizens to assess the fairness of legal procedures. *Law and Society Review*, 22(1), 301–355.

Tyler, T. R. (2006). Legitimacy and legitimation. *Annual Review of Psychology*, 57, 375–400.

Tyler, T. R., Boeckmann, R. J., Smith, H. J., & Huo, Y. J. (1997). *Social justice in a diverse society*. Boulder, CO: Westview Press.

Underwood, T. L., & Edmunds, C. (2003). *Victim assistance: Exploring individual practice, organizational policy, and societal responses*. New York, NY: Springer Publishing.

Victims of Crime Act of 1984, Pub. L. No. 98–473, 98 Stat. 2170 (1984), *codified as amended at 42 U.S.C. 10601 et seq.* (2015).

Villmoare, E., & Neto, V. (1987). *NIJ research in brief: Victim appearances at sentencing under California's victims' bill of rights*. Washington, DC: U.S. Department of Justice.

Violence against Women Act of 1994, Pub. L. No. 103–322, 108 Stat, 2835 (codified as amended at scattered sections of the U.S.C.).

Wakelin, A., & Long, K. M. (2003). Effects of victim gender and sexuality on attributions of blame to rape victims. *Sex Roles*, 49(9/10), 477–487.

Wallin, I. (2010). *Rights for victims of crimes: Rebalancing justice.* Lanham, MD: Rowman & Littlefield.

Walmsley, R. (2012). *World prison population list* (9th ed.). London: International Center for Prison Studies.

Weinstein, J. (1992). First amendment challenges to hate crime legislation: Where's the speech? *Criminal Justice Ethics*, 11(2), 6–20.

Wemmers, J., & Cyr, K. (2006). What fairness means to crime victims: A social psychological perspective on victim–offender mediation. *Applied Psychology in Criminal Justice*, 2(2), 102–128.

Widor, A. L. (1996). Fact or fiction? Role-reversal sexual harassment in the modern workplace. *University of Pittsburg Law Review*, 58, 225–254.

Wilson, A. (1976). *The naughty nineties.* London: Eyre Methuen.

Wilson, M. M. (2014). *Hate crime victimization, 2004–2012 – Statistical tables.* Washington, DC: U.S. Department of Justice, Office of Justice Programs, Bureau of Justice Statistics. Retrieved from http://www.bjs.gov/content/pub/pdf/hcv0412st.pdf

Wilson, W. J. (2012). *The truly disadvantaged: The inner city, the underclass, and social policy* (2nd ed.). Chicago, IL: University of Chicago Press.

Wolfgang, M. E. (1967). Victim precipitated criminal homicide. In M. E. Wolfgang (Ed.), *Studies in homicide* (pp. 72–87). New York, NY: Harper & Row.

Wood, J. K. (2005). Balancing innocence and guilt: A metaphorical analysis of the US Supreme Court's rulings on victim impact statements. *Western Journal of Communication*, 69(2), 129–146. doi: 10.1080/10570310500076817.

Worrall, J. L. (2008). *Crime control in America: What works?* (2nd ed.) Boston, MA: Pearson/Allyn & Bacon.

Yun, I., Johnson, M., & Kercher, G. (2005). *Victim impact statements: What victims have to say.* Huntsville, TX: Sam Houston State University Crime Victims' Institute.

Zaykowski, H. (2014). Mobilizing victim services: The role of reporting to the police. *Journal of Traumatic Stress*, 27(3), 365–369.

Zernova, M. (2007). *Restorative justice: Ideals and realities.* Abingdon: Ashgate.

Zurbriggen, E. L. (2010). Rape, war, and the socialization of masculinity: Why our refusal to give up war ensures that rape cannot be eradicated. *Psychology of Women Quarterly*, 34(4), 538–549. doi: 10.1111/j.1471-6402.2010.01603.x.

Zweig, J., & Yahner, J. (2013). Providing services to crime victims. In R. C. Davis, A. J. Lurigio, & S. Herman (Eds.), *Victims of crime* (4th ed., pp. 325–348). Thousand Oaks, CA: Sage Publications.

Cases

Booth v. Maryland, 482 U.S. 496 (1987).

Bowers v. Hardwick, 478 U.S. 186 (1986).

Commonwealth v. Shelley, 373 N.E. 2d 951 (Mass. 1978).

Gideon v. Wainwright, 372 U.S. 335 (1963).

Katz v. United States, 389 U.S. 347 (1967).

Lawrence v. Texas, 539 U.S. 558 (2003).

Mapp v. Ohio, 367 U.S. 643 (1961).

Miranda v. Arizona, 384 U. S. 436 (1966).

Payne v. Tennessee, 501 U.S. 808 (1991).

People v. Parisie, 287 N.E. 2d 310 (Ill. Ct. App. 1972).

People v. Schmitz, 586 N.W.2d 766 (Mich. Ct. App. 1998).

Salazar v. State, 90 S.W.3d 330 (Tex. Ct. Crim. App. 2002).

South Carolina v. Gathers, 490 U.S. 805 (1989).

State v. Lotter, 669 N.W.2d 438 (Neb. 2003).

State v. McKinney, Crim. Action No. 6381 (2d Jud. Dist. Ct., Albany Cnty., Wyo. 1999).

State v. Nissen, 560 N.W.2d 157 (Neb. 1997).

State v. Sibley, 33 S.W. 167 (Mo. 1895).

State v. Thornton, 532 S.W.2d 37 (Mo. Ct. App. 1975).

Wisconsin v. Mitchell, 508 U.S. 476 (1993).

INDEX

Taylor & Francis eBooks

Helping you to choose the right eBooks for your Library

Add Routledge titles to your library's digital collection today. Taylor and Francis ebooks contains over 50,000 titles in the Humanities, Social Sciences, Behavioural Sciences, Built Environment and Law.

Choose from a range of subject packages or create your own!

Benefits for you

» Free MARC records
» COUNTER-compliant usage statistics
» Flexible purchase and pricing options
» All titles DRM-free.

Benefits for your user

» Off-site, anytime access via Athens or referring URL
» Print or copy pages or chapters
» Full content search
» Bookmark, highlight and annotate text
» Access to thousands of pages of quality research at the click of a button.

REQUEST YOUR **FREE** INSTITUTIONAL TRIAL TODAY

Free Trials Available
We offer free trials to qualifying academic, corporate and government customers.

eCollections – Choose from over 30 subject eCollections, including:

Archaeology	Language Learning
Architecture	Law
Asian Studies	Literature
Business & Management	Media & Communication
Classical Studies	Middle East Studies
Construction	Music
Creative & Media Arts	Philosophy
Criminology & Criminal Justice	Planning
Economics	Politics
Education	Psychology & Mental Health
Energy	Religion
Engineering	Security
English Language & Linguistics	Social Work
Environment & Sustainability	Sociology
Geography	Sport
Health Studies	Theatre & Performance
History	Tourism, Hospitality & Events

For more information, pricing enquiries or to order a free trial, please contact your local sales team:
www.tandfebooks.com/page/sales

Routledge
Taylor & Francis Group

The home of
Routledge books

www.tandfebooks.com

Made in the USA
Monee, IL
24 August 2021

76439981R10286